Innovative Research in Attention Modeling and Computer Vision Applications

Rajarshi Pal
Institute for Development and Research in Banking Technology, India

A volume in the Advances in Computational
Intelligence and Robotics (ACIR) Book Series

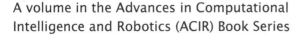

Information Science
REFERENCE
An Imprint of IGI Global

Published in the United States of America by
   Information Science Reference (an imprint of IGI Global)
   701 E. Chocolate Avenue
   Hershey PA, USA 17033
   Tel: 717-533-8845
   Fax: 717-533-8661
   E-mail: cust@igi-global.com
   Web site: http://www.igi-global.com

                          Library of Congress Cataloging-in-Publication Data

Innovative research in attention modeling and computer vision applications / Rajarshi Pal, editor.
     pages cm
 Includes bibliographical references and index.
  ISBN 978-1-4666-8723-3 (hardcover) -- ISBN 978-1-4666-8724-0 (ebook) 1. Computer vision. 2. Robot vision. 3. Tracking (Engineering) I. Pal, Rajarshi, 1982-
   TA1634.I5456 2015
   006.3'7--dc23
                          2015019731

This book is published in the IGI Global book series Advances in Computational Intelligence and Robotics (ACIR) (ISSN: 2327-0411; eISSN: 2327-042X)

British Cataloguing in Publication Data
A Cataloguing in Publication record for this book is available from the British Library.

All work contributed to this book is new, previously-unpublished material. The views expressed in this book are those of the authors, but not necessarily of the publisher.

For electronic access to this publication, please contact: eresources@igi-global.com.

Advances in Computational Intelligence and Robotics (ACIR) Book Series

ISSN: 2327-0411
EISSN: 2327-042X

MISSION

While intelligence is traditionally a term applied to humans and human cognition, technology has progressed in such a way to allow for the development of intelligent systems able to simulate many human traits. With this new era of simulated and artificial intelligence, much research is needed in order to continue to advance the field and also to evaluate the ethical and societal concerns of the existence of artificial life and machine learning.

The **Advances in Computational Intelligence and Robotics (ACIR) Book Series** encourages scholarly discourse on all topics pertaining to evolutionary computing, artificial life, computational intelligence, machine learning, and robotics. ACIR presents the latest research being conducted on diverse topics in intelligence technologies with the goal of advancing knowledge and applications in this rapidly evolving field.

COVERAGE

- Evolutionary computing
- Artificial life
- Add/Edit Topics Covered
- Cognitive Informatics
- Natural Language Processing
- Intelligent control
- Artificial Intelligence
- Computational Intelligence
- Fuzzy Systems
- Computational Logic

IGI Global is currently accepting manuscripts for publication within this series. To submit a proposal for a volume in this series, please contact our Acquisition Editors at Acquisitions@igi-global.com or visit: http://www.igi-global.com/publish/.

Titles in this Series

For a list of additional titles in this series, please visit: www.igi-global.com

www.igi-global.com

701 E. Chocolate Ave., Hershey, PA 17033
Order online at www.igi-global.com or call 717-533-8845 x100
To place a standing order for titles released in this series, contact: cust@igi-global.com
Mon-Fri 8:00 am - 5:00 pm (est) or fax 24 hours a day 717-533-8661

Table of Contents

Section 2
Other Computer Vision Applications

Detailed Table of Contents

Section 1
Visual Attention Modeling and Applications

Chapter 1

Vincent Ricordel, University of Nantes, France
Junle Wang, University of Nantes, France
Matthieu Perreira Da Silva, University of Nantes, France
Patrick Le Callet, University of Nantes, France

Visual attention is one of the most important mechanisms deployed in the human visual system (HVS) to reduce the amount of information that our brain needs to process. An increasing amount of efforts has been dedicated to the study of visual attention, and this chapter proposes to clarify the advances achieved in computational modeling of visual attention. First the concepts of visual attention, including the links between visual salience and visual importance, are detailed. The main characteristics of the HVS involved in the process of visual perception are also explained. Next we focus on eye-tracking, because of its role in the evaluation of the performance of the models. A complete state of the art in computational modeling of visual attention is then presented. The research works that extend some visual attention models to 3D by taking into account of the impact of depth perception are finally explained and compared.

Chapter 2

Rajarshi Pal, Institute for Development and Research in Banking Technology (IDRBT)
Hyderabad, India

Selective visual attention is an amazing capability of primate visual system to restrict the focus to few interesting objects (or portions) in a scene. Thus, primates are able to pay attention to the required visual content amidst myriads of other visual information. It enables them to interact with the external environment in real time through reduction of computational load in their brain. This inspires image and computer vision scientists to derive computational models of visual attention and to use them in varieties of applications in real-life, mainly to speed up the processing through reduction of computational burden which often characterizes image processing and vision tasks. This chapter discusses a wide variety of such applications of visual attention models in image processing, computer vision and graphics.

Chapter 3

A rich stream of visual data enters the cameras of a typical artificial vision system (e.g., a robot) and considering the fact that processing this volume of data in real-rime is almost impossible, a clever mechanism is required to reduce the amount of trivial visual data. Visual Attention might be the solution. The idea is to control the information flow and thus to improve vision by focusing the resources merely on some special aspects instead of the whole visual scene. However, does attention only speed-up processing or can the understanding of human visual attention provide additional guidance for robot vision research? In this chapter, first, some basic concepts of the primate visual system and visual attention are introduced. Afterward, a new taxonomy of biologically-inspired models of attention, particularly those that are used in robotics applications (e.g., in object detection and recognition) is given and finally, future research trends in modelling of visual attention and its applications are highlighted.

Chapter 4

Scene understanding and object recognition heavily depend on the success of visual attention guided salient region detection in images and videos. Therefore, summarizing computer vision techniques that take the help of visual attention models to accomplish video object recognition and tracking, can be helpful to the researchers of computer vision community. In this chapter, it is aimed to present a philosophical overview of the possible applications of visual attention models in the context of object recognition and tracking. At the beginning of this chapter, a brief introduction to various visual saliency models suitable for object recognition is presented, that is followed by discussions on possible applications of attention models on video object tracking. The chapter also provides a commentary on the existing techniques available on this domain and discusses some of their possible extensions. It is believed that, prospective readers will benefit since the chapter comprehensively guides a reader to understand the pros and cons of this particular topic.

Chapter 5

Displaying a large image in a small screen of a handheld gadget is a challenging task. Simple down-scaling of the image may reduce some objects too small to be perceptible. This gives rise to content-aware retargeting of the image. Important contents are allotted more screen space as compared to relatively less important contents of the image. Various types of content-aware image retargeting approaches have been proposed in a span of just over a decade. Another challenging area is to estimate importance of importance of the contents. Lot of researches has been carried out in this direction too to identify the important contents in the context of image retargeting. Equally important aspect is evaluation of these retargeting methods. This article contains a brief survey of related research in all of these aspects.

Chapter 6

Adrita Barari, Defence Institute of Advanced Technology, India
Sunita V. Dhavale, Defence Institute of Advanced Technology, India

The aim of this chapter is to review the application of the technique of Visual cryptography in non-intrusive video watermarking. The power of saliency feature extraction is also highlighted in the context of Visual Cryptography based watermarking systems for videos. All schemes in literature related to Visual cryptography based video watermarking, have been brought together with special attention on the role of saliency feature extraction in each of these schemes. Further a novel approach for VC based video watermarking using motion vectors (MVP Algorithm) as a salient feature is suggested. Experimental results show the robustness of proposed MVP Algorithm against various video processing attacks. Also, compression scale invariance is achieved.

Chapter 7

Anwesha Sengupta, Indian Institute of Technology Kharagpur, India
Sibsambhu Kar, Samsung India Software Operations, India
Aurobinda Routray, Indian Institute of Technology Kharagpur, India

Electroencephalogram (EEG) is widely used to predict performance degradation of human subjects due to mental or physical fatigue. Lack of sleep or insufficient quality or quantity of sleep is one of the major reasons of fatigue. Analysis of fatigue due to sleep deprivation using EEG synchronization is a promising field of research. The present chapter analyses advancing levels of fatigue in human drivers in a sleep-deprivation experiment by studying the synchronization between EEG data. A Visibility Graph Similarity-based method has been employed to quantify the synchronization, which has been formulated in terms of a complex network. The change in the parameters of the network has been analyzed to find the variation of connectivity between brain areas and hence to trace the increase in fatigue levels of the subjects. The parameters of the brain network have been compared with those of a complex network with a random degree of connectivity to establish the small-world nature of the brain network.

Section 2
Other Computer Vision Applications

Chapter 8

Chaman L. Sabharwal, Missouri University of Science and Technology, USA
Jennifer L. Leopold, Missouri University of Science and Technology, USA

The intersection between 3D objects plays a prominent role in spatial reasoning, and computer vision. Detection of intersection between objects can be based on the triangulated boundaries of the objects, leading to computing triangle-triangle intersection. Traditionally there are separate algorithms for cross and coplanar intersection. For qualitative reasoning, intersection detection is sufficient, actual intersection is not necessary; in contrast, the precise intersection is required for geometric modeling. Herein we present a complete design and implementation of a single integrated algorithm independent of the type of intersection. Additionally, this algorithm first detects, then intersects and classifies the intersections using barycentric coordinates. This work is directly applicable to: (1) VRCC-3D+, which uses intersection detection between 3D objects as well as their 2D projections essential for occlusion detection; and (2) CAD/CAM geometric modeling where curves of intersection between a pair of surfaces are required for numerical control machines. Experimental results are provided.

Chapter 9

Kumar S. Ray, Indian Statistical Institute, India
Soma Ghosh, Indian Statistical Institute, India
Kingshuk Chatterjee, Indian Statistical Institute, India
Debayan Ganguly, Indian Statistical Institute, India

This chapter presents a multi-object tracking system using scale space representation of objects, the method of linear assignment and Kalman filter. In this chapter basically two very prominent problems of multi object tracking have been resolved; the two prominent problems are (i) irrespective of the size of the objects, tracking all the moving objects simultaneously and (ii) tracking of objects under partial and/or complete occlusion. The primary task of tracking multiple objects is performed by the method of linear assignment for which few cost parameters are computed depending upon the extracted features of moving objects in video scene. In the feature extraction phase scale space representation of objects have been used. Tracking of occluded objects is performed by Kalman filter.

Chapter 10

Ruchira Naskar, National Institute of Technology Rourkela, India
Pankaj Malviya, National Institute of Technology Rourkela, India
Rajat Subhra Chakraborty, Indian Institute of Technology Kharagpur, India

Digital forensics deal with cyber crime detection from digital multimedia data. In the present day, multimedia data such as images and videos are major sources of evidence in the courts of law worldwide. However, the immense proliferation and easy availability of low-cost or free, user-friendly and powerful image and video processing software, poses as the largest threat to today's digital world as well as the legal industry. This is due to the fact that such software allow efficient image and video editing, manipulation and synthesis, with a few mouse clicks even by a novice user. Such software also enable formation realistic of computer-generated images. In this chapter, we discuss different types of digital image forgeries and state-of-the-art digital forensic techniques to detect them. Through these discussions, we also give an idea of the challenges and open problems in the field of digital forensics.

Chapter 11

Ramesh Chand Pandey, Indian Institute of Technology (BHU), Varanasi, India
Sanjay Kumar Singh, Indian Institute of Technology (BHU), Varanasi, India
K. K. Shukla, Indian Institute of Technology (BHU), Varanasi, India

With increasing availability of low-cost video editing softwares and tools, the authenticity of digital video can no longer be trusted. Active video tampering detection technique utilize digital signature or digital watermark for the video tampering detection, but when the videos do not include such signature then it is very challenging to detect tampering in such video. To detect tampering in such video, passive video tampering detection techniques are required. In this chapter we have explained passive video tampering detection by using noise features. When video is captured with camera it passes through a Camera processing pipeline and this introduces noise in the video. Noise changes abruptly from authentic to forged frame blocks and provides a clue for video tampering detection. For extracting the noise we have considered different techniques like denoising algorithms, wavelet based denoising filter, and neighbor prediction.

Chapter 12

Y. L. Malathi Latha, Swami Vivekananda Institute of Technology (SVIT), India
Munaga V. N. K. Prasad, Institute for Development and Research in Banking Technology, India

The automatic use of physiological or behavioral characteristics to determine or verify identity of individual's is regarded as biometrics. Fingerprints, Iris, Voice, Face, and palmprints are considered as physiological biometrics whereas voice and signature are behavioral biometrics. Palmprint recognition is one of the popular methods which have been investigated over last fifteen years. Palmprint have very large internal surface and contain several unique stable characteristic features used to identify individuals. Several palmprint recognition methods have been extensively studied. This chapter is an attempt to review current palmprint research, describing image acquisition, preprocessing palmprint feature extraction and matching, palmprint related fusion and techniques used for real time palmprint identification in large databases. Various palmprint recognition methods are compared.

Chapter 13

Santosh Kumar, Indian Institute of Technology (BHU), Varanasi, India
Shubam Jaiswal, Indian Institute of Technology (BHU), Varanasi, India
Rahul Kumar, Indian Institute of Technology (BHU), Varanasi, India
Sanjay Kumar Singh, Indian Institute of Technology (BHU), Varanasi, India

Recognition of facial expression is a challenging problem for machine in comparison to human and it has encouraged numerous advanced machine learning algorithms. It is one of the methods for emotion recognition as the emotion of a particular person can be found out by studying his or her facial expressions. In this paper, we proposes a generic algorithms for recognition of emotions and illustrates a fundamental steps of the four algorithms such as Eigenfaces (Principal Component Analysis [PCA]), Fisherfaces, Local Binary Pattern Histogram (LBP) and SURF with FLANN over two databases Cohn-kanade database and IIT BHU student face images as benchmark database. The objective of this book chapter is to recognize the emotions from facial images of individuals and compare the performances of holistic algorithms like Eigenfaces, Fisherfaces, and texture based recognition algorithms LBPH, hybrid algorithm SURF and FLANN. Matching efficiency of individual emotions from facial expression databases are labeled for training and testing phases. The set of features is extracted from labeled dataset for training purpose and test images are matched with discriminative set of feature points. Based on that comparison, we conclude that Eigenfaces and Fisherfaces yields good recognition accuracy on the benchmark database than others and the efficiency of SURF with FLANN algorithm can be enhanced significantly by changing the parameters.

Chapter 14

This proposed work deals with the uses and techniques of 3D range images for facial expression recognition. A 3D range image is basically a depth image (also called a 2.5D image), which contains depth information at each (x, y) pixel of the image. In the future, computer vision will become a part of our everyday life because of all of its extensive applications. Hence, the interactions between users and computers need to be more natural, and emphasizing as well as enumerating human-to-human communication to a larger extent. That is the reason why facial expressions find importance. Facial expression is an important factor of communication, and they reveal unknown facts about a person's feelings and emotions. There comes the need of a real facial expression detection system. Also, changes in expression are of great importance for the interpretation of human facial behavior as well as face recognition.

Chapter 15

In recent times, enormous advancement in communication as well as hardware technologies makes the video communication very popular. With the increasing diversity among the end using media players and its associated network bandwidth, the requirement of video streams with respect to quality, resolution, frame rate becomes more heterogeneous. This increasing heterogeneity make the scalable adaptation of the video stream in the receiver end, a real problem. Scalable video coding (SVC) has been introduced as a countermeasure of this practical problem where the main video stream is designed in such a hierarchical fashion that a set of independent bit streams can be produced as per requirement of different end using devices. SVC becomes very popular in recent time and consequently, efficient and secure transmission of scalable video stream becomes a requirement. Watermarking is being considered as an efficient DRM tool for almost a decade. Although video watermarking is regarded as a well focused research domain, a very less attention has been paid on the scalable watermarking in recent times. In this book chapter, a comprehensive survey on the scalable video watermarking has been done. The main objective of this survey work is to analyse the robustness of the different existing video watermarking scheme against scalable video adaptation and try to define the research problems for the same. Firstly, few existing scalable image watermarking schemes are discussed to understand the advantages and limitations of the direct extension of such scheme for frame by frame video watermarking. Similarly few video watermarking and some recent scalable video watermarking are also narrated by specifying their pros and cons. Finally, a summary of this survey is presented by pointing out the possible countermeasure of the existing problems.

Chapter 16

This chapter proposes a watermarking technique using Ridgelet and Discrete Wavelet Transform (DWT) techniques. A wavelet transform is the wavelet function representation. A wavelet is a mathematical function which divides a continuous time signal into different scale components, where each scale components is assigned with a frequency range. Wavelets represent objects with point singularities, while ridgelets represents objects with line singularities. The Ridgelet transform Technique is a multi-scale representation for functions on continuous spaces that are smooth away from discontinuities along lines. The proposed technique applies Ridgelet transform on the cover image to obtain ridgelet coefficients. These coefficients are transformed by using 2-level DWT to get low frequency sub-bands – LL1 and LL2. The mutual similarities between LL1 and LL2 sub-bands are considered for embedding watermark. The obtained watermarked image has better quality when compared to a few exiting methods.

Preface

Last few decades have witnessed a tremendous growth of image processing and computer vision. Improvement in sensor technologies coupled with efficient and effective algorithm development for image processing and computer vision has led to wide-spread usage of images and videos in several areas. It ranges from secret sharing through visual cryptography to surveillance and robotics. These later two require real-time intelligence to analyze surrounding images. Even image based technologies have been in use in sensitive domain like banking. For example, image based cheque clearing in banking system has emerged as a new phenomenon. So integrity of images has become a concern. In fact, it is not possible to codify all possible aspects of image processing and computer vision theories and their applications within a single book.

This edited book puts an effort to hold few of the application areas of image processing and computer vision. Many of these applications are benefited by theories from a psycho-visual phenomenon, called selective visual attention. Visual attention is a psycho-visual mechanism through which primates select only a few of the incoming sensory inputs for deeper analysis and recognition in brain. Though primate brains are very efficient, they cannot process the entire spectrum of sensory information in real-time. In order to carry out real-time interaction with external surrounding, primates pay attention to only selected stimuli, discarding myriads of other inputs. Which portions in a visual scene they focus has become a research problem. It has been observed that primate vision is guided by two kinds of attention mechanism – bottom-up and top-down. Bottom-up mechanism is purely stimulus driven. For example, a bright color tends to attract our vision. Top-down mechanism is a task-driven approach. This is guided by the task which an individual is performing.

Computer vision tasks also feel the burden of processing a bulk amount of image or video data. The capability of primates in efficiently dealing with dynamic surrounding through selective attention mechanism motivates computer vision researchers to develop efficient computer vision systems. They emulate this attention mechanism of primate vision to find out portions of importance in the visual scene. Processing based on only these selected portions in the scene increases speed as well as quality of outcome.

Beside these attention guided applications, many other interesting research areas in computer vision and image processing have also been presented in this book. Thus, this book is a compilation of research efforts in a wide spectrum of areas. Alongside highlighting usefulness of visual attention models in image processing and computer vision, this book sets up a platform of cross-disciplinary exchange of knowledge. Hopefully, these discussions will further open up new research directions.

This book contains few survey articles which give a good overview of the research that have been or still being carried out in some of these fields. Putting a good amount of existing research outcomes under one umbrella, these chapters are able to spot the lacunas which are still present there. Few new techniques have also been proposed in some of the chapters of this book to bring forward recent innovations.

This book has been divided into two sections. The first section, which consists of seven chapters (Chapter 1 to Chapter 7), speaks about visual attention models and how various applications in computer vision and image processing benefit from these visual attention models. The second section of this book (Chapter 8 to Chapter 16) discusses numerous other techniques in computer vision and image processing.

Chapter 1 discusses the conceptual theories related to visual attention mechanism. Then, it discusses various visual attention models. Both 2D and 3D models of visual attention have been presented. Chapter 2 highlights the usefulness of visual attention in image processing, computer vision and graphics through a thorough listing of applications which are benefited from theories of visual attention. Chapter 3 to Chapter 8, then, discusses few of these application areas in details. Chapter 3 sketches how attention is an important topic for robotic vision. A review on biologically-inspired models of attentive robot vision is presented in this chapter. Visual attention guided object detection and tracking has been discussed in Chapter 4. Chapter 5 is a compilation of phenomenal research efforts in the area of content-aware (based on identification of attentive regions) image retargeting. Image retargeting is useful in fitting an image of sufficiently high resolution in relatively small displays. Chapter 6 showcases the power of saliency for visual cryptography based watermarking. It proposes a novel visual cryptography based watermarking scheme using motion vector as a salient feature. Chapter 7 reports an electroencephalogram (EEG) based study of loss of alertness and fatigue of a driver using a visibility graph synchronization approach.

The second section (Chapter 8 to Chapter 16) of this book suggests that there are lot more in image processing and computer vision which do not intersect with visual attention theories. Chapter 8 describes a generic implementation for triangle-triangle intersection and its applications. Chapter 9 explains how some of the important problems in multi-object tracking can be tackled using scale-space representation of the objects, the method of linear assignment and Kalman filter. Chapter 10 discusses state-of-the-art research in digital image forensics and highlights few of the research challenges which must draw importance from research community. Chapter 11 discusses how noise feature can be used for video tampering detection. Chapter 12 provides an overview of existing palmprint based biometric recognition systems. Chapter 13 discusses techniques of emotion recognition from facial expressions. A novel technique of recognizing expression faces is proposed in Chapter 14 using 3D range images. Chapter 15 provides a survey of research in the area of scalable video watermarking. Chapter 16 proposes a technique of image watermarking based on fractal image coding.

Section 1
Visual Attention Modeling and Applications

Chapter 1
2D and 3D Visual Attention for Computer Vision:
Concepts, Measurement, and Modeling

Vincent Ricordel
University of Nantes, France

Matthieu Perreira Da Silva
University of Nantes, France

Junle Wang
University of Nantes, France

Patrick Le Callet
University of Nantes, France

ABSTRACT

Visual attention is one of the most important mechanisms deployed in the human visual system (HVS) to reduce the amount of information that our brain needs to process. An increasing amount of efforts has been dedicated to the study of visual attention, and this chapter proposes to clarify the advances achieved in computational modeling of visual attention. First the concepts of visual attention, including the links between visual salience and visual importance, are detailed. The main characteristics of the HVS involved in the process of visual perception are also explained. Next we focus on eye-tracking, because of its role in the evaluation of the performance of the models. A complete state of the art in computational modeling of visual attention is then presented. The research works that extend some visual attention models to 3D by taking into account of the impact of depth perception are finally explained and compared.

INTRODUCTION

In everyday life, we are constantly receiving an abundant amount of information through various senses. Among the senses, sight is considered to be the most dominant one (Wandell, 1995). However, our sensory system for vision, the human visual system (HVS), continually receives a really large amount of visual data and it is beyond our brain's capability to process all of them (Borji & Itti, 2013). To cope with this large amount of information, visual attention is one of the most important mechanisms deployed in the HVS to reduce the complexity of the analysis of visual scene (Wolfe, 2000). Driven by visual attention, viewers can selectively focus their attention on specific areas of interest in the scene.

DOI: 10.4018/978-1-4666-8723-3.ch001

In the last decades, extensive efforts have been dedicated to the study of visual attention. Neurologists, psychologists, vision scientists, and computer scientists have taken part in, and contributed to various aspects of visual attention. These efforts from different disciplines made the research on visual attention become a highly interdisciplinary field; different relevant disciplines deal with the research on visual attention from different points of view, and profit from each other.

In recent years, the use of visual attention mechanisms in image processing systems has found increasing interest by computer scientists. Taking into account visual attention information becomes an effective way for improving various existing algorithms in image processing. A variety of areas, including compression (Parkhurst, Law, & Niebur, 2002), retargeting (D. Wang, Li, Jia, & Luo, 2011), image retrieval (Vu, Hua, & Tavanapong, 2003), quality assessment (H. Liu & Heynderickx, 2011), have been benefiting of being provided information about the locations that attracts viewer's attention in the visual scene.

When visual attention is taken into account by the signal-processing community, the two terms, "salience" and "importance", have traditionally been considered synonymous. It is true that both of visual salience and visual importance denote the most visually "relevant" parts of the scene. However, from the vision scientist's point of view, they are two different concepts, since they come from two different mechanisms of visual attention: bottom-up and top-down. The two mechanisms are driven by different types of stimuli, and are formed in different visual pathways that go through different areas of the brain. Therefore, it would be worth identifying the two terms in the context of image processing.

In recent years, another problem faced by researchers in the field of visual attention is the impact of 3D. During the viewing of 3D content, depth perception of the scene is enhanced. This change of depth perception also largely changes human viewing behavior (Hakkinen, Kawai, Takatalo, Mitsuya, & Nyman, 2010; Huynh-Thu, Barkowsky, Le Callet, & others, 2011). Because of the emergence of 3D content and recent availability of 3D-capable display equipments, studies related to 3D visual attention have been gaining an increasing amount of attention in the last few years.

In this chapter we propose to clarify the last advancements in computational modeling of visual attention.

The first section details the concepts of visual attention including the latest research results linking visual salience and visual importance. The main characteristics of the human visual system involved in the process of visual perception are explained in section 2. Because of their substantial role in the evaluation of the performances of the models, eye-tracking systems are presented in section 3. A complete state of the art in computational modeling of visual attention is then presented in section 4. The research works that extend some visual attention models to 3D by taking into account of the impact of depth perception are finally explained in section 5.

1. VISUAL ATTENTION

It would be difficult to go directly into specific studies without a general introduction of some background knowledge on visual attention. So in this section, we first introduce concepts of visual attention as well as various mechanisms of attention. Secondly, we present a brief introduction of the HVS and of different types of eye movements as well as the technique for measuring eye movements, i.e. eye-tracking. Finally, we introduce some typical state-of-the-art computational models of visual attention.

The oldest and most famous definition of attention, which is provided by the psychologist William James (James, Burkhardt, & Skrupskelis, 1980), dates back to year 1890: "Everyone knows what attention is. It is the taking possession by the mind, in clear and vivid form, of one out of what seem several simultaneously possible objects or trains of thought. Focalization, concentration, consciousness are of its essence. It implies withdrawal from some things in order to deal effectively with others".

In the HVS, attention plays an important role in visual processing by keeping only the essential visual information. Tsotsos et al. (1995) proposed that visual attention is a mechanism having at least the following basic components:

1. The selection of a region of interest in the visual field;
2. The selection of feature dimensions and values of interest;
3. The control of information flow through the network of neurons that constitutes the visual system; and
4. The shifting from one selected region to the next in time. Driven by visual attention, viewers can therefore selectively focus their attention on specific areas of interest in the scene.

1.1 Overt Attention and Covert Attention

There are two types of attention, namely overt attention and covert attention. These two types of attention are differentiated based on their relation with eye movements.

Overt attention is usually associated with eye movements. This type of attention is easy to observe: when we focus our attention to an object, our eyes move to fixate this object. One of the earliest studies of overt attention came from Yarbus (1967). In particular, he studied the correlation between visual attention and eye movements during the viewing of human faces.

In addition to overt attention, William James et al. (1980) found that human are able to attend to peripheral locations of interest without moving the eyes; this type of attention is named as covert attention. An advantage of covert attention is its independence to motor commands (Frintrop, 2006). Since the eyes do not need to be moved to focus attention on a certain region, covert attention is much faster as compared to overt attention. An example of covert attention is driving, where a driver keeps his eyes on the road while simultaneously covertly monitoring the status of signs and lights (Borji & Itti, 2013).

Overt attention and covert attention are not independent. Humans cannot attend to one location while moving their eyes to a different location (Deubel & Schneider, 1996). The covert shift of attention to a location is linked to eye movement by setting up a saccade to that location (Peterson, Kramer, & Irwin, 2004).

Most of current studies, especially the studies of computational modeling of visual attention, are with respect to overt attention, since overt attention can be measured in a straightforward way by using eye-tracking. However, it is difficult to measure covert attention. A computational framework for covert attention is also still lacking.

1.2 Bottom-Up Attention and Top-Down Attention

A shift of attention can be caused by two categories of cues: one is referred to as bottom-up cue, and the other one is referred to as top-down cue.

Bottom-up attention is driven by the characteristics of a visual scene, i.e. the bottom-up cues. Bottom-up attention is hence also referred to as stimulus-driven attention or exogenous attention. Bottom-up attention is fast, involuntary, and most likely feed-forward (Borji & Itti, 2013). Since bottom-up attention is usually driven by low-level features (e.g. intensity, color, and orientation), in order to attract human's bottom-up attention, an area must be sufficiently distinctive compared to the surrounding area with respect to these low-level visual features.

On the other hand, top-down attention is based on "higher level" information, such as knowledge, expectations and current goals (Desimone & Duncan, 1995). Top-down attention is thus also referred to as concept-driven attention, goal-driven or endogenous attention. As compared to bottom-up attention, top-down attention is slow, voluntary and driven by the task demands. A famous illustration of top-down attention comes from Yarbus's work in 1967 (Yarbus, 1967). He demonstrated how eye movements varied depending on the question asked during the observation of the same scene (see Figure 1).

1.3 The Feature Integration Theory

One of the best-known and most accepted theories of visual attention is the "Feature Integration Theory", which was proposed by Treisman and Gelade (1980). This theory has been the basis of many computational models of visual attention.

Figure 1. An example that eye movements depend on observer's viewing task
(Yarbus, 1967). (Image from Lucs-kho at en.wikipedia [Public domain] via Wikimedia Commons.).

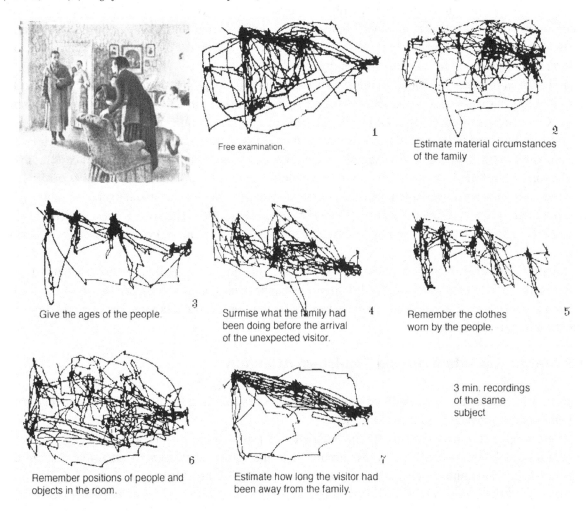

Treisman and Gelade (1980) claimed that "different features are registered early, automatically and in parallel across the visual field, while objects are identified separately and only at a later stage, which requires focused attention". According to the Feature Integration Theory (FIT), the different features of stimuli are firstly encoded in areas partially independent. In addition, our hierarchical cortical structures are organized in order to make the detection of these features relatively independently of their positions in the visual scene.

The FIT introduced a concept of "feature maps", which are topographical maps that highlight salience according to the respective feature. Information of the feature maps is then collected in a "master map of location". This map indicates the location of the objects, but does not provide information about what the objects are.

Finally, to construct a coherent representation of the scene, selective attention is used. The scene is scanned by an attentional beam of variable size (see Figure 2). This beam blocks the information that is not located within its radius. It is thus possible to match all the features found in this area in order to build a coherent representation. By moving the beam over time, our brain gradually constructs a global perception of the scene.

1.4 Linking Visual Salience and Visual Importance

Visual salience (Koch & Ullman, 1987; Itti, Koch, & Niebur, 1998) and visual importance (Osberger & Maeder, 1998; Maeder, 1995; Etz & Luo, 2000; Kadiyala, Pinneli, Larson, & Chandler, 2008) come

Figure 2. Illustration of the Feature Integration Theory
(Perreira Da Silva, 2010).

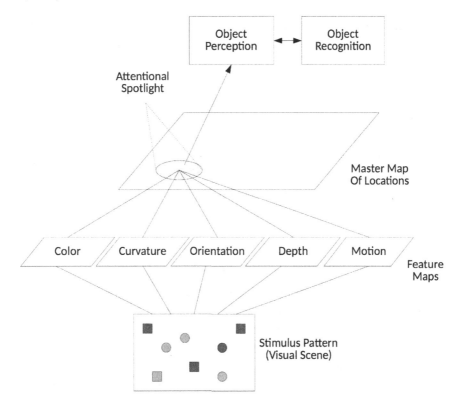

from the two different mechanisms of visual attention, the bottom-up mechanism and the top-down mechanism, respectively. Both visual salience and visual importance can provide important insights into how the human visual system addresses the image-analysis problem. Both of them are also believed to denote the most visually "relevant" parts of the scene. However, despite the differences in the way (bottom-up) visual salience and (top-down) visual importance are determined in terms of human visual processing, both salience and importance have traditionally been considered synonymous in the signal-processing community.

Experimental Study

A study measuring the similarities and differences between visual salience and visual importance has been conducted. We present the results of these two psychophysical experiments and the associated computational analyses designed to quantify the relationship (and its evolution over time) between visual salience and visual importance:

- A first experiment was performed to obtain visual importance maps for a large database of images. A visual importance map is an object-level map that specifies the visual importance of each object in an image relative to the other objects in the image (including what would normally be considered as the background). The object(s) that receive(s) the greatest visual importance is/are traditionally considered as the image's main subject. By using images from the Berkeley Image Segmentation Dataset, importance ratings were collected for each object in the 300 database images. Such importance ratings are generally believed to result from top-down visual processing, since the decisions used to rate each object typically involve scene interpretation, object recognition, and often consideration of artistic intent.

- In a second experiment, visual gaze patterns were measured for 80 of the images from the same Berkeley Image Segmentation Dataset. Using an eye-tracker, visual gaze locations were recorded under task-free viewing. Whereas importance maps are driven primarily by top-down processing, visual gaze patterns are generally believed to be driven by bottom-up, signal-based attributes, at least for early gaze locations. Bottom-up saliency (Koch & Ullman, 1987) is one particular signal-based attribute, which has been shown to correlate well with early gaze locations. An image region is considered visually salient if it "stands out" from its background in terms of one or more attributes (e.g., contrast, color, orientation). When visual gaze patterns are measured in task-free viewing, one can consider the locations to denote the salient regions in the image. Thus, from the gaze patterns, one can construct an experimental saliency map.

Results and Analysis

Qualitative Observations of Importance Maps and Saliency Maps

A qualitative comparison of the saliency maps and importance maps reveals some distinct similarities and differences between the two. Figure 3 depicts some representative examples.

First of all, one can notice that both importance maps and saliency maps are centrally biased, because source content is itself centrally biased by the photographer (the region of interest typically tends to be in the center of the photos that people take).

Figure 3. Representative results from the experiments

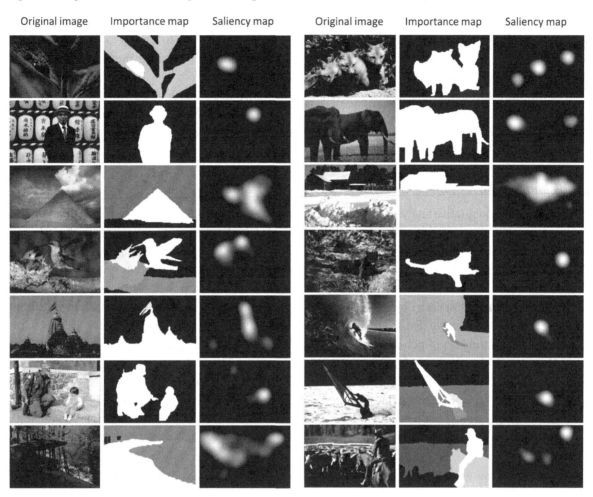

Tatler (2007) has proposed a method to correct data in very specific cases by using a centrally biased sampling distribution (from fixations from same observers of other images) when sampling non-fixated points for ROC computation. This helps evaluating the real values of a saliency prediction model without the effect of central bias. In our case, this method in not applicable since we don't evaluate the performance of a visual attention prediction model, but we compare using a fair approach, visual salience (namely here, salience and central bias) and visual importance maps.

The importance maps suggest that object category plays a bigger role than most other factors in determining subjective importance. In general, we found that observers tended to rate objects containing human faces and/or animals (for instance, consider in Figure 3, the image at the left second line, or the one at the right first line) to be of greatest importance. Background objects such as sky and grass were generally rated to be of least importance (for instance, consider in Figure 3, the image at the left 5th line, or the one at the right 4th line). Occlusion, whether an object is in the foreground vs. the background (for instance, consider in Figure 3, the image at the right 7th line), also seems to be an important factor for perceived importance.

The saliency maps generally suggest that regions that possess a distinguished shape, color, contrast, or other local spatial features attract attention. However, observers always gazed upon the image's main subject(s): Gaze position samples tended to occur on objects which belong to animal faces, human faces, or other subjects, which represent the region of interest in the image. The background, such as sky and ground, always attracted the least attention.

Yet, despite these similarities, the saliency maps and importance maps do not always agree. Although we employed a relatively long viewing period, the saliency maps never yielded an object-level segregation that is enforced in the importance maps. For example, whenever a face occurred in an image, whether an animal face or a human face, the observers' gaze positions always occurred on the face.

Predicting the Main Subject, Secondary Subject, and the Background

The results of the qualitative analysis suggest a relationship between saliency maps and importance maps. One way to quantify this relationship is to attempt to predict the importance maps from the saliency maps using the object-level segmentations as side-information. To predict the importance maps from the saliency maps (given the segmentations), the following two approaches were tested:

1. **Mean Saliency:** For each object, we summed those values of the saliency map that occurred within the object, and then we divided this value by the total number of pixels in the object. For each image, the resulting set of per-object saliency values was then normalized to span the range [0, 1].
2. **Coverage Saliency:** For each object, we summed those values of the saliency map which occurred within the object, and then we divided this value by the number of pixels in the object that were gazed upon (specifically, the number of pixels that were covered by the fovea). For each image, the resulting set of per-object coverage saliency values was then normalized to span the range [0, 1].

To facilitate the prediction, each importance map was quantized into three classes based on the importance values:

- **Main Subject:** Consisted of objects that received an importance value ranging from 2/3 to 1;
- **Secondary Subject:** Consisted of objects that received an importance value ranging from 1/3 to 2/3;
- **Background:** Consisted of objects that received an importance value ranging from 0 to 1/3.

The results of the prediction by the two approaches, namely Mean Saliency and Coverage Saliency are provided in Table 1 and Table 2, respectively. The prediction accuracy is presented in the form of confusion matrices. Each row of each matrix represents the actual (importance) class, and each column represents the predicted class. An ideal prediction would yield a diagonal matrix with 100% values, which means that all the objects belonging to each actual class are successfully predicted. As shown in Table 1, Mean Saliency can successfully predict the main subject 80.5% of the time. In other words, 80.5% of the objects predicted as main subject are really the main subject of the scene; so 19.5% of the objects predicted as main subject actually belong to secondary subject or background. Similarly, the background is successfully predicted approximately 47% of the time. We also found that, Coverage Saliency (shown in Table 2) yields lower prediction accuracy for main subject, but slightly higher accuracy for background.

Table 1. Confusion matrices for predicting each subject's importance from gaze data, and using the Mean Saliency approach

		Predicted		
		Main Subject	Secondary Subject	Background
Actual	**Main Subject**	**80.5%**	29.8%	12.6%
	Secondary Subject	12.5%	**42.6%**	40.7%
	Background	7.1%	27.6%	**46.7%**

Table 2. Confusion matrices for predicting each subject's importance from gaze data, and using the Coverage Saliency approach

		Predicted		
		Main Subject	Secondary Subject	Background
Actual	**Main Subject**	**56.5%**	38.6%	8.2%
	Secondary Subject	13.0%	**40.4%**	24.7%
	Background	30.5%	21.1%	**67.1%**

Temporal Analysis

During normal viewing, because visual attention shifts from one object to another, the number of gaze position samples that occur on each subject varies over time. For each of the three levels of importance (main subject, secondary subject, background), we analyzed this time dependence. Specifically, we computed the number of gaze position samples per importance class which occurred within each 100-ms interval during the 15-second viewing time. The resulting three time curves, summed across all observers, are shown in Figure 4.

Figure 4. Total number of gaze position samples in (a) main subjects, (b) secondary subjects, and (c) background computed in each 100-ms interval of the 15-second viewing time; note that the scale for the vertical axis in the first graph is 10x that of the other two graphs.

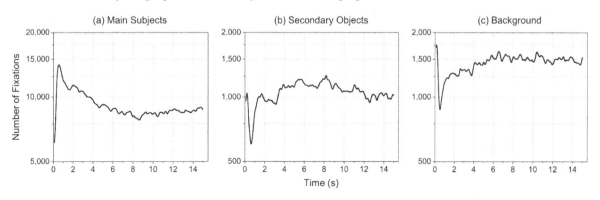

The plots in Figure 4 clearly indicate that, on average, subjects from different importance classes attract considerably different amounts of visual attention. Specifically, throughout the 15-second viewing time, the main subject always received the greatest number of gaze position samples, approximately 7-8 times greater than the number of samples for secondary subject and background.

Within 0-500 ms, the number of gaze position samples for the main subject (see Figure 4 (a)) was already 4-6 times greater than the number of samples for secondary subject (see Figure 4 (b)) and background (see Figure 4 (c)). This observation suggests bottom-up mechanisms can be effective at locating the main subject in these images; this might result from the fact that photographers tend to increase the saliency of the main subject via retouching, selective focusing, or other photographic techniques. Between 500-2000 ms, there was a pronounced increase in the number of gaze position samples for the main subject (see Figure 4 (a)), while the number for the other two importance classes decreased in this period (see Figures 4 (b) and (c)). These changes potentially indicate the influence of top-down mechanisms that might force observers to attend to the main subject. After this process, the number of gaze position samples for the main subject slightly decreased, and those for the other two classes slightly increased. This latter change may imply that the observers attempt to explore the whole image, but their attention is still held by the main subject.

These three time curves suggest that the relationship between visual salience and visual importance may be time dependent. In particular, the fact that the main subject attracts the most attention within 0-2000ms suggests that these early gaze position samples might be a better predictor of visual importance for the main subject than previously achieved using all samples. Accordingly, we predicted the importance maps by using the samples taken from only the first 0-2000ms. Table 3 lists the resulting confusion matrix computed (using Mean Saliency approach) based on gaze data of the first 2 seconds. Figure 5 depicts representative importance maps predicted from the data taken from all 15 seconds (see in Figure 5 the maps of the 3rd column) and from only the first two seconds (see in Figure 5 the maps of the 4th column). By using only these early gaze data, better prediction is achieved for the main subject.

This section presented the results of two psychophysical experiments and an associated computational analysis designed to quantify the relationship between visual salience (namely here, visual salience and central bias) and visual importance. We found that saliency maps and importance maps are related, but perhaps less than one might expect. The saliency maps were shown to be effective at predicting the main subjects. However, the saliency maps were less effective at predicting the subject of secondary importance and the unimportant one. We also found that the vast majority of early gaze position samples (0-2000 ms) were made on the main subject. This suggests that a possible strategy of the human visual system is to quickly locate the main subject in the scene.

Table 3. Confusion matrix (using Mean Saliency approach) for predicting importance from the first 2 seconds of gaze samples

		Predicted		
		Main Subject	**Secondary Subject**	**Background**
	Main Subject	**89.0%**	43.5%	12.4%
Actual	**Secondary Subject**	3.3%	**43.5%**	27.2%
	Background	7.7%	13.0%	**60.5%**

Figure 5. Representative results of using all gaze samples vs. only those from the first two seconds to predict the importance maps

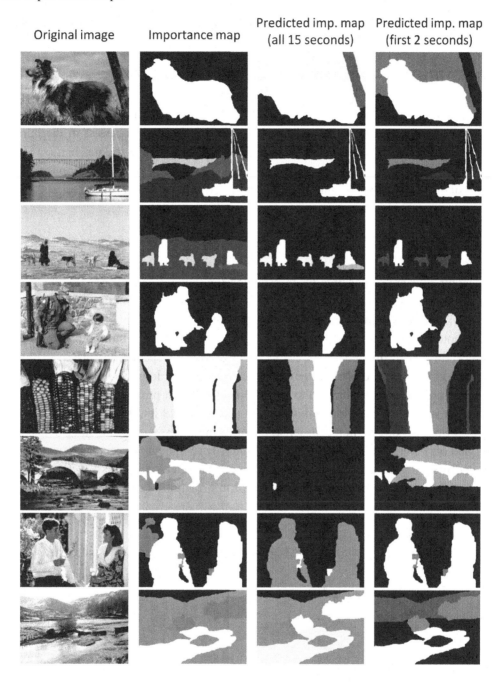

The implications of the findings presented in this chapter are quite important for image processing. Several algorithms have been published which can successfully predict gaze patterns, e.g. (Itti et al., 1998; Le Meur, Le Callet, Barba, & Thoreau, 2006). These results suggest that these predicted patterns can be used to predict importance maps when coupled with a segmentation scheme. In turn, the importance maps can then be used to perform importance-based processing such as auto-cropping, enhancement, compression, unequal error protection, and quality assessment.

Removing the central bias in the analysis of the relationship between visual salience and visual importance is not a simple task, and it was not done in this initial work (J. Wang, Chandler, & Le Callet, 2010) on which this part of this chapter is based. This issue is for the moment left for further investigations.

2. VISUAL ATTENTION AND THE HUMAN VISUAL SYSTEM

Since visual attention is a mechanism involved in the process of visual perception, it is of importance to introduce also the knowledge regarding how visual information is processed in the human visual system. While being far from an exhaustive explanation of the HVS and the mechanisms involved in the processing of visual information, we briefly present in this section an introduction of the retina and different areas of the visual cortex (Figure 6) that allow determining the main characteristics of the HVS.

2.1 The Retina

The retina is a light-sensitive surface, which has over 100 million photoreceptor cells (Mather, 2009). The photoreceptor cells are responsible for transducing light energy into neural signals. Note that the retina is not of uniform spatial resolution. The density of photoreceptor cells is higher at the center, which enables vision to be more accurate at the center (i.e. the fovea) than at the periphery. There are two types of photoreceptor cells: rods and cones, which are sensitive to light and color, respectively. Cone photoreceptors can be divided into three classes based on their spectral sensitivity: "Blue" or short wavelength (S); "Green" or medium wavelength (M); and "Red" or long wavelength (L).

The photoreceptor cells are connected to Ganglion cells, which provide the output signal from the retina. The receptive field of ganglion cell is circular and separated into two areas: a center area and a surround area. Two types of ganglion cells exist: the on-center cells, which respond excitatorily to light at the center and off-center cells, which respond inhibitorily to light at the center (Frintrop, 2006). The center area and the surround area always have opposite characteristics. This is why center-surround filtering is used as a mechanism for processing visual information in many computational models of visual attention.

Figure 6. The human visual system: from the retina to different areas of the visual cortex
Adapted from Kandel et al. (2000).

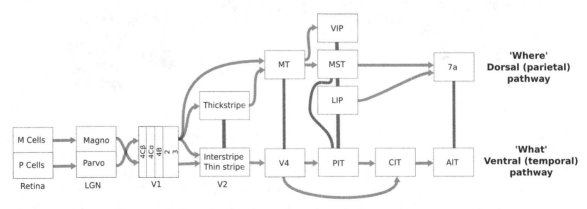

2.2 Visual Pathway

From the retina the optic nerve transmits visual information to the optic chiasm. From the optic chiasm, two visual pathways go to different areas of brain (see Figure 6). In primates, the majority (approximately 90%) of the visual information is transmitted by the retino-geniculate pathway to the Lateral Geniculate Nuclei (LGN); the remaining 10% goes to the superior colliculi. LGN cell fibers then transmit visual information to the cortical receiving area for vision, known as primary visual cortex or V1, which is located at the very back of the brain. From the primary visual cortex, the visual information is sent to higher brain areas, namely extrastriate cortex. The extrastriate cortex includes: V2, V3, V4, the infero-temporal cortex, the middle temporal area and the posterior-parietal cortex (Frintrop, 2006).

There is evidence that the connections between extrastriate areas segregate into two pathways after area V2: a ventral path way and a dorsal pathway. The dorsal pathway, which concerns the motion and depth information, runs via V3 to the middle temporal area (MT), then to the medial superior temporal area (MST) and the parieto occipale area (PO) and finally to the posterior-parietal cortex (PP). The dorsal pathway is also named as the "where pathway", since it mainly deals with the question of "where" something is in a scene. The ventral pathway, which processes color and form information, runs to V4 and finally in infero-temporal cortex (IT). Since the area IT responds to the recognition of objects, this pathway is also named as the "what pathway".

2.3 Attentional Mechanisms in the Brain

So far, it is believed that visual attention is not guided by any single brain area. Several areas have been found to be involved in the attentional process, but the accurate task and behavior of each area, as well as the interplay among these areas, still remain an open questions (Frintrop, 2006). Nevertheless, several findings have been claimed. It was proposed that the posterior-parietal cortex responds to disengaging the focus of attention from its present location (inhibition of return); the superior colliculus (SC) is responsible for shifting the attention to a new location (Posner & Petersen, 1990). The Frontal Eye Field area of the prefrontal cortex is found to be involved in guiding the eye movements. Additionally, this area is also the place where a kind of saliency map is located, which is affected by both bottom-up and top-down information (Bichot, 2001).

3. EYE MOVEMENTS AND EYE-TRACKING

Eye tracking is a technique which records the eye movements so that researchers can obtain precise information about

1. Where an observer is looking at any given time, and
2. The sequence in which his eyes are shifting from one location to another.

Eye tracking plays a substantial role in the research of psychology, biology, computer vision, and especially the computational modeling of visual attention. Given the strong link between overt visual attention and eye movements (Itti & Koch, 2001; Wolfe & Horowitz, 2004), eye movements data collected by means of eye tracking experiment are used as the ground truth to evaluate the performance of computational models.

3.1 Measures of Eye-Movements

Just and Carpenter (1976) assumed that what a person is looking at indicates what is at the "top of the stack" in cognitive processes. This "eye-mind" hypothesis implies that the eye movements provide a trace about where a person's (overt) attention is being directed. There exist various types of eye movements. Two basic ones are "fixation" and "saccade". From these two basic eye movements, another measurement, "scanpath", is stemmed. Moreover, pupil size and blink rate are also two types of eye movements usually studied. Introduction of each type of eye movement as well as metrics based on these basic types of eye movement are presented below.

Fixations

A fixation means that the visual gaze is approximately stationary on a single location. Fixations last for 218 milliseconds on average, with a range of 66 to 416 milliseconds (Poole & Ball, 2006). Based on fixations, several metrics can be derived:

- **Fixations per Area of Interest:** Experiments show that more fixations on a particular area indicate a greater interest or importance of a target (J. Wang, Chandler, & Le Callet, 2010). And it may also mean that the target is complex in some way and difficult to encode (Just & Carpenter, 1976). Jacob and Karn (2003) suggest that, in a search task, a higher number of fixations often means a greater uncertainty in recognizing a target item.
- **Fixations Duration:** A longer fixation can be interpreted in two ways, it may imply that information is difficult to extract, or the object is more engaging in some way (Just & Carpenter, 1976).
- **Fixation Spatial Distribution:** Cowen et al. (2002) suggested that highly concentrated fixations in a small area mean a focused and efficient searching, and evenly spread fixations indicate a widespread and inefficient searching. It was also found that if an object contains an area with highly concentrated fixations, the object tends to be considered as of high importance (J. Wang et al., 2010).
- **Repeat Fixations or "Post-Target Fixations":** A higher number of off-target fixations after the target has been fixated (i.e., a lower number of repeat fixations) means that the target lacks meaningfulness or visibility (Goldberg & Kotval, 1999).
- **Time to First Fixation On-Target:** A shorter time to first-fixation on an object or area indicates that the object or area has better attention-getting properties (Byrne, Anderson, Douglass, & Matessa, 1999).

Note that in the studies of computational modeling of visual attention, fixation spatial density is the metric mostly used, by means of computing a so-called "fixation density map".

Saccades

Saccades are those quick, simultaneous movements of both eyes in the same direction (Cassin, Solomon, & Rubin, 1990). They are fast movements of eyes occurring between fixations. It is generally believed that no encoding takes place in the human visual system during saccades, so vision is suppressed and it is difficult for us to get any clues about the complexity or salience of an object from the saccades. However, information about visual perception can be still extracted from several saccade metrics:

- **Number of Saccades:** A larger number of saccades indicates that more searching takes place during the observation (Goldberg & Kotval, 1999).
- **Saccade Amplitude:** Saccade amplitude is computed by measuring the distance between one saccade's start point (a fixation) and its end point (another fixation). Larger amplitude indicates the existence of more meaningful cues, since the attention is drawn from a distance (Goldberg, Stimson, Lewenstein, Scott, & Wichansky, 2002).

Scanpaths

Scanpath is a metric derived from the measurement of both fixations and saccades. A scanpath means a complete saccade-fixate-saccade sequence. The area covered by scanpath indicates the area observed. A longer scanpath means a less efficient searching (Goldberg et al., 2002). Additionally, we can compare the time spent for searching (saccades) to the time spent for processing (fixation) in a scanpath. A higher saccade/fixation ratio means more searching or less processing.

Blink Rate and Pupil Size

The blinking of eyes and the variation of pupil size are two eye movements that could also be recorded during eye tracking experiments. They can be considered as a cue that indicates cognitive workload. A lower blink rate is assumed to indicate a higher cognitive workload (Bruneau, Sasse, & McCarthy, 2002), and a higher blink rate may indicate visual fatigue (Brookings, Wilson, & Swain, 1996). The changing of pupil size also indicates some kinds of cognitive effort (Marshall, 2000). However, the blink rate and the pupil size can be easily affected by many factors during the observation, e.g. the luminance of environment. Due to this reason, blink rate and pupil size are not widely used in the researches related to visual attention.

3.2 Eye-Tracking

Eye tracking is a technique which records eye movements so that the researchers can obtain precise information about

1. Where an observer is looking at any given time, and
2. The sequence in which his eyes are shifting from one location to another.

Eye tracking has thus been deployed in a variety of disciplines to capture and analyze overt visual attention of human observers, including neuroscience, psychology, medicine, human factors, marketing, and computer science (Duchowski, 2002).

The common goal amongst all these disciplines is to capture human viewing behavior when performing specific visual tasks in a given context. For instance, in marketing research it is of interest to determine what products customers attend to in order to maximize profit (Wedel & Pieters, 2007). In medical research it is of interest to identify the search patterns of radiologists when investigating mammograms for improved breast cancer detection (Wedel & Pieters, 2007). In image and video quality assessment, taking into account the attention of viewers to artifacts may lead to enhanced quality prediction models (Engelke, Kaprykowsky, Zepernick, & Ndjiki-Nya, 2011). In the context of computational modeling of visual attention, eye-tracking results are usually post-processed into scanpaths or so-called fixation density maps (FDM), which are considered to be a reliable ground truth for developing computational models of visual attention.

Background of Eye Tracking Technique

The technology of eye tracking appeared more than 100 years ago in reading research (Rayner, Pollatsek, Ashby & Clifton, 2012). Since, different techniques have been applied to eye tracking. For instance, the "electro-oculographic techniques" needs to put electrodes on the skin around the eye so that eye movements can be detected by measuring the differences in electric potential. Some other methods rely on wearing large contact lenses. The lenses cover the cornea (the transparent front part of the eye) and sclera (the white part of the eye), while a metal coil is embedded around the lens so it moves along with the eye. The eye movements can thus be measured by fluctuations in an electromagnetic field when the eye is moving (Duchowski, 2007). However, these historical methods affect observers' eye-movement and are inconvenient to implement.

Video-based techniques are used by modern eye-trackers to determine where a person is looking at (i.e., the so-called "gaze point" or "point-of-regard"). These eye-trackers achieve the detection of point-of-regard based on the eye's features extracted from video images of the eye, such as corneal reflections (i.e. Purkinje images), iris-sclera boundary, and the apparent pupil shape (Poole & Ball, 2006; Duchowski, 2007).

Most state-of-the-art commercial eye trackers use the "corneal-reflection/pupil-centre" method to measure the point-of-regard. The corneal reflection is also known as (first) Purkinje image. During the eye-tracking recording, a camera focuses on one or both eyes to get images. Contrast is then used to get the location of the pupil, and infrared light is used to create a corneal reflection. By measuring the movements of corneal reflection relative to the pupil, it is then possible to know the head movement, eye rotation, the direction of gaze and consequently the point-of-regard.

Algorithms for Eye-Movement Identification

Given the information about eye-movement type (e.g. fixations, saccades) and their characteristics (e.g. duration, spatial distribution), various subsequent analyses can then be performed depending on the particular context and application of the research. However, the raw eye-movement data output from eye-tracking experiments are usually presented by means of a stream of sampled gaze points. Post-processings need to be performed to identify different types of eye movements from the gaze points.

Fixation detection algorithms extract and label fixations and saccades from raw eye-tracking data (i.e. sample points). These algorithms can identify the fixations, the saccades taking place between two successive fixations, and those smaller eye movements occurring during fixations, such as tremors, drifts, and flicks (Salvucci & Goldberg, 2000). Note that the fixation identification is a critical aspect of eye-movement data analysis, since its result can significantly affect later analyses. Evidences have showed that different identification algorithms could produce different interpretations even when analyzing the same eye-tracking data (Karsh & Breitenbach, 1983).

Salvucci and Goldberg (2000) suggested that most fixation identification algorithms took advantage of the following spatial or temporal features:

- **Velocity:** Some algorithms take advantage of the fact that fixation points have much lower velocities compared to the saccades. Generally, the sampling rate of an eye-tracker is constant, so the velocity equals to the distance between sample points.
- **Dispersion:** Some algorithms emphasize the spread distance (i.e. dispersion) of fixation points. It assumes that the sample points belonging to a fixation generally occur near one another, but saccades are far away from others.
- **Duration Information:** This criterion is based on the fact that fixations are rarely less than 100 ms and usually in the range of 200-400 ms.
- **Local Adaptivity:** This criterion means that the interpretation of a given point is influenced by the interpretation of temporally adjacent points.

Based on the different features selected, various fixation identification algorithms have been proposed. The two main types of fixation identification algorithms are introduced below.

Velocity-Based Algorithms

The velocity information of eye movements shows two distributions of velocities: low velocities for fixations, and high velocities for saccades. This velocity-based discrimination is straightforward and robust.

Among various velocity-based algorithms, Velocity-Threshold Identification (I-VT) is the simplest one to implement (Salvucci & Goldberg, 2000). I-VT calculates firstly point-to-point velocities for each point. Each velocity is computed as the distance between the current point and the next (or previous) point. Each point is then classified as a saccade point or fixation point based on a velocity threshold: if the velocity is higher than the threshold, it becomes a saccade, otherwise it becomes a fixation point. Finally, I-VT translate each fixation group into a $<x, y, t, d>$ representation. $<x, y>$ represent the centroid of the points, t and d means the time of the first point and the duration of the points respectively.

A more sophisticated type of velocity-based algorithm is Hidden Markov Model fixation Identification (I-HMM) (Salvucci, 1999; Salvucci & Anderson, 1998). I-HMM applies a two-state HMM in which the two states represent the velocity distributions for saccade and fixation points, respectively. Generally, I-HMM can perform more robust identification than fixed-threshold methods (e.g. I-VT) (Salvucci & Goldberg, 2000).

Dispersion-Based Algorithms

Dispersion-based Algorithms use the fact that fixation points tend to cluster closely together because of their low velocity. Dispersion-Threshold Identification (I-DT) is a typical type of the dispersion-based algorithms. I-DT identifies fixations as groups of consecutive points within a particular dispersion. A dispersion threshold is thus essential for I-DT algorithms. Moreover, a minimum duration threshold is also required, which is used to help alleviate equipment variability. The minimum duration threshold normally ranges from 100 ms to 200 ms (Widdel, 1984).

An implementation of I-DT algorithm is proposed by Widdel et al. (1984). They use a moving window to cover consecutive data points. The moving window begins at the start of the protocol. It initially contains a minimum number of points which is determined by a given duration threshold. The I-DT then computes the dispersion of the points in the window by summing the differences between the points' maximum and minimum x and y: $D=[max(x) - min(x)] + [max(y) - min(y)]$.

If the dispersion is above a dispersion threshold, the window moves to the following point. If the dispersion is below the threshold, the window represents a fixation and will be expended until the window's dispersion is above the threshold. The final window is marked as a fixation that centers at the centroid of the points and has a given onset time and duration.

4. COMPUTATIONAL MODELING OF VISUAL ATTENTION

Eye-tracking experiments can be considered as a reliable way to acquire the distribution of human's attention on a specific scene. However, conducting eye-tracking experiments is usually cumbersome, time consuming, and hence, expensive. In order to automatically predict the distribution of human's attention, extensive research efforts have been dedicated to computational modeling of visual attention. In our study, we particularly focus on the models that compute saliency maps. The results of this type of model, the saliency maps, indicate where the most visually interesting regions are located.

In the past years, a body of models using various mathematical tools has been proposed. According to the taxonomy introduced by Le Meur and Le Callet (2009), most of the computational models can be grouped into three main categories: hierarchical model, statistical model, and Bayesian model.

4.1 Main Computational Models

Hierarchical Models

This kind of model is characterized by the use of a hierarchical decomposition, whether it involves a Gaussian, a Fourier-based or wavelet decomposition. Various feature maps are then computed. Different strategies are then used to integrate information across sub-bands to create a final saliency map.

The Model of Itti

One of the most famous models of this category is the model proposed by Laurent Itti et al. (1998). It is the first computational and biologically plausible model of bottom-up visual attention, and it serves as a basis in many studies. The architecture of this model (see Figure 7) is based on the following principle

Figure 7. Architecture of Itti's model
Adapted from Itti et al. (1998).

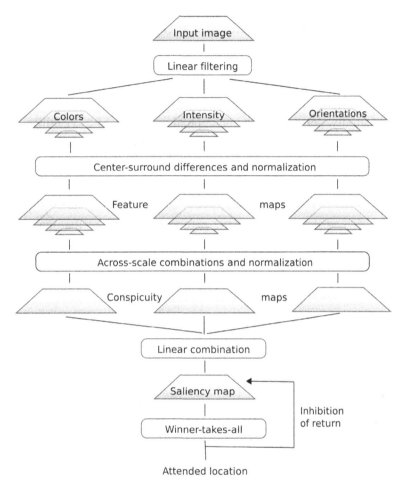

steps. The original image is firstly decomposed into three different perceptual channels: intensity, color and orientation. A multi-scale representation is constructed from the various channels. A set of linear center-surround operations akin to visual receptive fields is performed to obtain feature maps. These feature maps are

1. Normalized by an operator N, which enhances the feature maps containing a small number of peaks of saliency, and
2. Then summed to create the conspicuity maps (intensity, color, and orientation).

These three conspicuity maps are also normalized and summed to obtain a unique saliency map. In this model, the selection of focuses of attention (FOA) is achieved by a "winner-take-all" network, which selects the most salient area in the saliency map and contains an "inhibition of return" mechanism to temporarily prevent the FOA return immediately to the areas already visited.

The Model of Le Meur

Another representative model comes from Le Meur et al. (2006). It is also a bottom-up model based on Treisman's Feature Integration Theory (Treisman & Gelade, 1980) and the biologically plausible architecture proposed by Koch and Ullman (1987). This model was first described by Le Meur et al. (2006) and then modified in (Le Meur, Le Callet, & Barba, 2007), in order to take into account motion. We introduce here the original version of the model.

Le Meur's model (see Figure 8) builds on a coherent psychovisual space. Three aspects of the vision process are tackled: visibility, perception, and perceptual grouping. The "visibility" process simulates the limited sensitivity of the human visual system. For an input image, RGB luminance is first transformed into the Krauskopf's color space (A, C_{r1} and C_{r2}), which simulates the three channels used by retina for visual information encoding. The first channel, A, transforms achromatic perceptual signals; the second channel, C_{r1}, transforms chromatic perceptual signals of the opponent colors of red-green; and the third channel, C_{r2}, transforms chromatic perceptual signals of the opponent colors of blue-yellow. A contrast sensitivity function is then applied to each of the three channels. These contrast

Figure 8. Architecture of Le Meur's model
(Le Meur et al., 2006).

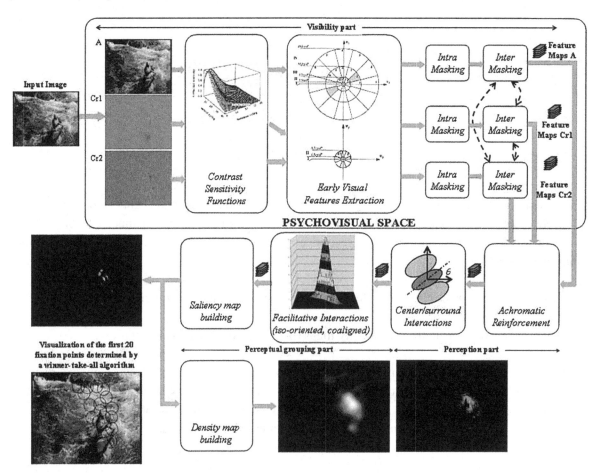

sensitivity functions show how the sensitivity of human eye varies as a function of spatial frequency and orientation. A hierarchical decomposition is then applied to each of the three channels. The decomposition consists in splitting the 2D spatial frequency domain both in spatial radial frequency and in orientation. In this model, each channel is considered as the feature map corresponding to a specific set of neurons. A "perception" process is then applied, in which a center-surround mechanism is performed to simulate the HVS for selecting relevant areas and reducing the redundant incoming visual information. The third process of the model is "perceptual grouping". It refers to the human visual ability which groups and binds visual features to organize a meaningful higher-level structure. Finally, this computational model sums the output of the different channels to obtain a two-dimensional spatial saliency map. Note that Le Meur et al. (2007) proposed a computational model for video, in which motion is considered as an additional visual channel. The result of the motion channel is a temporal saliency map, which is finally combined with the spatial saliency map to get a final saliency map.

Statistical Models

This kind of model utilizes probabilistic methods to compute the saliency. The probabilistic framework is deduced from the content of the current image. The measure of saliency of each location is based on various features, and is defined as the deviation of these features between the current location and its surrounding region. Note that

1.   The features used in statistical models refer not only to the low level visual features (e.g. color, intensity or orientation) but also some features derived by Independent Component Analysis (ICA) or Principal Component Analysis (PCA) algorithms; and
2.   Even the whole image might be considered as the "surrounding region" in these models.

The Model of Bruce and Tsotsos

Bruce and Tsotsos (2009) proposed a model of saliency computation based on the premise that localized saliency computation serves to maximize information sampled from one's environment. The framework of this model is depicted in Figure 9.

The first step of this model is the independent feature extraction. For each location *(i, j)* in the image, the response of various learned filters that simulate V1 cortical cells are computed. This operation is considered as measuring the response of various cortical cells coding for content at each individual spatial location. Gabor-like cells that respond to orientation structure within a specific spatial frequency band and cells that respond to color opponency are taken into account. This step yields a group of coefficients for each local neighborhood of the scene $C_{i,j}$.

The second stage is density estimation. The content of each local neighborhood $C_{i,j}$ of the image is characterized by several coefficients a_k. These coefficients, a_k, correspond to the various basis filters coding for that location. At one spatial location and in the surrounding regions of that location, there is a set of coefficients for a same filter type. Based on a non-parametric or histogram density estimate, the coefficients in the surround form a distribution that can be used to predict the likelihood of the coefficients of $C_{i,j}$. Any given coefficient can be then converted to a probability by looking up its likelihood

Figure 9. Architecture of the model of Bruce and Tsotsos
Adapted from Bruce & Tsotsos (2009).

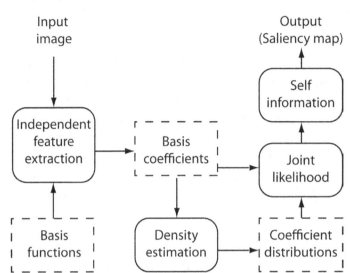

from the probability distribution derived from the surround. Based on the probabilities, joint likelihood of each location can be computed, which is then translated into Shannon's measure of Self-information. The resulting information map serves as the output of the model, the spatial saliency map.

The Model of Gao et al.

The model proposed by Gao et al. (2008) computes a so-called "discriminant center-surround saliency" by combining

1.   The classical assumption that bottom-up saliency is a center-surround process, and
2.   A discriminant saliency hypothesis.

The computation of saliency is formulated as a binary classification problem. For each location l in the input image, the saliency is defined with respect to two classes of stimuli: stimuli of interest and null hypothesis. Stimuli of interest refer to the observations within a neighborhood of l, (i.e. W_l^1, which is referred to as the center); null hypothesis refers to the observations within a surrounding window, (i.e. W_l^0, which is referred to as the surround). The saliency of each location is thus equal to the discriminant power, which is quantified by mutual information, for the classification of the observed features that comes from the center area and the surround.

Bayesian Models

In addition to information from the current image, the Bayesian framework is applied in this type of models to also take into account prior knowledge. This prior knowledge concerns, for instance, the statistic of visual features in natural scenes, including its distribution or its spectral signature. Since prior knowledge from the perceptual learning process would help the human visual system to understand the visual environment, the integration of prior knowledge into computational models could be compared to a visual priming effect that would facilitate the scene perception (Le Meur & Le Callet, 2009).

The Model of Zhang et al.

The model proposed by Zhang et al. (2008) is based on the assumption that one goal of human visual system is to find potential targets by estimating the probability of a target at every location given the visual features. The proposed model relies on a Bayesian probabilistic framework, in which bottom-up saliency is regarded as the self-information of visual features; when searching for a target, the overall saliency is considered as the point-wise mutual information between the features and the target. By

1. Letting the binary variable C denote whether a point belongs to a target class,
2. Letting the random variable L denotes the location,
3. Letting the random variable F denote the visual features, the computation of saliency of specific location z (e.g. a pixel) is formulated by:

$$S_z = p\left(C = 1 \mid F = f_z, L = l_z\right)$$

where f_z represents the feature observed at z, and l represents the location (i.e. pixel coordinates) of z.

Compared to other bottom-up saliency measures, which are defined solely in terms of the image currently being viewed, this model is defined based on natural statistics collected from a set of images of natural scenes. And this is the reason why it is named SUN. Besides, compared to the others, it involves only local computation on images, without calculation of global image statistics or saliency normalization or winner-take-all competition.

Due to the assumptions that

1. Features and location are independent and conditionally independent given C = 1, and
2. The distribution of a feature does not change with location, the formulation is given by:

$$\log S_z = -\log p(F = f_z) + \log p(F = f_z, C = 1) + \log p(F = f_z, L = l_z).$$

The first term on the right side of this equation, $-\log p(F = f_z)$, is the self-information. The rarer the visual features are, the more informative they are. The second term, $\log p(F = f_z, C = 1)$, is a log-likelihood term which favors feature values consistent with our knowledge of the target. It corresponds to the top-down effect when searching for a known target. The third term in the equation, $\log p(F = f_z, L = l_z)$, is independent of visual features and represents any prior knowledge of where the target is likely to appear. In the free-viewing condition, both the location prior knowledge and the log-likelihood term are unknown, so the bottom-up saliency is equal to the self-information, $-\log p(F = f_z)$.

4.2 Features for Visual Saliency Detection

The selection of visual features is of great importance in the computational modeling of visual attention. According to the feature integration theory (Treisman & Gelade, 1980), three features have been widely used in existing computational models of visual attention: intensity, color and orientation (Borji & Itti, 2013). Intensity is usually processed by a center-surround process, which is inspired by neural responses in lateral geniculate nucleus (LGN) and V1 cortex. To extract this feature, two types of filter are used to simulate the response of visual cells that have a center ON (resp. OFF) and a surround OFF (resp. ON). Color is usually taken into account by means of the red/green and the blue/yellow color pairs, which is inspired by color-opponent neurons in V1 cortex. Orientation is usually implemented as a convolution with oriented Gabor filters or by the application of oriented masks. Motion is also used in the models for video (in the primate brain motion is derived by the neurons at MT an MST regions which are selective to direction of motion (Borji & Itti, 2013). In addition to the basic visual features introduced previously, some other specific features that direct human's attention have been used in the modeling of visual attention (Borji & Itti, 2013), including: faces (Cerf, Harel, Einhäuser, & Koch, 2008), horizontal lines (Oliva & Torralba, 2001), wavelets (Li, Tian, Huang, & Gao, 2010), gist (Torralba, 2003), center-bias (Tatler, 2007), spatial resolution (Hamker, 2005), optical flow (Vijayakumar, Conradt, Shibata, & Schaal, 2001), flicker (Itti, Dhavale, & Pighin, 2004), crosses or corners (Privitera & Stark, 2000), entropy (Kadir & Brady, 2001), ellipses (Lee, Buxton, & Feng, 2005), symmetry (Kootstra, Nederveen, & De Boer, 2008), texture contrast (Parkhurst et al., 2002), depth (Maki, Nordlund, & Eklundh, 2000), components derived by ICA or PCA algorithms (L. Zhang et al., 2008; Bruce & Tsotsos, 2009).

5. EXTENSION TO THE COMPUTATIONAL MODELING OF STEREOSCOPIC 3D VISUAL ATTENTION

After introducing the studies regarding the ground truth of 3D visual attention and the impact of depth perception on visual attention, we particularly focus on the modeling of 3D visual attention. A new 3D visual attention model relying on both 2D visual features and features extracted from depth information is proposed and evaluated in this section.

We first introduce and summarize previous works on 3D visual attention. A taxonomy of computational models of 3D visual attention is proposed. After that, we introduce a depth-saliency-based model of 3D visual attention. To get benefit from psychophysical studies, we propose to apply Bayes's theorem on the result of an eye-tracking experiment using synthetic stimuli to model the correlation between depth features and the level of depth saliency. We also introduce and discuss two ways of combining depth saliency map with 2D saliency map.

During the viewing of stereoscopic 3D content, disparity information is used by the brain to retrieve the 3D layout of the environment, it leads to a stereoscopic perception of depth. This change of depth perception also largely modifies human's visual attention when watching stereoscopic 3D images/videos (Hakkinen, Kawai, Takatalo, Mitsuya, & Nyman, 2010b; Quan Huynh-Thu, Barkowsky, & Le Callet, 2011). Predicting the salient areas of a 3D scene becomes thus a challenging task due to the additional depth information.

Several challenges, importance and new applications of visual attention for 3D content viewing were introduced by Huynh-Thu et al. (2011). They described the conflicts that the human visual system has to deal with during watching 3D-TV. They also explained how these conflicts might be limited, and how visual comfort could be improved by knowing how visual attention is deployed. Several new application areas that can benefit from being provided the location (including depth) of salient areas were also introduced. These candidate applications exist in the different steps of a typical 3D-TV delivery chain, e.g. 3D video capture, 2D to 3D conversion, reframing and depth adaptation, and subtitling in 3D movie.

The increasing demand of visual-attention-based applications for 3D content highlights the importance of computationally modeling 3D visual attention. However, two questions need to be figured out for developing a 3D visual attention model:

- The influence of 2D visual features (e.g. color, intensity, orientation, and center-bias) in 3D viewing condition.
- The influence of depth on visual attention deployment in 3D viewing condition. For instance, it is necessary to figure out how the bias of fixations according to depth (i.e. the depth-bias), and the visual features based on depth information (e.g., the orientation of surface, the contrast of depth) affect the deployment of human's visual attention.

In the last decade, a large number of 2D visual attention models have been created. Therefore, the first question concerns the possibility of adapting this large amount of existing 2D models into the 3D case. On the other hand, the second question concerns the means by which the additional information, depth, can be taken into account.

The research on 3D visual attention modeling is also facing another problem: the lack of published eye-tracking database of 3D images. In addition to the lack of quantitative evaluation of performance, another consequence of the lack of ground truth is that most of the existing 3D visual attention models only take into account, in a qualitative way, the results of psychophysical experiments about depth's influence or the variation of 2D features' effects. Any model that quantitatively integrates experimental observation results is still missing so far. Moreover, there is still no strong conclusion on the means by which depth information should be used in 3D visual attention modeling: whether the depth should be used to weight 2D saliency map; or alternatively it should be considered as an additional visual dimension to extract depth features and create depth saliency map.

5.1 How 3D Visual Attention Is Affected by Various Visual Features

Based on observations from psychophysical experiments, several studies have started to examine both qualitatively and quantitatively how visual attention may be influenced by the 2D visual features and additional binocular depth cues.

One of the early works was done by Jansen et al. (2009) who investigated the influence of disparity on viewing behavior in the observation of 2D and 3D still images. They conducted a free-viewing task on the 2D and 3D versions of the same set of images. They found that additional depth information led to an increased number of fixations, shorter and faster saccades, and increased spatial extent of exploration. However, no significant difference was found between the viewing of 2D and 3D stimuli in terms of saliency of several 2D visual features including mean luminance, luminance contrast, and texture contrast. This consistence of the influence of 2D low-level visual features implied:

1. The importance of 2D visual feature detection in the design of 3D visual attention model, and
2. The possibility of adapting existing 2D visual attention models in the modeling of 3D visual attention.

Liu, Cormack and Bovik (2010) examined visual features at fixated positions for stereo images with natural content. They focused on comparing visual features extracted from fixations and random locations in the viewing of 3D still images. On one hand, they demonstrated that some 2D visual features including luminance contrast and luminance gradient were generally higher at fixated areas. On the other hand, their results also indicate that disparity contrast and disparity gradient of fixated locations are lower than randomly selected locations. This result is inconsistent with the result from Jansen et al (2009) who found that observers consistently look more at depth discontinuities (high disparity contrast areas) than at planar surfaces. One limitation of Liu et al.'s study might rely on the quality of ground truth disparity map. The disparity maps they used came from a simple correspondence algorithm rather than any depth range sensing systems or any sophisticated depth estimation algorithms. The final results might thus be affected by a considerable amount of noise in the estimated disparity maps.

Hakkinen et al. (2010) examined the difference in eye movement patterns between the viewing of 2D and 3D versions of the same video content. They found that eye movements are more widely distributed for 3D content. Compared to the viewing of 2D content, viewers did not only look at the main actors but also looked at some other targets on typical movie content. Their result shows that depth information from the binocular depth cue provides viewers additional information, and thus creates new salient areas in a scene. This result suggests the existence of a saliency map from depth, and a potential "summation" operation during the integration of 2D and depth saliency information. In opposite, Ramasamy et al.'s study (Ramasamy, House, Duchowski, & Daugherty, 2009), which is related to stereo-filmmaking, showed that observers' gaze points could be more concentrated when viewing the 3D version of some content (e.g. the scenes containing long deep hallway).

In terms of the depth plane where fixations tend to be located, Wang, Le Callet, Ricordel and Tourancheau (2011) examined a so-called "depth-bias" in task-free viewing of still stereoscopic synthetic stimuli. They found that objects closest to the observer always attract most fixations. The number of fixations on each object decreases as the depth order of the object increases, except that the furthest object receives a few more fixations than the one or two objects in front of it. The number of fixations on objects at different depth planes was also found to be time dependent. This result is consistent with the result of Jansen et al. (2009). Considering the influence of center-bias in 2D visual attention, these results indicate the existence of a location prior according to depth in the viewing of 3D content. This location prior indicates the possibility of integrating depth information by means of doing a weighting.

Wismeijer, Erkelens, van Ee and Wexler (2010) examined if saccades were aligned with individual depth cues or with a combination of depth cues by presenting stimuli in which monocular perspective cues and binocular disparity cues conflicted. Their results indicate a weighted linear combination of cues when the conflicts are small, and a cue dominance when the conflicts are large. They also found that vergence is dominated only by binocular disparity. Their result implies that the interocular distance recorded by binocular eye-tracking experiment for 3D content should be compensated by taking into account the local disparity value.

5.2 Previous Works on 3D Visual Attention Modeling

As introduced previously, great efforts have been put into the study of viewing behavior of 3D content. However, only a few computational models of 3D visual attention have been proposed as compared to the body of 2D visual attention models. Experimental results have demonstrated strong influences of 2D visual features, in the viewing of 3D content. However, due to the addition of new depth cues, depth features, and their combination or conflicts with other monocular cues (Hoffman, Girshick, Akeley, & Banks, 2008; Okada et al., 2006), a direct use of 2D visual attention model for 3D content is neither biologically plausible nor effective.

Furthermore, the disparity between two views can raise serious challenges on collecting 3D gaze points and creating fixation density maps, which are used as ground-truth, since the gaze data need to be extrapolated or processed to provide a notion of depth in relation with gaze direction or location (Quan Huynh-Thu et al., 2011).

In the literature, a few computational models of 3D visual attention have been proposed. All of these models contain a stage in which 2D visual features are extracted and used to compute 2D saliency maps. According to the ways they use depth information, these models can be classified into three different categories: depth-weighting model, depth-saliency model, and stereovision model.

Depth-Weighting Models

This type of model (Maki, Nordlund, & Eklundh, 1996; Y. Zhang, Jiang, Yu, & Chen, 2010; Chamaret, Godeffroy, Lopez, & Le Meur, 2010) do not contain any depth-map-based feature-extraction processes. Apart from detecting salient areas by 2D visual features, these models share a same step in which depth information is used as the weighting factor of 2D saliency. The saliency of each location (e.g. pixel, target or depth plane) in the scene is directly related to its depth. Both 2D scene and depth map are taken as input. Note that depth maps used in these models can be a ground truth depth map provided by depth detection equipment, or come from depth estimation algorithms which use two or multiple views.

Depth-Saliency Models

The models (Ouerhani & Hugli, 2000; Potapova, Zillich, & Vincze, 2011) in this category take depth saliency as additional information. This type of model relies on the existence of "depth saliency maps". Depth features are first extracted from depth map to create additional feature maps, which are used to generate the depth saliency maps. These depth saliency maps are finally combined with 2D saliency maps (e.g. from 2D visual attention models using color, orientation or intensity) by using saliency map pooling strategy to obtain a final 3D saliency map. This type of model takes as input 2D scene and depth map.

Stereovision Models

Instead of directly using depth map, this type of model takes into account the mechanisms of stereoscopic perception in the human visual system. Bruce and Tsotsos (2005) extend the 2D models that use a visual pyramid processing architecture by adding neuronal units for modeling stereo vision. Images from both views are taken as input, from which 2D visual features can be considered. In addition, the model takes into account the conflicts between two eyes resulting from occlusions or large disparities.

Summary of the Previous Studies

Table 4 introduces the main properties of the models belonging to each of the three categories. So far, most of the existing computational models of 3D visual attention belong to the first or the second category. Figure 10 summarizes the two different ways by which depth information is taken into account in these two types of model.

5.3 Recent Works: Depth-Saliency-Based Computational Model of 3D Visual Attention

Depth features have demonstrated their contribution in predicting saliency map of 3D images. Several depth features (e.g. surface curvature, depth gradient, relative surface orientation) have been proposed and used in previous 3D models. In this section, the way of creating depth map from which depth features can be extracted is first introduced. In a second step, we introduce a new method for generating a so-call "depth saliency map". The depth saliency map is computed based only on depth features (i.e. depth contrast) by using a Bayesian framework.

Depth Map Creation

We propose that a depth map providing the information of a scene's perceived depth needs to be computed at the first step of modeling 3D visual attention. In the literature, the disparity map is usually directly adopted as depth information (Chamaret et al., 2010). We propose that a transformation from disparity

Table 4. Main features of computational models of 3D visual attention

Depth Weighting	Depth Information	Operation	Validation
Maki, Nordlund and Eklundh (2000)	Relative depth	Assigned the target closer to observers with highest priority	Qualitative assessment; no quantitative comparison to eye-tracking data
Zhang et al. (2010)	Perceived depth, pop-out effect	Irregular space conversion. Pixels closer to observers and in front of screen is considered to be higher salient	Qualitative assessment; no quantitative comparison to eye-tracking data
Chamaret et al. (2010)	Relative depth	Weight each pixel in 2D saliency map by its depth value	Qualitative assessment; no quantitative comparison to eye-tracking data
Depth Saliency	**Depth Information**	**Operation**	**Validation**
Ouerhani and Hugli (2000)	Absolute depth (distance), surface curvature, depth gradient	Extract depth features from depth map. Compute additional conspicuity maps based on depth features. Pool all the conspicuity maps (from 2D features and depth features)	Qualitative assessment; no quantitative comparison to eye-tracking data
Potapova et al. (2011)	Surface height, relative surface orientation, occluded edges	Compute one saliency map for each (2D and depth) feature, then sum all the saliency maps	Qualitative assessment and quantitative comparison to labeled ROIs
Stereovision	**Depth Information**	**Operation**	**Validation**
Bruce and Tsotsos (2005)	Disparity	Take two views as input. Add interpretive neuronal units for stereo-vision modeling into 2D computational model which use visual pyramid processing architecture [34].	Qualitative assessment; no quantitative comparison to eye-tracking data

Figure 10. Two different ways of using depth in the depth-weighting models (left), and the depth-saliency models (right); note that the main difference between these two types of model is the existence of a stage for extracting depth features and creating depth saliency map.

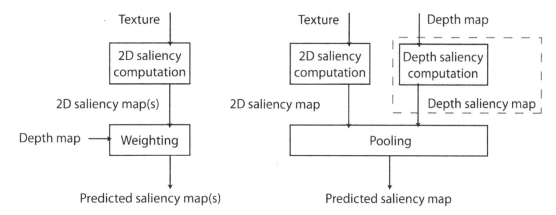

map to depth map which represents perceived depth in unit of length should be added in the chain of 3D visual attention modeling, since even the same disparity value corresponds to different perceived depth depending on the viewing condition.

From the view of display system, disparity is measured in unit of pixels. The relationship between disparity (in pixel) and perceived depth can be modeled by the following equation (see also Figure 11):

$$D = \frac{V}{\left(1 + \frac{I \cdot R_x}{P \cdot W}\right)}, \tag{1}$$

Figure 11. The relationship between disparity and perceived depth (top view)

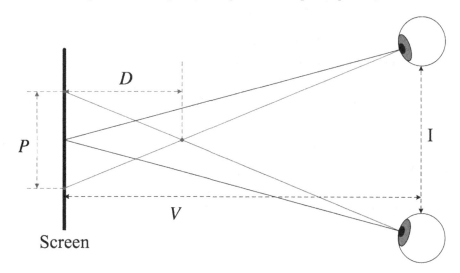

where D represents the perceived depth, V represents the viewing distance between observer and screen plane, I represents the interocular distance, P is the disparity in pixels, W and R_x represent, respectively, the width (in cm) and the horizontal resolution of the screen.

According to this Equation 1, perceived depth is not only a function of disparity but also influenced by the viewing conditions (the viewing distance and the properties of the display). For instance, an 8-pixel negative disparity can create a perceived depth of about 3.5 cm behind the screen when it is presented on a 24-inch full-HD stereoscopic display with 1-meter viewing distance (3 times of the screen's height). However, the same disparity corresponds to a perceived depth of infinite on a 2k-cinema screen with 8-meter screen height and 8-meter viewing distance. When the viewing condition varies, the change of perceived depth from even a same disparity value might make some areas of a 3D scene impossible to fuse. Consequently, the saliency distribution can be different. In this study, we adopt Equation 1 to compute the depth map for each image, the interocular distance is set to 6.3 cm, while the screen property parameters are set according to the setup of the eye-tracking experiment conducted for building the Bayesian based model presented below).

A Bayesian Approach of Depth Saliency Map Generation

In the area of saliency map creation, Bayes's theorem has been widely applied in various ways (L. Zhang, Tong, Marks, Shan, & Cottrell, 2008; Chikkerur, Serre, Tan, & Poggio, 2010; Pinneli & Chandler, 2008). In this chapter, we propose a new approach of Bayes's theorem for computing a depth saliency map based on features extracted from a depth map. The proposed approach correlates depth features with the level of depth saliency, by using data from a psychophysical experiment.

We firstly introduce the proposed definition of depth saliency: the depth saliency (S) of each location (a pixel) equals to the probability of this point being gazed at, given depth features observed at this point and the spatial location of this point:

$$S = P\left(C = 1 \mid \overline{f_{dep}}, l_z\right), \tag{2}$$

where C is a binary random variable denoting whether or not a point is gazed at. The random variable vector $\overline{f_{dep}}$ denotes depth features observed at this point, l_z denotes its location in depth. Note that the term about 'features', $\overline{f_{dep}}$, stands for not only the local visual features such as relative depth (i.e. disparity) and absolute depth (i.e. distance to observer), but also some higher order features considering the information from neighborhood, such as the result of applying Difference of Gaussian kernel (DoG) on feature maps.

Regarding to the right side of equation 2, $P\left(C = 1 \mid \overline{f_{dep}}, l_z\right)$, we make the assumptions that 1) the depth features of each point are independent of its distance to the viewer, and 2) P(C=1) is simply a constant.

By using Bayes' rule, this probability can be thus transformed to:

$$S = P\left(C = 1 \mid \overline{f_{dep}}\right) \cdot P\left(C = 1 \mid l_z\right) \cdot const. \tag{3}$$

The first term in equation 3, $P\left(C=1\mid \overline{f_{dep}}\right)$, represents the probability of a point to be gazed at, given only the features extracted from depth information at this point. By computing this probability, the saliency map from depth channel can be obtained. The second term in this equation, $P\left(C=1\mid l_z\right)$, represents the probability of a point to be gazed at given its distance to the viewer. This probability reflects observers' viewing strategy, the bias of eyes position, or the prior knowledge about at which distance potential targets are likely to appear. Compared to the well known 'center-bias' regarding to the location prior in the viewing of 2D image (Tatler, 2007; Tseng, Carmi, Cameron, Munoz, & Itti, 2009), relatively little of this preference of observation in depth is known and studied. Recently, this preference was quantified and named as 'depth-bias' by Wang et al. (2011). Therefore, based on the proposed model of depth saliency, the saliency value of each point in a three dimensional scene can be considered as a combination of visual saliency from depth features and depth prior. However, studying depth-bias is not in the scope of this chapter. In the following part, we focus on the introduction of modeling $P\left(C=1\mid \overline{f_{dep}}\right)$, omitting the depth prior part.

By using Bayes' rule, we can get:

$$P\left(C=1\mid \overline{f}_{dep}\right)=\alpha\cdot\frac{P\left(\overline{f}_{dep}\mid C=1\right)}{P\left(\overline{f}_{dep}\right)}, \tag{4}$$

where α is a constant value representing the probability P(C=1). The function $P\left(C=1\mid \overline{f}_{dep}\right)$ represents how depth features observed at a point, influence the probability of the human visual system of deciding whether to fixate this point or not. This probability is proportional to the feature distribution at a gaze point, normalized by the rarity of features in the context (see equation 4). Note that the use of the likelihood, $P\left(\overline{f}_{dep}\mid C=1\right)$ in the proposed approach differs from the way in which it is usually used by many models in the literature applying also Bayes's theory. We are not doing any binary classification to make a decision that a point is a fixation or not. Instead, we define the result (i.e. depth saliency map) as a distribution of probability of the points being gazed at as a function of depth features.

To achieve the computation of depth saliency map, the proposed approach consists of two stages:

1. Depth feature extraction, and
2. Probability distribution modeling.

Depth Feature Extraction

The proposed model uses depth contrast as feature for depth saliency map prediction. In most situations, depth contrast can be an efficient indicator of interesting targets. For example, the HVS might consider a region protruding above a flat plane as a potential target (Potapova et al., 2011); or might consider a hole as a place where potential target might exist.

Difference of Gaussians (DoG) filter was applied to the depth map for feature extraction (i.e. depth contrast). DoG filter has been widely used by computational models in the literature due to its resemblance to the receptive fields of neurons, and its capability of simulating the center-surround mechanism in the human visual system. The DoG filters used in the proposed model were generated by:

$$f(x,y) = \frac{1}{2\pi\sigma^2} \exp\left(-\frac{x^2+y^2}{2\sigma^2}\right) - \frac{1}{2\pi K^2\sigma^2} \exp\left(-\frac{x^2+y^2}{2K^2\sigma^2}\right), \tag{5}$$

where (x,y) is the location in the filter. σ and K were used to control the scales of DoG and the ratio between the 'center' area and 'surround' area. In this chapter, we selected a scale as $\sigma = 32$ pixels (approximately corresponding to 1 degree of visual angle in our experiment) and a center/surround ratio of 1/1.6 (the same value as the one used in (L. Zhang et al., 2008)).

Probability Distribution Modeling

In the proposed model, the function $P\left(C=1\,|\,\overline{f}_{contrast}\right)$ models the relationship between the depth contrast of each position in a scene and the probability that this position is gazed. We propose to model this function based on a probability-learning of eye movement data collected from an eye-tracking experiment.

An important factor that can affect modeling is the stimuli used in the eye-tracking experiment. In this study, eye movement data are obtained from an eye-tracking experiment using synthetic stimuli. These stimuli consisted of 3D scenes in which a background and some similar objects were deliberately displayed at different depth positions. The details of this experiment have been introduced in our previous study (J. Wang et al., 2011).

The probability distribution $P(f_{contrast})$ can be obtained based on the depth contrast maps of the synthetic stimuli. By considering the probability distribution of depth contrast at gaze points recorded during the viewing, $P\left(\overline{f}_{contrast}\,|\,C=1\right)$ can be then obtained. Therefore, the likelihood $P\left(C=1\,|\,\overline{f}_{contrast}\right)$ which models the relationship between depth contrast and the probability of being fixated, can be obtained by Equation 4. In Figure 12, we illustrate the resulting likelihood distribution $P\left(C=1\,|\,\overline{f}_{contrast}\right)$.

For the implementation of the proposed model, the modeled $P\left(C=1\,|\,\overline{f}_{contrast}\right)$ is applied on the depth feature map. By taking the depth contrast value at each pixel as input, the saliency value of each pixel in an image can be thus computed.

A Framework of Computational Modeling of 3D Visual Attention

In this section, we introduce the framework which integrates the depth saliency map with the saliency maps computed based on 2D visual features, and achieves the prediction of the final 3D saliency map. The general architecture of the proposed framework is presented in Figure 13.

Figure 12. The distribution $P\left(C = 1 \mid \bar{f}_{contrast}\right)$ *resulting from the eye-tracking experiment using synthetic stimuli*

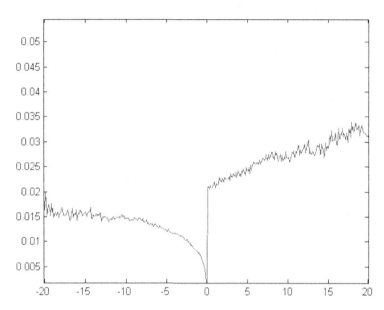

Figure 13. Overview diagram of the proposed framework

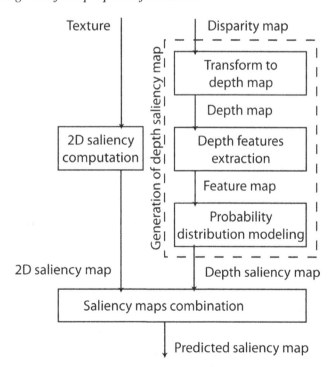

2D Saliency Map Generation

Since developing a completely new computational model of 2D visual attention is not in the scope of the present chapter, we leave the work of 2D visual features detection and 2D saliency map creation to existing models. Three bottom-up visual attention models using quite different mechanisms were used to perform the 2D saliency prediction, and involved in the final performance evaluation:

1. Itti's model (Itti, Koch, & Niebur, 1998) (obtained from http://www.saliencytoolbox.net/),
2. Bruce's AIM model (Bruce & Tsotsos, 2009) (obtained from http://www-sop.inria.fr/members/Neil.Bruce/), and
3. Hou's model (Hou & Zhang, 2007) (obtained from http://www.klab.caltech.edu/~xhou/).

In the proposed framework, 2D saliency computation is only performed based on the image from the left view which is selected arbitrarily, since the images from the two views are quite similar, and the difference in 2D features between the two views' images has thus only marginal influence on visual attention deployment. Computing a 2D saliency map based on only one view instead of both views can be beneficial to decrease the computational complexity of the model.

Saliency Maps Combination

In the literature, although several approaches combining conspicuity maps of 2D visual features have been proposed, there are still not any specific and standardized approach to combine saliency maps from depth and 2D visual features. In the proposed model, we adopt a straightforward approach which is the same as the one used in the work of Potapova et al. (2011) to merge the depth saliency map SM_{dep} and 2D saliency map SM_{2D}: the final saliency map SM_S is equal to the sum of both maps (see Equation 6):

$$SM_S(i, j) = \omega_1 SM_{dep} + \omega_2 SM_{2D}, \tag{6}$$

where $\omega_1 = \omega_2 = 0.5$.

5.4 Performance Assessment

Both qualitative and quantitative comparisons between the fixation density map and the output of the proposed model are performed in this section. All the results are obtained and based on our 3D image eye-tracking database which is introduced in (J. Wang, Da Silva, Le Callet, & Ricordel, 2013).

Qualitative Assessment

Figure 14 gives some examples of the performance of depth saliency maps (the predicted saliency maps created based on only depth map) and predicted saliency maps based on only 2D visual features (from the three 2D visual attention models introduced previously). The fixation density maps generated by eye-tracking data are also provided to be the ground-truth for the qualitative assessment. In each saliency map, brighter areas correspond to areas with higher saliency.

Figure 14. Examples of the performance of different models including from left to right: (a) original image, (b) human saliency map, (c) the depth saliency maps created by the proposed model, and the saliency maps created by (d) Itti's model, (e) Bruce's model, (f) Hou's model

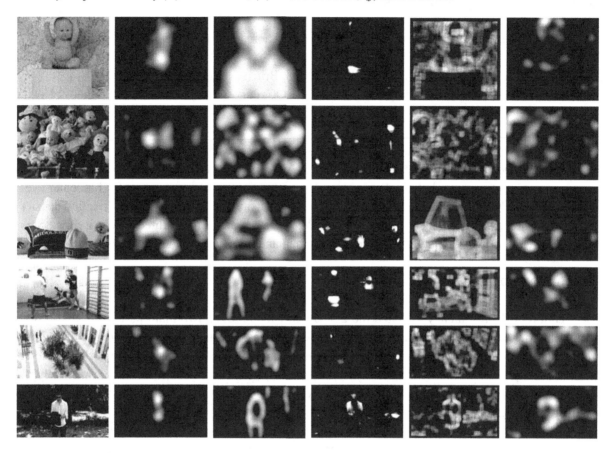

Qualitatively speaking, the proposed approach creates depth saliency maps that well predict salient areas in the 3D images. All the potential salient areas are depicted to be salient in the depth saliency maps. Compared to the depth saliency maps, the contribution of 2D visual features in predicting saliency of a 3D image largely depends on the model selected: Itti's model usually predicts some most salient areas, while it misses many areas of middle level saliency; Bruce's model significantly highlights the edges; Hou's model (as well as Bruce's model) is largely affected by the appearance of the large amount of texture in the background. For instance, in the image on the last row, the trees in the background are assigned high saliency by both these models.

Quantitative Metrics of Assessment

The goal of quantitative assessment is to quantify how well the proposed computational model of visual attention predicts fixation density maps coming from eye-tracking experiments. So far, there are no specific and standardized measures to compare the similarity between fixation density maps and the saliency maps created by computational models in 3D situation. Nevertheless, there exists a range of different measures that are widely used to perform the comparison between saliency maps for 2D content. The most common ones include:

1. Correlation coefficient (Le Meur, Le Callet, Barba, & Thoreau, 2006; Engelke, Maeder, & Zepernick, 2010),
2. Kullback-Leibler divergence (Le Meur et al., 2006; Bruce & Tsotsos, 2009), and
3. Area under the receiver operating characteristics (ROC) curve (L. Zhang et al., 2008; Zhao & Koch, 2011).

The former two are directly applicable to a comparison between a fixation density map and a predicted saliency map, whereas the area under the ROC curve (AUC) is usually used to compare the actual fixation (or gaze) points to a predicted saliency map. Since the disparity compensation for binocular eye-tracking data has been done during the process of fixation density map creation, the two fixation density maps from both views have been merged to one. We therefore adopt these three similarity measures to quantitatively compare a merged fixation density map and a predicted saliency map from one view.

Performance of Depth Saliency Map

The creation of depth saliency map and the 2D saliency map are the two main parts of the proposed model. In order to assess the extent to which these two sources of saliency maps can predict the salient areas in a scene, the performance of the depth saliency map only is compared with the performance of the 2D saliency maps that come from three state-of-the-art 2D visual attention models, respectively.

The results (see Table 5) from all the three objective metrics show that the depth saliency map has a significantly higher performance than Itti's model. Compared to Bruce's model and Hou's model, the performance of the depth saliency map is still higher, but without significant difference (except that the KL divergence value shows that the depth saliency map significantly outperforms Hou's model). These results demonstrate a great influence of the depth contrast on the distribution of visual attention in the viewing of 3D content.

Table 5. Performance of depth saliency map (noted as DSM in the table) only and three state-of-the-art 2D models; note that a smaller KLD score means a better performance.

	PLCC	KLD	AUC
DSM only	0.368	0.708	0.656
Itti's model	0.141*	2.809*	0.540*
Bruce's model	0.325	0.735	0.638
Hou's model	0.291	0.802*	0.630

* Means that it is significantly different from the performance of the DSM (paired t-test, $p < 0.1$).

Added Value of Depth Saliency Map

The proposed model in the present chapter belongs to the category "depth-saliency model", which highlights the existence of a depth saliency map. To compare the two different ways of taking advantage of depth information, the performance of the following methods was measured and compared:

- **No-Depth Method:** This is a direct deployment of 2D computational model, no depth information is taken into account.
- **Depth-Weighting (DW) Method:** We adopt Chamaret's method (Chamaret et al., 2010), which weights each pixel in the 2D saliency map by multiplying it with the depth value of the corresponding pixel in the depth map. Since we do not have the code to apply exactly the same 2D computational model used in their paper, the 2D saliency map creation part is replaced here by the models of Itti, Bruce, or Hou.
- **Depth-Saliency (DS) Method:** i.e. the proposed computational model in this section. It creates a depth saliency map and a 2D saliency map respectively, then combines the resulting saliency map from both paths to get the final result.

The performance of these three methods is shown in Table 6. Large added values of the depth saliency map are demonstrated for all the three 2D visual attention models. The proposed model outperforms both the DW method and the 2D models in predicting salient areas of 3D images. As it is difficult to have an idea of what a good performance is, we remind here the performance of these three state-of-the-art 2D models which has been validated on different 2D-image databases: Itti's model has a PLCC value ranging from 0.27 to 0.31 (Perreira Da Silva, 2010); Bruce's model has a PLCC value ranging from 0.40 to 0.45 (Perreira Da Silva, 2010); and Hou's model has an AUC value staying around 0.69 (Le Meur & Chevet, 2010). Compared to the performance of these state-of-the-art 2D models on 2D content, the proposed model (DS method) is demonstrated to have a comparable level of performance on 3D content.

Table 6. Contribution of the depth information on 2D models; note that a smaller KLD score means a better performance

		PLCC	KLD	AUC
Itti's model	2D model only	0.141	2.809	0.540
	Chamaret's method	0.140	2.892	0.540
	Proposed method	0.356*	0.701*	0.656*
Bruce's model	2D model only	0.325	0.735	0.638
	Chamaret's method	0.311	0.810	0.639
	Proposed method	0.423*	0.615	0.674
Hou's model	2D model only	0.291	0.802	0.630
	Chamaret's method	0.290	0.878	0.633
	Proposed method	0.409	0.603*	0.669

* Means that it is significantly different from the performance of the corresponding 2D model (paired t-test, $p < 0.1$).

The proposed model contains a depth saliency map creation part that is based on a probability-learning from the experimental data. By integrating the depth saliency map with the results of 2D visual feature detection, the proposed model provides a good prediction of salient areas. On the other hand, it is demonstrated that the performance of depth saliency map and its added value to 2D model vary across different types of scene. When too many areas (or no area) can be indicated as salient based on 2D visual features, depth becomes the dominant cue that directs viewer's attention. But the depth saliency map does not perform well in showing the salient areas that are caused by only 2D visual features.

Two different ways of applying depth information in 3D visual attention models are compared in our study. Our results show that, creating a depth saliency map based on depth contrast achieves a higher performance than a simple depth-weighting method (a multiplication of 2D saliency map and depth map). This result indicates the importance of a depth saliency map in modeling 3D visual attention. Nevertheless, this result should not lead to a strong conclusion that a depth-saliency model is definitely better or worse than a depth-weighting model, since depth-weighting models also have various advantages, such as a low computational complexity, or comparable performances for some types of scenes. On the other hand, it would be reasonable to suggest that an efficient 3D visual attention model can be an integration of both types of models: depth information is treated as an additional visual dimension from which depth features are extracted to create depth saliency maps; as a possible extension, the location information (e.g. center-bias or depth-bias) is also used as weighting information to relate the distribution of attention and the distance between the observer and each object in the scene.

6. CONCLUSION

In this chapter, we detail advancements in computational modeling of visual attention by presenting studies focusing on several aspects of the research of visual attention.

We quantitatively identify the similarities and differences between visual saliency maps and importance maps, which are two widely used ground truths for attention-related applications. By comparing the importance maps with the saliency maps, we show that the two types of maps are related, and demonstrate that saliency maps can be effective at predicting the main subject of a scene.

The main characteristics of the human visual system involved in the process of visual perception are also explained. A focus on eye-tracking systems is done because of their role in the research for evaluating the performances of the models, and a complete state of the art in computational modeling of visual attention is presented.

Lastly, a depth-saliency-based model of 3D visual attention is described where Bayes's theorem is applied for learning from previous eye-tracking data in order to compute the depth saliency map. The results demonstrate a large added value of depth saliency map and a good performance of the proposed depth-saliency model. Two different ways of applying depth information in 3D visual attention model are compared. Results show that, creating a depth saliency map based on depth feature achieves a higher performance than a simple depth-weighting method. But the proposed model still has limitations: for instance it takes into account only one depth feature, or a simple pooling strategy is used to combine the depth saliency map and 2D saliency map. In future works, one might consider including more depth features (e.g. surface curvature or depth gradient) and to use a more sophisticated pooling strategy, to improve the performance of such model. This chapter also does not present any practical application of the proposed 3D stereoscopic visual attention model. However, as mentioned for example in (Q. Huynh-Thu, Barkowsky, Le Callet, & others, 2011), potential applications of 3D models are numerous, not only for 3DTV but also for a wider range of domains (e.g. robotics). As a consequence, future works might focus on applications of our model.

REFERENCES

Bichot, N. P. (2001). Attention, eye movements, and neurons: Linking physiology and behavior. *Vision and Attention*, 209–232.

Borji, A., & Itti, L. (2013). State-of-the-art in Visual Attention Modeling. *IEEE Transactions on Pattern Analysis and Machine Intelligence*, *35*(1), 185–207. doi:10.1109/TPAMI.2012.89 PMID:22487985

Brookings, J. B., Wilson, G. F., & Swain, C. R. (1996). Psychophysiological responses to changes in workload during simulated air traffic control. *Biological Psychology*, *42*(3), 361–377. doi:10.1016/0301-0511(95)05167-8 PMID:8652753

Bruce, N. D. B., & Tsotsos, J. K. (2005). An attentional framework for stereo vision. In *Computer and Robot Vision, 2005. Proceedings. The 2nd Canadian Conference on*, (pp. 88–95). IEEE. doi:10.1109/CRV.2005.13

Bruce, N. D. B., & Tsotsos, J. K. (2009). Saliency, attention, and visual search: An information theoretic approach. *Journal of Vision, 9*(3).

Bruneau, D., Sasse, M. A., & McCarthy, J. (2002). The eyes never lie: The use of eye tracking data in HCI research. In *Proceedings of the CHI*, (vol. 2, p. 25). ACM.

Byrne, M. D., Anderson, J. R., Douglass, S., & Matessa, M. (1999). Eye tracking the visual search of click-down menus. In *Proceedings of the SIGCHI conference on Human Factors in Computing Systems*, (pp. 402–409). ACM. doi:10.1145/302979.303118

Cassin, B., Solomon, S., & Rubin, M. L. (1990). *Dictionary of eye terminology*. Wiley Online Library.

Cerf, M., Harel, J., Einhäuser, W., & Koch, C. (2008). Predicting human gaze using low-level saliency combined with face detection. *Advances in Neural Information Processing Systems*, 241–248.

Chamaret, C., Godeffroy, S., Lopez, P., & Le Meur, O. (2010). *Adaptive 3D rendering based on region-of-interest. In IS&T/SPIE Electronic Imaging* (p. 75240V). SPIE.

Chikkerur, S., Serre, T., Tan, C., & Poggio, T. (2010). What and where: A Bayesian inference theory of attention. *Vision Research*, *50*(22), 2233–2247. doi:10.1016/j.visres.2010.05.013 PMID:20493206

Cowen, L., Ball, L. J., & Delin, J. (2002). An eye movement analysis of web page usability. In People and Computers XVI-Memorable Yet Invisible, (pp. 317–335). Springer.

Desimone, R., & Duncan, J. (1995). Neural mechanisms of selective visual attention. *Annual Review of Neuroscience*, *18*(1), 193–222. doi:10.1146/annurev.ne.18.030195.001205 PMID:7605061

Deubel, H., & Schneider, W. X. (1996). Saccade target selection and object recognition: Evidence for a common attentional mechanism. *Vision Research, 36*(12), 1827–1837. doi:10.1016/0042-6989(95)00294-4 PMID:8759451

Duchowski, A. T. (2002). A breadth-first survey of eye-tracking applications. *Behavior Research Methods, Instruments, & Computers, 34*(4), 455–470. doi:10.3758/BF03195475 PMID:12564550

Duchowski, A. T. (2007). *Eye tracking methodology: Theory and practice.* Springer Science & Business Media New York.

Engelke, U., Kaprykowsky, H., Zepernick, H.-J., & Ndjiki-Nya, P. (2011). Visual Attention in Quality Assessment. *Signal Processing Magazine, IEEE, 28*(6), 50–59. doi:10.1109/MSP.2011.942473

Engelke, U., Maeder, A., & Zepernick, H. J. (2010). Analysing inter-observer saliency variations in task-free viewing of natural images. In *Image Processing (ICIP), 2010 17th IEEE International Conference on,* (pp. 1085–1088). IEEE.

Etz, S. P., & Luo, J. (2000). Ground truth for training and evaluation of automatic main subject detection. *Electronic Imaging,* 434–442.

Frintrop, S. (2006). *VOCUS: A visual attention system for object detection and goal-directed search* (Vol. 3899). Springer-Verlag New York. doi:10.1007/11682110

Gao, D., Mahadevan, V., & Vasconcelos, N. (2008). On the plausibility of the discriminant center-surround hypothesis for visual saliency. *Journal of Vision, 8*(7).

Goldberg, J. H., & Kotval, X. P. (1999). Computer interface evaluation using eye movements: Methods and constructs. *International Journal of Industrial Ergonomics, 24*(6), 631–645. doi:10.1016/S0169-8141(98)00068-7

Goldberg, J. H., Stimson, M. J., Lewenstein, M., Scott, N., & Wichansky, A. M. (2002). Eye tracking in web search tasks: design implications. In *Proceedings of the 2002 symposium on Eye tracking research & applications,* (pp. 51–58). ACM. doi:10.1145/507072.507082

Hakkinen, J., Kawai, T., Takatalo, J., Mitsuya, R., & Nyman, G. (2010). What do people look at when they watch stereoscopic movies?. *Electronic Imaging, 7524,* 75240E.

Hamker, F. H. (2005). The emergence of attention by population-based inference and its role in distributed processing and cognitive control of vision. *Computer Vision and Image Understanding, 100*(1), 64–106. doi:10.1016/j.cviu.2004.09.005

Hoffman, D. M., Girshick, A. R., Akeley, K., & Banks, M. S. (2008). Vergence–accommodation conflicts hinder visual performance and cause visual fatigue. *Journal of Vision (Charlottesville, Va.), 8*(3), 33. doi:10.1167/8.3.33 PMID:18484839

Hou, X., & Zhang, L. (2007). Saliency detection: A spectral residual approach. In *Computer Vision and Pattern Recognition, 2007. CVPR'07. IEEE Conference on,* (pp. 1–8). IEEE.

Huynh-Thu, Q., Barkowsky, M., & Le Callet, P. et al. (2011). The Importance of Visual Attention in Improving the 3D-TV Viewing Experience: Overview and New Perspectives. *Broadcasting. IEEE Transactions on, 57*(2), 421–431.

Itti, L., Dhavale, N., & Pighin, F. (2004). Realistic avatar eye and head animation using a neurobiological model of visual attention. In *Optical Science and Technology, SPIE's 48th Annual Meeting*, (pp. 64–78). SPIE.

Itti, L., & Koch, C. (2001). Computational modeling of visual attention. *Nature Reviews. Neuroscience, 2*(3), 194–203. doi:10.1038/35058500 PMID:11256080

Itti, L., Koch, C., & Niebur, E. (1998). A model of saliency-based visual attention for rapid scene analysis. *Pattern Analysis and Machine Intelligence. IEEE Transactions on, 20*(11), 1254–1259.

Jacob, R. J. K., & Karn, K. S. (2003). Eye tracking in human-computer interaction and usability research: Ready to deliver the promises. *Mind, 2*(3), 4.

James, W., Burkhardt, F., & Skrupskelis, I. K. (1980). *The principles of psychology* (Vol. 1). Harvard Univ Press.

Jansen, L., Onat, S., & König, P. (2009). Influence of disparity on fixation and saccades in free viewing of natural scenes. *Journal of Vision, 9*(1).

Just, M. A., & Carpenter, P. A. (1976). Eye fixations and cognitive processes. *Cognitive Psychology, 8*(4), 441–480. doi:10.1016/0010-0285(76)90015-3

Kadir, T., & Brady, M. (2001). Saliency, scale and image description. *International Journal of Computer Vision, 45*(2), 83–105. doi:10.1023/A:1012460413855

Kadiyala, V., Pinneli, S., Larson, E. C., & Chandler, D. M. (2008). *Quantifying the perceived interest of objects in images: effects of size, location, blur, and contrast. In Electronic Imaging* (p. 68060S). SPIE.

Kandel, E. R., Schwartz, J. H., & Jessell, T. M. (2000). *Principles of Neural Science* (Vol. 4). McGraw-Hill New York.

Karsh, R., & Breitenbach, F. (1983). Looking at looking: The amorphous fixation measure. *Eye Movements and Psychological Functions: International Views*, 53–64.

Koch, C., & Ullman, S. (1987). Shifts in selective visual attention: towards the underlying neural circuitry. In Matters of intelligence, (pp. 115–141). Springer.

Kootstra, G., Nederveen, A., & De Boer, B. (2008). Paying attention to symmetry. In *Proceedings of the British Machine Vision Conference (BMVC2008)*, (pp. 1115–1125). BMVC.

Le Meur, O., & Chevet, J. C. (2010). Relevance of a feed-forward model of visual attention for goal-oriented and free-viewing tasks. *Image Processing. IEEE Transactions on, 19*(11), 2801–2813.

Le Meur, O., & Le Callet, P. (2009). What we see is most likely to be what matters: visual attention and applications. In *Image Processing (ICIP), 2009 16th IEEE International Conference on*, (pp. 3085–3088). IEEE.

Le Meur, O., Le Callet, P., & Barba, D. (2007). Predicting visual fixations on video based on low-level visual features. *Vision Research*, *47*(19), 2483–2498. doi:10.1016/j.visres.2007.06.015 PMID:17688904

Le Meur, O., Le Callet, P., Barba, D., & Thoreau, D. (2006). A coherent computational approach to model bottom-up visual attention. *Pattern Analysis and Machine Intelligence. IEEE Transactions on*, *28*(5), 802–817.

Lee, K. W., Buxton, H., & Feng, J. (2005). Cue-guided search: A computational model of selective attention. *Neural Networks. IEEE Transactions on*, *16*(4), 910–924.

Li, J., Tian, Y., Huang, T., & Gao, W. (2010). Probabilistic multi-task learning for visual saliency estimation in video. *International Journal of Computer Vision*, *90*(2), 150–165. doi:10.1007/s11263-010-0354-6

Liu, H., & Heynderickx, I. (2011). Visual Attention in Objective Image Quality Assessment: Based on Eye-Tracking Data. *Circuits and Systems for Video Technology. IEEE Transactions on*, *21*(7), 971–982.

Liu, Y., Cormack, L. K., & Bovik, A. C. (2010). Natural scene statistics at stereo fixations. *Proceedings of the 2010 Symposium on Eye-Tracking Research & Applications*, 161–164. ACM. doi:10.1145/1743666.1743706

Maeder, A. J. (1995). Importance maps for adaptive information reduction in visual scenes. In *Intelligent Information Systems, 1995. ANZIIS-95. Proceedings of the Third Australian and New Zealand Conference on*, (pp. 24–29). IEEE. doi:10.1109/ANZIIS.1995.705709

Maki, A., Nordlund, P., & Eklundh, J. O. (1996). A computational model of depth-based attention. *Pattern Recognition, 1996, Proceedings of the 13th International Conference on*, (vol. 4, pp. 734–739). IEEE.

Maki, A., Nordlund, P., & Eklundh, J. O. (2000). Attentional scene segmentation: Integrating depth and motion. *Computer Vision and Image Understanding*, *78*(3), 351–373. doi:10.1006/cviu.2000.0840

Marshall, S. P. (2000). *Method and apparatus for eye tracking and monitoring pupil dilation to evaluate cognitive activity*. Google US Patents.

Mather, G. (2009). *Foundations of sensation and perception* (Vol. 10). Psychology Press.

Okada, Y., Ukai, K., Wolffsohn, J. S., Gilmartin, B., Iijima, A., & Bando, T. (2006). Target spatial frequency determines the response to conflicting defocus-and convergence-driven accommodative stimuli. *Vision Research*, *46*(4), 475–484. doi:10.1016/j.visres.2005.07.014 PMID:16198392

Oliva, A., & Torralba, A. (2001). Modeling the shape of the scene: A holistic representation of the spatial envelope. *International Journal of Computer Vision*, *42*(3), 145–175. doi:10.1023/A:1011139631724

Osberger, W., & Maeder, A. J. (1998). Automatic identification of perceptually important regions in an image. In *Pattern Recognition, 1998. Proceedings. Fourteenth International Conference on*, (vol. 1, pp. 701–704). IEEE.

Ouerhani, N., & Hugli, H. (2000). Computing visual attention from scene depth. In *Pattern Recognition, 2000. Proceedings. 15th International Conference on*, (vol. 1, pp. 375–378). IEEE.

Parkhurst, D., Law, K., & Niebur, E. (2002). Modeling the role of salience in the allocation of overt visual attention. *Vision Research*, *42*(1), 107–123. doi:10.1016/S0042-6989(01)00250-4 PMID:11804636

Perreira Da Silva, M. (2010). *Modèle computationnel d'attention pour la vision adaptative*. Université de La Rochelle.

Peterson, M. S., Kramer, A. F., & Irwin, D. E. (2004). Covert shifts of attention precede involuntary eye movements. *Attention, Perception & Psychophysics, 66*(3), 398–405. doi:10.3758/BF03194888 PMID:15283065

Pinneli, S., & Chandler, D. M. (2008). A Bayesian approach to predicting the perceived interest of objects. In *Image Processing, 2008. ICIP 2008. 15th IEEE International Conference on*, (pp. 2584–2587). IEEE.

Poole, A., & Ball, L. J. (2006). *Eye tracking in HCI and usability research. In Encyclopedia of Human Computer Interaction* (Vol. 1, pp. 211–219). IGR. doi:10.4018/978-1-59140-562-7.ch034

Posner, M., & Petersen, S. (1990). The attention system of the human brain. *Annual Review of Neuroscience, 13*(1), 25–42. doi:10.1146/annurev.ne.13.030190.000325 PMID:2183676

Potapova, E., Zillich, M., & Vincze, M. (2011). Learning What Matters: Combining Probabilistic Models of 2D and 3D Saliency Cues. In Computer Vision Systems, (pp. 132–142). Springer.

Privitera, C. M., & Stark, L. W. (2000). Algorithms for defining visual regions-of-interest: Comparison with eye fixations. *Pattern Analysis and Machine Intelligence. IEEE Transactions on, 22*(9), 970–982.

Ramasamy, C., House, D. H., Duchowski, A. T., & Daugherty, B. (2009). *Using eye tracking to analyze stereoscopic filmmaking. In SIGGRAPH'09: Posters* (p. 28). ACM.

Rayner, K., Pollatsek, A., Ashby, J., & Clifton, C. Jr. (2012). *Psychology of Reading*. Psychology Press.

Salvucci, D. D. (1999). *Mapping eye movements to cognitive processes*. Carnegie Mellon University.

Salvucci, D. D., & Anderson, J. R. (1998). *Tracing eye movement protocols with cognitive process models*. Lawrence Erlbaum Associates, Inc.

Salvucci, D. D., & Goldberg, J. H. (2000). Identifying fixations and saccades in eye-tracking protocols. In *Proceedings of the 2000 symposium on Eye tracking research & applications*, (pp. 71–78). ACM. doi:10.1145/355017.355028

Tatler, B. W. (2007). The central fixation bias in scene viewing: Selecting an optimal viewing position independently of motor biases and image feature distributions. *Journal of Vision, 7*(14).

Torralba, A. (2003). Modeling global scene factors in attention. *JOSA A, 20*(7), 1407–1418. doi:10.1364/JOSAA.20.001407 PMID:12868645

Treisman, A. M., & Gelade, G. (1980). A feature-integration theory of attention. *Cognitive Psychology, 12*(1), 97–136. doi:10.1016/0010-0285(80)90005-5 PMID:7351125

Tseng, P.-H., Carmi, R., Cameron, I. G. M., Munoz, D. P., & Itti, L. (2009). Quantifying center bias of observers in free viewing of dynamic natural scenes. *Journal of Vision, 9*(7).

Tsotsos, J. K., Culhane, S. M., Kei Wai, W. Y., Lai, Y., Davis, N., & Nuflo, F. (1995). Modeling visual attention via selective tuning. *Artificial Intelligence, 78*(1), 507–545. doi:10.1016/0004-3702(95)00025-9

Vijayakumar, S., Conradt, J., Shibata, T., & Schaal, S. (2001). Overt visual attention for a humanoid robot. In *Intelligent Robots and Systems, 2001. Proceedings. 2001 IEEE/RSJ International Conference on*, (vol. 4, pp. 2332–2337). IEEE.

Vu, K., Hua, K. A., & Tavanapong, W. (2003). Image retrieval based on regions of interest. *Knowledge and Data Engineering. IEEE Transactions on*, *15*(4), 1045–1049.

Wandell, B. A. (1995). *Foundations of vision*. Sinauer Associates.

Wang, D., Li, G., Jia, W., & Luo, X. (2011). Saliency-driven scaling optimization for image retargeting. *The Visual Computer*, *27*(9), 853–860. doi:10.1007/s00371-011-0559-x

Wang, J., Chandler, D. M., & Le Callet, P. (2010). *Quantifying the relationship between visual salience and visual importance. In IS&T-SPIE Electronic Imaging* (p. 75270K). SPIE.

Wang, J., Da Silva, M. P., Le Callet, P., & Ricordel, V. (2013). A Computational Model of Stereoscopic 3D Visual Saliency. *Image Processing. IEEE Transactions on*, *22*(6), 2151–2165.

Wang, J., Le Callet, P., Ricordel, V., & Tourancheau, S. (2011). Quantifying depth bias in free viewing of still stereoscopic synthetic stimuli. In *Proceedings of 16th European Conference on Eye Movements*.

Wedel, M., & Pieters, R. (2007). A review of eye-tracking research in marketing. *Review of Marketing Research*, *4*, 123–147. doi:10.1108/S1548-6435(2008)0000004009

Widdel, H. (1984). Operational problems in analysing eye movements. *Advances in Psychology*, *22*, 21–29. doi:10.1016/S0166-4115(08)61814-2

Wismeijer, D., Erkelens, C., van Ee, R., & Wexler, M. (2010). Depth cue combination in spontaneous eye movements. *Journal of Vision (Charlottesville, Va.)*, *10*(6), 25. doi:10.1167/10.6.25 PMID:20884574

Wolfe, J. M. (2000). Visual attention. *Seeing*, *2*, 335–386. doi:10.1016/B978-012443760-9/50010-6

Wolfe, J. M., & Horowitz, T. S. (2004). What attributes guide the deployment of visual attention and how do they do it?. *Nature Reviews. Neuroscience*, *5*(6), 495–501. doi:10.1038/nrn1411 PMID:15152199

Yarbus, A. L. (1967). *Eye movements and vision*. New York: Plenum. doi:10.1007/978-1-4899-5379-7

Zhang, L., Tong, M. H., Marks, T. K., Shan, H., & Cottrell, G. W. (2008). SUN: A Bayesian framework for saliency using natural statistics. *Journal of Vision (Charlottesville, Va.)*, *8*(7), 32. doi:10.1167/8.7.32 PMID:19146264

Zhang, Y., Jiang, G., Yu, M., & Chen, K. (2010). Stereoscopic Visual Attention Model for 3D Video. In *Advances in Multimedia Modeling*, (pp. 314–324). Springer Berlin.

Zhao, Q., & Koch, C. (2011). Learning a saliency map using fixated locations in natural scenes. *Journal of Vision (Charlottesville, Va.)*, *11*(3), 9. doi:10.1167/11.3.9 PMID:21393388

Chapter 2
Applications of Visual Attention in Image Processing, Computer Vision, and Graphics

Rajarshi Pal

Institute for Development and Research in Banking Technology (IDRBT) Hyderabad, India

ABSTRACT

Selective visual attention is an amazing capability of primate visual system to restrict the focus to few interesting objects (or portions) in a scene. Thus, primates are able to pay attention to the required visual content amidst myriads of other visual information. It enables them to interact with the external environment in real time through reduction of computational load in their brain. This inspires image and computer vision scientists to derive computational models of visual attention and to use them in varieties of applications in real-life, mainly to speed up the processing through reduction of computational burden which often characterizes image processing and vision tasks. This chapter discusses a wide variety of such applications of visual attention models in image processing, computer vision and graphics.

INTRODUCTION

Primates have an amazing capability of dealing with dynamic surrounding in real-time. They receive myriads of sensory information at a constant basis. Their course of action is based on what they sense. The load of real-time processing of this sensory information is enormous. But they effectively handle such a huge processing requirement. There is no doubt that primate brain is the most efficient, in terms of sheer processing power, of all creations existing as of now. But still brain cannot handle all sensory information coming at a particular instant of time. It only selects a few of this sensory information and processes them deep inside the brain, where activities like recognition and decision making take place. Most of the other information is discarded before it reaches to the deeper brain. This psycho-neurological phenomenon is known as selective attention.

DOI: 10.4018/978-1-4666-8723-3.ch002

Like primates, computer vision tasks also face the difficulty of handling this huge amount of sensory input (Tsotsos, 1990). To tackle this problem, computer vision researchers draw inspiration from the selective attention component of primate brain to restrict the computation in certain areas of input. As a result, computational modeling of visual attention has grown as an active research problem since last two decades. It requires a collective approach of theories from psychology, neurobiology of human visual system and other related topics. Psycho-visual experiments have provided some theoretical reasoning for saliency of a location or an object. Computer vision researchers try to fit various types of mathematical, statistical, or graph-based models on acquired eye-tracking data on the basis of these psycho-visual experiments.

There are two types of attention mechanism, i.e., bottom-up and top-down. Bottom-up attention is purely driven by external stimuli. It involuntarily attracts our gaze to salient portions in a scene (Itti and Koch, 2001). It models attractiveness of scene components at early stage of vision in the absence of semantic or context dependent knowledge about the scene being viewed. It is primarily driven by the unusualness in stimulus (in terms of one or more features) with respect to surroundings of a location or an object. In other words, this bottom-up mechanism of attention guides our vision towards distinguishable items in a scene. On the other hand, top-down mechanism of attention is driven by the demand of the task to be performed (Pelz and Canosa, 2001; Yarbus, 1967). This type of attention is controlled by semantic, context-dependent, or task-specific knowledge.

In the context of computer vision tasks, selective attention to a few pertinent salient portions in a scene has various advantages. It reduces the computational burden by decreasing the amount of data to be processed. Tasks such as searching a target object in a scene draws immense benefit from this attention-driven reduction of processing load. Moreover, suppression of irrelevant information ensures influence of only the relevant locations of the scene in the outcome of the system. As an example, tracking of an object in a scene or navigating a pilotless vehicle with the help of artificial vision system are examples of this category. In certain applications, indiscriminative treatment is given based on the saliency of individual contents of the scene. Visual attention guided compression is one such example. Here higher compression ratio is applied for less salient components of the image. On the contrary, salient image components are not compressed much. Underlying assumption behind this kind of compression techniques is that distortion due to lossy compression will not be perceptible, if they are restricted to less salient portions in the image.

Thus, a wide range of activities draw benefit from visual attention. This chapter, at first, briefly mentions computational models of two different categories of attention, i.e., bottom-up and top-down. Then, it focuses on wide range of applications of visual attention in image processing, computer vision, and graphics. These are discussed under various categories, such as

- Image and video processing (intelligent capturing of photos, compression, retargeting, watermarking, image quality assessment, color modification to guide attention and many more)
- Computer vision (object detection and tracking, scene classification, scene understanding, etc.)
- Robotics (self-localization and mapping, environment understanding and navigation for humanoid robots, pilotless vehicle navigation through artificial vision system, etc)
- Graphics (rendering and exploring virtual environments, improving 3D TV viewing experience, etc.)

COMPUTATIONAL MODELS OF VISUAL ATTENTION

Bottom-Up Attention

Feature integration theory of attention (Treisman and Gelade, 1980) provides the foundation for many of the widely acclaimed computational models of attention. It suggests that visual scene is separately encoded using various features at an early-stage of processing of visual sensory information. A detailed discussion on features which may or may not contribute to saliency can be found in (Wolfe and Horowitz, 2004). According to the feature integration theory (Treisman and Gelade, 1980), various features are registered in parallel across the visual field. In a location of a scene where attentional spotlight focuses, corresponding features integrate to present a perception of the object.

One of the earliest guidelines of computational model of attention is found in (Koch and Ullman, 1985). It provides a framework for the computational models based on feature-integration theory (Treisman and Gelade, 1980) and bottom-up mechanism of attention. Locations of the scene which are clearly different from their surrounding, in terms of each individual feature, contribute to conspicuity maps for each of these features. Then, these conspicuity maps are merged to produce a single saliency map. This saliency map conveys the relative saliency of the locations in the visual scene. A Winner-Take-All (WTA) mechanism selects various locations one-by-one in the decreasing order of their relative saliency starting from the most salient location.

The model in (Itti et al, 1998) directly implements the framework in (Koch and Ullman, 1985). According to (Itti et al, 1998), center-surround differences are estimated as the difference between finer and coarser scale in a multiple scale representation of various low-level features, such as color, intensity and orientation. Gaussian pyramid is used for multi-scale representation. (Milanese at al, 1994) uses difference-of-oriented-Gaussian (DoG) operator at multiple scales to compute saliency.

Computational models in (Ma and Zhang, 2003; Wu et al, 2009) encode saliency as a contrast of a pixel. Contrast, in these pixel based models, are measured using feature differences with neighboring pixels. As an alternative of capturing the difference between a pixel and its neighbors, (Vikram et al, 2011) considers the differences of a pixel with a set of randomly selected pixels. On the contrary to pixel-based approaches, region-wise difference estimations are also reported in (Luo and Singhal, 2000; Backer et al, 2001).

Information-theoretic approaches of determining saliency are reported in (Bruce, 2005; Bruce and Tsotsos, 2009; Qiu et al, 2007). The underlying philosophy, here, is that the information is inversely proportional to the likelihood of observing a particular feature in the image.

Graph based models of attention have been proposed in (Harel et al, 2006; Gopalakrishnan et al, 2009). In these graph based models, a node in the graph represent a pixel. Edge-weights are made proportional to feature difference of concerned pixels. These weights are also proportional to positional proximity of these pixels, when feature distances are same. Random walks on such graphs model shift of gaze through various pixels in the image. Markov chains from such graphs represent probabilities of shifting gaze from one pixel-to-other. Saliency is obtained through the equilibrium distribution on these Markov chains. A completely different kind of graph-based model is proposed in (Pal et al, 2010). A simple concept of degree of each node encodes the difference of underlying block of pixels with other blocks of pixels in the image.

(Kienzle et al, 2006) has trained a support vector machine (SVM) to classify a location as salient or non-salient. Gaze points were captured from observers while they were asked to view a set of training images. A 13-by-13 square patch around each pixel (at fixated gaze location or at any other random location) forms the feature vector. The support vector machine works with these feature vectors.

Several other notable models of visual attention include spectral residual based ((Hou and Zhang, 2007), rule-based (Yu and Wong, 2007), and edge detection based (Rosin, 2009) approaches. Apart from these static models of attention, various other models also deal with spatio-temporal characteristics of a video. The work in (Rapantzikos et al, 2004) is just a spatio-temporal extension of the static attention model in (Itti et al, 1998). At first, the video is split into constituent shots. Then, each shot is processed separately to construct a spatio-temporal saliency map. Frame-wise application of static model along with attention due to motion contributes to saliency. Many more saliency models can be found in (Guironnet et al, 2005; Zhai and Shah, 2006; Qiu et al, 2007; Li and Lee 2007; Chen et al, 2008; Longfei et al, 2008). A detailed review of various computational models can be found in (Frintrop et al, 2010; Pal, 2013).

Top-Down Attention

Top-down attention is driven by the task at hand. Sometimes, prior knowledge (or familiarity) of certain objects controls attention mechanism too. It prioritizes specific features based on the requirement of a task. A few computational models of top-down attention are mentioned here in brief.

In (Milanese et al, 1994), distributed associative memory (DAM) is used to recognize familiar objects. It provides the cue for the top-down model. The output of the DAM, i.e., the top-down attention map is integrated with several other bottom-up attention maps (derived from various features) using a relaxation based map combination strategy.

(Tsotsos et al, 1995) proposes the selective tuning model to selectively tune parts of the computation by a top-down hierarchy of winner-take-all processes embedded within a pyramidal processing architecture. Unwanted locations are inhibited or suppressed by identifying the feature values which are different from those of the target features. (Ramstrom and Christensen, 2002) proposes a game theoretic approach based on this selective tuning model. Game theory is adopted, here, for distributed control of attention.

(Driscoll et al, 1998) proposes a feature-gate based model to find out task-specific targets. Feature gate is described as a pyramidal artificial neural network. At each level of the feature gate, several networks exist for various feature channels. This model combines both bottom-up and top-down components of attention. Similar to bottom-up component of attention, it enhances locations having distinctive feature values with respect to their neighbors. The top-down mechanism suppresses saliency of a location in the presence of target-like objects in its neighborhood.

An attention model is proposed in (Tagare et al, 2001) which is more suitable for visual search using top-down attention mechanism. As the features of target objects are known, top-down attention plays an important role here. The basic assumption made by this work is that an object is constituted of several parts and each part is characterized by a set of features. This model finds out parts of objects which have a higher likelihood of becoming a target object by comparing features of the object part and the target feature.

In (Choi et al, 2004), attention is modeled as integration of bottom-up saliency and adaptive resonance theory (ART) network. ART network is a neural network model that is used to find patterns in input data. Supervised classification of salient and non-salient areas helps to train an ART network about characteristics of unwanted areas. Bottom-up saliency is computed using center-surround operations acting upon various features. A trained ART network is used to identify important areas among those specified by the bottom-up component.

In (Begum et al, 2006), a dynamically constructed Gaussian adapted resonance theory is employed to learn the features for attended locations. Then it guides attention to desired locations when performing desired task.

To incorporate the top-down bias in computing saliency, the model in (Peters and Itti, 2007) proposes to learn relation between gaze patterns and low-level signatures computed from features to represent image gist (Siagian and Itti, 2007). For a new scene, linear least-square best fit mechanism is employed to search for a suitable gist and corresponding gaze pattern is followed.

When the task is to search for objects with given features, a dissimilarity based top-down model is proposed in (Jing et al, 2009). At first, salient maps are constructed using a bottom-up model for each of the considered features. Manhattan distance is estimated between the task map and each of the generated bottom-up saliency maps. Each map is then boosted by a weight multiplier which is inversely proportional to its estimated distance.

In (Navalpakkam and Itti, 2006), top-down bias is controlled by the ratio of saliency of a target and that of distractors. Features that maximize this signal-to-noise ratio are chosen for search related tasks.

APPLICATIONS IN IMAGE AND VIDEO PROCESSING

Intelligent Capturing of Photos

Improvement in sensor technologies has delivered cameras with acceptable resolution with almost every hand-held electronic gadget. Mobile phones, tablet PCs are the simplest of those camera-enabled hand-held devices we can think of. So, everyone wants to be a good photographer. But can everyone master this art? Continuous technological progress towards this aim has brought smarter cameras to meet the eternal quest of the photographers to capture a perfect photo. Computational photography is a recent addition in this field. Programmability at the pixel level accompanied by smaller transistor size has contributed in increasingly more functionality in the cameras. One major aspect of a good photography is the captured photo should accurately convey the central theme of the photo (as perceived by the photographer) to the viewer. No other distracting object should unnecessarily occupy attention of the viewer. In this direction, (Pal et al, 2008) conceptualizes an intelligent camera to automatically capture the photo in such a way that the intended object automatically draws viewer's attention. It uses selective visual attention models to estimate which portions of the photograph will quickly attract viewers' gaze. Then this camera intelligently adjusts its parameters so that it highlights the intended portions of the photograph. Thus interested objects have maximum attention values. Rendering the objects of interest as more salient, this attention-based camera succeeds to attract viewers' gaze on the intended objects.

Image Modification for Guiding Attention

Apart from intelligent capturing of the image (as described above), specific objects (or portions) in the image (or video) are highlighted through changes in the media (image or video). For example, a panoramic 3D system for navigation in the city likes to draw tourists' attention towards landmark locations or places of tourists' interest. It can highlight the interesting contents using arrows or other highlighting effects. But, these approaches may distract the tourists from their tasks by exacerbating perceptual issues inherent to the task. Therefore, the viewers' attention must be automatically guided towards a target without disturbing their current visual attention.

(Kokui et al, 2013) proposes an approach to modify an image in such a fashion that viewers are automatically attracted towards the intended target. The proposed method iteratively adjusts the intensity and color so that the visual saliency of the intended target increases while the saliency decreases for other contents. The iteration is carried out until the target becomes the most salient within the image. As a result, viewers' attention can be silently guided to the intended target. Any artificially injected highlighting tool does not disturb the viewers' gaze here.

Image Watermarking

In image watermarking, some private information (i.e., watermark) is secretly embedded in the image by modifying pixel values of the image. Robustness of the watermarking scheme ensures that the watermark signal will not be destroyed due to various intentional or unintentional attacks on the watermarked image. But an increase in robustness may result in the increased visibility of the watermark. However, this perceptual distortion of the image is not directly related to the magnitude of the watermark signal. It has been demonstrated in (Sur et al, 2009) that a watermark in visually less salient locations causes less perceptual distortion in the image as compared to the same watermark being embedded in salient locations. For this purpose, the biologically-inspired visual attention model in (Itti et al, 1998) has been used in (Sur et al, 2009) to find less salient locations. Even, it has been reported for most of the cases that the least salient pixels in the original image remain least salient even after embedding watermark. Therefore, (Sur et al, 2009) introduces a new image watermarking technique by embedding the watermark in the less salient pixels.

Color-to-Gray Conversion

Converting a color image to gray-scale is necessary in several situations – for example, monochrome printing, single channel image processing, and many more. Conventional techniques consider a simple or weighted average of the red, green and blue values. But this conversion of 3-dimensional information to 1-dimension causes information loss. Moreover, it fails to retain the viewing pleasure as with the original color image.

This color-to-gray transformation is also immensely benefited by the theories of color perception by human visual system. Human vision is attracted towards regions with higher contrast. Moreover, the perceived color depends on color contrast in the neighborhood. Regions with the same color values may be perceived differently depending on their surrounding colors. This provides the basis in (Du et al, 2015) for developing a saliency-preserving color-to-gray transformation model. Unlike traditional methods, it does not always map the same color to same gray value. But this method maintains the same saliency for the region in the gray-scale image as with that in the original color image, thus leading to similar viewing experience.

Image and Video Browsing on Small Displays

Last decade has also witnessed a dramatic growth in mobile device technologies and Internet browsing. These concurrent growths lead to image and video browsing in small displays like mobile phones. But fitting high resolution images and videos into small displays poses a challenge. Simple down-sampling of the media does not result in pleasant viewing experience. Small objects become almost unrecognizable in small displays.

Several intelligent retargeting methods have come into rescue in this context. Visual attention model is at the core of these solutions. Attention model helps to identify important contents in the media. Discriminative treatment based on importance of each individual content is the fundamental theme of these methods.

Cropping a rectangular window of suitable size encompassing the important contents in an image is proposed in (Suh et al, 2003; Luo, 2007; Ciocca ct al, 2007). All other contents lying outside this rectangle are not selected for viewing. But these cropping based techniques produce good result when there is only one important object in the image or multiple important contents are closely located in the image. But these methods are not very effective when important objects are sparsely distributed in the image.

(Chen et al, 2003) proposes an effective image browsing technique based on rapid serial visual presentation. According to this method, important contents are displayed one-after-another. Here, time is compromised but viewers get pleasant viewing experience of all important contents.

Seam carving (Avidan and Shamir, 2007) is an effective method irrespective of spatial distribution of important contents within the image. Seam carving fits an image to the target display by iteratively removing seams those pass through less important contents of the image. But removing excessive number of seams to fit the image in small display often induces distortion. Later on, controlled seam carving (Hwang and Chien, 2008; Utsugi et al, 2009) methods have been introduced to control such distortions. Another retargeting approach based on optimized scale-and-stretch warping (Wang et al, 2008) iteratively computes local scaling factors for each local region. This technique is also proved effective, even if important contents are sparsely distributed in the image.

(Pal et al, 2011) proposes a rectangular partition based retargeting approach where relative enlargement of important rectangular partitions holds the key. At first, the original image space is partitioned into non-overlapping rectangles based on the importance of the contents in the image. Then similar partitioning of the target space maintains a one-to-one correspondence between the partitions in the input space and the target space. Then important rectangles are enlarged in the target space following a set of constraints as mentioned here: (i) Uniform enhancement for all important rectangles while maintaining their respective aspect ratios. (ii) Relative ordering of these important rectangles is maintained as same as the original image.

Another retargeting strategy has been proposed in (Pal et al, 2012) based on a well-calculated shrinkage of rectangular strips form the image. At first, the image is partitioned into rectangular strips containing important and unimportant contents, alternatively. Unimportant rectangular strips are shrinked more as compared with important rectangular strips.

Image and Video Compression

The fact that only a few salient locations draw human observer's attention helps in image and video compression. A high resolution representation of these locations of gaze fixations is formed in our retina.

Other regions are represented with decreasing resolution with distances from the fixation points. As a result, even a major degradation in visual quality remains unnoticed in these non-salient regions. This suggests that the visual scene can be represented using a non-uniform coding scheme.

This above discussion lays the foundation of visual attention based compression schemes (Stentiford, 2001). Visual attention model specifies a set of salient portions in the image (or video). (Stentiford, 2001) introduces a visual attention guided image compression scheme, where differential compression is applied based on this perceived importance of the regions. Higher compression rate is applied in less salient regions. Salient regions are subjected to lesser compression. Therefore, this scheme does not degrade the perceived quality of the image in spite of achieving an acceptable level of compression.

(Lee et al, 2011) applies similar concepts in the context of video compression. Moreover, they have adopted an audio-visual attention model. The basic assumption, here, is that the sound source and its neighboring region in the video attract viewers' attention. Therefore, a labeling of certain objects with the audio-channel is carried out using an audio-visual source localization algorithm. Basically, those objects are the focal points of attention (according to the underlying audio-visual attention model). Each frame in the video is partitioned into several regions based on their spatial distance from the sound source. Different quantization parameters are used to encode these regions depending on their distance form sound source. Large values for this quantization parameter are used for the regions which are away from the sound source. Therefore, such distant regions (less-salient) can be encoded with less number of bits as compared to regions which maintain spátial proximity with the sound source.

Image Quality Assessment

Image quality assessment is used in the context of a wide range of visual systems, e.g., optimizing digital imaging systems, benchmarking of image and video coding algorithms, measuring the loss of perceptual quality in watermarking. These metrics quantify the perceived quality of the image.

Traditional metrics, such as mean-squared error (MSE) and peak signal-to-noise ratio (PSNR), account for the pixel-by-pixel difference between the original and the distorted image. But these metrics do not correlate well with human perception. An artifact appearing on a region of interest is more visible compared to its presence in a less salient location. But these traditional metrics do not reveal this fact. As, human visual system is the ultimate evaluator of the image quality, researchers (Liu and Heynderickx, 2011) have proposed objective quality assessment metrics which also account for where we look more. The basic assumption is that a distortion in a highly attentive area is more annoying than in any other areas. Therefore, local distortions are weighted with corresponding local saliency. Basically, the natural scene saliency and the measured distortions in the image are estimated separately. Then, these two are combined to assess the quality of the image. Independence of underlying computational model of visual attention is one major characteristics of the work in (Liu and Heynderickx, 2009; 2011). Clearly, the researchers, here, wanted that deficiency of an underlying computational model should not demoralize the task of quality assessment. So, their work was directly based on human eye-tracking data. Human gaze behavior was recorded to understand the components in an image where more attention is being paid. A saliency score was estimated based on this eye-tracking data and this score is used in this work to assess image quality. The work in (You et al, 2010) has also demonstrated the usefulness of visual attention in assessing image quality.

Texture Description

Texture is defined as repetitive patterns with regular frequency. The work in (Mancas et al, 2006) tries to establish the relation between texture and visual attention. A rarity based attention model has been proposed in this work. It is an information theoretic approach. It is based on counting of similar pixels. Saliency is modeled as log-inversely proportional to pixel occurrence frequency. Rare pixels obtain a very high attention score, but repeatitive pixels get lower scores. So, a repeatitive or regular texture is less salient because it repeats itself more number of times. A homogenous area can be considered as the most regular texture. As a consequence, it is paid the least attention. For more irregular textures, attention is less. Thus, attentiveness to regions can directly be linked to the texture regularity. More salient a region is, less regular is its texture.

Furthermore, in (Mancas et al, 2006), this saliency map is thresholded using Otsu's method. This divides the image into foreground and background portions. Portions more salient than the threshold is considered as foreground, whereas portions less salient than the threshold is thought as background. Further, the foreground and the background regions are divided into several equally important parts. Then following two parameters are estimated for each of these parts:

1. Saliency levels (from 1 to 10), and
2. Spatial density of these levels.

A high density signifies a texture with a simple pattern as all the gray-levels of the pattern are quite close. If the density is not very high and the regions are spread over several saliency levels, it indicates that the texture pattern is quite complex and it is composed from very different gray levels. Thus visual attention model is utilized in texture characterization, i.e., there is a direct relation between visual attention and the texture regularity.

Image and Video Retrieval

In Content Based Image Retrieval (CBIR), an entire image repository is searched based on information about the actual contents of the images. Query information can be taken in various forms. One way is to query based on a similar image. A query engine, then, translates this image in some way as to query the database (based on previously extracted information from images in the repository) and retrieve the candidate images which have similar content like the input image.

Object-based approaches of CBIR rely on image segmentation techniques. But accurate segmentation of various kinds of images to decompose them into meaningful segments is a challenging task itself. (Marques et al, 2006) determines the regions of interest within an image based on a biologically-inspired model of visual attention in (Itti et al, 1998). According to this model, the salient regions within an image are extracted in a purely unsupervised approach. These salient regions indicate the important objects in the image. A feature extraction module then extracts the features from these regions, and the results are indexed and clustered with those of other similar regions from other images in the repository. Therefore, visual saliency reduces the task in such a way that only visually salient objects become center of processing in CBIR system. Similarly, attention can be applied in the context of video retrieval.

Image Mosaics

In traditional sense, a mosaic is a visible pattern which is designed using small pieces of colored stone, ceramic or glass tiles. An image mosaic is the digital correspondence of the traditional mosaic. In this context, tiles are basically small images which are called tile images. When these tile images are looked at separately, each of them appear to be a unique image. But, a collective view of these tile images which are specially arranged to form the mosaic, suggests a whole large image.

In a lifestyle image mosaic, the target image is a lifestyle image of a person, and the tile images are selected from his personal collection of lifestyle images. Based on saliency, a content-aware technique to generate such a lifestyle image mosaic is proposed in (Guo et al, 2015). There are three key issues of lifestyle image mosaics: tile decomposition of the target image, tile image retrieval and database formation. Visual saliency is used for target image decomposition and retrieval of tile images. Features like saliency weighted color histogram and saliency weighted texture histogram have been used for retrieving constituent tile images to form the mosaic.

Video Shot Matching

Shot-based similarity matching is a necessary step for any video indexing and retrieval systems. Traditionally, low-level features such as texture or color histograms of frames were used for this task. But lack of correlation between these low-level features and high-level semantics was a major valid concern against these approaches. (Li and Lee, 2007) presents an alternative way of video understanding by simulating the visual attention mechanism. An attention-driven shot matching method is proposed in (Li and Lee, 2007) where more attention is paid to the attentive regions.

Video Summarization

With the advances in multimedia technologies and due to the emergence of application areas like surveillance, a bulk amount of video data is generated every day. The large volume of data requires efficient video content management scheme for effective browsing. Automatic video summarization provides the basis for efficient management of bulk video data. The summary enables the viewer to grasp the gist of the video in minimal effort. The summary also helps the viewers to quickly find out a relevant portion in the large video. There are two kinds of representation of video summaries: key frames and video skims. Key frame based representation is a static summary comprising of a collection of the important frames from the video. A video skim is a much shorter video comprising a collection of important subclips from the video. The key-frame based static summary is useful in many contexts, though it does not preserve the time-varying nature of the video. On the other hand, a video skim, though computationally expensive to produce, provides a better preview of the entire video.

A good understanding of the semantic contents of the video is essential to produce a summary of the video. Automatic semantic understanding of a general video is a largely unsolved problem, as yet. Modeling of viewer's attention provides the capability to understand which portions of the video will be attended by the viewers. Therefore, (Ma et al, 2002) has proposed an attention-guided video summarization framework. It shows how a video summary can be generated without a semantic understanding of the underlying semantic. By assigning an attention score to each frame, this method finds out which set of frames are more likely to attract viewers' gaze. Then, the video skims are also generated based on the crests of the attention curve. An efficient attention-guided key frame extraction framework is also found in (Ejaz et al, 2013).

Video Hashing

Popularity of spatio-temporal video hashes is due to their ability to identify a video via both the spatial and temporal features. The video hashes, which are derived from the temporal representative frames (TRF), have received much of the interest. A video hashing scheme based on a temporally visual weighting (TVW) method is proposed in (Liu et al, 2013). The temporal variation of visual attention is utilized to weight the frames during the generation of the temporal representative frames (TRF).

Content Insertion in Video

Content insertion is an emerging application of video processing in the context of advertisement insertion. Advertisement insertion in videos (movie, sports, and other television programs) provides much more advertising opportunity to the advertisers. However, this task requires a lot of time and hard work for the large chunk of video data. Automatic content insertion techniques have been proposed to tackle this problem. While inserting contents, emphasis is given on following two points:

1. The inserted contents should be easily noticeable by the audience, and
2. The inserted contents should not disturb the audience's viewing experience to the original content.

Therefore, the contents should be at a time when the video attracts more attention from the audience. On the other hand, it should be inserted at a region in the frame where it will draw less attention as compared to the original contents of the frame. As a result, highly attentive shots are detected as the insertion time and less salient regions in the frames of those shots are selected as the insertion place.

Based on visual attention modeling, a generic content insertion system is presented in (Liu et al, 2008). The system uses temporal attention analysis to determine the highly attentive shots. It also selects the insertion place by detecting less salient regions through spatial attention analysis of the frames in the highly attentive shots. Thus, (Liu et al, 2008) draws a balance between the attentiveness of the inserted content and disturbance of the viewing experience to the original content.

APPLICATIONS IN COMPUTER VISION

Scene Analysis

Humans are adept at real-time analysis of complex scenes around them. Through attention, a subset of the available sensory information is selected for further processing at deeper brain. It reduces the complexity of scene analysis. It scans the scene both in a rapid, bottom-up, saliency-driven, and task-independent manner as well as in a slower, top-down, volition-controlled, and task-dependent manner. Basically, attention is guided as a combination of both bottom-up and top-down approaches.

(Itti et al, 1998) proposes one biologically-influenced computational model of visual attention on the basis of feature integration theory (Treisman and Gelade, 1980) and the works of (Koch and Ullman, 1985). The scene is decomposed into a set of topographic feature maps. Various spatial locations compete for saliency within each map. Only locations which are remarkably different from their surroundings are highlighted in the feature-specific conspicuity map. All such conspicuity maps combine to obtain a single saliency map. This saliency map conveys conspicuity of the locations over the entire visual scene.

Thus, (Itti et al, 1998) comes up with a massively parallel method for quick selection of a small number of interesting locations in the scene. Only those locations, then, can be analyzed by more complex and time consuming processes, such as object recognition and scene understanding. (Navalpakkam et al, 2005) provides a detailed explanation of how visual attention contributes in scene understanding. Even this approach provides immense advantage in searching activities. Confining the search process in highly salient locations reduces search time. Moreover, knowledge about the target object can be utilized to highlight certain feature maps such that only those can reach at higher levels of brain.

Target Search and Detection

Feature-integration theory (Treisman & Gelade, 1980) suggests that the search for an object is carried out through a slow serial scanning over various regions as attention binds low-level features into single objects. This theory inspires researchers to come up with visual attention models based on saliency maps. It realizes simple and direct implementation of task-independent bottom-up mechanism of attention. As an example, (Itti et al, 2001) implements a pre-attentive selection mechanism based on human visual system. They have shown how low-level features like intensity, orientation and color are encoded in a center-surround fashion at different spatial scales to produce a saliency map. This kind of models based on low-level features is adopted to perform target search in the absence of semantic information. The implementation was able to emulate human performance on a number of search experiments.

Visual context information also plays a major role in the search for a specific object in a complex scene. Our gaze is directed by the context information. (Oliva et al, 2003), proposes an attention model incorporating the relevance of the visual context of the object being searched. The work has revealed that the statistics *of* low-level features across the scene is strongly correlated with the location of a specific object. A simple model of saliency has been developed based on the distribution of local features in the image and a model of contextual priors. Contextual priors are driven by the relationship between context features and the location of the target as observed in the past. This paper suggests that pre-attentive heuristics based on the context within which an object is embedded speeds up the object detection through pre-selection of relevant regions in the image. Experimental validation of the scheme has been carried out with the task of locating possible locations of people in scenes.

(Torralba et al, 2006) represents the structure of a scene using the mean of global image features at a coarse spatial resolution. This representation eases the task of object detection without the help from segmentation and object recognition. Image saliency and context features are combined here. Task-guided top-down component influences the selection of relevant regions through context features for exploration.

Another visual attention model has been proposed in (Fang et al, 2011) for object detection in natural scenes through integration of bottom-up and top-down attention. The model uses the orientation features for top-down component of attention. Based on the statistical knowledge of orientation features in images, this model guides the search towards few potential locations in the image.

(Wang et al, 2012) decomposes the task as the process of visual information extraction and visual attention guiding. The visual attention guiding layer promotes the key feature of the target to guide the formation of saliency map. Thus this model improves the efficiency of search task.

(Hou et al, 2013) proposes an attention-guided ship detection method from Synthetic Aperture Radar (SAR) images. SAR is an active microwave sensor which can work irrespective of lighting and weather conditions. So it is heavily used for target detection and resource monitoring. (Hou et al, 2013) partitions the the ship detection process into two parts: water segmentation and ship detection. In water segmentation, the bottom-up and the top-down visual attention mechanisms are used to obtain water segmented image. Then, in ship detection part, the interested regions are extracted by estimating the conspicuity of visual attention in the water segments.

Object Tracking

(Li et al, 2003) proposes an object tracking method based on visual attention. At first, this method finds out the salient regions based on orientation and color. Then, these extracted features from the object being tracked are used to track the object in subsequent frames. The preliminary identification of salient regions helps to improve the processing speed.

Object Recognition

Visual attention, even, has been used to speed up the task of object recognition by restricting analysis to regions having significant information. In (Lee et al, 2010), top-down attention is guided by the concept of familiarity. Familiarity is thought of a measure of the resemblance between features extracted from the input image and features of trained object models. A high familiarity is perceived as evidence of the presence of the object. Therefore, this concept of familiarity guides attention to portions in the scene where presence of a known object is highly likely. A unified visual attention model has been proposed in (Lee et al, 2010) to incorporate both stimulus-driven bottom-up and goal-driven top-down components of attention. The saliency-model in (Itti et al, 1998) has been used here to model bottom-up attention. Reduction of recognition time has been substantial as it has been demonstrated in this work.

Face Recognition

Even this speed up is achieved in the context of face recognition too. (Bonaiuto and Itti, 2006) proposes the usage of visual attention for face recognition. The authors also suggest that the previous location of the face provides helps in recognizing the face. The basic assumption is that a person's location typically very little in consecutive frames. Therefore, bottom-up visual attention along with face prioritization by location provides better results for face recognition.

Scene Classification

Self-localization and navigation are two essential components in robotics. These activities require the capability to classify the scene based on its constituents. This is a challenge for outdoor scenes as outdoor environment can vary tremendously. Moreover, various other effects, such as different lighting conditions at different time of a day, dynamic background, make the task very difficult. Computer vision researchers have drawn the inspiration for human brain which is amazingly efficient in outdoor localization and navigation. Human visual system focuses attention only to those regions within the field of view which appear as interesting. Simultaneously, human brain is very efficient in capturing the gist of a scene. (Siagian and Itti, 2007) has proposed a scene classification technique by computing the gist of a scene through the use of same set of features which are used to compute saliency. Moreover, the model uses salient cues to create distinct signatures for individual scenes.

ROBOTICS

Visual attention modeling finds an important role in developing robotic vision. Enormous amount of research is directed towards how attention component of primate vision can be emulated in robot vision. Therefore, a separate section, in this chapter, is allotted to discuss application of visual attention in this particular field of computer vision.

Humanoid-Robots

Humanoid robots are designed to comprehend real-time instructions from a person. For this, such a robot has to be capable of processing visual and auditory sensory inputs in real time. Specifically, it understands human communication in the form of hand gestures and speech. Based on received instruction, the robot performs a well-defined task. In order to real-time comprehension of sensory signal inputs, the humanoid robot deploys a model of visual attention to focus on the necessary input (Driscoll et al, 1998).

The humanoid robot must also understand its dynamic surrounding to respond to the human interaction. The robot vision requires an attention component for real-time analysis of dynamic scene (Breazeal et al, 2001; Vijayakumar et al, 2001). It is to be noted that the robot is not static. It also changes its position through body movement as a result of its interaction with its instructor and the surrounding.

Real-time perception of dynamic scene poses two basic challenges:

1. Efficiently shifting the gaze, i.e., attentional spotlight, to important objects in the visual scene, and
2. Determining which objects are important and, as a consequence, where to look next.

(Orabona et al, 2005) employs a concept of saliency based on proto-objects (defined as blobs of uniform color) to control the gaze fixation points of a robot head. The robot, even, can build a statistical model of the features of the attended objects. These proto-objects and their relative spatial locations can then bias attention toward known objects. It is experimentally demonstrated how the top-down attention guides the the robot to find out specific objects among other objects lying on a table.

Ability to focus on task relevant information is crucial for most robotic applications. The capability of focusing on task-relevant and/or visually demanding information helps a robot to efficiently process the incoming visual information. A Bayesian model of visual attention for a behaving robot can be found in (Begum et al, 2006; 2010). Bayes filter along with a dynamically constructed adaptive resonance theory is considered to recursively estimate the focus of attention in a dynamic environment.

(Begum and Karray, 2011) presents a comprehensive survey on visual attention modeling for robot vision.

Robot Self-Localization and Mapping

Self-localization and mapping based on visual data is an important topic in robotics. It generates a map of the environment and stays localized within the map. The map keeps track of the landmarks and their relative position to each other and also with respect to the robot. This internal representation of the environment serves as guide for the robot in the environment. Selecting easily-tractable visual landmarks is required for visual localization and mapping. An attention guided landmark detection mechanism has been proposed in (Frintrop et al, 2007). Considering salient regions as landmark is essential for easy detection and tracking.

Control of Robot Vehicle

Pilotless autonomous robot vehicles decide its movement by analyzing the image of the road ahead. Road edges are identified to keep the vehicle on track. Lane markings guide it to proper direction. There are obstacles on the road in the form of other vehicles and pedestrians. The autonomous vehicle needs to make its way through the clutter of these obstacles. Moreover, presence of roadside trees, pedestrians and other vehicles may block its view to localize road edges and landmarks. Additionally, in a complex real-world road scene, myriads of other objects make the analysis difficult.

Driven by the challenge of attending to relevant important inputs for decision making (about the direction and speed to navigate the vehicle) among distracting obstacles, (Baluja and Pomerleau, 1997a; 1997b) has proposed a task-specific focus of attention based on predicting the expected location of the relevant objects in next time step. Inputs which do not match with these expectations can be de-emphasized from processing. This reduces the effects of distractions by unavoidable obstacles. But not all unexpected inputs are ignored. Surprise presence of another car on the road (though unexpected) is identified to properly navigate the vehicle on the road. Therefore, (Baluja and Pomerleau, 1997a; 1997b) used two modules of processing logic to deal with unexpected inputs in two different ways – one module de-emphasizes them to reduce distraction, and the other module emphasizes the attention on them to avoid collision, i.e., better navigation.

Tele-Operation System

In a vision guided teleoperation system, human operators remotely control the robots, or the teleoperators, to remotely perform the tasks. The visual signal is sent back to the remote operators through wireless communication channels. But wireless communication suffers from sudden drop of signal strength and, hence, non-uniform bandwidth distribution in the navigation zone. Since the video feedback is crucial component of the system and needs high bandwidth, an effective compression method is required to transmit the data over a limited and unstable bandwidth. Representation of the video using a space-variant resolution of is essential as the resolution around the attended location in retinal fovea is the highest. It decreases as the distance from fovea increases. (Teng et al, 2013) considers these aspects while generating the image sequences. As less space is required for the outer parts of an image if compressed with foveated multi-resolution method, visual feedback can capture wider focus of vision. A saliency-based visual attention mechanism is used to automatically identify the regions of interest where the operators must look at. Thus, (Teng et al, 2013) proposes a teleoperation system which helps operators in controlling the remote robots.

APPLICATIONS IN COMPUTER GRAPHICS

Synthetic Vision in a Virtual Environment

Many computer graphics based applications simulate a virtual environment. Video games are examples of such applications. In these games, new scenes are explored through the eyes of an autonomous actor, i.e., virtual humanoid. (Courty et al, 2003) develops a visual attention model for these virtual scenes and demonstrates how saliency maps can be utilized to guide the humanoid vision in new situations. The saliency map represents the conspicuity of every location in the visual field. Humanoid vision is guided based on this conspicuity information of those locations. (Hillaire et al, 2012) proposes a visual attention model specifically to explore 3D virtual environments.

Rendering of Dynamic Environments

In Virtual Environments (VE), prior estimation of regions, where attention will be focused, provides the developers several advantages to efficiently render a high-quality virtual scene. Thus, a better utilization of computational resources is possible while elegantly rendering a virtual scene. For example, proper illumination of a scene requires accurate calculation of lighting at every point in the scene. It is computationally expensive process, even for static environments. Obviously, it is more computationally challenging for dynamic environments. It is proportional to number of images used for the animation. Moreover, presence of moving objects increases the computation. Global illumination can be estimated a priori for a lighting solution in static environments. On the contrary, every moving object or light source influences every other object in the dynamic environments. Based on two psychophysical concepts – spatio-temporal sensitivity and visual attention, (Yee et al, 2001) proposes a technique to extensively reduce this computational burden. Spatio-temporal sensitivity specifies the amount of tolerable error. It helps in saving computation in less sensitive areas. Visual attention guides our gaze. Areas selected through visual attention must be accurately rendered as compared to less salient regions. Thus, this work exploited the limitations of the human visual system in perceiving moving spatial patterns. Efficacy of this method has been experimentally demonstrated with animation sequences.

(Cater et al, 2003) proposes to render scene objects which are not related to the task with lower resolution. As it is experimentally observed that the task influences the attended regions in a scene, viewers so not feel any reduction in quality in this case. A computational framework has been developed to use high-level task information to derive the error visibility in each frame of a progressively rendered animation. Thus, high quality animated sequences are generated at a constant frame rate within a very short span of time. It is to be noted that this technique only depends on the task, not on the viewer. This is because viewers participating in the same task will resort to similar visual processes to focus on same regions. Thus, inattentional blindness has been exploited for accelerate rendering by reducing quality in regions that are not directly related to the given task.

Improving 3D TV Viewing Experience

Three-dimensional (3D) television (TV) is the next buzzword in consumer electronics. A good visual experience by the viewer will be crucial in wider acceptance of 3D-TV. Viewers, generally, pay attention to specific interesting areas in the image. Visual attention, hence, is a key factor in determining the overall visual experience. In (Huynh-Thu et al, 2011), authors discusses how the 3D visual attention models can be used to improve the overall 3D TV viewing experience.

CONCLUSION

As it can be found throughout this chapter, visual attention models improve the performance of wide range of applications in image processing, computer vision, and graphics. This is, indeed, inspired by this phenomenal capability of primate vision system to focus on selected contents in the scene. This chapter attempts to compile a good number of these applications as found in literature. Putting enormous amount of related research efforts within one article, this chapter enlightens us about the utility of visual attention models.

REFERENCES

Avidan, S., & Shamir, A. (2007). Seam carving for content-aware image resizing. *ACM Transactions on Graphics*, *26*(3), 10. doi:10.1145/1276377.1276390

Backer, G., Mertsching, B., & Bollmann, M. (2001). Data- and model-driven gaze control for an active-vision system. *IEEE Transactions on Pattern Analysis and Machine Intelligence*, *23*(12), 1415–1429. doi:10.1109/34.977565

Baluja, S., & Pomerleau, D. (1997b). Dynamic relevance: Vision-based focus of attention using artificial neural networks. *Artificial Intelligence*, *97*(1-2), 381–395. doi:10.1016/S0004-3702(97)00065-9

Baluja, S., & Pomerleau, D. A. (1997a). Expectation-based selective attention for visual monitoring and control of a robot vehicle. *Robotics and Autonomous Systems*, *22*(3-4), 329–344. doi:10.1016/S0921-8890(97)00046-8

Begum, M., & Karray, F. (2011). Visual attention for robotic cognition: A survey. *IEEE Transactions on Autonomous Mental Development*, *3*(1), 92–105. doi:10.1109/TAMD.2010.2096505

Begum, M., Karray, F., Mann, G. K. I., & Gosine, R. G. (2010). A probabilistic model of overt visual attention for cognitive robots. *IEEE Transactions on Systems, Man, and Cybernetics. Part B, Cybernetics*, *40*(5), 1305–1318. doi:10.1109/TSMCB.2009.2037511 PMID:20089477

Begum, M., Mann, G. K. I., & Gosine, R. G. (2006). A biologically inspired Bayesian model of visual attention for humanoid robots. In *Proc. of 6th IEEE-RAS International Conference on Humanoid Robots*, (pp. 587–592). doi:10.1109/ICHR.2006.321333

Bonaiuto, J., & Itti, L. (2006). The use of attention and spatial information for rapid facial recognition in video. *Image and Vision Computing*, *24*(5), 557–563. doi:10.1016/j.imavis.2005.09.008

Breazeal, C., Edsinger, A., Fitzpatrick, P., & Scassellati, B. (2001). Active vision for sociable robots. *IEEE Transactions on Systems. Man and Cybernetics: Part A*, *31*(5), 443–453. doi:10.1109/3468.952718

Bruce, N. D. B. (2005). Features that draw visual attention: An information theoretic perspective. *Neurocomputing, 65-66*, 125–133. doi:10.1016/j.neucom.2004.10.065

Bruce, N. D. B., & Tsotsos, J. K. (2009). Saliency, attention and visual search: An information theoretic approach. *Journal of Vision (Charlottesville, Va.), 9*(3), 1–24. doi:10.1167/9.3.5 PMID:19757944

Cater, K., Chalmers, A., & Ward, G. (2003). Detail to attention: exploiting visual tasks for selective rendering. In *Proc. of 14th Eurographic Workshop on Rendering*.

Chen, D.-Y., Tyan, H.-R., Hsiao, D.-Y., Shih, S.-W., & Liao, H.-Y. M. (2008). Dynamic visual saliency modeling based on spatiotemporal analysis. In *Proc. of IEEE International Conference on Multimedia and Expo*.

Chen, L.-Q., Xie, X., Fan, X., Ma, W.-Y., Zhang, H.-J., & Zhou, H.-Q. (2003). A visual Attention model for adapting images on small displays. *Multimedia Systems, 9*(4), 353–364. doi:10.1007/s00530-003-0105-4

Choi, S.-B., Ban, S.-W., & Lee, M. (2004). Biologically motivated visual attention system using bottom-up saliency map and top-down inhibition. *Neural Information Processing-Letters and Reviews, 2*.

Ciocca, G., Cusano, C., Gasparini, F., & Schettini, R. (2007). Self-adaptive image cropping for small displays. *IEEE Transactions on Consumer Electronics, 53*(4), 1622–1627. doi:10.1109/TCE.2007.4429261

Courty, N., Marchand, E., & Arnaldi, B. (2003). A new application for saliency maps: synthetic vision of autonomous actors. In *Proc. of International Conference on Image Processing*. doi:10.1109/ICIP.2003.1247432

Driscoll, J. A., Peters, R. A. II, & Cave, K. R. (1998). A visual attention network for a humanoid robot. In *Proc. of IEEE/RSJ International Conference on Intelligent Robots and Systems*. doi:10.1109/IROS.1998.724894

Du, H., He, S., Sheng, B., Ma, L., & Lau, R. W. H. (2015). Saliency-guided color-to-gray conversion using region-based optimization. *IEEE Transactions on Image Processing, 24*(1), 434–443. doi:10.1109/TIP.2014.2380172 PMID:25531949

Ejaz, N., Mehmood, I., & Baik, S. W. (2013). Efficient visual attention based framework for extracting key frames from videos. *Signal Processing Image Communication, 28*(1), 34–44. doi:10.1016/j.image.2012.10.002

Fang, Y., Lin, W., Lau, C. T., & Lee, B.-S. (2011). A visual attention model combining top-down and bottom-up mechanisms for salient object detection. In *Proc. of IEEE International Conference on Acoustics, Speech and Signal Processing*. doi:10.1109/ICASSP.2011.5946648

Frintrop, S., Jensfelt, P., & Christensen, H. (2007). Simultaneous robot localization and mapping based on a visual attention system. *Attention in Cognitive Systems, Lecture Notes on Artificial Intelligence, 4840*.

Frintrop, S., Rome, E., & Christensen, H. I. (2010). Computational visual attention systems and their cognitive foundations: a survey. *Transactions on Applied Perceptions, 7*(1).

Gopalakrishnan, V., Hu, Y., & Rajan, D. (2009). Random walks on graphs to model saliency in images. In *Proc. of IEEE Computer Society Conference on Computer Vision and Pattern Recognition*. doi:10.1109/CVPR.2009.5206767

Guironnet, M., Guyader, N., Pellerin, D., & Ladret, P. (2005). Spatio-temporal Attention Model for Video Content Analysis. In *Proc. of IEEE International Conference on Image processing*. doi:10.1109/ICIP.2005.1530602

Guo, D., Tang, J., Cui, Y., Ding, J., & Zhao, C. (2015). Saliency-based content-aware lifestyle image mosaics. *Journal of Visual Communication and Image Representation*, 26, 192–199.

Harel, J., Koch, C., & Perona, P. (2006). Graph-based visual saliency. *Advances in Neural Information Processing Systems*, 19, 2006.

Hillaire, S., Lecuyer, A., Regia-Corte, T., Cozot, R., Royan, J., & Breton, G. (2012). Design and application of real-time visual attention model for the exploration of 3D virtual environments. *IEEE Transactions on Visualization and Computer Graphics*, 18(3), 356–368. doi:10.1109/TVCG.2011.154 PMID:21931178

Hou, B., Yang, W., Wang, S., & Hou, X. (2013). SAR image ship detection based on visual attention model. In *Proc. of IEEE International Geoscience and Remote Sensing Symposium*, (pp. 2003-2006). doi:10.1109/IGARSS.2013.6723202

Hou, X., & Zhang, L. (2007). Saliency detection: a spectral residual approach. In *Proc. of IEEE Conference on Computer Vision and Pattern Recognition*.

Huynh-Thu, Q., Barkowsky, M., & Callet, P. L. (2011). The importance of visual attention in improving the 3D-TV viewing experience: Overview and new perspectives. *IEEE Transactions on Broadcasting*, 57(2), 421–431. doi:10.1109/TBC.2011.2128250

Hwang, D. S., & Chien, S. Y. (2008). Content-aware image resizing using perceptual seam carving with human attention model. In *Proc. of IEEE International Conference on Multimedia and Expo*.

Itti, L., Gold, C., & Koch, C. (2001). Visual attention and target detection on cluttered natural scenes. *Optical Engineering (Redondo Beach, Calif.)*, 40(9), 1784–1793. doi:10.1117/1.1389063

Itti, L., & Koch, C. (2001). Computational modeling of visual attention. *Nature Reviews. Neuroscience*, 2(3), 194–203. doi:10.1038/35058500 PMID:11256080

Itti, L., Koch, C., & Niebur, E. (1998). A model of saliency-based visual attention for rapid scene analysis. *IEEE Transactions on Pattern Analysis and Machine Intelligence*, 20(11), 1254–1259. doi:10.1109/34.730558

Jing, Z., Li, Z., Jingjing, G., & Zhixing, L. (2009). A study of top-down visual attention model based on similarity distance. In *Proc. of 2nd International Congress on Image and Signal Processing*.

Kienzle, W., Wichmann, F. A., Scholkopf, B., & Franz, M. O. (2006). A non-parametric approach to bottom-up visual saliency. *Advances in Neural Information Processing Systems*, 19.

Koch, C., & Ullman, S. (1985). Shifts in selective visual attention: Towards the underlying neural circuitry. *Human Neurobiology*, 4, 219–227. PMID:3836989

Kokui, T., Takimoto, H., Mitsukura, Y., Kishihara, M., & Okubo, K. (2013). Color image modification based on visual saliency for guiding visual attention. In *Proc. of the 22nd IEEE International Symposium on Robot and Human Interactive Communication*. doi:10.1109/ROMAN.2013.6628548

Lee, J.-S., Simone, F. D., & Ebrahimi, T. (2011). Efficient video coding based on audio-visual focus of attention. *Journal of Visual Communication and Image Representation, 22*(8), 704–711. doi:10.1016/j. jvcir.2010.11.002

Lee, S., Kim, K., Kim, J.-Y., Kim, M., & Yoo, H.-J. (2010). Familiarity based unified visual attention model for fast and robust object recognition. *Pattern Recognition, 43*(3), 1116–1128. doi:10.1016/j. patcog.2009.07.014

Li, S., & Lee, M.-C. (2007). An efficient spatiotemporal attention model and its application to shot matching. *IEEE Transactions on Circuits and Systems for Video Technology, 17*(10), 1383–1387. doi:10.1109/ TCSVT.2007.903798

Li, Y., Ma, Y.-F., & Zhang, H.-J. (2003). Salient region detection and tracking in video. In *Proc. of International Conference on Multimedia and Expo*.

Liu, H., & Heynderickx, I. (2009). Studying the added value of visual attention in objective image quality metrics based on eye movement data. In *Proc. of 16th IEEE International Conference on Image Processing*. doi:10.1109/ICIP.2009.5414466

Liu, H., & Heynderickx, I. (2011). Visual attention in objective image quality assessment: Based on eye-tracking data. *IEEE Transactions on Circuits and Systems for Video Technology, 21*(7), 971–982. doi:10.1109/TCSVT.2011.2133770

Liu, H., Jiang, S., Huang, Q., & Xu, C. (2008). A generic virtual content insertion system based on visual attention analysis. In *Proc. of the 16th ACM International Conference on Multimedia*. doi:10.1145/1459359.1459410

Liu, X., Sun, J., & Liu, J. (2013). Visual attention based temporally weighting method for video hashing. *IEEE Signal Processing Letters, 20*(12), 1253–1256. doi:10.1109/LSP.2013.2287006

Longfei, Z., Yuanda, C., Gangyi, D., & Yong, W. (2008). A computable visual attention model for video skimming. In *Proc. of Tenth IEEE Symposium on Multimedia*. doi:10.1109/ISM.2008.117

Luo, J. (2007). Subject content-based intelligent cropping for digital photos. *IEEE International Conference on Multimedia and Expo*. doi:10.1109/ICME.2007.4285126

Luo, J., & Singhal, A. (2000). On measuring low-level saliency in photographic images. In *Proc. of IEEE Conference on Computer Vision and Pattern Recognition*. doi:10.1109/CVPR.2000.855803

Ma, Y.-F., Lu, L., Zhang, H.-J., & Li, M. (2002). A user attention model for video summarization. In *Proc. of the 10th ACM International Conference on Multimedia*. doi:10.1145/641007.641116

Ma, Y.-F., & Zhang, H.-J. (2003). Contrast-based image attention analysis by using fuzzy growing. In *Proc. of 11th ACM International Conference on Multimedia*. doi:10.1145/957013.957094

Mancas, M., Mancas-Thillou, C., Gosselin, B., & Macq, B. (2006). A rarity-based visual attention map – application to texture description. In *Proc. IEEE International Conference on Image Processing*. doi:10.1109/ICIP.2006.312489

Marques, O., Mayron, L. M., Borba, G. B., & Gamba, R. H. (2006). Using visual attention to extract regions of interest in the context of image retrieval. In *Proc. of the 44th Annual Southeast Regional Conference*. doi:10.1145/1185448.1185588

Milanese, R., Wechsler, H., Gil, S., Bost, J., & Pun, T. (1994). Integration of bottom-up and top-down cues for visual attention using nonlinear relaxation. In *Proc. of IEEE Computer Society Conference on Computer Vision and Pattern Recognition*. doi:10.1109/CVPR.1994.323898

Navalpakkam, V., Arbib, M., & Itti, L. (2005). Attention and scene understanding. In L. Itti, G. Rees, & J. K. Tsotsos (Eds.), *Neurobiology of Attention* (pp. 197–203). doi:10.1016/B978-012375731-9/50037-9

Navalpakkam, V., & Itti, L. (2006). Optimal cue selection strategy. *Advances in Neural Information Processing Systems, 19*, 987–994.

Oliva, A., Torralba, A., Castelhano, M. S., & Henderson, J. M. (2003). Top-down control of visual attention in object detection. In *Proc. of International Conference on Image Processing*. doi:10.1109/ICIP.2003.1246946

Orabona, F., Metta, G., & Sandini, G. (2005). Object-based Visual Attention: a Model for a Behaving Robot. In *Proc IEEE Computer Society Conference on Computer Vision and Pattern Recognition*. doi:10.1109/CVPR.2005.502

Pal, R. (2013). Computational models of visual attention: a survey. In R. Srivastava, S. K. Singh, & K. K. Shukla (Eds.), *Recent Advances in Computer Vision and Image Processing: Methodologies and Applications* (pp. 54–76). IGI Global.

Pal, R., Mitra, P., & Mukherjee, J. (2012) Image retargeting using controlled shrinkage. In: *Proc. of ICVGIP*. doi:10.1145/2425333.2425404

Pal, R., Mitra, P., & Mukhopadhyay, J. (2008). ICam: maximizes viewers attention on intended objects. In *Proc. of Pacific Rim Conference on Multimedia* (LNCS), (vol. 5353, pp. 821-824). Berlin: Springer. doi:10.1007/978-3-540-89796-5_90

Pal, R., Mukherjee, A., Mitra, P., & Mukherjee, J. (2010). Modelling visual saliency using degree centrality. *IET Computer Vision, 4*(3), 218–229. doi:10.1049/iet-cvi.2009.0067

Pal, R., Mukhopadhyay, J., & Mitra, P. (2011). Image retargeting through constrained growth of important rectangular partitions. In *Proc. of 4th International Conference on Pattern Recognition and Machine Intelligence*. doi:10.1007/978-3-642-21786-9_19

Pelz, J. B., & Canosa, R. (2001). Oculomotor behavior and perceptual strategies in complex tasks. *Vision Research, 41*(25-26), 3587–3596. doi:10.1016/S0042-6989(01)00245-0 PMID:11718797

Peters, R. J., & Itti, L. (2007). Beyond bottom-up: incorporating task-dependent influences into a computational model of spatial attention. In *Proc. of IEEE Conference on Computer Vision and Pattern Recognition*. doi:10.1109/CVPR.2007.383337

Qiu, G., Gu, X., Chen, Z., Chen, Q., & Wang, C. (2007). An information theoretic model on spatiotemporal visual saliency. In *Proc. of IEEE International Conference on Multimedia and Expo*. doi:10.1109/ICME.2007.4285023

Ramstrom, O., & Christensen, H. I. (2002). *Visual attention using game theory*. Biologically Motivated Computer Vision.

Rapantzikos, K., Tsapatsoulis, N., & Avrithis, Y. (2004). Spatiotemporal visual attention architecture for video analysis. In *Proc. of IEEE 6th Workshop on Multimedia Signal Processing*. doi:10.1109/MMSP.2004.1436423

Rosin, P. L. (2009). A simple method for detecting salient regions. *Pattern Recognition*, *42*(11), 2363–2371. doi:10.1016/j.patcog.2009.04.021

Siagian, C., & Itti, L. (2007). Rapid biologically-inspired scene classification using features shared with visual attention. *IEEE Transactions on Pattern Analysis and Machine Intelligence*, *29*(2), 300–312. doi:10.1109/TPAMI.2007.40 PMID:17170482

Stentiford, F. (2001). An estimator for visual attention through competitive novelty with application to image compression. In *Proc. Picutre Coding Symposium*.

Suh, B., Ling, H., Bederson, B. B., & Jacobs, D. W. (2003). Automatic Thumbnail Cropping and Its Effectiveness. In *Proc. of 16th Annual Symposium on User Interface Software and Technology*. doi:10.1145/964696.964707

Sur, A., Sagar, S. S., Pal, R., Mitra, P., & Mukhopadhyay, J. (2009). A new image watermarking scheme using saliency based visual attention model, In *Proc. of IEEE Indicon*. doi:10.1109/INDCON.2009.5409402

Tagare, H. D., Toyama, K., & Wang, J. G. (2001). A maximum-likelihood strategy for directing attention during visual search. *IEEE Transactions on Pattern Analysis and Machine Intelligence*, *23*(5), 490–500. doi:10.1109/34.922707

Teng, W.-C., Kuo, Y.-C., & Tara, R. Y. (2013). A teleoperation system utilizing saliency-based visual attention. In *Proc. of IEEE International Conference on Systems, Man, and Cybernetics*.

Torralba, A., Oliva, A., Castelhano, M. S., & Henderson, J. M. (2006). Contextual guidance of eye-movements and attention in real-world scenes: The role of global features in object search. *Psychological Review*, *113*(4), 766–786. doi:10.1037/0033-295X.113.4.766 PMID:17014302

Treisman, A. M., & Gelade, G. (1980). A feature integration theory of attention. *Cognitive Psychology*, *12*(1), 97–136. doi:10.1016/0010-0285(80)90005-5 PMID:7351125

Tsotsos, J. K. (1990). Analyzing vision at the complexity level. *Behavioral and Brain Sciences*, *13*(03), 423–469. doi:10.1017/S0140525X00079577

Tsotsos, J. K., Culhane, S. M., Wai, W. Y. K., Lai, Y., Davis, N., & Nuflo, F. (1995). Modeling visual attention via selective tuning. *Artificial Intelligence*, *78*(1-2), 507–547. doi:10.1016/0004-3702(95)00025-9

Utsugi, K., Shibahara, T., Koike, T., & Naemura, T. (2009). Proportional constraint for seam carving. In *Proc. of International Conference on Computer Graphics and Interactive Techniques*.

Vijayakumar, S., Conradt, J., Shibata, T., & Schaal, S. (2001) Overt visual attention for a humanoid robot. In *Proc IEEE/RSJ International Conference on Intelligent Robots and Systems*. doi:10.1109/IROS.2001.976418

Vikram, T. N., Tscherepanow, M., & Wrede, B. (2011). A random center-surround bottom-up visual attention model useful for salient region detection. In *Proc. of IEEE Workshop on Applications of Computer Vision*. doi:10.1109/WACV.2011.5711499

Wang, H., Liu, G., & Dang, Y. (2012). The target quick searching strategy based on visual attention. In *Proc. of International Conference on Computer Science and Electronics Engineering*. doi:10.1109/ICCSEE.2012.442

Wang, Y.-S., Tai, C.-L., Sorkine, O., & Lee, T.-Y. (2008). Optimized scale-and-stretch for image resizing. *ACM Transactions on Graphics*, 27(5), 1. doi:10.1145/1409060.1409071

Wolfe, J. M., & Horowitz, T. S. (2004). What attributes guide the deployment of visual attention and how do they do it? *Nature Reviews. Neuroscience*, 5(6), 495–501. doi:10.1038/nrn1411 PMID:15152199

Wu, C.-Y., Leou, J.-J., & Chen, H.-Y. (2009). Visual attention region determination using low-level features. In *Proc. of IEEE International Symposium on Circuits and Systems*. doi:10.1109/ISCAS.2009.5118478

Yarbus, A. L. (1967). *Eye movements and vision*. New York: Plenum Press. doi:10.1007/978-1-4899-5379-7

Yee, H., Pattanaik, S., & Greenberg, D. P. (2001). Spatiotemporal sensitivity and visual attention for efficient rendering of dynamic environments. *ACM Transactions on Graphics*, 20(1), 39–65. doi:10.1145/383745.383748

You, J., Perkis, A., & Gabbouj, M. (2010). Improving image quality assessment with modeling visual attention. In *Proc. of 2nd European Workshop on Visual Information Processing*. doi:10.1109/EU-VIP.2010.5699102

Yu, Z., & Wong, H.-S. (2007). A rule based technique for extraction of visual attention regions based on real time clustering. *IEEE Transactions on Multimedia*, 9(4), 766–784. doi:10.1109/TMM.2007.893351

Zhai, Y., & Shah, M. (2006). Visual attention detection in video sequences using spatiotemporal cues. In *Proc. of the 14th Annual ACM International Conference on Multimedia*. doi:10.1145/1180639.1180824

KEY TERMS AND DEFINITIONS

Bottom-Up Attention: In the absence of prior knowledge about the scene being viewed, our gaze is attracted towards salient objects (or locations), of the scene. The saliency, here, is computed in terms of low-level visual features like color, intensity, orientation, size, motion, etc.

Top-Down Attention: Sometimes context-specific, task-driven or semantic guided knowledge about the scene guides our vision. This component of attention is known as top-down attention.

Visual Attention: Visual attention is the mechanism of primate vision system to pay attention only to selected set of visual stimuli at a particular time. This selective attention capability reduces the processing burden of the brain so that it can efficiently interact with the surrounding.

Visual Saliency: Saliency of an object (or a location) of scene specifies the propensity of the object (or the location) to capture attention.

Chapter 3
Biologically–Inspired Models for Attentive Robot Vision:
A Review

Amirhossein Jamalian
Technical University of Chemnitz, Germany

Fred H. Hamker
Technical University of Chemnitz, Germany

ABSTRACT

A rich stream of visual data enters the cameras of a typical artificial vision system (e.g., a robot) and considering the fact that processing this volume of data in real-rime is almost impossible, a clever mechanism is required to reduce the amount of trivial visual data. Visual Attention might be the solution. The idea is to control the information flow and thus to improve vision by focusing the resources merely on some special aspects instead of the whole visual scene. However, does attention only speed-up processing or can the understanding of human visual attention provide additional guidance for robot vision research? In this chapter, first, some basic concepts of the primate visual system and visual attention are introduced. Afterward, a new taxonomy of biologically-inspired models of attention, particularly those that are used in robotics applications (e.g., in object detection and recognition) is given and finally, future research trends in modelling of visual attention and its applications are highlighted.

INTRODUCTION

Machine vision is used in many real world applications such as surveillance systems, robotics, sport analysis and other new technologies. Obviously, processing of all visual data may not be necessary and using current technology a deep image analysis is quite impossible in real-time. Hence, a clever mechanism is required to select useful, desirable and relevant data while omitting others. When we inspire machine vision from biology, one of the mechanisms in the primate's brain which determines which part of the sensory data is currently the most relevant part is *selective attention* or briefly attention. Focusing the resources only on some parts of the whole visual scene, information flow is controlled to improve vision.

DOI: 10.4018/978-1-4666-8723-3.ch003

First, vision modules compute features of the scene (such as color, intensity, etc.) rather independently, but then they will have to be integrated for further processing. Attention has been first described as a *spotlight of attention* (Posner et al., 1980). A spotlight prefers a particular region of interest for further processing. In human vision, the highest resolution belongs to the center of the retina (fovea). Hence, when a human looks at a certain object, it is like using a spotlight to highlight this object within a dark room (Shulman et al., 1979). It is possible to get an impression of the whole visual scene by scanning it using saccades (quick eye movements) exactly like one can realize the content of a dark room using a shifting spotlight.

Many computational models of visual attention have been proposed in literature. Koch & Ullman (1985) proposed a winner-takes-all (WTA) strategy on a *saliency map* to determine a location of interest, a concept on which more sophisticated models have been developed (Itti et al., 1998; Frintrop, 2005). In general, this model suggests transforming the complex problem of scene understanding into a sequential analysis of image parts. Although such spatial selection is computationally efficient (Tsotsos, 1990; Ballard, 1991), other crucial issues of efficiency should be considered as well. For instance, it may be not ideal to scan too many salient items before the relevant one. Besides, by focusing the processing only on salient items, other important parts might be missed. In this case, the methodology should incorporate high-level signals (e.g., knowledge about a desired object) into the selection process. Moreover, attention mechanisms should not only select points in space, but also should facilitate further processing of the scene. For example, if an attention mechanism only determines a few salient points in space, it would not be useful for high level tasks such as object recognition. Thus, additionally, it must enhance the relevant features for object recognition to indicate the salient regions (Hamker, 2005a).

The majority of attention models in machine vision applications only specify the regions of interest (RoI), either by bottom-up or by merging bottom-up and top-down factors. However, attention can be used for the *binding problem* as well (Tsotsos, 2008). Binding refers to the problem of relating features to each other that are processed independently and are represented in different maps (e.g., shape and location). Tsotsos (2008) described a set of four binding processes (convergence binding, full recurrence binding, partial recurrence binding and iterative recurrence binding) which use attentive mechanisms to achieve recognition and claimed that these four are enough for solving recognition, discrimination, localization, and identification tasks solving the binding problem. In each process, attention is involved somehow, e.g., in the first process, attention is used to search for a maximum response within a neural representation arranged in hierarchical layers. Besides, in a localization task (full recurrence binding), top-down stimulus segmentation and localization as well as local maximum selection on the top-down traversal have to be performed.

Models of visual attention have many applications in various machine vision problems such as pedestrian detection (Miau et al., 2001), handwritten digit recognition (Salah et al., 2002), traffic sign recognition (Ouerhani, 2003), object tracking (Walther et al., 2004, Mahadevan & Vasconcelos, 2013), motion detection (Barranco et al., 2009) and segmentation of 3D scenes (Potapova et al., 2012). Meanwhile, there are several attempts to apply attention models for Robot Vision. This may be one of the most important and interesting branches of machine vision at least from the viewpoint of biologically inspired vision.

Robot Vision

The term Robot Vision is used ambiguously. Often, it is applied to the theoretical aspects of robot control as well as to the study of practical systems. There is no precise definition for robot vision in the literature. However, robot vision could be considered as a branch of machine vision in which the machine is replaced by a robot (a device with input sensors to perceive its environment and actions to interact with the environment). In robot vision, the main input sensor is at least one camera used for capturing pictures or entire video streams. The single, or for stereo vision, the two cameras shall be able to actively scan the visual scene. Since a robot interacts with its environment, it is expected that it would be able to perform its tasks in real-time or near-real-time. Although it is harder to develop appropriate (near) real-time artificial vision algorithms, the trend of new research in artificial vision is toward robot vision. Perhaps the main reason for the popularity of robot vision is that it would be desirable to develop robots which are able to perform many separate physical tasks (like humans) based on a set of flexible algorithms for image analysis and action selection.

Since a subset of research is inspired by the primate visual system, we provide a brief introduction into this field. Consequently, the concept of visual attention, which originally came from psychology, is introduced. Apart from previous classifications of computational models of attention (e.g., Frintrop et al., 2010), a new taxonomy of biologically-inspired models of attention in robotic application is given. The viewpoint for this new taxonomy is the structure and functionality of the models to implement general purpose vision systems. Finally, some conclusion and future trends of this research field are discussed.

PRIMATE VISUAL SYSTEM

In this section, an introduction to the anatomy, physiology and functionality of the primate visual system is given. Figure 1 illustrates a typical primate visual system, its areas and connections. The light enters the eye and is projected onto the *retina*. Then, 90% of the visual information is transmitted via optic nerve toward the *Lateral Geniculate Nucleus (LGN)* and the rest of them to the Superior Colliculus. From the LGN, the signals are further projected to V1 (primary visual cortex) at the back of the brain. From V1, information is transmitted to the other areas of the brain via different pathways such as ventral and dorsal streams. In Figure 1, green arrows show the ventral stream which is involved in object recognition tasks and is the basic path for many of biologically-inspired models of attention to compute features and proto-objects whereas blue arrows belong to the dorsal stream which has been typically considered to contribute to the saliency map formation. Cells in higher levels (V2-V5, IT, PP or Posterior Parietal cortex, etc.) are more complex and combine the results received from their previous areas (Rousselet et al., 2004).

- **Retina and LGN:** Retinal ganglion and LGN cells are either *ON cells* or *OFF cells* as defined by their receptive fields. In ON cells, light in the center of the receptive field causes the neuron to fire and light in the circular region around the center suppresses the cell. In OFF cells the effect is reversed, light in the center deactivates the neuron and in the periphery activates the neuron (Hubel, 1995). This behavior can be described by difference of Gaussians (DoG) (Cai et al., 1997).
- **Primary Visual Cortex (V1):** V1 is the biggest part of the visual cortex and processes static and moving edges (DeAngelis et al., 1995). V1 neurons have different tuning properties and based on their responses small changes in visual orientations, spatial frequencies and colors can be distinguished. In addition, in primates and other animals with binocular vision, V1 provides depths information about the processed stimulus relative to the fixated depth plane (Read, 2005). A set

Figure 1. The primate visual system; the green and blue pathways are regarding to ventral and dorsal streams, respectively. The former is involved in object recognition task and used for biologically-inspired models of attention whereas the latter is responsible for the saliency map formation.

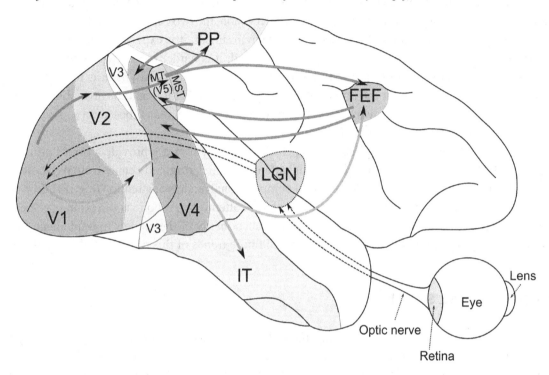

of selective spatio-temporal filters composes the initial responses of V1 neurons. The functionality of V1 is very similar to local spatial functions, complex Fourier transforms, or more precisely Gabor transforms. These filters can perform many spatio-temporal features such as orientations and motion directions.

- **Visual Area V2:** V2 receives its input from V1 and sends out its output to V3, V4 and V5. It also has feedback connection to V1. Multiple orientations in different sub-regions within a single receptive field can drive neurons in V2 (Friston & Büchel, 2000; Bender & Youakim, 2001).

- **Visual Area V3:** Van Essen et al. (1986) divided V3 into *Dorsal* (located in upper part of hemisphere) and *Ventral* (located in lower part) sections. These two separate sections have different connections and different neuronal responses. However, the functionality of V3 is presently not well understood.

- **Visual Area V4:** V4 is located between V2 and the IT area. It receives its input from V2 and is sending signals to the IT and FEF. V4 is tuned at the level of orientation, spatial frequency, and color and seems to be well suited for feature extraction of shapes with an intermediate degree of complexity (Cadieu et al., 2007) but not for sophisticated objects such as a face.

- **Infero Temporal Cortex (IT):** Complex object features such as global shape, face, recognition of numbers, etc. are processed in this area. It receives its input from V4.

- **Medial Temporal and Medial Superior Temporal Area (MT/MST):** The MT and MST regions lie in the dorsal stream. MT (also known as visual area V5) receives its input from V1, V2 and dorsal V3 (Ungerleider & Desimone, 1986; Felleman & Van Essen, 1991) and sends a part of its output to MST. Although both areas are involved in the detection and perception of motion (Born & Bradley, 2005), some computations such as optic flow are particularly performed in MST.

- **Frontal Eye Field (FEF):** The FEF is the cortical site of eye movement control, but also appears to be involved in selective attention (Schall, 2004). Electrical stimulation in the FEF elicits saccadic eye movements, but below threshold excitation leads to attention effects in visual areas such as V4 (Moore et al., 2003). The FEF determines saccade targets in retinotopic coordinates by its activity (Bruce et al., 1985).
- **Posterior Parietal Cortex (PP):** The PP receives its input from sensory systems (e.g., visual system) and plays a key role in the visual representation of the location of action relevant objects in different coordinate systems, such as eye, head or body centered ones (Cohen & Andersen, 2002). It also represents locations of salient or task relevant objects (Goldberg et al., 2006).

VISUAL ATTENTION

Although many things in our environment attract our attention, our visual system analyzes in detail only parts of a visual scene, which are usually the things that we look at (Resnik et al., 1997; Simons, 2000). Normally, attention is intertwined by eye movements and it precedes the gaze shift in time (Deubel and Schneider, 1996). O*vert attention* describes the preferred processing of parts by shifting gaze. However, it is possible to attend to a peripheral location without shifting gaze, known as *covert attention*.

In the visual attention literature terms such as *bottom-up* and *top-down* factors, are frequently used. The former are derived from contents of the visual scene (Nothdurft, 2005). Using bottom-up factors, *salient* regions of the scene could be determined. These salient regions have one or more features which are sufficiently different from their surrounding ones, e.g., a red item among green ones. Top-down factors, however, are based on expectations or prior knowledge about an object. Intraparietal cortex and frontal cortex in the brain are responsible for goal-driven (top-down) attention (Corbetta & Shulman, 2002).

At the neurobiological level the effect of attention it typically an increase in the neural response towards the attended stimulus and a decrease in response to unattended stimuli (Desimone & Duncan, 1995). This effect is particularly strong if multiple stimuli are presented within the same receptive field. If a single stimulus is presented alone in the receptive field the neural response is strong, but it depends on the contrast of the stimulus. Adding a second distracting stimulus reduces the response if attention is directed away. However, if attention is directed to the initial stimulus, the response recovers as if the distracting stimulus is not in the receptive field. These competitive effects have been observed in several visual areas such as V4, IT and MT (Chelazzi et al., 1998; Reynolds et al., 1999; Lee & Maunsell, 2010).

The main ingredients of such competitive interactions are now well understood and have been modelled by gain normalization and suppression (Lee & Maunsell, 2009; Reynolds & Heeger, 2009). Thus, local circuits of attentive competition require a biasing or gain increase signal which can be spatial or feature specific arriving from another part of the brain. In addition, such local circuits also implement suppression. Some neuro-computational models addressed the systems level of attention, in particular the interplay of the eye movement system and attention (Hamker, 2005b) and proposed that areas involved in the planning of eye movements project back into visual areas. This feedback projection locally increases the gain of neurons, so that stimuli around the location of the future saccade target are processed more intensively. The search for particular features irrespective of their location in the scene has been modelled as a feature-specific top down signal.

CLASSIFICATION OF BIOLOGICALLY-INSPIRED MODELS FOR ATTENTIVE ROBOT VISION

In computer vision and robotics, there is increasing interest in a selection mechanism which determines the most relevant parts within the large amount of visual data. As mentioned before, visual attention is such a selection mechanism and therefore, many *artificial* attention models have been built during the last three decades. We used the term *artificial models* (versus psychophysical models) to indicate that such models are designed and implemented in engineering problems e.g., computer vision, object recognition, robotics and etc.

As it can be seen in the literature, biologically plausible models of attention are increasingly used in engineering problems. Most of these biologically plausible models follow the idea of a saliency map which is depicted in Figure 2 (Frintrop et al., 2010). It is inspired from psychological theories such as Feature Integration Theory (Treisman & Gormican, 1988) and the Guided Search model (Wolfe, 1994). Several features are initially computed in parallel and then their conspicuities are fused into a single *saliency map*. The saliency map is a two-dimensional scalar map which shows which region in the corresponding visual scene is deserved to be attended as determined by a winner-take-all competition. This concept was introduced by Koch and Ullman (1985) and was further developed by Itti et al (1998).

Although most of the saliency systems consider only bottom-up computations of saliency, top-down is examined and implemented in several systems as well. Top-down information is based on knowledge about the environment. For example, all objects that would be expected to be in the scene are investigated in advance and their special features are extracted (Fritz et al., 2004; Pessoa & Exel, 1999). Another approach in top-down attention is context information which means visual search should operate only in a relevant region, e.g., the search for a car in the street and not in the sky. In visual search, top-down knowledge is used to guide attention only to properties of the searched object, e.g., only to all red items. The simplest solution is to construct a saliency map and then weight channels that match the target information stronger than others (Milanese et al., 1994; Frintrop et al., 2005; Navalpakkam & Itti, 2006a).

Hereinafter, we propose a new categorization of visual attention models which are used in object recognition and robotics. All of the following categories are linked to the term saliency maps, even if some models may focus explicitly on models of particular brain areas. Saliency maps have been found in several brain areas but typically the FEF and areas in the parietal cortex correspond well to the computational concept of a saliency map. The difference among the different models of attention is their behaviour in linking attention to object recognition and binding. The basic structure of these three categories is illustrated in Figure 3(a-c).

1. **Simple Saliency-Based Models:** The general structure of models of this class is depicted in Figure 3(a). A saliency map is constructed based on basic features such as intensity, orientation and color using some standard process. A top-down signal in this class of models helps the process to construct a more goal-driven saliency map. Hence, the most salient region in a saliency map (yellow point in Figure 3(a)) provides the output of such saliency models. It indicates directly the proposed

Figure 2. General structure of bottom-up attention systems basic features (e.g., color, intensity, orientation, etc.) are extracted from an input image and center-surround operations lead to a saliency map. Then, often a winner-take-all strategy is used for finding the maximum to determine the Focus of Attention (FoA).

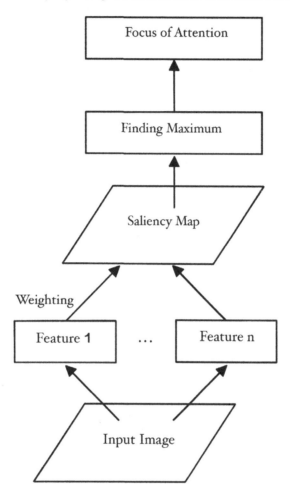

location of attention or gaze in image coordinates. Obviously in this kind of models, generating the saliency map is based on basic features and object recognition is not considered. Thus, these models primarily address the potential speedup of processing using the output of the saliency-based model to determine a preferred processing around the selected location.

2. **Proto-Object-Based Models:** Visual attention is not only responsible for serializing visual information, but also for recognizing one object at a time in a complex scene. However, saliency models offer only a selection of a location without specifying the size of a focus of attention (FoA) or any access to a particular object at the selected location. The human brain groups related picture elements into integrated regions which are called *proto-objects*. Hence, a proto-object could be either part of an object or may represent the whole object. The saliency is linked to a proto-object. Models of this class (Figure 3(b)) provide a proto-object map besides the saliency map, and a spatial selection on the saliency map points towards a proto-object. Therefore, proto-objects may be organized in a hierarchical way. Models of this class use the saliency map and allow pointing to a proto-object which may facilitate its further processing.

Figure 3. (a): Simple Saliency-Based Models: A saliency map is generated mostly using bottom-up process (sometimes a top-down signal is used in goal-driven scenarios). However, the MSR (yellow point) directly indicates the focus of attention in visual space, regardless of the possible objects in it. (b): Proto-Object-Based Models: A proto-object map is constructed either simultaneously or prior to the saliency map. The MSR indicates the most salient proto-object. (c): Iterative Models: A top-down signal is used to construct both saliency and proto-object maps. The most salient object is recognized and localized concurrently as result of an iterative process.

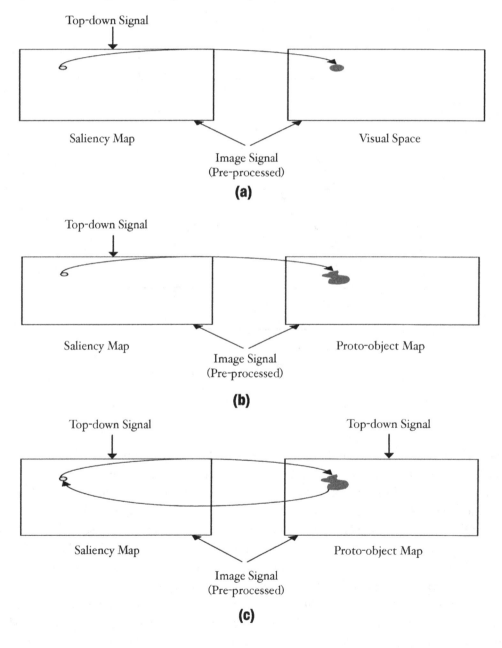

3. **Iterative Models:** Proto-object based models try to construct a proto-object map in parallel with the saliency map for object recognition. Proto-object formation and object recognition, however, is outside the loop of attentional selection. For recognizing a searched object in a scene, the object must first be located and recognized which, however, is only possible if the object has been recognized well. Such a "Chicken-egg-problem" could be solved using attention in a way where object detection and spatial selection depend on each other (Hamker, 2005a). In such iterative models of visual attention, spatial attention links to proto-objects, but equally well proto-objects to attention. When a particular object is searched, the top-down signal reinforces the activation of all cells (neurons) that encode a view of such an object and suppress the activation of other cells. This process is iterated such that an object of interest or a region of space is processed with preference.

In the next three sections, we will describe important examples of three aforementioned categories in more detail.

SIMPLE SALIENCY-BASED MODELS

A typical example of a saliency model of attention used in robot vision is Frintrop's VOCUS (Visual Object detection with a CompUtational attention System) model (Frintrop, 2005). The bottom-up model of VOCUS is shown in Figure 4. VOCUS is based on the model proposed by Itti et al. (1998) known as the *Neuromorphic Vision Toolkit* (NVT) which inspired several saliency-based models. In the NVT model, a linear filtering phase applies on the input image to extract three basic features: color, intensity and orientation. *Image pyramids*, which are typical tools for feature detection on different scales, have been used for related computations. The results of this filtering and feature extraction are basic inputs for generating feature maps. A fast and simple *Center-surround* mechanism on these pyramids subtracts the different scales of the image pyramid to construct the conspicuity maps. These conspicuity maps are combined by a linear or by alternative combination methods and result in the saliency map. Based on the suggestion of Koch and Ullman (1985), a WTA network determines the Most Salient Region (MSR) which yields the Focus of Attention (FoA). In a newer work, Navalpakkam & Itti (2006a) developed a derivative of the NVT with the capability of dealing with top-down cues and visual search. Similar as in NVT, VOCUS computes image pyramids and scale maps for the three aforementioned basic features, intensity (I), orientation (O) and color (C). In next step, saliencies are computed in multiple scales. As it can be seen in Figure 4, the saliency map is constructed gradually and in each step important aspects are enhanced while others are suppressed. As far as color is concerned, VOCUS imitates the human perception by transforming the input image to a human-inspired color space (LAB). The LAB color space is substantially uniform and very near to the color perception system of human (Forsyth & Ponce, 2003), i.e., if in coordinate space the distance between two near colors is less than some threshold, these colors are indistinguishable by the human's visual system.

A color pyramid P_{LAB} is constructed and using it, color pyramids P_R, P_G, P_B and P_Y are created. Then, based on image pyramids, *scale maps* I″, O″ and C″ are computed. Scale maps determine saliencies on different scales and for various feature types. I″, O″ and C″ are fused to construct *feature maps* I′, O′ and C′, respectively. In the next step, feature maps are combined into *conspicuity maps* I, O and C. Using a proper weighting mechanism for the combination of conspicuity maps, the final saliency map is constructed. Based on the saliency map, MSR and consequently Foci of Attention are extracted. In scenarios

Figure 4. Bottom-up model of Frintrop's VOCUS system; input image is converted to LAB color image to construct color pyramids. On the other hand, image pyramids for intensity and orientation images are constructed. Then, scale maps, feature maps and conspicuity maps are generated, respectively. The final saliency map is the result of combination of conspicuity maps with a proper weighting mechanism.

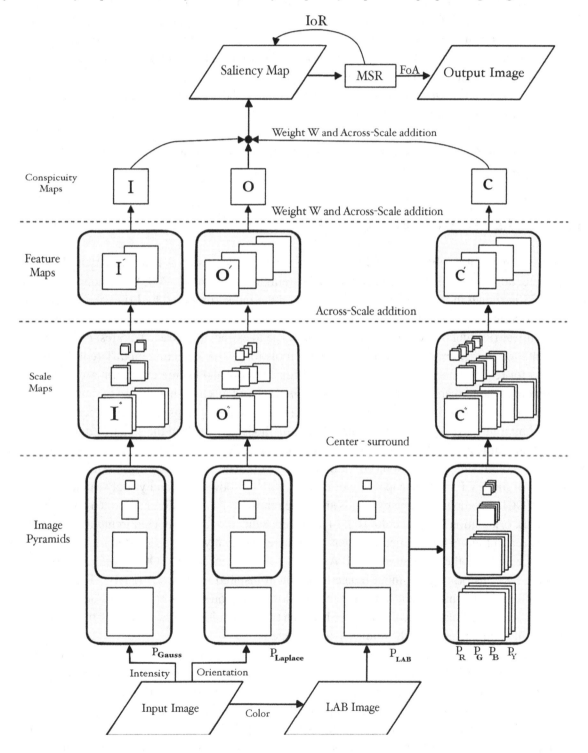

with more than one MSR, the IoR (inhibition of return) resets the selected region in the saliency map and the next MSR appears. This cycle runs until enough foci are determined. The algorithmic description of VOCUS (bottom-up part) can be found in Table 1.

Although VOCUS consists of bottom-up and top-down parts, the bottom-up part mentioned before is sufficient for some robotic applications such as SLAM (Simultaneous Localization And Mapping) as introduced in a robot implementation (Frintrop & Jensfelt, 2008). Here, the bottom-up part of VOCUS finds salient regions that are used as landmarks. A Scale-Invariant Feature Transform (SIFT) descriptor matches and tracks salient regions in the image sequence to obtain the 3D location of the landmark. When the robot closes a loop and returns to the previously visited position, the algorithm stops.

In addition to the bottom-up part, VOCUS has a top-down mechanism as well. After generating the saliency map, the model has two modes: a learning mode (realizing the properties of a specified target) and a search mode. In the learning mode, usually a user determines the region of interest manually and VOCUS finds the MSR within this region. The system learns the features which discriminate the target from other parts of the image. A weight value is assigned to each feature and these results in a weight vector which will be used in the search mode. In such a search mode, a top-down signal modulates the weight vector and excites or inhibits features dependent on the search task.

VOCUS uses no proto-object in its architecture. Instead, simply after the computation of the global saliency map, the MSR will be highlighted in the output image. Hence, it belongs to the class of simple saliency-based models which is depicted in Figure 3(a). Another usage of VOCUS in robotics has been

Table 1. The algorithmic description of VOCUS; bottom-up part

Algorithm 1: Bottom-Up Part of VOCUS	
Input: RGB_Image	**Output:** Saliency Map with Focus of Attention
Feature Computations	
Pre-processing: Convert RGB_Image to a gray-scale and a LAB image	
Image pyramids generation: • Compute Gaussian image pyramids $P_{Gauss} = \{S_0, S_1, S_2, S_3, S_4\}$ using 2D-Convolution of gray-scale image and 3×3 Gaussian filter mask ($S_0 - S_4$ are scales) • Compute $P_{LAB} = \{S_0, S_1, S_2, S_3, S_4\}$ like P_{Gauss} and then P_R, P_G, P_B and P_Y using LAB image and P_{LAB} • Compute Laplacian image pyramids $P_{Laplace} = \{S_0, S_1, S_2, S_3, S_4\}$ from P_{Gauss} by subtracting two adjacent levels	
Scale maps generation: • Construct 12 intensity scale maps $I''_{i,s,\sigma}$ (for i in {(on), (off)}, s in $\{S_2, S_3, S_4\}$, σ in $\{3, 7\}$) using center-surround operation • Construct 12 orientation scale maps $O''_{s,\theta}$ (s in $\{S_2, S_3, S_4\}$, θ in $\{0°, 45°, 90°, 135°\}$) by applying Gabor filter of θ on pyramid s • Construct 24 color scale maps $C''_{\gamma,s,\sigma}$ (γ in {(R), (G), (B), (Y)}, s in $\{S_2, S_3, S_4\}$, σ in $\{3, 7\}$) using center-surround operation	
Feature maps generation: • Resize all maps to scale S_2 • $I'_i := \sum_{s,\sigma} (I''_{i,s,\sigma})$ $O'_\theta := \sum_s (O''_{s,\theta})$ $C'_\gamma := \sum_{s,\sigma} (C''_{\gamma,s,\sigma})$ which $\sum$ means pixel by pixel addition	
Fusing Saliencies	
Conspicuity maps generation: • $I := \sum_i W(I'_i)$ $O := \sum_\theta W(O'_\theta)$ $C := \sum_\gamma W(C'_\gamma)$ which W is a weighting function • Normalize I in $[0, max(I'_i)]$, O in $[0, max(O'_\theta)]$ and C in $[0, max(C'_\gamma)]$	
Saliency maps generation: S = W(I) + W(O) + W(C) which W is a weighting function	
FoA computation: • *Seed* := The brightest pixel in S • FoA := All neighbours of *Seed* which their values differ less than 25%	

proposed by Mitri et al. (2005). They used a combination of bottom-up and top-down parts of VOCUS for ball detection in RoboCup. VOCUS finds regions of interest for possible locations of the ball and then a fast classifier tries to detect balls in regions of interest.

A more recent saliency-based model, called NLOOK, has been proposed by Heinen and Engel (2009). Its structure and functionality is very similar to VOCUS and NVT, but more emphasis is given on the run-time. The input data of NLOOK could be either static images or a color video stream. At each time instant, three basic features (intensity, color and orientation) are computed by set of center-surround operations to generate feature maps. One of the differences between NLOOK and NVT appears here: NLOOK normalizes the resulting feature maps by subtraction of their mean and division by their standard deviation.

Afterward, the feature maps are used to create a saliency scale-space and then a unique saliency map. Again a winner-take-all neural network is used to identify the MSR. The second difference of NLOOK and NVT lies in the implementation of the center-surround operation. Heinen and Engel (2009) compared NLOOK to NVT and conclude that NLOOK is less sensitive to 2D similarity transforms such as a rotation of the image. Whereas in NLOOK the FoA is stable, even if the image has been rotated, in NVT the resulting FoA's depend on the rotation of the input image. NLOOK uses DoG filters over scale-spaces and this makes NLOOK less sensitive in terms of 2D similarity transform. Another difference appears in creation of the unique saliency map. NVT produces the saliency map at the coarsest level whereas NLOOK makes it at the finest level.

NLOOK is a fast biologically plausible model of attention which is suitable for robotic applications. Its whole process can be performed on 30 images per second input stream. It has been implemented on a Pioneer 3-DX robot for several experiments using natural images and the results show that it outperforms some previous models especially NVT.

It is worth noting that, there are many other models which belong to the simple saliency-based class. Remarkable works could be found in (Miau et al., 2001; Salah et al., 2002; Ouerhani, 2003). However, they have not been applied to any robotic application yet.

PROTO-OBJECT-BASED MODELS

Many models of bottom-up attentional selection assume that elementary image features, like intensity, color and orientation, attract attention. According to Gestalt psychology, however, humans perceive whole objects before analyzing features. Inspired by this theory, many attempts have been made to develop proper attentional systems so called object-based attention systems (e.g. Walther & Koch, 2006).

Obviously in this class of models, the most important novel aspect is the computation of a proto-object map. There are many attempts to produce a proper proto-object map in the literature. A recent method has been proposed by Russel et al (2014) which estimates the location and the spatial-scale of proto-objects in the input image. The core of this model is a feedforward grouping mechanism, depicted in Figure 5. Object edges are extracted in the first step using 2D Gabor filters inspired by the receptive field of simple cells in area V1. From a simple cell response pair, a complex cell response is computed which is more phase and contrast invariant. Assigning an edge to a figure or ground, the model uses center-surround mechanisms of both polarities using a DoG: ON-center receptive fields which determine bright objects on a dark background and OFF-center for vice versa. In the next step, by modulating complex cell re-

Figure 5. The architecture proposed by Russel et al. (2014) to construct a proto-object map; this feed-forward grouping mechanism used in Figure 6. 2D Gabor filters are applied for edge extraction and then a center-surround mechanism assigns an edge to a figure or ground to group parts together within each level of the pyramid.

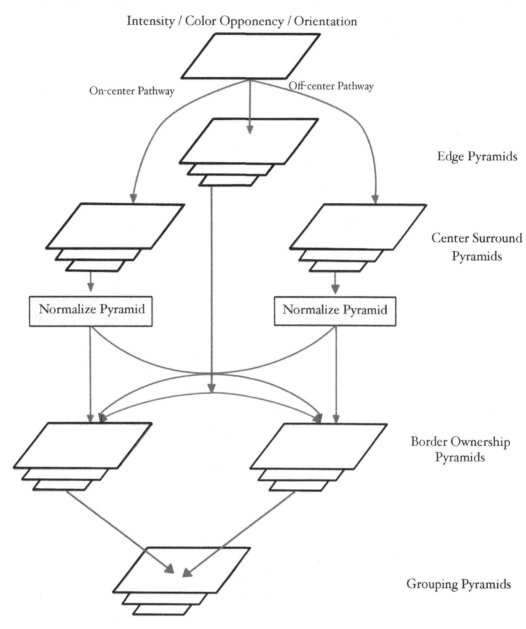

sponses with the activity from the center-surround pyramids, border ownership responses for a given angle are calculated. Finally, border ownership activity is used annularly to generate a grouping pyramid.

In Figure 6 the proto-object saliency algorithm is illustrated. An input image is divided into Intensity, Color Opponency and Orientation channels. Then, each channel runs its proper grouping mechanism (Figure 5). For proto-objects of similar size and feature composition, a normalization operator is performed for better decision making as follows: the grouping activity of maps with few proto-objects gives higher priority in comparison with grouping activity of maps with multiple proto-objects. Afterward, the results of the grouping mechanism is normalized and merged to generate conspicuity maps. After some normalization, that is an enhancement of the activity channels with unique proto-objects and suppression of activity channels with multiple proto-objects, the different maps are summed linearly to construct the proto-object saliency map.

Yanulevskaya et al (2013) used a hierarchical image segmentation algorithm to extract proto-objects. They used *rarity-based* and *contrast-based* saliency to achieve saliency at the proto-object level. Rarity-based saliency is based on the idea that rare features in an image deserve to be attended more whereas contrast-based saliency provides salient regions based on differences in contrast. In their work, proto-objects are created using graph-based hierarchical image segmentation (van de Sande et al., 2011). In the next step, the algorithm identifies the saliency of the proto-objects using contrast-based and rarity-based methodologies. The idea underlying the contrast-based methodology is that, the contrast of a salient proto-object is one which remarkably differs from its surroundings. However, there are some exceptions: The contrast of a bright sky differs from the rest of the image while it is not salient. Dealing with this problem, the average difference among all segments within a proto-object are estimated and used to suppress the saliency of such a proto-object. On the other hand, the idea underlying the rarity-based methodology is that, a rare object deserves more for attention as it is unique. To calculate the rarity of a typical proto-object a measure of entropy is calculated and the final proto-object-based saliency map is obtained from the summation of the outputs of contrast-based and rarity-based modules.

Although methods provided by Russel et al. (2014) and Yanulevskaya et al. (2013) for proto-object map generation are new and interesting, they have not been applied in any robotic application. Palomino et al. (2011) have proposed an object-based attention system for social robots with a stereo camera (Figure 7). Since in dynamic scenarios the task of the robot may change during time, their model considers this aspect for recognizing the most salient object. Their triad system is composed of pre-attentive, semi-attentive and attentive stages. Salient proto-objects are implemented in a pre-attentive module whereas task-based items are identified and tracked in a semi-attentive stage. The third stage is responsible for fixing the FoA to the most salient object regarding the current task.

The computation of salient proto-objects in the pre-attentive stage is based on four bottom-up features and a top-down signal. Proto-objects are constructed from blobs of uniform colors which are bounded by edges. The four bottom-up features are color, luminosity contrasts between the proto-object and its surrounding, mean disparity and the probability of the proto-object to be a face or a hand, based on its colour. The last feature is specific for a human gesture detection scenario of the social robot. To create the saliency map, features are summed other using proper normalized weights. These weights depend on the current task of the robot.

Yu et al. (2008), (2010) and (2013) developed models of attention based on the proto-object concept in three robotic applications. The model in (Yu et al., 2010), which is an extension of (Yu et al., 2008), works

Figure 6. After the decomposition of the input image into intensity, color and orientation channels, the grouping mechanism shown in Figure 5 is applied and after normalization and merging steps a proto-object map is obtained.
(Russel et al., 2014).

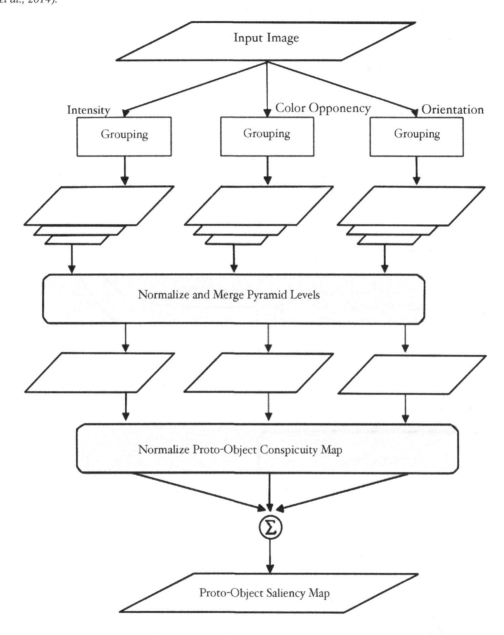

Proto-object-based Saliency Model

in two phases: The attending phase and the learning phase. The attending phase consists of the modules preattentive processing, top–down biasing, bottom–up competition, mediation between top–down and bottom–up ways, generation of saliency maps, and perceptual completion processing. The preattentive processing module has two steps: extraction of low-dimensional preattentive features and preattentive

Figure 7. Biologically inspired attention mechanism of Palomino et al. (2011); a pre-attentive module is responsible for salient proto-object generation. The semi-attentive and attentive stages are used for tracking already attended objects and task-based target selection.

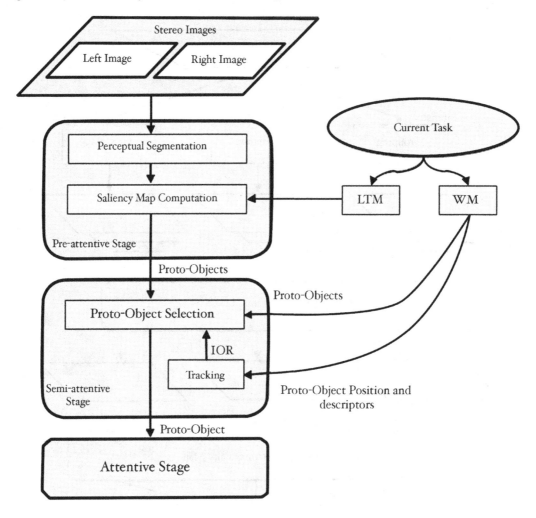

segmentation which divides the scene into different proto-objects and background. For recognizing a specific object, the top–down biasing module constructs the attentional template(s) by using features such as appearance (shape information), color, intensity, orientation or motion. The conspicuity of the input scene is estimated in a bottom–up competition module. Cooperation of location-based top–down biases and bottom–up conspicuity yield a location-based saliency map. Combining the saliency map within each proto-object, proto-object-based saliency is achieved. Finally, the most salient proto-object is chosen for attention and be given to perceptual completion processing module for the sake of object recognition.

In more recent work, Yu et al. (2013) proposed a pure-bottom-up proto-object-based model which involves four modules (Figure 8): Extraction of preattentive features, preattentive segmentation, estimation of space-based saliency, and estimation of proto-object-based saliency. Intensity, red-green, blue-yellow and orientation energy are preattentive features in the first module. The first three features are extracted at multiple scales using Gaussian pyramid (Burt & Adelson, 1983) whereas an Oriented Laplacian Pyramid (Greenspan et al., 1994) is used to extract multi-scale orientation energy. In the pre-attentive segmentation module, the scene is partitioned into proto-objects preattentively using the BIP (Bhattacharyya distance based Irregular Pyramid) algorithm proposed by the authors. In fact, BIP is a *split-and-merge* image segmentation algorithm which uses an *irregular pyramid* method. Robustness against noise and spatial transformation, self-determination of the number of proto-objects and efficient computational complexity are the main characteristics of the BIP algorithm. This algorithm assigns a node to each segment and considers nodes in higher pyramidal levels as a probabilistic distribution. These nodes could be assumed as the receptive field of neurons with the corresponding spatial size. Robustness of the BIP algorithm against noise (in comparison with some known segmentation algorithms e.g., graph-based segmentation (GBS) and hierarchical K-means (HKM)) is relatively high because of using Bhattacharyya distance to estimate the intralevel similarity (the similarity of nodes in the same pyramidal level). In addition, BIP applies an adaptive neighbor search strategy to realize the number of proto-objects automatically. First, based on graphic constraint, a set of candidate nodes are selected for a center node (*proximity-driven*) and then, each candidate node which satisfies a similarity condition would be selected as neighbor (*similarity-driven*). It has been shown that the computational complexity of the BIP is $O(N_0)$ where N_0 is the number of nodes in level 0 pyramid (original size)

At the end, these proto-objects are resized to the original scale. Since the proto-objects are obtained at the original scale, space-based saliency is interpolated from the saliency scale to the original scale. The usage of mean function on the space-based saliency and the proto-object results in a proto-object-based saliency map. Obviously, the FoA is the proto-object with the maximal proto-object-based saliency. The algorithmic description of (Yu et al., 2013) is demonstrated in Table 2.

ITERATIVE MODEL

The iterative model is strongly grounded in neuro-physiological observations (Hamker, 2005b). A first version to deal with natural scenes demonstrated goal-directed search in images where the task was to find a previously shown object (Hamker, 2005a). This model has been further developed for modelling attentive vision in neuro-robotics within the EU research project EYESHOTS (Antonelli et al., 2014). It has been demonstrated that a target object can be detected among other objects using a top-down object-selective bias towards learned high-level filters. While the previous version (Hamker, 2005a) used multiple feature cues, the latter improved model operates at the level of learned proto-objects. The cognitive and biologically plausible architecture for object recognition used in this kind of work consists of three modules: V1 for feature analysis, High Visual Area (HVA) for proto-object representation and the Frontal Eye Field (FEF) for gaze direction and spatial attention illustrated in Figure 9. The architecture consists of several neural networks. Each neural network models a cortical region. The main difference to the proto-object based models discussed before is that here attention is the emergent result of competition between a proto-object representation and the Frontal Eye Field (FEF), and not just the result of competition on a single saliency map.

Considering the functionality of this model in general, V1 encodes simple features by computing V1 complex cell responses from stereo images to obtain features like the orientation of edges, local contrast differences and retinal disparity. The responses of V1 cells are delivered to HVA which mimics cells

Figure 8. The model proposed by Yu et al. (2013) to construct a proto-object map; preattentive features (intensity, color and orientation) are extracted at multiple scales. Then, the BIP algorithm is performed in a pre-attentive segmentation stage to construct the proto-object map. Finally, a combination of the proto-object map and space-based saliency results in a proto-object based saliency map.

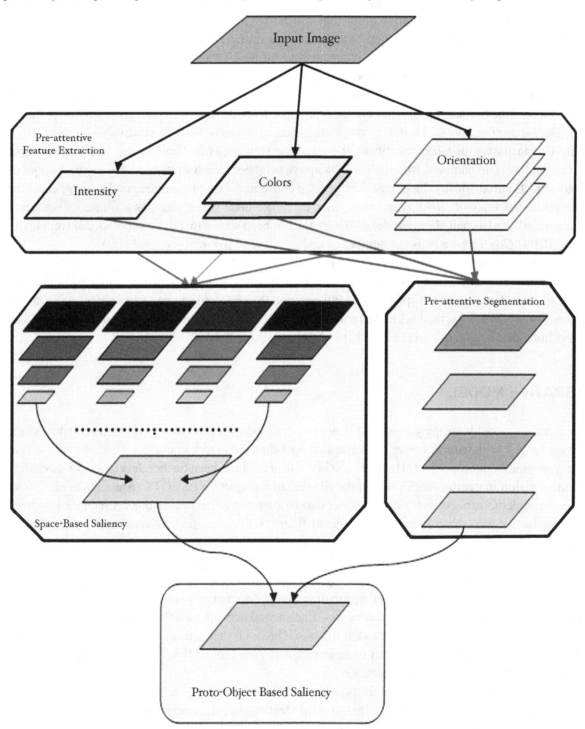

Table 2. The algorithmic description of method used in (Yu et al., 2013)

Algorithm 2: Proto-Object-Based Algorithm Developed in (Yu et al., 2013)	
Input: RGB_Image	**Output:** Saliency Map with Focus of Attention on Proto-Object

Extraction of Pre-Attentive Features
Extract color components (r, g and b) from RGB_Image <ul><li>$F_{int} = (r + g + b) / 3$ // Intensity feature</li><li>$F_{rg} = R - G$ where $R = r - (g + b) / 2$ and $G = g - (r + b) / 2$ // Red–Green feature</li><li>$F_{by} = B - Y$ where $B = b - (r + g) / 2$ and $Y = (r + g) / 2 - |r - g| / 2 - b$ // Blue–Yellow feature</li><li>Compute Gaussian pyramids to estimate intensity and color features at 9 scales.</li><li>Compute Laplacian pyramids to estimate orientation feature ($F_{o\theta}$) at 9 scales. θ in {0°, 45°, 90°, 135°}</li></ul>

Pre-Attentive Segmentation
Extract proto-objects (R_g) using BIP algorithm (Yu et al., 2013)   **Space-Based Saliency:** Θ denotes across-scale subtraction in following lines. <ul><li>Calculate center–surround difference $F'_{int}(c, s) = \|F_{int}(c) \Theta F_{int}(s)\|\ c$ in {2,3,4}, $s = c + \alpha$, α in {3, 4}</li><li>Calculate center–surround difference $F'_{rg}(c, s) = \|F_{rg}(c) \Theta F_{rg}(s)\|\ c$ in {2,3,4}, $s = c + \alpha$, α in {3, 4}</li><li>Calculate center–surround difference $F'_{by}(c, s) = \|F_{by}(c) \Theta F_{by}(s)\|\ c$ in {2,3,4}, $s = c + \alpha$, α in {3, 4}</li><li>Calculate center–surround difference $F'_{o\theta}(c, s) = \|F_{o\theta}(c) \Theta F_{o\theta}(s)\|\ c$ in {2,3,4}, $s = c + \alpha$, α in {3, 4}</li><li>Conspicuity maps generation: $\sum$ denotes across-scale addition and $N(.)$ is normalization operator to</li><li>[0, 255] in following lines.</li></ul>

$$F_{int}^{cp} = \frac{1}{6} \sum_{c=2}^{4} \sum_{s=c+3}^{c+4} N\left(F'_{int}\left(c,s\right)\right) \quad F_{rg}^{cp} = \frac{1}{6} \sum_{c=2}^{4} \sum_{s=c+3}^{c+4} N\left(F'_{rg}\left(c,s\right)\right)$$

$$F_{by}^{cp} = \frac{1}{6} \sum_{c=2}^{4} \sum_{s=c+3}^{c+4} N\left(F'_{by}\left(c,s\right)\right) \quad F_{o\theta}^{cp} = \frac{1}{6} \sum_{c=2}^{4} \sum_{s=c+3}^{c+4} N\left(F'_{o\theta}\left(c,s\right)\right)$$

Space-Based Saliency Map:

$$S_p = N\left(F_{int}^{cp}\right) + N\left(\frac{N\left(F_{rg}^{cp}\right) + N\left(F_{by}^{cp}\right)}{2}\right) + N\left(\sum_{\theta} \frac{N\left(F_{o\theta}^{cp}\right)}{4}\right)$$

Proto-Object Based Saliency
$S'_p :=$ Interpolate S_p from saliency scale to the original scale

$$S\left(R_g\right) = \sum_{r_i \in R_g} \frac{S'_p\left(r_i\right)}{N_g} \quad \text{where } r_i \text{ is a pixel and } N_g \text{ is number of pixels in proto-object } R_g \text{ at original scale}$$

encoding parts of objects similar to the idea of proto-objects. HVA is organized in several maps where each map encodes a different (learned) proto-object. Learning the connections from V1 to HVA takes place in an off-line training phase using unsupervised learning. The idea is that on the short time scale of stimuli presentations, the visual input is more likely to originate from the same object under the same view, rather than from different objects or views. These view-tuned cells can be related to brain areas V4 and IT (Logothetis et al., 1994; MIT AI Memos., 1995). Using weight sharing, the HVA is organized in different retinotopic maps where each map encodes the feature selectivity of a proto-object (green shapes in Figure 9). The FEF is simulated by two maps: *FEFv* and *FEFvm* representing the visual and

Figure 9. Biologically plausible iterative model used in (Antonelli et al., 2014); simple features (e.g., orientation of edges) are computed by V1 cells using input stereo images. The responses of V1 cells are combined into invariant object views at the level of HVA cells. The learning of object views has been done off line. A top-down attention signal from Object Memory increases the sensitivity of the HVA cells to a particular to be searched object. Simultaneous localization and recognition are performed iteratively using circular path between HVA and FEF where the FEF computes the next gaze shift towards the object of interest.

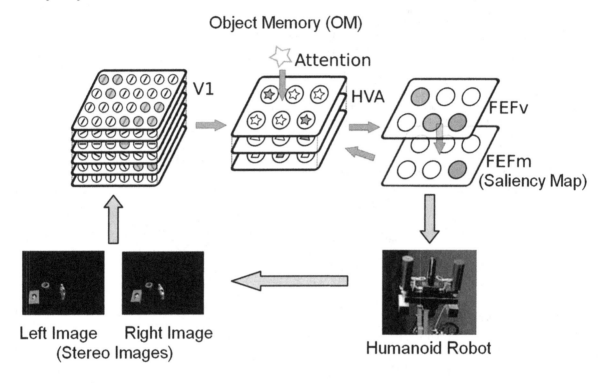

visuomovement cell types respectively. The former is a kind of saliency map and indicates the places where a searched object is probably located and the latter is responsible for providing the saccade target location. However, this map also projects back to visual areas to increase the visibility of the proto-object at the saccade target prior to any shift in gaze. Biological background of the process can be found in (Hamker, 2005b). The model is based on a rate coded neuron model for all neurons in the model.

As mentioned before, the iterative model links spatial attention to proto-objects but equally well proto-objects to attention. The top-down signal reinforces the activation of all neurons related to a typical object (HVA cells) during the search process of it. The activation of other cells is suppressed. This process is iterated such that an object of interest or a region of space is processed with preference. This method may help to solve the chicken-egg recognition and localization problem: object recognition depends on localization and localization depends on object recognition. Furthermore, the back projection from *FEFvm* to HVA implements spatial attention. In general, *feature-based attention* is defined as attending a certain feature or object over the whole scene whereby *spatial attention* is defined as attending a certain location. This double connection between *FEFvm* (decision on the saliency map) and HVA (as proto-object map) fits to the Figure 3(c). Table 3 describes the steps of the iterative model using a high-level algorithmic description.

Table 3. The algorithmic description of Beuth & Hamker model

Algorithm 3: Iterative Model of Beuth-Hamker	
Input: Stereo_RGB_Images, Searched_Object	**Output:** Saliency Map with Location of Searched Object
Training Phase (Off-Line)	
Generating proto-objects for each object in HVA layer	
Learn the connection weights from V1 population (input layer of neural network) to HVA layer	
Operational Phase (On-Line)	

Bottom-up stage:
  • From Stereo_RGB_Images, extract local features like orientation of edges and disparities
  • Set these local features as V1 neurons, send the output to HVA	

Top-down stage and iteration:
  While (output of FEFm neurons reach 0.96 of maximum) do
    • In HVA layer, encode single views of the Searched_Object, send the output to the object memory and FEF
    • In FEF layer, Encode the spatial information to construct the saliency map, send the feedback to HVA
    • In HVA, receive the feedback (attention/suppression signals for recognition) from object memory to enhance the target responses
    • In HVA, receive the feedback (attention/suppression signals for localization) from FEF
    • Update the output of the HVA neurons using the attention/suppression signals: excite the attended features and locations and inhibit the unattended ones
  End While	

(Antonelli et al., 2014).

The aforementioned cognitive architecture was implemented on the humanoid robotic torso Tombatossal (Antonelli et al., 2014). The head of the robot had a stereo camera with resolution 1024×768 and frame rate 30 fps. However, the images have been converted to resolution 320×240 pixels. For software implementation several parallel modules based on YARP middle-ware were used to manage the communication among them. The experimental results showed the benefits obtained by implementing such models on a robot platform, e.g., capability of executing a set of tasks such as recognizing, gazing and reaching target objects.

An investigation about the impact of suppression in the biologically plausible object recognition system is another recent work performed in (Beuth et al., 2014). It has been shown that it is not only important to select the target information, but also it is important to explicitly suppress the distracting sensory data. Simple suppression of the neurons encoding distractors is not sufficient to achieve robust recognition; rather suppressing the location of each one has an additional remarkable effect.

CONCLUSION AND FUTURE RESEARCH DIRECTIONS

In this chapter we introduced some important biologically-inspired models of attention which have been implemented on robots. Considering the term biologically-inspired, the need for basic knowledge about the primate visual system is evident.

We classified such models into three separate classes: simple saliency-based, proto-object-based and iterative. Although all of these classes incorporate the concept of saliency maps, models belonging to third class rely on competition within the whole network. Normally, a saliency map is constructed using basic features e.g., intensity, color and orientation. In this case, the FoA is object-independent. In other words, the result of attention would be a point in the image which may or may not be a part of an object. Although the construction process of the proto-object maps varies in different models, they all link saliency to a corresponding proto-object. However, the formation of the proto-object is a preattentive, attention-independent process.

The model belonging to the iterative model class tries to solve the chicken-egg problem in object recognition and object localization: For recognizing a searched object in a scene, the object must first be located and recognized which, however, is only possible if the object has been recognized well. Using a top-down attention signal, activations of all neurons that encode a view of a typical object are reinforced whereas the activations of other neurons are suppressed. This process is iterated such that an object of interest or a region of space is processed with preference.

Future Research Trend

Heretofore, most of the previous modeling research has been focused on the bottom-up component of visual attention. This is because of their simplicity in design and implementation. However, for object recognition we need more than a simple saliency-map. Hence, the future trend of computational visual attention (especially biologically-inspired models) should be toward the development of more top-down-based and task-driven models.

Obviously, one of the most important usages of visual attention is in robotic applications. Regardless of the models mentioned in this chapter, there is not a vast volume of literature on the subject of biologically-inspired attention-based robot vision. Many models are just designed on normal computers but have not been implemented on any robot. Perhaps one reason is that they are not suitable for (near) real-time applications whereas, normally, an efficient robot algorithm should be (near) real-time. However, the demand of robot vision is growing and undoubtedly we will see more implemented models of attention on robots in the future.

A new more fundamental research direction in biologically-inspired models for attentive robot vision could be focused on the role of binding. Most work deals just with the question of speeding up processing by an analysis of only parts of an image. Attention may also facilitate object recognition. However, a more fundamental role of attention is to bind image contents to cognition. Currently, vision and cognition are rather different systems that are not well integrated. Particularly in the field of robotics vision serves for the extraction of information for the task at hand and cognitive systems should be able to tune the visual system to extract and bind the relevant information to cognitive processes.

Finally, it is worth noting that a lack in the field of attention-based object recognition is the absence of a good dataset for comparison of existing models especially in robotic applications. Every research group developed their model for a specific application without performing any comparison with other models across a small range of applications. Hence, developing a test bench and a reliable dataset for such comparisons (at least in a specific problem e.g., attention-based robots object recognition) could be a worthy future attempt.

ACKNOWLEDGMENT

This work has been supported by the European Union's Seventh Framework Programme (FET, Neuro-Bio-Inspired Systems: Spatial Cognition) under grant agreement $n°$ 600785.

REFERENCES

Antonelli, M., Gibaldi, A., Beuth, F., Duran, A. J., Canessa, A., Solari, F., & Sabatini, S. P. et al. (2014). A hierarchical system for a distributed representation of the peripersonal space of a humanoid robot. *IEEE Transactions on Autonomous Mental Development*, 6(4), 259–273. doi:10.1109/TAMD.2014.2332875

Ballard, D. (1991). Animate vision. *Artificial Intelligence*, 48(1), 57–86. doi:10.1016/0004-3702(91)90080-4

Barranco, F., Díaz, J., Ros, E., & del Pino, B. (2009). Visual System Based on Artificial Retina for Motion Detection. *IEEE Transactions on Systems, Man, and Cybernetics. Part B, Cybernetics*, 39(3), 752–762. doi:10.1109/TSMCB.2008.2009067 PMID:19362896

Bender, D. B., & Youakim, M. (2001). Effect of attentive fixation in macaque thalamus and cortex. *Journal of Neurophysiology*, 85(1), 219–234. PMID:11152722

Beuth, F., Jamalian, A., & Hamker, F. H. (2014). How Visual Attention and Suppression Facilitate Object Recognition? In *Proceedings of 24th International Conference on Artificial Neural Networks (ICANN)* (pp. 459-466). Hamburg, Germany: Springer. doi:10.1007/978-3-319-11179-7_58

Born, R. T., & Bradley, D. C. (2005). Structure and function of visual area MT. *Annual Review of Neuroscience*, 28(1), 157–189. doi:10.1146/annurev.neuro.26.041002.131052 PMID:16022593

Bruce, C. J., Goldberg, M. E., Bushnell, M. C., & Stanton, G. B. (1985). Primate Frontal Eye Fields. II. Physiological and Anatomical Correlates of Electrically Evoked Eye Movements. *Journal of Neurophysiology*, 54(3), 714–734. PMID:4045546

Burt, P. J., & Adelson, E. H. (1983). The laplacian pyramid as a compact image code. *IEEE Transactions on Communications*, 31(4), 532–540. doi:10.1109/TCOM.1983.1095851

Cadieu, C., Kouh, M., Pasupathy, A., Connor, C. E., Riesenhuber, M., & Poggio, T. (2007). A model of V4 shape selectivity and invariance. *Journal of Neurophysiology*, 98(3), 1733–1750. doi:10.1152/jn.01265.2006 PMID:17596412

Cai, D., DeAngelis, G. C., & Freeman, R. D. (1997). Spatiotemporal receptive field organization in the LGN of cats and kittens. *Journal of Neurophysiology*, 78, 1045–1061. PMID:9307134

Chelazzi, L., Duncan, J., Miller, E. K., & Desimone, R. (1998). Responses of Neurons in Inferior Temporal Cortex During Memory-Guided Visual Search. *Journal of Neurophysiology*, 80, 2918–2940. PMID:9862896

Cohen, Y. E., & Andersen, R. (2002). A common reference frame for movement plans in the posterior parietal cortex. *Nature Reviews. Neuroscience*, 3(7), 553–562. doi:10.1038/nrn873 PMID:12094211

Corbetta, M., & Shulman, G. L. (2002). Control of goal-directed and stimulus-driven attention in the brain. *National Review*, 3(3), 201–215. doi:10.1038/nrn755 PMID:11994752

DeAngelis, G., Ohzawa, I., & Freeman, R. D. (1995). Receptive-field dynamics in the central visual pathways. *Trends in Neurosciences*, 18(10), 451–458. doi:10.1016/0166-2236(95)94496-R PMID:8545912

Desimone, R., & Duncan, J. (1995). Neural mechanisms of selective visual attention. *Annual Review of Neuroscience, 18*(1), 193–222. doi:10.1146/annurev.ne.18.030195.001205 PMID:7605061

Deubel, H., & Schneider, W. X. (1996). Saccade target selection and object recognition: Evidence for a common attentional mechanism. *Vision Research, 36*(12), 1827–1837. doi:10.1016/0042-6989(95)00294-4 PMID:8759451

Felleman, D. J., & Van Essen, D. C. (1991). Distributed hierarchical processing in the primate cerebral cortex. *Cerebral Cortex, 1*(1), 1–47. doi:10.1093/cercor/1.1.1 PMID:1822724

Forsyth, D. A., & Ponce, J. (2003). *Computer Vision: A Modern Approach*. Berkeley, CA: Prentice Hall.

Frintrop, S. (2005). *VOCUS: a visual attention system for object detection and goal-directed search*. (Ph.D. thesis). Rheinische Friedrich-Wilhelms-Universität Bonn, Germany.

Frintrop, S., & Jensfelt, P. (2008). Attentional Landmarks and Active Gaze Control for Visual SLAM. *IEEE Transactions on Robotics, 24*(5), 1054–1065. doi:10.1109/TRO.2008.2004977

Frintrop, S., Rome, E., & Christensen, H. I. (2010). Computational Visual Attention Systems and their Cognitive Foundations: A Survey. *ACM Transactions on Applied Perception, 7*(1), 1–46. doi:10.1145/1658349.1658355

Friston, K. J., & Büchel, C. (2000). Attentional modulation of effective connectivity from V2 to V5/MT in humans. *Proceedings of the National Academy of Sciences of the United States of America, 97*(13), 7591–7596. doi:10.1073/pnas.97.13.7591 PMID:10861020

Fritz, G., Seifert, C., & Paletta, L. (2004). Attentive object detection using an information theoretic saliency measure. In *Proceedings of 2nd Int'l Workshop on Attention and Performance in Computational Vision (WAPCV)* (pp 136–143). Prague, Czech Republic: WAPCV.

Goldberg, M. E., Bisley, J. W., Powell, K. D., & Gottlieb, J. (2006). Saccades, salience and attention: The role of the lateral intraparietal area in visual behavior. *Progress in Brain Research, 155*, 157–175. doi:10.1016/S0079-6123(06)55010-1 PMID:17027387

Greenspan, A. G., Belongie, S., Goodman, R., Perona, P., Rakshit, S., & Anderson, C. H. (1994). Overcomplete steerable pyramid filters and rotation invariance. In *Proceedings of IEEE International Conference on Computer Vision Pattern Recognition (CVPR)* (pp. 222–228). doi:10.1109/CVPR.1994.323833

Hamker, F. H. (2005a). The emergence of attention by population-based inference and its role in distributed processing and cognitive control of vision. *Computer Vision and Image Understanding, 100*(1-2), 64–106. doi:10.1016/j.cviu.2004.09.005

Hamker, F. H. (2005b). The reentry hypothesis: The putative interaction of the frontal eye field, ventrolateral prefrontal cortex, and areas V4, IT for attention and eye movement. *Cerebral Cortex, 15*(4), 431–447. doi:10.1093/cercor/bhh146 PMID:15749987

Heinen, M. R., & Engel, P. M. (2009). NLOOK: A computational attention model for robot vision. *Journal of the Brazilian Computer Society, 15*(3), 3–17. doi:10.1007/BF03194502

Hubel, D. H. (1995). *Eye, Brain and Vision*. New York, NY: Scientific American Library.

Itti, L., Koch, C., & Niebur, E. (1998). A model of saliency-based visual attention for rapid scene analysis. *IEEE Transactions on Pattern Analysis and Machine Intelligence*, *20*(11), 1254–1259. doi:10.1109/34.730558

Koch, C., & Ullman, S. (1985). Shifts in selective visual attention: Towards the underlying neural circuitry. *Human Neurobiology*, *4*, 219–227. PMID:3836989

Lee, J., & Maunsell, J. H. R. (2009). A Normalization Model of Attentional Modulation of Single Unit Responses. *PLoS ONE*, *4*(2), e4651. doi:10.1371/journal.pone.0004651 PMID:19247494

Lee, J., & Maunsell, J. H. R. (2010). Attentional Modulation of MT Neurons with Single or Multiple Stimuli in Their Receptive Fields. *The Journal of Neuroscience*, *30*(8), 3058–3066. doi:10.1523/JNEUROSCI.3766-09.2010 PMID:20181602

Logothetis, N. K., Pauls, J., Bülthoff, H. H., & Poggio, T. (1994). View-dependent object recognition by monkeys. *Current Biology*, *4*(5), 401–414. doi:10.1016/S0960-9822(00)00089-0 PMID:7922354

Mahadevan, V., & Vasconcelos, N. (2013). Biologically-inspired Object Tracking Using Center-surround Mechanisms. *IEEE Transactions on Pattern Analysis and Machine Intelligence*, *35*(3), 541–554. doi:10.1109/TPAMI.2012.98 PMID:22529325

Miau, F., Papageorgiou, C., & Itti, L. (2001). Neuromorphic algorithms for computer vision and attention. In *Proceedings of Annual Int'l Symposium on Optical Science and Technology* (pp 12–23). Academic Press.

Milanese, R., Wechsler, H., Gil, S., Bost, J., & Pun, T. (1994). Integration of bottom-up and top-down cues for visual attention using non-linear relaxation. In *Proceedings of IEEE International Conference on Computer Vision and Pattern Recognition (CVPR'94)* (pp 781–785). doi:10.1109/CVPR.1994.323898

Mitri, S., Frintrop, S., Pervolz, K., Surmann, H., & Nuchter, A. (2005). Robust Object Detection at Regions of Interest with an Application in Ball Recognition. In *Proceedings of IEEE International Conference on Robotics and Automation (ICRA)* (pp 125–130). Barcelona, Spain: IEEE. doi:10.1109/ROBOT.2005.1570107

Moore, T., Armstrong, K. M., & Fallah, M. (2003). Visuomotor origins of covert spatial attention. *Neuron*, *40*(4), 671–683. doi:10.1016/S0896-6273(03)00716-5 PMID:14622573

Navalpakkam, V., & Itti, L. (2006a). An integrated model of top-down and bottom-up attention for optimizing detection speed. In *Proceedings of International Conference on Computer Vision and Pattern Recognition (CVPR)*. doi:10.1109/CVPR.2006.54

Nothdurft, H. C. (2005). Salience of feature contrast. In L. Itti, G. Rees, & J. K. Tsotsos (Eds.), *Neurobiology of Attention* (pp. 233–239). Amsterdam, Netherlands: Elsevier Academic Press. doi:10.1016/B978-012375731-9/50042-2

Ouerhani, N. (2003). *Visual attention: From bio-inspired modeling to real-time implementation.* (Ph.D. thesis). Institut de Microtechnique Université de Neuchâtel, Switzerland.

Palomino, A. J., Marfil, R., Bandera, J. P., & Bandera, A. (2011). A Novel Biologically Inspired Attention Mechanism for a Social Robot. *EURASIP Journal on Advances in Signal Processing, 2011*, 1–10. doi:10.1155/2011/841078

Pessoa, L., & Exel, S. (1999). Attentional strategies for object recognition. In *Proceedings of International Work-Conference on Artificial and Natural Neural Networks (IWANN '99)* (Vol. 1606, pp. 850–859). Alicante, Spain: Springer.

Posner, M. I., Snyder, C. R., & Davidson, B. J. (1980). Attention and the detection of signals. *Journal of Experimental Psychology. General, 109*(2), 160–174. doi:10.1037/0096-3445.109.2.160 PMID:7381367

Potapova, E., Zillich, M., & Vincze, M. (2012). Attention-driven segmentation of cluttered 3D scenes. In *Proceedings of International Conference on Pattern Recognition (ICPR 2012)*, (pp 3610-3613). ICPR.

Read, J. C. A. (2005). Early computational processing in binocular vision and depth perception. *Progress in Biophysics and Molecular Biology, 87*(1), 77–108. doi:10.1016/j.pbiomolbio.2004.06.005 PMID:15471592

Rensink, R. A., O'Regan, J. K., & Clark, J. J. (1997). To see or not to see: The need for attention to perceive changes in scenes. *Psychological Science, 8*(5), 368–373. doi:10.1111/j.1467-9280.1997.tb00427.x

Reynolds, J. H., Chelazzi, L., & Desimone, R. (1999). Competitive Mechanisms Subserve Attention in Macaque Areas V2 and V4. *The Journal of Neuroscience, 19*(5), 1736–1753. PMID:10024360

Reynolds, J. H., & Heeger, D. J. (2009). The normalization model of attention. *Neuron, 61*(2), 168–185. doi:10.1016/j.neuron.2009.01.002 PMID:19186161

Rousselet, G. A., Thorpe, S. J., & Fabre-Thorpe, M. (2004). How parallel is visual processing in the ventral pathway? *Trends in Cognitive Sciences, 8*(8), 363–370. doi:10.1016/j.tics.2004.06.003 PMID:15335463

Russel, A. R., Mihalaş, S., von der Heydt, R., Niebur, E., & Etienne-Cummings, R. (2014). A model of proto-object based saliency. *Vision Research, 94*, 1–15. doi:10.1016/j.visres.2013.10.005 PMID:24184601

Salah, A., Alpaydin, E., & Akrun, L. (2002). A selective attention based method for visual pattern recognition with application to handwritten digit recognition and face recognition. [PAMI]. *IEEE Transactions on Pattern Analysis and Machine Intelligence, 24*(3), 420–425. doi:10.1109/34.990146

Schall, J. D. (2004). On the role of frontal eye field in guiding attention and saccades. *Vision Research, 44*(12), 1453–1467. doi:10.1016/j.visres.2003.10.025 PMID:15066404

Shulman, G., Remington, R., & McLean, J. (1979). Moving attention through visual space. *Journal of Experimental Psychology. Human Perception and Performance, 5*(3), 522–526. doi:10.1037/0096-1523.5.3.522 PMID:528957

Simons, D. J. (2000). *Change blindness and visual memory.* Philadelphia, PA: Psychology Press.

Logothetis, N. K., Pauls, J., & Poggio, T. (1995). Spatial reference frames for object recognition, tuning for rotations in depth. Cambridge, MA: MIT.

Treisman, A. M., & Gormican, S. (1988). Feature analysis in early vision: Evidence from search asymmetries. *Psychological Review, 95*(1), 15–48. doi:10.1037/0033-295X.95.1.15 PMID:3353475

Tsotsos, J. K. (1990). Analyzing vision at the complexity level. *Behavioral and Brain Sciences, 13*(03), 423–445. doi:10.1017/S0140525X00079577

Tsotsos, J. K. (2008). What Roles can Attention Play in Recognition? In *Proceedings of 7th IEEE International Conference on Development and Learning (ICDL)* (pp. 55–60). IEEE. doi:10.1109/DEVLRN.2008.4640805

Ungerleider, L. G., & Desimone, R. (1986). Cortical connections of visual area MT in the macaque. *The Journal of Comparative Neurology, 248*(2), 190–222. doi:10.1002/cne.902480204 PMID:3722458

van de Sande, K. E. A., Uijlings, J. R. R., Gevers, T., & Smeulders, A. W. M. (2011). Segmentation as selective search for object recognition. In *Proceedings of International Conference on Computer Vision* (pp. 1879– 1886). Barcelona, Spain: IEEE. doi:10.1109/ICCV.2011.6126456

Van Essen, D. C., Newsome, W. T., Maunsell, J. H. R., & Bixby, J. L. (1986). The projections from striate cortex (V1) to areas V2 and V3 in the macaque monkey: Asymmetries, areal boundaries, and patchy connections. *The Journal of Comparative Neurology, 244*(4), 451–480. doi:10.1002/cne.902440405 PMID:3958238

Walther, D., Edgington, D. R., & Koch, C. (2004). Detection and tracking of objects in underwater video. In *Proceedings of International Conference on Computer Vision and Pattern Recognition (CVPR)*, (pp 544–549). doi:10.1109/CVPR.2004.1315079

Walther, D., & Koch, C. (2006). Modeling attention to salient proto-objects. *Neural Networks, 19*(9), 1395–1407. doi:10.1016/j.neunet.2006.10.001 PMID:17098563

Wolfe, J. M. (1994). Guided search 2.0: A revised model of visual search. *Psychonomic Bulletin & Review, 1*(2), 202–238. doi:10.3758/BF03200774 PMID:24203471

Yanulevskaya, V., Uijlings, J., Geusebroek, J. M., Sebe, N., & Smeulders, A. (2013). A proto-object-based computational model for visual saliency. *Journal of Vision, 13*(27), 1-19.

Yu, Y., Gu, J., Mann, G. K. I., & Gosine, R. G. (2013). Development and Evaluation of Object-Based Vosual Attention for Automatic Perception of Robots. *IEEE Transactions on Automation Science and Engineering, 10*(2), 365–379. doi:10.1109/TASE.2012.2214772

Yu, Y., Mann, G. K. I., & Gosine, R. G. (2008). An Object-based Visual Attention Model for Robots. In *Proceedings of IEEE International Conference on Robotics and Automation (ICRA)* (pp. 943–948). Pasadena, CA: IEEE.

Yu, Y., Mann, G. K. I., & Gosine, R. G. (2010). An Object-based Visual Attention Model for Robotic Applications. *IEEE Transactions on Systems, Man, and Cybernetics, 40*(5), 1398–1412. doi:10.1109/TSMCB.2009.2038895 PMID:20129865

ADDITIONAL READING

Andreopoulos, A., Hasler, S., Wersing, H., Janssen, H., Tsotsos, J. K., & Körner, E. (2011). Active 3D Object Localization Using a Humanoid Robot. *IEEE Transactions on Robotics, 27*(1), 47–64. doi:10.1109/TRO.2010.2090058

Aragon-Camarasaa, G., Fattah, H., & Siebert, J. P. (2010). Towards a unified visual framework in a binocular active robot vision system. *Robotics and Autonomous Systems, 58*(3), 276–286. doi:10.1016/j.robot.2009.08.005

Belardinelli, A., Pirri, F., & Carbone, A. (2007). Bottom-Up Gaze Shifts and Fixations Learning by Imitation. *IEEE Transactions on Systems, Man, and Cybernetics. Part B, Cybernetics, 37*(2), 256–271. doi:10.1109/TSMCB.2006.886950 PMID:17416155

Beuter, N., Lohmann, O., Schmidt, J., & Kummert, F. (2009). Directed attention - A cognitive vision system for a mobile robot. In *Proceedings of 18th IEEE International Symposium on Robot and Human Interactive Communication* (pp. 854-860), Toyama, Japan:IEEE. doi:10.1109/ROMAN.2009.5326156

Beuth, F., Wiltschut, J., & Hamker, F. H. (2010). Attentive stereoscopic object recognition. In *Proceedings of Workshop New Challenges in Neural Computation* (pp. 41-48).

Borji, A., & Itti, L. (2013). State-of-the-Art in Visual Attention Modelling. [PAMI]. *IEEE Transactions on Pattern Analysis and Machine Intelligence, 35*(1), 185–207. doi:10.1109/TPAMI.2012.89 PMID:22487985

Boynton, G. M. (2009). A framework for describing the effects of attention on visual responses. *Vision Research, 49*(10), 1129–1143. doi:10.1016/j.visres.2008.11.001 PMID:19038281

Carlson, N. R., Carver, C. S., Scheier, M., & Aronson, E. (2007). *Physiology of behavior* (9th ed.). Boston, MA: Allyn & Bacon.

Chang, C. K., Siagian, C., & Itti, L. (2010). Mobile Robot Vision Navigation & Localization Using Gist and Saliency. In *Proceedings of IEEE/RSJ International Conference on Intelligent Robots and Systems* (pp. 4147–4154), Taipei, Taiwan:IEEE.

Choi, S. B., Ban, S. W., & Lee, M. (2004). Biologically motivated visual attention system using bottom-up saliency map and top-down inhibition. *Neural Information Processing-Letters and Reviews, 2*(1), 19–25.

Crespo, J. L., Faina, A., & Duro, R. J. (2009). An adaptive detection/attention mechanism for real time robot operation. *Neurocomputing, 72*(4-6), 850–860. doi:10.1016/j.neucom.2008.06.023

Draper, B. A., & Lionelle, A. (2005). Evaluation of selective attention under similarity transformations. *Journal of Computer Vision and Image Understanding, 100*(1-2), 152–171. doi:10.1016/j.cviu.2004.08.006

Einhorn, E., Schröter, C., & Gross, H. M. (2011). Attention-driven monocular scene reconstruction for obstacle detection, robot navigation and map building. *Robotics and Autonomous Systems, 59*(5), 296–309. doi:10.1016/j.robot.2011.02.008

Findlay, J. M., & Gilchrist, I. D. (2001). Visual Attention: The Active vision Perspective. In M. Jenkin & L. R. Harris (Eds.), *Vision & Attention* (pp. 83–103). New York, NY: Springer New York. doi:10.1007/978-0-387-21591-4_5

Frintrop, S., Rome, E., Nüchter, A., & Surmann, H. (2005). A bimodal laser-based attention system. *Journal of Computer Vision and Image Understanding, 100*(1-2), 124–151. doi:10.1016/j.cviu.2004.08.005

Gazzaniga, M. S., Ivry, R. B., & Mangun, G. R. (2002). *Cognitive neuroscience: the biology of the mind.* New York, NY: W. W. Norton & Company.

Herrmann, K., Montaser-Kouhsari, L., Carrasco, M., & Heeger, D. J. (2010). When size matters: Attention affects performance by contrast or response gain. *Nature Neuroscience, 13*(12), 1554–1559. doi:10.1038/nn.2669 PMID:21057509

Johansson, R., Westling, G., Backstrom, A., & Flanagan, J. (2001). Eye-hand coordination in object manipulation. *The Journal of Neuroscience, 21*(17), 6917–6932. PMID:11517279

Kandel, E. R., Schwartz, J. H., & Jessell, T. M. (1996). *Essentials of Neural Science and Behavior. Norwalk, CT: McGraw-Hill.* Appleton: Lange.

Lee, K., Buxton, H., & Feng, J. (2003). Selective attention for cue-guided search using a spiking neural network. In *Proceedings of International Workshop on Attention and Performance in Computer Vision (WAPCV)* (pp 55–62), Graz, Austria.

Livingstone, M. S., & Hubel, D. H. (1987). Psychophysical evidence for separate channels for the perception of form, color, movement, and depth. *The Journal of Neuroscience, 7*(11), 3416–3468. PMID:3316524

Navalpakkam, V., & Itti, L. (2006b). Top-down attention selection is fine-gained. *Journal of Vision (Charlottesville, Va.), 6*(11), 1180–1193. doi:10.1167/6.11.4 PMID:17209728

Nicholls, J. G., Martin, A. R., Wallace, B. G., & Fuchs, P. A. (2001). *From neuron to brain.* Sunderland, MA: Sinauer Associates.

Olshausen, B., Anderson, C. H., & Van Essen, D. C. (1993). A neurobiological model of visual attention and invariant pattern recognition based on dynamic routing of information. *The Journal of Neuroscience, 13*(11), 4700–4719. PMID:8229193

Palmer, S. E. (1999). *Vision Science, Photons to Phenomenology.* Cambridge, MA: The MIT Press.

Palmer, S. M., & Rosa, M. G. P. (2006). A distinct anatomical network of cortical areas for analysis of motion in far peripheral vision. *The European Journal of Neuroscience, 24*(8), 2389–2405. doi:10.1111/j.1460-9568.2006.05113.x PMID:17042793

Rao, R., Zelinsky, G., Hayhoe, M., & Ballard, D. (2002). Eye movements in iconic visual search. *Vision Research, 42*(11), 1447–1463. doi:10.1016/S0042-6989(02)00040-8 PMID:12044751

Rasolzadeh, B., Björkman, M., Huebner, K., & Kragic, D. (2010). An Active Vision System for Detecting, Fixating and Manipulating Objects in the Real World. *The International Journal of Robotics Research, 29*(2-3), 133–154.

Rensink, R. A. (2000). The dynamic representation of scenes. *Visual Cognition, 7*(1–3), 17–42. doi:10.1080/135062800394667

Riesenhuber, M., & Poggio, T. (1999). Are cortical models really bound by the "binding problem"? *Neuron, 24*(1), 87–93. doi:10.1016/S0896-6273(00)80824-7 PMID:10677029

Rosenblatt, F. (1961). *Principles of Neurodynamics: Perceptions and the Theory of Brain Mechanisms.* Washington, DC: Spartan Books.

Rothenstein, A. L., & Tsotsos, J. (2008). Attention links sensing to recognition. *Image and Vision Computing, 26*(1), 114–126. doi:10.1016/j.imavis.2005.08.011

Sincich, L. C., Park, K. F., Wohlgemuth, M. J., & Horton, J. C. (2004). Bypassing V1: A direct geniculate input to area MT. *Nature Neuroscience, 7*(10), 1123–1128. doi:10.1038/nn1318 PMID:15378066

Spratling, M. W. (2005). Learning viewpoint invariant perceptual representations from cluttered images. *IEEE Transactions on Pattern Analysis and Machine Intelligence, 27*(5), 753–761. doi:10.1109/TPAMI.2005.105 PMID:15875796

Teichmann, M., Wiltschut, J., & Hamker, F. H. (2012). Learning invariance from natural images inspired by observations in the primary visual cortex. *Neural Computation, 24*(5), 1271–1296. doi:10.1162/NECO_a_00268 PMID:22295987

Treisman, A., & Gelade, G. (1980). A feature integration theory of attention. *Cognitive Psychology, 12*(1), 97–136. doi:10.1016/0010-0285(80)90005-5 PMID:7351125

Tsotsos, J. K., Culhane, S. M., Wai, W. Y. K., Lai, Y., Davis, N., & Nuflo, F. (1995). Modeling visual attention via selective tuning. *Artificial Intelligence, 78*(1–2), 507–545. doi:10.1016/0004-3702(95)00025-9

Wersing, H., & Körner, E. (2003). Learning optimized features for hierarchical models of invariant object recognition. *Neural Computation, 15*(7), 1559–1588. doi:10.1162/089976603321891800 PMID:12816566

Zeki, S. (1993). *A Vision of the Brain.* Oxford, UK: Blackwell Scientific.

Chapter 4
Visual Attention Guided Object Detection and Tracking

Debi Prosad Dogra
Indian Institute of Technology Bhubaneswar, India

ABSTRACT

Scene understanding and object recognition heavily depend on the success of visual attention guided salient region detection in images and videos. Therefore, summarizing computer vision techniques that take the help of visual attention models to accomplish video object recognition and tracking, can be helpful to the researchers of computer vision community. In this chapter, it is aimed to present a philosophical overview of the possible applications of visual attention models in the context of object recognition and tracking. At the beginning of this chapter, a brief introduction to various visual saliency models suitable for object recognition is presented, that is followed by discussions on possible applications of attention models on video object tracking. The chapter also provides a commentary on the existing techniques available on this domain and discusses some of their possible extensions. It is believed that, prospective readers will benefit since the chapter comprehensively guides a reader to understand the pros and cons of this particular topic.

INTRODUCTION

Attention of a person toward a particular portion of an object in a stationary scene is guided by various features such as intensity, color, contrast, texture, size, and other salient characteristics of the scene (Sun, 2003). Regions that attract human attention are popularly known as salient regions of a given image or scene. Scientists have proposed several methods that are based on psychological as well as statistical parameters to localize such regions. These methods are quite popular amongst the researchers of this community for carrying out various basic as well as advanced level image processing tasks, namely image segmentation, object recognition, content based image retrieval, and pattern recognition applications.

Visual attention model finds application in video processing too. For example, detection and tracking of objects in videos is often aided by visual attention guided models. Object detection which is considered to be one of the preliminary steps of several computer vision tasks is often carried out with the help of

DOI: 10.4018/978-1-4666-8723-3.ch004

localizing salient regions in a given scene. Since, deformation of a shape can be better understood in temporal domain, localization of salient regions representing a particular shape is extended for a sequence of frames. Therefore, visual attention becomes quite important in localizing these salient regions to be used further for tracking. Similarly, various parameters related to the movement of an object can be better understood using visual attention based models. It is a well-known fact that human visual attention is often influenced by movement patterns. Therefore, it is necessary to give sufficient importance to this parameter to accurately track moving objects in videos where multiple objects are interacting with each other. This can be understood from the below mentioned hypothesis. Assume, a group of people moving voluntarily in an environment without any knowledge about their movements being closely monitored by observers. In such a scenario, it is expected that an observer will give equal importance to all the moving persons unless something unusual activity is noticed by the observer. Here, unusual movements can be of following types: sudden quick movement, slow movement, unusual trajectory, and several other variations that are easily detectable by a human. This happens because humans are trained to recognize them as unusual activities happening within its field of view. Similar reasoning can be applied to support the influence of visual attention in situations when humans pay more attention toward a particular person or a group of persons due to their change in appearance, e.g. height, clothing, spatial locations, etc. Therefore, human attention model must not be ignored while designing robust object tracking algorithms if it is desired to act quite accurately.

However, the requirements of object detection and tracking and its applicability vary largely from task to task. If the object to track is known in advance, model-based trackers may be applied which require an initial training phase. In some applications however, the object of interest is not known in advance. A user might for example react to an object to the system for various reasons. A long training phase is usually inacceptable in such applications. Therefore, online learning methods are often called in such situations. In systems with a static camera, it is possible to apply methods like background subtraction. If interest is for example in counting people or other statistical investigations which do not require immediate response, it is possible to process the data offline which extends the range of applicable algorithms considerably. On the other hand, systems which shall operate on a mobile platform usually have to operate in real-time and have to deal with more difficult settings. The background changes, illumination conditions vary, and platforms are often equipped with low-resolution cameras. Such conditions require robust and flexible tracking mechanisms. Mostly, feature-based tracking approaches are applied in such areas which track an object based on simple features such as color cues or corners. However, in all of the above situations, visual attention guided techniques can play a crucial role.

Several research articles have already been published in this context and techniques proposed in those articles cover statistical and heuristic based models for applying human attention to achieve higher accuracy in common as well as application specific computer vision related tasks. To begin with, a comprehensive review on all such existing techniques that focus more on object detection and tracking is presented in the following section. Next, a brief introduction to visual attention model that is appropriate in the context of object recognition is presented. How such models can be applied on a sequence of images is discussed consequently that is followed by a philosophical explanation of possible techniques to improve video object tracking algorithms. It is believed that the readers will benefit from the technical commentary of the chapter since it presents the basic but important technical knowhow of the said topic in a well understandable form.

A BRIEF REVIEW ON EXISTING TECHNIQUES

There are a variety of visual tasks that cannot be completed using typical static model based computer vision paradigm. As an example, navigation and object identification through a sequence of frames becomes truly important to be guided by visual attention model that essentially helps to decide about what and where to look on a frame by frame basis. Therefore, it is utmost necessary to understand the importance of visual attention model from the right perspective so that it can be applied in computer vision related tasks. In this section, segment of the literature that mainly talks about one particular task popularly known as video object detection and tracking is presented. However, to understand specialized models of visual attention that are suitable for object detection and tracking, it is necessary to have a little knowledge on the generic models. Therefore, a small portion of the text is dedicated for describing such generic models that are often used in computer vision applications.

As per the published documents available till date, visual attention based tracking has actually gained pace from past few decades. For example, Mori, Inaba, and Inoue (1996) have proposed a method that is based on an attention window to track multiple objects present in a video. Since then, various research groups have come up with new techniques to improve video object tracking with the help of visual attention models. However, the ability to accurately detect and keep track of objects is of larger interest in machine vision as well as in mobile robotics. Example applications are surveillance systems, mobile robots which shall guide or follow people, or human-robot interaction in which a robot shall interact with a human and both have to concentrate on the same objects. Generating saliency map of a given image is considered as an important step toward developing applications mentioned earlier. Significant contributions have been made by various research groups in this context. For example, Ouerhani, N., and Hugli (2003) have proposed a model to compute the dynamic visual attention using a static saliency map which discriminates salient scene locations based on static features and a dynamic saliency map that highlights moving scene constituents. The saliency maps are then combined into a final map of attention that is also called the final saliency map. Region tracking based on color correlograms proposed by Galdino and Borges (2000) also uses visual attention model for extracting trajectories. Similarly, motion saliency has been used in designing algorithms for surveillance and security applications. For example, Li and Lee (2007) have proposed a novel method to estimate the motion saliency by using the rank deficiency of grey scale gradient tensors within the local region neighborhoods of video frame. In the next step, they have used this information for tracking regions in a video. Another interesting application of visual attention based tracking is to detect unusual/eye catching activity from a set of activities that are happening within the field of view of a camera. As an example, in a crowded scene, if majority of the objects except a few of them are moving or following a particular pattern, it often catches the attention of an observer. Therefore, considerable deviation from the usual pattern of movement can be considered as unusual and we as human being are capable of detecting such events without much difficulty. One such methodology has been discussed in the work proposed by Guler, S., Silverstein, J., and Pushee (2007). The authors have proposed a method to detect stationary foreground objects in naturally busy surveillance video scenes with several moving objects. As the authors claimed, their approach is inspired by human's visual cognition processes and builds upon a multi-tier video tracking paradigm with main layers being the spatially based "peripheral tracking" loosely corresponding to the peripheral vision and the object based "vision tunnels" for focused attention and analysis of tracked objects. Biologically inspired attention models are also becoming popular in solving computer vision related problems. For example, Sun, Fisher, Wang, and Gomes (2008) have proposed a computational framework for modelling visual object based attention and attention driven eye movements. Very recently, Mahadevan, and Vasconcelos (2013) have proposed a biologically inspired discriminant object tracker that tracks objects based on center-surround saliency mechanism. They have proposed a focus of attention (FoA) mechanism and a bottom-up saliency model to maximize the chance of selection of good features for object detection. Next, using the feature-based attention mechanism and a target-tuned top-down discriminant saliency detector, they have detected the target. Finally, the tracker iterates between learning discriminant features from the target location in a video frame and detecting the location of the target in the next frame. Recently, visual attention has also been used in video coding and its applications. For example, Cheni, Zhang, Zhengi, Gu, and Lini (2013) have shown in their work that, if visual attention model is applied in selection of the region on interest (ROI) while encoding a frame, it can produce sufficiently high subjective quality of experience (QoE).

VISUAL ATTENTION IN OBJECT TRACKING

In this section, attention models suitable for object detection and tracking are discussed in details. One of the most challenging tasks in designing robotic systems is to process data acquired through visual sensors attached with a device. Inputs from the visual sensors are equally important as compared to other sensors to achieve acceptable accuracy in automatic navigation. However, human visual system is a very complex model, therefore, reproducing a similar system with electronic sensors and processing units is not realistic at present day technology. Thus, scientists always look for alternative solutions that can closely match with the human visual system. If such a system is available, it can be used successfully for designing robotic systems. In this context, it has been observed that object recognition and tracking are two most important components of a vision system to start with. Firstly, importance of object recognition has been explained in the context of visual attention. Next, how any prior knowledge about an object can help the user to track it in successive frames has been discussed in details. To present the whole idea in a systematic way, factors that heavily affect the visual attention in the context of object tracking are mainly divided into three domains namely, appearance based object recognition, appearance of object in temporal domain, and shape of object trajectory. In the forthcoming sections, all of the above three factors are discussed in the context of visual attention.

Visual Attention and Object Recognition

At the beginning, it is indeed necessary to understand the importance of visual attention in the context of object recognition before going into further details on how visual attention is affected by object tracking and related features. As pointed out by Kelley, Serences, Giesbrecht, and Yantis (2008), visual attention plays a crucial role in the control and sequence of eye movements and visual perception. Attention filters out visual backgrounds and ensure that eye movements are programmed solely on the objects, features, locations, or groups selected by attention. In continuation to this, Sun, Fisher, Wang, and Gomes (2008) have shown in their work that a biologically-plausible framework based on visual-object-based attention for integrating attentional shifts and eye movements through overlapped circuits and shared control can be developed. The authors have shown that, the proposed framework is inspired by psychophysical research on multiple attentional selectivity and their relationships with eye movements. They have evaluated the performance of the system using natural scenes and the results show the ability to effectively reduce the shift times and search errors to select useful objects, regions, and structured groups, and the ability to flexibly select visual-objects whether they are located in the foveal field or in visual periphery.

Therefore, presence of an object in a scene at different locations usually influences the visual attention of the observer. In a scene that contains multiple objects, attention toward a specific region or object is therefore guided by its shape, location, relative size, and several other scene specific contexts. However, attention shift is different from gaze shift. Assuming the visual sensors used to capture a scene are static, it is more important to concentrate on attention shift than the gaze shift. Thus, the hierarchical model used by Sun et al. (2008) to demonstrate the visual attention hierarchy is quite relevant in the present context. Objects or segments are dynamically formed as a hierarchy of grouped regions, objects and other components. An example of a hierarchical grouping is shown in Figure 1.

Therefore, it is important to understand that, human visual system analyzes a scene at various levels. In some cases, a particular shape of an object can attract a user more than any other feature. Similarly, contrasting appearance can also be a distinguishing factor. However, to recognize an object present in a scene, a user must pay attention. As Kelley et al. (2008) pointed out, though the cortical mechanism is mainly responsible behind shifting the gaze for attention, feedback mechanism through the sensors is quite important to stabilize the attention of the user toward a particular region of interest. This can be explained with an example. Let, the object of interest be a circular object such as a football inside a soccer match. A user often tries to shift the gaze to locate the ball inside the field. Once the ball is located, the user can easily track it based on spatio-temporal relation. Therefore, any prior knowledge about the shape of an object is quite important. However, it may be difficult to locate the ball if the user is not familiar with its shape. In addition to that, even if the user is quite familiar with the shape of the object that is being tracked, it needs to shift the gaze for searching the object inside field of view of human eyes. In such cases, human visual attention plays an important role. A user may scan the whole scene and try to match probable segments taken out of the scene with some of the shape priors that are presumed to

Figure 1. Hierarchical structure of a scene taken from the Berkeley[1] image segmentation dataset

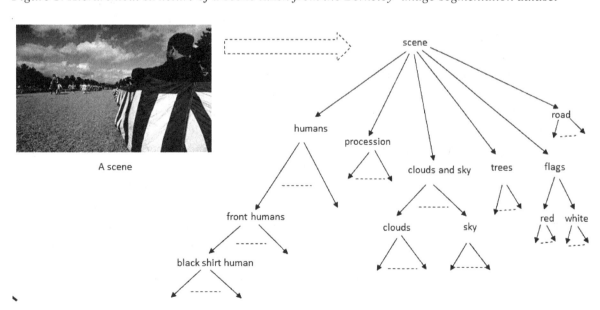

be stored inside the human memory during the learning process. Therefore, recognition of an object of interest is very important to follow it in future. Several models have been proposed by various scientists to represent human visual attention in the context of object recognition. However, all such models can easily be divided into two groups namely, bottom-up and top-down approaches. Bottom-up approaches are often referred to as task-independent components which are typically based on low-level and image-based outliers and conspicuities. On the other hand, the top-down approaches usually look into features that can correlate the movement of eyes due to external influences. As an example, according to the philosophy of top-down approaches, attention can also be guided by memory-dependent, or anticipatory mechanisms such as, when a person is looking ahead of moving objects or sideways before crossing streets. Combination of top-down and bottom-up approaches also find application in determining the salient regions or a given image. For example, Navalpakkam and Itti (2006) have proposed a model that first computes the naive, bottom-up salience of every scene location for different local visual features such as colors, orientations and intensities at multiple spatial scales. Next, a top-down component is used to learn statistical knowledge of the local features of the target and distracting clutter for optimizing the relative weights of the bottom-up maps such that the overall salience of the target is maximized relative to the surrounding clutter. Such an optimization efficiently renders a target that is more salient than the distractors, thereby maximizing target detection speed. However, pure top-down methods are preferred by the researchers at large while designing algorithms that are suitable for saliency based object recognition. In this context, several methods have been proposed. Research in this direction has gradually advanced from simple low level features to complex high level features such as joint Condition Random Field (CRF) models. For example, the top-down control model of visual attention for object recognition proposed by Oliva, Torralba, Castelhano, and Henderson (2003) uses a simple model of image saliency based on the distribution of local features in the image and a model of contextual priors (that learns the relationship between context features and the location of the target during past experience) in order to select interesting regions of the image. They have mentioned in their work that, human observers use a top-down mechanism to find regions of interest where an object should be located, independent of the presence of the physical features of the object. More recently, advanced features such as CRF proposed by Yang and Yang (2012) has been found applications in detecting objects present in an image based on user attention. The authors argue that, top-down saliency models can learn from training examples to generate probability maps for localizing objects of interest (e.g. car, bicycle, person, etc.) in a query image. According to their research, saliency formulation can be considered as a latent variable model by training a CRF classifier jointly with dictionary learning. Very recently, Karthikeyan, Jagadeesh, and Manjunath (2013) proposed a novel object context based visual attention model that incorporates co-occurrence of multiple objects in a scene for visual attention modeling. The regression based algorithm uses several high level object detectors to identify human faces, people, cars, text, and it also tries to understand how presence of multiple objects affects the visual attention of a person. The authors argue that, scene context features are more accurate in determining visual attention regions when compared with low, mid, and high level features. This can be explained with the toy example shown in Figure 2. The figure contains three scenes comprises with two objects, e.g. OBJECT 1 and OBJECT 2 at different scales and orientations. Though the effect of orientation may not be shown in any of the images, it can be assumed that appearance of these objects in different scenes is governed by natural rule of scale and orientation depending on the viewing distance and angle of the observer's eye.

The first scene demonstrate the presence of OBJECT 1 as a small object as compared to its appearance in scene 3 whereas second scene contains OBJECT 2 of a relatively large size as compared to OBJECT

Figure 2. Illustration of the effect of scene context in determining locations of visual attention

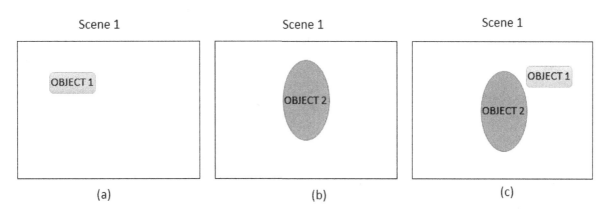

1 of scene 1. Experimentally, it has been observed that, when similar situations occur in real life images, attention of an observer is usually affected by several factors such as presence of any other objects in the scene, size of the object, and sometimes any prior knowledge about the objects present in a scene. For example, though the size of OBJECT 1 in Figure 2 (a) is comparatively smaller than the size of OBJECT 2 in Figure 2 (b), both the objects can attract similar amount of attention due to absence of any other objects in these scenes. On the other hand, attention density in a large sized object such as OBJECT 2 of scene 3 usually remains relatively unchanged due to the presence of the small object (OBJECT 1 in scene 3), as depicted in Figure 2 (c). However, the co-presence of a relatively larger object contributes significantly to attention loss in case of the smaller object (OJECT 1). Such phenomenon has been observed while Karthikeyan et al. (2013) have experimented with natural images with similar appearance of objects. This illustrates the requirement to cluster the attention loss cause and effect features with different metrics. Scientists have also observed that, objects which cause a large attention shift are typically those objects which have a large overall attention sum contained within them (e.g. objects which occupy a large portion of viewing area, e.g. OBJECT 3 in Figure 3 (c). Also, the objects which take the greatest impact or effect have high concentration or attention density in small prominent objects, e. g. OBJECT 1 in Figure 3 (c). Therefore, it is necessary to give due importance to appearance of an object in a scene if the aim is recognize the presence of an object and track its movement in temporal sequence. It is anticipated that, if the recognition of an object is done with higher accuracy, an object tracking algorithm will be more accurate in associating the features describing the object in successive frames. However, this is only the one leg of the success story of an object tracking algorithm, whereas it has two other important dimensions namely, change in appearance which deals with any change in the appearance of an object in time domain, and the shape of the trajectory of a moving object. In the successive sections, these two are discussed in details.

Visual Attention Guided Search

As mentioned in the previous section, appearance of an object plays an important role in guiding the attention of a user. However, this is not only true in the case of static images, however, similar phenomenon may be observed in videos, e.g. sequence of image frames captured by focusing on the object of interest in predefined time intervals. The appearance of a moving object has great importance in this context.

Figure 3. Presence of salient regions in a frame and its presence in translated, rotated or scaled form in subsequent frames

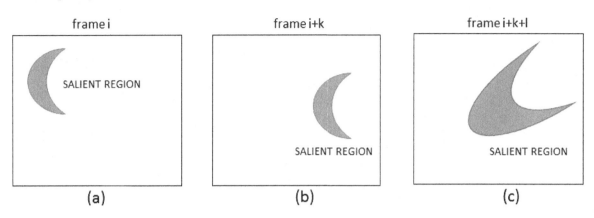

For example, an object which appears as an eye catching one in one frame may not appear as attractive in some of the other frames separated by a slight time interval. Therefore, it is also necessary to impact of such changes in objects on the visual attention of a user since tracking of an object in temporal domain is highly dependent on the localization of the object in individual frame.

One of the ways of associating the appearance of an object in the context of tracking is by localizing the salient regions of an image in each frame and then try to correlate them in temporal domain. However this is very much computation intensive since determining locations of interest in each frame consumes considerable amount of processing power and memory. Therefore, researchers usually detect the location of interest or salient regions in the initial frame and then use some heuristics or statistical parameters to reduce the search space for localizing the salient regions in subsequent frames. One such method has been proposed by Frintrop and Kessel (2009) which is known as most salient region tracker. The authors have proposed a top-down guided visual search module to favor features that fit to a previously learned target object. Appearance of an object is learned online within the first image in which it is detected and in subsequent images, the attention system searches for the target features and builds a top-down, target-related saliency map. This has enabled the authors to focus on most relevant features of an object without knowing anything about a particular object model or scene in advance.

The concept can be understood from the image shown in Figure 3. It has been assumed in the demonstration that an object of interest (e.g. salient region) has been identified in one frame, say *frame i*, as depicted in Figure 3 (a). Detection such regions can be done in many ways. For example, the methods described in the previous sections can easily be adopted to identify such regions in static scene. However, the salient region marked or detected in one of the preceding frames can be translated due to the movement of the object e.g. *frame i+k*, as depicted in Figure 3 (a). Therefore, the knowledge gathered about this region in the previous instances can be used to localize it in the successive frames. Similarly, if the region is rotated or scaled due to motion artefact or any change in viewing angle, it may not always be easy to localize only with the knowledge gained through the previous steps. However, the whole method can be split into several important tasks namely determining the saliency map (feature extraction), detecting the salient regions in an image, determining a feature vector representing the salient region, visual searching of the feature vectors in successive frames, and applying the motion model to finalize the attention regions in temporal domain. Out of these five steps, the final one deals with how the trajectory of a moving object can influence the visual attention of the observer in the tracking process. In the next section, this has been elaborated with various examples.

Visual Attention and Object Trajectory

The basic idea is to exploit the information provided by the visual attention algorithm based on static or individual scene to correct the trajectory of the moving object by tracking the salient features or locations. Therefore, the detected spots of attention are first characterized by determining their discriminating features and then such spots are tracked over time. In these algorithms, tracking algorithms usually start with creating a few initial trajectories, each of which contains some detected spots of attention in the first frame. Next, a new detected spot of attention is either inserted into an existing trajectory or gives rise to a new one, depending on its similarity with the last inserted spot or the head element- of already existing trajectories. However, most of these algorithms heavily depend on the detection of initial salient regions in earlier frames and then track such regions to get the trajectories or modify the already detected tracks. On the contrary, understanding importance of visual attention solely based on the shape of a trajectory is also an important area of research; however, it has not been exploited much till date. In this section, some of the possible models and theories related to this are presented in a systematic way which can be considered as the main contribution of this chapter.

To begin with, it is indeed necessary to understand the importance of the trajectory of a moving object in the context of visual attention. This is explained with a series of pictorial demonstrations which will guide through a reader to understand of the topic. Let, the movements of a set of objects are being recorded from a given location. The location can be considered as the position of the human observer with respect to whom the visual attention model will be explained. An observer's eye movement pattern with respect to a moving target can definitely give valuable information to understand the change in attention at each time instance. However, any hypothesis related to this needs to be supported by evidences. Though, it may not always be possible to provide experimental validation to some of the claims, theoretical explanation and existing prior-art references can be recalled to support such a theory. In this section, this is explained and the necessary supporting theories are also provided so that the reader can verify them A set of trajectories corresponding to moving objects are shown in Figure 4. These synthetic trajectories can be used to explain the importance of visual attention along with the help of a few more that are shown later in this chapter. Though, the trajectories shown in this figure have been generated synthetically, they can be used to explain the real life events without loss of generality. If the canvas of the figure is considered as the boundary of the image captured by a fixed camera with respect to which these trajectories have been recorded, then the relative patterns of such trajectories can be of good importance to understand the behavioural pattern of the moving targets. For example, it may be recalled that, first two trajectories, e.g. Trajectory-1 and Trajectory-2 are of similar type where both the objects move in horizontal direction until they take opposite turns after a long stretch. On the contrary, other two objects move in circular or near-circular paths as depicted through Trajectory-3 and Trajectory-4. Therefore, classifying these four trajectories into two categories is not a bad idea. However, which trajectory(s) will attract a user attention amongst these four is a topic of interest in the present context. It is highly possible that, a user observing these trajectories will distinguish those which catches more attention to the

Figure 4. A set of trajectories showing the movement pattern with respect to a fixed camera or observer

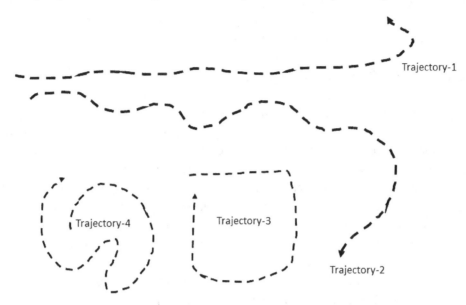

user. For example, if a user is interested in searching objects that usually move in circular, spiral, or any other paths of interest, he or she will definitely give more importance to such types of trajectories. This is entirely context dependent and sometimes it may be user dependent too. However, for a sufficiently large population, such variations may be negligible and an average estimation can be done. To apply any generic model, it is indeed necessary to extract some generic features which can be useful while understanding the observer's visual attention in the context of a trajectory from practical perspectives.

Feature Extraction

This section describes a generalized approach of feature extraction to aid in the process of visual attention guided tracking. It has already been mentioned that, type and pattern of movement highly influences the visual attention of an observer. Therefore, understanding the pattern of movement from a trajectory is essential. This has been explained with an example. Given a trajectory, say p_k, various features can be extracted from it to understand the underlying behaviour of the target object in the perception of the observer. Let, the trajectory of a chosen target be represented as in (1) where k represents the size of the trajectory and $\langle x_i, y_i \rangle$, represents the spatial coordinate of the target at a given instant of time, say p_i.

$$p_k = \left\{ \langle x_1, y_1 \rangle, \langle x_2, y_2 \rangle, \langle x_3, y_3 \rangle, \ldots, \langle x_k, y_k \rangle \right\} \tag{1}$$

The trajectory p_k can be processed to extract relevant information for analysing the dynamics of the target movement. For example, instantaneous velocity of the target at a given time, can be computed with the help of the uniformly sampled points of p_k and this can be used for extracting important features related to the dynamics of the moving object that influence the visual attention of an observer.

In addition to that, segmentation of a larger trajectory can be done to extract local features. This is important in the context of the influences of local information such as presence of an interest point on the path of the target, physical condition of the target, colocation of other targets etc. Also, local statistics may vary significantly from the global statistics depending on the above mentioned features. Therefore, an observer getting attracted to a particular segment than others is not an unusual behaviour. In such cases, sudden change in eye gaze and movement may be observed.

An example of segmentation of a trajectory has been shown in Figure 5. In this figure, the trajectory is segmented into five non-overlapping segments based on several predefined criteria. However, characteristics of a trajectory segment, say segment-1, bounded by t_A and t_B remains unchanged during the interval. At this point of discussion, it must be mentioned that, segmentation of a trajectory can be done differently depending on the features used. For example, if instantaneous velocity is used as a feature, a trajectory can be divided into several non-overlapping segments based on the velocity of a running averaging window. Similarly, if the pattern of movement is important than the velocity of the moving object, curvature analysis may be used. In some cases, velocity can be combined with curvature to get complex features. The typical segments shown in Figure 5 are not of any particular type. They are indicative of the markers corresponding to non-overlapping segments of a sufficiently large trajectory. Segmentation of a trajectory can be done with respect to the presence of other moving objects also. In such cases, instead of segmenting a single trajectory, segmentation of a group of trajectories can be done. This is explained with an example shown in Figure 6. In this case, segmentation of a scene is done with the help of a set of trajectories over the same spatial space. For example, in Figure 6, a total of fourteen synthetic trajectories are plotted over the scene. If these trajectories are assumed to be the movement paths of fourteen independent objects, several observations can be done from the features extracted from these set of trajectories. As an example, a classification of the trajectories based on the resultant

Figure 5. Partitioning of a large trajectory into small segments for extraction of local features

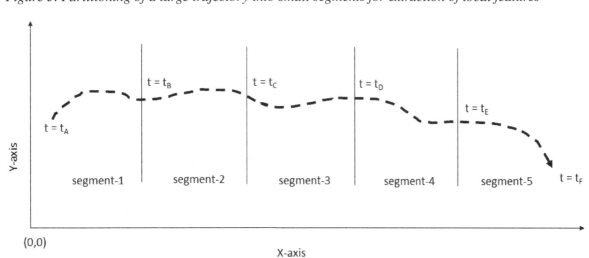

Figure 6. Demonstration of flow segmentation in the context of visual attention

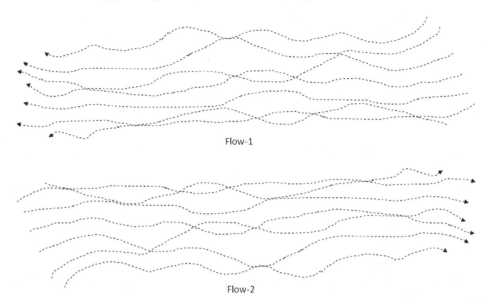

direction can easily be obtained. It is evident from the figure that, some of the objects moved in left-to-right and some moved in right-to-left directions. However, detecting such flows may not be trivial in all situations, especially when the trajectories are mixed altogether. In such cases, individual trajectory can be processed and segmented and a complex feature vector representing similar trajectories can be constructed to separate flows. This can be achieved using the below mentioned technique. Let, there be N trajectories given on a particular scene and they are represented using a set, say P_N as given in (2).

$$P_N = \left\{ p_1, p_2, p_3, ..., p_N \right\} \tag{2}$$

Each of these trajectories can be represented using vectors as shown in Equation (1). The analysis depicted in Figure 5 can be done as follows. Let there be a set of parameters that represents a segment of a given trajectory using (3),

$$S_{\langle t_i, t_j \rangle} = \left[v_{max}, v_{min}, v_{avg}, f_{max}, f_{min}, f_{avg}, dir_{avg} \right] \tag{3}$$

where the parameters represent velocity, acceleration, and direction of a particular segment. A segment can be identified by incrementally adding successive points and computing the feature vector repetitively.

Once all trajectories under consideration are segmented, a classification of the trajectories can be done. Therefore, every trajectory is now represented by a set of feature vectors and the whole set of trajectories can be represented using (4).

$$P_N = \begin{pmatrix} S_{p_{1,1}} & \cdots & S_{p_{1,q}} \\ \vdots & \ddots & \vdots \\ S_{p_{n,1}} & \cdots & S_{p_{n,q}} \end{pmatrix} \qquad (4)$$

$S_{p_{i,j}}$ represents the coefficient corresponding to the pth type of segment of the ith trajectory at j^{th} position. Now, classification of the trajectories can be performed with the help of P_N.

Assume a user is observing the movement of a group of people along a path. It is quite natural that the observer will concentrate on the overall flow of the people instead of focusing on a single object movement. However, in exceptional cases, the user may give more attention to a particular object of set of objects which will be discussed in the next part of the discussion. In this section, it is assumed that none of the target objects has distinguishable feature or pattern of movement. Therefore, in such cases, visual attention of an observer usually goes to the overall flow of the crowd rather than a single object. In Figure 6, one such situation is depicted. This can be observed that, there are two distinguishable flows in opposite directions. Therefore, even if these flows are separated by a small spatial distance, an observer usually gives equal attention to both flows unless they are distinguishably separate. For example, if one these flows suddenly changes its characteristics such as getting very slow or fast in quick time, an observer may get attracted toward that. However, if a single object or a small set of objects deviates from the normal flow, an observer's attention may be diverted toward that which has been explained in the next part of the discussion.

Improving Object Tracking with Visual Attention

Till this point, it has been discussed how attention of an observer is influenced by several distinguishable features of the movement of an object or group of objects. Therefore, now the reverse process can be examined to check whether the underlying visual attention model can help to improve the existing tracking algorithms by accurately localizing the target in successive video frames. Prior-art related to object detection and tracking has already been discussed in the preceding section. It has been observed that a large number of the existing object tracking algorithms rely on parameters related to motion and appearance of the moving object. However, recall that the basic idea of tracking is to successfully localize a moving object by an observer in each video frame. Therefore, any prior knowledge about the movement pattern and context of the scene usually helps the observer to adjust its gaze which results in successful tracking on the object. In machine vision, the observer's eyes are usually replaced with vision sensors such as camera. Thus, if the prior knowledge about an object trajectory is available to the computing system, conventional tracking algorithms can be improved. This has been explained in this section with pictorial demonstration.

In Figure 7, an example of visual attention getting attracted toward a distinguishable trajectory with respect to a usual flow is presented. This can be used to explain the importance of incorporating prior knowledge about the movement of the target in tracking. Assume an observer is well aware about the usual flow (F). Several algorithms exist in literature that can successfully determine the type and magnitude of such flows given a video sequence. Therefore, the statistical parameters of the flow such as velocity, acceleration, and energy can be computed to estimate the instantaneous dynamics of the system. In such a scenario, any single target that significantly deviates from the usual path can be detected and

Figure 7. Depiction of a distinguishable trajectory which deviates considerably from the usual flow and thus may get addition attention by an observer

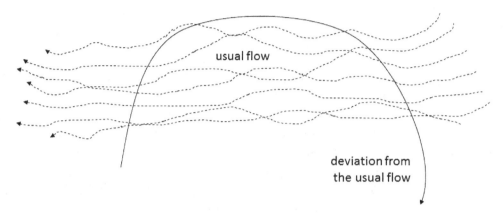

tracked if the knowledge about the usual flow is taken into consideration. Visual attention model of the observer toward an isolated trajectory can be used to correct the path of the target. For example, if experiments are carried out in situations depicted in Figure 7, it is anticipated that a suitable model of visual attention for the said context can be found and it can be used in correcting the trajectory of the target in complex environment.

FUTURE RESEARCH DIRECTIONS

Details of the visual attention models suitable for a particular situation is beyond the scope of this chapter. However, the readers can build models that are very much suitable to the type of the applications to be dealt with. Some of the immediate research extensions can be designing visual models for segmenting opposite flows as shown in Figure 6. This has several applications in traffic monitoring and crowd management in social and political rallies. Similarly, tracking individual object or a set of moving objects in sports can be done more efficiently and accurately if appropriate visual attention model is used. As an example, summarization or highlight generating in soccer videos can be aided with visual attention models suitable for the type of the object.

CONCLUSION

The chapter outlines the basic philosophy of applying visual attention models in the context of object recognition and tracking. This has been discussed at the beginning that, performance of object recognition is highly correlated with observer's visual attention model. Therefore, if the object recognition algorithms are designed with the knowledge of visual attention, accuracy can be improved. However, experimental validations are necessary for justifying the claim which can be done whenever necessary.

Similarly, it has also been demonstrated with pictorial demonstration and subsequent descriptions that automatic tracking of a moving target can be aided by visual attention guided approaches. No specific approach has been discussed in this chapter since it depends on the type and necessity of the application and therefore left to wisdom of the readers.

REFERENCES

Cheni, X., Zhang, J., Zhengi, X., Gu, Z., & Lini, N. (2013). *A New Modeling for Visual Attention Calculation in Video Coding.* Paper presented at ICMEW. doi:10.1109/ICMEW.2013.6618329

Doran, M. D., & Hoffman, J. E. (2010). The Role of Visual Attention in Multiple Object Tracking: Evidence from ERPs. *Attention, Perception & Psychophysics, 72*(1), 33–52. doi:10.3758/APP.72.1.33 PMID:20802834

Frintrop, S., & Kessel, M. (2009). *Most Salient Region Tracking.* Paper presented at IEEE International Conference on Robotics and Automation, Kobe, Japan.

Galdino, L., & Borges, D. (2000). *A Visual Attention Model for Tracking Regions Based on Color Correlograms.* Paper presented at CGIP. doi:10.1109/SIBGRA.2000.883892

Guler, S., Silverstein, J., & Pushee, I. (2007). *Stationary Objects in Multiple Object Tracking.* Paper presented at AVSS. doi:10.1109/AVSS.2007.4425318

Karthikeyan, S., Jagadeesh, V., & Manjunath, B. S. (2013). *Learning top down Scene context for Visual Attention modeling in Natural Images.* Paper presented at IEEE International Conference on Image Processing. doi:10.1109/ICIP.2013.6738044

Kelley, T. A., Serences, J. T., Giesbrecht, B., & Yantis, S. (2008). Cortical mechanisms for shifting and holding visuospatial attention. *Cerebral Cortex, 18*(1), 114–125. doi:10.1093/cercor/bhm036 PMID:17434917

Li, S., & Lee, M. (2007). *Fast Visual Tracking Using Motion Saliency in Video.* Paper presented at ICASSP. doi:10.1109/ICASSP.2007.366097

Mahadevan, V., & Vasconcelos, N. (2013, March). Biologically Inspired Object Tracking Using Center-Surround Saliency Mechanisms. *IEEE Transactions on Pattern Analysis and Machine Intelligence, 35*(3), 541–554. doi:10.1109/TPAMI.2012.98 PMID:22529325

Mori, T., Inaba, M., & Inoue, H. (1996). *Visual Tracking Based on Cooperation of Multiple Attention Regions.* Paper presented at ICRA. doi:10.1109/ROBOT.1996.509156

Navalpakkam, V., & Itti, L. (2006). *An Integrated Model of Top-Down and Bottom-Up Attention for Optimizing Detection Speed.* Paper presented at International Conference on Computer Vision and Pattern Recognition. doi:10.1109/CVPR.2006.54

Oliva, A., Torralba, A., Castelhano, M. S., & Henderson, J. M. (2003). *Top down control of visual attention in object detection.* Paper presented at IEEE International Conference on Image Processing. doi:10.1109/ICIP.2003.1246946

Ouerhani, N., & Hugli, H. (2003). *A Model of Dynamic Visual Attention for Object Tracking in Natural Image Sequences*. Paper presented at CMNM. doi:10.1007/3-540-44868-3_89

Sun, J. (2003). *Hierarchical object-based visual attention for machine vision*. Edinburgh, UK: University of Edinburgh.

Sun, Y., Fisher, R., Wang, F., & Gomes, H. (2008). A Computer Vision Model for Visual-object-based Attention and Eye Movements. *Computer Vision and Image Understanding*, *112*(2), 126–142. doi:10.1016/j.cviu.2008.01.005

Yang, J., & Yang, M. (2012). *Top-Down Visual Saliency via Joint CRF and Dictionary Learning*. Paper presented at International Conference on Computer Vision and Pattern Recognition. doi:10.1109/CVPR.2012.6247940

ADDITIONAL READING

Yaoru, S. (2003). *Hierarchical Object-Based Visual Attention for Machine Vision*. (Ph. D. Thesis). Institute of Perception, Action and Behavior, School of Informatics, University of Edinburgh.

KEY TERMS AND DEFINITIONS

Trajectory: Trajectory of a moving object is the sequence of location of the object at successive video frames in temporal domain.

ENDNOTE

[1] http://www.eecs.berkeley.edu/Research/Projects/CS/vision/bsds/BSDS300/html/dataset/images/color/145086.html

Chapter 5
Content–Aware Image Retargeting:
A Survey

Rajarshi Pal
Institute for Development and Research in Banking Technology, India

Prasun Chandra Tripathi
Institute for Development and Research in Banking Technology, India & University of Hyderabad, India

ABSTRACT

Displaying a large image in a small screen of a handheld gadget is a challenging task. Simple down-scaling of the image may reduce some objects too small to be perceptible. This gives rise to content-aware retargeting of the image. Important contents are allotted more screen space as compared to relatively less important contents of the image. Various types of content-aware image retargeting approaches have been proposed in a span of just over a decade. Another challenging area is to estimate importance of importance of the contents. Lot of researches has been carried out in this direction too to identify the important contents in the context of image retargeting. Equally important aspect is evaluation of these retargeting methods. This article contains a brief survey of related research in all of these aspects.

INTRODUCTION

Twenty first century has witnessed, so far, breakthrough technological advances in digital handheld gadgets. Usage of tablet PCs and mobile phones has increased significantly due to their availability in affordable prices. These devices have good quality displays to provide the users a pleasant experience of viewing personal photos, music videos, and even movies. Moreover, availability of high-resolution cameras with these devices and revolutionary ways of connecting with people through social media have added a new dimension in how people express themselves through images and videos.

As these images and videos are viewed using variety of gadgets having wide range of display resolutions, adaptation of these images/videos to each individual display is essential for good viewing experi-

DOI: 10.4018/978-1-4666-8723-3.ch005

ence. If an image is captured with a high resolution camera and the image is viewed in a smaller display, then certainly some mechanism is needed to fit the image with the display size. This has opened a new area of research in image processing, namely image retargeting for fitting the image in the display size.

Simple down-scaling an image to fit into the smaller display is the rudimentary solution. This approach shrinks every object in the image equally. But down-scaling makes a small object even smaller and, in certain cases, viewers may find it difficult to recognize those objects. Researchers have found a solution to this problem based on importance of each individual content in the image. Idea, here, is that the important contents are allotted more space in the target area as compared to the unimportant contents. A wide spectrum of content-aware solutions is available in literature, like cropping, seam carving, warping, growth and shrinkage of rectangles, etc.

Researchers, hence, have faced another challenge in identifying important contents in an image, which is the first step of content-aware image retargeting as depicted in Figure 1. In this context, visual attention/saliency models have played a crucial role to signify importance of the contents in the image. Apart from visual saliency models, use of various energy estimation functions (gradient-based or entropy-based) can be found in literature. Often, face and/or text recognition techniques have been used to identify human faces and texts to capture semantically important contents.

This article attempts to compile a significant amount of these research efforts. It provides a comprehensive view of the works which have been carried out in this field. At first, this article focuses on how importance of the contents in an image is measured. Then, various retargeting approaches have been summarized. Key aspects of each category of these approaches have been highlighted. Evaluating a method is also an integral component of proposing any new method. Therefore, this article discusses various evaluating strategies of image retargeting approaches. Though majority of the researchers resorted to subjective evaluation, few recent researches demonstrate the objective evaluation of these methods. Thus, this article provides a good overview of the current status in the field of content-aware image retargeting. It is to be noted that a comparative study of various image retargeting approaches can also be found in (Rubinstein et al, 2010).

ESTIMATING IMPORTANCE

Content-aware image retargeting approaches suggest discriminative treatments to the contents of an image based on their importance. While reducing the size of the entire image to fit it into a smaller display, these approaches allot a bigger space in the display for the important contents as compared to the space

Figure 1. Components of content-aware image retargeting

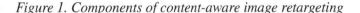
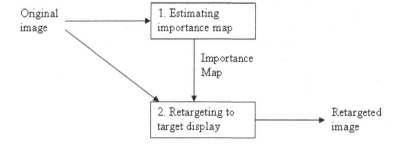

allotted to the unimportant contents. Thus, important contents maintain their recognizability. It helps the image to correctly convey its main theme and also leads to pleasant viewing experience for the viewer.

Visual attention models have been extensively used to find out important contents in an image. Extensive experiments, reported in (Elazary & Itti, 2008), also indicate that saliency leads to interesting objects in a scene.

Several image retargeting techniques (Fan et al, 2003; Chen et al, 2003; Setlur et al, 2005; Li and Ling, 2009; Yan et al, 2014) propose to use a visual attention model, as in (Itti et al, 1998), to find out salient contents in an image. A saliency map is generated using low-level features like intensity, color and orientation. Gaussian pyramids are formed to represent these features at multiple scales. Conspicuity maps are obtained by computing the center-surround differences, which are computed as difference of feature representations between finer and coarser scales. Finally, a saliency map, which is a two-dimensional representation of saliency of every pixel in the image, is found by combining the conspicuity maps from individual features. Binarization of this saliency map provides a set of interesting regions. As people tend to attend regions which are close to the center of an image, a Gaussian template centered at the image is used in some of these methods (Fan et al, 2003; Chen et al, 2003; Setlur et al, 2005) for weighting the attentional importance based on their positions in the image.

Apart from low-level saliency, some of these retargeting methods also consider face (Fan et al, 2003; Chen et al, 2003; Setlur et al, 2005) and text (Fan et al, 2003; Chen et al, 2003) as important semantic components in the image. The methods in (Li et al, 2002) and (Chen & Zhang, 2001) have been used here to detect faces and text regions, respectively. Importance of face is calculated by considering the size of the facial region weighted by positional weight. Bigger the size of the facial region, it is more likely to draw attention. The importance of regions containing text is estimated by considering the size, aspect ratio and positional weight of the regions. Finally, the importance maps from low-level visual attention, face and text are integrated into a single importance map for the image.

The retargeting method in (Ciocca et al, 2007a; 2007b) performs a categorization of an image as – landscape image, close-up image, or other image. Different approaches are adopted to derive the importance map according to the category of the image. No separate region is differentiated as important for a landscape image, i.e., all portions in the image are treated as equally important. The saliency map using the visual attention model in (Itti et al, 1998) is used to find importance of the contents in a close-up image. Other categories of images are further classified depending on the presence of faces using a face detector as in (Viola and Jones, 2004). In the absence of faces in the image, an attention model (Itti et al, 19998) based on low-level features provides information about importance, as same as the close-up images. For an image containing faces, skin color detector is applied to generate a skin color map, in addition to the saliency map and face regions. Then, a combination of saliency map, face regions, and skin color map produce the importance map in these images.

Visual attention models other than the one in (Itti et al, 1998) are also used for this purpose. The contrast-based attention model in (Ma and Zhang, 2003) is used to compute the saliency map in (Liu & Gleicher, 2005; Guo et al, 2009). According to the attention model in (Ma and Zhang, 2003), saliency value of a pixel is estimated as the weighted sum of differences between the pixel and other pixels in its neighborhood. A face detector using Adaboost method (Viola & Jones, 2001) is also used in (Liu & Gleicher, 2005; Guo et al, 2009) to provide face regions which have high semantic importance. Apart form low-level saliency and face detector, the retargeting approach in (Guo et al, 2009) also assumes the human body part as equally important. An iterative graph cut based approach to determine the body position from the location of the face (as proposed in (Wang et al, 2006)) is used here for this purpose.

A multi-scale contrast-based saliency map generation method has also been proposed in (Liu et al, 2010). Here, each pixel is represented using a vector of length five using red, green, blue, yellow, and luminance channels. Contrast of a pixel at a particular scale is defined, here, as the difference of average feature vectors of the center region and the surrounding region. For each pixel, a small rectangular window centering at the pixel is considered as the center region. Whereas, a larger rectangular window encompassing the center region (but excluding the center region in the middle) constitutes the surrounding region. Finally, the average of the contrast measures at multiple scales is considered as the saliency of the pixel.

Image retargeting methods in (Liang et al, 2012; 2013) propose to compute the importance map as a weighted sum of a saliency map and an edge map. A graph based model in (Harel et al, 2006), which models gaze shift as a random walk and the equilibrium distribution over the random walk as the propensity of being salient, is used here to generate the saliency map. Sobel operator is used to derive the edge map. As saliency map highlights the areas which are more likely to attract our vision, edge map promotes pixels which are more sensitive to the contour of the important objects.

Another graph based saliency model (Pal et al, 2010) has been used as an estimate of importance in the retargeting methods in (Pal et al, 2011; 2012). According to this graph based model of saliency (Pal et al, 2010), an image is represented as a graph, where a block of homogeneous pixels is represented by a node in this graph. Degree of each node captures the saliency for the concerned block of pixels by encoding the feature difference (weighted by positional proximity) of the concerned block with all other blocks in the image.

Saliecny map from a frequency-tuned saliency model (Achanta et al, 2009) is combined with face regions (as found in (Viola and Jones, 2004)) to derive the importance map in the retargeting approach in (Ren et al, 2010).

A context-aware saliency map (Goferman et al, 2012) is considered as the importance map in stereoscopic image retargeting (Lin et al, 2014).

In another approach, (Achanta & Susstrunk, 2009) generates a saliency map by measuring the Euclidean distance of the average color vector of the image with each pixel of a Gaussian blurred version of the same image. The computation is carried out in a perceptually uniform CIE Lab color space. This saliency map is combined with an energy map to produce a better importance map.

(Ding et al, 2011) uses a visual attention based model in (Montabone & Soto, 2010) along with a face detector (Viola & Jones, 2004) to generate a saliency map. But this saliency map does not reflect the underlying geometrical structure in the image. In order to maintain the minimum distortion in the image structure at the time of retargeting, shift in the pixels from the same object should be similar. As the shift of the pixels is decided by their importance, the pixels in same object should have similar importance values. Therefore, (Ding et al, 2011) argues that saliency map generated using a visual attention based model along with a face detector does not perform well to preserve the underlying geometrical structure in the image. Henceforth, the authors improve the saliency map under the guidance of the original image using a guided filter method in (He et al, 2010).

In a completely different style of finding salient regions, (Marchesotti et al, 2009) assumes that a set of images having similar visual appearance has similar salient regions. Banking on the availability of an annotated image database, authors retrieve few most similar images to the target image. Finally, a simple classifier is developed to generate the saliency map based on the similar looking images.

(Ma & Guo, 2004) proposes entropy as a measure of importance. Entropy is computed in each of the planes of HUV color space. A region with larger entropy contains more information and therefore, of more importance to the viewer.

A simple energy function involving gradient of intensities and histogram of oriented gradients is proposed as measure of importance in (Avidan & Shamir, 2007). Even the retargeting methods in (Huang et al, 2009; Kim et al, 2009) adopt this gradient based energy function as measure of importance. This energy function basically signifies the presence of structures in the image. It assigns higher importance to textured areas and edges, whereas smooth salient regions obtain low importance.

An energy function (as proposed in (Avidan & Shamir, 2007)) fails to highlight the importance of human beings which are often present in an image. (Subramanian et al, 2008) improves this energy estimation by incorporating, beside this gradient based energy function, a neural network based skin detector to enhance the energy value of skin pixels. According to this method, an image segmentation is carried out, at first, based on a fuzzy c-means clustering based algorithm. A multilayer perceptron is used, then, as skin detector. The back propagation algorithm to train the multilayer perceptron is trained with skin and non-skin pixels. Working with RGB color map fails to detect the red tones as non-skin. Similarly, working with HSV color map fails to detect dark wood brown as non-skin. Therefore, the network is trained with both color maps. The intersection of both results is considered to remove these tones. Similarly, (Subramanian et al, 2008) also suggests the usage of YCbCr color map to reduce the effect of ambient light, but the results with RGB and HSV color maps are reported as sufficiently satisfactory.

Moreover, the retargeting methods in (Wang et al, 2008; Hwang & Chien, 2008) combine the gradient based energy map (as in (Avidan & Shamir, 2007)) and the saliency map (as obtained from (Itti et al, 1998)) to determine the significance of each pixel. The gradient highlights the presence of structure in the image, whereas the saliency map dignifies the attractiveness of the content. Thus, they complement each other to promote meaningful salient structures in the image as important. Same strategy of combining gradient energy with low-level saliency map has also been adopted in (Roberto et al, 2011). But a line-wise measure of importance is required in this springs-based retargeting strategy (Roberto et al, 2011). Hence, a projection along the desired direction is considered and either the max or the mean operator is applied in this direction. Additionally, the methods in (Hwang & Chien, 2008; Roberto et al, 2011) also mention about usage of a face detector (Viola & Jones, 2001; 2004).

(Murthy et al, 2010) estimates importance as the gradient map computed using the DCT coefficients of the 8×8 blocks. This is very effective for retargeting JPEG compressed images, as decompression of the image can be avoided here.

In the symmetry-preserving retargeting approach (Wu et al, 2010), emphasis is given to preserve the structure, shape and illumination distribution of symmetrical structures. Therefore, symmetrical structures in the image are treated as important. (Wu et al, 2010) proposes a novel technique to detect such symmetrical structures. The basic elements for the symmetrical structure, termed as cells, are detected based on the maximally stable extremal region (MSER) (Matas et al, 2002). Affine invariant MSERs ensure that cells with similar pattern can be identified irrespective of viewing perspective. MSERs are not also influenced much by illumination. This guarantees that similar patters can be identified over different lighting conditions. A symmetry structure is generally having multiple similar looking cells. Therefore, clustering is performed to identify the major clusters of MSERs and outliers are filtered out. Then, a lattice is formed for each cluster connecting the center of the cells in the cluster.

Domain knowledge helps to extract semantically important regions in images from a game of basketball (Wu et al, 2012). Knowing that the most of the images from basketball game are captured as a long shot, a major portion of such an image is assumed to be occupied by the playing court. Hence, a dominant color in the image is identified through clustering of hues (H) in HSV color model. Identification of dominant color leads to a segmentation of the playing court. The boundaries of the playing court are identified as semantic edges. Then, orientation of each pixel with respect to these semantic edges decides whether the pixel belongs to important region or not.

Several other notable approaches of capturing importance are also found in literature. Usage of high order statistics at a nonlinear diffusion space of the image (Kim & Kim, 2011) is the most noteworthy among other approaches.

Face detection to identify semantically important faces in the image is used by various retargeting approaches as discussed above. The notable approach for face detection in (Viola & Jones, 2001; 2004) is widely accepted in literature. But the retargeting approach in (Kiess et al, 2012) moves one step ahead by differentiating in-focus and out-of-focus faces. The main philosophy of this classification approach is that each face has characteristic edges due to nose, mouth, eyes and eyebrows. For an in-focus face, very strong edges are visible. Edge pixels are identified using gradients. Based on the gradient magnitude, if one of the edges are identified as a strong edge, then the face is considered as in-focus face. Other faces are considered out-of-focus. Only the in-focus faces are considered as important in (Kiess et al, 2012).

Actually, finding the importance of the contents in an image without proper understanding of their semantic is a challenging problem in image processing. Various researchers have resorted to various methods as it can be found in above discussion. In a nutshell, most of them utilize a visual attention-based saliency map. Some of the widely-used saliency models are center-surround based (Itti et al, 1998) and contrast-based (Ma and Zhang, 2003) models. Usage of graph-based saliency models (Harel et al, 2006; Pal et al, 2010), frequency-tuned saliency model (Achanta et al, 2009), context-aware saliency model (Goferman et al, 2012), the model in (Montabone & Soto, 2010) and several other models can be found in few of these retargeting approaches. Apart from these visual attention models, a gradient map has also been widely used in many of the works (Avidan & Shamir, 2007; Wang et al, 2008; Subramanian et al, 2008; Murthy et al, 2010). An entropy-based measure of importance is proposed in (Ma & Guo, 2004). As it is observed in various studies, these low-level feature based estimations of importance, often, lack in highlighting the semantically important regions. Face images are identified to incorporate semantic importance in this context. Face detector, as proposed in (Viola and Jones, 2001; 2004), is widely accepted in this context. (Kiess et al, 2012) advances one more step to differentiate among in-focus (semantically important) and out-of-focus (semantically not-so-important) faces. Even detection of text regions, as proposed in (Chen and Zhang, 2001), adds semantic value in the importance map. (Wu et al, 2012) uses domain knowledge about a basketball court to derive importance of the contents in an image from a basketball game.

RETARGETING APPROACHES

Various types of retargeting approaches are available in the literature. This section discusses the state-of-the-art methods in each of these types of approaches.

Rapid Serial Visual Presentation

Human eyes rapidly shift over the important portions in a scene which they wish to look at. At a time, attention is paid to only one of those portions for its better understanding. Similarly, rapid serial visual presentation (RSVP) mechanism selects one portion of the image at a time based on a decreasing order of importance and projects it in the target display. At first, the most important portion is projected into the target display, and then the second most important portion is projected, and so on. Thus, the viewer gets a good view of the entire image. Here, time is compromised to tackle the space constraint of a small display. (Fan et al, 2003; Liu et al, 2003) propose this RSVP mechanism for image retargeting. Additionally, (Liu et al, 2003) introduces minimum perceptible time (i.e., the duration of projecting in the display) for each of the important content.

Cropping

Several researchers (Suh et al, 2003; Ma & Guo, 2004; Santella et al, 2006; Luo, 2007) have suggested to crop a tight-bound rectangle containing all important contents in the image and to fit it into the target display. This strategy performs well if there is only one important object in the image. Even it is an effective method, if multiple important objects are densely located at one portion of the image. But if the important contents are sparsely distributed in the image, the tight-bound rectangle will be large as compared to the area of the target display. Then, there is a possibility that some of these important contents will reduce in size too much to be perceptible in the retargeted image. (Chen et al, 2003) adopts various strategies to tackle this problem depending on the minimal perceptible size for each of the important contents. The minimal perceptible size of an object is defined as the minimally required area to represent the object. According to (Chen et al, 2003), the cropping rectangle can be expanded to include few more less important contents for some images. But for other images, it is better to maintain the tight-bound rectangle as the cropping rectangle so that the important contents can occupy slightly larger area in the target display. Even, it has been suggested (Chen et al, 2003) that, at times, better results can be achieved if the target display (and the cropping rectangle) is rotated by 90 degrees.

The retargeting approach in (Ciocca et al, 2007a; 2007b) identifies a landscape image and suggest to fit the entire image in the target area through down-scaling. The underlying assumption is that any particular object is not focused in these landscape images. Image cropping around the important contents is suggested for all other kinds of images

Warping

Contrary to cropping-based methods, which completely discard all unimportant contents falling outside the tight-bound rectangular window encompassing important contents, warping techniques retain those unimportant contents. A non-linear function, which maps positions in the source image to positions in the target image, is used in these techniques to de-emphasize the unimportant contents. A fish-eye view warping based retargeting method has been proposed in (Liu & Gleicher, 2005). Fish-eye warping is a popular method in information visualization which highlights the focus area as well as retains its context. At first, size and position of the important region is estimated in such a way that the important region occupies the maximum area in the target display while maintaining its original aspect ratio. As the aspect ratio for the important region is being maintained, some space in the target display may still be left as unoccupied. Those are filled by contents from unimportant regions using the fish-eye warping method. Size of the unimportant objects reduces with the distance from the center of the focal point (i.e., important region) due to radial distortion in a fish-eye.

In another kind of warping technique, (Wang et al, 2008) puts a grid mesh on the image. The edges in the mesh form vertical and horizontal grid lines which partition the image into quads. Then, an optimal local scaling factor is estimated for each of the quads so that quads with high importance scales uniformly in both directions (maintaining the aspect ratio), whereas distortions are introduced in less important contents in other quads. One drawback of this method is that some of the unimportant quads may become a line or a point due to shrinkage. Hence, the contents of those quads vanish from the retargeted image.

Growth of Important Rectangles

(Pal et al, 2011) proposes a retargeting method based on uniform growth of important contents in the target area. According to this method, each important portion in the image is encompassed with a separate tight-bound rectangle. Their size and position is estimated in the target area assuming a uniform down-scaling for the entire image. The portions outside these important rectangles can be treated as a rectangle (due to rectangular shape of an image and the target display) with rectangular holes (due to rectangular encompassing of important contents). These areas in both the original image and the target space are partitioned into a minimum number of rectangular partitions. Same partitioning scheme is applied for both spaces (image and target) to ensure one-to-one correspondence of the rectangles between them. Then, the important rectangles in the target space are incrementally enlarged ensuring the following conditions:

- All-important rectangles are enlarged by a uniform factor.
- Aspect ratios of the important rectangles are preserved.
- Relative spatial ordering of these important rectangles is maintained.
- Moreover, enlargement of important rectangles causes reduction of unimportant rectangular partitions. But any of these unimportant rectangles must not diminish to non-existence, unlike (Wang et al, 2008).

Therefore, important rectangles are grown in the target space (and automatically unimportant rectangles shrink) until the above stated conditions are violated. At the end, one-to-one correspondence of these rectangles (both important and unimportant) between the original image and the target space helps to map the contents from the original image to the target display.

Unequal Shrinkage of Rectangular Partitions

(Pal et al, 2012) treats the image retargeting as a problem of fitting a square-shaped object of non-uniform elasticity into a small box by applying uniform pressure from all directions. This object has varying elasticity at different parts of it. As a result, some parts (unimportant) shrink more as compared to other parts (important). At first, the image is partitioned into horizontal strips containing important and unimportant contents, respectively. Then amount of shrinkage for each of the important and the unimportant horizontal strips are estimated based on the dimensions of the image and the target area and a shrinkage control factor. Shrinkage control factor is defined as the ratio of the amount of shrinkage in unimportant strip to that of important strip (assuming both strips are of equal height). Hence, the shrinkage control factor controls the disparity of shrinkage among important and unimportant strips. Then, the image is reduced in height by applying the estimated amount of shrinkage in each of the horizontal strips. Similarly, partitioning the image in vertical strips having important and unimportant contents, alternatively, will result in reduction in the width of the image. It is to be noted that the distortion can be controlled by choosing an appropriate value for the shrinkage control factor.

Seam Carving

A seam is defined as an 8-connected path of less important pixels crossing the entire image either from top to bottom or left to right. (Avidan & Shamir, 2007) conceptualizes this seam carving method for image retargeting. The size of the image is reduced through iteratively removing the seams. Seams are removed in the increasing order of their importance starting from the least important seam until the image reduces to a desired size. Removal of horizontal seams (spreading left to right of the image) shrinks the image in height, whereas reduction in width of the image occurs due to removal of vertical seams (spreading top to bottom of the image). This seam carving technique is also adopted by other researchers ((Subramanian et al, 2008)).

As iteratively searching for the least important seam and its removal is a time consuming process, (Srivastava and Biswas, 2008) proposes methods to speed up the seam carving technique. It is suggested that a chunk of seams can be removed at every iteration without degrading the outcome. Chunk of these seams can be selected as (i) the least important seam and few other seams spatially adjacent to it, (ii) few (suggested number 3) least adjacent seams irrespective of their spatial location, or (iii) few seams from each partition of the image. Thus, (Srivastava and Biswas, 2008) improves the execution time over the basic seam carving in (Avidan & Shamir, 2007). (Huan et al, 2009) also reports a faster seam carving method using a matching relation between adjacent rows or columns.

Moreover, an excessive removal of seams (in case of the target area being much smaller than the original image) introduces unwanted perceptible distortions in an image. Therefore, (Hwang & Chien, 2008) suggests to stop any further removal of seams when the importance score of the least important seam at an iteration becomes higher then a certain threshold. A simple down-scaling is applied at that stage to fit the remaining image to the target display.

Another approach adopts seam searching based pixel fusion (Yan et al, 2014) to control this distortion. Seam carving is applied based on an estimated number of searched seams. Then, the pixels are assigned into various groups. An inter-row importance filtering is carried out in order to ensure spatial coherence between adjacent rows. Ultimately, pixel fusion is carried out according to an estimated scaling factor for each of the groups to produce the retargeted image. This method claims to reduce unwanted artifacts in the retargeted image as compared to basic seam carving in (Avidan & Shamir, 2007).

Retargeting for Stereoscopic Images

This subsection contains a brief mention of major approaches to retarget stereoscopic images. Rapid development in stereoscopic equipments has led the emergence of stereoscopic image retargeting. According to (Niu et al, 2012), a pair of stereoscopic images are optimally cropped and fitted to the display in order to maximize the aesthetic value whose estimation is guided by the principles of stereoscopic photography. Similar to cropping in normal images, this method does not perform well if the important contents are sparsely distributed in the images.

Success of seam carving based techniques for image retargeting (originally introduced by (Avidan & Shamir, 2007) and later improved by several other researchers) has encouraged the adoption of these methods for stereoscopic image retargeting too (Utsugi et al, 2010; Basha et al, 2011). These methods remove a pair of seams of least importance from each of the input images. Similar to normal images, removal of seams in excessive number leads to unpleasant artifacts in these images too.

Warping based methods are also applied for stereoscopic images. Warping methods to map these source images to the target display have been formulated as an optimization problem in (Chang et al, 2011; Lee et al, 2012). These approaches aim to preserve the disparities and shapes of objects of high importance. An object coherence warping (Lin et al, 2014) further improves the results. Information about matching objects is considered in this method, in stead of using information about matching pixels. Hence, object correspondences generate object importance maps. Thus, it results in better preservation of disparity and shapes of important objects.

Other Approaches

In (Setlur et al, 2005), important objects are removed, at first, from the original image. The resulting gaps are filled by the content from the background. Then, the obtained image (without the important objects) is resized to fit in the target display. Then the important objects are placed at appropriate positions in the target image. While positioning these important objects in the target image, the following points are taken care of:

- Relative ordering in the positions of important objects is not changed from that in the original image.
- Aspect ratio of each important object is maintained the same as in the original image.
- There is no change of the background for each important object. Each of them are placed at the same background as in the original image.

(Simakov et al, 2008) argues that an ideal retargeted image must have the following properties:

1. It must preserve as much as content from the original image, and
2. It must preserve visual coherence of the original image.

A bidirectional similarity measure between the original and the retargeted image is proposed to capture these requirements. Then, retargeting is perceived as an optimization problem. A retargeted image is obtained which maximizes this similarity measure.

EVALUATION STRATEGIES FOR RETARGETING APPROACHES

Correct evaluation of any method is important before adopting it for any practical purpose. It is also equally important for the researchers to understand the acceptability of their new retargeting method amidst a clutter of already existing methods. This section discusses the retargeting approaches adopted by several researchers to establish their retargeting methods.

Subjective Evaluation

In the absence of methods to quantitatively measure the correctness of retargeting approaches, researchers mainly resort to user study which is subjective in nature. A set of volunteers are shown the results from various competitive methods and their opinions are recorded to compare the concerned methods.

For example, questions such as "Do the fixated regions really present interesting areas?" and "Does the approach facilitate image browsing on a small screen?" were asked to the volunteers to evaluate the RSVP based image retargeting in (Fan et al, 2003; Liu et al, 2003). The expected answer of the first question was binary in nature. For the second question, volunteers were asked whether the proposed approach is better, equivalent, or worse than the other known methods. Similar practices were adopted for (Chen et al, 2003).

(Liu and Gleicher, 2005) randomly selected two retargeting methods at a time from the set of comparative methods and their results for a certain input image were displayed side by side as simulated cell phone displays on web pages. Volunteers were asked to select the result that they would prefer. Repeating this experiment over a set of images with a number of volunteers revealed the retargeting methods which were preferred over few other retargeting methods. Similarly, a binary selection between two comparative methods was also reported in (Setlur et al, 2005). In (Luo, 2007), volunteers were given more freedom to select neither, either, or both images to specify their acceptance of the results. Additionally, (Setlur et al, 2005) conducted two separate user studies for two different display resolutions: (154×171 pixels) and (320×320 pixels), whereas the resolution of the original images was 640×480 pixels. Hence, they could study how the preference of retargeting methods changes with the size of the target display.

Volunteers were asked to rank the comparative results in (Zund et al, 2013). An aggregation of ranks given by a set of volunteers over a set of images provides a qualitative measure of relative performance of the retargeting methods.

Results from subjective user studies involving more or less of the same procedures described above are also reported by several other researchers (Ciocca et al, 2007a; 2007b; Subramanian et al, 2008; Pal et al, 2011; 2012; Liang et al, 2013; Yan et al, 2014).

Objective Evaluation

Recently, a few objective assessment methods have been devised and used by several researchers. This subsection discusses these methods for objective evaluation of the retargeting techniques.

Non-uniform scaling of important and unimportant contents in content-aware retargeting introduces geometric distortions (such as distorted lines, shapes, or textures) in the resultant image. Therefore, perceptibility of these distortions as well as of the information loss is quantified to assess the quality of retargeting (Hsu et al, 2013; 2014). The geometric distortion in the retargeted image is estimated using the local variance of SIFT flow vector fields (Liu et al, 2011) between the original and the retargeted image. A visual attention model is used to derive the weights of patch-wise geometric distortions depending on the visual importance of these patches. Moreover, an attention guided estimation of information loss is also considered in the proposed metric. Information loss is estimated as the ratio of the amount of saliency value lost in retargeting to the total saliency value of the original image. But to compute this loss of saliency value, the saliency map of the original image is warped to the size of the retargeted image base on the pixel correspondences (as guided by the SIFT flow map). Finally, a weighted combination of these two metrics produces a single quality measure for image retargeting. An adaptive weighted combination based on automatic determination of the weights also adds novelty in (Hsu et al, 2014) as compared to (Hsu et al, 2013).

A structural similarity based image retargeting assessment method is proposed in (Fang et al, 2014). This method is inspired by the structural similarity based image quality metric as proposed in (Wang et al, 2004). At each spatial location in the original image, the structural similarity map reveals how the structural information is preserved in the retargeted image. A spatial pooling method involving both bottom-up and top-down saliency is, then, used to obtain an overall assessment of the retargeted image. This is a useful metric as image content-aware retargeting methods aim to preserve the salient local structures of the original image.

Moreover, execution time is one crucial factor for real-time deployment of the retargeting methods. Therefore, (Srivastava and Biswas, 2008) measured the execution time to demonstrate how their method achieves a speed up through intelligently removing seams as compared to original seam carving (Avidan and Shamir, 2007).

FUTURE RESEARCH DIRECTIONS

Though a lot of research efforts have been put in this field, few gaps are still not closed. For example, estimation of importance is still an open problem. Researchers have attempted various methods as discussed in this chapter. But none of these methods performs equally well in all kinds of images. Ideally, one should understand the semantic of the contents in the image to resolve this problem. But semantic understanding of an image is far from achieved.

Distortions in the retargeted images are introduced due to over-emphasizing of important contents as compared to unimportant contents in the image. Researchers is still trying to draw a thin line of margin between the emphasizing and over-emphasizing of important contents. Loss of contextual information is also must be minimized. This is again a contradiction of goals as the main aim of content-aware retargeting is to give more priority to important contents. These points lead to frequent emergence of new retargeting methods.

Research on quantification of objective assessment of the retargeting strategies is a new topic too. Only few initial approaches have been proposed in (Hsu et al, 2013; 2014; Fang et al, 2014).

CONCLUSION

This article is a compilation of research efforts on various aspects of content-aware image retargeting. Major aspects which have been highlighted here are: estimation of importance of contents in an image, various retargeting approaches, and assessment (both subjective and objective) of these approaches. Thus, by summarizing the state-of-the-art researches under one umbrella, this chapter will help present and future researchers a lot. Achievements being put together, limitations and potential research avenues have come into focus.

REFERENCES

Achanta, R., Hemami, S., Estrada, F., & Susstrunk, S. (2009). Frequency-tuned salient region detection. In *Proc. of International Conference on Computer Vision and Pattern Recognition*.

Achanta, R., & Susstrunk, S. (2009). Saliency detection for content-aware image resizing. In *Proc. of 16th IEEE International Conference on Image Processing*.

Avidan, S., & Shamir, A. (2007). Seam Carving for Content-Aware Image Resizing. *ACM Transactions on Graphics*, *26*(3), 10. doi:10.1145/1276377.1276390

Basha, T., Moses, Y., & Avidan, S. (2011). Geometrically consistent stereo seam carving. In *Proc. of IEEE International Conference on Computer Vision*.

Chang, C.-H., Liang, C.-K., & Chuang, Y.-Y. (2011). Content-aware display adaptation and interactive editing for stereoscopic images. *IEEE Transactions on Multimedia*, *13*(4), 589–601. doi:10.1109/TMM.2011.2116775

Chen, L.-Q., Xie, X., Fan, X., Ma, W.-Y., Zhang, H.-J., & Zhou, H.-Q. (2003). A visual Attention model for adapting images on small displays. *Multimedia Systems*, *9*(4), 353–364. doi:10.1007/s00530-003-0105-4

Chen, X. R., & Zhang, H. J. (2001). Text area detection from video frames, In *Proc. of 2nd IEEE Pacific-Rim Conference on Multimedia*.

Ciocca, G., Cusano, C., Gasparini, F., & Schettini, R. (2007a). Self-adaptive Image Cropping for Small Displays. In *Proc. of International Conference on Consumer Electronics*.

Ciocca, G., Cusano, C., Gasparini, F., & Schettini, R. (2007b). Self-Adaptive Image Cropping for Small Displays. *IEEE Transactions on Consumer Electronics*, *53*(4), 1622–1627. doi:10.1109/TCE.2007.4429261

Ding, Y., Xiao, J., & Yu, J. (2011). Importance filtering for image retargeting. In *Proc. of IEEE Conference on Computer Vision and Pattern Recognition*.

Elazary, L., & Itti, L. (2008). Interesting objects are visually salient. *Journal of Vision, 8*(3), 1-15.

Fan, X., Xie, X., Ma, W.-Y., Zhang, H.-J., & Zhou, H.-Q. (2003). Visual Attention Based Image Browsing on Mobile Devices. In *International Conference on Multimedia and Expo*.

Fang, Y., Zeng, K., Wang, Z., Lin, W., Fang, Z., & Lin, C.-W. (2014). Objective quality assessment for image retargeting based on structural similarity. *IEEE Journal on Emerging and Selected Topics in Circuits and Systems*, *4*(1), 95–105. doi:10.1109/JETCAS.2014.2298919

Goferman, S., Zelnik-Manor, L., & Tal, A. (2012). Context-aware saliency detection. *IEEE Transactions on Pattern Analysis and Machine Intelligence*, *34*(10), 1915–1926. doi:10.1109/TPAMI.2011.272 PMID:22201056

Guo, Y., Liu, F., Shi, J., Zhou, Z.-H., & Gleicher, M. (2009). Image retargeting using mesh parameterization. *IEEE Transactions on Multimedia*, *11*(5), 856–867. doi:10.1109/TMM.2009.2021781

Harel, J., Koch, C., & Perona, P. (2006). *Graph-based visual saliency*. Proc. of Neural Information Processing Systems.

He, K., Sun, J., & Tang, X. (2010). Guided image filtering. In *Proc. of European Conference on Computer Vision*.

Hsu, C.-C., Lin, C.-W., Fang, Y., & Lin, W. (2013). *Objective quality assessment for image retargeting based on perceptual distortion and information loss*. Proc. of Visual Communications and Image Processing. doi:10.1109/VCIP.2013.6706443

Hsu, C.-C., Lin, C.-W., Fang, Y., & Lin, W. (2014). Objective quality assessment for image retargeting based on perceptual geometric distortion and information loss. *IEEE Journal of Selected Topics in Signal Processing*, *8*(3), 377–389. doi:10.1109/JSTSP.2014.2311884

Huang, H., Fu, T., Rosin, P. L., & Chun, Q. (2009). Real-time content-aware image resizing. *Science in China Series F: Information Sciences*, *52*(2), 172–182. doi:10.1007/s11432-009-0041-9

Hwang, D.-S., & Chien, S.-Y. (2008). Content-aware image resizing using perceptual seam curving with human attention model. In *Proc. of IEEE International Conference on Multimedia and Expo*.

Itti, L., Koch, C., & Niebur, E. (1998). A model of saliency-based visual attention for rapid scene analysis. *IEEE Transactions on Pattern Analysis and Machine Intelligence*, *20*(11), 1254–1259. doi:10.1109/34.730558

Kiess, J., Gracia, R., Kopf, S., & Effelsberg, W. (2012). Improved image retargeting by distinguishing between faces in focus and out of focus. In *Proc. of IEEE International Conference on Multimedia and Expo Workshops*. doi:10.1109/ICMEW.2012.32

Kim, J.-S., Kim, J.-H., & Kim, C.-S. (2009). Adaptive image and video retargeting technique based on fourier analysis. In *Proc. of IEEE Conference on Computer Vision and Pattern Recognition*.

Kim, W., & Kim, C. (2011). A texture-aware salient edge model for image retargeting. *IEEE Signal Processing Letters*, *18*(11), 631–634. doi:10.1109/LSP.2011.2165337

Lee, K.-Y., Chung, C.-D., & Chuang, Y.-Y. (2012). Scene warping: Layer based stereoscopic image resizing. In *Proc. of IEEE Conference on Computer Vision and Pattern Recognition*.

Li, S. Z., Zhu, L., Zhang, Z. Q., Blake, A., Zhang, H. J., & Shum, H. (2002). Statistical learning of multi-view face detection, In *Proc. of 7th European Conference on Computer Vision*.

Li, X., & Ling, H. (2009). Learning based thumbnail cropping. In *Proc. of IEEE International Conference on Multimedia and Expo*.

Liang, Y., Liu, Y.-J., Luo, X.-N., Xie, L., & Fu, X. (2013). Optimal-scaling-factor assignment for patch-wise image retargeting. *IEEE Computer Graphics and Applications*, *33*(5), 68–78. doi:10.1109/MCG.2012.123 PMID:24808083

Liang, Y., Su, Z., & Luo, X. (2012). Patchwise scaling method for content-aware image resizing. *Signal Processing*, *92*(5), 1243–1257. doi:10.1016/j.sigpro.2011.11.018

Lin, S.-S., Lin, C.-H., Chang, S.-H., & Lee, T.-Y. (2014). Object-coherence warping for stereoscopic image retargeting. *IEEE Transactions on Circuits and Systems for Video Technology*, *25*(5), 759–768.

Liu, C., Yuen, J., & Torralba, A. (2011). SIFT flow: Dense correspondence across scenes and its applications. *IEEE Transactions on Pattern Analysis and Machine Intelligence, 33*(5), 978–994. doi:10.1109/TPAMI.2010.147 PMID:20714019

Liu, F., & Gleicher, M. (2005). Automatic image retargeting with fisheye-view warping. In *Proc. of the 18th Annual ACM Symposium on User Interface Software and Technology*. doi:10.1145/1095034.1095061

Liu, H., Xie, X., Ma, W.-Y., & Zhang, H.-J. (2003). Automatic browsing of large pictures on mobile devices. In *Proc. of 11th ACM International Conference on Multimedia*. doi:10.1145/957013.957045

Liu, Z., Yan, H., Shen, L., Ngan, K. N., & Zhang, Z. (2010). Adaptive image retargeting using saliency-based continuous seam carving. *Optical Engineering (Redondo Beach, Calif.), 49*(1).

Luo, J. (2007). Subject content- based intelligent cropping for digital photos. In *IEEE International Conference on Multimedia and Expo*. doi:10.1109/ICME.2007.4285126

Ma, M., & Guo, J. K. (2004). Automatic Image Cropping for Mobile Devices with Built-in Camera. In *First IEEE Consumer Communications and Networking Conference*. doi:10.1109/CCNC.2004.1286964

Ma, Y.-F., & Zhang, H.-J. (2003). Contrast-based image attention analysis by using fuzzy growing. In *Proc. ACM Multimedia*. doi:10.1145/957013.957094

Marchesotti, L., Cifarelli, C., & Csurka, G. (2009). A framework for visual saliency detection with applications to image thumbnailing. In *Proc. of IEEE 12th International Conference on Computer Vision*. doi:10.1109/ICCV.2009.5459467

Matas, J., Chum, O., Urban, M., & Pajdla, T. (2002). Robust wide baseline stereo from maximally stable extremal regions. In *Proc. of British Machine Vision Conference*. doi:10.5244/C.16.36

Montabone, S., & Soto, A. (2010). Human detection using a mobile platform and novel features derived from a visual saliency mechanism. *Image and Vision Computing, 28*(3), 391–402. doi:10.1016/j.imavis.2009.06.006

Murthy, O. V. R., Muthuswamy, K., Rajan, D., & Tien, C. L. (2010). Image retargeting in compressed domain. In *Proc. of 20th International Conference on Pattern Recognition*.

Niu, Y., Liu, F., Feng, W. C., & Jin, H. (2012). Aesthetics-based stereoscopic photo cropping for heterogeneous displays. *IEEE Transactions on Multimedia, 14*(3), 783–796. doi:10.1109/TMM.2012.2186122

Pal, R., Mitra, P., & Mukherjee, J. (2012). Image retargeting using controlled shrinkage. In *Proc. of the Eighth Indian Conference on Vision, Graphics, and Image Processing*.

Pal, R., Mukherjee, A., Mitra, P., & Mukherjee, J. (2010). Modeling visual saliency using degree centralita. *IET Computer Vision, 4*(3), 218–229. doi:10.1049/iet-cvi.2009.0067

Pal, R., Mukhopadhyay, J., & Mitra, P. (2011). Image retargeting through constrained growth of important rectangular partitions. In *Proc. of 4th International Conference on Pattern Recognition and Machine Intelligence*. doi:10.1007/978-3-642-21786-9_19

Ren, T., Liu, Y., & Wu, G. (2010). Rapid image retargeting based on curve-edge grid representation. In *Proc. of IEEE 17th International Conference on Image Processing*. doi:10.1109/ICIP.2010.5654031

Roberto, G., Ardizzone, E., & Pirrone, R. (2011). Springs-based simulation for image retargeting. In *Proc. of 18th IEEE International Conference on Image Processing.*

Rubinstein, M., Gutierrez, D., Sorkine, O., & Shamir, A. (2010). A comparative study of image retargeting. *ACM Transactions on Graphics, 29*(6), 1. doi:10.1145/1882261.1866186

Santella, A., Agrawala, M., DeCarlo, D., Salesin, D., & Cohen, M. (2006). Gaze-based interaction for semi-automatic photo cropping. In *Proc. of the SIGCHI Conference on Human Factors in Computing Systems.* doi:10.1145/1124772.1124886

Setlur, V., Takagi, S., Raskar, R., Gleicher, M., & Gooch, B. (2005). Automatic Image Retargeting. In *Proc. of 4th International Conference on Mobile and Ubiquitous Multimedia.* doi:10.1145/1149488.1149499

Simakov, D., Caspi, Y., Shechtman, E., & Irani, M. (2008). Summarizing visual data using bidirectional similarity. *Proc. of IEEE Conference on Computer Vision and Pattern Recognition.*

Srivastava, A., & Biswas, K. K. (2008). Fast content aware image retargeting. In *Proc. of Sixth Indian Conference on Computer Vision, Graphics, & Image Processing.* doi:10.1109/ICVGIP.2008.44

Subramanian, S., Kumar, K., Mishra, B. P., Banerjee, A., & Bhattacharya, D. (2008). Fuzzy logic based content protection for image resizing by seam curving. In *Proc. of IEEE Conference on Soft Computing and Industrial Applications.*

Suh, B., Ling, H., Bederson, B. B., & Jacobs, D. W. (2003). Automatic thumbnail cropping and its effectiveness. In *Proc. of 16th Annual Symposium on User Interface Software and Technology.* doi:10.1145/964696.964707

Utsugi, K., Shibahara, T., Koike, T., Takahashi, K., & Naemura, T. (2010). Seam carving for stereo images. In *Proc. of 3DTV-Conference.* doi:10.1109/3DTV.2010.5506316

Viola, P., & Jones, M. (2001). Rapid object detection using a boosted cascade of simple features. In *Proc. of International Conference on Computer Vision and Pattern Recognition.* doi:10.1109/CVPR.2001.990517

Viola, P., & Jones, M. J. (2004). Robust real-time face detection. *International Journal of Computer Vision, 57*(2), 137–154. doi:10.1023/B:VISI.0000013087.49260.fb

Wang, J., Ying, Y., Guo, Y., & Peng, Q. (2006). Automatic foreground extraction of head shoulder images. In *Proc. of 24th Computer Graphics International Conference.* doi:10.1007/11784203_33

Wang, Y.-S., Tai, C.-L., Sorkine, O., & Lee, T.-Y. (2008). Optimized scale-and-stretch for image resizing. *ACM Transactions on Graphics, 27*(5), 1. doi:10.1145/1409060.1409071

Wang, Z., Bovik, A. C., Sheikh, H. R., & Simoncelli, E. P. (2004). Image quality assessment: From error visibility to structural similarity. *IEEE Transactions on Image Processing, 13*(4), 600–612. doi:10.1109/TIP.2003.819861 PMID:15376593

Wu, H., Wang, Y.-S., Feng, K.-C., Wong, T.-T., Lee, T.-Y., & Heng, P.-A. (2010). Resizing by symmetry-summarization. *ACM Transactions on Graphics, 29*(6), 1. doi:10.1145/1882261.1866185

Wu, L., Gong, Y., Yuan, X., Zhang, X., & Cao, L. (2012). Semantic aware sports image resizing jointly using seam carving and warping. *Multimedia Tools and Applications.*

Yan, B., Li, K., Yang, X., & Hu, T. (2014). Seam searching based pixel fusion for image retargeting. *IEEE Transactions on Circuits and Systems for Video Technology*.

Zund, F., Pritch, Y., Sorkine-Hornung, A., Mangold, S., & Gross, T. (2013). Content-aware compression using saliency-driven image retargeting. In *Proc. of 20th IEEE International Conference on Image Processing*.

KEY TERMS AND DEFINITIONS

Cropping: Cropping is an image retargeting technique which retains a rectangular region containing the important contents while discarding all other contents in the retargeted image.

Image Retargeting: Image retargeting refers to the process of fitting an image to a target display whose resolution is different from that of the image. The problem which is addressed in this chapter, arises due to fitting a large image in a smaller display.

Seam Carving: Seam carving is a retargeting method which iteratively removes low energy seams to fit the image in a desired size.

Seam: Seam is an 8-connected path of pixels crossing the image either from top to bottom (vertical seam) or from left to right (horizontal seam).

Visual Attention: Visual attention is the mechanism of primate vision system to pay attention only to selected set of visual stimuli at a particular time. This selective attention capability reduces the processing burden of the brain so that it can efficiently interact with the surrounding.

Visual Saliency: Saliency of an object (or a location) of scene specifies the propensity of the object (or the location) to capture attention.

Warping: Warping is an image retargeting technique which applies a non-linear mapping of the contents from the original image to the target display depending on the importance of the contents.

Chapter 6
Video Saliency Detection for Visual Cryptography– Based Watermarking

Adrita Barari
Defence Institute of Advanced Technology, India

Sunita V. Dhavale
Defence Institute of Advanced Technology, India

ABSTRACT

The aim of this chapter is to review the application of the technique of Visual cryptography in non-intrusive video watermarking. The power of saliency feature extraction is also highlighted in the context of Visual Cryptography based watermarking systems for videos. All schemes in literature related to Visual cryptography based video watermarking, have been brought together with special attention on the role of saliency feature extraction in each of these schemes. Further a novel approach for VC based video watermarking using motion vectors (MVP Algorithm) as a salient feature is suggested. Experimental results show the robustness of proposed MVP Algorithm against various video processing attacks. Also, compression scale invariance is achieved.

1. INTRODUCTION

The rapid growth in digital video editing technologies has become a threat to the authenticity and integrity of video data. In case of wide range of applications, such as video surveillance, video broadcast, DVDs, video conferencing, and video-on-demand applications, protection of intellectual property rights of transmitted video data is vital. Digital watermarking technology has emerged in last decade as a well-known solution for video copyright protection (Hartung & Kutter, 1999). In digital watermarking technique (Hartung & Kutter, 1999; Petitcolas, F.A.P, 2000), a watermark representing the copyright information (w) is embedded into the cover video (x) to obtain new watermarked signal $\hat{x} = x + w$, practically indistinguishable from x, by people, in such a way that an eavesdropper cannot detect the presence of w in $\hat{x}$. At the time of ownership dispute, the embedded watermark is extracted ($\hat{w}$) from

DOI: 10.4018/978-1-4666-8723-3.ch006

the watermarked video ($\hat{x}$) and used for verification. Almost all digital video data today is distributed and stored in the compressed format. Hence, existing approaches in video watermarking can be categorized as uncompressed domain video watermarking (Sun & Liu, 2005; Chen & Leung, 2008; Blanchi & Piva, 2013) and compressed domain video watermarking (Ardizzone, E., La Cascia, M., Avanzato, A., & Bruna, A., 1999; Lin, Eskicioglu, Reginald, & Edward, 2005; Fang & Lin, 2006; Sejdic, Djurovic & Stankovic 2011; Aly, H., 2011).

A well-designed video watermarking system must offer both perceptual transparency and robustness (Petitcolas, F.A.P, 2000). Perceptual transparency means that the watermarked video should be perceptually equivalent to the original video. Robustness refers to a reliable extraction of the watermark even if the watermarked video is degraded during different intentional and non-intentional attacks. Assuring perceptual transparency is difficult in video compared to that with still images, due to the temporal dimension existing in video. Embedding different watermarks into video frames independently without taking the temporal dimension into account usually yields a flicker effect in video. This is due to the fact that the differences exist between the intensities of pixels at the same position in two successive video frames.

Of late, visual cryptography (VC) has come up as one of the novel solution for image and video watermarking which is capable of providing zero perceptual distortion along with good robustness towards attacks. VC is a cryptographic technique which allows visual information (for example images, text, etc.) to be split into n different shares with the help of simple mathematical techniques (Naor & Shamir, 1995). In case of watermarking, a secret watermark image w is split into master share M and ownership share O using VC technique. The master share M is generated based on the unique salient features of the host data h which needs to be watermarked. The ownership share O depends on both binary watermark secret w as well as master share M and is registered with certified authority CA. At the time of dispute over the rightful ownership of the attacked host data $\hat{h}$, ownership is identified by stacking the master share $\hat{M}$ (estimated based on $\hat{h}$) and ownership share O kept by the CA. Generation of master share M affects the robustness and security of VC based watermarking. As M is generated based on the unique salient features of the host data h, video saliency detection plays an important role in VC based watermarking.

This chapter provides a brief introduction to VC and application of VC in watermarking. The chapter also provides detail overview of existing VC based video watermarking techniques. In case of non-intrusive VC based video watermarking approaches, the importance of video saliency detection stage in generation of master share M is analyzed. Finally, a novel approach is suggested for VC based video watermarking techniques using motion vectors.

2. VISUAL CRYPTOGRAPHY IN WATERMARKING

In 1995, a novel visual secret sharing concept called Visual Cryptography (VC) was proposed by Moni Naor and Adi Shamir. VC is a technique which allows visual information (for example images, text, etc.) to be split into n different *shares* with the help of simple mathematical techniques. These shares are nothing but pseudo random noise-like structures which reveal no meaningful information if viewed in isolation as seen in Figure 1(a) and 1(b). However, when all the required shares are printed upon transparencies and overlaid one upon the other, they reveal the secret image as illustrated in Figure 1(c). The reconstruction of the secret visual information in this case can be done only with the help of the Human Visual System (HVS). This is the reason why the technique is called *visual* cryptography.

Figure 1a. Shares created by VC technique

Figure 1b. Shares created by VC technique

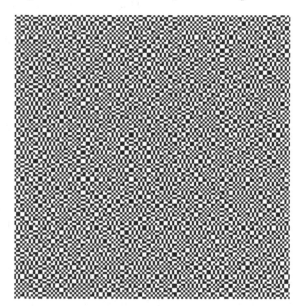

Figure 1c. Overlapping of shares to reveal watermark

The basic model of VC as suggested in (Naor & Shamir, 1995) is as follows. It consists of a printed page of *cipher text* (which can be sent by mail or faxed) and a printed transparency (which serves as a secret key). The original *clear text* is revealed by placing the transparency with the key over the printed page of the cipher text. Both the cipher text and the clear text are random noise-like structures. In a more general way, these pseudo random noise-like structures are called *shares*.

This model can be extended to the k out of n secret sharing problem. In this scheme, the secret image is split into n different shares. The secret information can be retrieved by overlaying $k\left(k \leq n\right)$ or more than k shares but any $(k-1)$ shares give absolutely no information about the secret image.

The basic model can be considered to be a particular case of the (k, n) model described above. It can be considered to be a 2 out of 2 secret sharing scheme. The $(2,2)$ VSS scheme can be explained as follows. A secret image with size $(M \times N)$ is divided into two shares with size $(2M \times 2N)$ where every pixel of the secret image is represented by a block of (2×2) pixels. In the encryption process, every secret pixel is turned into two blocks, and each block belongs to the corresponding share image. In the process, two share images are obtained. In the decryption process, two corresponding blocks of a pixel are simply stacked together to retrieve the secret pixel. Two share blocks of a white secret pixel are similar while share blocks of a black secret pixel are complementary. Figure 2 shows the concept of $(2,2)$ VSS scheme.

Figure 2. Concept of (2, 2) VSS scheme
(Rawat and Balasubramanian, 2012).

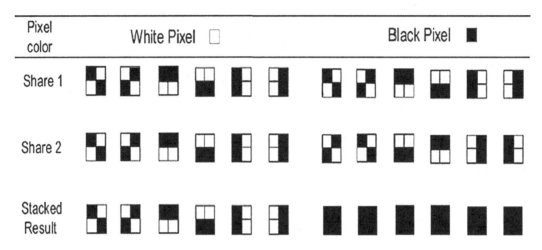

This visual secret sharing scheme shares the secret into a predetermined number of shares so that the cooperation of the legitimate group of shareholders reveals the secret information. The retrieval of the secret information is impossible by an unauthorized group of shareholders.

The VC technique is gaining momentum and acceptance in the field of information hiding and security because of its benefits over normal cryptography and traditional watermarking techniques. The advantages of using visual cryptography in watermarking are as follows:

- VC based watermarking schemes are non-intrusive and do not alter the contents of the host image or video. Thus, VC does not deteriorate the quality of the host.
- VC based watermarking techniques can achieve large embedding capacity, that is, it can embed a large watermark (an image) into the cover images
- It can achieve high security.
- It has the ability to share a secret image between multiple users.
- The VC based scheme is easy to implement where preparation of shares does not require any complex cryptographic computations unlike normal cryptography where a lot of mathematical calculations need to be performed.
- VC requires no previous knowledge or experience of cryptography on the part of the person decoding the message since decoding can be done by the Human Visual System (HVS). By means of the shares, visual information is encrypted such that decryption becomes a mechanical operation.
- It is equally difficult for an unauthorized user to decode the message since secret message can be deciphered only if all shares are available to the attacker. The probability of this happening is very less since one of the shares has to be registered with a higher Certified Authority (CA).

As seen from above, one of the major advantages of the VC technique is that it does not modify the cover data at all. This property of VC makes VC based watermarking techniques an absolutely lossless procedure. VC based watermarking may be used in applications where the cover image or video contains sensitive information whose integrity needs to be preserved. Though traditional watermarking techniques have been successful in proving the rightful ownership of a multimedia content, the process embedding of the watermark has been found to seriously degrade the quality of the host image or video. This is particularly undesirable in defence, military and medical sectors where classified information is conveyed through multimedia. For this reason, there was a need to develop a non-intrusive watermarking technique which would preserve the integrity of the host as well as successfully establish the ownership. This could be achieved with Visual Cryptography (VC) based watermarking techniques where a single image or text is split into Master share M and Ownership Share O. When M and O are overlaid one upon the other, the secret watermark information is revealed. VC based watermarking schemes have been developed by researchers worldwide for watermarking images and videos (Lou, Tso & Liu, 2007; Wang & Chen, 2009; Liu & Wu, 2011). Thus, VC finds some great applications in watermarking as will be discussed in the next section.

3. EXISTING VC BASED VIDEO WATERMARKING TECHNIQUES

Video watermarking schemes are used for various video applications such as copyright protection, copy control, fingerprinting, broadcast monitoring, video authentication, enhanced video coding etc. Here, a video is nothing but a sequence of images yet image watermarking techniques cannot be directly applied to videos owing to their three dimensional characteristics. In addition to their special preprocessing techniques, the temporal nature of videos has to be taken into account (Hartung & Kutter, 1999). Redundancy between frames and a large volume of data makes it all the more difficult to perform watermarking in videos. Further, real time implementations of video watermarking techniques are generally much more complex than that of image watermarking which becomes an important issue.

Some common forms of attack on videos are frame swapping, frame averaging, frame dropping, statistical analysis, interpolation etc. which are unknown to the domain of image watermarking. Inter-video collusion attacks and intra-video collusion attacks are also major issues in case of video fingerprinting applications. In collusion attacks, several compromised buyers can come together and use their authorized copies to generate a new copy. This process can remove the watermark from new copy thus making them evade punishment.

Almost all traditional video watermarking approaches modify the content of the host video which in turn affects the host video quality. Thus, instead of the traditional watermarking schemes, we can use VC based non-intrusive video watermarking approaches effectively for copyright protection. In this section, we present some of the existing VC based watermarking schemes for videos.

3.1 Work by Houmansadr and Ghaemmaghami, (2006)

One of the earliest VC based video watermarking approaches was proposed by Houmansadr and Ghaemmaghami, (2006). This approach was in the spatial domain and proved to be robust to collusion attacks and geometrical attacks. The proposed scheme is based on Naor and Shamir's (2,2) visual secret sharing scheme (Naor & Shamir, 1995) and can be broadly categorized into Embedding of Watermark and Detection of Watermark stages.

Within the embedding stage, the algorithm begins with the share creation phase wherein the binary watermark image is split into two noise-like pseudo random shares. The binary format (0,1) of the watermark information is converted to the (-1, +1) signed format which gives a pseudo-random watermark sequence which is approximately zero mean. In the following phase of the proposed algorithm, the frames of the video are temporally scrambled by the use of a Linear Feedback Shift Register (LFSR) as illustrated in Figure 3. Initial condition of the LFSR serves as the private key in the watermark detection stage.

A one to one mapping is maintained between the frames of the original video and the temporally scrambled video. The next phase which is the share insertion phase scales the shares by a parameter (α) that determines the strength of the watermark and combines them with the scrambled video frames. The final watermarked video sequence is produced by the inverse temporal scrambling process. The watermark detection stage, shown in Figure 4, begins with passing the watermarked video through a high pass filter (HPF) which preserves the high frequency components in the noise- like watermark sequence. Subsequently, the video is temporally scrambled once again such that the frames containing

Figure 3. Embedding of watermark
(Houmansadr and Ghaemmaghami, 2006).

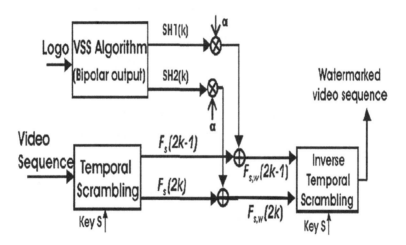

Figure 4. Retrieval of watermark
(Houmansadr and Ghaemmaghami, 2006).

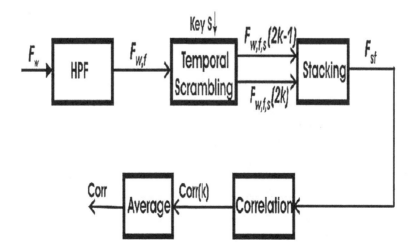

the shares now lie adjacent to each other. As a result $\dfrac{L}{2}$ stacked frames are obtained where a pixel by pixel comparison between the stacked frames are done, followed by a reduction of the stacked image from $(2M \times 2N)$ pixels to $(M \times N)$ pixels. The detection algorithm uses the principle that stacking frames, containing corresponding shares of the logo, makes higher correlation with the logo, as compared to stacked frames containing non- relevant shares of the logo. The correlation between the $\dfrac{L}{2}$ stacked frames and the binary watermark is calculated to check the presence of the watermark.

In this simple and effective spatial domain method (Houmansadr and Ghaemmaghami, 2006), the inserted watermark shows high resilience against some attacks, such as geometrical distortions and collusion attacks. However, the scheme is in spatial domain which provides a lower robustness to steganalysis in comparison to VC based watermarking techniques of the transformed domain. Further, since the shares are embedded into the host video in the watermark embedding stage, the process alters the contents of the host and hence degrades it.

The strength of the algorithm is tested by performing several attacks. As mentioned above, the correlation between the $\dfrac{L}{2}$ stacked frames and the binary watermark is calculated to check the presence of the watermark. Tables 1-3 (Houmansadr and Ghaemmaghami, 2006) show a decrement in the correlation coefficient after performing attacks such as frame cropping, frame rotating and changing the aspect ratio of the watermarked video sequence . Also, the watermarked sequence is found to have good robustness against geometric distortions. Table 4 shows resistance of this scheme to frame scaling. Table 5 demonstrates the average true to false ratio detection ratio when the watermarked sequence is M-JPEG compressed with different quality factors.

Table 1. Decrement of correlation coefficient after frame cropping (keeping middle of frames)

Cropping Percentage	Decrement of Correlation Coefficient(%)
10	8
20	10
30	6
40	11
50	16

Table 2. Decrement of correlation coefficient after frame rotation

Rotation Angle	Decrement of Correlation Coefficient(%)
10	8
20	10
30	6
40	11
50	16

*Table 3. Decrement of correlation coefficient after changing the AR of 240 * 360 pixels watermarked frames*

New Size Pixels	Decrement of Correlation Coefficient(%)
240 * 180	15
240 * 90	12
480 * 360	29

Table 4. Decrement of correlation coefficient after frame scaling

Scaling Ratio	Decrement of Correlation Coefficient(%)
2	29
4	31
8	39

Table 5. Average true to false detection ratio after M-JPEG compression for different quality factors

Quality Factor	Average True to False Detection Ratio
100	7.83
90	5.20
80	2.75
60	1.72
40	1.53

3.2 Work by Zeng and Pei, (2008)

Later, Zeng and Pei, (2008), suggested a novel video diagnosing method where the generation of crypto watermarks was carried out by using the concept of visual cryptography. Here, significant information in the form of crypto-watermarks is embedded into the video through a Dual Domain Quaternary Watermarking Algorithm which lends robustness to the scheme. The proposed method can identify the attack category (frame attack and temporal attack) and the video authentication type (whether video is a watermarked video or non-watermarked video).

The first stage of the algorithm is the generation of such crypto- watermarks while the next stage embeds the crypto-watermarks using the quaternary watermarking algorithm. The crypto-watermarks are generated through visual cryptography from binary images and have different resistances against different attacks. Four crypto-watermarks, namely first watermark (w_1), second watermark (w_2), intra-watermark (w_3) and inter-watermark (w_4) are generated as shown in Figure 5. Here, w_1 and w_2 form the quaternary watermark w_q. This quaternary watermark is added into the intra frame in the DCT domain in the embedding stage. During the watermark extraction stage at the receiver end, the data stream is divided into (8×8) non overlapping blocks and then w_q is extracted by calculating sample values in the DCT domain.

The bit-error-rate (BER) between the extracted watermarks of the suspected video and the original crypto watermarks is measured. Analysis of BER determines the nature of attack on the video. Based on a comparison of BER's between the first, second, intra and inter watermarks, status of frame attack is assigned. The status can be used to diagnose a video to be a non-watermarked video, authorized video, recompressed video and unauthorized frame inserted video.

Important applications of this methodology include dispute resolving, content identity verification and prevention of illegal video editing. However, the decryption process is not done by merely overlaying the shares. Since the watermark extraction process involves computations in the DCT domain followed by calculation of sample, it causes a computational overhead. Thus the inherent advantage of visual cryptography that is, extracting the secret information directly by the human visual system without the use of any complex computational process, is compromised. Also, similar to the method proposed by Houmansadr and Ghaemmaghami, (2006), this is an intrusive method and operates by directly embedding the watermark into the contents of the host.

Figure 5. Generation of crypto-watermarks
Zeng and Pei, (2008).

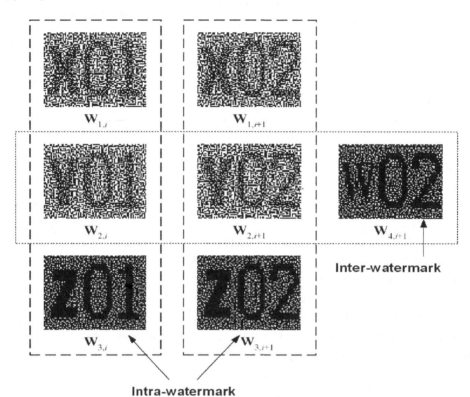

3.3 Work by Vashistha, Nallusamy, Das, & Paul (2010)

In both previous mentioned techniques, content of host audio is modified. Vashistha et.al (2010) proposed a method that employs $(2,2)$ visual cryptography, scene change detection and extraction of features from scene to create *Verification Information* (VI). The authors' have rightly coined the term *'non-intrusive watermarking'* for visual cryptographic schemes since the information of the watermark has been extracted by creation of shares applying the principles of visual cryptography rather than embedding watermark information directly into the cover content (host image or video). This is indeed a major advantage over the previously mentioned schemes of Houmansadr and Ghaemmaghami, (2006) and Zeng and Pei, (2008).

The process to generate VI for watermark pattern (w) of size $(h \times l)$ and an original 256 gray-leveled image (I) of size $(m \times n)$ with the help of a secret key (S) and by the rule shown in Figure 6. The VI is constructed by assembling all the (VI_1, VI_2) pairs. In the verification process, the authenticity of the image $\left(\hat{I}\right)$ is assessed by using the inverse process. The above process is used in the context of videos by first performing scene change detection and then by forming a scene averaged image which is converted into grey scale for computing the VI. The number of scenes detected decides the number of VI vectors since these two values have to be necessarily equal. The VI vector is thus one of the shares generated from the watermark pattern and the secret image.

Figure 6. Rules for retrieval of watermark
Vashistha et.al (2010).

Color of ith pixel in W	The MSB of R_i^{th} pixel of image I	Assign (V_{i1}, V_{i2}) of VI to be
Black	1	(0,1)
Black	0	(1,0)
White	1	(1,0)
White	0	(0,1)

Since no data is embedded into the host video in this technique, the method is resilient to attacks aimed at distorting the data embedded into videos. The method is particularly effective against frame averaging, frame dropping, frame swapping and interpolation attacks. All watermarked scenes, and not just individual frames, need to be dropped for an effective attack. Dropping of scenes makes illegal copying and distribution pointless and thus automatically discourages malpractices. A major contribution of this scheme is that it can survive as much as a 50% frame drop attacks. However, the scheme is in the spatial domain which makes it less robust than its transform domain counterparts.

3.4 Work by Singh, R., Singh, M. & Roy (2011)

Singh et al. (2011) implemented VC based scheme based on DWT transform domain and scene change detection. Here, 1- level Discrete Wavelet Transform (DWT) is applied on averaged frame and features are extracted from LL sub band. The watermark is split into sub-watermarks, the number of sub-watermarks being equal to the number of detected scenes. Frame mean μ_k of all k frames in a scene and global mean (μ) of the frame mean in a scene are found by taking the average of all corresponding pixel values in all frames in the same scene and the average of all pixel values in the frame mean in the same scene respectively.

Next, the construction of owner's share is done by checking the pixel value of the binary watermark and comparing the pixel value of the frame mean of same scene of the video with the global mean. Since, different parts of a single watermark are used in different scenes while the same sub-watermark is used for the different frames of a same scene the algorithm becomes robust to frame attacks like frame averaging, frame dropping, frame swapping and interpolation attacks. The identification share is generated by comparing the frame mean $\hat{\mu}_k$ of the suspected video with the global mean μ of this frame mean. The stacking of both the shares reveals copyright information. An overview of this scheme is demonstrated in Figures 7(a) and 7(b). The robustness of DWT to noise attacks and the security and simplicity of VC makes this technique easy to implement.

Though all above mentioned VC based video watermarking schemes have tried to achieve high imperceptibility and robustness, they suffer from limitations imposed by VC technique itself. For any VC scheme, resolution of extracted secret watermark binary image is degraded due to pixel expansion (Naor & Shamir, 1995). Here, pixel expansion increases apparent randomness and security but often leads to a poorer quality of extracted watermark. Therefore, a compromise between security and resolution

Figure 7a. Overview of the watermarking process by Singh et.al (2011): generation of owner's share

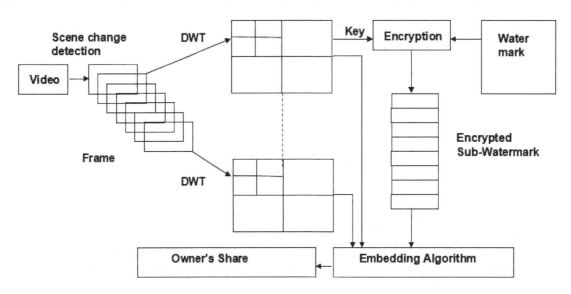

Figure 7b. Overview of the watermarking process by Singh et.al (2011): generation of identification share

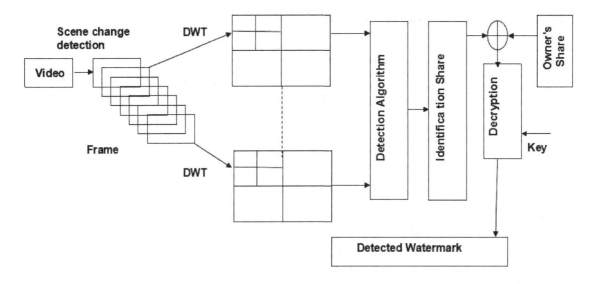

should be made for successful implementation of these VC based schemes. Also, certain VC schemes operate by dividing the host image or video into non-overlapping blocks and then by selecting only a few blocks on which the feature extraction techniques are applied (Singh et. al., 2011). When a smaller block size is chosen, the number of blocks obviously increases. Thus, there is more randomness in selecting the blocks which enhances the security of the scheme (Barari & Dhavale, 2013). On the other hand, a larger block size captures the features of the host more effectively as compared to a smaller block size. Therefore, a tradeoff needs to be achieved in between level of security and feature extraction accuracy too. A thorough performance comparison is given in Table 6.

Table 6. Performance comparison of various VC based watermarking schemes for videos

S. No.	Proposed Scheme	Year	No. of Shares	Domain	Intrusive /Non-Intrusive	Techniques Used	Performance Mentioned in Related Work
1	Houmansadr and Ghaemmag hami	2006	2	Spatial	intrusive	Temporal Scrambling, Stacking, Correlation	For 50% frame cropping decrement in correlation coefficient 16%; For 8 times frame scaling, decrement in correlation coefficient 39%;
2	Zeng and Pei	2008	4	Dual Domain (DCT and Spatial)	intrusive	Inter-Frame and Intra-Frame Crypto watermark generation	Average PSNR found to be 52.78 dB for original frames and 42.18 dB for watermark; capable of identifying different types of attacks.
3	Vashistha et al.	2010	2	Spatial	non-intrusive	Construction of Verification Information, Scene change detection by segmentation based on colour difference histogram, Scene averaging.	Survives as much as a 50% frame drop
4	Singh et al.	2013	2	DWT	non-intrusive	Scene change detection, scene averaging	NC above 0.95 for all kinds of frame attacks

Visual Cryptography has proven to be a simple, robust and non-intrusive video watermarking technique. Utilizing the power of visual secret sharing methods for may offer a very attractive and robust solution for different sectors like defence or military video based communication services, music industries to establish their rightful copyright ownerships, digital video forensic applications etc.

In VC based techniques, identifying the salient features is a primary task, which helps in creation of the Master share M. Thus, saliency detection in videos in case of VC based video watermarking techniques is an important consideration. The following section explains the importance of video saliency detection in video watermarking schemes.

4. IMPORTANCE OF VIDEO SALIENCY DETECTION IN WATERMARKING

Saliency detection is widely used to extract regions of interest (ROIs) in images or in video frames for various image and video processing applications such as segmentation, classification, watermarking etc. The number of image saliency detection models proposed in literature is many during the last decade (Hou & Zhang., 2007; Guo & Zhang, 2010). Compared to image saliency detection, video saliency detection algorithms are much more computationally intensive since they have to account for motion in between video frames since motion features attract the Human Visual System. Currently, several studies have tried to detect salient regions in video (Guo & Zhang, 2010; Shuai, Zhang, Liu, Liu, Feng, 2011).

As mentioned previously saliency detection plays a vital role in video watermarking. Video watermarking schemes use perceptually salient regions to embed the watermark information. According to some schemes suggested in literature (Fang, Lin,Chen, Tsai & Lin, 2013), a watermark must be placed in the perceptually significant components of the host signal for it to be robust to distortions and malicious attacks. Thus, the perceptually most significant components are the salient regions of the host signal and must be explicitly identified and extracted. In contrast to this view, a few other schemes claim that modification of perceptually significant components of the host signal may result in faster perceptual distortions. Thus, the watermark should be placed in the perceptually insignificant portions of the host image or video. Consequently, many watermarking schemes that focus on extracting the perceptually significant features were developed by researchers. Such techniques which aim at extracting regions of perceptual significance in images and videos are known as *Saliency Region Extraction* techniques (Fang et. al., 2013).

Previous schemes are based on uncompressed domain but most of the videos on the internet are available in compressed format. A few techniques have been developed in the recent years which perform video watermarking in the compressed domain. A scheme proposed in (Ding-Yu & Long-Wen, 2006) uses the phase angle of the motion vectors in the inter-frame as the salient features to embed data in a video. A different approach has been suggested in (Aly, 2011) to achieve a lesser distortion to prediction error and lower data size overhead in comparison to (Ding-Yu & Long-Wen, 2006). Here, motion vectors whose associated macroblocks prediction error is high are taken to be candidate motion vectors (CMV). The CMVs which become the salient features are then used to hide a bit of data in their horizontal and vertical components.

Shanableh (2012) later proposed two novel approaches to which gave a higher message extraction accuracy and payload. In the first approach message bits are concealed by modifying the quantization scale of the MPEG video. Feature extraction is performed by for individual macroblocks and a second order regression model is computed to predict the content of the hidden message. Though this procedure has a high level of prediction accuracy the payload is restricted to one bit per macroblock. The second approach proposed in (Shanableh, 2012) benefits from a high message payload with negligible drop in the PSNR levels. This solution uses Flexible Macroblock Ordering (FMO) to direct the encoder to create slice groups (independently coded and decoded units). This approach is compatible with H.264/AVC standards and is independent of the frame type being used (Intra frame Predicted frame or Bidirectional Frame), so it is advantageous from the point of view of implementation.

All of these schemes modify the content of the host video which in turn affects the host video quality. Instead of mentioned traditional watermarking schemes, we can use VC based techniques effectively for copyright protection. In VC based watermarking techniques, creating Master share M using the salient video features adds more robustness towards different kinds of video attacks. Thus, saliency detection in videos becomes an important consideration.

In the following section, we present a novel approach that uses motion vectors in the MPEG domain as salient features for generating master share for VC based video watermarking. Randomly selected motion vectors from the available motion vectors are used to create the Master Share M. M is further used to generate Ownership Share O.

5. PROPOSED VC BASED VIDEO WATERMARKING APPROACH USING MOTION VECTORS AS SALIENT FEATURES

All of the above VC based video watermarking techniques, depict watermarking of uncompressed videos wherein share creation is usually done by using pixel values of the individual frames or by applying some transform operations on the pixel values of frames. These techniques are good for the purpose of authentication, copyright protection or patenting a video. However, they fail to suggest a technique, where the required data can be hidden and retrieved by using the features of the video in compressed domain itself. Extraction of compressed domain features is expected increase the resilience towards compression attacks, thus making it compression invariant. Although the existing schemes show a good amount of robustness against most attacks, it is observed that their resilience against attacks involving the change of compression scale decreases rapidly with increase in the number of attacked frames of the video. To overcome this disadvantage of the above mentioned existing schemes, the salient features of the video in the compressed MPEG domain is targeted in the proposed work.

The novelty of the proposed scheme arises from the fact that it uses the salient MPEG domain motion features derived from the host video for the purpose of share creation. Here, the unique motion features that are extracted from the host video are the motion vectors. The reason for selecting motion vectors as unique features is that they are processed internally during the video encoding/decoding which makes it hard to be detected by image and video steganalysis methods. Also, motion vectors are loss less coded, thus they are not prone to quantization distortions (Shuai et. al. 2011). Hence, more robustness of the watermark against different malicious and non-malicious attacks, and more specifically against compression scale attacks, is ensured. Motion vectors are coded in the compressed stream and allow to reconstruct motion compensated macroblocks. Their extraction is very simple and fast and does not require a full decompression of the video stream which makes the algorithm computationally efficient (Shuai et. al. 2011). Further computational economy comes from having only one motion vector for each (16 x 16) macroblock.

In the following sections, the different modules of the proposed MVP Algorithm have been explained. The MPEG encoder flowchart is presented in the Figure 8. The MPEG encoder converts the video in raw Y4M/YUV format to compressed MPEG format.

Figure 8. MPEG encoder

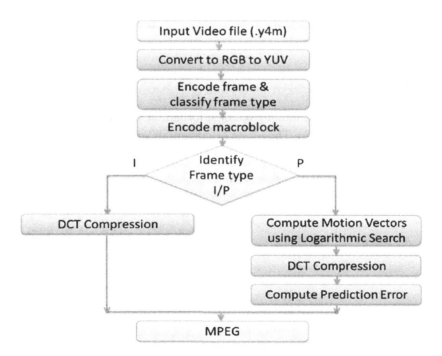

5.1 Motion Feature Extraction

The proposed schemes use two distinct features of the motion vectors:

1. Length or magnitude, and
2. Phase of the motion vectors as its salient features.

The magnitude of a motion vector MV_i is computed as follows:

$$MV_i = \sqrt{MV_{iH}^2 + MV_{iV}^2} \tag{1}$$

where MV_{iH} is the horizontal component and MV_{iV} is the vertical component of the ith motion vector of a P frame. A large magnitude of a motion vectors indicates a fast moving object the modification of a motion vector with large magnitude is less perceivable than that of a smaller magnitude motion vector (Shuai et. al. 2011). The phase of a motion vector ϑ_i is computed as follows:

$$\theta_i = \arctan\left(\frac{MV_{iV}}{MV_{iH}}\right) \tag{2}$$

Figure 9 gives a diagrammatic representation of the phase of a motion vector MV_i.

Since phase angle of a motion vector gives us an impression of the change in the position of blocks from one frame to the next, a less phase angle changed motion vector indicates that the shapes of the objects in the next frame are same as the previous frame. The motion vectors are computed in the MPEG encoder during the motion estimation stage. They are retrieved through computer programming before the share creation phase. Following this, the magnitude and phase parameters of the selected motion vectors are computed for share creation.

5.2 Share Creation Module

As discussed in the previous section, motion vector information such as phase and magnitude is extracted from the MPEG encoded video. The phase or magnitude information of the randomly selected

Figure 9. Representation of phase of a motion vector

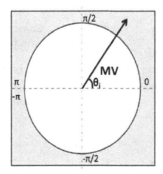

motion vectors is converted to a binary matrix B as per the rules which will be discussed in this section. The binary matrix B and the binary watermark image W are now compared on a pixel to pixel basis. B and W are the inputs to the Share Creation Module which creates the Master Share (M) according to the following rules:

If B_i is a white pixel, then $M_i = \begin{bmatrix} 1 & 0 \\ 0 & 1 \end{bmatrix}$

If B_i is a black pixel, then $M_i = \begin{bmatrix} 0 & 1 \\ 1 & 0 \end{bmatrix}$

The *M* generated is of the size *(2m x 2n)* . After generating the *M*, we generate an Owner Share (*O*) by combining the *M* and the pixels of *W*. The construction of the *O* is as follows:

If $W_i = 1$ and $M_i = \begin{bmatrix} 1 & 0 \\ 0 & 1 \end{bmatrix}$ then $O = \begin{bmatrix} 1 & 0 \\ 0 & 1 \end{bmatrix}$

If $W_i = 1$ and $M_i = \begin{bmatrix} 0 & 1 \\ 1 & 0 \end{bmatrix}$ then $O = \begin{bmatrix} 0 & 1 \\ 1 & 0 \end{bmatrix}$

If $W_i = 0$ and $M_i = \begin{bmatrix} 1 & 0 \\ 0 & 1 \end{bmatrix}$ then $O = \begin{bmatrix} 0 & 1 \\ 1 & 0 \end{bmatrix}$

If $W_i = 0$ and $M_i = \begin{bmatrix} 0 & 1 \\ 1 & 0 \end{bmatrix}$ then $O = \begin{bmatrix} 1 & 0 \\ 0 & 1 \end{bmatrix}$

The O again is of the size *(2m x 2n)*. O should be registered with a higher authority for further authentication.

During creation of the share, the proposed scheme assumes that the binary watermark image W represents the ownership information like company logo image etc. In order to extend the usability of proposed algorithm for fingerprinting applications i.e. buyer specific watermarking, a secret unique key K_s can be maintained for recognizing each buyer. During share creation module, K_s will decide the selection of the motion vectors or/and will permute the binary watermark image W before creating share. In this case, the created Owner Share O can able to identify the compromised buyer among the set of legitimate buyers.

5.3 Watermark Extraction Module

At the receiving end, the watermark may be revealed by stacking M generated at the receiver end and the O retrieved from the CA. However, the size of this watermark is *(2m x 2n)* since both M and O are of this size. Thus, we need to reduce the extracted watermarks to get the original watermark. This is achieved by dividing the watermark obtained into *(2 x 2)* non-overlapping blocks. Let us denote these blocks by w'. Then, the reduced secret image W'' is

$$W''_{ij} = \left\{ 0 \, for \sum_i \sum_j w'_{i,j} < 2 \right\}$$

$$W''_{ij} = \left\{ 1 \, for \sum_i \sum_j w'_{i,j} \geq 2 \right\} \tag{3}$$

5.4 Proposed MVP Algorithm

In the proposed algorithm, initially Motion Vector Magnitude is used as the salient features of the MPEG domain. However, this algorithm was not able to sustain different types of attacks since a small variation in the magnitude of the selected motion vectors was enough to change the mean value of motion vectors. Consequently, there was a drop in the value of Normalized Correlation (NC). To overcome this drawback, Motion Vector Phase was used as a salient feature from the MPEG domain. Motion Vector Phase was able to overcome small perturbations in the value of motion features due to attacks. This made it much more robust to different kinds of attacks. However, on careful observation it was found that the outline of the watermark image was visible in the generated Owner Share. This was because while creating the shares, the phase values of motion vectors are used directly without any preprocessing and compared with the pixels of the watermark image on a one to one basis. This is dangerous in a situation where the malicious user has even the slightest hint or information about the watermark image. Thus, there was a need to devise an algorithm where the watermark information would be completely inconspicuous.

The proposed *MVP algorithm* stands for the Motion Vector Phase based VC video watermarking scheme. The salient features from the MPEG domain are motion vector phase features. MVP attempts to improve on the shortcomings of both the previous approaches by preprocessing the motion feature matrix instead of using the feature values directly. Here, the motion feature matrix is obtained by randomly selecting $\left(4 \times (m \times n)\right)$ number of motion vectors. The motion feature matrix is then split into blocks of size (4 x 1) each. The blocks are transformed to the DFT domain. Following this, SVD is used on each of the blocks so that a single value is obtained for each of the four motion vector phase values in the motion feature matrix. This single value represents features of each of the 4 values of the block. While DFT prevents us from using the motion vector phase information directly, SVD gives us a single value for one to one comparison in the Share Creation Module. MVP has been explained in details in this section.

Preprocessing Stage:

1. The uncompressed video in YUV/Y4M video is converted to a compressed format as per MPEG coding standards.

    Share creation stage:

1. Extract motion vectors from all P-Frames of the compressed host video h.
2. Select $\left(4 \times (m \times n)\right)$ motion vectors, using a pseudo-random number generator. The randomly selected motion vector positions are now appended to form the secret key K, which has to be transmitted to the authenticated personnel at the receiver end, through a secured channel.
3. Enter the randomly selected motion vector phase values in a $\left(4 \times (m \times n)\right)$ matrix called $MVPhase$.
4. Split $MVPhase$ into blocks of (4×1) size. Perform DFT followed by SVD on each block. Store the first singular value obtained from each block in $SVDFirstValmatrix$.
5. Calculate the binary matrix B from the matrix $SVDFirstValmatrix$ as

$$B_{ij} = 0 \text{ if } SVDFirstValmatrix < 180$$

$$B_{ij} = 1 \text{ } otherwise$$

Here 180 is used to decide the pixel of B_{ij}, since on inspection it is found that the entire range of transformed values is between 0 and 360.

6. Generate the M and the O according to the rules given in the Share Creation Module.
7. The O is registered with a higher Certified Authority (CA) for retrieval in case of any dispute regarding the ownership.

    The Share Creation Process of MVP has been shown in Figure 10.
    Watermark Extraction Stage:
    At the receivers end, HV' is the video received which may have been subjected to various malicious and non-malicious attacks. To establish rightful ownership, the watermark W needs to be extracted. The steps for watermark extraction are given as follows:

1. Retrieve Key K from secure channel.
2. Using K, identify the locations of the selected $\left(4 \times (m \times n)\right)$ number of motion vectors from HV and retrieve the magnitude of the corresponding locations from HV'.
3. Store the selected motion vector phase values in an $\left(4 \times (m \times n)\right)$ matrix called $MVAttPhase$.
4. Split $MVAttPhase$ into blocks of (4 x 1) size. Perform DFT followed by SVD on each block. Store the first singular value obtained from each block in $SVDFirstValAttMatrix$.
5. Calculate the binary matrix B from the matrix $SVDFirstValAttMatrix$ as

Figure 10. Share creation process of the proposed approach

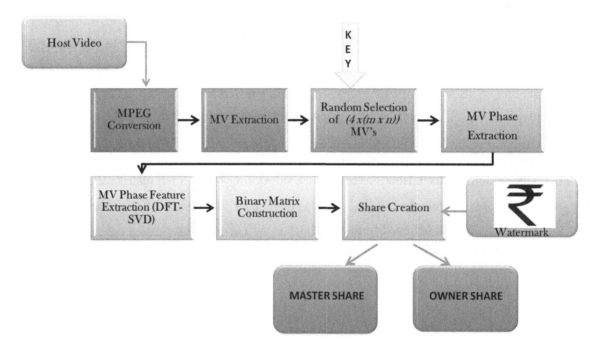

$$B_{ij} = 0 \text{ if } SVDFirstValAttMatrix < 180$$

$$B_{ij} = 1 \ otherwise$$

6. Again, the M' and the O' are created from B_{ij} and W_{ij} according to the rules explained in the Share Creation Module.
7. The O is retrieved from the CA and O and M' are stacked together to reveal the watermark W' by the process explained in Watermark Extraction Module. The size of W' is *(2m x 2n)*.
8. The secret image is reduced to *(m x n)* to get the retrieved watermark image.

The Watermark Extraction process in MVP has been shown in Figure 11.

The proposed MVP algorithm uses motion vector phase as its salient feature from the MPEG domain. MVP uses 4 times more the number of features from the host video. Following this, the use of DFT to convert each (4 x 1) block to the transform domain and the application of SVD to extract the robust feature from each block has ensured that imperceptibility of the watermark in the shares is preserved. Besides, the MVP algorithm also achieves a high value of NC for various kinds of attacks for the extracted watermark. The next chapter on experimental results and analysis validates all the proposed schemes against attacks.

This experiments carried by simulating the proposed algorithm in the MATLAB 2012 Platform. MPEG- 2 standards have been encoded and the code for MPEG-2 encoder (Steve Hoelzer) has been customized for implementing the VC based video watermarking schemes. Here, a source movie can be encoded into MPEG format and then can be decoded back into a MATLAB movie. A standard test video

Figure 11. Watermark extraction stage of the proposed approach

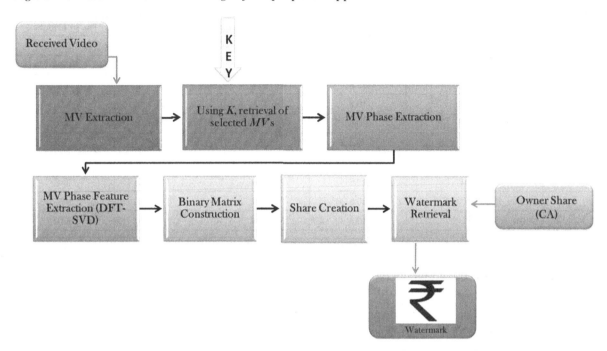

database consisting of movie sequences of the YUV and Y4M formats were selected for our analysis. The following video sequences which were used in the experiments as shown in Figure 12 are *Akiyo, Bowing, Carphone, Container, Coastguard, Flower, Foreman, Hall_Monitor, Mother_daughter* and *Silent*. The information regarding the format, height, width, size and number of frames has been tabulated in Table 7. Each of these videos is played at a frame rate of 30 frames per second (fps).

Figure 12. Standard video database

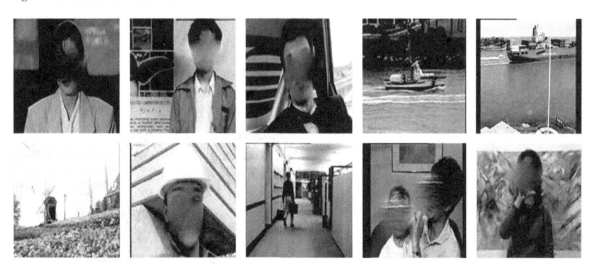

Table 7. Information regarding standard video database

S. No.	Video	Size (MB)	Width	Height	No. of Frames
1	Akiyo_qcif	10.8	176	144	300
2	Bowing_qcif	10.8	176	144	300
3	Carphone	13.8	176	144	382
4	Container_qcif	10.8	176	144	300
5	Coastguard_qcif	10.8	176	144	300
6	Flower_cif	36.2	352	288	250
7	Foreman_qcif	7.25	176	144	300
8	Hall_monitor_qcif	10.8	176	144	300
9	Mother_Daughter_qcif	10.8	176	144	300
10	Silent_qcif	10.8	176	144	300

In our simulations, these raw uncompressed videos are encoded using a GOP of 10 frames length with a frame pattern of *"IPPPPPPPP"*. The scaling factor used in MPEG compression module is set to the fixed value of 31 and has been varied only while performing compression scaling attacks on the proposed schemes.

In these videos, the frame resolution is either (176 x 144) pixels or (352 x 288) pixels. Each frame is divided into macroblocks of the size (16 x16). The one to one correspondence in between the number of macroblocks and motion vectors has already been observed. Hence, the number of macroblocks and correspondingly the number of motion vectors is obtained by dividing the resolution with the macroblock size. For instance, in a video frame with frame resolution of (176 x 144), a set of 99 motion vectors per frame are extracted. The motion vectors which have been encoded from random frames of the test video sequence *carphone* have been plotted as shown in Figure 13.

According to the proposed schemes, the salient features from the test video sequences are extracted, randomly selected, stored in a matrix and then compared on a pixel to pixel basis with the binary water-

Figure 13a. Motion vectors from random frames of carphone: Frame 2

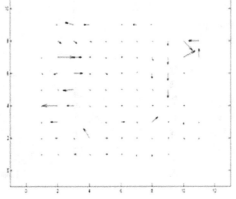

Figure 13b. Motion vectors from random frames of carphone: Frame 9

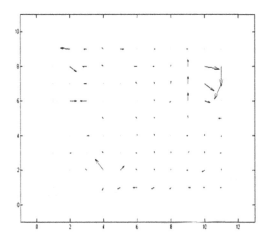 

mark image. This forms the basis for share creation. At the receiving end, *M'* and *O* are overlaid upon each other to reveal the watermark. The retrieved watermark is then evaluated on the basis of standard parameters which are discussed in the next subsection.

5.5 Watermark Evaluation Parameters

A watermarking scheme is evaluated on the basis of criteria like perceptibility, reliability, robustness, capacity, speed of implementation and statistical detectability. MSE (Mean Square Error), PSNR (Peak Signal to Noise Ratio) and NC (Normalized Correlation) are some of the popular metrics which are used for evaluating a watermark scheme (Petitcolas, F.A.P, 2000). While implementing the proposed algorithms, the algorithm was validated for robustness to various attacks based on these metrics.

Peak signal to noise ratio (PSNR) is used in this paper to analyze the visual quality of the extracted watermark W in comparison to the original watermark W. PSNR gives us a measure of the degree of distortion to the watermark and given as in Equation (4).

$$PSNR = 10 \log_{10} \left(\frac{255^2}{MSE} \right) db \qquad (4)$$

where MSE is the mean-square error given as

$$MSE = \frac{1}{MN} \sum_{i=0}^{M-1} \sum_{j=0}^{N-1} \left[W_{i,j} - \hat{W}_{i,j} \right]^2 \qquad (5)$$

Normalized Correlation (NC) is the measure of similarity between the original and extracted watermarks. The closer NC value is to 1, more is the similarity between W and W. The expression for NC is given in Equation (3).

$$NC = \frac{\sum_{i=0}^{m}\sum_{j=0}^{n}\overline{W_{i,j} \oplus \hat{W}_{i,j}}}{(m \times n)} \tag{6}$$

where denotes the exclusive-or (XOR) operation and *(m × n)* is the size of the watermark.

5.6 Performance against Attacks

In the following section, the performance of the watermark against various kinds of attacks is evaluated against these watermark evaluation parameters. MVP Algorithm is tested for robustness against various different types of attacks. NC, PSNR and MSE values are calculated to obtain a comprehensive quantitative analysis. The generated shares and retrieved watermarks for Frame drop attack and Gaussian noise attack have been shown.

5.6.1 Frame Drop Attack

An attacker can attempt to distort the video and yet conserve its visual quality by dropping a few frames. A large percentage of frame drops may create unnecessary suspicion for the attacker. Here in in Figure 14, the quality of the extracted watermark has been shown for a frame drop attack where 10 frames are dropped from a 300 frame video sequence. Figures 14 (a) and 14 (b), shows the generated Master shares and Owner shares while 14 (c) shows the extracted watermark retrieved by overlaying the two shares. The corresponding NC, MSE and PSNR values have also been shared.

Figure 14a. Master share
NC = 0.9404; MSE = 0.0596; PSNR = 54 db

Figure 14b. Owner share
NC = 0.9404; MSE = 0.0596; PSNR = 54 db

Figure 14c. Extracted watermark for frame drop attack for MVP
NC = 0.9404; MSE = 0.0596; PSNR = 54 db

5.6.2 Gaussian Noise Attack

To validate the proposed algorithms against Gaussian noise attack, frames of the video were subjected to Gaussian noise at zero mean and different local variances ranging from 0.01 to 0.1. The results for a Gaussian noise attack of 10 frames out of a 300 frame video being subjected to a Gaussian noise with a noise variance of 0.01, have been shown in Figure 15. Figures 15 (a) and 15 (b), shows the generated Master shares and Owner shares while 15 (c) shows the extracted watermark obtained after overlaying the two shares. Also, the corresponding NC, MSE and PSNR values have also been shared.

A graphical representation of the performance MVP against 15 different types of attacks has been shown.

Here, the NC values for different attacks is plotted against the number of frames being subjected to that attack. It is observed that MVP sustains as much as 20% of frame attack without causing any severe

Figure 15a. Master share
NC = 0.9504; MSE = 0.0496; PSNR = 53 db

Figure 15b. Owner share
NC = 0.9504; MSE = 0.0496; PSNR = 53 db

Figure 15c. Extracted Watermark for Gaussian noise attack for MVP
NC = 0.9504; MSE = 0.0496; PSNR = 53 db

distortion to the watermark. A high value of Normalized Correlation (NC) of the extracted watermark for attacks, particularly for frame drop, scaling, averaging and sharpening attacks, proves that MVP has a good amount of robustness against these attacks. See Figure 16 (a)-(p).

Table 8 tabulates the average values of NC and PSNR for all attacks when performed using the Standard Binary Test Image Database with images of size (64 x 64 size) shown in Figure 17. An important observation here is the MPEG Compression scale change attack which has been performed by varying the compression scale of the MPEG video from 1 to 112. It is observed that in spite of varying the compression through the entire range, there is no severe degradation in the quality of the extracted watermark. Thus, we may say that Compression Scale Invariance is achieved in the proposed algorithm.

Figure 16a.

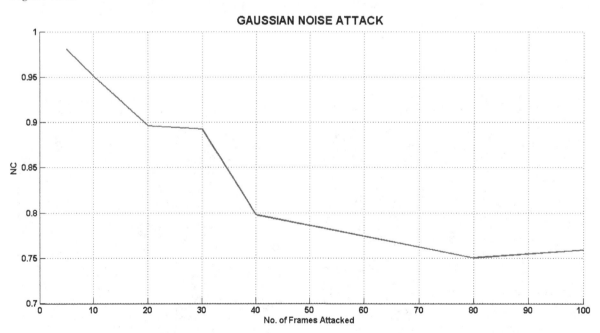

Figure 16b. Graphical analysis of performance of MVP algorithm against following attacks: frame drop

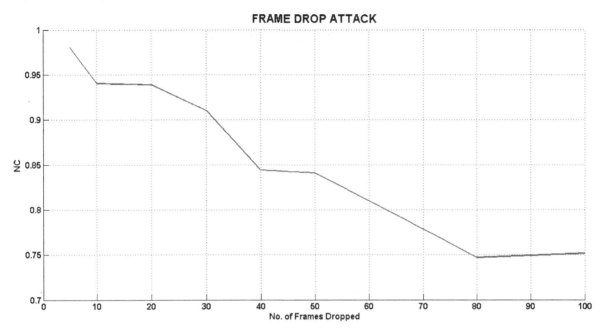

Figure 16c. Graphical analysis of performance of MVP algorithm against following attacks: averaging attack

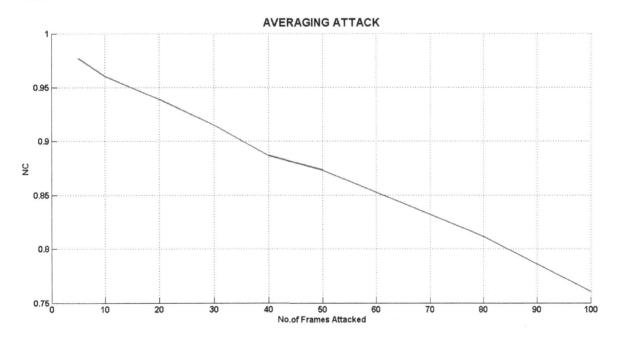

Figure 16d. Graphical analysis of performance of MVP algorithm against following attacks: salt & pepper noise

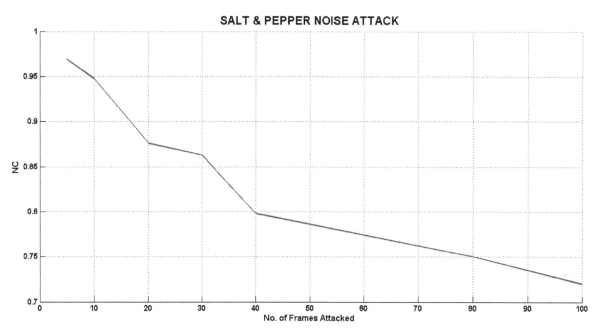

Figure 16e. Graphical analysis of performance of MVP algorithm against following attacks: Gaussian noise

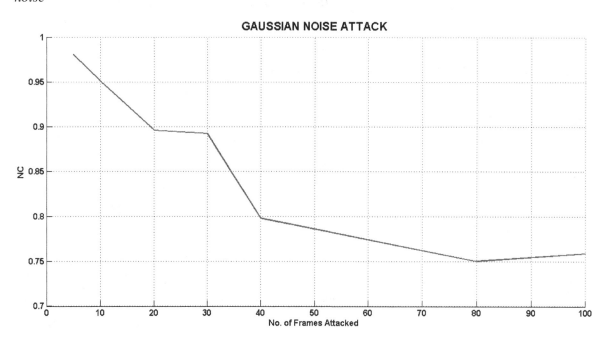

Figure 16f. Graphical analysis of performance of MVP algorithm against following attacks: motion blur

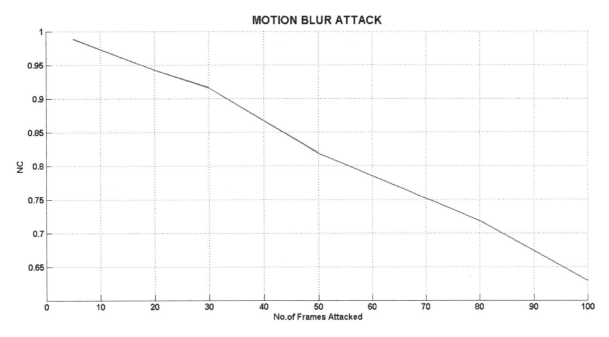

Figure 16g. Graphical analysis of performance of MVP algorithm against following attacks: sharpening attack

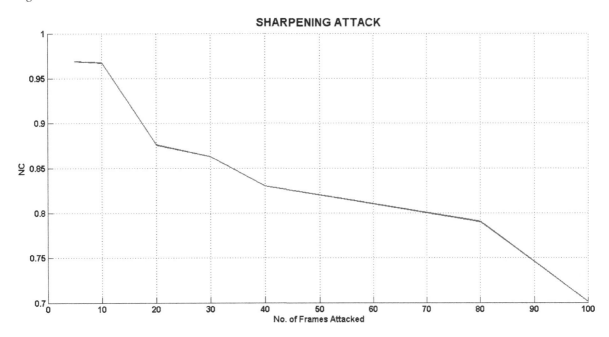

Figure 16h. Graphical analysis of performance of MVP algorithm against following attacks: blurring attack

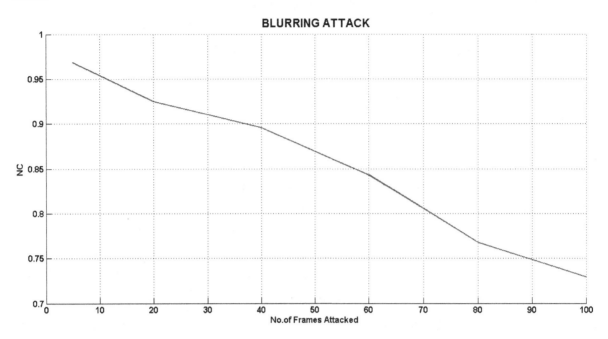

Figure 16i. Graphical analysis of performance of MVP algorithm against following attacks: histogram equalization

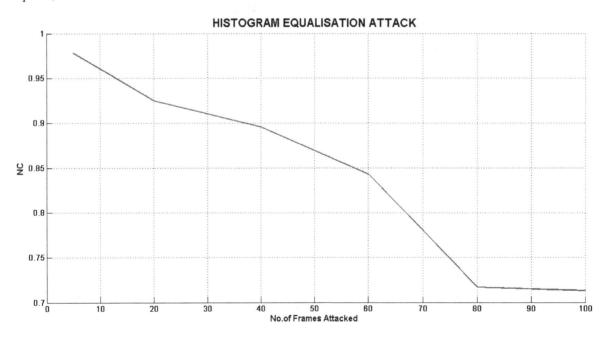

Figure 16j. Graphical analysis of performance of MVP algorithm against following attacks: cropping

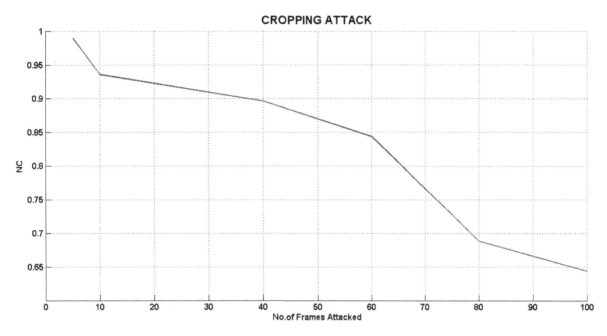

Figure 16k. Graphical analysis of performance of MVP algorithm against following attacks: image negative attack

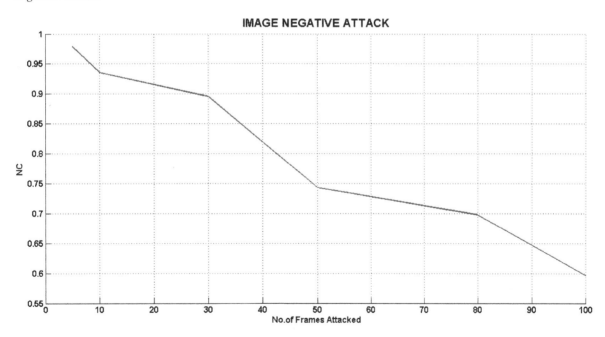

Figure 16l. Graphical analysis of performance of MVP algorithm against following attacks: rotation attack

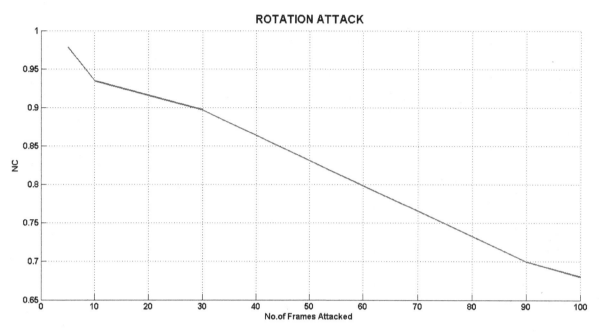

Figure 16m. Graphical analysis of performance of MVP algorithm against following attacks: scaling attack

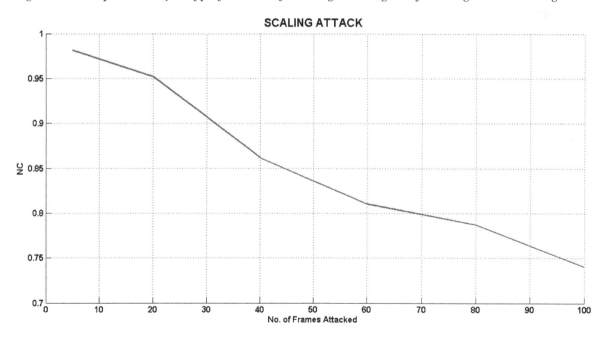

Figure 16n. Graphical analysis of performance of MVP algorithm against following attacks: gamma correction attack

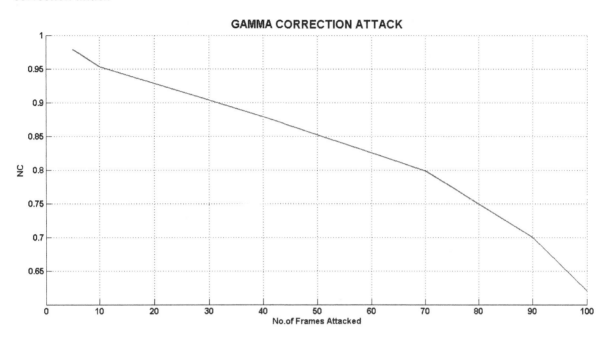

Figure 16o. Graphical analysis of performance of MVP algorithm against following attacks: median filtering attack

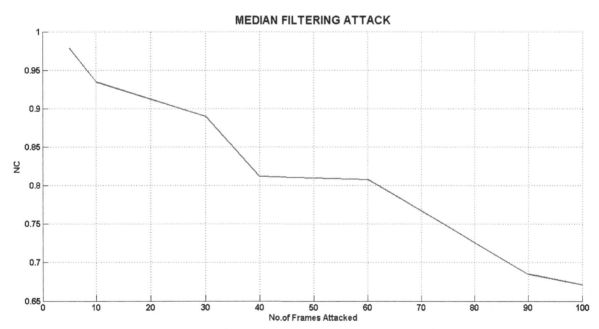

Figure 16p. Graphical analysis of performance of MVP algorithm against following attacks: MPEG compression scale change

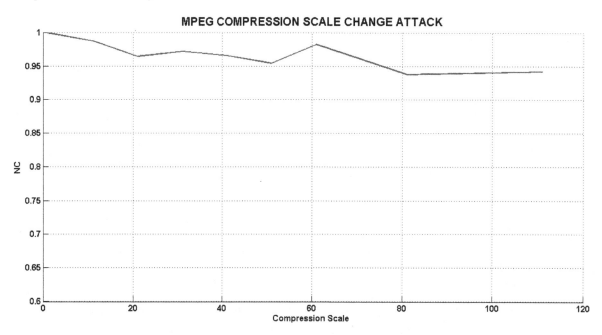

Table 8. Average NC and PSNR values for watermark retrieved using algorithm MVP

Attacks	MVP	
	NC	PSNR (dB)
Frame Drop	0.9379	54.17
Averaging Attack	0.9645	48.73
Salt & Pepper Noise	0.9457	53.78
Gaussian Noise	0.9553	53.05
Motion Blur	0.9420	54.87
Sharpening Attack	0.9645	49.73
Blurring	0.9278	57.63
Histogram Equalization	0.9271	57.78
Cropping	0.9369	56.01
Image Negative Attack	0.9271	56.08
Rotation Attack	0.9308	56.84
Scaling Attack	0.9817	43.08
Gamma Correction Attack	0.9364	55.67
Median Filtering Attack	0.9604	47.80
Compression Scale Change Attack	0.9845	41.73

Figure 17. Standard binary test image database (all of 64 x 64 size)

5.7 Performance Analysis

A payload of 1 bits per macro block is achieved in MVP Algorithm. The validation of the proposed scheme has been carried out by conducting 15 different types of attacks on the host video. It is found that the retrieved watermark is visually recognizable after all attacks which prove the robustness of the algorithm. Also, it is observed that change of quality scale of the MPEG from 1 to 112 by the attacker does not render the watermark unidentifiable as seen in Figure 16(p). Thus, compression scale invariance is also achieved. Since the feature extraction module is based on general MPEG coding, the proposed algorithms can be integrated in the MPEG Encoder for real time applications. Furthermore, the retrieval of the hidden data by an unauthorized person or malicious attacker is extremely difficult because the Ownership Share is registered with a CA. The proposed also method provides a good tradeoff between ease of implementation and security.

6. FUTURE RESEARCH DIRECTIONS

In all VC based video watermarking schemes, each host video corresponds to a secret image that is registered to a certified authority (CA). When the number of cover videos is large, it will be a heavy burden for the CA to store all the secret images. Hence in future a solution to this problem needs to be addressed.

Also a robust salient features need to be extracted from the video data in order to create the master share and hence to increase the robustness of the algorithm further. From simulation results of MVP Algorithm, it has been observed that as more number of salient features i.e. motion vectors are selected from the available motion vector set, there is a decrease in the robustness of the extracted watermark. This is because with increase in selected motion vectors, the randomness of watermark embedding decreases. Research may be carried out in future to increase the robustness of the proposed algorithms for a higher percentage of frame attacks.

7. CONCLUSION

In this chapter, importance of visual cryptography technique in non-intrusive video watermarking is evaluated. The chapter also states the pros and cons of the existing research works for non-intrusive video watermarking. Further the importance of saliency detection in general video watermarking and creation of master share in VC based watermarking has been discussed. Finally, a novel robust visual cryptography based video watermarking approach (MVP Algorithm) has been proposed which uses motion vector phase features of the video from the MPEG domain as salient features for creation of master share. Experimental results shows that the proposed MVP Algorithm provides a good trade off among different parameters like robustness, embedding payload capacity, ease of implementation and security.

REFERENCES

Aly, H. (2011). Data Hiding in Motion Vectors of Compressed Video Based on Their Associated Prediction Error. *IEEE Transactions on Information Forensics and Security*, 14-18.

Barari, A., & Dhavale, S. (2013). An Overview of Visual Cryptography based Video Watermarking Schemes: Techniques and Performance Comparison. In *Proceedings of International Conference on Advances in Computer Science, Association of Computer Electronics and Electrical Engineers*.

Bianchi, T., & Piva, A. (2013). Secure watermarking for multimedia content protection: A review of its benefits and open issues. *Signal Processing Magazine, IEEE*, *30*(2), 87–96. doi:10.1109/MSP.2012.2228342

Chen, S., & Leung, H. (2008). Chaotic watermarking for video authentication in surveillance applications. *Circuits and Systems for Video Technology. IEEE Transactions on*, *18*(5), 704–709.

Fang, D. Y., & Chang, L. W. (2006, May). Data hiding for digital video with phase of motion vector. In *Circuits and Systems, 2006. ISCAS 2006. Proceedings. 2006 IEEE International Symposium on*. IEEE.

Fang, Y., Lin, W., Chen, Z., Tsai, C. M., & Lin, C. W. (2014). A video saliency detection model in compressed domain. *Circuits and Systems for Video Technology. IEEE Transactions on*, *24*(1), 27–38.

Guo, C., & Zhang, L. (2010). A novel multiresolution spatiotemporal saliency detection model and its applications in image and video compression. *Image Processing. IEEE Transactions on*, *19*(1), 185–198.

Hartung, F., & Kutter, M. (1999). Multimedia watermarking techniques. *Proceedings of the IEEE*, *87*(7), 1079–1107. doi:10.1109/5.771066

Hou, X., & Zhang, L. (2007, June). Saliency detection: A spectral residual approach. In *Computer Vision and Pattern Recognition, 2007. CVPR'07. IEEE Conference on* (pp. 1-8). IEEE. doi:10.1109/CVPR.2007.383267

Houmansadr, A., & Ghaemmaghami, S. (2006, April). A novel video watermarking method using visual cryptography. In *Engineering of Intelligent Systems, 2006 IEEE International Conference on* (pp. 1-5). IEEE. doi:10.1109/ICEIS.2006.1703171

Liu, F., & Wu, C. K. (2011). Robust visual cryptography-based watermarking scheme for multiple cover images and multiple owners. *IET Information Security, 5*(2), 121-128.

Lou, D. C., Tso, H. K., & Liu, J. L. (2007). A copyright protection scheme for digital images using visual cryptography technique. *Computer Standards & Interfaces*, *29*(1), 125–131. doi:10.1016/j.csi.2006.02.003

Naor, M., & Shamir, A. (1995). Visual cryptography. In Advances in Cryptology—EUROCRYPT'94 (pp. 1-12). Springer Berlin/Heidelberg. doi:10.1007/BFb0053419

Petitcolas, F. A. (2000). Watermarking schemes evaluation. *Signal Processing Magazine, IEEE, 17*(5), 58–64. doi:10.1109/79.879339

Rawat, S., & Raman, B. (2012). A blind watermarking algorithm based on fractional Fourier transform and visual cryptography. *Signal Processing, 92*(6), 1480–1491. doi:10.1016/j.sigpro.2011.12.006

Shanableh, T. (2012). Data hiding in MPEG video files using multivariate regression and flexible macroblock ordering. *Information Forensics and Security. IEEE Transactions on, 7*(2), 455–464.

Shuai, B., Zhang, Q., Liu, J., Liu, X., & Feng, X. (2011, October). Saliency region extraction for MPEG video method based on visual selective attention. In *Image and Signal Processing (CISP), 2011 4th International Congress on* (Vol. 1, pp. 560-564). IEEE. doi:10.1109/CISP.2011.6099990

Singh, T. R., Singh, K. M., & Roy, S. (2013). Video watermarking scheme based on visual cryptography and scene change detection. *AEÜ. International Journal of Electronics and Communications, 67*(8), 645–651. doi:10.1016/j.aeue.2013.01.008

Sun, J., & Liu, J. (2005, September). A temporal desynchronization resilient video watermarking scheme based on independent component analysis. In *Image Processing, 2005. ICIP 2005. IEEE International Conference on* (Vol. 1, pp. I-265). IEEE.

University of Illinois at Chicago (UIC). (n.d.). Retrieved from http://www.cs.cf.ac.uk/Dave/Multimedia/ Lecture_Examples/Compression/ mpegproj/

Vashistha, A., Nallusamy, R., Das, A., & Paul, S. (2010, July). Watermarking video content using visual cryptography and scene averaged image. In *Multimedia and Expo (ICME), 2010 IEEE International Conference on* (pp. 1641-1646). IEEE. doi:10.1109/ICME.2010.5583256

Wang, M. S., & Chen, W. C. (2009). A hybrid DWT-SVD copyright protection scheme based on k-means clustering and visual cryptography. *Computer Standards & Interfaces, 31*(4), 757–762. doi:10.1016/j. csi.2008.09.003

Xu, C., Ping, X., & Zhang, T. (2006, August). Steganography in compressed video stream. In *Innovative Computing, Information and Control, 2006. ICICIC'06. First International Conference on* (Vol. 1, pp. 269-272). IEEE.

Zeng, Y. C., & Pei, S. C. (2008, May). Automatic video diagnosing method using embedded crypto-watermarks. In *Circuits and Systems, 2008. ISCAS 2008. IEEE International Symposium on* (pp. 3017-3020). IEEE.

ADDITIONAL READING

Al-Qaheri, H., Mustafi, A., & Banerjee, S. (2010). Digital Watermarking using Ant Colony Optimization in Fractional Fourier Domain. *Journal of Information Hiding and Multimedia Signal Processing, 1*(3).

Ardizzone, E., La Cascia, M., Avanzato, A., & Bruna, A. (1999, July). Video Indexing Using MPEG Motion Compensation Vectors, *IEEE International Conference on Multimedia Computing and Systems*, 2,(725–729) doi:10.1109/MMCS.1999.778574

Ateniese, G., Blundo, C., De Santis, A., & Stinson, D. R. (1996). Visual cryptography for general access structures. *Information and Computation*, *129*(2), 86–106. doi:10.1006/inco.1996.0076

Bo, W., Ming, X., & Zhang, C.-C. (2011). Realization of Digital Image Watermarking Encryption Algorithm Using Fractional Fourier Transform, *The 6th International Forum on Strategic Technology.*

Chang, C. C., & Chuang, J. C. (2002). An image intellectual property protection scheme for gray-level images using visual secret sharing strategy. *Pattern Recognition Letters*, *23*(8), 931–941. doi:10.1016/S0167-8655(02)00023-5

Choudhary,S., Yadav, S., Sen,N., & Nasreen, G. (2012). A Study of Image Fingerprinting by Using Visual Cryptography, Computer Engineering and Intelligent Systems, 3(7).

Fang, W. P., & Lin, J. C. (2006). Progressive viewing and sharing of sensitive images. *Pattern Recognition and Image Analysis*, *16*(4), 638–642. doi:10.1134/S1054661806040080

Faragallah, O. S. (2013). Efficient video watermarking based on singular value decomposition in the discrete wavelet transform domain. *International Journal of Electronics.And Communication.*, *67*(3), 189–196. doi:10.1016/j.aeue.2012.07.010

Ghouti, L., Bouridane, A., Ibrahim, M. K., & Boussakta, S. (2006). Digital Image Watermarking Using Balanced Multiwavelets. *IEEE Transactions on Signal Processing*, *54*(4), 1519–1536. doi:10.1109/TSP.2006.870624

Gonzalez, R., & Woods, R. (2002). *Digital image processing* (2nd ed.). Upper Saddle River, N.J.: Prentice Hall.

Hadizadeh, H., & Baji'c, I. V. (2014, January). Saliency-Aware Video Compression. *IEEE Transactions on Image Processing*, *23*(1), 19–33. doi:10.1109/TIP.2013.2282897 PMID:24107933

Hou, Y.-C., & Quan, Z.-Y. (2011, November). Progressive Visual Cryptography with Unexpanded Shares. *IEEE Transactions on Circuits and Systems for Video Technology*, *21*(11), 1760–1764. doi:10.1109/TCSVT.2011.2106291

Hwang, R.-J. (2000). A Digital Image Copyright Protection Scheme Based on Visual Cryptography. *Tamkang Journal of Science and Engineering*, *3*(2), 97–106.

Jianga, M., Maa, Z., Niua, X., & Yanga, Y. (2011). Video Watermarking Scheme Based on MPEG-2 for Copyright Protection, *3rd International Conference on Environmental Science and Information Application Technology (ESIAT 2011)*. doi:10.1016/j.proenv.2011.09.136

Lee, K.-H. & Chiu,P.L.(2012). An Extended Visual Cryptography Algorithm for General Access Structures, *IEEE Transactions On Information Forensics And Security*, 7(1).

Lin, C.-C., & Tsai, W.-H. (2003). Visual cryptography for gray-level images by dithering techniques. *Pattern Recognition Letters*, *24*(1-3), 349–358. doi:10.1016/S0167-8655(02)00259-3

Lin, E.-T., Eskicioglu, A. H., Reginald, L. L., & Edward, J. D. (2005, January). Advances in Digital Video Content Protection. *Proceedings of the IEEE, 93*(1), 171–183. doi:10.1109/JPROC.2004.839623

Lin, S.-F, & Chung,W.-H.(2012). A Probabilistic Model of *(t,n)* Visual Cryptography Scheme With Dynamic Group, *IEEE Transactions On Information Forensics And Security,* 7(1).

Ling, H., Wang, L., Zou, F., Lu, Z., & Li, P. (2011). Robust video watermarking based on affine invariant regions in the compressed domain. *Signal Processing, 91*(8), 1863–1875. doi:10.1016/j.sigpro.2011.02.009

Mehta, S., Vijayaraghavan, V., & Nallusamy, R. (2012). On-the-fly Watermarking of Videos for Real-time Applications, *IEEE International Conference on Multimedia and Expo Workshops.* doi:10.1109/ICMEW.2012.17

Oakes, M., & Abhayaratne, C. (2012, May). Visual saliency estimation for video. In Image Analysis for Multimedia Interactive Services (WIAMIS), 2012 13th International Workshop on (pp. 1-4). IEEE. doi:10.1109/WIAMIS.2012.6226751

Patel, S., & Yadav, A. R. (2011). Invisible Digital Video Watermarking Using 4-level DWT, *National Conference on Recent Trends in Engineering & Technology.*

Paul, R.T. (2011). Review of Robust Video Watermarking Techniques, *International Journal of Computer Applications Special Issue on "Computational Science - New Dimensions & Perspectives"..*

Sejdic, E., Djurovic, I., & Stankovic, L. (2011). Fractional Fourier transform as a signal processing tool:An overview of recent developments. *Signal Processing, 91*(6), 1351–1369. doi:10.1016/j.sigpro.2010.10.008

Shamir, A. (1979, November). How To Share A Secret. *Communications of the Association for Computer Machinery, 22*(11), 612–613. doi:10.1145/359168.359176

Wang, C.-C., & Lin, Y.-C. (2010). An automated system for monitoring the visual quality and authenticity of satellite video streams using a fragile watermarking approach. *Digital Signal Processing, 20*(3), 780–792. doi:10.1016/j.dsp.2009.10.005

Wang,L., Ling,H., Zou,F., & Lu,Z.(2012). Real-Time Compressed- Domain Video Watermarking Resistance to Geometric Distortions, *Multimedia in Forensics, Security, and Intelligence.*70-79.

Yang, C.-N., Shih, H.-W., Wu, C.-C., & Harn, L. (2012). k Out of n Region Incrementing Scheme in Visual Cryptography. *IEEE Transactions on Circuits and Systems for Video Technology, 22*(5), 799–810. doi:10.1109/TCSVT.2011.2180952

Zheng, L., Shi, D., & Zhang, J. (2013). *CAF–FrFT: A center-affine-filter with fractional Fourier transform to reduce the cross-terms of Wigner distribution.* Signal Processing Elsevier Journals.

KEY TERMS AND DEFINITIONS

Compression Scale Change Invariance: The phenomenon where there is no degradation in the quality of the extracted watermark even after the MPEG Compression Scale is varied over the entire permissible range.

Digital Watermarking: The method of embedding data into digital multimedia content. This is used to verify the credibility of the content or to recognize the identity of the digital content's owner.

Motion Feature Extraction: The process of extraction of salient motion features from a video. These motion features may be motion vector magnitude features or motion vector phase features.

Normalized Correlation: The similarity between the extracted watermark and the original watermark.

Saliency Detection: The process of identifying visually or perceptually significant or salient regions in an image or video.

Visual Cryptography: A cryptographic technique which allows visual information (pictures, text, etc.) to be encrypted in such a way that decryption becomes a mechanical operation which does not require complex calculations. Decryption can be done visually.

Chapter 7
Study of Loss of Alertness and Driver Fatigue Using Visibility Graph Synchronization

Anwesha Sengupta
Indian Institute of Technology Kharagpur, India

Sibsambhu Kar
Samsung India Software Operations, India

Aurobinda Routray
Indian Institute of Technology Kharagpur, India

ABSTRACT

Electroencephalogram (EEG) is widely used to predict performance degradation of human subjects due to mental or physical fatigue. Lack of sleep or insufficient quality or quantity of sleep is one of the major reasons of fatigue. Analysis of fatigue due to sleep deprivation using EEG synchronization is a promising field of research. The present chapter analyses advancing levels of fatigue in human drivers in a sleep-deprivation experiment by studying the synchronization between EEG data. A Visibility Graph Similarity-based method has been employed to quantify the synchronization, which has been formulated in terms of a complex network. The change in the parameters of the network has been analyzed to find the variation of connectivity between brain areas and hence to trace the increase in fatigue levels of the subjects. The parameters of the brain network have been compared with those of a complex network with a random degree of connectivity to establish the small-world nature of the brain network.

INTRODUCTION

Maintenance of a performance level over time, such as that required during driving calls for sustained vigilance, selective attention and complex decision-making abilities. Long hours of continuous work, a monotonous working environment, or working hours that interfere with the circadian rhythm may bring about degradation in performance of the individual. The link between changes in behavioral arousal and

DOI: 10.4018/978-1-4666-8723-3.ch007

the EEG spectrum is strong enough for the EEG spectrum to be used as a direct indicator of arousal level. In general, EEG features in the frequency domain have been found to be more efficient and reliable than those in the time domain for prediction of the behavioral alertness level. Changes in EEG with vigilance have generally shown that distribution, amplitude and frequency of alpha waves in the EEG spectrum change with the onset of drowsiness. A change in the pattern of alpha wave distribution during driver fatigue has been reported (Lal & Craig, 2001) A positive relation between EEG power and cognitive performance in the alpha frequency range has been reported (Klimesch, 1999) and alpha band was found to be the most important component for judging alertness level in an expectancy task (Gale et al, 1971).

EEG has widely been used to judge the alertness level of an individual during monotonous tasks or tasks requiring sustained attention or response to specific stimuli. A study of fluctuation in attention of participants in a vigilance task examines the possibility of periodicity in the pattern (Smith et al, 2003). Participants were required to listen to the letters of the alphabet arranged randomly and were required to press a button when two consecutive letters appeared.

A considerable body of work has been carried out on EEG-based fatigue detection and various methods have been reported to find the changes in EEG signal characteristics during the onset of fatigue. Relative energy of different energy bands (alpha, beta, beta/alpha ratio and (alpha+theta)/beta ratio) has often been used as an indicator of fatigue (Eoh et al, 2005). The relative energy parameter (alpha+theta)/beta has been found to decrease with a decrease in alertness level (De Waard & Brookhuis, 1991).

Another significant domain of fatigue study using EEG includes entropy as the indicator of fatigue. Shannon Entropy, Renyi entropy, Tsallis entropy, Kullback–Leibler Entropy and Cross-Approximate Entropy have often been employed as indicators of fatigue (Papadelis et al., 2006; 2007). A method based on Shannon Entropy and Kullback-Leibler Entropy measures and alpha band relative energy for relative quantification of fatigue during driving has been proposed (Kar et al, 2010).

Alertness detection procedures based on the spectral analysis of EEG signal have also been proposed (Alvarez Rueda, 2006; Jung et al, 1997). In (Makeig & Jung, 1995), minute-scale fluctuations in the normalized EEG log spectrum during drowsiness have been correlated with concurrent changes in level of performance for a sustained auditory detection task. Almost identical linear relationships have been found to exist between normalized EEG log spectra and minute-scale changes in auditory detection probability during single and dual-task experiments alike. An algorithm has been developed for automatic recognition of alertness level using full-spectrum EEG recording in (Kiymik et al, 2004). Time-frequency analysis of EEG signals and independent component analysis have been employed (Huang et al, 2008) to analyze the tonic and phasic dynamics of EEG activities during a continuous compulsory tracking task. Relative spectral amplitudes in alpha and theta bands, as well as the mean frequency of the EEG spectrum, have been used to predict alertness level in an auditory response test (Huang et al, 2001). The mean frequency of the beta band was used for the visual task study.

Parameter-based EEG analysis approaches based on energy, entropy and other statistical measures involving EEG frequency bands commonly used in brain state monitoring (Jap et al, 2009) involve information from individual electrodes and hence fail to characterize the interaction (integration and segregation) of two or more cortical regions. Any mental and physical activity happens as a result of rhythmic neuronal oscillation at various frequencies. The communication of cortical areas through rhythmic oscillations is marked by a tendency of these regions to synchronize or desynchronize (Klimesch, 1996). The degree or nature of such interaction needs to be analyzed to have an idea about the gradual development of fatigue as well as sleepiness in human subjects.

A number of synchronization measures such as correlation (Chialvo, 2004), phase synchronization (Rosenblum et al, 1996), synchronization likelihood (SL) (Montez et al, 2006; Stam & Dijk, 2002) etc. have been employed to find the connectivity between different cortical areas of the brain. However, correlation computes the linear dependency between signals, and hence is not a suitable measure for non-stationary EEG signals. Phase synchronization considers only the distribution of the phase difference between two time series, but omits the amplitude information and is suitable only for oscillatory systems. SL measures both linear and non-linear interdependencies between two time series and is suitable for non-stationary signals like EEG (Montez et al., 2006; Stam & Dijk, 2002). (Ahmadlou & Adeli, 2012) have recently proposed the Visibility Graph Similarity (VGS), a generalized measure of synchronization that converts a time series into an undirected graph. Their work also showed that VGS gives more accurate measure of synchronization as compared to SL. In this work, a weighted Visibility Graph Similarity (WVGS) technique has been proposed to measure synchronization between two EEG time series. This work is a development on the earlier use of the Visibility Graph technique for EEG-based diagnosis of Alzheimer's Disease (Ahmadlou et al, 2010).

Synchronization between different brain areas can be formulated in terms of a complex network (Stam, 2005; Strogatz, 2001). A network may be defined by a set of vertices (nodes) and edges between each pair of vertices (links). Nodes in large-scale brain networks usually correspond to brain regions, while links represent anatomical, functional, or effective connections (Friston, 1994). Anatomical connections typically correspond to white matter tracts between pairs of brain regions. Functional connections correspond to magnitudes of temporal correlations (linear or nonlinear interactions, as well as interactions at different time scales) and may occur between pairs of anatomically unconnected regions. Effective connections denote direct or indirect causal influences of one region on another and may be estimated from measures of directed information flow (Rubinov & Sporns, 2010).

Such networks are extensively used in different research areas as task classification, disease detection, sleep study etc. (Stam et al, 2007; Stam, 2004; Van Dongen & Dinges, 2000). Literature suggests the presence of a small-world structure in brain networks in terms of anatomical and functional connectivity (Strogatz, 2001). Various brain functions, including the cognitive, depend on the effective integration of brain networks and the functional interactions between different areas of the brain (Stam & Reijneveld, 2007). Brain networks can be weighted or un-weighted; two nodes are taken to be connected in an un-weighted network if the synchronization exceeds a threshold value. In case of weighted networks, the strength of each branch is either taken to be equal to, or assumed to be a function of, the degree of synchronization between the corresponding nodes.

BACKGROUND

Fatigue in drivers has been widely reported as the cause behind 20-30% of road accidents across the world ("DRIVER FATIGUE AND ROAD ACCIDENTS," n.d., "Fatigue is a Major Cause in Truck Crashes," n.d.; Lal & Craig, 2001). Fatigue has also been pointed out as a major contributing factor behind air crashes ("Airplane crashes are very often caused by fatigue l L.A.Fuel," n.d.).Since fatigue in drivers often prove fatal and can lead to loss or damage of lives and property, it is important that fatigue in drivers be detected early, so that appropriate countermeasures can be designed and employed.

Fatigue is characterized by the lack of alertness and associated with drop in mental and physical performance and a reduced inclination to work (Grandjean, 1979). Driving involves a number of activities including perception, psychomotor skills, reasoning abilities, auditory and visual processing, decision making and reaction to stimuli. Continuous execution of these skills may induce physical, mental and visual fatigue (Macdonald, 1985). Activities such as changing of clutches and gear, moving the steering wheel, pulling of brakes etc., are likely to induce physical fatigue. Physical fatigue is characterized by declined muscle activities and efficiency in terms of movement, power and co-ordination, whereas visual fatigue is concerned with stress developed in the eyes. Since mental fatigue happens as a result of mental processes and physical activities and is characterized by a state of decreased cognitive performance (Matthews et al, 2000), a driving task involves reasoning, decision making, perception and decision making skills and hence is likely to induce mental fatigue as well.

Driving at night is likely to induce stress on the eyes (visual fatigue) due to the intermittent glare of light from the opposite direction. Visual fatigue is reflected in eye blink rate, PERCLOS and other ocular parameters. Sleep deprivation may increase visual fatigue, leading to an increase in blinking frequency and long duration blink (Caffier et al, 2003; Schleicher et al, 2008). Fatigue in drivers is affected by sleep disorders, circadian disruption, sleep deprivation, irregular working hours, long and monotonous driving etc. Environmental stimuli and psychological factors like anxiety, mood, expectation etc. (Lal & Craig, 2001) are also known to bring about fatigue in drivers. Driving performance is also affected by circadian rhythm and is known to be the worst between 02.00am at night to 06.00am in the morning (Lenné et al, 1997). (Maycock, 1997) found that the sleep related accidents take a peak in the afternoon.

A boring view or a monotonous highway can lead to an illusory state called highway hypnosis (Williams, 1963) which slows down the reaction time of the driver. Subjective factors as age, gender, medication, stress, mood; personality etc. of the driver are also effective variables in fatigue generation. Fatigue in drivers may also be induced by extrinsic factors such as steering, brakes, tires etc., comfort inside the vehicle, music, cell phone, passengers and environmental factors such as road condition, traffic, weather, surroundings etc.

Fatigue may be detected by examining the direct manifestation of fatigue (facial or behavioral or physiological changes) or indirect manifestation of fatigue (effect on performance). Driver's fatigue may manifest itself in the form of eye closure, yawning or nodding of head. Notable changes in physiological signals as EEG, ECG, EMG and composition of blood parameters have also been observed as result of fatigue. Among the physiological signals which reflect changes in driving due to fatigue, the EEG is considered to be the most significant index of fatigue (Lal & Craig, 2001). Functions like body movement, visual processing along with cognition, decision making etc. involved in driving are associated with specific changes in the nature of the EEG signal.

MAIN FOCUS OF THE CHAPTER

This chapter analyses the results of an experiment designed to induce fatigue gradually through a set of tasks and activities continued for a long time along with sleep deprivation. Requisite ethical clearance was obtained prior to the experiment. Information was collected along various channels to find a correlation among changes in various kinds of physiological data during the course of the experiment. The experiment was conducted at Indian Institute of Technology, Kharagpur, India.

Experiment Design

12 healthy male drivers were involved in the experiment. All the subjects were reported to have no sleep disorders. They were asked to refrain from any type of medicine and stimulus like alcohol, tea or coffee during the experiment. The experiment was conducted in 2 sessions with 6 subjects in each session.

The duration of the experiment was divided into 12 identical stages of 3 hours each. Each stage involved activities meant to induce mental, physical and visual fatigue in the subject. EEG data were recorded at the beginning of the experiment and at the final phase of each stage. The condition of the subject was monitored by a medical practitioner at the beginning of each stage. After the subject was declared fit, he was asked to perform the following predefined tasks.

- Physical exercise on a treadmill for 2-5 minutes to generate physical fatigue;
- Simulated driving for about 30 minutes to generate physical, visual, and mental fatigue;
- Auditory and visual tasks for 15 minutes to generate mental and visual fatigue;
- A computerized game related to driving for about 20 minutes.

A single stage of experiment lasted for about 3 hours. The subjects were allowed to read books or newspapers in the interval between two stages in order to keep them awake. Closed circuit cameras were used to monitor the subjects throughout the duration of the experiment. The stages were continued for about 36 hours (12 stages) when most subjects complained of extreme fatigue.

Three sets of EEG were recorded in each stage, i.e.

- For 3 minutes during the computer game
- For 2 minutes after the game with open eyes and no activity condition
- For 2 minutes with closed eyes and no activity.

Nineteen scalp electrodes (Ag/AgCl, RMS, India) were used for EEG recording, in addition to reference and ground to collect the signals from locations Fp1, Fp2, F3, F4, F7, F8, Fz, T3, T4, T5, T6, C3, C4, Cz, P3, P4, Pz, O1, and O2 following the international 10–20 system. In this study, the 3 minute EEG recording during simulated computer driving game has been chosen for analysis.

In addition to the EEG recording, several physiological parameters were recorded during the various stages of the experiment.

1. **Video Recording:** Video images of each subject were recorded at all the stages using a digital color camera (model: JN-2019P) at 30 fps, synchronized with the EEG recordings.
2. **Blood Sample Collection:** Blood samples were collected from each subject at five instances during 36 hours (For example, blood samples were collected for subject 1 at the following instants: Day1: 08.30 hrs; 16.30 hrs; Day2:01.30 hrs; 10.30 hrs and 19.30 hrs).
3. **Speech Recording:** Speech data were collected by vocal response of the sentence "Now the time is -------", at all stages of the experiment. This sentence was selected to find the voiced, unvoiced and silence parts, as well as the response time, which is the time gap between 'is' and the time spoken by the subjects, measured with a clock.
4. **Subjective Assessment:** Subjective feedback was obtained from the drivers in course of the experiment.

5. **PVT Data:** The subjects were asked to respond to four different auditory inputs (up, down, left and right) and movement of an object (up, down, left and right), generated randomly in a computer, and accordingly respond by pressing the four arrows in the keyboard. In both the tests, the response time (the time gap between command generation and response from the subjects) was computed.
6. ECG, Spirometry, and Oximetry data were also recorded for correlation analysis.

The experiment works with the objective of establishing a correlation of EEG-based fatigue measurement with other methods such as ocular measures, subjective assessment, blood bio-chemicals, PVT, etc. The present chapter deals with the analysis of the EEG data to establish the efficacy of EEG synchronization methods.

EEG Preprocessing

The raw EEG signal is passed through a band pass filter with cutoff frequencies of 0.5Hz and 30Hz followed by normalization (conversion into a dataset with zero mean and unity standard deviation). This operation removes the power-line artifacts and ensures removal of any unwanted bias that might have been introduced during experimental recording. The EEG is then decomposed into various bands using the Discrete Wavelet Transform approach.

Visibility Graph Construction

The visibility graph (VG) is a tool in time series analysis that maps a time series to a network (Lacasa, Luque, Ballesteros, Luque, & Nuño, 2008). This tool uses techniques of graph theory to characterize time series and a node in the VG corresponds to a point in the time series. The resultant network inherits dynamical behavior of the time series from which it is generated and can be used to obtain information about the time series. The nodes of the visibility graph being arranged in the same order as the points in the time series, a visibility graph-based measure can be proposed to study the similarity or the nature of synchronization between coupled dynamic systems as EEG signals.

A time series and its corresponding visibility graph are shown in Figure 1 and Figure 2 respectively. The i-th node of the graph a_i corresponds to the i-th point in the time series x_i. The nodes a_m and a_n of the graph will be connected if and only if

$$x_{m+j} < x_n + \left(\frac{n - (m + j)}{n - m} \right) (x_m - x_n), j < (n - m) \tag{1}$$

Visibility Graph Synchronization

The Visibility Graph Synchronization (VGS) is a generalized synchronization method that may be used to find the interdependencies of time series by reconstruction of trajectories in a state–space (Takens, 1993) to measure the interdependencies of the dynamics of the systems generating the time series (Ahmadlou & Adeli, 2012).

Figure 1. Time series

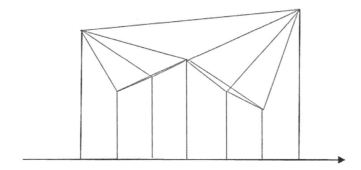

Figure 2. Corresponding visibility graph

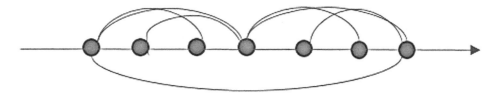

In the VGS method, each time series is first reconstructed as a trajectory in a state space. M number of time series $x_{k,i}$, each of length N may be considered, where $k = 1, 2, 3, ..., M$ and $i = 1, 2, 3, ..., N$. From each time series a state vector $X_{k,i}$ is formed as

$$X_{k,i} = \left(x_{k,i}, x_{k,i+l}, x_{k,i+2l}, ..., x_{k,i+(m-1)l} \right) \tag{2}$$

$$i = 1, 2, 3, ..., N - (m-1)l$$

where l is the lag and m is known as embedding dimension (Cao et al, 1998; Cao, 1997). The time lag is generally chosen as the first zero of the autocorrelation function or the minimum of the mutual information (Akaike, 1974; Albano & Mees, 1987). Embedding is a process to convert a scalar time series to a vector time series (Judd & Mees, 1998). The time-delay embedding (Takens, 1981)is used to generate a non-intersecting reconstruction of the time series in a high-dimensional space that captures the connectivity and directivity of the underlying dynamics of the system. An optimum choice of the time lag is essential as a small value of the lag would restrict the attractor to the diagonal of the reconstructed phase space and a large value would give rise to uncorrelated components and the reconstructed attractor would no longer represent the true dynamics. The embedding dimension must be sufficiently large to capture the dynamics of the system, but not too large to avoid over-fitting.

Vectors $X_{k,i}$ form an m-dimensional phase space (known as lagged phase space) of which $X_{k,i}$ is a point. $X_{k,i}$ is the i-th state of the k-th trajectory X_k. In other words, for each time series a matrix is constructed as

$$X_k = \begin{bmatrix} x_{k,1} & x_{k,1+l} & \cdots & x_{k,1+(m-1)l} \\ . & . & \cdots & . \\ x_{k,N-(m-1)l} & x_{k,N-(m-1)l+l} & \cdots & x_{k,N} \end{bmatrix} \quad (3)$$

For example, if $x_{5,1}$ is the first element of the 5th time series x_5 of length 100, the corresponding state vector will be

$$X_{5,1} = \left(x_{5,1}, x_{5,1+l}, x_{5,1+2l}, \ldots, x_{5,1+(m-1)l} \right) \quad (4)$$

Hence the matrix for time series x_5 will be

$$X_5 = \begin{bmatrix} x_{5,1} & x_{5,1+l} & \cdots & x_{5,1+(m-1)l} \\ . & . & \cdots & . \\ x_{5,100-(m-1)l} & x_{5,100-(m-1)l+l} & \cdots & x_{5,100} \end{bmatrix} \quad (5)$$

N_t identical instances are selected on each time series. For each time series k and each reference instance t, two windows w_1 and w_2 are defined as $w_1 \ll w_2 \ll N$. The m-dimensional distance vector $D_{i,j,m}$ between $X_{k,i}$ and $X_{k,j}$, $\left(\dfrac{w_1}{2} \ll |i-j| \ll \dfrac{w_2}{2} \right)$ is computed as

$$D_{i,j,m} = \left| X_{k,i} - X_{k,j} \right| \quad (6)$$

This forms the m-dimensional distance time series (DTS) that is required to find the visibility of the nodes at each time instant.

For each node, the visibility is observed along each dimension. Two nodes of the graph are connected along the dimension m if and only if:

$$d_{i,j+q,m} < d_{i,p,m} + \left(\frac{p-(q+j)}{p-q} \right)(d_{i,q,m} - d_{i,p,m}), \forall j \in Z^+ \quad (7)$$

where $j < (n-m)$. Visibility along different dimensions and the corresponding visibility graphs have been shown in Figure 3 and Figure 4 respectively.

The weighted visibility graph (WVG) (as shown in Figure 5) is obtained by calculating the mean visibility of each pair of nodes as

$$w_{i,j} = \frac{\sum actual\ visibility\ in\ each\ dimension}{m} \tag{8}$$

The degree of each node is calculated as a sum of weights connected to that node. This generates a degree sequence (DS) for each node at each instant t. The steps have been summarized in Figure 6.

The synchronization $S_{(k_1,k_2)}^t$ between two signals $x_{(k_1,t)}$ and $x_{(k_2,t)}$ at instant t is measured as cross-correlation of the degree sequences of the pair of signals. The overall synchronization of the signals is measured as a mean of synchronization values obtained at different time instances.

Figure 3. Visibility along different dimensions

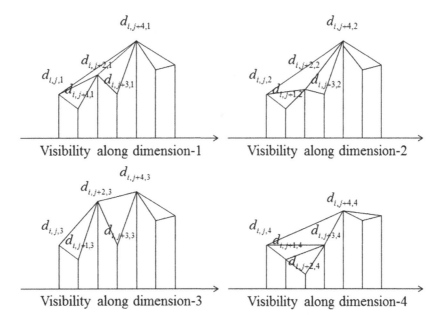

Figure 4. Visibility graphs along different dimensions

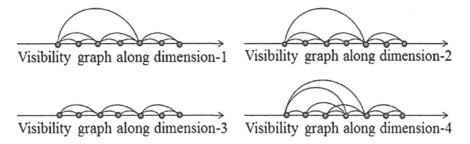

Figure 5. Weighted visibility graph

Figure 6. Formation of degree sequence from time series

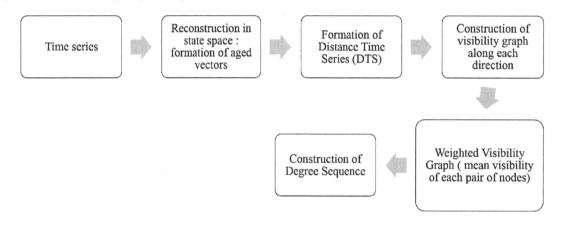

$$S_{k_1,k_2} = \frac{\sum_t S^t_{(k_1,k_2)}}{N_t} \tag{9}$$

The process is summarized in Figure 7.

In the present case, EEG record for each subject and stage for each frequency band consists of 19 time series, one for each channel. Synchronization values between each pair of electrodes are stored in a 19 × 19 symmetric matrix called visibility matrix.

Figure 7. Computation of visibility graph synchronization for two time series from degree sequence

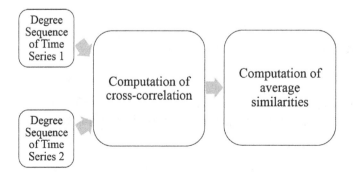

Construction of a Complex Network from Synchronization Values

For construction of the brain network, each electrode is considered as a node. For construction of the adjacency matrix, if an entry of the synchronization matrix is greater than a threshold, it is replaced by 1, else 0 replaces it. In the present case, the mean synchronization across all subjects and stages is taken as the threshold. A connection (link) is assumed to exist between two nodes in the network if the corresponding entry in the adjacency matrix happens to be 1, and no connection exists otherwise.

Computation of Network Parameters

Brain networks may be quantified using a small number of network measures that are neuro-biologically significant and easy to compute (Sporns & Zwi, 2004; Bassett & Bullmore, 2006). Literature reports that the brain adheres to the twin principles of functional integration and functional segregation; functional segregation requires that cells with common functional properties be grouped together, and functional integration handles the interactions among specialized neuronal populations.

The nature of interactions between brain regions depends upon sensorimotor (Sporns & Zwi, 2004) or cognitive faculties (Bassett & Bullmore, 2006). A number of network parameters have been suggested in literature to help describe and define these activities; for example, characteristic path length and density degree are taken to be the measures of integration between brain areas, whereas segregation between areas of the brain is indicated by the clustering coefficient (Rubinov & Sporns, 2010).

Measures of Integration

Functional integration measures indicate how fast the specialized information from various brain regions can be combined and are mostly based upon the concept of a path.

Characteristic Path Length $\left(L\right)$: It is a global structural characteristic and indicates the functional integration of the graph. The smaller the length, better is the integration and hence easier is the information transfer. For un-weighted networks, the characteristic path length is defined as (Rubinov & Sporns, 2010)

$$L = \frac{1}{n}\sum_{i \in N}L_i = \frac{1}{n}\frac{\sum_{j \in N, \, j \neq i}d_{ij}}{n-1} \tag{10}$$

where N is the set of all nodes in the network and n is the number of nodes. L_i is the average distance between node i and all other nodes.

Measures of Segregation

Functional segregation refers to specialized information processing that occurs within groups of brain regions (referred to as clusters or modules) that are densely interconnected.

Clustering Coefficient $\left(C\right)$: The clustering coefficient is a measure of local structure of the network. For a node i, it is defined as the ratio of number of existing branches connected to i and the number of maximum possible branches between neighbors of node i. The mean clustering coefficient for the network reflects, on average, the prevalence of clustered connectivity around individual nodes. For an un-weighted network clustering coefficient is defined as (Rubinov & Sporns, 2010)

$$C = \frac{1}{N} \sum_{i \in N} C_i = \sum_{i \in N} \frac{2t_i}{k_i (k_i - 1)} \tag{11}$$

Here C_i is the clustering coefficient of node i and $t_i = \frac{1}{2} \sum_{j,h \in N_e} a_{ij} a_{ih} a_{jh}$ is the geometric mean of triangles around node i. k_i is the degree of node i.

Small-World Nature of the Brain Network

The values of clustering coefficient are high for regular networks $\left(C \approx 3 / 4 \right)$ and low for random graphs $\left(k / N \right)$, while those for path length are large for regular networks $\left(L \approx N / 2k \right)$ and low for random networks $\left(L \approx \ln(N) / \ln(k) \right)$ (Stam, 2004). An anatomical structure that meets the opposing requirements of functional integration and segregation is commonly called small-world, and has higher clustering coefficient than and characteristic path length approximately equal to that of a random network. (Strogatz, 2001). That is to say, the clustering coefficient for a small-world network would be close to that of a regular network and the path length would be close to that for a random network (Watts & Strogatz, 1998). Such a network structure, which is neither regular nor random, has been suggested for networks in the brain (Stam et al., 2009).

Results

The adjacency matrices and the corresponding brain networks have been shown in Figure 8 and Figure 9 respectively. The first stage of the experiment is taken as a practice stage in which the subject is acquainted with the experiment settings and hence is omitted from analysis. Therefore, stages 2-12 of the experiment become stages 1-11 for the analysis. Since the alpha frequency band is more sensitive to variation in consciousness or alertness of human subjects, only the alpha band has been considered for the analysis of fatigue and sleepiness.

The synchronization was found to increase along the stages of the experiment in the first few cases in most of the electrode pairs for all the subjects. More significant synchronization was observed in the parietal and occipital lobes. This may be explained by the fact that an important role is played by the parietal and occipital lobes in movement, cognition and visual information processing – the skills involved in execution of the experiment. Synchronization values in successive stages show an increasing trend for most electrode pairs.

Variation of network parameters along the stages has been shown in Figure 10. The characteristic path length $\left(L \right)$ shows a decreasing trend over successive stages. This corresponds to the increase in

Figure 8. Adjacency matrices over 11 stages for all subjects

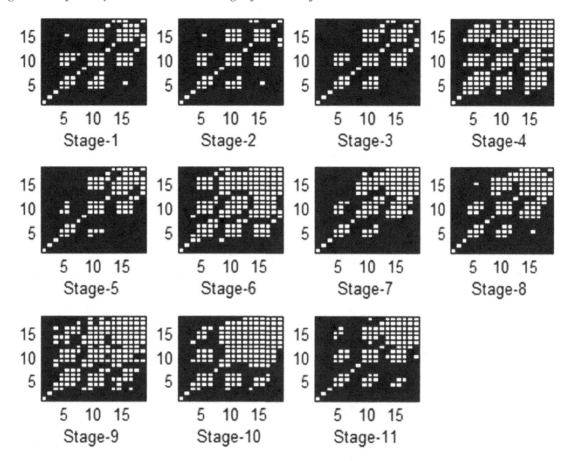

synchronization values between electrodes in successive stages of the experiment. The connection strength between the electrodes increases with an increase in the synchronization and this facilitates the information transfer between different areas of the brain. The increasing trend in clustering coefficient (C) is indicative of tight coupling between the corresponding electrode regions that increases in successive stages with an increase in fatigue. However, some non-uniformity is also observed, since the effect of sleep deprivation and fatigue is also influenced by natural circadian rhythm of the subjects. The distortion in the trend may be attributed to the effect of variation of circadian rhythm upon the change in fatigue levels of the subjects.

The values for clustering coefficient and mean path length (Stam et al., 2009) of the network proposed from the synchronization values is compared with that of a random network obtained by shuffling the non-diagonal elements of adjacency matrix (Kar et al., 2010). This would be equivalent to rewiring some of the connections in the network. Finally, the parameters (C / C_r), (L / L_r) and the small world metric $(C / C_r) / (L / L_r)$ have been computed (C and L represent the clustering coefficient and mean path length of the brain network and C_r and L_r stand for the clustering coefficient and the mean path

Figure 9. Brain networks over 11 stages for all subjects

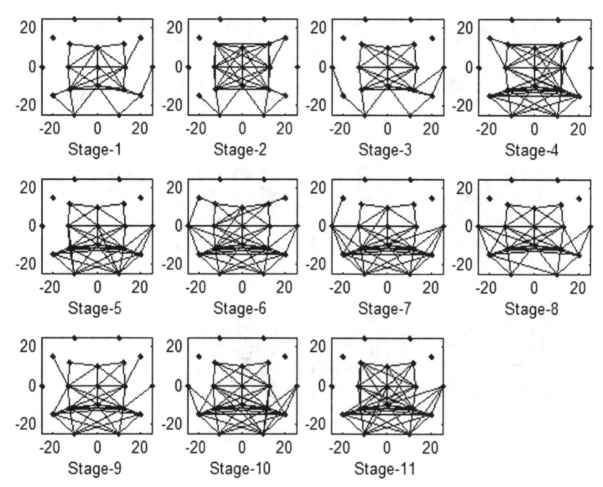

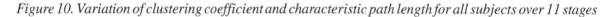

Figure 10. Variation of clustering coefficient and characteristic path length for all subjects over 11 stages

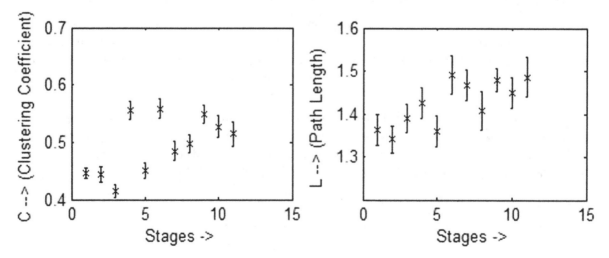

length, respectively, for the random network). The values for clustering coefficient C are found to lie between the limits in all stages, indicating a small-world structure in the network. The ratio $\left(C \, / \, C_{r} \right)$ shows a gradual increase, and the ratio $\left(L \, / \, L_{r} \right)$ shows a gradual decrease over the stages, as shown in Figure 11. The dip in intermediate stages may be attributed to the effect of circadian rhythm on the fatigue and sleepiness of the subjects.

FUTURE RESEARCH DIRECTIONS

The present work deals with the analysis of variation of fatigue of human subjects die to sleep deprivation using a Weighted Visibility Graph Similarity-based synchronization measure. However, possible extensions/augmentations of the present work include

- Analysis of the variation of entropy of various regions of the brain with increase in fatigue due to sleepiness.
- **Dynamic Model of the Brain with Gradual Change in Fatigue:** The present study uses 3-minute EEG recordings at 3-hour intervals. An improvement on this work can be to devise a dynamic model for tracing the continuous variation of fatigue throughout the duration of the experiment.
- **Use of Horizontal Visibility Graph (HVG) Technique:** The HVG is a recent development on the visibility graph technique (Zhu et al, 2014) which may employed to analyze the variation in fatigue of the experiment. A comparison between weighted VG and HVG is another possibility.

CONCLUSION

The present chapter deals with the formulation of a complex brain network structure for study of fatigue, sleepiness and circadian rhythm at different stages of a sleep-deprivation experiment. A weighted visibility graph synchronization technique is employed to compute EEG synchronization between brain areas and the values of network parameters for the brain network have been compared against those of a complex network with a random degree of connectivity to examine the small-world nature of the brain

Figure 11.

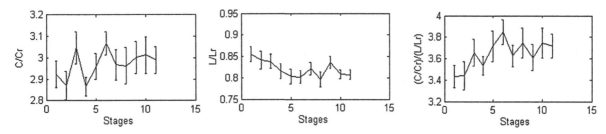

network. The connectivity in the network has been found to increase with an increase in the fatigue levels in successive stages of the experiment, indicating an increase in the synchronization. The increase is more pronounced in the parietal and occipital regions because of degradation in visual information processing ability and other cognitive functions due to fatigue.

REFERENCES

Ahmadlou, M., & Adeli, H. (2012). Visibility graph similarity: A new measure of generalized synchronization in coupled dynamic systems. *Physica D. Nonlinear Phenomena, 241*(4), 326–332. doi:10.1016/j.physd.2011.09.008

Ahmadlou, M., Adeli, H., & Adeli, A. (2010). New diagnostic EEG markers of the Alzheimer's disease using visibility graph. *Journal of Neural Transmission, 117,* 1099–1109. doi:10.1007/s00702-010-0450-3

Airplane crashes are very often caused by fatigue | L.A.Fuel. (n.d.). Retrieved May 26, 2014, from http://www.lafuel.com/2013/04/-3&d=78

Akaike, H. (1974). A new look at the statistical model identification. *IEEE Transactions on Automatic Control, 19*(6), 716–723. doi:10.1109/TAC.1974.1100705

Albano, A., & Mees, A. (1987). Data requirements for reliable estimation of correlation dimensions. *Chaos in Biological....* Retrieved from http://link.springer.com/chapter/10.1007/978-1-4757-9631-5_24

Álvarez Rueda, R. (2006, November 1). *Assessing alertness from EEG power spectral bands.* Retrieved from http://bibdigital.epn.edu.ec/handle/15000/9872

Bassett, D. S., & Bullmore, E. (2006). Small-world brain networks. *The Neuroscientist, 12*(6), 512–523. doi:10.1177/1073858406293182 PMID:17079517

Caffier, P. P., Erdmann, U., & Ullsperger, P. (2003). Experimental evaluation of eye-blink parameters as a drowsiness measure. *European Journal of Applied Physiology, 89,* 319–325. doi:10.1007/s00421-003-0807-5

Cao, L. (1997). Practical method for determining the minimum embedding dimension of a scalar time series. *Physica D. Nonlinear Phenomena, 110*(1-2), 43–50. doi:10.1016/S0167-2789(97)00118-8

Cao, L., Mees, A., & Judd, K. (1998). Dynamics from multivariate time series. *Physica D. Nonlinear Phenomena, 121*(1-2), 75–88. doi:10.1016/S0167-2789(98)00151-1

Chialvo, D. R. (2004). Critical brain networks. *Physica A: Statistical Mechanics and its Applications* (Vol. 340, pp. 756–765). doi:10.1016/j.physa.2004.05.064

De Waard, D., & Brookhuis, K. A. (1991). Assessing driver status: A demonstration experiment on the road. *Accident; Analysis and Prevention, 23*(4), 297–307. doi:10.1016/0001-4575(91)90007-R PMID:1883469

Driver Fatigue and Road Accidents. (n.d.). Retrieved May 26, 2014, from http://www.rospa.com/road-safety/info/fatigue.pdf

Eoh, H. J., Chung, M. K., & Kim, S. H. (2005). Electroencephalographic study of drowsiness in simulated driving with sleep deprivation. *International Journal of Industrial Ergonomics*, *35*(4), 307–320. doi:10.1016/j.ergon.2004.09.006

Fatigue is a Major Cause in Truck Crashes. (n.d.). Retrieved May 26, 2014, from http://www.optalert.com/news/truck-crashes-fatigue

Friston, K. J. (1994). Functional and effective connectivity in neuroimaging: A synthesis. *Human Brain Mapping*, *2*(1-2), 56–78. doi:10.1002/hbm.460020107

Gale, A., Haslum, M., & Penfold, V. (1971). EEG correlates of cumulative expectancy and subjective estimates of alertness in a vigilance-type task. *The Quarterly Journal of Experimental Psychology*, *23*(3), 245–254. doi:10.1080/14640746908401818

Grandjean, E. (1979). Fatigue in industry. *British Journal of Industrial Medicine*, *36*, 175–186. doi:10.2105/AJPH.12.3.212 PMID:40999

Huang, R. S., Jung, T. P., Delorme, A., & Makeig, S. (2008). Tonic and phasic electroencephalographic dynamics during continuous compensatory tracking. *NeuroImage*, *39*(4), 1896–1909. doi:10.1016/j.neuroimage.2007.10.036 PMID:18083601

Huang, R. S., Tsai, L. L., & Kuo, C. J. (2001). Selection of valid and reliable EEG features for predicting auditory and visual alertness levels. *Proceedings of the National Science Council, Republic of China. Part B, Life Sciences*, *25*, 17–25. PMID:11254168

Jap, B. T., Lal, S., Fischer, P., & Bekiaris, E. (2009). Using EEG spectral components to assess algorithms for detecting fatigue. *Expert Systems with Applications*, *36*(2), 2352–2359. doi:10.1016/j.eswa.2007.12.043

Judd, K., & Mees, A. (1998). Embedding as a modeling problem. *Physica D. Nonlinear Phenomena*, *120*(3-4), 273–286. doi:10.1016/S0167-2789(98)00089-X

Jung, T. P., Makeig, S., Stensmo, M., & Sejnowski, T. J. (1997). Estimating alertness from the EEG power spectrum. *IEEE Transactions on Bio-Medical Engineering*, *44*(1), 60–69. doi:10.1109/10.553713 PMID:9214784

Kar, S., Bhagat, M., & Routray, A. (2010). EEG signal analysis for the assessment and quantification of driver's fatigue. *Transportation Research Part F: Traffic Psychology and Behaviour*, *13*(5), 297–306. doi:10.1016/j.trf.2010.06.006

Kiymik, M. K., Akin, M., & Subasi, A. (2004). Automatic recognition of alertness level by using wavelet transform and artificial neural network. *Journal of Neuroscience Methods*, *139*(2), 231–240. doi:10.1016/j.jneumeth.2004.04.027 PMID:15488236

Klimesch, W. (1996). Memory processes, brain oscillations and EEG synchronization. *International Journal of Psychophysiology*, *24*(1-2), 61–100. doi:10.1016/S0167-8760(96)00057-8 PMID:8978436

Klimesch, W. (1999). EEG alpha and theta oscillations reflect cognitive and memory performance: A review and analysis. *Brain Research. Brain Research Reviews*, *29*(2-3), 169–195. doi:10.1016/S0165-0173(98)00056-3 PMID:10209231

Lacasa, L., Luque, B., Ballesteros, F., Luque, J., & Nuño, J. C. (2008). From time series to complex networks: The visibility graph. *Proceedings of the National Academy of Sciences of the United States of America*, *105*(13), 4972–4975. doi:10.1073/pnas.0709247105 PMID:18362361

Lal, S. K. L., & Craig, A. (2001). A critical review of the psychophysiology of driver fatigue. *Biological Psychology*, *55*(3), 173–194. doi:10.1016/S0301-0511(00)00085-5 PMID:11240213

Lenné, M. G., Triggs, T. J., & Redman, J. R. (1997). Time of day variations in driving performance. *Accident; Analysis and Prevention*, *29*(4), 431–437. doi:10.1016/S0001-4575(97)00022-5 PMID:9248501

Macdonald, W. A. (1985). *Human factors & road crashes - A review of their relationship*. Academic Press.

Makeig, S., & Jung, T. P. (1995). Changes in alertness are a principal component of variance in the EEG spectrum. *Neuroreport* (Vol. 7, pp. 213–216). doi:10.1097/00001756-199512290-00051

Matthews, G., Davies, D. R., Westerman, S. J., & Stammers, R. B. (2000). Human performance: Cognition, stress, and individual differences. Psychology Press East Sussex Cap 9 – 12 (p. 416).

Maycock, G. (1997). Sleepiness and driving: The experience of U.K. car drivers. *Accident; Analysis and Prevention*, *29*(4), 453–462. doi:10.1016/S0001-4575(97)00024-9 PMID:9248503

Montez, T., Linkenkaer-Hansen, K., van Dijk, B. W., & Stam, C. J. (2006). Synchronization likelihood with explicit time-frequency priors. *NeuroImage*, *33*(4), 1117–1125. doi:10.1016/j.neuroimage.2006.06.066 PMID:17023181

Papadelis, C., Chen, Z., Kourtidou-Papadeli, C., Bamidis, P. D., Chouvarda, I., Bekiaris, E., & Maglaveras, N. (2007). Monitoring sleepiness with on-board electrophysiological recordings for preventing sleep-deprived traffic accidents. *Clinical Neurophysiology*, *118*(9), 1906–1922. doi:10.1016/j.clinph.2007.04.031 PMID:17652020

Papadelis, C., Kourtidou-Papadeli, C., Bamidis, P. D., Chouvarda, I., Koufogiannis, D., Bekiaris, E., & Maglaveras, N. (2006). Indicators of sleepiness in an ambulatory EEG study of night driving. In *Conference Proceedings : ... Annual International Conference of the IEEE Engineering in Medicine and Biology Society. IEEE Engineering in Medicine and Biology Society* (vol. 1, pp. 6201–6204). doi:10.1109/IEMBS.2006.259614

Rosenblum, M., Pikovsky, A., & Kurths, J. (1996). Phase synchronization of chaotic oscillators. *Physical Review Letters*, *76*(11), 1804–1807. doi:10.1103/PhysRevLett.76.1804 PMID:10060525

Rubinov, M., & Sporns, O. (2010). Complex network measures of brain connectivity: Uses and interpretations. *NeuroImage*, *52*(3), 1059–1069. doi:10.1016/j.neuroimage.2009.10.003 PMID:19819337

Schleicher, R., Galley, N., Briest, S., & Galley, L. (2008). Blinks and saccades as indicators of fatigue in sleepiness warnings: Looking tired? *Ergonomics*, *51*(7), 982–1010. doi:10.1080/00140130701817062 PMID:18568959

Smith, K. J., Valentino, D. A., & Arruda, J. E. (2003). Rhythmic oscillations in the performance of a sustained attention task. *Journal of Clinical and Experimental Neuropsychology*, *25*(4), 561–570. doi:10.1076/jcen.25.4.561.13869 PMID:12911107

Sporns, O., & Zwi, J. D. (2004). The small world of the cerebral cortex. *Neuroinformatics*, *2*(2), 145–162. doi:10.1385/NI:2:2:145 PMID:15319512

Stam, C. J. (2004). Functional connectivity patterns of human magnetoencephalographic recordings: A "small-world" network? *Neuroscience Letters*, *355*(1-2), 25–28. doi:10.1016/j.neulet.2003.10.063 PMID:14729226

Stam, C. J. (2005). Nonlinear dynamical analysis of EEG and MEG: Review of an emerging field. *Clinical Neurophysiology*, *116*(10), 2266–2301. doi:10.1016/j.clinph.2005.06.011 PMID:16115797

Stam, C. J., de Haan, W., Daffertshofer, A., Jones, B. F., Manshanden, I., van Cappellen van Walsum, A. M., & Scheltens, P. et al. (2009). Graph theoretical analysis of magnetoencephalographic functional connectivity in Alzheimer's disease. *Brain. Journal of Neurology*, *132*, 213–224. doi:10.1093/brain/awn262 PMID:18952674

Stam, C. J., Jones, B. F., Nolte, G., Breakspear, M., & Scheltens, P. (2007). Small-world networks and functional connectivity in Alzheimer's disease. *Cerebral Cortex*, *17*(1), 92–99. doi:10.1093/cercor/bhj127 PMID:16452642

Stam, C. J., & Reijneveld, J. C. (2007). Graph theoretical analysis of complex networks in the brain. *Nonlinear Biomedical Physics*, *1*(1), 3. doi:10.1186/1753-4631-1-3 PMID:17908336

Stam, C. J., & Van Dijk, B. W. (2002). Synchronization likelihood: An unbiased measure of generalized synchronization in multivariate data sets. *Physica D. Nonlinear Phenomena*, *163*(3-4), 236–251. doi:10.1016/S0167-2789(01)00386-4

Strogatz, S. H. (2001). Exploring complex networks. *Nature*, *410*(6825), 268–276. doi:10.1038/35065725 PMID:11258382

Takens, F. (1981). Detecting strange attractors in turbulence. In Dynamical Systems and Turbulence, Lecture Notes in Mathematics (pp. 366– 381). Springer-Verlag. doi:10.1007/BFb0091924

Takens, F. (1993). Detecting nonlinearities in stationary time series. *International Journal of Bifurcation and Chaos*. Retrieved from http://www.worldscientific.com/doi/pdf/10.1142/S0218127493000192

Van Dongen, H. P. A., & Dinges, D. F. (2000). Circadian Rhythms in Fatigue, Alertness and Performance. In *Principles and Practice of Sleep Medicine* (pp. 391–399). Retrieved from http://www.nps.navy.mil/orfacpag/resumepages/projects/fatigue/dongen.pdf

Watts, D. J., & Strogatz, S. H. (1998). Collective dynamics of "small-world" networks. *Nature*, *393*(6684), 440–442. doi:10.1038/30918 PMID:9623998

Williams, G. W. (1963). Highway hypnosis: An hypothesis. *The International Journal of Clinical and Experimental Hypnosis*, *11*(3), 143–151. doi:10.1080/00207146308409239 PMID:14050133

Zhu, G., Li, Y., & Wen, P. P. (2014). Analysis and Classification of Sleep Stages Based on Difference Visibility Graphs from a Single Channel EEG Signal. *IEEE Journal of Biomedical and Health Informatics*, (99), 1–1. doi:10.1109/JBHI.2014.2303991

ADDITIONAL READING

Ahadpour, S., Sadra, Y., & ArastehFard, Z. (2014). Markov-binary visibility graph: A new method for analyzing complex systems. *Information Sciences*, *274*, 286–302. doi:10.1016/j.ins.2014.03.007

Belyavin, A., & Wright, N. A. (1987). Changes in electrical activity of the brain with vigilance. *Electroencephalography and Clinical Neurophysiology*, *66*(2), 137–144. doi:10.1016/0013-4694(87)90183-0 PMID:2431878

Bhaduri, S., & Ghosh, D. (2014). Electroencephalographic Data Analysis With Visibility Graph Technique for Quantitative Assessment of Brain Dysfunction. *Clinical EEG and Neuroscience*, 1550059414526186. PMID:24781371

Bullmore, E., & Sporns, O. (2009). Complex brain networks: Graph theoretical analysis of structural and functional systems. *Nature Reviews. Neuroscience*, *10*(3), 186–198. doi:10.1038/nrn2575 PMID:19190637

Cajochen, C., Brunner, D. P., Kräuchi, K., Graw, P., & Wirz-Justice, A. (2000). EEG and subjective sleepiness during extended wakefulness in seasonal affective disorder: Circadian and homeostatic influences. *Biological Psychiatry*, *47*(7), 610–617. doi:10.1016/S0006-3223(99)00242-5 PMID:10745053

Fioriti, V., Tofani, A., & Di Pietro, A. (2012). Discriminating Chaotic Time Series with Visibility Graph Eigenvalues. *Complex Systems*, *21*(3).

Franken, P. A. U. L., Dijk, D. J., Tobler, I. R. E. N. E., & Borbely, A. A. (1991). Sleep deprivation in rats: Effects on EEG power spectra, vigilance states, and cortical temperature. *American Journal of Physiology. Regulatory, Integrative and Comparative Physiology*, *261*(1), R198–R208. PMID:1858947

Hanke, S., Oberleitner, A., Lurf, R., & König, G. (2013). *A Wearable Device for Realtime Assessment of Vigilance*. Biomedical Engineering/Biomedizinische Technik.

Horne, J. A., & Baulk, S. D. (2004). Awareness of sleepiness when driving. *Psychophysiology*, *41*(1), 161–165. doi:10.1046/j.1469-8986.2003.00130.x PMID:14693012

Jagannath, M., & Balasubramanian, V. (2014). Assessment of early onset of driver fatigue using multimodal fatigue measures in a static simulator. *Applied Ergonomics*, *45*(4), 1140–1147. doi:10.1016/j.apergo.2014.02.001 PMID:24581559

Jiang, Z., Yanting, H., & Chongqing, H. (2013). Prediction of Epileptic Disease Based on Complex Network. In *Sixth International Symposium on Computational Intelligence and Design*, pp. 395-398. doi:10.1109/ISCID.2013.211

Kamzanova, A. T., Kustubayeva, A. M., & Matthews, G. (2014). Use of EEG Workload Indices for Diagnostic Monitoring of Vigilance Decrement. *Human Factors: The Journal of the Human Factors and Ergonomics Society, 0018720814526617.*

Kircher, A., Uddman, M., & Sandin, J. (2002). *Vehicle control and drowsiness*. Linköping: Swedish National Road and Transport Research Institute.

Knyazeva, M. G., Carmeli, C., Fornari, E., Meuli, R., Small, M., Frackowiak, R. S., & Maeder, P. (2011). Binding under conflict conditions: State-space analysis of multivariate EEG synchronization. *Journal of Cognitive Neuroscience*, *23*(9), 2363–2375. doi:10.1162/jocn.2010.21588 PMID:20946055

Lin, C. T., Wu, R. C., Liang, S. F., Chao, W. H., Chen, Y. J., & Jung, T. P. (2005). EEG-based drowsiness estimation for safety driving using independent component analysis. *IEEE Transactions on Circuits and Systems. I, Regular Papers*, *52*(12), 2726–2738. doi:10.1109/TCSI.2005.857555

Mantini, D., Perrucci, M. G., Del Gratta, C., Romani, G. L., & Corbetta, M. (2007). Electrophysiological signatures of resting state networks in the human brain. *Proceedings of the National Academy of Sciences of the United States of America*, *104*(32), 13170–13175. doi:10.1073/pnas.0700668104 PMID:17670949

Mardi, Z., Ashtiani, S. N. M., & Mikaili, M. (2011). EEG-based Drowsiness Detection for Safe Driving Using Chaotic Features and Statistical Tests. *Journal of medical signals and sensors, 1(2), 130.*

Mehar, N., Zamir, S., Zulfiqar, A., Farouqui, S., Rehman, A., & Rashdi, M. A. (2013). Vigilance Estimation Using Brain Machine Interface. *World Applied Sciences Journal*, *27*(2), 148–154.

Molina, E., Correa, A., Sanabria, D., & Jung, T. P. (2013). Tonic EEG dynamics during psychomotor vigilance task. In *6th International IEEE/EMBS Conference on Neural Engineering*, *pp.* 1382-1385. doi:10.1109/NER.2013.6696200

Routray, A., & Kar, S. (2012). Classification of brain states using principal components analysis of cortical EEG synchronization and HMM. In *IEEE International Conference on Acoustics, Speech and Signal Processing*, *pp.* 641-644. doi:10.1109/ICASSP.2012.6287965

Sanei, S., & Chambers, J. A. (2008). *EEG signal processing*. John Wiley & Sons.

Sengupta, A., Routray, A., & Kar, S. (2013). Complex Brain Networks Using Visibility Graph Synchronization. In *Annual IEEE India Conference*, *pp.* 1-4. doi:10.1109/INDCON.2013.6726126

Shi, L. C., & Lu, B. L. (2008). Dynamic clustering for vigilance analysis based on EEG. In *30th Annual International Conference of the IEEE Engineering in Medicine and Biology Society, pp. 54-57.* doi:10.1109/IEMBS.2008.4649089

Sporns, O., Chialvo, D. R., Kaiser, M., & Hilgetag, C. C. (2004). Organization, development and function of complex brain networks. *Trends in Cognitive Sciences*, *8*(9), 418–425. doi:10.1016/j.tics.2004.07.008 PMID:15350243

Sporns, O., Honey, C. J., & Kötter, R. (2007). Identification and classification of hubs in brain networks. *PLoS ONE*, *2*(10), e1049. doi:10.1371/journal.pone.0001049 PMID:17940613

Sporns, O., & Kötter, R. (2004). Motifs in brain networks. *PLoS Biology*, *2*(11), e369. doi:10.1371/journal.pbio.0020369 PMID:15510229

Yan, J., Zhang, J., Wang, R., Kuang, H., & Wang, Y. (2014). On New Indexes to Judge Synchronization of EEG. In *2014 International Conference on e-Education, e-Business and Information Management*. doi:10.2991/iceeim-14.2014.89

Yeo, M. V., Li, X., Shen, K., & Wilder-Smith, E. P. (2009). Can SVM be used for automatic EEG detection of drowsiness during car driving? *Safety Science*, *47*(1), 115–124. doi:10.1016/j.ssci.2008.01.007

Zhang, C., Wang, H., & Fu, R. (2014). Automated Detection of Driver Fatigue Based on Entropy and Complexity Measures. *IEEE Transactions on Intelligent Transportation Systems*, *15*(1), 168–177. doi:10.1109/TITS.2013.2275192

Zhang, C., Yu, X., Yang, Y., & Xu, L. (2014). Phase Synchronization and Spectral Coherence Analysis of EEG Activity during Mental Fatigue. *Clinical EEG and Neuroscience*, 1550059413503961. PMID:24590874

Zhang, J. Y., Qiu, W. W., Fu, H. J., Zhang, M. T., & Ma, Q. G. (2014). Review of Techniques for Driver Fatigue Detection. *Applied Mechanics and Materials*, *433*, 928–931. doi:10.4028/www.scientific.net/AMM.651-653.928

Zhou, C., Zemanová, L., Zamora, G., Hilgetag, C. C., & Kurths, J. (2006). Hierarchical organization unveiled by functional connectivity in complex brain networks. *Physical Review Letters*, *97*(23), 238103. doi:10.1103/PhysRevLett.97.238103 PMID:17280251

Zhu, G., Li, Y., & Wen, P. P. (2014). Epileptic seizure detection in EEGs signals using a fast weighted horizontal visibility algorithm. *Computer Methods and Programs in Biomedicine*, *115*(2), 64–75. doi:10.1016/j.cmpb.2014.04.001 PMID:24768081

KEY TERMS AND DEFINITIONS

Characteristic Path Length: Measure of functional integration in brain networks. The average shortest path length between all pairs of nodes in the network.

Circadian Rhythm: Physical, mental and behavioral changes following an approximately 24-hour cycle, in response to light and darkness in an organism's environment. Influences sleep-wake cycles, hormone release, body temperature and other important bodily functions. Widely observed in plants, animals, fungi, cyanobacteria etc.

Clustering Coefficient: Measure of segregation in brain networks. The fraction of triangles around an individual mode in the network; equivalent to the fraction of the node's neighbors that are also neighbors of each other.

EEG: The electrical activity of the brain, recorded for a short period of time along the scalp. Measure of fluctuation of voltage resulting from ionic current flows within the neurons of the brain.

Fatigue: A physical and/or mental state of being tired and weak. May be caused by overwork, lack of sleep, anxiety, boredom, over/underactive thyroid glands, depression or certain medications.

Graph Theory: Study of graphs, mathematical structures used to model pairwise relations between objects. Used to model relations and processes in computer science, linguistics, chemistry, physics, sociology, biology etc.

Small-World Network: A network that combines the high degree of clustering of a regular network and small characteristic path length of a random graph. Hence facilitates regional specialization and easy information transfer. Example: social networks.

Visibility Graph: A graph for a set of points in the Euclidean plane, where each node stands for the location of a point, and each edge represents a visible connection between them.

Section 2
Other Computer Vision Applications

Chapter 8

A Generic Design for Implementing Intersection between Triangles in Computer Vision and Spatial Reasoning

Chaman L. Sabharwal
Missouri University of Science and Technology, USA

Jennifer L. Leopold
Missouri University of Science and Technology, USA

ABSTRACT

The intersection between 3D objects plays a prominent role in spatial reasoning, and computer vision. Detection of intersection between objects can be based on the triangulated boundaries of the objects, leading to computing triangle-triangle intersection. Traditionally there are separate algorithms for cross and coplanar intersection. For qualitative reasoning, intersection detection is sufficient, actual intersection is not necessary; in contrast, the precise intersection is required for geometric modeling. Herein we present a complete design and implementation of a single integrated algorithm independent of the type of intersection. Additionally, this algorithm first detects, then intersects and classifies the intersections using barycentric coordinates. This work is directly applicable to: (1) VRCC-3D+, which uses intersection detection between 3D objects as well as their 2D projections essential for occlusion detection; and (2) CAD/CAM geometric modeling where curves of intersection between a pair of surfaces are required for numerical control machines. Experimental results are provided.

INTRODUCTION

Triangular mesh is used to represent the boundary of freeform 3D objects. The intersection between 3D objects plays a prominent role in spatial reasoning, geometric modeling, and computer vision. Detection of possible intersection between objects can be based on the objects' boundaries (approximate triangulations of objects) in region connection calculi (RCC8), leading to computing triangle-triangle intersection. Traditionally there are specialized algorithms for cross intersection and coplanar intersection. The

DOI: 10.4018/978-1-4666-8723-3.ch008

intersection detection is a byproduct of actual intersection computations. Most of the time intersection detection is done prior to the determination of the actual intersection so that the non-intersecting objects can be discarded. For example, in qualitative spatial reasoning, intersection detection is sufficient, actual intersection is not required; however in geometric applications, it is desirable to have actual intersections. For early intersection detection, we present a complete uniform integrated algorithm that is independent of cross and coplanar intersection. Herein we illustrate this with an algorithm, and with a Python implementation where the output is displayed with tables and figures.

The ability to detect the existence of possible intersection between pairs of objects is important in a variety of problem domains such as geographic information systems (Egenhofer & Golledge, 1998), real-time rendering (Tropp, Tal & Shimshoni, 2006), collision-detection, geology (Caumon, Collon, Le Carlier de Veslud, Viseur, & Sausse, 2009), surface modeling (Houghton, Emnett, Factor, & Sabharwal,1985), computer vision, networking and wireless computing. Typically, the boundary of each object is represented as a triangulated surface and a triangle-triangle intersection is the computational basis for determining intersection between objects. Since an object boundary may contain thousands of triangles, algorithms to speed up the intersection detection process are still being explored for various applications, sometimes with a focus on innovations in processor architecture (Elsheikh & Elsheikh, 2012).

For pairs of triangles, there are three types of intersections: zero dimensional (single point), one dimensional (line segment), and two dimensional (area) intersection. In the past, almost all attention has been devoted to determining the cross intersections, which resulted in an absence of analysis in two dimensional intersections. Coplanar triangle intersections are unique because an intersection may be any of the aforementioned three types. If the triangles cross intersect, only zero or one dimensional intersection is possible. If the planes are parallel and distinct, the triangles do not intersect. If the triangles are coplanar, then there is a possibility of intersection. Even when the cost of intersecting a triangle pair is constant, the cost of intersecting a pair of objects A and B is order $O(T_A * T_B)$ where T_A is the number of triangles in object A, and T_B is the number of triangles in object B.

In qualitative spatial reasoning, spatial relations between regions are defined axiomatically using first order logic (Randell, Cui, & Cohn, 1992), or the 9-Intersection model (Egenhofer & Franzosa, 1991). Using the latter model, the spatial relations are defined using the intersections of the interior, boundary, and exterior of one region with those of a second region. It has been shown in (Sabharwal & Leopold, 2011) that it is sufficient to define the spatial relations by computing 4-Intersection predicates, (namely, Interior–Interior (IntInt), Boundary–Boundary (BndBnd), Interior–Boundary (IntBnd), and Boundary–Interior (BndInt)) instead of 9-Intersections. Since IntBnd and BndInt are the converse of each other, only three algorithms are necessary for these predicates. In order to implement these algorithms, we must first implement the triangle-triangle intersection determination. The triangle-triangle intersection is a lower level problem that must be solved in order to determine the 4-Intersection predicates which, in turn, determine the qualitative spatial relation between two objects.

In geometric modeling, the surface-surface intersection problem occurs frequently. In CAD/CAM, Numerical Control (NC) machines use automated tooling for parts and automated machines use algorithms for cutting sheet metal parts. The parts are represented as 3D objects using the ANSI (Brep) model. Since the surface is represented as triangulated mesh, intersection between 3D objects amounts to detecting and computing intersection between 3D triangles. Herein the triangle-triangle intersection is required for such applications. The algorithm presented here is extremely useful for geometric modeling where intersection between objects occurs thousands of times. For geometric applications, cross intersection is the most often used approach to determine curves of intersection between surfaces (Houghton et al., 1985).

Most of the algorithms use code optimization of same or similar cross intersection algorithms. In order to realize this for cross or coplanar intersection, we must design a criteria that will work for all cases unambiguously. Thus here we present new algorithms that are different from previous approaches.

This chapter is organized as follows. First we briefly review the background: vector concepts and vector equation solutions, and related inequalities resulting from an intersection framework. Then we discuss the types of possible cross and coplanar intersections between a pair of triangles. We then describe the cross intersection, coplanar area intersection algorithm, and composite algorithms for general triangles. Finally we develop the overall generic algorithm for triangle-triangle intersection, and classify the intersections. Later we describe experiments, the timing results, and two of the applications where this approach is directly applicable.

BACKGROUND

Vector Notation and Terminology

Vector analysis is the foundation for the intersection problems. The relevant definitions can be found in any book on calculus. The terms such as *position* vector, *localized* vector, scalar multiplication, *dot* or *scalar* or *inner* product, *cross* or *vector* product, *unit* vector, *collinear* vectors, *coplanar* vectors, and vector equation of a line are standard.

We do review some of the terminology here. The vector A is a geometric entity defined by its components, $[a_1, a_2, a_3]$. A vector is conventionally denoted by bold letter, **A**, or with an arrow over it, $\vec{A}$, but for convenience, we will use the same symbol A for vector and point. The vector $A = [a_1, a_2, a_3]$ is a row vector; equivalently, a vector can be represented by a column vector as $\begin{bmatrix} a_1 \\ a_2 \\ a_3 \end{bmatrix}$ or $[a_1, a_2, a_3]^t$, the transpose of row vector $[a_1, a_2, a_3]$. It is a *position* vector of a point (a_1, a_2, a_3) if the start point is the origin of the coordinate system and the terminal point is the position of point (a_1, a_2, a_3). The length of vector is $\sqrt{(a_1^2 + a_2^2 + a_3^2)}$, and the direction is from the origin to the point A. Conventionally i, j, and k denote unit vectors along the principal axes (i.e. x-,y-, and z-axis). If A and B are position vectors, then AB is a vector from position A to position B and $AB = \begin{bmatrix} b_1 - a_1 \\ b_2 - a_2 \\ b_3 - a_3 \end{bmatrix}$. The vector A is a *free* vector if it refers to any line segment with same length and direction, i.e. a free vector is free from the coordinates of the start point and the terminal point which may be different depending on the location of the vector.

The two operations on vectors are *dot* product and *cross* product. The *dot* product of two vectors A and B is denoted by as A•B and is defined as $A•B \equiv a_1b_1 + a_2b_2 + a_3b_3$ or simply $A•B \equiv A^tB$. The dot product is commutative (*symmetric*). The *cross* product of vector A with B is denoted by AxB and is defined as $A \times B = \begin{bmatrix} a_2b_3 - a_3b_2 \\ a_3b_1 - a_1b_3 \\ a_1b_2 - a_2b_1 \end{bmatrix}$ or simply AxB = A IxB = AxI B where I is the 3x3 identity matrix.

The cross product is *anti-symmetric*. Geometrically, it is a vector perpendicular to A and B so that A, B, and AxB form a right-handed system.

Two vectors A and B are *orthogonal* if A•B = 0. Two vectors A and B are *parallel* if AxB = 0. Two vectors A and B are *collinear* if they are parallel and have a point in common, i.e., they are located along the same line. The vector equation of a line through a point P along a direction U is given by R(u) = P + u U, -∝ < u < ∝. Two lines R(a) = P + a A and R(b) = Q + b B are *coplanar* if AxB•PQ = 0. The position vectors of points A and B are always coplanar, two localized vectors need not be coplanar.

We use the following three identities very frequently in our derivations. If A, B, C, and D are vectors, then: (1) AxB•C = A•BxC, (2) Ax(BxC)= A•C B – A•B C, and (3) (AxB)x(CxD) = AxB•D C - AxB•C D.

If A and B are coplanar and non-collinear vectors, any vector X in the plane of A and B can be expressed as X = a A + b B, where a, b are the components of the vector X with respect to vectors A and B.

If A, B and C are non-coplanar vectors in 3D, any vector X in the 3D space can be expressed as X = a A + b B + c B, where a, b, and c are the components of the vector X with respect to vectors A, B, and C.

USING VECTORS TO SOLVE EQUATIONS AND PITFALLS

In this section, we present a method for solving the vector equations and ensuring the accuracy of the solution. This is the backbone of the generic algorithm we present in later sections.

Let U, V (non-collinear) and W be 3D vectors. We solve the following equation for u and v where

u U + v V = W

The general technique to solve this equation is to define two vectors Ux(UxV) and Vx(UxV) orthogonal to U and V, respectively. When we dot multiply this equation with Vx(UxV) and Ux(UxV), we quickly get u, v as

$$u = \frac{W \cdot V \times (U \times V)}{U \cdot V \times (U \times V)} = -\frac{W \times (U \times V)}{(U \times V) \cdot (U \times V)} \cdot V$$

and

$$v = \frac{W \cdot U \times (U \times V)}{V \cdot U \times (U \times V)} = -\frac{W \times (U \times V)}{(U \times V) \cdot (U \times V)} \cdot U$$

We will encounter this vector equation frequently when we analyze the triangle-triangle intersection problem in later sections. This quick solution looks like a perfect solution, when in fact it is not robust. This innocent looking solution is treacherous. We need to be very careful. There is a short coming in this solution. This solution (u, v) may or may not be valid, i.e., if we plug it into the equation it may or may not satisfy the equation. If it does not satisfy the equation, then either the solution is inconsistent or the equation is inconsistent. For example, let x i + y j = k. Applying the above method, we get x = y = 0, which does not satisfy the equation because k is a unit vectors. This complicates overfitting because the equation is inconsistent. This equation is consistent if and only if UxV•W=0.

To make the implementation code robust, additional testing is necessary. A test UxV•W=0 has to be made to ascertain that the equation is consistent. We want a solution that satisfies the constraints of the given equation.

USING VECTORS TO REPRESENT TRIANGLES

A triangle (three angles) ABC is a shape (more accurately the boundary of a shape) defined with three non-collinear points A, B, and C. The shape consists of infinitely many points represented by (compressed into) three points. It is a polygon with three vertices, three sides, and three angles. More accurately, it is a trigon. The sum of the interior angles of a triangle is equal to 180 degrees, the angles may be acute, obtuse or right angles. The orientation of a triangle ABC is right handed if one moves along the sides, AB, BC, and CA so that the interior of the triangle is always to its left. More formally, if the direction of the head is represented by a normal vector N, then the triangle ABC is oriented counter clockwise if ABxAC•N > 0.

There are various types of triangles: equilateral, isosceles, and scalene. There are various properties associated with a triangle: interior, exterior, boundary, area, perimeter, centroid, orthocenter, incenter, etc. Interestingly triangles have been used as symbols to represent various phenomena. For example, Egyptians used triangles to design pyramids, the department of transportation uses triangles as a warning symbol on highways, a "yellow" triangle is used as a biological hazard symbol in hazardous environments and for weak WIFI wireless signals, and a "pink" triangle symbol was used as gay rights protest symbol on badges in Nazi concentration camps.

In this exposition, we are interested in the representation and intersection of a pair of triangles devoid of any other properties. Thus we represent the terms, *vertex, edge, edgeInterior, and triangleInterior* in terms of parametric coordinates. A triangle can be represented in Cartesian coordinates or parametric coordinates. The parametric representation is succinct and more useful in complex geometric computations. The parametric representation of a *plane* is determined by three non-collinear points A, B, C in 2D/3D, as

$$R(b, c) = A + b(B - A) + c(C - A)$$

where $-\infty < b, c < \infty$, or

$$R(b, c) = (1-b-c)A + bB + cC$$

where $-\infty < b, c < \infty$.

Since a triangle has infinitely many points represented by (or compressed into) three points A, B, C in 3D, any point in the triangle can be parametrically represented as

R(a, b, c)= a A + b B + c C where $0 \leq$ a, b, c ≤ 1, a + b + c =1.

The parameters a, b and c are called the *barycentric* coordinates of a point in the triangle. Since a, b, c are not independent, the equation of a triangle alternately can be written as

R(b, c)= (1- b – c) A +b B + c C where $0 \leq$ b, c, b+c ≤ 1

or

R(b, c) $\equiv$ A +b (B – A) + c (C – A) with $0 \leq$ b, c, b+c ≤ 1.

Associated with a triangle, the terms *vertex, edge, edgeInterior* and *triangleInterior* are parametrically defined here.

- **Vertex:** The parametric values (b, c) are the barycentric coordinates corresponding to a point in the triangle ABC. In particular, R(0, 0) represents the *vertex A*, R(1, 0) represents the *vertex B*, and R(0, 1) represents the *vertex C*.
- **Edge:** In addition, R(b, 0) $\equiv$ A +b (B – A) where $0 \leq b \leq 1$ is the *side* AB, R(0,c) $\equiv$ A + c (C – A) where $0 \leq c \leq 1$ is the *side* AC, and R(b, c) $\equiv$ A +b (B – A) + c (C – A) where $0 \leq$ b, c ≤ 1 and b+c = 1 is the *side* BC. The sides of the triangles are also referred to as the *edge*s.
- **edgeInterior:** R(b,0), R(c,0), with $0 <$ b, c < 1 are *interior*s of edges AB and AC, and where R(b, c) with b+c =1, $0 <$ b, c < 1 is the *interior* of edge BC.
- **triangleInterior:** If $0 <$ b, c, b+c < 1, then R(b, c) is *interior point* of triangle ABC.

In particular if a triangle ABC is parameterized with R_1(b,c), a triangle PQR is parameterized with R_2(q,r) and X is a point such that X= R_1(1,0) or R_1(0,1) or R_1(0,0), and X= R_2(1,0) or R_2(0,1) or R_2(0,0), then X is a **vertex** common to both of the triangles ABC and PQR.

SOLVING INEQUALITIES AND PITFALLS

The inequalities of the form below appear as part of intersection algorithms.

m $\leq$ ax + by $\leq$ n

M $\leq$ Ax + By $\leq$ N

The following example explains why one should beware of the pitfalls when solving these inequalities:

- 1 $\leq$ x + y $\leq$ 1 (a)

- 1 ≤ x - y ≤ 1 (b)

Adding (a) and (b) yields −1 ≤ x ≤ 1, and subtracting (b) from (a) yields - 1 ≤ y ≤ 1 which is the area enclosed by dotted boundary in Figure 1(a). This is an inaccurate solution to the inequalities (a), and (b). But the accurate solution is in the shaded area in Figure 1(a), which is |x| ≤ 1, and |y| ≤ (1 - |x|).

If we modify the coefficients in (b) so that (b) becomes (b'): 0 ≤ x -y ≤ 0, then on adding (a) and (b'), it yields −1/2 ≤ x ≤ 1/2, and (b') yields x=y, and the result is a straight line as seen in Figure 1(b).

Further, if we further modify the coefficients in (a) so that (a) becomes (a'): 0 ≤ x + y ≤ 0, and we have y=x from (b'), then (a') yields y=x=0, and the result is a single point as seen in Figure 1(c).

Thus to accurately solve these inequalities - 1 ≤ x + y ≤ 1, and - 1 ≤ x - y ≤ 1, we first solve these for one variable x, then use that value to solve for the other variable y; otherwise, we run the risk of an inaccurate solution due to the additional extraneous part in the solution displayed in the box, but not included in the diamond in Figure 1(a).

Solving Two General Inequalities

The most general form of the two inequalities in x and y is:

$$m \le ax + by \le n \tag{1}$$

$$M \le Ax + By \le N \tag{2}$$

Solving the inequalities of this form will be of paramount importance in the generic algorithm presented later. These inequalities may or may not have a solution. For example, the inequalities 0≤x+y≤1 and 4≤2x+2y≤6 do not have a solution. Algorithm 1 determines:

Figure 1. (a) Solution to inequalities: - 1 ≤ x + y ≤ 1 and -1 ≤ x - y ≤ 1; using brute force method of elimination of variables yields the area enclosed by the dotted boundary, but the accurate solution is enclosed by the shaded area. (b) Solution to inequalities: - 1 ≤ x + y ≤ 1, and 0 ≤ x - y ≤ 0; the solution results in a shaded line segment. (c) Solution to inequalities: 0 ≤ x + y ≤ 0 and 0 ≤ x - y ≤ 0; the solution results in a shaded single point.

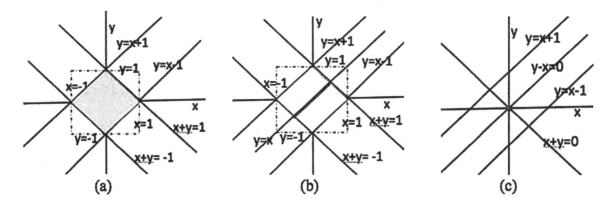

Algorithm 1. The existence and evaluation of x values

Input: coefficients of the two inequalities m, a, b, n, M, A, B, N

Output: If a solution does not exist, return false; otherwise, return true and x_m, x_M such that for each x in $[x_m, x_M]$, the inequalities are satisfied.

Pseudocode:

boolean solve_x (m, a, b, n, M, A, B, N, x_m, x_M)

First assume b and B are non-negative. If not, multiply the inequalities by -1 to update them as non-negative. Now multiplying (1) by B and (2) by b, subtraction leads to

(mB - Nb) ≤ (aB - Ab)x ≤ (nB - Mb)

If (mB - Nb) ≤ (nB - Mb), then there exists a solution in x, else the inequalities do not have a solution.

This inequality yields a range [$\mathbf{x_m}$, $\mathbf{x_M}$] for ξ ϖαλυεσ provided aB-Ab ≠ 0, otherwise any arbitrary value x satisfies the inequality and we may assign x_m = - ∝, x_M = ∝, hence the solution in x is unbounded.

1. **Existence:** whether a solution exists or not; and
2. If a *solution* exists, then it determines the range of x, and computes x_m, x_M such that for each x in $[x_m, x_M]$, the inequalities hold.

Assuming aB-Ab ≠ 0, once x_m, x_M have been determined, for each x in $[x_m, x_M]$ in the inequalities, we similarly determine the range $[y_m(x), y_M(x)]$ for y(x). That is, after the range $[x_m, x_M]$ is determined, only then for each x in $[x_m, x_M]$, if a solution in y exists, the range for y is determined for the selected value x (Algorithm 2).

These two algorithms solve a pair of inequalities completely. The result is either no solution, a single point, a line segment, or an area.

Algorithm 2. The existence and evaluation of y values

Input: coefficients of the two inequalities *m, a, b, n, M, A, B, N; the range for* x: [x_m, x_M] is determined from the above algorithm.

Output: If a solution is not found, return false; otherwise, return true and a range for y [$y_m(x)$, $y_M(x)$] for each x in [x_m, x_M], for which the inequalities hold. In the process, the values of [x_m, x_M] may be updated to retain those x values for which the solution in y exists.

Pseudocode:

boolean solve_y (m, a, b, n, M, A, B, N, x, y_m, y_M)

Given that x_m ≤ x ≤ x_M are known, it solves the inequalities for y_m, y_M.

Now for an x such that x_m ≤ x ≤ x_M, the inequalities become

m − ax ≤ by ≤ n − ax and

M − Ax ≤ By ≤ N − Ax.

If m − ax > n − ax or M − Ax > N − Ax the solution does not exist because the inequalities are inconsistent. Assume b and B are non-negative, otherwise multiply the inequalities by -1 and update b, and B to non-negative. The solution is determined as follows.

if b>0 and B>0 then

$$y_m(x) = \max\left(\frac{m-ax}{b}, \frac{M-Ax}{B}\right)$$

and

continued on following page

Algorithm 2. Continued

$$y_M(x) = \max\left(\frac{n-ax}{b}, \frac{N-Ax}{B}\right)$$

```
elseif b>0 then
```

$$y_m(x) = \frac{m-ax}{b}$$

```
and
```

$$y_M(x) = \frac{n-ax}{b}$$

```
elseif B>0 then
```

$$y_m(x) = \frac{M-Ax}{B}$$

```
and
```

$$y_M(x) = \frac{N-Ax}{B}$$

```
else y is arbitrary
```

```
y (x) = - ∝ and y (x) = ∝,
 m                    M
```

```
hence the solution in y is unbounded.
```

THE CONVENTIONAL TRIANGLE-TRIANGLE INTERSECTION STRATEGIES

There is an abundance of papers devoted to the intersection between a pair of triangles ((Möller, 1997), (Didier, 1990), (Guigue & Devillers, 2003), (Sabharwal & Leopold, 2013)). Interestingly, most of this work concentrates on *cross* intersection; the authors simply reinvent the algorithm and optimize the code to implement it slightly differently and more efficiently, with no innovation. In these approaches, attempts are made to compute the intersection immediately, rather than first trying to determine whether an intersection even exists. The paper (Sabharwal & Leopold, 2013) surveyed various approaches for determining the cross intersection detection, and developed a fast vector version of the cross intersection detection, as well as classification of the type of intersection. The papers (Möller, 1997) and (Guigue & Devillers, 2003) also compare hardware implementation of their algorithm based on the number of arithmetic $+$, $-$, $*$, $/$ operations. Another paper (Guigue & Devillers, 2003) also compares the optimized intersection times. Recent papers (Didier, 1990) and (Guigue & Devillers, 2003) considered an approach for determining the intersection detection covering coplanar intersection. These approaches, (Didier, 1990), (Guigue & Devillers, 2003), and (Sabharwal & Leopold, 2013), lead to one composite algorithm that uses two separate algorithms, one for cross intersection and one for coplanar intersection. Our approach follows (Sabharwal, Leopold, & McGeehan, 2013) and is exhaustive and analytically more rigorous than the previous approaches of (Möller, 1997), (Held, 1997), (Didier, 1990), (Guigue & Devillers, 2003), and (Sabharwal & Leopold, 2013). It computes intersection in terms of barycentric coordinates. Logical rather than computational tests are used to detect whether the intersection is a single point, or a line, or an area. The algorithms in (Sabharwal, Leopold & McGeehan, 2013) are not robust completely as they are missing critical steps for $(t_m(s), t_M(s))$ yielding an approximate solution and there are exposition errors in the derivation of the triangle-triangle intersection algorithm. Herein we address those errors and provide the implementation for accurately solving the inequalities. Consequently, we give a robust algorithm and clear exposition in this paper overcoming all the shortcomings in the previous papers. Our approach is different from previous ones in that we depend on only one equation rather than different ones for each special case. We show that it is possible to detect the existence of intersection before the precise intersection computations are performed. Two triangles may not intersect (as seen in Figure 2), or may cross intersect or may coplanar intersect.

Figure 2. Disjoint triangles: planes supporting the triangles may be crossing or coplanar. The triangles do not have anything in common.

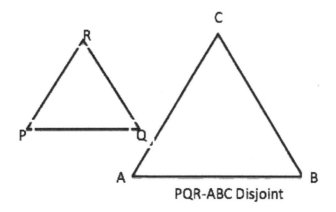

PQR-ABC Disjoint

It should be noted that the precise intersection of coplanar triangles is a little more complex because it can result in area intersection as well. For *coplanar* triangles, the intersection can be classified as:

1. Single point intersection (*vertex-vertex, vertex-edgeInterior*) shown in Figure 3(a, b);
2. Line segment Intersection (*edge-edgeCollinear*) shown in Figure 4(a), and (3) area intersection bounded by 3 edges, shown in Figure 5(a, b); bounded by 4, 5, 6 edges, shown in Figure 6(a, b, c).

A triangle may be entirely contained in the other triangle, see Figure 6(d). Note that coplanar or crossing triangles in Figure 3(a, b) and Figure 4(b), look alike when projected in a plane. There are 4 versions of Figure 6(c).

If the triangles *cross intersect*, the intersection can be classifies as:

1. Single point intersection (*vertex-vertex, vertex-edgeInterior, edgeInterior-edgeInterior, vertex-triangleInterior*), shown in Figure 3(a, b, c, d), or
2. Line segment intersection (*edge-edge, edge-triangleInterior, triangleInterior-triangleInterior*), shown in Figure 4(a, b, c).

Figure 3. Triangles intersect at a single point; the intersections between triangles ABC and PQR are JEPD (Jointly Exhaustive and Pairwise Distinct) cases of Single Point intersection between triangles. (a) vertex-vertex and (b) vertex-edgeInterior can occur in both cross and coplanar intersections. However, (c) vertex-triangleInterior and (d) edgeInterior-edgeInterior intersection point can occur in cross intersection only.

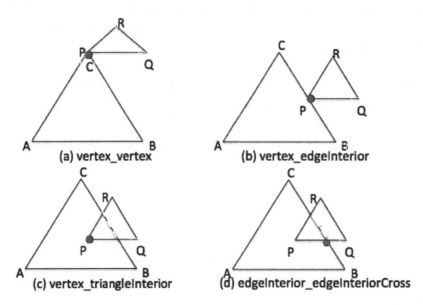

Figure 4. Triangles intersect in a line segment; (a) edge-edgeCollinear intersection can occur in both cross and coplanar intersections. However, (b) edge-triangleInterior and (c) triangleInterior-triangleInterior intersection segment occur in cross intersection only.

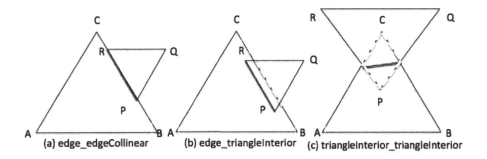

Figure 5. Triangles intersect in an area (shaded); (a) one edge of triangle PQR and two edges AB and AC of triangle ABC intersect, vertex A is in the interior of PQR. (b) One edge of triangle PQR with three edges of ABC, and vertex A in the interior of PQR. The common area is bounded by three edges. The intersections vertex-triangleInterior, edge_triangle, and edgeInterior-triangleInterior hold.

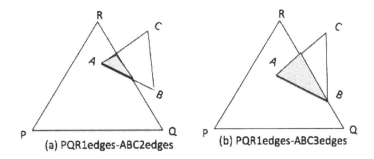

It is possible that two triangles cross intersect in a line segment even when a triangle is on one side of the other triangle. In that case, it may be desirable to know which side of the other triangle is occupied. In Figure 4(b), the triangle PQR (except QR which is in ABC) is on the positive side of triangle ABC. So PQR does not intersect the interior of object of triangle ABC.

CATEGORIZING OF TRIANGLE-TRIANGLE INTERSECTION

The intersection between a pair of triangles can be abstracted as: Cross (C) intersection or Parallel (P) coplanar triangles intersection. For taxonomy of cross and parallel coplanar triangles, the conceptual intersections are supported with figures presented here. The specific cases are as follows:

Figure 6. Triangles intersect in an area (continued); the coplanar triangle intersections are bounded by four, five, and six edge segments. (a) Two edges of triangle PQR and two edges AB and AC of triangle ABC intersect, vertex A is in the interior of PQR, and vertex R is in the interior of triangle ABC. The intersection area is bounded by four edges. (b) Two edges of triangle PQR and three edges of triangle ABC intersect; vertex C is in the interior of PQR. The intersection area is bounded by five edges. (c) Three edges of triangle PQR and three edges of triangle ABC intersect; every vertex of one triangle is outside the other triangle. The intersection is bounded by six edges. (d) No edge of triangle PQR intersects any edge of triangle ABC; vertices P, Q, R are in the interior of triangle ABC. The intersection area is the triangle PQR.

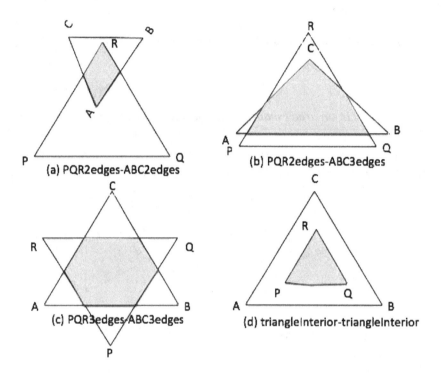

- **No Intersection:**
  - *disjoint* (C, P) (see Figure 2)
- **Single Point Intersection:**
  - *vertex-vertex* Intersection (C, P) (see Figure 3(a))
  - *vertex-edgeInterior* Intersection (C, P) (see Figure 3(b))
  - *vertex-triangleInterior* Intersection (C) (see Figure 3(c))
  - *edgeInterior-edgeInteriorCross* Intersection (C) (Figure 3(d))
- **Line Intersection:**
  - *edge-edgeCollinear* Intersection (C, P) (see Figure 4(a))
  - *edge-triangleInterior* Intersection (C) (see Figure 4(b))
  - *triangleInterior-triangleInterior* Intersection (C) (Figure 4(c))

- **Area Intersection:**
    - ○ *vertex-triangleInterior* Intersection (P) (see Figure 5(a,b), Figure 6(a, b, d))
    - ○ *edgeInterior-edgeInterorCross* Intersection (P) (Figure 5(a,b), Figure 6(a, b, c))
    - ○ *edge-triangleInterior* Intersection (P) (see Figure 5(a, b), Figure 6(d))
    - ○ *triangleInterior-triangleInterior* Intersection (P) (see Figure 5(a,b), Figure 6(a, b, c, d))

It is possible that two triangles cross intersect in a line segment even when a triangle is on one side of the other triangle. In that case, it may be desirable to know which side of the other triangle is occupied. In Figure 4(b), the triangle PQR (except QR which is in ABC) is on the positive side of triangle ABC. So PQR does not intersect the interior of object of triangle ABC.

It should be noted that the vertex-edge intersection encompasses vertex-vertex and vertex-edgeInterior intersection, whereas the vertex-triangle intersection encompasses vertex-vertex, vertex-edgeInterior, and vertex-triangleInterior. Thus 1D jointly exhaustive and pairwise disjoint (JEPD) cross intersection between ABC and PQR can be one of the three possibilities:

1. Collinear along edges,
2. An edge of PQR lying in the plane of triangle ABC, or
3. Triangles "pierce" through each other yielding an intersection segment.

EXAMPLE FIGURES FOR INTERSECTION BETWEEN A PAIR OF TRIANGLES

In this paper, we present a detailed integrated analytical study of the intersection of coplanar as well as cross intersecting triangles, which previously has not been explored. We will use this concept development in the section where we discuss our generic algorithm. Here we display some representative figures for intersection between a pair of triangles (See Figure 2).

It should be noted that the vertex-edge intersection encompasses vertex-vertex and vertex-edgeInterior intersections, whereas the vertex-triangle intersection encompasses vertex-vertex, vertex-edgeInterior, and vertex-triangleInterior intersections. Thus 1D JEPD cross intersection between ABC and PQR can be one of the three possibilities:

1. Collinear along edges,
2. An edge of PQR lying in the plane of triangle ABC, or
3. The triangles may "pierce" through each other yielding an intersection segment.

The examples Figure 3–6 show that there can be various types of intersections for both cross intersection and coplanar intersection between the triangles. All other configurations are homeomorphic to the figures presented in this paper. For qualitative spatial reasoning, in some cases (when the knowledge of cross intersection is insufficient), we resort to coplanar intersection to distinguish the externally or tangentially connected objects.

SPECIALIZED INTERSECTION METHODS AND ALGORITHMS

Here we describe the conventional approach to triangle-triangle intersection in terms of two algorithms, one for cross intersection and one for coplanar intersection. Then we derive the composite algorithm for triangle-triangle intersection. First we give the supporting algorithms for special cases (Algorithm 3).

The vector $\frac{(U \times V)}{(U \times V) \cdot (U \times V)}$ is computed only once and used repeatedly. As a result $\gamma = \frac{AX \times (U \times V)}{(U \times V) \cdot (U \times V)}$ is calculated with one cross product, and u, v are calculated with one dot product. The parameters u, v naturally lend themselves to classification of intersections. Similarly for $\gamma' = \frac{PX \times (S \times T)}{(S \times T) \cdot (S \times T)}$.

Classification of Intersection Point

In order to determine whether the vertex X of triangle PQR is a *vertex* of ABC, or on the *edge* of ABC, or an *interior point* of triangle ABC, no extra computational effort is required now. Logical tests are sufficient to establish the classification of this intersection. Since $0 \leq u, v, u + v \leq 1$, we can classify point X relative to ABC in terms of the following parametric coordinates:

- **Vertex ((u, v)):** If $(u, v) \in \{ (0, 0), (0, 1), (1, 0)\}$, then X is one of the vertices of ABC. In particular, parameter (0,0) corresponds to parametric coordinates of vertex A, (1,0) corresponds to parametric coordinates of vertex B, and (0,1) corresponds to parametric coordinates of vertex C.
- **Edge ((u, v)):** If $(u = 0, 0 \leq v \leq 1)$ or $(v = 0, 0 \leq u \leq 1)$ or $(u + v = 1, 0 \leq u \leq 1)$, then X is an edge of ABC. In particular $(u = 0, 0 \leq v \leq 1)$ is the parametric representation of edge AC, $(v = 0, 0 \leq u \leq 1)$ is the parametric representation of edge AB, $(u + v = 1, 0 \leq v \leq 1)$ is the parametric representation of edge BC, and $(u + v = 1, 0 \leq u \leq 1)$ is the parametric representation of edge CB.
- **edgeInterior ((u, v)):** If $(u = 0, 0 < v < 1)$ or $(v = 0, 0 < u < 1)$ or $(u + v = 1, 0 < u < 1)$, then X is on an edge of ABC, excluding vertices. In particular, $(u = 0, 0 < v < 1)$ is the parametric representation of the interior of edge AC, $(v = 0, 0 < u < 1)$ is the parametric representation of the interior of edge AB, $(u + v = 1, 0 \leq v \leq 1)$ is the parametric representation of the interior of edge BC, and $(u + v = 1, 0 \leq u \leq 1)$ is the parametric representation of the interior of edge CB.
- **triangleInterior ((u, v)):** If $(0 < u < 1$ and $0 < v < 1$ and $0 < u + v < 1)$, then X is an interior point (excluding the boundary) of the triangle ABC.

Similarly, as above we can classify vertex X of triangle ABC as the *vertex, edgeInterior,* or *triangleInterior* point of triangle PQR. Single point intersection may result from cross intersection of edges as well. An edge point may be a vertex or an interior point of the edge.

Algorithm 3. Single point intersection (0D)

We first analyze the vertices of the triangle PQR with respect to triangle ABC to determine if a vertex P or Q or R is common to the ABC triangle and conversely.

Input: A vertex X of triangle PQR and a triangle ABC

Output: return false if X lies outside ABC; otherwise, return true and in addition, classify if X is vertex, or edge interior or triangleInterior point.

PseudoCode:

vertex-triangleTest (X, tri = ABC)

To determine the relation of X ∈{P, Q, R} to the triangle ABC, we solve

A + u U + v V = X for 0 ≤ u, v, u + v ≤ 1,

Rearranging the equation, we get

u U + v V = AX

Let N = UxV, then NxU and NxV are orthogonal to U and V. To eliminate one of the parameters u, v in this equation, we dot product the equation with vectors NxV and NxU .

Let $\gamma = \dfrac{AX \times \left(U \times V\right)}{\left(U \times V\right)\bullet\left(U \times V\right)}$

then u = - γ•V and v = γ•U

continued on following page

Algorithm 3. Continued

```
if 0 ≤ u, v, u + v ≤ 1


return true // X of PQR, intersects the triangle ABC.


else


return false


/*end of algorithm*/
```

The Edge-Edge Cross Intersection Point

If two triangles cross intersect across an edge, the edge-to-edge intersection results in a single point. The edge-edge cross intersection *algorithm* is presented below followed by the algorithm for edge-edge cross intersection with a single point classification (Algorithm 4).

Edge-Edge Cross Intersection Single Point Classification

If u_m, s_m, be the pair of parametric coordinates of the 3D intersection of an edge of ABC and an edge of PQR.

If $u_m = 0$ or $u_m = 1$, the it is *vertex* of ABC
Elseif $0 < u_m < 1$, then it is edge interior of an edge of ABC
Else no edge-edge cross intersection.
If $s_m = 0$ or $s_m = 1$, the it is *vertex* of PQR
Elseif $0 < s_m < 1$, then it is *edgeInterior* of an edge of PQR
Else no edge-edge cross intersection.

Composite Classification of Single Point Intersection

Here we represent the intersection point uniformly for both the algorithms. Let A_m, P_m, be the pair of bilinear parametric coordinates (u_m, v_m) and (s_m, t_m) of the 3D intersection points $R_1(u_m, v_m)$ and $R_2(s_m, t_m)$ with respect to triangles ABC and PQR, respectively. When there is no confusion, we will refer to the points as A_m and P_m instead of 3D points $R_1(u_m, v_m)$ and $R_2(s_m, t_m)$. From vertex-triangle intersection, we have

P_m is a vertex of PQR, and $A_m = (u_m, v_m)$,

where u_m and v_m are $u_m = -\gamma \bullet V$, $v_m = \gamma \bullet U$, or

Algorithm 4.

Input: An edge of triangle ABC and an edge of triangle PQR

Output: Return false if the edges do not cross intersect; otherwise, return true and classify the intersection point.

Pseudocode:

edge_edgeCrossIntersection (edge1, edge2)

Let the two edges be AB and PQ. Then the edges are represented with equations

X = A + u U with U = B - A, $0 \leq u \leq 1$

X = P + s S with S = Q - P, $0 \leq s \leq 1$

if UxS•AP≠0, return false //non - coplanar lines

elseif UxS = 0, return false //lines are parallel

else UxS ≠0, // lines cross

/* solve for u_P, s_A values for the intersection point*/

$A + u_P U = P + s_A S$

$u_P U - s_A S = P - A$

$u_P U - s_A S = AP$

continued on following page

Algorithm 4. Continued

$$u_P = \frac{S \cdot PA \times (U \times S)}{(U \times S) \cdot (U \times S)}$$

$$s_A = \frac{U \cdot AP \times (U \times S)}{(U \times S) \cdot (U \times S)}$$

```
if (u_p < 0) or (u_p > 1), return false //no cross intersection,

elseif (s_A < 0) or (s_A > 1),

return false //no cross intersection,

else

return true and (u_p, s_A) //there is edge-edge cross intersection.

endif

/* end of algorithm*/
```

A_m is a vertex of ABC, and $P_m = (s_m, t_m)$,

where s_m and t_m are $s_m = -\gamma' \bullet T$, $t_m = \gamma' \bullet S$.
From edge-edge cross intersection, we have

$A_m = (u_m, v_m) = (0, u_P)$ or $(u_P, 0)$ or $(u_P, 1 - u_P)$ or $(1 - u_P, u_P)$

$P_m = (s_m, t_m) = (0, s_A)$ or $(s_A, 0)$ or $(s_A, 1 - s_A)$ or $(1 - s_A, s_A)$

If A_m is a vertex of ABC and P_m is vertex of PQR, then it is *vertex-vertex* intersection. If A_m is a vertex of ABC and P_m is an edgeInterior of PQR, then it is *vertex-edgeInterior* intersection. If A_m is an edgeInterior point of ABC and P_m is a vertex of PQR, then it is *edgeInterior-vertex* intersection. If

A_m is an edgeInterior point of ABC and P_m is an edgeInterior point of PQR, then it is *edgeInterior-edgeInterior* intersection. If A_m is a vertex of ABC and P_m is an triangleInterior point of PQR, then it is *vertex-triangleInterior* intersection.

This completes the discussion of single point intersection classification and parameters for the corresponding 3D points.

Line Intersection (1D)

Besides edge-edge cross intersection, edge-edge collinear intersection is a possibility, independent of crossing or coplanar triangles. In this section we discuss algorithms that result in a segment (1D) intersection; see Figure 4.

Intersection Algorithm and Parametric Coordinates

Here we derive an edge-edgeCollinear intersection algorithm. This algorithm is seamlessly applicable to both cross intersecting and coplanar triangles. The following algorithm implements intersection of edges of the triangles ABC and PQR (Algorithm 5).

Algorithm 5.

```
Input: Two line segments, edges from each triangle


Output: If they do not intersect, return false otherwise return true and the
intersection segment, degenerate or non-degenerate


PseudoCode:


boolean edge-edgeCollinearTest (edge1, edge2)
```

First we compute the linear parameter coordinates u_P, u_Q, s_A, s_B for intersection of X = A + u (B − A), for X = P, Q and X = P + s (Q − P), for X = A, B. Similarly we can compute the intersection of other edges of triangle ABC with any edge of triangle PQR. Then we update the parameters for the common segment. This algorithm is standard, straightforward, follows quickly from the vertex-edge intersection algorithm, and hence is omitted.

Uniform Representation of Edge-Edge Intersection

Again we first represent the intersection parameters uniformly as $A_m = (u_m, v_m)$, $A_M = (u_M, v_M)$ and $P_m = (s_m, t_m)$, and $P_M = (s_M, t_M)$. Now we have the linear coordinates for intersection points u_P, u_Q and s_A, s_B. We map the linear parameters for intersection points to bilinear parameter coordinates (u, v) and (s, t). If u_P, u_Q are known along an edge and the edge is AB, let $u_m = u_P$, $u_M = u_Q$, $v_m = 0$, $v_M = 0$. Similarly for AC, let $u_m = 0$, $u_M = 0$, $v_m = u_P$, $v_M = u_Q$; and for BC, let $u_m = u_P$, $u_M = u_Q$, $v_m = 1 - u_P$, $v_M = 1 - u_Q$.

Thus ABC triangle bilinear coordinates for the intersection points are:

$$A_m = (u_m, v_m), A_M = (u_M, v_M),$$

where $v_m = v_M = 0$ or $u_m = u_M = 0$ or $u_m + v_m = u_M + v_M = 1$

Similarly for the triangle PQR, the linear coordinates s_A, s_B of intersection translate into bilinear coordinates

$$P_m = (s_m, t_m), P_M = (s_M, t_M),$$

where $t_m = t_M = 0$ or $s_m = s_M = 0$ or $s_m + t_m = s_M + t_M = 1$.

Now we have the bilinear parametric coordinates u, v, s, t for the intersection segment. The common 3D segment is denoted by $[R_1(A_m), R_1(A_M)]$ which is $[R_2(P_m), R_2(P_M)]$ or $[R_2(P_M), R_2(P_m)]$. It is possible that the intersection segment is equal to both edges, or it overlaps both edges, or it is entirely contained in one edge. Since the intersection is a part of the edges, it cannot properly contain any edge.

Composite Classification of Line Intersection

For collinear edge intersection A_m and A_M are normally distinct and similarly P_m, P_M may be distinct. Though the intersection segment is given by $[R_1(A_m), R_1(A_M)] = [R_2(P_m), R_2(P_M))$ or $[R_1(A_m), R_1(A_M)] = [R_2(P_m), R_2(P_M)]$, it is not necessary that parameter coordinates $[A_m, A_M] = [P_m, P_M]$ or $[A_m, A_M] = [P_M, P_m]$. The predicate for edge-edge collinear intersection segment becomes

edge-edgeCollinear (edge1, edge2) = $[A_m, A_M] \subseteq$ edge1(ABC)

and

$[P_m, P_M] \subseteq$ edge2(PQR) and $[R_1(A_m), R_1(A_M)] == [R_2(P_m), R_2(P_M)]$

or

$[R_1(A_m), R_1(A_M)] == [R_2(P_M), R_2(P_m)]$.

Also it may be noted that for cross intersecting triangles, an *edge-triangleInterior* intersection may result in a segment intersection, see Figure 4(b). For cross intersecting planes we have:

edge-triangle (edge, triangle) = $[A_m, A_M] \subseteq$ edge(ABC) and

$[P_m, P_M] \subseteq triangle(PQR)$ and $[R_1(A_m), R_1(A_M)] == [R_2(P_m), R_2(P_M)]$

or

$[R_1(A_m), R_1(A_M)] == [R_2(P_M), R_2(P_m)]$.

This completes the classification of segment intersection (1D) in 3D for both *cross* and *coplanar* triangle intersections.

Philosophy of Previous Cross Intersection Approaches

We briefly review three approaches for determining intersection detection that are relevant to our discussion herein, starting with Moller's algorithm (Möller, 1997). For two triangles T_1 and T_2, two planes P_1 and P_2 that support the triangles are determined. Then it is determined whether triangle T_1 and plane P_2 overlap, and triangle T_2 and plane P_1 overlap. If all vertices of triangle T_1 lie on the same side of plane P_2, and no vertex of triangle T_1 lies in plane P_2, then triangle T_1 and plane P_2 do not overlap; hence the triangles do not intersect. The same test is repeated for triangle T_2 and plane P_1. If the two tests succeed, then the algorithm computes the intersection segment S_{12} of triangle T_1 and plane P_2, as well as segment S_{21} of triangle T_2 and plane P_1. Further, a line-line 3D intersection algorithm is used to test whether the two segments S_{12} and S_{21} overlap; see Figure 7(a). If they do intersect, the triangles are guaranteed to cross intersect. It should be noted that this algorithm does not address additional questions related to the classification of intersection points, information that would be useful for spatial reasoning.

The second approach (Held, 1997) reviewed here starts out similar to the above approach for solving the triangle-triangle intersection problem. If the above preliminary test succeeds, now instead of computing segment S_{21} of the intersection between triangle T_2 and plane P_1, the solution is approached slightly differently. It will be determined whether intersection segment S_{12} of triangle T_1 and plane P_2 overlap. If segment S_{12} and triangle T_2 overlap, the intersection algorithm succeeds, and the determination is made that the two triangles intersect; see Figure 7(b). Unfortunately this approach has the same problems as the previous algorithm for degenerate cases.

A third approach in (Didier, 1990) differs in its strategy from the previous two algorithms: if the edges of one triangle intersect the surface of the other triangle, it can be concluded that the triangles intersect. In this case, six such intersection tests are performed: three to test triangle ABC against the edges of triangle PQR, and three tests where the roles of ABC and PQR are reversed. This technique solves the six sets of linear equations associated with the problem and exploits the relations between these sets to speed up their solution. Like the other algorithms, it does not answer the related intersection classification questions. Notably, Badouel's algorithm (Didier, 1990) uses a vector approach in preference to Cartesian coordinates, yet still performs the same tests as the aforementioned algorithms.

Our intersection outcome is closer to that of (Held, 1997), but our approach is more direct and different from the previous strategies.

Figure 7. (a) S_{12} is the intersection of T_1 and P_2, S_{21} is the intersection of T_2 and P_1; intersection of S_{12} and S_{21} is the intersection of T_1 and T_2. (b) $I_2 I_1$ is the intersection S_{12} and P_2.

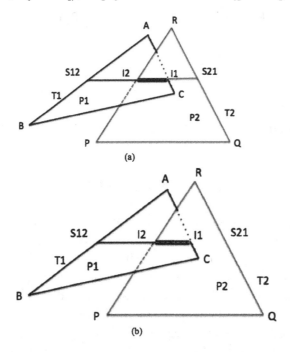

THE TRIANGLE-TRIANGLE INTERSECTION ALGORITHMS

Here we give the line intersection for cross intersection and area intersection for coplanar triangles separately and combine the two into one algorithm as is conventionally done. In the next section we present our new algorithm, which employs a more singular, seamless approach instead of combining the separate algorithms.

The Triangle-Triangle Line Intersection Algorithm

The cross intersection algorithm encompasses the single point and edge intersection cases. Here we give a solution which is *different* from previous approaches (Algorithm 6). The algorithm has been implemented in Python 3.3.3.

The Triangle-Triangle Area Intersection Algorithm

For coplanar triangles only, the area intersection is possible. The input, output, method prototype and pseudo code are given in Algorithm 7.

Algorithm 6. Cross intersection, line intersection

Input: Two triangles ABC and PQR

Output: Determine if they cross intersect. Return true if they intersect, otherwise return false.

PseudoCode:

boolean crossInt (tr1 = ABC, tr2 = PQR)

The vector equations for two triangles ABC and PQR are

$R_1(u, v) = A + u U + v V, 0 \leq u, v, u + v \leq 1$

$R_2(s, t) = P + s S + t T, 0 \leq s, t, s + t \leq 1$

where U = B - A, V = C - A, and S = Q - P, T = R - P are direction vectors along the sides of triangles.

Let N_1 = UxV, N_2 = SxT be normals to the planes supporting the triangles. The triangles intersect if there exist some barycentric coordinates (u, v) and (s, t) satisfying the equation

A + u U + v V = P + s S + t T

Since N_1x$N_2 \neq 0$ for cross intersecting triangles, and S and T are orthogonal to N_2, the dot product of this equation with N_2 eliminates S and T from the above equation to yield

$u U \cdot N_2 + v V \cdot N_2 = AP \cdot N_2$

continued on following page

Algorithm 6. Continued

This is the familiar equation of a line in the uv - plane for real variables u, v. The vector equation using real parameter λ becomes

$$\left(u,v\right) = AP{\bullet}N_2 \frac{\left(U{\bullet}N_2, V{\bullet}N_2\right)}{U{\bullet}N_2^2 + V{\bullet}N_2^2} + \lambda\left(V{\bullet}N_2, -U{\bullet}N_2\right)$$

Then parameter values u, v are explicitly written as

$$u = AP{\bullet}N_2 \frac{U{\bullet}N_2}{U{\bullet}N_2^2 + V{\bullet}N_2^2} + \lambda V{\bullet}N_2$$

$$v = AP{\bullet}N_2 \frac{V{\bullet}N_2}{U{\bullet}N_2^2 + V{\bullet}N_2^2} - \lambda U{\bullet}N_2$$

$$u + v = AP{\bullet}N_2 \frac{\left(U{\bullet}N_2 + V{\bullet}N_2\right)}{U{\bullet}N_2^2 + V{\bullet}N_2^2} + \lambda\left(V{\bullet}N_2 - U{\bullet}N_2\right)$$

If there is a λ satisfying three equations such that $0 \leq u$, v, $u + v \leq 1$, then the triangles are ensured to intersect. The solution in λ is the range of values of λ satisfying $\lambda_m \leq \lambda \leq \lambda_M$ for some λ_m and λ_M. This detects whether the two triangles cross intersect only.

In fact, for precise intersection, using λ_m, λ_M, as parameter values, we compute (u_m, v_m) from λ_m and (u_M, v_M) from λ_M for the end points of the segment of intersection in triangle ABC. Similarly the values (s_m, t_m) and (s_M, t_M) represent the segment of intersection in triangle PQR. There are two ways to solve this problem. The first approach is to compute (s_m, t_m) and (s_M, t_M) from scratch. The precise intersection between the two triangles is the common segment of these two segments (Möller, 1997), (Sabharwal & Leopold, 2013). The second approach is to compute (s_m, t_m) using (u_m, v_m), and (s_M, t_M) using (u_M, v_M) in the main equation. This can be simplified, and we can compute the subsegment of the precomputed segment for triangle ABC (Held, 1997). If the segment degenerates into a single point, the parameter values also can be used to classify the intersection as a vertex, an *edgeInterior* point or *triangleInterior* point in the triangles ABC and PQR.

Algorithm 7. Area intersection

Input: Two triangles ABC and PQR coplanar

Output: If they do not intersect, then return false; otherwise, return true and the intersection area.

PseudoCode:

boolean coplanarInt (tr1 = ABC, tr2 = PQR)

For coplanar triangles, there may be no intersection (Figure 2), a single point (Figure 3(a, b)), a segment (Figure 4(a)) or an area (Figure 5, Figure 6(a, b, c)), including one triangle contained in another, (Figure 6(d)). An area can result from two edges of one triangle and one, two, or three edges of another triangle, or three edges from both triangles creating a star shaped figure. The resulting area is bounded by 3, 4, 5, or 6 edges. All other configurations are homeomorphic to the figures presented earlier in this paper. The derivation of the algorithm is based on extensive use of the intersections of the edges of one triangle with the edges of the second triangle and the collection of the relevant interaction points to form the area if any (Guigue & Devillers, 2003). If the triangles ABC and PQR are coplanar and a vertex of PQR is in the interior of ABC (or the converse is true), then an area intersection occurs, (Figure 5(a, b), Figure 6(a,b,c,d)). If no two edges intersect and *vertex_triangleInterior (*vertex, triangle = tr2) is true for every vertex of a triangle tr1, then the triangle tr1 is contained in tr2, and conversely. If no *edge-edge* intersection takes place and no vertex of one triangle is inside the other triangle (or the converse is true), then they do not intersect, and hence they are disjoint.

Some of the previous methods may use edge-oriented techniques to determine the area of intersection; however, those will be lacking classification capability (Guigue & Devillers, 2003).

The Triangle-Triangle Traditional Composite Intersection Algorithm

A classical approach is to first determine whether two triangles are cross or coplanar, and then apply an appropriate algorithm (Algorithm 8).

Algorithm 8. Intersection between coplanar intersetion

Input: Two triangles ABC and PQR

Output: If they do not intersect, then return false; otherwise, return true and the intersection.

PseudoCode:

```
boolean compositeInt (tr1 = ABC, tr2 = PQR)
```

The vector equations for two triangles ABC and PQR are

$$R_1(u, v) = A + u U + v V, \ 0 \leq u, v, u + v \leq 1$$

$$R_2(s, t) = P + s S + t T, \ 0 \leq s, t, s + t \leq 1$$

where U = B - A, V = C - A, and S = Q - P, T = R - P are direction vectors along the sides of triangles.

```
if (UxV)x(SxT) ≠ 0 // planes supporting triangles are not parallel

    if crossInt (tr1, tr2) // cross intersect the triangles

        return true

    else

        return false

elseif (UxV)x(SxT) = 0, // triangles planes are parallel
```

continued on following page

Algorithm 8. Continued

```
if AP•(UxV) = 0, //the triangles are coplanar

if coplanarInt (tr1, tr2)

return true

else

return false

elseif AP•(UxV) ≠ 0, //the triangles are not coplanar,

no Intersection

return false

endif

endif

/*end of algorithm*/
```

GENERIC ALGORITHM FOR TRIANGLE-TRIANGLE INTERSECTION

We now present an algorithm that is more comprehensive, robust, and analytically rigorous; it is implicitly capable of handling any specific type of intersection, which may be a single point, a segment, or an area. The triangles may be coplanar or crossing. This single algorithm is not a modification of any previous algorithm, but rather a new approach different from the other strategies. Even existing methods that use somewhat similar alternate edge-oriented techniques to determine the area of intersection (Guigue & Devillers, 2003) are much more limited than what we present (Algorithm 9).

Algorithm 9. The generic algorithm for intersection between arbitrary triangles

Input: Two triangles ABC and PQR in 3D, triangles may be coplanar or crossing

Output: If the triangles do not intersect, return false; otherwise, return true and the intersection, which may be single point, a line segment, or an area.

PseudoCode:

boolean triTriIntersection (tr1 = ABC, tr2 = PQR)

The triangles ABC and PQR are

X = A + u U + v V with U = B - A, V = C - A, 0 ≤ u, v, u + v ≤ 1

X = P + s S + t T with S = Q - P, T = R - P, 0 ≤ s, t, s + t ≤ 1

The general set up for detecting intersections is to solve the equation

A + u U + v V = P + s S + t T

with 0 ≤ u, v, u + v, s, t, s + t ≤ 1,

Rearranging the equation, we have

u U + v V = AP + s S + t T   (1)

This is an underdetermined system of equations involving four parameters u, v, s, t and three equations in x, y, and z- coordinates of 3D vectors. This means one of the parameters can be arbitrarily assigned. The other three parameters can be determined in terms one parameter provided the system is consistent; otherwise, no solution can be found due to inconsistency. We need an

continued on following page

Algorithm 9. Continued

additional constraint to have a valid solution. Here the parameters u, v, s, t are bounded such that 0 ≤ u, v, u+v ≤ 1 and 0 ≤ s, t, s+t ≤ 1. In addition, the solution for u, v, s, and t must be consistent. This may be confirmed by checking that the (u, v)-intersection and the (s, t)-intersection correspond and satisfy the equation. It can be quickly determined that the point X = P + s S + t T lies in the uv-plane by checking the dot product AX•UxV=0, and vice versa.

For simplicity in solving (1), we use the following notation.

Let δ = (UxV)•(UxV) and AP = P - A be a vector. The vectors α, β, γ are explicitly defined as

$$\alpha = \frac{S \times (U \times V)}{\delta}, \beta = \frac{T \times (U \times V)}{\delta}, \gamma = \frac{AP \times (U \times V)}{\delta}$$

For intersection between triangles ABC and PQR, dot equation (1) with (UxV)xV and (UxV)xU, we quickly get u and v as

u = - (γ•V + s α•V + t β•V)

v = γ•U + s α•U + t β•U

Adding the two equations,

u + v = γ• (U - V) + s α• (U - V) + t β•(U - V)

The constraint 0 ≤ u, v, u + v ≤ 1 yields three inequalities in parameters s and t

1. - γ•U ≤ α•U s + β•U t ≤ 1 - γ•U

continued on following page

Algorithm 9. Continued

2. $- 1 - \gamma \bullet V \leq \alpha \bullet V\ s + \beta \bullet V\ t \leq - \gamma \bullet V$

3. $- \gamma \bullet (U - V) \leq \alpha \bullet (U - V)\ s + \beta \bullet (U - V)\ t \leq 1 - \gamma \bullet (U - V)$

These inequalities (a) - (c) are linear in s and t and are of the general form

$m \leq ax + by \leq n$

$M \leq Ax + By \leq N$

We developed a robust technique to solve a pair of inequalities in an earlier section. The robust solution to this system of inequalities is derived via two functions

solve_x $(m,a,b,n,M,A,B,N,\ x_m,\ x_M)$ and

solve_y $(m,a,b,n,M,A,B,N,\ x,\ y_m,\ y_M)$

This method of solution can be also applied to three linear inequalities. We apply these methods here in solving the inequalities pairwise (a),(b); (a),(c); and (b),(c).

Let $s_m = 0,\ s_M = 1$

If solve_x $(-\gamma \bullet U,\ \alpha \bullet U,\ \beta \bullet U,\ 1 - \gamma \bullet U,\ -1 - \gamma \bullet V,\ \alpha \bullet V,\ \beta \bullet V,\ - \gamma \bullet V,\ x_m,\ x_M)$ // (a), (b)

$s_m = \max (s_m,\ x_m),\ s_M = \min (s_M,\ x_M)$

continued on following page

Algorithm 9. Continued

```
If solve_x (-γ•U, α•U, β•U, 1 - γ•U, - γ•(U - V), α• (U - V), β•(U - V), 1 -
γ•(U - V), x_m, x_M) // (a), (c)


s_m = max (s_m, x_m), s_M = min (x_M, s_M)


If solve_x (- 1 - γ•V, α•V, β•V, - γ•V, - γ•(U - V), α•(U - V), β•(U - V), 1 -
γ•(U - V), x_m, x_M) // (a), (c)


s_m = max (s_m, x_m), s_M = min (x_M, s_M)


if s_m > s_M


return false


else


for s∈[s_m, s_M] // we solve the (a)-(c) inequalities for t


Let t_m(s) = 0; t_M(s) = 1;


if solve_y(- γ•U, α•U, β•U, 1 - γ•U, -1- γ•V, α•V, β•V, - γ•V, s, y_m, y_M) //
(a), (b)


t_m(s) = max (t_m(s), y_m), t_M(s) = min (t_M(s), y_M)


if solve_y(-γ•U, α•U, β•U, 1 - γ•U, - γ•(U-V), α•(U-V), β•(U-V), 1 - γ•(U-V),
s, y_m, y_M) //(a), (c)


t_m(s) = max (t_m(s), y_m), t_M(s) = min (t_M(s), y_M)
```

continued on following page

Algorithm 9. Continued

```
if solve_y(-1- γ•V, α•V, β•V, - γ•V, - γ•(U-V), α•(U-V), β•(U-V),1 - γ•(U-V),
s, y_m, y_M) //(b), (c)


t_m(s) = max (t_m(s), y_m), t_M(s) = min (t_M(s), y_M),


if t_m(s) > t_M(s)


return false, s_m = s;


else


t_m(s) ≤ t ≤ t_M(s)


return true


/* end of algorithm */
```

We first solved the three inequalities pairwise for a range of values for s, so that $s_m \leq s \leq s_M$ holds good simultaneously with three inequalities. Then from this range of s values, we solved for t(s) values as a function of s such that $t_m(s) \leq t(s) \leq t_M(s)$. There is no closed form function as such, it is a numerical solution to t(s) for each s. Thus if $s_m = s_M$ and if $t_m(s) = t_M(s)$, t(s) is constant, it results in a single point; otherwise, it is a line segment. Also if $s_m < s_M$ and $t_m(s) = t_M(s)$ for each s, it is a line segment. If $s_m < s_M$ and $t_m(s) < t_M(s)$ for some s, then it is an area intersection. The parametric bounding box for overall intersection is $[s_m, s_M] \times [t_m, t_M]$ where $t_m = \min\{ t_m(s): s_m \leq s \leq s_M\}$, and $t_M = \max\{ t_M(s): s_m \leq s \leq s_M\}$. The bilinear parameter coordinates for range of parameters are denoted by $p_m = (s_m, t_m)$, $p_M = (s_M, t_M)$ where the corresponding 3D points are denoted by $P_m = P + s_m S + t_m(s_m) T$, and $P_M = P + s_M S + t_M(s_M)$ T. In general, $P([s_m, s_M], t(s)) = P + s S + t(s) T$. This discussion may be summarized and the intersection points can be classified as follows:

if the algorithm returns false,
No Intersection
elseif ($s_m = s_M$ and ($t_m(s) = t_M(s)$ for $s_m \leq s \leq s_M$)
Single Point Intersection
elseif ($s_m = s_M$ or ($t_m(s) = t_M(s)$ for $s_m \leq s \leq s_M$)

Line segment intersection common to two triangles
else
Area Intersection common to two triangles

This will implicitly cover the case when a triangle is inside the other triangle as well. If triangles do not intersect, then the triangles are declared *disjoint*. This completes the discussion of the generic algorithm for intersection between triangles.

If required, we similarly can determine (u, v)-parameter values corresponding to triangle ABC. This algorithm detects whether the triangles intersect regardless of crossing or coplanar triangles, and we classify the intersection as a *vertex, edge-interior,* or *triangle-interior* point.

This algorithm may be used with any application (e.g., qualitative spatial reasoning, surface modeling, image processing etc.). The algorithm determines whether intersection exists or not (i.e., it returns true or false). If true, the parameter coordinates of intersection are readily available. Now we can derive all the classification information from the parametric coordinates; only logical tests are required for classification of the intersections. It is not the intent of this algorithm to determine whether the triangles are crossing or coplanar. This can be quickly determined as follows: if $UxV \bullet SxT \neq 0$, then the triangles cross; otherwise, the triangles are parallel, or if $AP \bullet UxV = 0$ or $AP \bullet SxT = 0$, then the triangles are coplanar.

In order to determine whether an intersection point $X=(u,v)$ is a *vertex* of ABC, or on the *edge* of ABC, or an *interior point* of triangle ABC, no extra computational effort is required now. Logical tests are sufficient to establish the classification of this intersection.

EXPERIMENTAL RESULTS

There are four possibilities for triangle-triangle intersection: no intersection, single point intersection, line segment intersection, and area intersection. There are *three* types of no intersection: parallel non-coplanar, parallel coplanar, and non-parallel triangles. There are *six* types of single point intersection: vertex-vertex parallel, vertex-vertex crossing, vertex-edgeInterior parallel, vertex-edgeInterior crossing, vertex-triangleInterior crossing, and edgeInterior-edgeInterior crossing. There are *four* types of line intersection: edge-edge parallel, edge-edge crossing, edge-triangleInterior crossing, and triangleInterior-triangleInterior crossing. Area intersection occurs only when the triangles are coplanar. There are *nine* types of area intersection: no edges intersect (0edge-0edge intersection), edge-2edge intersection, edge-3edge, 2edge-2edge, 2edge-3edge, and 3edge-3edge intersection (four cases). The converse cases are considered because the converse can be obtained by simply interchanging the parameters. Thus in all there are twenty-two triangle-triangle versions that could be considered for experiments.

The algorithm is implemented in MacPython 3.3.3. The test time results are obtained via the Python *timeit* utility. Time tests were performed on Apple Macintosh OS X processor (2.2 GHz intel Core i7). The average time for no intersection, single point intersection(0D), a line segment intersection (1D) and an area intersection (2D) intersection were measured in seconds. The program was executed 100 times on each of the twenty two sample triangle pairs. The intersection times shown in Table 1 are neither optimized nor hardware embedded, they also include classification of intersections. Times were shown as proof of concept that this single integrated algorithm works reliably on all triangle pairs. The test data domain consists of synthetic triangles that have every possible type of intersection. For example, the

Table 1. Execution average times of algorithm in second

Type of Intersection	Time in Seconds
No Intersection	0.000073
Single Point	0.000531
Line Segment	0.001483
Area	0.001962
overall	0.001353

times for no intersection were averaged over 100 runs with three samples. Similarly single point inter-section six sample pairs were averaged over 100 runs, then four samples were used for line segment and averaged over 100 runs, and finally nine sample triangle pairs were used and averaged. The composite average intersection time was computed. The test time statistics are displayed in Table 1. We also give three sample run output figures for examples of single point intersection, a line intersection and an area intersection. The Matlab software is used to draw the figures, see Figure 8-10. The Matlab user interface allows the user to select any of the possible triangle-triangle pairs for intersections and it displays the corresponding triangles and the intersection. For the sake of space consideration, one of the 0D (single point) intersections, (see Figure 8), one of the 1D line segment intersections, (see Figure 9), and one of 2D area intersections, (see Figure 10), are displayed here.

Figure 8. Single Point Intersection

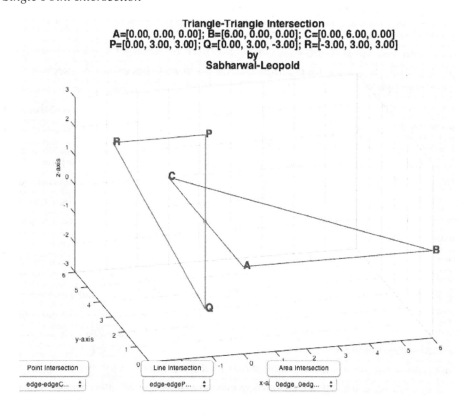

APPLICATIONS OF TRIANGLE-TRIANGLE INTERSECTION

Here we describe two of the applications where triangle-triangle intersection is used extensively: qualitative spatial reasoning and geometric modeling. It is not limited to these two applications; other applications include virtual reality, computer vision, and data mining (Lum, Singh, Lehman, Ishkanov, Vejdemo-Johansson, Alagappan, Carlsson & Carlsson, 2013).

Qualitative Spatial Reasoning

Qualitative Spatial Reasoning relies on intersections between objects whose boundaries are triangulated. The spatial relations are determined by the 9-Intersection/4-Intersection model (Egenhofer & Franzosa, 1991), (Sabharwal & Leopold, 2011). That is, for any pair of objects A and B, the interior-interior intersection predicate, IntInt(A, B), has true or false value depending on whether the interior of A and the interior of B intersect without regard to precise intersection. Similarly, IntBnd(A, B) represents the truth value for the intersection of the interior of A and the boundary of B, and BndBnd(A,B) represents the predicate for the intersection of the boundaries of A and B. These four qualitative spatial reasoning predicates are sufficient to define RCC8 spatial relations (Sabharwal & Leopold, 2011).

Figure 9. Line segment Intersection

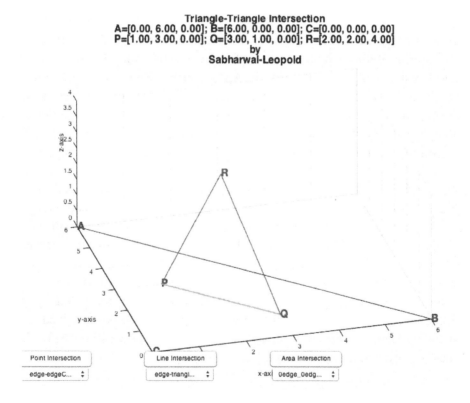

Figure 10. Area intersection

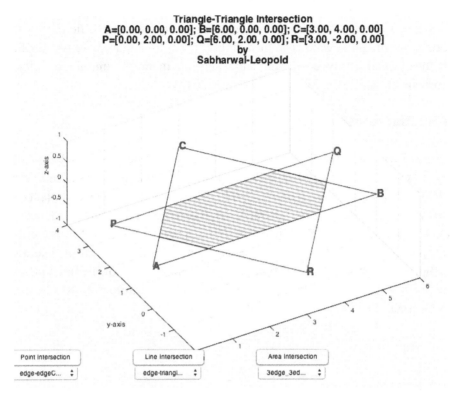

For spatial reasoning, we classify pairwise intersection based on the predicates IntInt(A,B) (intersection of Interior of object A and Interior of object B), IntBnd(A,B) (intersection of Interior of object A and Boundary of object B), BndInt(A,B), and BndBnd(A,B), without computing the precise extent of intersections. When cross intersection is insufficient to determine tangential intersection, some applications such as RCC8 and VRCC-3D$^+$ resort to coplanar intersection to support relations such as externally connected (EC) and tangentially connected (TPP, TPPconverse). The precise intersection of coplanar triangles is a little more complex because it can result in area intersection as well.

In the application VRCC-3D+ (Sabharwal, Leopold, and Eloe, 2011), the boundary of an object is already triangulated; that is, we will need to intersect pairs of only triangles. To reduce the computational complexity, the algorithm uses axis-aligned bounding boxes (AABB) to determine the closest triangles which may possibly intersect (Sabharwal, et al., 2011). For example, for objects A and B, if bounding boxes for triangles of A are disjoint from bounding boxes for triangles of B, either A is contained in B (BndInt, IntInt is true), or B is contained in A (IntBnd, IntInt is true), or A is disjoint from B. The test for such containment of objects can be designed by casting an infinite ray through the centroid of A. If the ray intersects B an odd number of times, then B is contained in A or A is contained in B. If A is not contained in B and B is not contained in A, then A and B are disjoint (i.e., IntInt(A, B), IntBnd(A, B), BndInt(A, B), and BndBnd(A, B) are all false).

Without the knowledge of BndBnd(A,B), BndInt(A,B), IntBnd(A,B), calculation of IntInt(A,B) is too costly. On the other hand, with this prior knowledge, it becomes quite inexpensive as the odd parity can be used for quick IntInt detection.

If the triangles cross intersect (e.g., *triangleInterior–triangleInterior* is true), then IntInt, IntBnd, BndInt, BndBnd will be true. However if the triangles are coplanar and intersect, only BndBnd(A, B) is true and IntInt(A, B), IntBnd(A, B), BndInt(A, B) are false for the objects; otherwise, BndBnd(A, B) is also false.

It is possible that two triangles cross intersect in a line segment even when a triangle is on one side of the other triangle, so *edgeInterior–triangleInterior* is true. In that case, it may be desirable to know which side of the other triangle is occupied. In Figure 3(b), the triangle PQR is on the positive side of triangle ABC. For example, if triangle1 of object A cross intersects the negative side of triangle2 of object B, then BndInt(A, B) is true.

For qualitative spatial reasoning, in some cases (when the knowledge of cross intersection is insufficient), we resort to coplanar intersection to distinguish the externally or tangentially connected objects. Some applications may even require the area of coplanar triangle-triangle intersection. Since intersection area is enclosed by 3, 4, 5,or 6 sides, it can be triangulated into 1, 2, 3, or 4, triangles, the intersection area will be the sum of the areas of the composing triangles.

Table 2 is a characterization of the intersection predicates, which subsequently can be used to resolve the eight RCC8 relations. Here we assume all normals are oriented towards the outside of the object. Each characterization in Table 2 describes when the associated predicate is true. If the truth test fails, then other triangles need to be tested. If no pair of triangles results in a true value, then the result is false.

This characterizes the intersection predicates that help in resolving the RCC8 relations.

Geometric Modeling

In geometric modeling, the surface-surface intersection problem occurs frequently. In CAD/CAM, the objects are represented with enclosing surface boundaries using the ANSI (Brep) model. Intersection between 3D surfaces amounts to detecting and computing intersection between 3D triangles. Briefly, a pair of surfaces is subdivided using axis-aligned bounding boxes (AABB) until the surfaces are reasonably planar and bounding boxes intersect. Then the plane surfaces are triangulated and the triangles are tested for cross-intersection and the intersection computed. The intersection segments are linked together to form curves of surface-surface intersection. The curves may be open curves, 'flares' or closed curves,

Table 2. Characterization of intersection predicates

BndBnd	At least one pair of triangles (cross or coplanar) intersects.
BndInt	At least one pair tr1 and tr2 intersect, at least one vertex of tr1 is on the negative side of triangles of object 2. Or object 1 is contained inside object2, i.e. every vertex of object1 is on the negative side of triangles of object 2.
IntBnd	At least one pair tr1 and tr2 intersect, at least one vertex of tr2 is on the negative side of triangles of object 1. Or object 2 is contained inside object1, i.e. every vertex of object2 is on the negative side of triangles of object 1.
IntInt	At least one pair of triangles cross intersects (triangleInterior-triangleInterior) Or an object is contained in the other.

'loops' or even a combination of both (Houghton et al., 1985). The triangle-triangle intersection is required for such applications. The algorithm presented here is extremely useful for geometric modeling where intersection between objects occurs thousands of times. For geometric applications cross intersection is most often used to obtain the line segment of intersection. Detailed analysis and implementation of the most comprehensive surface/surface intersection algorithm may be found in (Houghton et al., 1985).

CONCLUSION

Triangle-Triangle intersection plays a prominent role in applications such as computer vision and spatial reasoning. Herein we presented a single algorithm for the complete design and a robust implementation of a complete framework for determining and characterizing the triangle-triangle intersections. In contrast to other combined algorithms, this approach is a generic technique to detect any type of cross or coplanar intersection using only one algorithm. The algorithm is independent of whether the triangles cross or are coplanar. The classification of intersections is based on logical tests on parametric coordinates rather than computational arithmetic tests in Cartesian coordinates. Thus our algorithm not only detects whether or not an intersection exists, but also classifies and computes the intersections as a single point, a line segment, or an area, whichever the case may be. The algorithm provides more information than required by applications such as spatial reasoning systems. Consequently, we hope the new ideas and additional information including classification of 3D intersection presented herein will be useful for a variety of spatial-based applications.

REFERENCES

Caumon, G., Collon-Drouaillet, P., Le Carlier de Veslud, C., Viseur, S., & Sausse, J. (2009). Surface - based 3D modeling of geological structures. *Math Geosci, 41*(8), 927–945. doi:10.1007/s11004-009-9244-2

Didier, B. (1990). *An Efficient Ray - Polygon Intersection. In Graphics Gems*. Academic Press.

Egenhofer, M. J., & Franzosa, R. (1991). Point-Set topological Relations, International Journal of *Geographical. Information Systems, 5*(2), 161–174.

Egenhofer, M. J., & Golledge, R. G. (1998). *Spatial and Temporal Reasoning in Geographic Information Systems*. Oxford University Press.

Eloe, N., Leopold, J. L., Sabharwal, C. L., & Yin, Z. (2012). Efficient Computation of Boundary Intersection and Error Tolerance in VRCC-3D+. In *Proceedings of the 18h International Conference on Distributed Multimedia Systems (DMS'12)*. Academic Press.

Elsheikh, A. H., & Elsheikh, M. (2012). A reliable triangular mesh intersection algorithm and its application in geological modeling. *Engineering with Computers*, 1–15.

Guigue, P., & Devillers, O. (2003). Fast and robust triangle - triangle overlap test using orientation predicates. *Journal of Graphics Tools, 8*(1), 25–42.

Held, M. (1997). ERIT a collection of efficient and reliable intersection tests. *Journal of Graphics Tools*, *2*(4), 25–44. doi:10.1080/10867651.1997.10487482

Houghton, E. G., Emnett, R. F., Factor, J. D., & Sabharwal, C. L. (1985). Implementation of A Divide and Conquer Method For Surface Intersections. *Computer Aided Geometric Design*, *2*, 173–183. doi:10.1016/0167-8396(85)90022-6

Lum, P. Y., Singh, Lehman, Ishkanov, Vejdemo-Johansson, Alagappan, Carlsson, & Carlsson. (2013). Extracting insights from the shape of complex data using topology. *Scientific Reports*, *3*(1236). DOI: 10.1038/srep01236

Möller, T. (1997). A fast triangle - triangle intersection test. *Journal of Graphics Tools*, *2*(2), 25–30. doi:10.1080/10867651.1997.10487472

Randell, D. A., Cui, Z., & Cohn, A. G. (1992). A Spatial Logic Based on Regions and Connection. *KR*, *92*, 165–176.

Sabharwal, Leopold, & McGeehan. (2013). Triangle-Triangle Intersection Determination and Classification to Support Qualitative Spatial Reasoning, Polibits. *Research Journal of Computer Science and Computer Engineering with Applications*, (48), 13–22.

Sabharwal, C. L., & Leopold, J. L. (2013). A Fast Intersection Detection Algorithm For Qualitative Spatial Reasoning. In *Proceedings of the 19h International Conference on Distributed Multimedia Systems*. Academic Press.

Sabharwal, C. L., & Leopold, J. L. (2011). Reducing 9-Intersection to 4-Intersection for Identifying Relations in Region Connection Calculus. In *Proceedings of the 24th International Conference on Computer Applications in Industry and Engineering* (CAINE 2011). IEEE.

Sabharwal, C. L., Leopold, J. L., & Eloe, N. (2011). A More Expressive 3D Region Connection Calculus. In *Proceedings of the 2011 International Workshop on Visual Languages and Computing (in conjunction with the 17th International Conference on Distributed Multimedia Systems (DMS'11)*. Academic Press.

Tropp, O., Tal, A., & Shimshoni, I. (2006). A fast triangle to triangle intersection test for collision detection. *Computer Animation and Virtual Worlds*, *17*(50), 527–535. doi:10.1002/cav.115

Chapter 9
Multiple Object Tracking by Scale Space Representation of Objects, Method of Linear Assignment, and Kalman Filter

Kumar S. Ray
Indian Statistical Institute, India

Kingshuk Chatterjee
Indian Statistical Institute, India

Soma Ghosh
Indian Statistical Institute, India

Debayan Ganguly
Indian Statistical Institute, India

ABSTRACT

This chapter presents a multi-object tracking system using scale space representation of objects, the method of linear assignment and Kalman filter. In this chapter basically two very prominent problems of multi object tracking have been resolved; the two prominent problems are (i) irrespective of the size of the objects, tracking all the moving objects simultaneously and (ii) tracking of objects under partial and/or complete occlusion. The primary task of tracking multiple objects is performed by the method of linear assignment for which few cost parameters are computed depending upon the extracted features of moving objects in video scene. In the feature extraction phase scale space representation of objects have been used. Tracking of occluded objects is performed by Kalman filter.

INTRODUCTION

Object tracking is a sequential method of object detection, feature selection, object representation using selected features in each frame of a video. Finally detected object(s) in each current frame is matched with object(s) of previous frame to locate an object's position in every frame of the video and thus the trajectory of an object is generated as it moves around the area under surveillance or any computerized vision system. Fast and reliable object tracking is very important in vision based systems such as

DOI: 10.4018/978-1-4666-8723-3.ch009

1. Surveillance systems,
2. Human computer interaction,
3. Traffic monitoring,
4. Vehicle navigation,
5. Action recognition,
6. Navigation of autonomous robots, etc.

Tracking of objects is very complex in nature due to several problems such as presence of different noise in video, unpredictable motion of objects, non-rigid or articulated nature of objects, partial and full object occlusion, change in scene illumination, changes in background etc. Usually, tracking is simplified by imposing constraints on the motion or appearance or both of the objects. For example, almost all the tracking algorithms assume that the object motion is smooth with no abrupt changes. For most of the systems, area under operation is not exactly unknown; i.e. some prior knowledge about the type and the size of the objects or the object appearance and shape are used to simplify the problem.

In this chapter, a multiple object tracking method for surveillance system is described. This system will detect objects under partial and /or complete occlusion and track all the objects simultaneously without putting any restriction on the size/dimension of the objects, i.e., objects may be cars or persons or whatever. The concept described in this chapter can be applied with some modifications, for the surveillance of any other public places like daily market place, railway station, meeting hall, parking space etc.

BACKGROUND

Several approaches of object tracking have been presented so far (Yilmaz, Javed, & Shah, 2006). They differ from each other with respect to object representation methods, features used for tracking, tracking methods employed etc. For instance objects can be represented as point i.e. the centroid (Veenman, Reinders, & Backer, 2001) or set of points (Serby, Koller-Meier, & Gool, 2004), primitive geometric shapes such as rectangles and ellipses (Comaniciu, Ramesh, & Meer, 2003),object contour which is used to represent non rigid objects (Yilmaz, Li, & Shah, 2004) and others. Objects also can be represented as scale space blobs, corners, ridges and edges (Lindeberg, 1996a, 1996b). The blobs in a video frame are related to the contrast between the spatial feature and its neighbourhood. The important features used for tracking the objects are colour in different colour spaces such as RGB, YCbCr, HSV. But none of these colour spaces are unanimously accepted as all of them are affected by noise (Song, Kittler, & Metrou, 1996). Feature like edge, which can be easily detected because of its distinct change in intensity can also be used for tracking. Edges have the advantage that it is not susceptible to illumination changes, like colour. Tracking algorithms that track on the basis of object boundaries use the edge finding algorithms. The most popular algorithm among the existing edge finding algorithms is Canny's edge detection (Canny, 1986) algorithm. Similarly some approaches use the Optical flow of the objects as feature, which is a dense field of displacement vectors computed assuming constant brightness of corresponding pixels in consecutive frames (Horn & Schunk, 1981; Lucas & Kanade, 1981). The algorithms for object detection are numerous in nature; for instance, the popular techniques for object detection are interest point detectors which are usually unique to an object and they are not susceptible to illumination or camera view point changes. Harris interest point detector (Harris & Stephens, 1988) and SIFT detector (Lowe, 2004) belong to this category. Background subtraction can also be used for object detection .In this technique a background model is formed and each incoming frame is compared with the background to identify changes which represent the foreground objects. The most popular approach for background model is the mixture of Gaussian (Wren, Azarbayejani, & Pentland, 1997; Stauffer & Grimson, 2000). Segmentation is another technique for object detection. The aim of segmentation algorithm is to partition the image into similar regions. The most popular segmentation technique is mean shift clustering (Comaniciu & Meer, 2002). Next to object detection, the most important task is tracking of objects on the basis of the features extracted from one frame to the next. The tools employed to track objects depend on the features used to represent the objects. For instance objects represented by points are tracked based on their location and motion information. For this Kalman filter is a very popular tool which has been in use since 1986 (Broida & Chellappa, 1986). Kalman filter is used for estimation of object location when object states are assumed to have Gaussian distribution. For non-Gaussian objects state particle filters are used (Kitagawa, 1987). Modification of the Kalman filter to an extended form has also been successfully employed in object tracking (Bar-Shalom & Foreman, 1988). Object represented by Kernel (i.e. basic geometrical shapes) use template matching which is the most simplest and popular technique to track object (Schweitzer, Bell, & Wu, 2002). Another very efficient method for tracking is kernel tracking algorithm. It uses the concepts of mean shift clustering which is developed by Comaniciu (Comaniciu, Ramesh, & Meer, 2003). In this approach the Kernel histogram information is used. Comaniciu combined the mean shift algorithm with the Kalman filter to give a faster solution to the tracking problem. Another tracking technique, very similar in operation to the kernel tracking technique, uses the object boundary along with the object histogram information to track objects (Kang, Cohen, & Medioni, 2004) which is known as silhouette tracking. From the above discussed tracking algorithms we experience that the assumptions used by these tracking algorithms such as prior object dimension information, minimal amount of occlusion, constant illumination, high contrast between foreground objects and background, arbitrary initialization of model parameters etc. do not always work in an efficient manner in the real world. In the present time using the previously stated techniques and some new techniques many multi object tracking algorithms has come into existence each with its set of advantages and disadvantages. (Wang, Wang, & Yang Li, 2010) uses Kalman filter to track multiple objects uses distance and dimension as features, the algorithm is fast but does not deal with static occlusion and moreover it consider dynamically merged objects as new objects. Some multi object tracking employed modified version of existing tracking technique to implement multi object tracking such as (Mishra, Chouhan, & Nitnawre, 2012) which employs a modified version of mean shift tracking; but here the objects to be tracked are needed to be identified manually. Moreover they do not deal with partial occlusion. There are algorithms which do multi object tracking using k-means algorithm (Berclaz, Fleuret, Turetken, & Fua, 2011). The tracking algorithm does not pose any restriction on the location colour or dimension of the objects but imposes restrictions such as objects neither appear or disappear but at certain locations, do not move quickly and cannot share place with any other objects. Khan, Gu, and Backhouse (2011) is one of the few papers that deal with long time occlusion. It uses anisotropic meanshift and particle filters but does not deal with multi object tracking. Particle swarm optimization has also been employed successfully in multi object tracking in the recent years (Hsu & Dai, 2012; Zhang, Hu, Qu, & Waybank, 2010). Multi-object tracking in non-stationary video has also been done (Nguyen & Bhanu, 2009). Pushpa and Sheshadri (2012) deals with multiple object tracking using greedy algorithm but the occlusion handling is not very robust.

In this chapter we aim to eliminate some of the above mentioned problems in multi object tracking. We aim to build a real time object tracking system which is capable of tracking objects in any given video sequence provided the video is an unedited continuous video from a static camera. Here, background model of the given video sequence is developed using Approximated Median Filter (AMF) algorithm. Then Frame differencing is used to detect objects. The features used to represent objects are its location, and curvature scale space representation of the object which is described later. The location of the detected objects in the next frame is estimated using Kalman filter. The Kalman filter is initialized properly so that it converges to the correct estimation quickly. Truth verification of the Kalman estimate is done to update the parameters of the Kalman Filter. A different Kalman filter is introduced for each new track identified. Objects identified in the next frame is assigned to a previously existing track using linear assignment approach. Partial and/or Complete occlusions are handled using Kalman estimates.

MAIN FOCUS OF THE CHAPTER

The proposed methodology consists of five basic steps. In the first step background estimation is done using Approximated Median Filtering (AMF) algorithm. In the second step object detection is done using frame differencing. In the third step feature extraction of the detected objects is performed. Then in the fourth step multiple objects tracking is treated as Linear Assignment Problem (LAP) and finally, in the fifth step, tracking of objects, under occlusion, if necessary, is dealt with Kalman filter.

Background Estimation

Moving objects identification from a video sequence is a fundamental and critical task in many computer-vision applications. A common approach to this problem is to perform background subtraction, which identifies moving objects from the portion of a video frame that differs significantly from a background model. There are many challenges in developing a good background subtraction algorithm. First, it must be robust against changes in illumination. Second, it should avoid detecting non-stationary background objects such as swinging leaves, rain, snow, and shadow cast by moving objects. Finally, the background model which is stored internally should react quickly to changes in background such as starting and stopping of vehicles. One popular technique is to model each pixel feature in a video frame with the Mixture Of Gaussians (MOG) method (Stauffer & Grimson, 2000). The MOG method can deal with periodic motions from a cluttered background, slow lighting changes, etc. However, it is not adaptive to the quick variations in dynamic environments (Javed, Shafique, & Shah, 2002). Other pixel-wise modeling techniques include kernel density estimation (Elgammal, Harwood, Davis, 2000; Sheikh & Shah, 2005) and code-book approach (Kim, Chalidabhongse, Harwood, & Davis, 2005), etc. Due to the large memory requirements of non-recursive filtering, McFarlane and Schofield proposed a simple recursive filter to estimate the background using the concept of median (Mcfarlane & Schofield, 1995) which requires less memory. This technique has been used in back-ground modeling for urban traffic monitoring (Remagnino, 1997). In this scheme, the running estimate of the median is incremented by one if the input pixel is larger than the estimate, and decreased by one if smaller. This estimate eventually converges to a value for which half of the input pixels are larger than and half are smaller than this value; that is the median.

For estimation of background we consider AMF. We start the process by considering the first frame of the video sequence as background frame and for each of the successive video frames following procedure is done: Each pixel in the background model is incremented by one if the corresponding pixel in the current frame is greater in value, i.e.

if $Fr(x_i, y_j) > Bg(x_i, y_j) \Rightarrow Bg(x_i, y_j) = Bg(x_i, y_j) + 1$ OR

Each pixel in the background model is decreased by one if the corresponding pixel in the current frame is smaller in value, i.e.

if $Fr(x_i, y_j) < Bg(x_i, y_j) \Rightarrow Bg(x_i, y_j) = Bg(x_i, y_j) - 1$;

where Fr=current frame, Bg= background frame and $i = 1...$No. of rows of the frame and $j = 1...$No. of columns of the frame. So far accuracy is concerned, AMF is not as good as MOG and median filter(MF). But it produces good performance with extremely simple implementation. Since the amount of background update (+1 or -1) is independent of the foreground pixels, it is very robust against moving traffic. It requires less memory and also it works faster than MOG and MF. The only drawback of this approximated scheme is that it adapts slowly towards a large change in background. That is why to compensate for large change in background, in object detection phase of the next section we use frame differencing.

Object Detection

In this section, object detection is done by means of a modified version of frame differencing. Frame differencing has been in use since the late 1970s (Jain & Nagel, 1979).The basic idea of the frame differencing technique is to subtract a temporarily adjacent frame from the current frame to identify the objects which are moving in the current frame. The advantage of frame differencing is that certain changes in background especially in an external scene such as illumination, a weather becoming cloudy or a car being parked can be incorporated as background very easily. But it is very difficult for the background estimation model to incorporate such phenomena immediately. However, there are some disadvantages of the frame differencing model, e.g. it evidently works only in particular conditions of objects' speed and frame rate and is very sensitive to the chosen thresholds which are ad hoc in nature. Hence, we modify the frame differencing method to remove the above said disadvantages. The most important disadvantage of the frame differencing technique is that if the movements of the objects are very slow then there is no significant change in the temporarily adjacent frames. A very easy solution to this problem is to increase the distance between the adjacent frames i.e. instead of using the adjacent frames we can use the frames which is a number of frames before the current frame so that we can also detect the motion of the slow objects.

Now we obtain an image which contains only the moving object of the current frame and devoid of any noise due to error in background estimation. Thus the moving objects are detected. In case any fragmentation of objects occur we use a distance based criteria which connects blobs very close to one another if they are within a certain threshold.

Feature Representation using Curvature Scale Space Image

Curvature Scale Space (CSS) image is a multi-scale, curvature-based shape representation technique for planar curves. It consists of several arch-shaped contours representing the inflection points of a shape as it is smoothed. The maxima of these contours are used to represent a shape. For an example, we have a frame of a video which contains an object in Figure 1.

Suppose after detecting the object using Approximate Median Filter as background subtraction method we get an image in Figure 2. Then using any edge detection algorithm the edge of the object is detected. Every object is represented by the x and y coordinates of its boundary points.

The boundary of the object (curve) is then smoothed repeatedly by a Gaussian function of monotonically increasing width and the locations of curvature zero-crossings on the smoothed curve are determined at different levels of scale (width of Gaussian). The location of curvature zero-crossings on the curve is the length of curve at which the zero-crossing is resulted.

Now, we have a set of zero-crossing points at each "σ" value (width of Gaussian filter). We can display the resulting points in (u,σ) plane, where u is the normalised arc length and σ is the width of the Gaussian kernel. This plotting is called as CSS Image.

As seen in Figure 3, there are two curvature zero-crossings on every concave or convex part of the shape, and as the curve becomes smoother, these points approach each other and create a contour in the CSS image of the shape (see Figure 4). When the segment is filled, the two points join and represent the maximum of the relevant contour. The height of this contour then reflects the depth and size of the concavity or convexity. The deeper and larger the segment, the higher the maximum. In other words, a contour maximum in the CSS image represents a segment of the shape. Now the maximum of each significant contour in Figure 4 are extracted. Usually there is a small gap at the neighbourhood of the maxima. As the curve flattens with increasing sigma, the slope is very close to zero, but not exactly zero;

Figure 1. A frame of a video sequence containing an object

Figure 2. A background subtracted image

therefore, two curvature zero-crossings on every concave or convex part of the shape comes very near to each other but do not converge. So, maximum of the contours are calculated as the mid-point of the line connecting two highest points. Thus, an object in an image can be represented by locations of its CSS contour maxima in CSS image $-(u_m, \sigma_m)$, where m =1, 2 ... the no. of maxima. Such as, the person in Figure 1 can be represented as three pairs of (u, σ) values (as per Figure 4).

Compactness is an aspect of the CSS representation. A shape is represented by about less than ten pairs of integer values (Abbasi, Mokhtarian, & Kittler, 1999). Another property of the CSS image is that it retains the local properties of the shape. Every contour of the CSS image corresponds to a concavity or a convexity of the shape. A local deformation of the shape mainly causes a change in the corresponding contour of the CSS image (Abbasi, Mokhtarian, & Kittler, 1999).

*Figure 3. The locations of curvature zero-crossings on the curve are pointed by "red *" and the "green *" denotes the starting point of measuring the length of the curve*

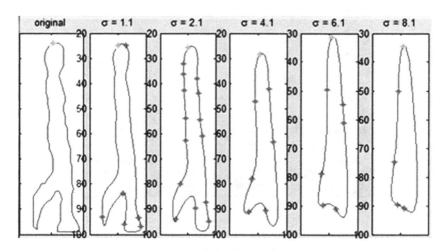

Feature Extraction

After object detection the next stage is feature extraction so that the detected objects can be represented and tracked in the next frame. Objects are represented as points (Veenman, Reinders, & Backer, 2001), kernels (having geometrical shape) (Serby, Koller-Meier, & Gool, 2004), contours (Yilmaz, Li, & Shah, 2004), and others. In addition to these, many features such as colour histogram of the object, its SIFT detectors etc. are used to represent objects. Here we primarily use three features to represent an object:

1. Curvature scale space representation of object detected,
2. The centroid of the object detected, and
3. Dimension of the bounding box.

SOLUTIONS AND RECOMMENDATIONS

In this section we solve the tracking problem under two considerations, viz., tracking of multiple objects which are not occluded and tracking of objects under occlusion. We empirically compare our method with some existing methods.

Multiple Object Tracking

The problem of multiple object tracking is considered as a linear assignment problem as stated below:

Let there be a set of existing tracks and a set of objects be identified in the next frame. The problem is to assign the detected objects in current frame either to the existing tracks or to the new tracks such that cost of assigning the object is minimum .The block diagram of this phase is shown in Figure 5.

Figure 4. Blue points are curvature zero-crossing points at each sigma value and red triangles denote the maximas of the contours

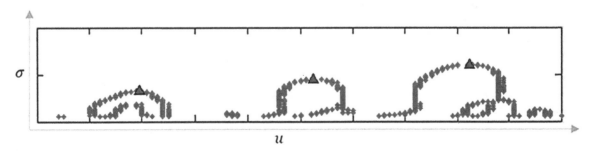

Figure 5. Steps involved in multiple object tracking

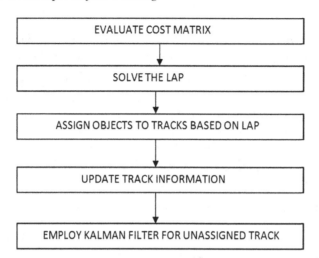

The cost that we calculate is as follows:

In the video sequence when, for the first time, there is a frame which contains an (some) object (objects) then there is no existing track. We introduce tracks where the features of the said object/objects are stored along with the track number. The features are:

1. The "centroid" of the objects,
2. "Width and height of the bounding box" of the objects,
3. "FeaturePoint" (mean of the object-shape's CSS contour maxima locations $-(u_m, \sigma_m)$, and
4. "Range" (difference between minimum and maximum of horizontal and vertical position of maximas respectively - (*Hrange, Vrange*)).

Now in the next frame a set of objects are detected among which some of the objects belong to the earlier frame and some are appearing for the first time. Here the question of linear assignment arises.

Other than the first frame, for each frame we create a cost matrix for each detected object in the frame. The cost of assigning each object from the detected set of objects in current frame to the existing track is calculated. As in Figure 6, there are two existing tracks in the previous frame and three detected objects in the current frame. We compute the Euclidian distance between the *centroid* value, stored in *track 1* and the *centroid* value of each object of the current frame. If this measure is greater than the *width or height of the bounding box* stored in *track 1*, then we assign *-1* value for the *Track_no* field and 999 in *cost* field of the cost matrix for the object which indicates no resemblance; otherwise, we proceed to calculate Euclidean distance of *FeaturePoint* and *Range* between the object and the *track 1*. If measured difference of *Range* is less than or equal to 3 then, the object is considered as a promising candidate to be assigned to the *track 1*. we assign Track No. for the *Track_no* field and measured Euclidean distance of *FeaturePoint* in the *cost* field of the cost matrix for the object. This process is repeated for all detected objects for each of the existing tracks and cost matrix of each object in the current frame is prepared. For example, Table1 is a sample cost matrix for a video frame like Figure 6.

Figure 6. Existing tracks of the previous frame (left) and detected objects in current frame (right)

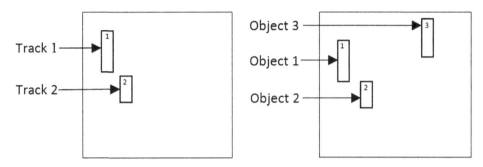

In the following paragraph the pseudo-code of creating cost matrix for linear assignment is stated as:

Remark: (x_i, y_i) is the centroid of $track_i$ and (x_j, y_j) is the centroid of the jth object ($Object_j$) in the current frame. $Width_j$ and $Height_j$ are the dimensions of the bounding box of $Object_j$. .. is the *FeaturePoint* of $track_i$ and (u_j, σ_j) is the *FeaturePoint* of $Object_j$. $(Hrange_i, Vrange_i)$ is the *Range* of $track_i$ and $(Hrange_j, Vrange_j)$ is the *Range* of $Object_j$. $Cos\,t_{ij}$ is the cost of assigning $Object_j$ to $track_i$ and $Track_{ij}$ is the track no which is either i or -1.

$$D = \sqrt{(x_i - x_j)^2 + (y_i - y_j)^2}$$

if $(D < Width_j) \,||\, (D < Height_j)$ % Resemblance between $track_i$ and $Object_j$

   then

$$FD = \sqrt{(u_i - u_j)^2 + (\sigma_i - \sigma_j)^2}$$

$$RD = \sqrt{(Hrange_i - Hrange_j)^2 + (Vrange_i - Vrange_j)^2}$$

Table 1. A sample cost matrix for a video frame

Object/Track	Track 1	Track 2
Object 1	Track no. = 1; Cost = 1.882	Track no. = 2; Cost = 19.43
Object 2	Track no. = 1; Cost = 28.79	Track no. = 2; Cost = 4.556
Object 3	Track no. = -1; Cost = 999	Track no. = -1; Cost = 999

if *(RD ≤ 3)*, then

$Track_{ij} = i$

$Cos\,t_{ij} = FD$

else

% No resemblance between $track_i$ and $Object_j$

$Track_{ij} = -1$

$Cos\,t_{ij} = 999$

and calculate the next cost.

We update the Track for each frame in the following process:

An object is decided to be a perfect match with a track with minimum cost. So, for each object, cost matrix is searched for minimum *cost* and corresponding *track_no* and the object is assigned to the Track of *track_no* with minimum *cost*. For example, as *object 1*, in Table 1 has minimum cost for *track 1*; *object 1* will be assigned to *track 1*. Thus all track data are updated with proper object data.

In any frame, there may be some objects which do not have any resemblance with any track, i.e. they may have -1 for *track_no* and 999 as *cost* for all the tracks in cost matrix; then these are new objects. We introduce *n* number of new tracks for *n* new objects and assign the new objects to those tracks. Such as, *Object 3* in Table 1 is a new object and will be assigned to new track *Track 3*. Some objects detected in earlier frames may be occluded in current frame. For these undetected objects kalman filter is applied to update the track information.

We will now discuss the above method using some pictorial examples from a video sequence. We will take any three frames from the video sequence; say $Frame_i$, $Frame_j$, $Frame_k$ at the *i, j* and *k* time instances where $i < j < k$.

For $Frame_i$:

Using the above mentioned object detection and feature extraction methods, the single object in the frame is represented by the features as in Figure 7. Suppose this is the first frame in the video sequence; so the object is directly assigned to the *Track1* as shown in the Table 2 and the next frame is processed.

For $Frame_j$:

This frame contains two objects whose features are as per Figure 8 and *Track1* in Table 2 is the existing track for this frame. From Figure 8 and the Table 2 it can be observed that difference between *centroid* of Object1 and Track1 (1) is less than both *width and height of object's bounding box* (16, 62), whereas difference between *centroid* of Object2 and Track1 (80.78) is greater than both *width and height of*

Figure 7. Detected object and its features in $Frame_i$ of a video

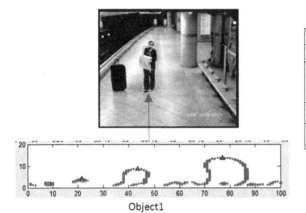

Features	Object1
Centroid	(66, 70)
Dimension of object's bounding box (width, height)	(15, 61)
FeaturePoint (u, σ)	(60.71, 8.67)
Range (*Hrange, Vrange*)	(84.00, 10.5)

Features of object detected in current frame

object's bounding box (6, 30). So, we will calculate *FeaturePoint* and *Range* of Object1 and Track1 and will mark Object2 as "no resemblance" with Track1. As per the Figure 8 and Table 2 difference between *Range* of Track1 and Object1 (0.80) is less than 3; so, cost matrix for Object1 will contain 1 as *Track_no* and difference between *FeaturePoints* of Track1 and Object1 (4.39) as *cost*. As per the pseudo code to calculate cost matrix described above, the cost matrix for $Frame_j$ is shown in Table 3.

Figure 8. Detected objects and their features in $Frame_j$ of a video

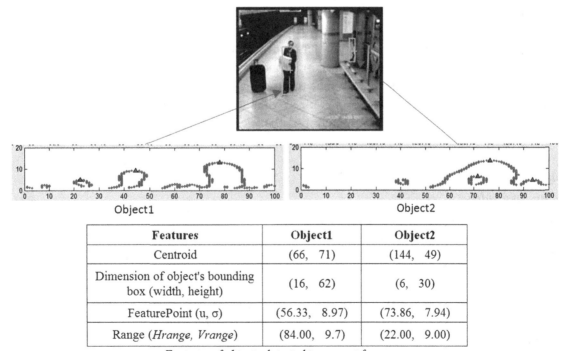

Features	Object1	Object2
Centroid	(66, 71)	(144, 49)
Dimension of object's bounding box (width, height)	(16, 62)	(6, 30)
FeaturePoint (u, σ)	(56.33, 8.97)	(73.86, 7.94)
Range (*Hrange, Vrange*)	(84.00, 9.7)	(22.00, 9.00)

Features of objects detected in current frame

Table 2. Assigned object in respective Track in Frame$_i$ of a video

Features	Track1
Centroid	(66, 70)
Dimension of object's bounding box (width, height)	(15, 61)
FeaturePoint (u, σ)	(60.71, 8.67)
Range (Hrange, Vrange)	(84.00, 10.5)

Table 3. The cost matrix for Frame$_j$

Object/ Track	Track 1
Object 1	Track no. = 1; cost = 4.39
Object 2	Track no. = -1; cost = 999

As per Table 3, *Object1* has minimum cost for *Track1*; so it is assigned to T*rack1* and *Object2* is assigned to a new Track- *Track2* and the next frame is processed. Table 4 depicts the assignment of features of individual objects in *Frame$_j$* to their respective tracks.

For *Frame$_k$*:

This frame contains two objects whose features are as per Figure 9 and *Track1* and *Track2* in Table 4 are the existing tracks for this frame. By observing Figure 9 and Table 4 and following the process-done for *Frame$_j$*, the cost matrix of this frame is as depicted in Table 5.

As per Table 5, *Object1* has minimum cost for *Track1* and *Object2* has minimum cost for *Track2*; so the *object1* is assigned to *Track1* and the *Object2* is assigned to *Track2*; as illustrated in Table 6.

Applying the described process to the whole video sequence we can obtain successful tracking results as shown in Figure 10.

Occlusion Problem

Kalman filter is used to solve the tracking problem under occlusion of object. When an object is detected for the first time and assigned a new track, its corresponding Kalman filter is initialized with the centroid values of the object assigned to the track. When that track is reassigned an object in the next frame then its corresponding Kalman filter is again reinitialized with the centroid and velocity information. Finally when the track is assigned an object for the 3rd time it is again initialized for the last time so that the

Table 4. Assigned objects in respective Tracks in Frame$_j$ of a video

Features	Track1	Track2
Centroid	(66, 71)	(144, 49)
Dimension of object's bounding box (width, height)	(16, 62)	(6, 30)
FeaturePoint (u, σ)	(56.33, 8.97)	(73.86, 7.94)
Range (Hrange, Vrange)	(84.00, 9.7)	(22.00, 9.00)

Table 5. The cost matrix for Frame$_k$ of a video

Object/ Track	Track 1	Track2
Object 1	Track no. = 1; Cost = 2.20	Track no. = -1; Cost = 999
Object 2	Track no. = -1; Cost = 999	Track no. = 2; Cost = 7.97

Figure 9. Detected objects and their features in $Frame_k$ of a video

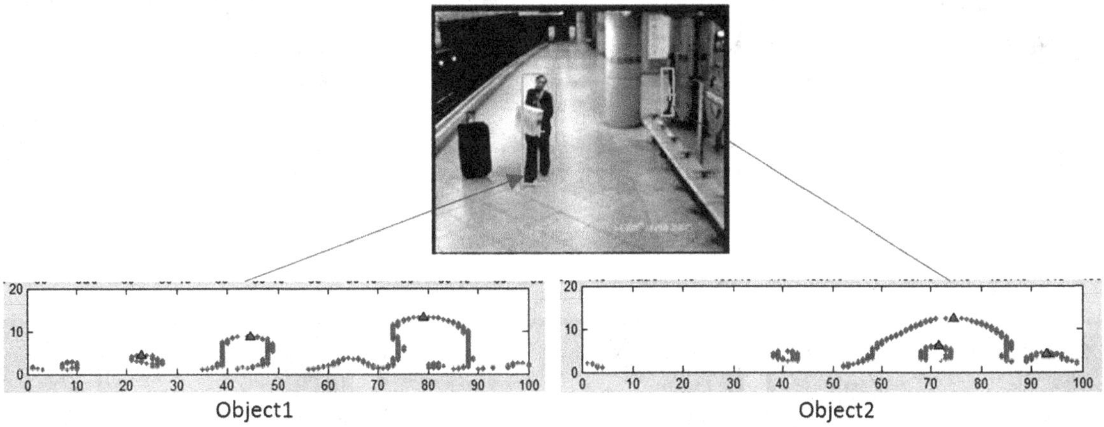

Features	Object1	Object2
Centroid	(66, 72)	(145, 49)
Dimension of object's bounding box (width, height)	(17, 62)	(6, 30)
FeaturePoint (u, σ)	(58.50, 9.34)	(81.79, 7.14)
Range (Hrange, Vrange)	(83.50, 10.2)	(21.5, 8.4)

Features of objects detected in current frame

Table 6. Assigned objects in respective Track in $Frame_k$ of a video

Features	Track1	Track2
Centroid	(66, 72)	(145, 49)
Dimension of object's bounding box (width, height)	(17, 62)	(6, 30)
FeaturePoint (u, σ)	(58.50, 9.34)	(81.79, 7.14)
Range (Hrange, Vrange)	(83.50, 10.2)	(21.5, 8.4)

centroid, velocity and acceleration values are properly initialized. The first two initializations are done so that if a track is not assigned an object for three frames, even then the Kalman filter will be able to predict a location even though the prediction may not be very accurate. This process of initialization is done, because a proper initialization of the Kalman filter enables it to predict the next location in the coming frames more accurately. Whenever a track is assigned an object the corrections are made to the Kalman filter parameters according to the previously stated rules and the next predicted location is determined. If an existing track is not assigned an object from the current frame we can assume that the object got occluded partially or completely by some other object; hence it is not detected. Here we use the Kalman filter prediction for that track if the Kalman prediction for the location of the object is within the image dimension. We assume that the occluded object is located in that particular location, and the centroid information of the corresponding track is updated. All other information remains the same. The kalman prediction for occluded objects are shown in Figure 11.

Figure 10. Successful tracking in indoor scene

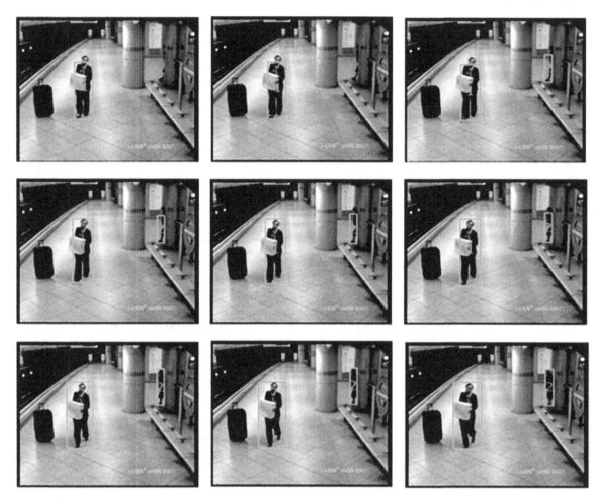

Results

The system is tested on four types of image sequences all of which are continuous unedited and from a static camera. The system is highly successful in all these types shown in Table 7. The result (Table 8) shows that the system is not that efficient only when its an outdoor scene with many objects present which is primarily due to the failure of the object detection part than the tracking part.

Comparative Study

In this section, we will present an empirical comparison of some well-known tracking algorithms and our presented algorithm. Before starting the comparison we will brief the compared processes:

- **Kalman Filter:** The Kalman filter has been extensively used in the computer vision for tracking. This method is composed of two steps- prediction and correction. The prediction step predicts new state of the variables using state models. In the correction step objects predicted state is up-

Figure 11. Shows successful tracking under partial occlusion

Table 7. Different types of videos used

Scene	Number of Videos	Number of Objects
Outdoor	1	Many
Outdoor	3	Few
Indoor	1	Many
Indoor	2	few

Table 8. Performance of tracking algorithm

Scene	Number of Objects	Number of Objects Present	Number of Objects Tracks Successfully	Percentage of Success
Outdoor	Many	26	18	69%
Outdoor	Few	12	10	83.3%
Indoor	Few	11	11	100%
Indoor	Many	9	7	77%

dated using current observations. But, Kalman filter falters in estimating the state variables that do not follow Gaussian distribution (Bar-Shalom & Foreman, 1988; Broida & Chellappa, 1986; Wang, Wang, & Yang Li, 2010).

- **Multiple Hypothesis Tracking (MHT):** This is an iterative algorithm. Iteration begins with a set of existing track hypothesis. Each hypothesis is a collection of disjoint tracks. For each hypothesis, a prediction of object's position in the following frame is made. The prediction are then compared with actual values by calculating a distance measure.

- **Mean Shift Method:** This is an efficient approach to tracking objects whose appearance is defined by histograms. Probabilistic distribution of Region Of Interest (ROI) in first frame is obtained using color feature. This distribution of first frame is compared with consecutive frame and the target is accurately localized using Chamfer distance transform (Broida & Chellappa, 1986).
- **Support Vector Machine (SVM):** SVM is a classification method which gives a set of positive and negative training values. For SVM, the positive samples contain tracked image object and the negative samples consists of all remaining things that are not tracked.
- **Shape Matching:** In this method, for each frame of the video a model is generated from the hypothesized object silhouette based on previous frame. Then the object silhouette and its associated model is searched in the current frame. But, this approach considers only translation of the silhouette from one frame to another, therefore non-rigid object motion is not explicitly handled.
- **Contour Tracking:** This method iteratively evolves an initial contour in the previous frame to its new position in the following frame. The contour evolution requires that some part of the object in the current frame overlap with object region in the previous frame. There are two approaches of contour tracking: using state space models to model the contour shape and motion. Another approach is to evolve the contour directly by minimizing the contour energy (see Table 9).

FUTURE RESEARCH DIRECTIONS

Significant progress has been achieved in object tracking during the last decade. There are many efficient and robust trackers which can track objects in simple scenarios (and/or with assumptions like, smoothness of motion, minimal occlusion, constant illumination, videos captured by single static camera

Table 9. An empirical comparison of tracking methodologies

	Tracking Method	Category	No. of Objects Tracked	Entry	Exit	Training	Initialization	Occlusion
1	Kalman Filter	Point Tracking	S	×	×	-	-	×
2	MHT	Point Tracking	M	√	√	-	-	√
3	Mean Shift	Kernel Tracking	S	-	-	×	√	√
4	SVM	Kernel Tracking	S	-	-	√	√	√
5	Shape Matching	Silhouette Tracking	S	-	-	×	-	×
6	Contour Matching	Silhouette Tracking	M	-	-	√	-	√
7	Presented Method	Silhouette + Point Tracking	M	√	√	-	-	√

(Yilmaz, Javed, & Shah, 2006).

(√: Required/Can handle, ×: Not required/Cannot handle, -: Not Applicable).

etc.). However, these assumptions does not hold in many realistic scenarios and hence the obstructions rein the effectiveness of the tracker in the applications like automated surveillance, traffic monitoring, vehicle navigation, video retrieval, human-computer interaction etc.

One of the challenges in tracking is to develop an algorithm to track objects in unconstrained videos which are noisy, compressed and unstructured (obtained from broadcast networks or captured by CCTV cameras). Due to noise in these videos differencing between the foreground and background is tough, hence detection of moving object difficult. Also due to non-clarity of data particular feature selection becomes tough. Other unconstrained videos are those captured by camera rotating on its axis and thus generating multiple views of same area or videos captured by camera installed on a vehicle. For the first type of video proper image registration is required to detect object properly and for the second type of video as background is not constant separating moving object and changing background is difficult. Another challenging video is of meetings where multiple people are in a small field of view. Thus, there is severe occlusion to hinder the tracking.

Thus, tracking (i.e. locating object position in each video frame and generating its trajectory) along with associated methods of object detection, feature selection and object representation, dynamic shape and motion estimation are still very active area of research and new ideas are continuously immerging. Researchers are actively working on these issues. In a general belief, additional sources of information, like contextual and prior information should be employed whenever possible. By the integration of different sources of information will result in a general tracker that can be employed successfully in a variety of applications.

CONCLUSION

The algorithm is successful in dealing with partial and complete occlusion. Only when we are dealing with very busy outdoor video sequences that the tracking rate falls primarily due to failure in distinct object detection. Many complicated techniques such as joint probability distribution etc. have been used to solve the multiple object tracking problem but linear assignment technique is successful in doing the tracking. Moreover proper initialization of Kalman filter ensures correct location determination under occlusion, The only place where this system fails is in the detection of partially occluded objects for the first time for e.g. a group of people is considered as a single object if they are very close together which leads to error in tracking. Perhaps use of better segmentation technique in the object detection phase may solve this problem.

REFERENCES

Abbasi, S., Mokhtarian, F., & Kittler, J. (1999). Curvature scale space image in shape similarity retrieval. *Multimedia Systems*, 7(6), 467–476. doi:10.1007/s005300050147

Bar-Shalom, Y., & Foreman, T. (1988). *Tracking and Data Association: Mathematics in Science and Engineering*. San Diego, CA: Academic Press.

Berclaz, J., Fleuret, F., Turetken, E., & Fua, P. (2011). Multiple Object Tracking Using K-Shortest Paths Optimization. *Institute Of Electrical And Electronics Engineers Transactions On Pattern Analysis And Machine Intelligence, 33*(9), 1806–1819. PMID:21282851

Broida, T., & Chellappa, R. (1986). Estimation of object motion parameters from noisy images. *Institute Of Electrical And Electronics Engineers Transactions on Pattern Analysis and Machine Intelligence, 8*(1), 90–99. PMID:21869326

Canny, J. A. (1986). Computational approach to edge detection. *Institute Of Electrical And Electronics Engineers Transaction Pattern Analysis and Machine Intelligence, 8*(6), 679–698. PMID:21869365

Comaniciu, D., & Meer, P. (2002). Mean shift: A robust approach toward feature space analysis. *Institute Of Electrical And Electronics Engineers Transactions on Pattern Analysis and Machine Intelligence, 24*(5), 603–619.

Comaniciu, D., Ramesh, V., & Meer, P. (2003). Kernel-based object tracking. *Institute Of Electrical And Electronics Engineers Transactions on Pattern Analysis and Machine Intelligence, 25*, 564–575.

Elgammal, A., Harwood, D., & Davis, L. (2000). Non-parametric Model for Background Subtraction. *European Conference on Computer Vision, 2 (June)*, (pp. 751-767).

Harris, C., & Stephens, M. (1988). A combined corner and edge detector. *4th Alvey Vision Conference*, (pp. 147–151).

Horn, B., & Schunk, B. (1981). Determining optical flow. *Artificial Intelligence, 17*(1-3), 185–203. doi:10.1016/0004-3702(81)90024-2

Hsu, C. C., & Dai, G. T. (2012). Multiple Object Tracking using Particle Swarm Optimization. *World Academy of Science. Engineering and Technology, 6*(8), 29–32.

Jain, R., & Nagel, H. (1979). On the analysis of accumulative difference pictures from image sequences of real world scenes. *Institute Of Electrical And Electronics Engineers Transactions on Pattern Analysis and Machine Intelligence, 1*(2), 206–214. PMID:21868850

Javed, O., Shafique, K., & Shah, M. (2002). A Hierarchical Approach to Robust Background Subtraction using Color and Gradient Information. *Institute Of Electrical And Electronics Engineers Workshop on Motion and Video Computing*, (pp. 22-27). doi:10.1109/MOTION.2002.1182209

Kang, J., Cohen, I., & Medioni, G. (2004). Object reacquisition using geometric invariant appearance, model. *International Conference on Pattern Recognition (ICPR)*, (pp. 759–762).

Khan, Z. H., Gu, I. Y. H., & Backhouse, A. G. (2011). Robust Visual Object Tracking Using Multi-Mode Anisotropic Mean Shift and Particle Filters. *Institute Of Electrical And Electronics Engineers Transactions On Circuits And Systems For Video Technology, 21*(1), 74–87.

Kim, K., Chalidabhongse, T. H., Harwood, D., & Davis, L. (2005). Real-time Foreground-Background Segmentation using Codebook Model. *Real-Time Imaging, 11*(3), 167–256. doi:10.1016/j.rti.2004.12.004

Kitagawa, G. (1987). Non-gaussian state-space modeling of nonstationary time series. *Journal of the American Statistical Association, 82*(400), 1032–1041.

Lindeberg, T. (1996a). *Feature detection with automatic scale selection. Technical Report.* Dept. of Numerical Analysis and Computing Science, Royal Institute of Technology.

Lindeberg, T. (1996b). *Edge detection and ridge detection with automatic scale selection. Technical report.* Dept. of Numerical Analysis and Computing Science, Royal Institute of Technology.

Lowe, D. (2004). Distinctive image features from scale-invariant keypoints. *International Journal of Computer Vision, 60*(2), 91–110. doi:10.1023/B:VISI.0000029664.99615.94

Lucas, B. D., & Kanade, T. (1981). An iterative image registration technique with an application to stereo vision. *7th International Joint Conference on Artificial Intelligence.*

Mcfarlane, N., & Schofield, C. (1995). Segmentation and tracking of piglets in images. *Machine Vision and Applications, 8*(3), 187–193. doi:10.1007/BF01215814

Mishra, R., Chouhan, M. K., & Nitnawre, D., Dr. (2012). Multiple Object Tracking by Kernel Based Centroid Method for Improve Localization. *International Journal of Advanced Research in Computer Science and Software Engineering, 2*(7), 137–140.

Nguyen, H., & Bhanu, B. (2009). Multi-Object Tracking In Non-Stationary Video Using Bacterial Foraging Swarms. *Proceedings of the 16th Institute Of Electrical And Electronics Engineers international conference on Image processing,* (pp. 873-876).

Pushpa, D., & Sheshadri, H. S. (2012). Multiple Object Detection and Tracking in Cluttered Region with Rational Mobile Area. *International Journal of Computers and Applications, 39*(10), 14–17. doi:10.5120/4855-7125

Remagnino, P. (1997). An integrated traffic and pedestrian model-based vision system. *Proceedings of the Eighth British Machine Vision Conference,* (pp. 380-389).

Schweitzer, H., Bell, J. W., & Wu, F. (2002) Very fast template matching. *European Conference on Computer Vision (ECCV).* (pp. 358–372).

Serby, D., Koller-Meier, S., & Gool, L. V. (2004). Probabilistic object tracking using multiple features. *Institute Of Electrical And Electronics Engineers International Conference of Pattern Recognition (ICPR),* (pp. 184–187).

Sheikh, Y., & Shah, M. (2005). Bayesian Modeling of Dynamic Scenes for Object Detection. *Institute Of Electrical And Electronics Engineers Transactions on Pattern Analysis and Machine Intelligence, 27*(11), 1778–1792. PMID:16285376

Song, K. Y., Kittler, J., & Petrou, M. (1996). Defect detection in random color textures. *Image and Vision Computing, 14*(9), 667–683. doi:10.1016/0262-8856(96)84491-X

Stauffer, C., & Grimson, W. E. L. (2000). Learning Patterns of Activity Using Real-Time Tracking. *Institute Of Electrical And Electronics Engineers Transactions on Pattern Analysis and Machine Intelligence, 22*(8), 747–757.

Veenman, C., Reinders, M., & Backer, E. (2001). Resolving motion correspondence for densely moving points. *Institute Of Electrical And Electronics Engineers Transactions on Pattern Analysis and Machine Intelligence, 23*(1), 54–72.

Wang, X. L. K., Wang, W., & Yang Li, A. (2010). Multiple Object Tracking Method Using Kalman Filter. *Proceedings of the 2010 Institute Of Electrical And Electronics Engineers International Conference on Information and Automation.*

Wren, C., Azarbayejani, A., & Pentland, A. (1997). Pfinder: Real-time tracking of the human body. *Institute Of Electrical And Electronics Engineers Transactions on Pattern Analysis and Machine Intelligence, 19*(7), 780–785.

Yilmaz, A., Javed, O., & Shah, M. (2006). Object tracking: A survey. Association for Computing Machinery Computer Survey, 38(4).

Yilmaz, A., Li, X., & Shah, M. (2004). Contour based object tracking with occlusion handling in video acquired using mobile cameras. *Institute Of Electrical And Electronics Engineers Transactions on Pattern Analysis and Machine Intelligence, 26*(11), 1531–1536. PMID:15521500

Zhang, X., Hu, W., Qu, W., & Maybank, S. (2010). Multiple Object Tracking Via Species-Based Particle Swarm Optimization. *Institute Of Electrical And Electronics Engineers Transactions On Circuits And Systems For Video Technology, 20*(11), 1590–1602.

ADDITIONAL READING

Avidan, S. (2001). Support vector tracking. *Institute Of Electrical And Electronics Engineers Conference on Computer Vision and Pattern Recognition (CVPR),* 184-191.

Bertalmio, M., Sapiro, G., & Randall, G. (2000). Morphing active contours. *Institute Of Electrical And Electronics Engineers Transactions on Pattern Analysis and Machine Intelligence, 22*(7), 733–737.

Bowyer, K., Kranenburg, C., & Dougherty, S. (2001). Edge detector evaluation using empirical roc curve. *Computer Vision and Image Understanding, 84*(1), 77–103. doi:10.1006/cviu.2001.0931

Chen, Y., Rui, Y., & Huang, T. (2001). JPDAF based HMM for real-time contour tracking. *Institute Of Electrical And Electronics Engineers Conference on Computer Vision and Pattern Recognition (CVPR),* 543–550.

Comaniciu, D., & MEER, P. (1999). Mean shift analysis and applications. *Institute Of Electrical And Electronics Engineers International Conference on Computer Vision (ICCV),* 2, 1197–1203.

Comaniciu, D. (2002). Bayesian kernel tracking. *Annual Conference of the German Society for Pattern Recognition,* 438–445.

Cox, I., & Hingorani, S. (1996). An efficient implementation of reid's multiple hypothesis tracking algorithm and its evaluation for the purpose of visual tracking. *Institute Of Electrical And Electronics Engineers Transactions on Pattern Analysis and Machine Intelligence, 18*(2), 138–150.

Han, J., & Bhanu, B. (2006). Individual recognition using gait energy image. *Institute Of Electrical And Electronics Engineers Transactions on Pattern Analysis and Machine Intelligence, 28*(2), 316–322. PMID:16468626

Hu, W., Tan, T., Wang, L., & Maybank, S. (2004). A Survey on Visual Surveillance of object motion and behaviours. *Institute Of Electrical And Electronics Engineers Transactions on Systems, Man and Cybernetics. Part C, 34*(3), 334–352.

Huttenlocher, D., Noh, J., & Rucklidge, W. (1993). Tracking nonrigid objects in complex scenes. *Institute Of Electrical And Electronics Engineers International Conference on Computer Vision (ICCV)*, 93–101.

Isard, M., & Blake, A. (1998). Condensation - conditional density propagation for visual tracking. *International Journal of Computer Vision, 29*(1), 5–28. doi:10.1023/A:1008078328650

Javed, O., Rasheed, Z., Shafique, K., & Shah, M. (2003). Tracking across multiple cameras with disjoint views. *Institute Of Electrical And Electronics Engineers International Conference on Computer Vision (ICCV)*, 952–957. doi:10.1109/ICCV.2003.1238451

Jepson, A., Fleet, D., & Elmaraghi, T. (2003). Robust online appearance models for visual tracking. *Institute Of Electrical And Electronics Engineers Transactions on Pattern Analysis and Machine Intelligence, 25*(10), 1296–1311.

Li, B., Chellappa, R., Zheng, Q., & Der, S. (2001). Model-based temporal object verification using video. *Institute Of Electrical And Electronics Engineers Transaction on Image Processing, 10*(6), 897–908.

Li, G., Zhang, J., Lin, H., Tu, D., & Zhang, M. (2004). A moving object detection approach using Integrated Background template for smart video sensor. *Institute Of Electrical And Electronics Engineers Instrumentation and Measurement Technology Conference, 21(1)*, 462-466.

Maccormick, J., & Blake, A. (2000). Probabilistic exclusion and partitioned sampling for multiple object tracking. *International Journal of Computer Vision, 39*(1), 57–71. doi:10.1023/A:1008122218374

Mokhtarian, F., & Suomela, R. (1998). Robust Image Corner Detection Through Curvature Scale Space. *Institute Of Electrical And Electronics Engineers Transactions On Pattern Analysis And Machine Intelligence, 20*(12), 1376–1381.

Nillius, P., Sullivan, J., & Carlsson, S. (2006). Multi-target tracking-linking identities using Bayesian Network inference. *Institute Of Electrical And Electronics Engineers Computer Society Conference on Computer Vision and Pattern Recognition*, 2187-2194. doi:10.1109/CVPR.2006.198

Park, S., & Aggarwal, J. K. (2003). Recognition of two-person interactions using a Hierarchical Bayesian Network. *International Workshop on Video Surveillance*, 65-76. doi:10.1145/982452.982461

Park, S., & Aggarwal, J. K. (2004). A hierarchical Bayesian network for event recognition of human actions and interactions. *Multimedia Systems, 10*(2), 164–179. doi:10.1007/s00530-004-0148-1

Rasmessen, C., & Hager, G. D. (2001). Probabilistic Data Association methods for tracking complex visual objects. *Institute Of Electrical And Electronics Engineers Transactions on Pattern Analysis and Machine Intelligence, 23*(6), 560–576.

Sarkar, S., Phillips, J., Liu, Z., Vega, I. R., Grother, P., & Bowyer, K. W. (2005). The HumanID Gait Challenge Problem: Data Sets, Performance, and Analysis. *Institute Of Electrical And Electronics Engineers Transactions on Pattern Analysis and Machine Intelligence*, *27*(2), 162–177. PMID:15688555

Sato, K., & Aggarwal, J. (2004). Temporal spatio-velocity transform and its application to tracking and interaction. *Computer Vision and Image Understanding*, *96*(2), 100–128. doi:10.1016/j.cviu.2004.02.003

Sheikh, Y., & Shah, M. (2005). Bayesian modelling of dynamic scenes for object detection. *Institute Of Electrical And Electronics Engineers Transactions on Pattern Analysis and Machine Intelligence*, *27*(11), 1778–1792. PMID:16285376

Zhong, J., & Sclaroff, S. (2003). Segmenting foreground objects from a dynamic textured background via a robust kalman filter. *Institute Of Electrical And Electronics Engineers International Conference on Computer Vision (ICCV)*, 44–50. doi:10.1109/ICCV.2003.1238312

Zhou, S., Chellapa, R., & Moghadam, B. (2003). Adaptive visual tracking and recognition using particle filters. *Institute Of Electrical And Electronics Engineers International Conference on Multimedia and Expo (ICME)*. 349–352.

KEY TERMS AND DEFINITIONS

Background Subtraction: This is a process of detecting foreground or moving objects in a scene captured using static camera. In this process, a reference frame/image which contains the stationary stuffs like pillar, window, door, furniture etc. is called as background model. Moving objects are detected by differentiating the current frame and the model frame.

Comparison of the Present Method with Some of the State-of-Art: This is a process of performance evaluation of the present method . Performance of the present method is compared with some existing methods. Some general parameters of this comparison are if the methods need manual initialisation, training or methods can handle entry or exit of object(s), full/partial occlusion of object(s) etc.

Determination of Dimension of the Blobs: Dimension of the blob means height and width of the blob which captures the gross information of the objects.

Features of Detected Objects: In tracking, features are distinctive representation of the detected objects. Features can be shape, colour, texture or dimension of the detected objects. Features are used to differentiate/correlate between multiple objects during tracking.

Kalman Filter Technique: This is a set of mathematical equations that recursively estimates the state of a process. The filter is named for Rudolf (Rudy) E. Kálmán, one of the primary developers of its theory.

Linear Assignment Problem: It is the problem of assigning M jobs to N persons such that the cost of assigning the jobs is minimum. When N=M it is known as Symmetric Linear Assignment problem and when N $\neq$ M it is known as asymmetric Linear Assignment problem.

Multiple Object Tracking: Object tracking is a method of locating an object in each video frame and thus creating a trail of the moving object. This helps in observing behaviour of particular person(s) or car(s) for any threat to the security of a place.

Occlusion in Tracking: In Tracking occlusion is the obstruction in the field of view of the camera. If the moving object is partially or completely hidden by another object. For example, two persons walking past each other, car passing under a bridge etc.

Static Camera: This type of camera is stationary and has a fixed area of vision. Usually static cameras are installed on walls of airport, stations, malls etc. with an arm or tripod. Videos captured by static camera have a fixed background.

Chapter 10
Digital Forensics:
State-of-the-Art and Open Problems

Ruchira Naskar
National Institute of Technology Rourkela, India

Pankaj Malviya
National Institute of Technology Rourkela, India

Rajat Subhra Chakraborty
Indian Institute of Technology Kharagpur, India

ABSTRACT

Digital forensics deal with cyber crime detection from digital multimedia data. In the present day, multimedia data such as images and videos are major sources of evidence in the courts of law worldwide. However, the immense proliferation and easy availability of low-cost or free, user-friendly and powerful image and video processing software, poses as the largest threat to today's digital world as well as the legal industry. This is due to the fact that such software allow efficient image and video editing, manipulation and synthesis, with a few mouse clicks even by a novice user. Such software also enable formation realistic of computer-generated images. In this chapter, we discuss different types of digital image forgeries and state-of-the-art digital forensic techniques to detect them. Through these discussions, we also give an idea of the challenges and open problems in the field of digital forensics.

1. INTRODUCTION

In today's cyber world digital images and videos act as the most frequently transmitted information carriers. This has been made possible by the huge proliferation of low-cost, easy-to-use and efficient consumer devices such as high-resolution digital cameras for image acquisition and availability of high-speed transmission media such as the internet. Gone are the days when image acquisition was essentially an analog process. Photography and image formation was film dependent and could only be done by experts in dark rooms. With the advancement of analog to digital (A/D) converters, every step of digital image acquisition, formation and storage, is now well within the grip of the common man.

DOI: 10.4018/978-1-4666-8723-3.ch010

However, the present day easy availability of low-cost or free image and video processing software and desktop tools, having immense number of multimedia manipulating features, pose threat to the fidelity of digital multimedia data. Common image and video processing operations such as cropping, splicing, blurring etc., can be performed at the click of a mouse by an average user using such software. This situation compels us to question the trustworthiness of the digital images and videos. Since digital images and videos act as the major electronic evidences for law enforcement across the world, as they are the most effective and efficient means to collect digital evidences from crime scenes. Hence, maintenance of their trustworthiness and reliability is a major challenge in today's digital world. It is extremely crucial to preserve such digital evidences against cyber-crime for suitable presentation in court of law. The need for investigation and maintenance of the fidelity and reliability of digital images and videos, has given rise to the field of "Digital Forensics" (Sencar & Memon (eds.), 2013; Redi et. al., 2011). In the recent years, researchers have focused on the areas of digital image authentication, tampering detection, identification of image forgery as well as investigation of image sources. In this chapter, we shall focus on the basics of digital forensics and the need for research in this direction. The chapter contents will include two major topics:

1. **Image Forgery Detection:** Analysis of whether the image is *original*, or has it undergone any form of tampering. Image forgery detection is carried out with the aim of investigating whether the image under question represents the unmodified captured scene or has it been forged to deceive the viewer.
2. **Image Source Identification:** Forensic analysis to investigate which device (or class of device) captured or formed the image under question.

Since JPEG is currently the most commonly used digital image format, and it is the default image format in almost all current digital camera, in this chapter we shall majorly focus on JPEG images.

Rest of the chapter is organized as follows. In Section 2, we discuss the necessity of digital forensics in the relation to digital media content protection; we compare and contrast various pros and cons of digital forensic methods in comparison to other existing digital content protection tools and techniques. In Section 3, we present different classes of digital image forgeries and state-of-the-art digital forensic techniques to deal with those classes. In Section 3, we also present a forensic technique to detect JPEG forgery, in detail. In Section 4, we present state-of-the-art digital forensic techniques to identify the origin of an image. Finally we conclude with a discussion on the future of digital forensics, in Section 5.

2. DIGITAL CONTENT PROTECTION AND DIGITAL FORENSICS

The last couple of decades have seen rapid growth of research interest in the fields of *Digital Content Protection* and *Digital Rights Management* (Cox et. al., 2008), due to rapid increase of cyber-crime rate. The most widely used practices in this direction encompass digital techniques such as *Watermarking* and *Steganography* (Cox et. al., 2008). In this section we discuss the major difference and benefit of digital forensic techniques, over such traditional digital content protection measures.

In *Digital Watermarking* (Shih, 2007) techniques, the data to be protected (*cover data*) undergoes some form of pre-processing such as embedding, compression (lossless or lossy) etc., which later help to detect malicious third party interventions. The *watermark* is a piece of information that is kept embedded into the cover data and is used to provide security to the cover data. For example, the watermark may be authentication information such as hash computed over the cover data, which is subsequently extracted and matched for detecting modification attacks or tampering activities. The major purposes of digital watermarking are digital rights management, secure media distribution and authentication.

On the other hand, *Steganography* (Shih, 2007; Fridrich, 2010) refers to the act of hiding data into digital media without drawing any suspicion from an observer (either manual or automated).. The major purpose of Steganography is to protect sensitive data against eavesdropping while transmission over an insecure channel. This is achieved by embedding the sensitive data into a *stego-file* while transmission. It is assumed that no active attack is carried out on the stego-file while transmission. Steganography is sometimes discussed in the same breath as cryptography; however, they are essentially different arts. Cryptography scrambles a message, so an uninvited reader is unable to understand it. On the other hand, steganography is about secrecy, so a potential eavesdropper won't even have a reason to suspect there's a hidden message to be read, or if he does search for it, would be unable to recover it (Fridrich, 2010).

All such techniques belong to the class of *non-blind* cyber security measures. *Non-blind* security measures are those which mandatorily need some external information in addition to the data to be secured; and such external information is obtained by preprocessing the data in some form or the other. For example, the watermark (or hash) in Digital Watermarking is a form of pre-computed external data. However, such external data pre-computation is not possible in every situation. Also in Steganography, the cover-image into which the sensitive image is hidden, may be viewed as additional information. Securing multimedia data by Digital Watermarking or Steganography can only be enforced by means of special software, embedded into the devices forming the image or video. Considering that digital images and videos act as major evidences in court of law worldwide, it now becomes mandatory that all image and video capturing devices be designed to have special security capabilities such as encryption, watermarking and data embedding. However, these added capabilities usually increase the cost of such devices, which adversely affects the business of the camera manufacturing companies. This, along with ever-increasing cyber crime rates, has lead to the search of *blind* security measures with the expectation to reduce the need for pre-computing any additional information.

Digital forensics is a developing research field which aims at *blind digital forgery detection* (Mahadian & Saic, 2010). Digital forensic techniques provide security and protection to multimedia data in those situations where the user has neither any apriori information about that data to be secured, nor has carried out any computation on the data prior to forgery detection. Such techniques do not need any external information, apart from the data to be secured. The goal of digital forensics is cyber forgery detection without any requirement of preprocessing the data to be secured. Hence such techniques belong to the class of *blind* security measures for digital content protection. Block diagrams demonstrating the operation of digital forensic techniques, and traditional digital content protection measures, have been presented in Fig. 1.

Next in this chapter, we shall present the state-of-the-art digital forensic techniques for detection of cyber forgery in digital images, as well as identification of image origin counterfeit attacks.

3. DIGITAL IMAGE FORGERY AND FORENSICS

The major purpose of Digital Image Forensics is cyber forgery detection by identification of intentional tampering or manipulation of digital images, where the user has no prior reference to the image under

Figure 1. Block diagrams representing the broad operational steps of non-blind digital content protection techniques: (top) Digital Watermarking, (middle) Steganography; and (bottom) blind Digital Forensic technique

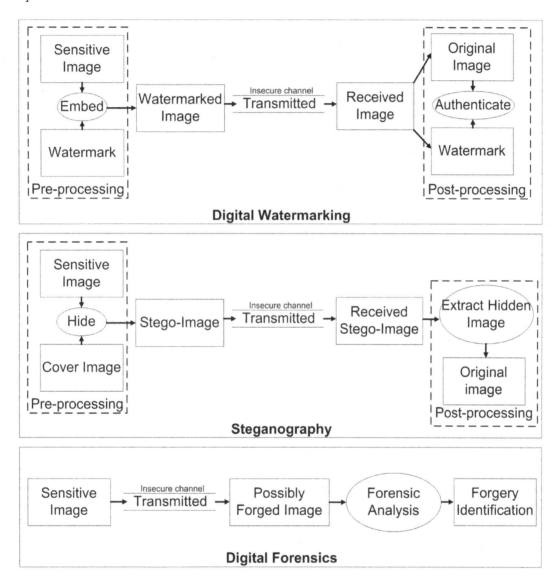

question. In this section we shall present state-of-the-art digital forensic methods (Farid, 2009, Sencar & Memon, 2008) to detect different kinds of digital image forgery. But first, we discuss the forms of digital image forgeries prevalent in today's cyber world. This background would be helpful in better understanding of their detection techniques

3.1. Digital Image Forgery

A digital image forgery may involve a single or multiple images. In a single image forgery, some portion of the image is replaced by some other portion. Hence some objects may be deleted from, modified or repeated in the image. Additionally such image modifications are usually accompanied by smoothening of the object edges by smudging or blurring selected regions of the image. As mentioned previously, in today's scenario, easy availability of user-friendly image processing tools has made such image manipulations extremely trivial, even for novice users.

In digital image forgeries involving multiple images, portion(s) of one image is maliciously transplanted into another, to give an idea to the viewers that the transplanted portion is a valid part of the latter image. This class of forgery is referred as "copy-move" forgery (Fridrich et. al., 2003; Huang et. al., 2008). Here also, the copy-move activities as well as smoothening of edges may be quite trivially carried out image manipulating softwares. This leaves little doubt why the rate of image forgery based cyber crimes, is increasing sharply with each passing day. The fidelity of any image we see today, even in television or newspapers, has become questionable, and hence image forgery is seen as a threat to the media world and broadcast industry. State-of-the-art digital image forensic methods aim at verifying the integrity and authenticity of such digital images under question.

Next, we shall present the various digital forensic methods that researchers have come up with in the recent years to combat the threats discussed above. In this chapter, we shall present the state-of-the-art of digital forensics, to pave the path for further research in this direction thereafter. The readers are requested to refer to the cited research papers for detailed working of the techniques.

3.2. Natural Images vs. Computer-Generated Images

Natural images refer to images of natural events or scenes. Many digital forensic methods exploit the statistical characteristics, inherently present in natural images (for e.g., very high pixel-value correlation) to identify forged or unnatural images. Image editing software is usually the major mean of producing such unnatural images, which the attackers generate with a target to deceive the viewer. In this section we present "visual descriptors", as means to differentiate between natural and unnatural (or computer-generated) images.

Visual descriptors are the characteristic features of a digital image that describes its visual appearance. In natural images, visual descriptors are used to quantify the visual stimulus that the image produces in the *Human Visual System* (*HVS*). One example of visual descriptors used in (Wu et. al., 2006) to identify natural images, is *color properties* of the image. The authors in (Wu et. al., 2006) have used the number of distinct colors comprising the image as well spatial variation of colors in the image. The other visual descriptor used in (Wu et. al., 2006) is *texture*. Specifically, the authors have used *Gabor Texture Descriptor* (Manjunath et. al., 2001) as well as intensity of edges in the image, as the visual descriptors to differentiate between natural and computer-generated images. *Regularity in color composition* is another statistical feature inherent in natural images that can be exploited for identification of forged computer-generated images (Lalonde & Efros, 2007). In this work, the authors have used the fact that in natural images the foreground (objects) and background are highly color-compatible.

Another characteristic image feature used in natural image identification is *Fractal Dimension* (Hutchison, 1981). Fractal dimension refers to a statistical measure of density of an image pattern, measured in different scales. Self-similarity property of a fractal makes it an inherent feature of natural images useful for digital forensic techniques. In (Pan et. al. 2009), the authors have proposed identification of natural images, based on fractal dimension computation on hue and saturation components of a color image, which provides 91% accuracy in distinguishing natural and unnatural images.

Examples of other natural image statistics used in digital image forensics are shadow texture, surface roughness or smoothness, power spectrum of image (Wang & Doube, 2011; Ng & Chang, 2004) etc. Wavelet domain coefficients and various moments of the wavelet distribution, such as mean and variance, are also used by some researchers (Farid & Lyu, 2003; Srivastava et. al., 2003) as natural image statistics in digital forensics. Detection of synthetic images based on analysis of natural image statistics has been proposed recently in (Ke et. al., 2014).

3.3. Image Forensics for Copy-Move/Copy-Paste Forgery

In copy-move forgery, one portion of an image is copied and moved to another region of the same image (as discussed in Section 3.1), with the intention to obscure the latter from the viewer. Copy-move attack is more prevalent in images having uniform texture or patterns, for e.g. sand, grass, water etc. There must be repetition of one or more regions in a copy-move forged image. This kind of repetition is termed as "cloning", and digital forensic techniques to identify copy-move forgery are based on identification of such repetitions or "cloning" activities in an image.

One of the earliest digital forensic techniques for copy-move attack, proposed by Fridrich et al. in (Fridrich et. al., 2003), is based on the principle of cloning identification. In (Fridrich et. al., 2003), the authors search for two image regions, having exactly identical pixel values. However standard images consisting of thousands of pixels, it is computationally quite infeasible to carry out a brute-force search to find such identical (image region) pairs. To make the searching efficient, the authors divide the entire image into fixed-sized blocks and then sort the blocks lexicographically. Post-sorting, extraction of identical image blocks from this sorted list is trivial. Note that in this case, there may be more than one pairs of identical blocks.

While transplanting an image block onto some other region of the image, many times the adversary needs to resize the block, to match the dimension of the region to obscure. One such forgery approach has been presented in (Popescu & Farid, 2005). Here, the attacker resizes the image by up-sampling or down-sampling the image signal. This kind of forgery is detected by searching for signal correlation among different image blocks. When a block is down-sampled by a factor of two, every alternate sample in the original block may be found in the re-sampled block. Alternatively, when a block is up-sampled by a factor of two, every sample in the original block may be found in the new block, along with alternate samples in the new block being linear combination of its neighbors. Re-sampling image blocks by any integer factor induces such periodic correlations among original and forged image blocks. Re-sampling (by an integer factor) induces such periodic correlations among original and forged image blocks. Such correlation among signal samples, a phenomenon not prevalent in natural images (Popescu & Farid, 2005), is exploited in digital forensics to detect transplantation of re-sampled image blocks.

The image blocks which are transplanted may also be geometrically transformed by the attacker in many situations, e.g. an image block may be rotated by some angle by the attacker before it is transplanted. In such case, duplicate image regions may be detected by matching SIFT (Scale-invariant feature transform) (Lowe, 2004) keypoints of the regions. Such forensic approaches to diagnose copy-move forgery having geometrically transformed image blocks, have been proposed in (Pan & Lyu, 2010; Huang et. al., 2008).

3.4. Forgery Involving Multiple Images and Related Forensic Analyses

A forged image formed by compositing multiple (different) images cannot be identified by the forensic analysis techniques applicable to single image forgery, such as cloning detection or detection of image regions re-sampling or transformation. However, there exist some differences in statistical features between the composed image regions, coming from distinct images. Those statistical differences are often helpful for digital forensic investigators to identify forgeries involving multiple images.

Detection of forgeries involving multiple images may be done by analysis of patterns, left within the image by the capturing device. Different cameras leave different unique patterns or fingerprints on the images they capture. When a composed image is analyzed based on such characteristic of the camera sensor, it gives clues regarding different regions of the image being captured by different devices. In (Zhan et. al., 2009) the authors propose to detect image composition by analysis of noise characteristics produced by the camera sensor. More details on digital image forensics by identification of source devices are presented in later part of this chapter.

Scene illumination analysis is one preliminary technique for image forgery detection involving multiple images. In (Lukas et. al., 2006), the authors analyze the directions of incident light on different objects comprising an image, to identifying image composition. If the incident light direction is found to be different in some object compared to the others, then the authors inferred that that object came from some other image. Moreover, the orientation of incident light reflection on the pupil of human eye (considering humans as objects in an image) may give indication of image composition.

Objects in a forged image coming from distinct images, may also be identified by studying the shadow of the objects. Authors in (Johnson & Farid, 2005) have proposed to study the differences in geometric properties of shadows, such as length, orientation etc. Other properties such as the characteristics of source of light (whether it is a point or an extended source), may also be matched to find objects coming from different images. A multiple forgery detection technique based on "median comparison of image blocks in the Region of Suspicion (RoS)" has been proposed in (Bacchuwar & Ramakrishnan, 2013).

Open problems in the field of digital forensics in multiple image forgery, includes consideration of forgeries involving multiple images under identical lighting environments or shadow orientations. In such cases, none of the above discussed techniques are applicable. Also there is need for consideration of more complex illumination conditions, where more than one source of light may be present.

In the next section we discuss format-dependent, forgery type independent digital forensics techniques.

3.5. Digital Forgery in JPEG Images

As mentioned previously, in most present-day digital camera the standard format for image storage is JPEG (Joint Photographic Experts Group). This standard is used due to the fact that JPEG format provides the best compression, hence optimal space requirement for image storage. The statistical as well as perceptual redundancy in natural images, are efficiently exploited in JPEG compression. Moreover, the JPEG format has an adaptive compression scheme that allows saving in varying levels of compression. However, every time we compress an image some space is saved but at the same time some information loss occurs. Also when the image is reconstructed from its JPEG compressed version, it contains degradations compared to the original image. Although the loss of information is disadvantageous while image forgery detection, various JPEG features are advantageous for identification of alteration or modification of JPEG images.

In this section, we present a state-of-the-art digital forensic technique for identification of JPEG image forgery, in detail (Farid, 2009; Zach et. al., 2012). In this technique, the phenomenon of multiple JPEG compressions in an image is exploited. Let us consider a modification attack carried out on a JPEG image. To deliver such tampering, the attacker first opens the image in an image editing software, manipulates some regions of the image, and finally resaves the image back in JPEG format. In this entire process, some regions of the image get compressed more than once. Hence, compression of the forged part is different from the rest of the image. This difference in compression provides evidence of image manipulation and is useful in the detection of forgery. *JPEG ghost classification* (Zach et. al., 2012) is a forensic analysis technique that enables detection of multiple JPEG compressions in an image. Multiple JPEG compressions limited to specific image regions are also detectable by investigation of JPEG ghosts. JPEG ghosts differentiate between the different compression ratio in the image while compressing the image more than once. A JPEG ghost is uncovered by comparing original and resaved versions of an image. The technique of JPEG image forgery detection through analysis of JPEG ghosts is beneficial in situations where some parts of the image is forged and it is very difficult to visually identify the tampering. Digital forensic techniques for JPEG forgery detection, based on analysis of JPEG ghosts are proposed in (Farid, 2009; Zach et. al., 2012).

The procedure followed in standard JPEG compression (Wallace, 1991) is as follows:

1. The image is divided into small blocks (of size 8×8 pixels).
2. The YCbCr color space is considered and chrominance components Cb, Cr are sub-sampled by a factor of two. This step exploits the fact that the chrominance components of a color image produce lower sensitivity in the HVS, compared to what the luminance component Y produces.
3. The 8×8 image blocks are transformed to frequency domain by application of 2D DCT (*2-Dimensional Discrete Cosine Transform*).
4. Now the set of DCT coefficients, *c*, is quantized by a factor *q* to produce the set of quantized values *c'*. This is represented by:

$$c' = round(c/q) \tag{1}$$

where the function *round*() maps every real number (belonging to the set of DCT coefficients) to its nearest integer.

Now, the procedure of JPEG image tampering detection by investigating JPEG ghosts may be broadly divided into the following steps:

1. Let the image be successively quantized by factors *q1* and *q2*. Let the initial set of DCT coefficients be represented by *c*, which produces the quantized set *c'* after quantization by *q1*, and *c"* be the second quantized set produced by quantizing *c'* by *q2*, i.e.,

$$c \rightarrow q1 \rightarrow c' \rightarrow q2 \rightarrow c'' \tag{2}$$

2. Now we consider the sum of squared differences between the elements of c and c'', as a function of $q2$ (where $q1$ is a constant). This function may be represented as:

$$f(q2) = \sum_i \left(c_i - c''_i \right)^2 \tag{3}$$

3. We find that this function (shown in Eq. 3) increases with increasing $q2$. We also find that function attains a global minimum at $q2 = q1$.

Now let us investigate the characteristics of the above function in case of a forged image which undergoes an additional step of illegal quantization.

1. Let the set of initial DCT coefficients be c. Consider that the forger has quantized c multiple times to yield c'. We look at the optimal case of two-step quantization on c:

$$c \to q0 \to q1 \to c' \tag{4}$$

Now, c' is quantized (as before) by factor $q2$ to yield c'':

$$c' \to q2 \to c'' \tag{5}$$

The entire process may be represented as:

$$c \to q0 \to q1 \to c' \to q2 \to c'' \tag{6}$$

2. Now, if we investigate the function $f(q2) = \sum_i \left(c_i - c''_i \right)^2$, (where $q1$ is constant), we shall again find a minima at $q2 = q1$.
3. Additionally, since the coefficients c were initially quantized by $q0$, we also find another minimum at $q2 = q0$. However this second minimum is not necessarily global. This second minima is referred to as the *JPEG ghost*. Multiple such ghosts may be found in a forged JPEG image which has been quantized more number of times. These JPEG ghosts indicate quantization, after each image manipulation.

Figure 2 demonstrates the formation of a JPEG ghost. In Figure 2 the sum of differences $\sum_i \left(c_i - c''_i \right)^2$, has been plot against $q2 \in [0,30]$. The values of $q0$ and $q1$ are constant.

In the previous section (Section 3), we had discussed various state-of-the-art digital forensic techniques, respective to different classes of digital image forgeries. In this section, we have presented digital forgery investigation mechanism for JPEG images. Next, in Section 5 we shall present another paradigm in digital forensics: *Image Source Identification*.

Figure 2. Formation of JPEG ghosts in multiply compressed JPEG Images

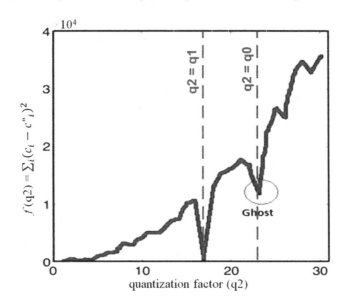

4. IMAGE SOURCE IDENTIFICATION

The origin of an image many times forms important evidence in the court of law. Image source identification deals with recognizing the device which is responsible for formation and storage of the image under question. In cases where an intruder tries to forge the image source, it may be useful for the forensic analyzer to indicate device or class of device captured the image, or at least which did not. The area of forensic research, discussed in this section, is dedicated for this kind of investigation and analysis (as discussed above).

In this section we shall present state-of-the-art digital forensic techniques for analysis of image origin and its source identification. First, we shall briefly discuss the various components of a present-day image capturing device: the digital camera.

4.1. Digital Camera Components

The two major components of an image capturing device are the *lens* and the *sensor*. Below we discuss their roles in image formation and storage, in a digital camera (Adams et. al., 1998):

1. **Taking Lens:** Forms an image of the scene (in front of the camera) on the surface of the sensor. The taking lens is responsible for bending and curving the path of incident radiation, so as to make it reach the sensor.
2. **Sensor:** Converts incident radiation into photocharges, which are subsequently digitized and stored as raw image data. Basic imaging element of a sensor is a "pixel" and a sensor is made up of a rectilinear grid of pixels. The sensor is responsible for sensing a sampled version of the image

formed. A good sensor forms generates photocharges at precise locations in the image and also prevents subsequent random dispersion of these charges, until they are read out. After capturing the incident radiation in form of photocharges in a digital camera sensor, what remains is to acquire the color information about the image. This is done by *color filters*.

3. **CFA:** *Color filters* are nothing but (single or multiple) thin layer(s) of different colorants, laid on the surface of the camera sensor. An array of pixel sized color filters, arranged over the sensor surface, enables detection of full color information of an image, using only a single sensor. This array is called *CFA* or *Color Filter Array*.

Since a color image can be fully digitally represented by three components, for e.g. RGB (Red Green Blue), precise capture of full color information of an image requires a set of at least three sensors at each pixel location. However this specification would highly increase the cost and complexity of manufacturing the device. Hence in conventional digital cameras, at each pixel location is designed to sample only one color. Hence the cost and complexity are reduced by the use of single color filter at each pixel location; the missing colors are interpolated from the neighboring pixel locations. CFA interpolation is often termed as *Demosaicing*. The Bayer pattern (Bayer, 1976), shown in Fig. 3, is one such example of arrangement strategy for color filters over a sensor CFA. The Bayer pattern uses 50% green filters and 25% filters to sense each of red and blue color, taking into account the fact that the HVS is more sensitive to the green component of a an RGB image. In this pattern, at each pixel location, one color is precisely recorded and other two colors are interpolated from the neighboring pixels (see Figure 3).

After collection of color information of an image is over and the interpolated image is available, some further image enhancement steps (Adams et. al., 1998), such as sensor noise reduction, color correction, edge enhancement etc. are carried out before the finished image is finally produced in the camera.

Information about the image and its source may be obtained from image metadata, such as the file header or EXIF (Exchangeable image file format). Such metadata include information such as camera make and model (but not the specific camera identity), manufacturer details, image size, date and time

Figure 3. Bayer Pattern arrangement of color filters

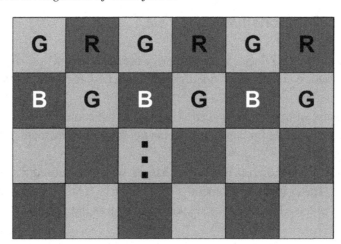

of image capture, compression ratio in JPEG images, etc. However, such information contained in the file header is highly vulnerable to modification attacks. Hence we need blind forensic techniques to throw some light on the origin of an image. Next, we shall present the state-of-the-art digital forensic techniques, proposed for image source investigation.

Blind forensic techniques exploit the different traces left behind in an image, as a result of various processing steps, while its formation and storage by a particular device. Those traces or artifacts are formed in an image in either one of two steps:

1. **Image Acquisition:** Image Acquisition artifacts are nothing but either the distortions generated by the camera lens while capturing a scene, or the sensor noise produced during color information acquisition (and interpolation) by the CFA.
2. **Image Storage:** Image storage artifacts are those patterns which are generated in an image while processing it for storage in a standard format. Such processing activities includes noise removal, image enhancement etc.

The image artifacts described above, function as means of distinguishing between different camera models, depending on their components such as the camera lens. Those artifacts may also provide specific device related information, utilizing the traces produced by the sensor.

4.2. Source Identification Based on Lens Aberration

The primary feature for distinguishing one camera model from another, is the camera lens. Model specific (photosensitive or geometric) properties of a lens cause some distortions to be created in its captured images. This kind of image distortions are collectively called *lens aberration*.

One example on lens aberration is *chromatic lens aberration*, which provides an efficient measure to identify digital forgery an image. *Chromatic lens aberration* refers to the lens imperfection that causes a point of incident light to form an image on an imprecise sensor location. The shift in position of the point of light (formed on the sensor surface), varies with the wavelength of incident radiation, due to difference in *angle of refraction*. Due to this fact, in an image, there must be some specific alignment between the locations at which the sensor receives lights from different color channels. However, if an adversary transplants some external data into an image, this color channel specific location alignment, is found to be different in the transplanted image region, compared to its neighborhood. This feature is exploited by Johnson et al. (Johnson & Farid, 2006) to identify forged images. Another lens feature used to identify image source device is *radial aberration*. *Radial aberration* is the geometric distortion produced by a lens which makes the straight lines in a scene to appear curved, in the image capture. The deviation of image (curved) lines from the original (straight) lines formed by a particular lens may be used as a camera fingerprint. Radial aberration artifacts have been used as image source device identifier by Choi et al. (Choi et. al., 2006). However, this feature cannot distinguish between distinct exemplars belonging to the same camera model, hence using identical lens.

4.3. Source Identification Based on Sensor Noise and Processing Artifacts

As discussed previously the sensor of camera converts incident radiation into photo-electric charges, which are subsequently converted to digital values and later stored into the memory. Before storage, the image undergoes other processing steps such as white balancing, gamma correction, noise reduction, image enhancement and JPEG compression. These processing steps induce some sort of unique pattern or fingerprint on the image, which may be used as sensor identifier by a forensic analyzer. Various digital forensic researchers (Chen et. al., 2006; Fridrich et. al., 2006; Gou et. al., 2007; Swaminathan et. al., 2008) have modeled the artifacts produced by the sensor and the subsequent processing steps, to identify the image origin. For example, the authors in (Chen et. al., 2006; Fridrich et. al., 2006) have modeled the camera sensor noise and processing artifacts, by analyzing a set of images formed by the camera. The noise model may be represented as:

$$I' = IK + N \tag{6}$$

where I is the distortion-free image, I' is the observed image having sensor noise and processing artifacts, K is the sensor-generated noise pattern called *Photo Response Non Uniformity* (*PRNU*), and N is the noise contribution of other processing steps.

The above model (Eq. 6) estimates the noise of an image for a specific camera. This estimate may be used for authenticating an image, claimed to be originating from a particular camera (Chen et. al., 2006; Fridrich et. al., 2006). Noise in an image, actually originating from the camera, will have high correlation with the estimated value; whereas low correlation indicates forgery, the where observed noise value largely deviates from the estimated value.

During the *demosaicing* phase of image acquisition (discussed previously in Section 5.1), characteristic artifacts are left on the image in form of specific pattern, which may serve the purpose of digital fingerprint or signature of the capturing device. *Demosaicing* involves interpolation of a particular (missing) color component, at a particular pixel location, from its neighboring pixels. For example, in Fig. 3 pixel at location (2,4) has the G (green) color component information only. The R (red) component at pixel location (2,4) is computed by interpolation of R values of pixels (1,4) and (3,4). Similarly, its B (Blue) component is computed by interpolation of B values at (2,3) and (2,5). Every demosaicing algorithm leaves behind a specific pattern on the final complete color image. This pattern represents nothing but a specific correlation among the precise and interpolated values, at various locations for a particular color channel. Such demosaicing algorithm based image artifacts have often served as indicators to the image source device in various digital forensic techniques such as (Bayram et. al., 2005; Popescu & Farid, 2005; Long & Huang, 2006; Kharrazi et. al., 2004). A digital forgery detection technique based on Neural Network Modelling of CFA has been developed by (Vinod & Gopi, 2013).

4.4. Image Storage Based

The final step of image formation is image storage. The image storage stage also provides cues to identify image source device. In this chapter we shall discuss the standard JPEG image format (Wallace, 1991). As discussed previously in Section 3.5, JPEG is used to compress an image so that it occupies less space in the memory. The JPEG standard applies DCT to each 8×8 image block and quantizes the DCT coefficients by a factor q. The quantized DCT coefficients are what actually represent the compressed JPEG image. However, JPEG is a *lossy compression* (Wallace, 1991) technique where some information is permanently lost in the process. The complete (original) image data cannot be retrieved by decompressing the JPEG image. JPEG compression produces permanent, camera-specific patterns or artifacts in the stored image, which are exploited by many forensic researchers as unique image source identifier (Farid, 2006).

Image *thumbnails* are also used by some forensic analyzers as fingerprints to identify the device (Kee & Farid, 2010). A thumbnail is a low-resolution representation of a complete image. It is mainly used for simultaneous preview of multiple images, stored in a device. Thumbnail formation encompasses various image processing steps such as JPEG compression, cropping, down-sampling and filtering, which generate device-specific artifacts in the thumbnails. Farid et al. (Kee & Farid, 2010), have used image thumbnails as identifiers to distinguish one imaging device from another. In

5. CONCLUSION AND FUTURE WORK

In this chapter we have focused on different classes of cyber-forgery on digital images and the need of research related to each class. We have presented state-of-the-art digital forensic techniques to deal with different classes of image forgery. We have specifically dealt with JPEG images, since it is the image format used by almost all present-day digital cameras; we have presented a digital forensic technique to identify forgery in JPEG images. Finally we have discussed the forensic techniques for identifying the source of an image.

With ever increasing rate of cyber-crimes and intelligent forgeries in the digital world, it would not take much to render the present digital forensic state-of-the-art, obsolete. With continuous effort by adversaries to break the existing forensic tools, an equally vigorous effort is mandatory to produce more and more efficient forensic techniques. In this respect an emerging field is that of *anti-forensics* or *counter-forensics* (Böhme & Kirchner, 2012). Counter-forensics is nothing but counter-measures to forensic analyzes. The set of technologies adopted by adversaries to hide their identities from forensic analyzers or compromise legal evidences, hence to mislead forensic analysis, is collectively referred to as counter-forensics. Detailed investigation of counter-forensic technologies such as source counterfeiting, tamper hiding, synthesis of traces of authenticity etc., is extremely important to cope with the ever increasing digital forgeries and cyber-crimes.

REFERENCES

Adams, J., Parulski, K., & Spaulding, K. (1998). Color processing in digital cameras. *IEEE Micro*, *18*(6), 20–30. doi:10.1109/40.743681

Bacchuwar, K. S., & Ramakrishnan, K. (2013). A Jump Patch-Block Match Algorithm for Multiple Forgery Detection. In *International Multi-Conference on Automation* (pp. 723–728). Computing, Communication, Control and Compressed Sensing. doi:10.1109/iMac4s.2013.6526502

Bayer, B. E. (1976). Color Imaging Array. *U.S. Patent 3971065.*

Bayram, S., Sencar, H. T., & Memon, N. (2005). Source camera identification based on CFA interpolation. In *IEEE Int. Conf. Image Processing*. doi:10.1109/ICIP.2005.1530330

Böhme, R., & Kirchner, M. (2012). Counter-forensics: Attacking image forensics. In Digital Image Forensics. Berlin, Germany: Springer.

Chen, M., Fridrich, J., Goljan, M., & Lukas, J. (2008). Determining image origin and integrity using sensor noise. *IEEE Transactions on Information Forensics and Security*, *3*(1), 74–90. doi:10.1109/TIFS.2007.916285

Choi, K. S., Lam, E. Y., & Wong, K. K. Y. (2006). Source camera identification using footprints from lens aberration. *Proceedings of the Society for Photo-Instrumentation Engineers*, 60690J, 60690J-8. doi:10.1117/12.649775

Cox, I. J., Miller, M. L., Bloom, J. A., Fridrich, J., & Kalker, T. (2008). *Digital Watermarking and Steganography* (2nd ed.). Burlington: Morgan Kaufmann.

Farid, H. (2006). *Digital image ballistics from JPEG quantization*. Dept. Computer Science, Dartmouth College, Tech. Rep. TR2006-583.

Farid, H. (2009). A Survey of image forgery detection. *IEEE Signal Processing Magazine*, *26*(2), 16–25. doi:10.1109/MSP.2008.931079

Farid, H. (2009). A Survey of image forgery detection. *IEEE Signal Processing Magazine*, *26*(2), 16–25. doi:10.1109/MSP.2008.931079

Farid, H., & Lyu, S. (2003). Higher-order wavelet statistics and their application to digital forensics. *IEEE Workshop on Statistical Analysis in Computer Vision*. doi:10.1109/CVPRW.2003.10093

Fridrich, A. J., Soukal, B. D., & Lukáš, A. J. (2003). Detection of copy-move forgery in digital images. *Proceedings of Digital Forensic Research Workshop*.

Fridrich, J. (2010). *Steganography in Digital Media*. Cambridge, UK: Cambridge University Press.

Fridrich, J., Chen, M., & Goljan, M. (2007). Imaging sensor noise as digital x-ray for revealing forgeries. *9th International Workshop on Information Hiding*.

Gou, H., Swaminathan, A., & Wu, M. (2007). Noise features for image tampering detection and steganalysis. *IEEE International Conference on Image Processing*. doi:10.1109/ICIP.2007.4379530

Huang, H., Guo, W., & Zhang, Y. (2008). Detection of copy-move forgery in digital images using SIFT algorithm. *IEEE Pacific-Asia Workshop on Computational Intelligence and Industrial Application*. doi:10.1109/PACIIA.2008.240

Hutchinson, J. E. (1981). Fractals and self-similarity. *Indiana University Mathematics Journal*, *3*(5), 713–747. doi:10.1512/iumj.1981.30.30055

Johnson, M., & Farid, H. (2005). Exposing digital forgeries by detecting inconsistencies in lighting. *Proc ACM Multimedia and Security Workshop*. doi:10.1145/1073170.1073171

Johnson, M. K., & Farid, H. (2006). Exposing digital forgeries through chromatic aberration. *ACM Multimedia and Security Workshop*.

Ke, Y., Min, W., Qin, F., & Shang, J. (2014). Image Forgery Detection based on Semantics. *International Journal of Hybrid Information Technology*, *10*(1), 109–124. doi:10.14257/ijhit.2014.7.1.09

Kee, E., & Farid, H. (2010). Digital image authentication from thumbnails. *SPIE Symposium on Electronic Imaging*.

Kharrazi, M., Sencar, H. T., & Memon, N. (2004) Blind source camera identification. *In Proceedings of the IEEE International Conference on Image Processing*.

Lalonde, J. F., & Efros, A. A. (2007). Using color compatibility for assessing image realism. *Proceedings of the International Conference on Computer Vision*. doi:10.1109/ICCV.2007.4409107

Long, Y., & Huang, Y. (2006). Image based source camera identification using demosaicing. *Proceedings of MSP*, 419–424.

Lowe, D. (2004). Distinctive image features from scale-invariant key-points. *International Journal of Computer Vision*, *60*(2), 91–110. doi:10.1023/B:VISI.0000029664.99615.94

Lukas, J., Fridrich, J., & Goljan, M. (2006). Detecting digital image forgeries using sensor pattern noise. *Proc of Security, Steganography, and Watermarking of Multimedia Contents VIII, part of EI SPIE*.

Mahdian, B., & Saic, S. (2010). A bibliography on blind methods for identifying image forgery. *Signal Processing Image Communication*, *25*(6), 389–399. doi:10.1016/j.image.2010.05.003

Manjunath, B. S., Ohm, J. R., Vasudevan, V. V., & Yamada, A. (2001). Color and Texture Descriptors. *IEEE Transactions on Circuits and Systems for Video Technology*, *11*(6), 703–715. doi:10.1109/76.927424

Ng, T. T., & Chang, S. F. (2004). *Classifying photographic and photorealistic computer graphic images using natural image statistics. Technical report, ADVENT Technical Report*. Columbia University.

Pan, F., Chen, J. B., & Huang, J. W. (2009). Discriminating between photorealistic computer graphics and natural images using fractal geometry. *Science in China Series F: Information Sciences*, *52*(2), 329–337. doi:10.1007/s11432-009-0053-5

Pan, X., & Lyu, S. (2010). Detecting image duplication using SIFT features. *Proceedings of IEEE ICASSP*.

Popescu, A. C., & Farid, H. (2005). Exposing digital forgeries by detecting traces of re-sampling. *IEEE Transactions on Signal Processing*, *53*(2), 758–767. doi:10.1109/TSP.2004.839932

Popescu, A. C., & Farid, H. (2005). Exposing digital forgeries in color filter array interpolated images. *IEEE Transactions on Signal Processing*, *53*(10), 3948–3959. doi:10.1109/TSP.2005.855406

Redi, J., Taktak, W., & Dugelay, J. L. (2011). Digital Image Forensics: A Booklet for Beginners. *Multimedia Tools and Applications*, *51*(1), 133–162. doi:10.1007/s11042-010-0620-1

Sencar, H. T., & Memon, N. (2008). Overview of state-of-the-art in digital image forensics. In *Indian Statistical Institute Platinum Jubilee Monograph series titled Statistical Science and Interdisciplinary Research*. Singapore: World Scientific. doi:10.1142/9789812836243_0015

Sencar, H. T., & Memon, N. (Eds.). (2013). *Digital Image Forensics: There is More to a Picture than Meets the Eye.* New York, NY, USA: Springer. doi:10.1007/978-1-4614-0757-7

Shih, F. Y. (2007). *Digital Watermarking and Steganography: Fundamentals and Techniques. BocaRaton.* CRC Press.

Srivastava, A., Lee, A. B., Simoncelli, E. P., & Zhu, S. C. (2003). On advances in statistical modeling of natural images. *Journal of Mathematical Imaging, 18*(1), 17–33. doi:10.1023/A:1021889010444

Swaminathan, A., Wu, M., & Liu, K. J. R. (2008). Digital image forensics via intrinsic fingerprints. *IEEE Transactions on Information Forensics and Security, 3*(1), 101–117. doi:10.1109/TIFS.2007.916010

Vinod, S., & Gopi, E. S. (2013). Neural Network Modelling of Color Array Filter for Digital Forgery Detection using Kernel LDA. *Proceedings of International Conference on Computational Intelligence: Modeling Techniques and Applications (CIMTA), 10,* 498-504.

Wallace, G. (1991). The JPEG still picture compression standard. *IEEE Transactions on Consumer Electronics, 34*(4), 30–44.

Wang, N., & Doube, W. (2011). How real is really a perceptually motivated system for quantifying visual realism in digital images. *Proceedings of the IEEE International Conference on Multimedia and Signal Processing 2,* 141–149. doi:10.1109/CMSP.2011.172

Wu, J., Kamath, M. V., & Poehlman, S. (2006). Detecting differences between photographs and computer generated images. *Proceedings of the 24th IASTED International conference on Signal Processing, Pattern Recognition, and Applications,* 268–273.

Zach, F., Riess, C., & Angelopoulou, E. (2012). Automated Image Forgery Detection through Classification of JPEG Ghosts. *Proceedings of the German Association for Pattern Recognition (DAGM 2012),* 185–194. doi:10.1007/978-3-642-32717-9_19

Zhan, W., Cao, X., Zhang, J., Zhu, J., & Wang, P. (2009). Detecting photographic composites using shadows. *IEEE International Conference on Multimedia and Expo,* 1042–1045.

ADDITIONAL READING

Bacchuwar, K. S., & Ramakrishnan, K. (2013). A Jump Patch-Block Match Algorithm for Multiple Forgery Detection. In *International Multi-Conference on Automation* (pp. 723–728). Computing, Communication, Control and Compressed Sensing. doi:10.1109/iMac4s.2013.6526502

Berger, S. B., & Cepelewicz, B. (1996). Medical-legal issues in teleradiology. *AJR. American Journal of Roentgenology, 166*(3), 505–510. doi:10.2214/ajr.166.3.8623616 PMID:8623616

Celik, M. U., Sharma, G., Tekalp, A., & Saber, E. (2003). Localized lossless authentication watermark (law). *International Society for Optical Engineering, 5020,* 689–698.

Elias, P. (1995). Coding for noisy channels. *IRE Convention Record, 3,* 37–46.

Fridrich, J., Goljan, M., & Du, R. (2001). Distortion free data embedding. *Proceedings of 4th Information Hiding Workshop, 2137,* 27–41.

Gonzalez, R. C., & Woods, R. E. (2002). *Digital Image Processing, New Jersey: Prentice Hall.*

Haralick, R. M., Sternberg, S., & Zhuang, X. (1987). Image analysis using mathematical morphology. *IEEE Transactions on Pattern Analysis and Machine Intelligence, 9*(4), 532–550. doi:10.1109/TPAMI.1987.4767941 PMID:21869411

Hunt, R. W. G. (1975). *The Reproduction of Color.* New York: John Wiley and Sons.

Jarvis, J. F., Judice, C. N., & Ninke, W. H. (1976). A survey of techniques for the display of continuous-tone pictures on bilevel displays. *Computer Graphics and Image Processing, 5*(1), 13–40. doi:10.1016/S0146-664X(76)80003-2

Ke, Y., Min, W., Qin, F., & Shang, J. (2014). Image Forgery Detection based on Semantics. *International Journal of Hybrid Information Technology, 10*(1), 109–124. doi:10.14257/ijhit.2014.7.1.09

Lee, C. S., & Kuo, Y. H. (2000). Fuzzy techniques in image processing. Studies in Fuzziness and Soft Computing, ch. Adaptive fuzzy filter and its application to image enhancement, New York: Springer–Verlag, 52, 172–193.

Lin, J., Weng, R. C., & Keerthi, S. S. (2008). Trust region newton method for large-scale logistic regression. *Journal of Machine Learning Research, 9,* 627–650.

Mitra, S., & Sicuranza, J. (2001). *Nonlinear Image Processing.* San Diego: Academic Press.

Stanberry, B. (2001). Legal ethical and risk issues in telemedicine. *Computer Methods and Programs in Biomedicine, 64*(3), 225–233. doi:10.1016/S0169-2607(00)00142-5 PMID:11226620

Vinod, S., & Gopi, E. S. (2013). Neural Network Modelling of Color Array Filter for Digital Forgery Detection using Kernel LDA. *Proceedings of International Conference on Computational Intelligence: Modeling Techniques and Applications (CIMTA), 10,* 498-504.

Xing, N., Wang, J., Zhang, X., & Zhang, J. (2014). Digital image identification based on generalized Gaussian model. *Proc. SPIE 9233, International Symposium on Photonics and Optoelectronics 2014, 923303, doi:*10.1117/12.206969

KEY TERMS AND DEFINITIONS

Color Filter Array: A mosaic of color filters, placed over camera sensors to capture color information of a scene image.

Copy Move Attack: A form of attack on digital images whereby a region of the images is pasted over another, primarily with the aim to obscure significant information.

Counter Forensics: Technology providing counter-measures to forensic analysis.

Cyber Forgery: Illegal usage or modification of information (especially in digital form) through exploitation of internet technologies.

Demosaicing: Also known as "Color Filter Array Interpolation". It is the act of producing complete color information of a scene, by the application of some interpolation algorithm to the partial color information output of a color filter array.

Digital Forensics: Technology and science aimed to protect digital content against any form of cybercrime, by investigation and analysis of evidences found in digital devices.

Synthetic Images: Artificial images generated through application of computer graphics.

Chapter 11
Passive Video Tampering Detection Using Noise Features

Ramesh Chand Pandey
Indian Institute of Technology (BHU), Varanasi, India

Sanjay Kumar Singh
Indian Institute of Technology (BHU), Varanasi, India

K. K. Shukla
Indian Institute of Technology (BHU), Varanasi, India

ABSTRACT

With increasing availability of low-cost video editing softwares and tools, the authenticity of digital video can no longer be trusted. Active video tampering detection technique utilize digital signature or digital watermark for the video tampering detection, but when the videos do not include such signature then it is very challenging to detect tampering in such video. To detect tampering in such video, passive video tampering detection techniques are required. In this chapter we have explained passive video tampering detection by using noise features. When video is captured with camera it passes through a Camera processing pipeline and this introduces noise in the video. Noise changes abruptly from authentic to forged frame blocks and provides a clue for video tampering detection. For extracting the noise we have considered different techniques like denoising algorithms, wavelet based denoising filter, and neighbor prediction.

INTRODUCTION

In recent years due to presence of sophisticated video editing software, network technologies, low cost multimedia devices and wide adaptation of digital multimedia coding standards, video tampering has become very easy. Due to digital nature of video file, it can be easily manipulated, synthesized and tampered numerous ways. Additionally there are no requirements of better technical skills to tamper the video. Internet is providing different tools and software without any cost, which is further increasing the ease of video tampering. People do video tampering to hide or expose some important scene or event

DOI: 10.4018/978-1-4666-8723-3.ch011

which was actually not present in the original video. Someone can create a fake video of any popular person and can defame them. Sometimes, Hollywood and Television celebrities are victimized by video tampering attacks. People are also using tampered video to get justice in their favor from court of law. Video tampering has proven the concept "Seeing is not believing". So it is important to bring out the truth to the world.

Video tampering can be categorized in spatial tampering and Temporal tampering domains. In Spatial domain only a single frame is affected with tampering, but in Temporal domain many frames are affected with tampering. Video tampering detection techniques are basically categorized in two categories, first one is Active video tampering detection technique and second one is Passive video tampering detection technique. In starting, people were using Digital Watermark (DW) and Digital Signature (DS) for video tampering detection which belongs to Active video tampering detection technique. Active video tampering detection technique requires pre embedding information in the video, but if the video does not contain pre-embedding information like DS and DW then it is very difficult to detect tampering in such video. Currently, the main challenge is to detect tampering through Passive video tampering detection technique which does not include pre-embedding information like Active video tampering detection technique. Passive video tampering detection technique utilizes the intrinsic properties of video like noise feature, camera response function, color filter arrays etc. In Blind and Passive video tampering detection technique we have no information of source from which the video has been taken and video does not contain any information like DS or DW, so Blind and Passive video tampering detection technique is much more complex in comparison to active video tampering detection technique.

BACKGROUND

In the early days of internet, Digital Signature and Digital Watermarking were the main video/image tampering detection technique (Lee & Jung., 2001). We should take care of inserting the Digital Watermark in the video/ image. Once the video/ image is available on the internet without Watermark then later enter the Watermark in the video/ image cannot prevent video/ image tampering. A few years back, a number of passive image tampering detection technique have been studied (Van Lanh et al., 2007). These techniques exploit inconsistency and abnormal behavior of the image features. Jonson and Farid used inconsistencies in lighting (Johnson & Farid, 2005) and chromatic aberration (Johnson, & Farid, 2006). (Lin et al., 2005) estimated camera response function and verified its uniformity across an image. (Lukas et al., 2006) extracted fixed pattern noise from an image and compared it with a reference pattern. (Fridrich et al, 2003) had computed correlation between segments in an image and detected cloned regions. (Ye et al., 2007) used JPEG quantization table for evaluation of video forgery. The different digital image forensic methods mentioned above help us to aggressively estimate the authenticity of digital images. (Liu et al., 2006) estimated the noise level function (NLF) from a single image, which relates the noise intensity with the image intensity. The spatial variance in an image contains the variance resulted in object's texture as well as the intensity of the noise. Obtaining the component of the real noise from NLF, we can disassociate the component of texture from the variance of the observation. They utilized the function not only for denoising but also for adaptive bilateral filtering and edge detection. Noise information is available for camera identification and forgery detection as well. Due to the sensor imperfections developed in a manufacturing process, the CCD camera contains pixels with different sensitivity to light. This spatial variation of sensitivity is temporally fixed and known as fixed pattern noise. Since this non-uniformity is inherent in a camera, we can exploit it as a fingerprint. (Lukas et al., 2005) determined the reference noise pattern of a camera by averaging the noise extracted from several images. They extracted fixed pattern noise from a given image using a smoothing filter and identified the camera that took the image.

The rest of the chapter is as follows: Video tampering, Camera pipeline processing, Noise Extraction Techniques, Importance of Noise features, Video tampering detection using Noise Features, Recommendation, Issue and Challenges, Application, Conclusion and Future Direction.

VIDEO TAMPERING

Illegal, improper or malicious intention of modifying video to conceal some important information, event or object is known as video tampering. However, not all types of modification are considered as malicious tampering. For example, a modification done to enhance the quality of the video is not considered as tampering. Video tampering attacks can be categorized in two ways: i) Spatial Tampering, ii) Temporal Tampering (see Figure 1).

Spatial Tampering

The content of video frame is modified by specialized crackers with malicious intentions. Spatial tampering includes copy-move, splicing, resampling etc. to manipulate the frame. Spatial tampering is also known as intra frame tampering (see Figure 2).

Copy-Move

Copy-Move is one of the most common video/image manipulations technique in which a part of the frame/ image itself is copied and pasted into another part of the same frame/image. When this is done carefully, it can be difficult to detect copy move visually. And since the copy move blocks can be of any shape and location, it is very difficult to search all possible frame/image locations and sizes (Farid, 2009). An example for this type of forgery can be seen in a video where static scenes from frames are duplicated to the same frames to cover unwanted object. This process can be done without any modifications on the

Figure 1. Categories of video tampering

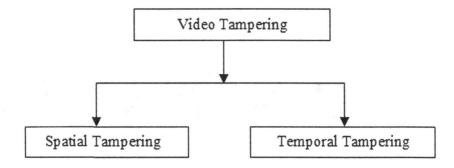

Figure 2. Spatial tampering

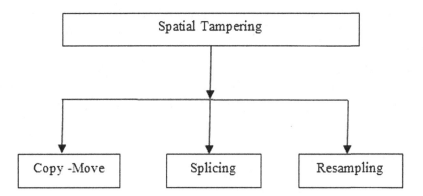

duplicated regions. As a result, the tampered region would exhibit the same characteristics as the rest of the frame which makes it hard to identify using the tools that are designed to detect the anomalies in the frame/image. Hence, to detect copy-move forgeries, we need techniques that can detect the frame/image regions which occur more than once in the frame/image. However, finding the very same region might not be enough in all cases, since an editor could use retouching tools, add noise, or compress the resulting frame/image. Furthermore, for better blending purposes, the copied area might be slightly rotated, scaled, or blurred without disturbing the image statistics, or revealing the forgery. Therefore, a good copy-move forgery technique should detect the duplicated frame/image regions, without getting affected by the slight modifications and/or operations such as noise addition, compression, rotation, scaling and illumination.

The copy-move forgery detection is one of the emerging problems in the field of digital video/image forensics. Many techniques have been proposed to address this problem. Copy-Move tampering detection techniques are facing challenge to detect the duplicated image/frame regions without getting affected by the common video/image processing operations, e.g. compression, noise addition, rotation, scaling, illumination etc . The other challenge is computational time, which becomes important when we are considering the large databases (see Figure 3).

Figure 3. Copy-Move tampering

Splicing

There are many methods of digital frame/image tampering, such as frame/image compositing, frame/image morphing, frame/image re-touching, frame/image enhancement, computer generating, and frame/image rebroadcast. Frame/Image compositing is the most common method and frame/image splicing is a basic operation in it. Frame/Image splicing is a technology of frame/image compositing by combining frame/image fragments from the same or different frame/images without further post processing such as smoothing of boundaries among different fragments. The steps of frame/image splicing process are shown in the Figure 4. Splicing is the most dangerous attack for the frame/ image in which we take two or more frames/images and create one composite frame/image. If we do splicing carefully then it is impossible to detect its visually.

The detection of image splicing has received considerable achievement; still, much work is left for frame/image splicing detection. Some of future works are as follows:

1. Splicing detection rates are still lower; therefore study of high detection rates is necessary.
2. To find out fast and robust algorithms.
3. Building large and realistic image and video database.
4. Splicing detection in video is less mature and required more work to be done in this area.
5. To make the forgery even harder to detect, one can use the feathered crop or the retouch tool to further mask any traces of the splicing segments. So, tampering other than splicing needs to be investigated.

Resampling

To create matching composite photograph sometimes it is necessary to resize, stretch, or rotate the portion of frame/image. For example when we are creating composite photograph of two persons in which one is fat and another is thin, then for making convincing composite photograph we must resize the first person (Farid, 2009). This process requires resampling of previous frame/image in new sampling lattice. The difference between resizing and resampling has to do with whether or not you're changing

Figure 4. Splicing process

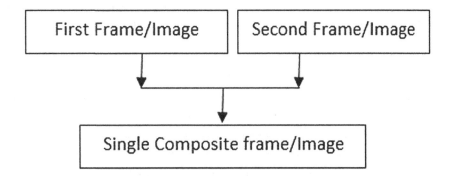

the number of pixels in the image/frame. If you are keeping the number of pixels in the image/frame the same and simply changing the size at which the image/frame will print, it is known as resizing. Further if anyone is changing the number of pixels in the image/frame, it is called resampling.

Temporal Tampering

In this tampering a sequence of frame is manipulated. Temporal attack mainly affects the time sequence of frames. The various temporal tampering attacks are as follows:

Adding New Frame

In this tampering we simply add new frame in the existing video which was not present before, to provide fake evidence or for any malicious activity. Adding new frame may change the structure of Group of pictures (GOP) and provide clue for tampering detection. When someone wants to add new frame in the video then they decode the video and after adding the frame in the video they re-encode the video. In this way double compression arise in the video which provide clue for video tampering.

Deleting Existing Frame

This involves intentionally deleting existing frame from the video to remove evidence or any other malicious activity. After deleting the frames from video, the structure of GOP may change which provide clue for tampering. Double compression is also an important clue of frame deletion from given video.

Duplication of Frame

In duplication of frame, people hide the unwanted frame by duplicated frame. Inter-frame correlation may provide clue for tampering detection. If many numbers of video frames contain same correlation coefficients then it indicates frame duplication. Considering suitable threshold on the basis of correlation coefficient, we can detect frame duplication in the video.

Shuffling of Frame

In shuffling of frame, people change the order of frame in the video which gives different meaning than actual. Double MPEG compression can provide clue for frame shuffling.

Modification of Frame

In modification of the frame people alter the content of frame by applying different video tampering technique like copy Move, Splicing and Resampling. For convincing temporal tampering these modifications affect a sequence of frame rather than single frame of video. Inter frame correlation based on some video features can provide clue for video tampering. This tampering affect both spatial and temporal domain of video so it is not pure temporal tampering, it can be known as spatial-temporal tampering.

CAMERA PIPELINE PROCESSING

When the video is taken from the camera it passes through different stage like lens, sensor, Color filter array (CFA), demosaicing, white balancing, gamma correction, post processing and data compression. In each stage, we get some modification in video frame which leads some intrinsic fingerprint to trace out the video frame. In many digital video/image based forensic application, the intrinsic fingerprint are focused, such as Camera Response Function (CRF), Color Filter Array (CFA), Sensor Noise, Compression Artefacts, etc. Sensor pattern noise play important role to find out camera sources and forgery detection (Hsu et al, 2008). Sensor pattern noises, extracted from digital frames/images as device fingerprints and it has been proved as an effective way for digital device identification (see Figure 5).

Lens

The camera lens is the most vital part of the image/video capturing process in a camera because it moulds and shapes the light that comes through external world to the sensor. Some of the features to be familiar with when looking for a camera lens are aperture, focal length, focus type, size. On single-lens reflex cameras, the lens can be changed to help the photographer achieve the perfect shot for image and video.

The aperture controls the falling light on the camera lens. In wider aperture, the more light can enter, and smaller is the aperture number. More light entering the camera allows for a faster shutter speed which gives the photographer the ability to freeze action and get blur free sharp image/video.

A camera lens can either have a fixed focal length or varying focal lengths, which is also known as a zoom lens. For example, a focal length between 40 and 60 mm represents the viewing range of the human eye. A telephoto lens of 200 mm can zoom in about four times as far.

Most cameras offer manual focus and automatic focus ability. This means that the photographer can set the focus or allow the camera to do it. Some cameras go a step even further and allow the photographer to adjust the manual focus without having to change the mode on the lens. Depending on the usage, a smaller, lighter lens may be more practical to buy than a larger one. Typically, the more powerful the zoom is, the larger is the lens. However, Canon has introduced lenses with the abbreviation DO, for "Diffractive Optic," that has significantly less length and weight from a conventional lens (http://www.ehow.com/facts_5179428_camera-lens-characteristics.html).

Figure 5. Camera pipeline processing

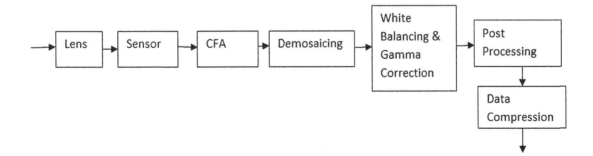

Sensor

Both CCD (charge-coupled device) and CMOS (complementary metal-oxide semiconductor) image/video sensors start work at the same point and convert light into electrons. Sensor used in a camcorder simply put, has a 2-D array of many thousands or millions of tiny solar cells, each of which transforms the light from one small portion of the image into electrons. CCD and CMOS devices perform this task using a variety of technologies.

Due to manufacturing differences, there are many noticeable differences between CCD and CMOS sensors.

- CCD sensors create high-quality, low-noise images/videos. CMOS sensors, traditionally, are more susceptible to noise and create low quality of images/videos.
- The light sensitivity of a CMOS chip tends to be lower.
- CMOS traditionally consumes little power so CMOS yields low power sensor.
- CCD consumes 100 times more power in comparison to CMOS sensor.
- CMOS sensor is extremely in expensive in compare to CCD.
- For a longer period of time CCD sensor has been mass produced, so they are more mature. They have more pixels and higher quality (http://electronics.howstuffworks.com/cameras-photography/digital/question362.htm).

CFA

A color filter array (CFA), or color filter mosaic (CFM), in photography is a mosaic of tiny color filters placed over the pixel sensors of an image/video sensor to capture color information. The typical photo sensors detect light intensity with little or no wavelength specificity, and therefore cannot separate color information. As a result Color filters are needed. Since sensors are made of semiconductors they obey solid-state physics.

The color filters filter the light by wavelength range, such that the separate filtered intensities include information about the color of light. For example, the Bayer filter gives information about the intensity of light in red, green, and blue (RGB) wavelength regions. The raw image data captured by the image sensor is then converted to a full-color image (with intensities of all three primary colors represented at each pixel) by a demosaicing algorithm which is tailored for each type of color filter (http://en.wikipedia.org/wiki/Color_filter_array). In passive image and video forgery detection CFA provides clue for tampering detection.

Demosaicing

A demosaicing process is a digital image process used to reconstruct a full color image from the incomplete color samples which are output from an image sensor overlaid with a color filter array (CFA). It is also known as interpolation of CFA or color reconstruction.

Most modern digital cameras acquire images using a single image sensor overlaid with a CFA, so demosaicing is part of the processing pipeline required to render these images into a viewable format. Demosaicing process aims to reconstruct a full color image from the spatially under sampled color channels output from the CFA. The process should have the following characteristics:

- Avoiding the introduction of false color artifacts, such as chromatic aliases, zippering (abrupt unnatural changes of intensity over a number of neighboring pixels) and purple fringing.
- Maximum image resolution preservation.
- Fast processing using low computational complexity.
- Robustness regarding accurate noise reduction

In passive image and video forgery detection demosaicing provides clue for tampering detection.

White Balancing and Gamma Correction

Color balance, in photography and image processing, is the global adjustment of the intensities of the colors which are mainly red, green, and blue primary colors. This adjustment aims to render specific colors – predominantly neutral colors correctly; hence, this method is called by various names such as gray balance, neutral balance, or white balance. Color balance changes the overall mixture of colors in an image and is used for color correction generalized versions of color balance are used to get colors other than neutrals to also appear correct or pleasing.

In video or still image systems, gamma correction, gamma nonlinearity, gamma encoding, or simply gamma, is a nonlinear operation used to code and decode luminance or tri-stimulus values. Gamma correction is defined by the following power-law expression:

$$V_{Out} = A V_{\text{In}}^{\gamma} \qquad (1)$$

where A is a constant and the input and output values are non-negative real values; in the common case of A = 1, inputs and outputs are typically in the range 0–1. A gamma value $\gamma < 1$ is sometimes called an encoding gamma, and the process of encoding with this compressive power-law nonlinearity is called gamma compression; conversely a gamma value $\gamma > 1$ is called a decoding gamma and the application of the expansive power-law nonlinearity is called gamma expansion (http://en.wikipedia.org/wiki/Gamma_correction).

Post-Processing

The term post-processing is used in the video/film business for quality-improvement, image processing methods used in video playback devices, and video player's software and transcoding software. It is also commonly used in real-time 3D rendering to add additional effects. Video post-processing is the process of changing the perceived quality of a video on playback. Image scaling routines such as linear interpolation, bilinear interpolation, or cubic interpolation can be performed when increasing the size of images; this involves either subsampling (reducing or shrinking an image) or zooming. This helps reduce or hide image artifacts and flaws in the original film material. It is important to understand that post-processing always involves a trade-off between speed, smoothness and sharpness.

Data Compression

Video data may be represented as a collection frames. The collection of frames contains spatial and temporal redundancy that video compression algorithms attempt to eliminate or try to code in a smaller size.

Similarities can be encoded by only storing differences between frames, or by using perceptual features of human vision. For example, small differences in color are more difficult to perceive than are changes in brightness. Compression algorithms can average a color across these similar areas to reduce space, in a manner similar to those used in JPEG image compression. Some of these methods are inherently lossy while others may preserve all relevant information from the original, uncompressed video. One of the most powerful techniques for compressing video is inter-frame compression. Inter-frame compression uses one or more earlier or later frames in a sequence to compress the current frame, while intra-frame compression uses only the current frame like JPEG image compression.

NOISE FEATURES EXTRACTION TECHNIQUES

Here we will discuss techniques to extract frame/image noise features for tampering detection. We can extract noise feature from frame/image using three techniques (Gou et al, 2007).In the first technique, we apply denoising algorithms for a frame/image to obtain frame/image noise. In the second technique, a set of noise features based on Gaussian fitting errors of wavelet coefficients is estimated. Finally, we use third technique for frame/image noise through neighborhood prediction and use the prediction error for extracting the noise features.

Denoising Algorithms Based on Noise Features

To extract frame/image noise features, we first utilize frame/image denoising algorithms. As shown in Figure 6, for a frame/image F is a given, denoising operation is applied to obtain its denoised version FD. The estimated frame/image noise NF at the pixel location (i, j) is then found by pixel-wise subtraction

$$NF\ (i, j) = F(i, j) - FD\ (i, j). \tag{2}$$

The mean and the standard deviation of noise feature form the first set of features. To capture the different aspects of noise, we apply four different denoising algorithms to a frame/image: linear filtering with an averaging filter, linear filtering with a Gaussian filter, median filtering, and Wiener adaptive image denoising. Low pass linear filtering using averaging or Gaussian filters helps model the high-frequency noise, non-linear median filtering addresses the "salt and pepper" noise, and adaptive methods such as Wiener filtering can tailor noise removal to the local pixel variance (Gou et al,.2007).

Noise Features from Wavelet Analysis

In this technique we get a set of noise features via wavelet analysis. After one stage 2 D wavelet decomposition, an input frame/image is decomposed to four sub bands as follows: low-low (LL), low-high (LH),

Figure 6. Denoised frame

high low(HL), and high-high (HH) sub bands. Among these four sub bands, the LL sub band contains low-frequency information, while the other three are for high-frequency information (Gou et al, 2007). In survey, it has been observed that for a large class of frames/images, the wavelet coefficients in the LH, HL, and HH sub bands do not follow a Gaussian distribution (Chang et al, 2000). This is because the spatial structure of these frames/images consists of smooth areas interspersed with occasional edges, and therefore coefficients in the high-frequency sub bands are sharply peaked at zero with broad tails. When applying tampering operations, such non-Gaussian property of the high-frequency wavelet coefficients may be affected. The noise strength may also be changed due to the tampering operations. Based on above analysis, we extract statistical noise feature in the wavelet domain. After that we perform a one stage 2-D wavelet decomposition to frame/image and obtain its three high-frequency sub bands HH, HL, LH. For each of these three sub bands, we calculate the mean (μ) and the standard deviation of the wavelet sub band coefficients. We take the standard deviation as our second statistical noise feature (Gou et al, 2007). First, we assume that the high-frequency wavelet coefficients can be modeled as the sum of a stationary white Gaussian noise and a noise-free image. After the decomposition, only high-frequency components (i.e., the LH $h(i, j)$, HL $v(i, j)$ and HH $d(i, j)$ sub bands) are used for processing. The local variance of each wavelet coefficient is estimated. For each wavelet coefficient, we define a window size of $W \times W$, where $W \in \{3, 5, 7, 9\}$.

Noise Features from Neighborhood Prediction

Most frames/images consist of some smooth regions, where pixel values can be estimated from certain neighboring pixels with high accuracy. However, when smooth regions of a frame are impured by noise, non-trivial prediction errors may be resulted in during the neighborhood prediction. Therefore, we characterize frame noise in terms of the neighborhood prediction error in the smooth regions, and then extract the third set of noise features from it (Gou et al, 2007).

IMPORTANCE OF NOISE FEATURES

In early period of digital camera, different survey has been done on the study of noise in signal and image processing. The main goal of this research is to remove noise from images. Many denoising techniques have been proposed and systematically classified for images (Motwani et al., 2004). On the other hand, some researchers have recently introduced interesting attempts to make effective use of noise features, rather than trying to remove it from images and videos (Kobayashi et al., 2009). Matsushita and Lin exploited the distribution of noise intensity for each scene irradiance to estimate the camera response functions (CRFs) (Matsushita & Lin, 2007). Noise distribution is by nature shown to be symmetric, but it is skewed by nonlinear CRFs. Conversely, the inverse CRF can be estimated by evaluating the degree of symmetry of back-projected irradiance distribution. Using the noise in a frame/image, the detection ability of the method is not degraded by noise and thus the method can be used under conditions of high-level noise. (Liu et al., 2006) estimated the noise level function (NLF) from a single image, which relates the noise intensity with the image intensity. The spatial variance in an image contains the variance resulted in objects texture as well as the intensity of the noise. Obtaining the component of the real noise from NLF, we can disassociate the component of texture from the variance of the observation. They utilized the function not only for denoising but also for adaptive bilateral filtering and edge detection.

Noise information is available for camera identification and forgery detection as well. Due to the sensor imperfections developed in a manufacturing process, the CCD camera contains pixels with different sensitivity to light. This spatial variation of sensitivity is temporally fixed and known as fixed pattern noise. Since this non-uniformity is inherent in a camera, we can exploit it as a fingerprint. (Lukas et al., 2005) determined the reference noise pattern of a camera by averaging the noise extracted from several images. They extracted fixed pattern noise from a given image using a smoothing filter and identified the camera that took the image. The authors also proposed a method for detecting forgeries in an image using the same approach (Lukas et al., 2006).

VIDEO TAMPERING DETECTION METHOD USING NOISE FEATURES

A. Using Noise Residue Feature

Noise residue features play important role in video tampering detection. (Hsu et al., 2008) proposed video forgery detection using correlation of noise residue features. The summary of proposed process is as follows (see Figure 7).

Summary of Proposed Process

The proposed method work as follows:

1. Fetch the video.
2. Extract frame from the video.
3. Denoised the frame using wavelet based denoising filter (Wiener).
4. Subtract the denoised frame from original frame to get the noise residue.

Figure 7. Process for video tampering detection

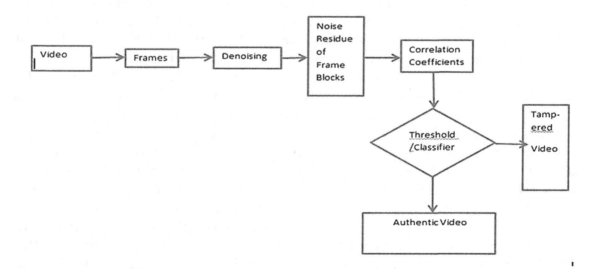

5. Calculate the noise residue of frame blocks.
6. Compute the correlation between noise residue of intra frame blocks (Spatial).
7. Compute the correlation of noise residue in inter frame blocks (Temporal).
8. Select the threshold value for tampering detection using Gaussian Mixture Model (GMM) based classifier.
9. Get forged or authentic video.
10. End.

Wavelet Based Denoising Filter

Authors (Hsu et al., 2008) are considering wavelet based denoising filter to get noise free frame from the video. It works as follows (see Figure 8):

1. Four levels of wavelet decomposition is performed on noisy frames to obtain its wavelet coefficients. Authors are considering only high frequency component for processing.
2. For each wavelet coefficient they have predefined window size and compute variance of each wavelet coefficient.
3. Weiner filter have been used for removing the noise.
4. Repeat the previous process for each wavelet coefficient until the process converges.
5. Apply inverse wavelet transform to get noise free frame of the video.

Estimation of Noise Correlation at Block Level

Let $n(i, j)$ denotes the noise residual at pixel coordinate (i, j). The correlation value R or r between previous frame and current frame on each block can be defined as

Figure 8. Wavelet decomposition of a noisy frame

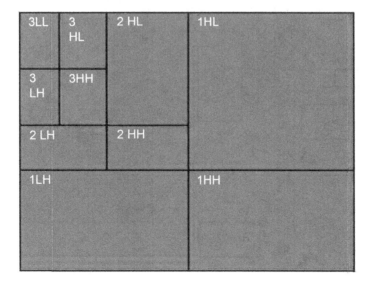

$$R = \frac{\sum_i \sum_j \left(n_{i,j}^t - \bar{n}^t\right)\left(n_{i,j}^{t-1} - \bar{n}^{t-1}\right)}{\sqrt{\sum_i \sum_j \left(n_{i,j}^t - \bar{n}^t\right)^2 \sum_i \sum_j \left(n_{i,j}^{t-1} - \bar{n}^{t-1}\right)^2}} \tag{3}$$

where t denotes the tth frame and $\bar{n}$ is the mean value of the noise residual at t^{th} frame. When a region is forged, the correlation value of temporal noise residue in the region is usually changed (increased or decreased) depending on the forgery scheme used. Intra frame and Interframe correlation coefficient is computed for spatial and temporal tampering detection (Hsu et al., 2008) (see Figure 9).

Forgery Detection by Statistical Analysis of Noise Residue

Tampered regions can be easily found by analyzing the statistical properties of block-level noise correlation. For a Gaussian distributed signal, the parameters can be estimated easily by calculating

$$\sigma_r^2 = \frac{1}{N} \sum_{n=1}^{N} \left(r_n - \bar{r}\right)^2 \tag{4}$$

In typical applications, in a forged video, the area of forged regions is usually much smaller than that of normal region. Based on this assumption, pre-classification result can be used to speed up the model adaptation in the fine-classification. The pre-classification is defined as follows:

Figure 9. Inter frame correlation of noise features

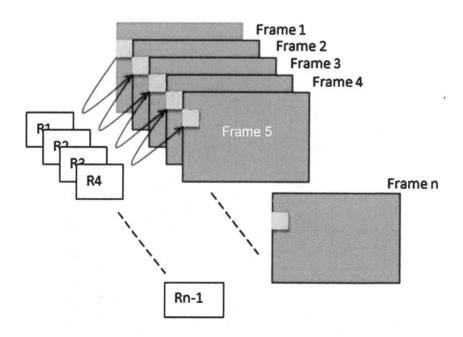

$$Class(n) = \begin{cases} 0 & \left| r_n - \overline{r} \right| < k.\sigma_r \\ 1 & else \end{cases} \tag{5}$$

where Class (n) denotes the binary classification mask for the nth block with a value of 1 indicating the block has been forged. A fine-classification process is performed to refine the detection result. Otherwise, the video frame is classified as a non-tampered frame, and no further detection process is performed. Based on the pre-classification, a GMM model is applied to characterize the statistical distributions of block-level noise correlations for the tampered and normal regions, respectively. The means and variances of the block-level noise correlation of the forged and normal classes are used as the initial values in the Expectation Maximization algorithm to speed up the iteration process. It is assumed that there are two Gaussian distributions in a forged video. For the two-class problem, the discriminate function can be defined as

$$g_i(R) = -\frac{1}{2}\ln 2\pi + \ln \sigma_r - \frac{(r - \overline{r})^2}{2\sigma_r^2} + \ln P(\omega_i) \tag{6}$$

where $P(w_i)$ denotes the prior of the $i\,th$ class, which can be approximated by the result of pre-classification (Hsu et al., 2008).

Limitations of Proposed Method

This method has following limitations:

- Proposed method is not well suited for video with high compression.
- Authors have considered static background.
- Performance depends on noise extraction techniques.

B. Using Noise Level Function (NLF)

Kobayashi et al, (2009) proposed video forgery detection based on noise features. In video capturing digital camera, several noise sources corrupt the video such as photon shot noise, dark current noise, thermal noise, read-out noise and quantization noise. Authors focus on photon shot noise among these noise sources because of the following two reasons: (1) photon shot noise is dominant noise in a scene except in an extremely dark environment, and (2) the relation between the brightness and the noise intensity is useful for forgery detection. The number of photons that enters a CCD element has temporal fluctuation (which are converted into electrons and finally into bits) and thus this variation behaves as noise. This fluctuation follows a Poisson distribution; the noise intensity depends on its mean – the noiseless irradiance. Unfortunately, the distribution of photons cannot directly be measured because photons are converted into electrons, electric voltage, and finally bit chains. However, instead the relation between the mean and the variance of the observed pixel value be computed which is considered as a measure of tampering. Let O be the noiseless observed intensity. Due to the effect of noise, the real observation has fluctuation and thus we obtain a random variable of observation O. Let μ and σ be the mean and the variance of the observed pixel intensity O, respectively, when the noiseless observation is $\hat{o}$. The relationship between variance and mean represents how the variance changes with respect to the mean of the observed pixel value. When we obtain the mean observation μ the variance is described by a function with respect to the mean (see Figure 10).

Summary of Proposed Process

The proposed process works as follow (Kobayashi et al., 2009).

1. Mean and variance of pixel value is calculated at each pixel.
2. NLF is estimated by fitting function to noise characteristic point (Mean & Variance).
3. Find out the distance of each pixel from NLF.
4. If the distance of pixel from NLF exceeds some threshold value then forgery is indicated else it is authentic.

Mean and Variance of Noise Features

If we have an image or a single frame of video sequence, NLF can be obtained by calculating spatial mean and variance. This approach, however, requires an assumption of the local uniformity of the objects reflectance and shading. If there is a textured object in a scene, we cannot obtain the noise component independently from the total variance because the spatial variation is mixed in the signal. The proposed method proves its merits in this case. In this method, the authors deal with a static scene where the

Figure 10. Relation between mean and variance (thick black line NLF)

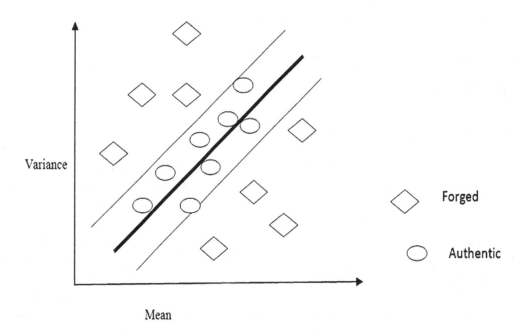

camera and the objects are fixed during recording. Therefore a conclusion is drawn that the temporal variation of each pixel value results entirely from noise. Operating statistical analysis along a time-line to the given video, the authors obtain the relation between μ and σ at each pixel (Kobayashi et al., 2009).

NLF Estimation

Analyzing observed intensity along a time-line, the authors obtain a dense set of points, as many as the resolution of the video. Then the authors fit a linear NLF $\tau\,(\mu)$ to the points using linear least squares method as follow:

$$\tau\,(\mu) = \alpha\mu + \beta, \tag{7}$$

where α and β are the estimated parameters. In order to eliminate the effect of the scale factor between the mean and the variance, they are normalized before estimation. Inconsistencies of the relation between the mean and the variance can be a clue to the forgery. Therefore, we can claim pixels whose noise characteristic is far from NLF to be from a tampering process (Kobayashi et al., 2009).

Tampering Detection

Once we obtain the NLF $\tau(\mu)$, the authenticity of each pixel in the video is evaluated based on the distance from the estimated NLF .The evaluation of the pixel *N* located at the position *r* is determined as follows:

$$N_r = \begin{cases} Tampered & if \; \left| \sigma^2\left(r\right) - \tau\left(\mu\left(r\right)\right) \right| > threhold\left(\epsilon\right) \\ Authentic & else \end{cases} \tag{8}$$

where ε is the constant threshold (Kobayashi et al., 2009).

Limitation of Proposed Method

This method has following limitations:

- Works for static scene video. It cannot detect tampering of moving object or person as shown in Figure 11.
- Assumes Linear Camera Response Function.
- Assumes Linear Noise Level Function.
- Does not utilize spatial pixel for forgery detection.
- Distribution of noise for video follows Gaussian distribution.

Authors in (Kobayashi et al., 2009) improved their work as in (Kobayashi et al., 2010) where they considered nonlinear NLF for video forgery detection. But the limitations of both methods are this that it detect tampering in static scene or object but not dynamic scene or object.

*Figure 11. Authentic and tampered frame
(Qadir et al, 2012).*

RECOMMENDATION

Noise residue plays important role in video tampering detection using noise features. Author Hsu et al. (2008) have used wavelet based video denoising technique using wiener filter. Video denoising using nonlinear thresholding with wavelet shrinkage can provide better noise residue. If we are able to find better noise residue then it will help to detect tampered location in high compressed video.

Further (Hsu et al., 2008) have implemented their method in MATLAB which consume more time for video tampering detection. Real time processing is less support by MATLAB, so video tampering detection in Open-CV is better option. The recommended method is as follow:

1. Fetch the video.
2. Extract frame from the video.
3. Denoised the frame using nonlinear thresholding (HARD and SOFT) with wavelet shrinkage.
4. Subtract the denoised frame from original frame to get the noise residue.
5. Calculate the noise residue of frame blocks.
6. Compute the correlation between noise residue of intra frame blocks (Spatial).
7. Compute the correlation of noise residue in inter frame blocks (Temporal).
8. Select the threshold value for tampering detection using GMM based Bayesian classifier.
9. Get forged or authentic video.
10. End.

Noise extraction using nonlinear thresholding with wavelet shrinkage and by proposing hybrid technique using existing methods in (Hsu et al., 2008) and (Kobayashi et al., 2010) can reduce the limitation and increase performance of both methods.

VIDEO SOURCE IDENTIFICATION USING NOISE FEATURES

There are basically two techniques for video source identification using noise features. First is based on Photo Response Non-uniformity and second is based on Pixels defects.

Using Photo Response Non-uniformity (PRNU) Estimation

Chen et al., (2007) proposed camcorder identification by considering two major statistical signal processing procedures, which are

1. Estimating the PRNUs from individual videos.
2. Determining the common origin by establishing the presence of the same PRNUs.

Consider two video-clips 1 and 2 were produced by the exact same camcorder. Let K1 and K2 be the PRNUs estimated from both clips. Because the PRNU is a unique signature of the camera, the task of origin identification is equivalent to discriminating K1 from K2. Due to estimation errors and varying quality and length of the video clips, the accuracy of the estimated PRNUs K1 and K2 might also vary. Apply normalize cross correlation between K1 and K2.If the correlation value approach to 1 that indicate both video clip are coming from same camcorder. Otherwise it is coming from different camcorder.

Using Pixel Defects

Geradts et al., (2001) examined the defects of CCD pixels and used them to match target images to source digital camera. Pixel defects include point defects, hot point defects, dead pixel, pixel traps, and cluster defects. To find the defective pixels, a couple of images with black background are taken by each of the 12 cameras, tested and compared to count the common defect points that appear as white. The result shows that each camera has distinct pattern of defective pixels.

ISSUE AND CHALLENGES IN VIDEO TAMPERING DETECTION

The various issue and challenge for video tampering detection is as follow:

New Tampering Attack

We have discussed different type of video tampering attacks but it does not imply that we have only this type of tampering attacks. A new video tampering attack can arise at any time and detection of such attack may be very difficult.

Hardware

Due to the continuous recording in surveillance video it requires huge memory and a lot of transmission power. If we try to make recording event wise then it would be tough to detect tampering in surveillance video because we would not have video frame sequence in continuous time space.

Passive Video

If we will not have digital signature and digital watermark in the video then proving authenticity of video or tampering detection will be very tough.

Source

If we have no information from which camera the particular video is taken then it would create problem to prove authenticity of source or tampering detection in video.

Tools

Video and image editing tool are so advance that they visually leave no clue for video / Image tampering detection. These tools are so advanced that they create same size frame/ image .Tampering detection in such frame / image requires analysis till pixel level.

Data Set

Video tampering is not as easy as image tampering, so creating and maintaining a data set of tampered video is very difficult.

Robust Feature Representation

One of the challenges in detecting video tampering is to find the robust representations of features for the video frame blocks, so that the duplicated blocks can be identified even after modifications.

Collocated Area

When a region is forged across the frames in a spatially collocated area, it may be very difficult to distinguish the forged regions and the authentic regions.

Small Patch Size

Detecting forgeries of small patch size such as a macro-blocks or of the order of few macro-blocks is a big challenge for video tampering detection.

High Compressed video

Feature extraction in videos of high compression is very challenging in comparison to videos with less compression. For example noise features can be easily extracted from a less compressed video in comparison to a high compressed one.

New video tampering attacks, passive video, low quality/high compressed video and different format of video are creating great challenge for researcher to detect video tampering.

APPLICATION

Video tampering detection techniques help to prove the authenticity of video & development of computer forensic tools for video. Video tampering detection tools are used by TV-Media, investigation of crime by police and some other government or private agencies to check the forgery of video. Everywhere in this world when we have doubt on a video we can use video tampering detection techniques and video forensic tools according to our requirements. Noise features based forensic scheme help in video tampering detection and camera source identification.

CONCLUSION AND FUTURE DIRECTION

In this chapter, we have presented passive video tampering detection technique based on noise features of the video. By analyzing the various video/image tampering that were presented in this chapter, we can say that the tampering detection techniques are very necessary for the surveillance video, film industry, medical, copyright, court of law. As the time passes, we are getting more involved with image and video applications in our daily life. Now our social media and news channels most depend on video/image applications. Various, wide range of tampering attacks, causes severe challenges for the video authenticity. Passive video tampering detection is challenging in comparison to active video tampering detection. A perfect passive video tampering detection algorithm that can detect all kinds of malicious manipulations and tolerate all non-malicious manipulations is yet to be discovered. In near future robustness and performance would be the key point for video tampering detection, so that it can differentiate the acceptable video processing operations from malicious tampering attacks. Passive video forensic is less mature in comparison to passive image forensic, a lot of research works are required to be done in this field.

REFERENCES

Chang, S. G., Yu, B., & Vetterli, M. (2000). Spatially Adaptive Wavelet Thresholding with Context Modeling for Image Denoising. *IEEE Transactions on Image Processing*, 9(9), 1522–1531. doi:10.1109/83.862630 PMID:18262990

Chen, M., Fridrich, J., Goljan, M., & Lukas, J. (2007). Source digital camcorder identification using sensor photo-response nonuniformity. In *Proc. of SPIE Electronic Imaging*. Photonics West.

Farid, H. (2009). A Survey of Image Forgery Detection. *IEEE Signal Processing Magazine*, 26(2), 16–25. doi:10.1109/MSP.2008.931079

Fridrich, J., Soukal, D., & Lukas, J. (2003). Detection of copy-move forgery in digital images. In *Proc. of Digital Forensic Research Workshop*.

Geradts, Z. J., Bijhold, J., Kieft, M., Kurosawa, K., Kuroki, K., & Saitoh, N. (2001). Methods for Identification of Images Acquired with Digital Cameras. In *Proc. of SPIE, Enabling Technologies for Law Enforcement and Security*, (vol. 4232). doi:10.1117/12.417569

Gou, H., Swaminathan, A., & Wu, M. (2007). Robust Scanner Identification based on Noise Features. *In Proc. of IS&TSPIE Conf on Security, Stego., and Watermarking ofMultimedia Contents IX*.

Gou, H., Swaminathan, A., & Wu, M. (2007). Noise Features For Image Tampering Detection And Steganalysis. In Proc. Of IEEE ICMP, (pp. 97-100). doi:10.1109/ICIP.2007.4379530

Hsu, C., Hung, T., Lin, C.-W., & Hsu, C. (2008). Video forgery detection using correlation of noise residue. In *Proceedings of IEEE 10th Workshop on Multimedia Signal Processing*. IEEE.

Johnson, M. K., & Farid, H. (2005). Exposing digital forgeries by detecting inconsistencies in lighting. In *Proc. of Workshop on Multimedia and security*. doi:10.1145/1073170.1073171

Johnson, M. K., & Farid, H. (2006). Exposing digital forgeries through chromatic aberration. In *Proc. of International Multimedia Conference*.

Kobayashi, M., Okabe, T., & Sato, Y. (2009). *Detecting Video Forgeries Based on Noise Characteristics*. *Pooc.of*. Springer-Verlag Berlin Heidelberg.

Kobayashi, M., Okabe, T., & Sato, Y. (2010). Detecting Forgery From Static-Scene Video Based on Inconsistency in Noise Level Functions. *IEEE Transactions on Information Forensics and Security*, *5*(4), 883–892. doi:10.1109/TIFS.2010.2074194

Lee, S.-J., & Jung, S.-H. (2001). A survey of watermarking techniques applied to multimedia. In *Proc. of IEEE International Symposium on Industrial Electronics*, (*vol. 1*, pp. 272–277). IEEE.

Lin, Z., Wang, R., Tang, X., & Shum, H.-Y. (2005). Detecting doctored images using camera response normality and consistency. In *Proc. of IEEE Computer Society Conference on Computer Vision and Pattern Recognition*, (vol. 1, pp. 1087–1092). IEEE.

Liu, C., Szeliski, R., Kang, S. B., Lawrence Zitnick, C., & Freeman, W. T. (2006). *Automatic estimation and removal of noise from a single image*. Technical Report MSR-TR-2006-180. Microsoft Research.

Luk'aˇs, J., Fridrich, J., & Goljan, M. (2006) Detecting digital image forgeries using sensorpattern noise. In *Proc. of Society of Photo-Optical Instrumentation Engineers Conference*, (vol. 6072, pp. 362–372).

Lukas, J., Fridrich, J., & Goljan, M. (2005). Determining digital image origin using sensor imperfections. In *Proc. of Society of Photo-Optical Instrumentation Engineers Conference*, (vol. 5685, pp. 249–260).

Matsushita, Y., & Lin, S. (2007). Radiometric calibration from noise distributions. In *Proc. of IEEE Computer Society Conference on Computer Vision and Pattern Recognition*, (pp. 1–8). IEEE.

Motwani, M. C., Gadiya, M. C., Motwani, R. C., & Harris, F. C. Jr. (2004). Survey of image denoising techniques. In *Proc. of Global Signal Processing Expo*.

Qadir, G., Yahay, S., & Ho, A. T. S. (2012). Surrey university library for forens ic analys is (SULFA) of video content. In *Proc. of IET Conference on Image Processing*.

Van Lanh, T., Chong, K.-S., Emmanuel, S., & Kankanhalli, M. S. (2007) A survey on digital camera image forensic methods. In *Proc. of IEEE International Conference on Multimedia and Expo*. doi:10.1109/ICME.2007.4284575

Ye, S., Sun, Q., & Chang, E.-C. (2007). Detecting digital image forgeries by measuring inconsistencies of blocking artifact. In *Proc. of IEEE International Conference on Multimedia and Expo*. doi:10.1109/ICME.2007.4284574

ADDITIONAL READING

Amerini, I., Ballan, L., Caldelli, R., Bimbo, A. D., & Serra, G. (2011). A SIFT based forensic method for copy move attack detection and information recovery, published in: IEEE Transactions on Information Forensics & Security, vol. 6, no.1.

Amerini, I. Barni, M., Caldelli, R. & Costanzo, A. (2013). Counter forensic of SIFT based copy-move detection by means of key point classification, published in: Springer-EURASIP Journal on Image and Video Processing. doi:.10.1186/1687-5281-18

Dong, Q., Yang, G., & Zhu, N. (2012). MCEA Based Passive Forensic Scheme for Detecting Frame Based Video Tampering.Elsevier Vol.9.Digital Investigation, Hunan University. *China*, 151–159.

Fridrich, J., Soukal, D., & Lukas, J. (2003). Detection of copy-move forgery in digital images.*Proc Digital Forensic Research Workshop*, Clevelan, OH.

Gonzalez, R. C., & Woods, R. E. (2002). Digital Image Processing, University of Tennesse, New Jersey 07458: Prentice Hall Upper Saddle River.

Guohui, L., Qiong, W., & Dan, T. & ShaoJie, S. (2007). A sorted neighborhood approach for detecting duplicated regions in image forgeries based on dwt and svd, Proc. of International Conference on Multimedia and Expo, pp.1750-1753.

Hsu, Y. F., & Chang, S. F. (2006). Detecting Image Splicing Using Geometry Invariants And Camera Characteristics Consistency. Paper presented at International Conference on Multimedia and Expo, Toranto, Canada. doi:10.1109/ICME.2006.262447

Johnson, M. K., & Farid, H. (2005). Exposing digital forgeries by detecting inconsistencies in lighting.In *Proc.ACM 7th Workshop on Multimedia and Security*. New York, pp.1–10. doi:10.1145/1073170.1073171

Mahdian, B., & Lavsac, S. (2007). Detection of copy–move forgery using a method based on blur moment invariants, Elsevier Vol. 171. *Forensic Science International*, *171*(2-3), 180–189. doi:10.1016/j.forsciint.2006.11.002 PMID:17161569

Ng, T. T., Chang, S. F., & Sun, Q. (2004). *A data set of authentic and spliced image blocks. Tech. Rep., DVMM*. Columbia University.

Popescu, A. C., & Farid, H. (2004). Exposing digital forgeries by detecting du- plicated image regions. Dept. Comput. Sci., Dartmouth College, Tech. Rep. TR2004-515.

Popescu, A. C., & Farid, H. (2005). Exposing digital forgeries in color filter array interpolated images. *IEEE Transactions on Signal Processing*, *53*(10), 3948–3959. doi:10.1109/TSP.2005.855406

Shi, Y. Q., Chen, C., & Chen, W. (2007). A Natural Image Model Approach to Splicing Detection, ACM Multimedia & security. New York. pp.51-62.

Su, Y., Jhang, J., & Liu, J. (2009). Exposing Digital Video Forgery by Detecting Motion Compensated edge Artefacts, IEEE Computational intelligence and software engineering.Wuhan, pp.1-4.

Theobalt, C., Ahmed, N., Aguiar, D., Ziegler, G., Lensch, H., Magnor, M., & Seidel, H. P. (2005). Joint Motion and Reflectance Capture for Creating Relightable 3D Videos. Technical Report MPI-I-2005-4-004.

Wang, W., Dong, J., & Tan, T. (2009). Effective image splicing detection based on image chroma. Presented in International Conference on Image Processing, Cario, Egypt. doi:10.1109/ICIP.2009.5413549

Wang, W., & Farid, H. (2007). Exposing digital forgeries in video by detecting duplication. In *Proceedings of the Multimedia and Security Workshop*, Dallas, TX. pp. 35-42. doi:10.1145/1288869.1288876

Xu, B., Liu, G., & Dai, Y. (2012). A Fast Image Copy-move Forgery Detection method using Phase Correlation, *IEEE Fourth International Conference on Multimedia Information Networking and Security*, China, pp.319-322. doi:10.1109/MINES.2012.18

Zhang, J., Feng, Z., & Su, Y. (2008). A new approach for detecting copy-move forgery in digital images, Published in: IEEE International conference on communication System.Guangzhou.pp.362-366.

Zhao, X., Li, J., Li, S., & Wang, S. (2011). Detecting Digital Image Splicing in Chroma Spaces. Springer IWDW. Verlag, Berlin, Heidelberg. pp.12-22. doi:10.1007/978-3-642-18405-5_2

KEY TERMS AND DEFINITION

Active Video Tampering Detection Technique: A video which contain pre-embedding information like digital signature and digital watermark is called active video. The technique used to detect tampering in such video is known an active video tampering detection technique.

Blind Video: A video which does not contain any information regarding source from which these video was taken then this is called blind video.

CFA: Color filter array is used for filtering the color which is measured by camera sensor. Generally we see three color filters in camera, Red, Green and blue.

Copy Move: Copy Move or cloning is an image or frame tampering technique in which we remove scene or object within that particular image/frame and fill the removed location with background color. Some time we perform copy of some scene from an image /frame and paste it different location of the same image /frame.

CRF: The camera response function measure image/frame irradiance at the image/frame plane to the measured intensity values. Various application like Color constancy, photometric stereo, and shape from shading, require object radiance rather than image/frame intensity.

Demosaicing: Demosaicing is a process to find out missing color from existing color sample with the help of Color filter array. Other name of demosaicing is color reconstruction or color filter array interpolation.

NLF: Noise level function, Relate mean and variance of noise features.

Passive Video Tampering Detection Technique: A Video which does not contain pre-embedding information like digital signature and digital watermark is called Passive video. The technique used to detect tampering in such video is called passive video tampering detection technique.

Sensor Noise: Noise produce by Camera sensor in image is known as sensor noise. A digital image/ frame moves from the camera sensor to the computer memory, it undergoes a series of processing's, Including: quantization, white balancing, De-mosaicking, color correction, gamma correction, these produce noise in image.

Splicing: Splicing is an image or frame tampering technique in which we create single composite image/ frame with the help of two or more images/frames.

Video Forensic: In video forensic we study regarding video tampering attacks and sources identification of video for authentication of the video.

Chapter 12
A Survey on Palmprint–Based Biometric Recognition System

Y. L. Malathi Latha
Swami Vivekananda Institute of Technology (SVIT), India

Munaga V. N. K. Prasad
Institute for Development and Research in Banking Technology, India

ABSTRACT

The automatic use of physiological or behavioral characteristics to determine or verify identity of individual's is regarded as biometrics. Fingerprints, Iris, Voice, Face, and palmprints are considered as physiological biometrics whereas voice and signature are behavioral biometrics. Palmprint recognition is one of the popular methods which have been investigated over last fifteen years. Palmprint have very large internal surface and contain several unique stable characteristic features used to identify individuals. Several palmprint recognition methods have been extensively studied. This chapter is an attempt to review current palmprint research, describing image acquisition, preprocessing palmprint feature extraction and matching, palmprint related fusion and techniques used for real time palmprint identification in large databases. Various palmprint recognition methods are compared.

INTRODUCTION

Today's electronically interconnected information society requires accurate automatic personal authentication schemes to authenticate a person's identity before giving an access to resources. The motivation behind such schemes is to guarantee that just a legitimate user and nobody else access the rendered resources. Cases of such applications incorporate secure access to personal computers (PCs), laptops, PDAs, network and applications, control entry to secure areas of a building and automatic teller machine (ATM) and debit transactions. Without solid individual recognition schemes, these systems are vulnerable against the wiles of an imposter.

Traditionally, user authentication systems use passwords or ID cards, which can be lost or forgotten. They are based on something one knows or something one has. Today, people using advance technology of forgery and passwords hacking techniques to gain illegal access to services of a legitimate user. So,

DOI: 10.4018/978-1-4666-8723-3.ch012

traditional approaches are no longer suitable for information society. Therefore there is need for accurate atomic computer aided personal authentication system in the information based world. Biometric technology has emerged as viable solution for personal identity and security.

The automatic use of physiological or behavioral characteristics (Jain et al., 2008) to determine or verify identity of individual's is regarded as biometrics. Fingerprints, Iris, Voice, Face, and palmprints are considered as physiological biometrics whereas voice and signature are behavioral biometrics. Among different sorts of biometric identifiers, hand-based biometrics draws in more attention due to their high user acknowledgement and comfort. In real time applications like UID enrolment and access control purpose widely used biometrics are iris and fingerprint. On the other hand it is hard to extract the small, unique feature from unclear fingerprint and iris input devices are costly, other biometric modularity's like face and voice are less accurate and easy to mimic. Alternatively, the palmprint has several advantages compared to other biometrics which are 1) capture device has cheaper cost 2) palm contains additional features like principal lines, wrinkles, ridges, and 3) Features can easily extracted from low resolution images Palmprint recognition is basically a pattern recognition that is utilized to distinguish or confirm user focused around his or her interesting physical charteristics.

Palmprint is the inner surface of a person's hand. For quite long time, palmprint have been used for predicting the future. The study of palmprint is ancient and has appeared much in Indian history. Chinese traditional medicine has long observed that the palm print is connected with health and characters, which is generally recognized by more dermatoglyphic experts. Recently, after extensive research, it has been found that the palmprint is related to nationality, geological race, age calculation, gender identification, health, security .intelligence and heredity and so forth. Palmprint is extensively used in security for person identification. China was the first country to use palmptint for forensic applications.

Palm contain many features like geometric features, delta point's features, principal lines features, minutiae, ridges and creases(Zhang, 2004). Principal lines are namely heart line, head line and life line. Figure 1 shows structure of palmprint. These features are useful for palmprint representation and can be extracted at different image resolutions. Low resolution images(such as 75or 150 dpi) can extract principle lines wrinkles and texture while high resolution images can extra ridges, singular points and minutia points in additional to principal line and wrinkles. High resolution images are suitable for

Figure 1. Structure of palmprint

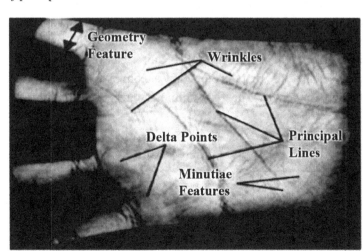

crime investigation and low resolution images are suitable for civil and commercial applications. At first palmprint exploration concentrated on high-resolution images (Dai & Zhou, 2011) however now all investigation is on low resolution images.

Palmprint recognition can be done in two ways: identification or verification. Identification is the process of one-to-many comparison to match the individual's data against all enrolled users in the database. Verification is the process of one-to-one comparison to verify that individual is who he/she claims to be. Palmprint recognition system has four stages that are image acquisition, pre-processing, feature extraction and matching. Figure 2 shows general block diagram of palmprint recognition system. In first stage, we captured the image of palmprint using different types of digital cameras and scanners. In second stage, noise present in the image can be removed using filters, align the palmprint image and segment. Feature extraction is to acquire effective features like principle lines, orientation fields, minutia, texture and density from the pre-processed palm prints can be extracted in third stage. Finally, the two palmprint features are matched to take decision.

BACKGROUND

This section presents overview of various techniques related to image acquisition, preprocessing palmprint feature extraction and matching, palmprint related fusion and palmprint identification in large databases. Various palmprint recognition methods are compared.

PALMPRINT ACQUISITION AND PREPROCESSING

Palmprint Acquisition

Generally, palmprint image can be acquired using offline and online methods. An offline palmprint are obtained from inked palmprints and are digitized by using digital scanner. This method is not suitable for real-time application and image quality is not satisfactory because the amount of the ink used (Zhang & Shu, 1999) affects the palmprint image.

Online palmprint image can be acquired by putting the hand on a scanner. Then the scanner captures the image and digitizes the data. CCD based palmprint scanner, Digital scanners, Digital cameras and digital video cameras are used to capture online palmprint images.CCD cameras uses pegs to align the palms and high quality image can be obtained. But it requires careful device setup.

CCD based palmprint scanner was first developed by a team of researchers (Zhang et al., 2003) from Hong Kong polytechnique University. The first online low-resolution palmprint recognition system

Figure 2. Palmprint recognition system

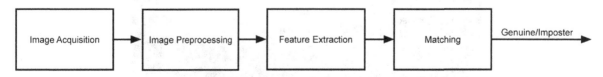

was proposed by Zhang et al. (2003) and published a public palmprint image database, *i.e.*, the PolyU database. Most of the palmprint system (Zhang et al., 2003; Su, 2009) utilized CCD scanner to acquire the palmprint Image.

Digital cameras and video cameras are used by the researches as they require less efforts for setting system design (Kumar &. Zhang, 2006).These collection approaches are mostly used because they did not use pegs, not require special lighting control, reduce maintenance efforts of system and higher user acceptance.

However, the palmprint quality may be low because of uncontrolled light and distortion. Kumar et al. (2006) and Ribaric et al. (2005) captured hand images using a digital camera in contact manner respectively. Apart from CCD scanners and digital camera/video camera, there was also research which employed digital scanner (Qin et al., 2006). For real-time applications digital scanner are not suitable as because of long scanning time and the images may be deformed due to the pressing effect of the hand on the platform surface.

Recently, contact-free palmprint acquisition system (Xin et al., 2011) are developed. Usually, web-cameras (Xin et al., 2011) cameras in smart phones, panel PCs, or notebook PCs were used to collect contact-free palmprint images.

Preprocessing

The pre-processing is a crucial step in palmprint recognition. At the point when palmprints are obtained using digital cameras without pegs, distortion including noise, rotation, shift and translation may be present in the palm image. Hence preprocessing is used to correct distortion, remove noise, align different palms and to segment region of interest for feature extraction. There are five steps involved in preprocessing 1) Binarizing the palm image 2) Boundary tracing 3) the key point detection 4) Establishing a coordinate system and 5) Extracting ROI. Most of the research uses Otsu's method for binarizing the hand image (Otsu, 1978). Otsu's method calculates the suitable global threshold value for every hand image. The boundary pixels of the hand image are traced utilizing boundary tracking algorithm (Doublet et al., 2007). The tangent(Zhang & Kong,2003), Bisector (Li et al., 2002 & Wu et al., 2004) and Finger based (Han, 2004) methods are used to detect the key points between fingers.

The tangent based strategy considers the edges of two fingers gaps on binary image which are to be traced and the common tangent of two fingers gaps is found to be axis. The middle point of the two tangent points is defined as the key points for establishing coordinate system .Tangent-based approaches have several advantages. It is robust to incomplete and the presence of rings.

Bisector-based method determines two centroids of each finger gaps for image alignment. After locating three finger gaps the center of gravity of the gaps can be calculated. The intersection of the line and the finger boundary is considered a key point to establish the coordinate system.

The multiple finger approach uses a wavelet and a set of predefined boundary points on the three fingers to construct three lines in the middle of the three fingers. The two lines from point and ring fingers are used to set the orientation of the coordinate system and the line from the middle finger is used to set its position. Han detects point in the middle of fingers and construct lines passing through fingertips to points to setup a coordinate system (Han et al., 2003). All these approaches utilize only the information on boundaries of fingers. While Kumar et al. (2003) propose to use all information in palm. They fit an ellipse to a binary palmprint image and set up the coordinate system according to the orientation of ellipse.

After obtaining the coordinate systems, the region of interest (ROI) of palmprints are segmented using three classes: Square based segmentation, Circle based segmentation and Elliptical based segmentation. Most of the researchers used square based regions for handling translation variation, while the circular and half elliptical regions may be easier for handling rotation variation. There are many schemes (Zhang & Kong, 2004; Poon et al., 2004; Li et al., 2009 & Kekre et al., 2012) were proposed to extract the ROI in palmprint images. In Figure 3. A squared ROI is extracted based on finger valley reference points. It is defined in such a way that it is parallel and centered to the line that crosses the two points (Kong et al., 2009).

Different ROI sizes are reported in the existing literature. Most of the researchers(Chen et al.,2010; Huang et al., 2008 & Zhang et al., 2010) utilized the PolyU Palmprint database and they extracted fixed size 128*128 ROI. Some of the researchers used the CASIA palmprint database and extracted ROI sizes are 135*135 & 128*128. The developers at the IIT Delhi Touchless Palmprint Database have extracted the ROI of size 150 x 150. The fixed size ROI has limitations. The fixed size ROI covers smaller area and valued information is missing. To avoid the limitations of fixed size ROI, research is focused on extraction of Dynamic Region Of Interest (ROI) from the palmprint image. Hemanth Kumar et al.,(2012) proposes dynamic ROI extraction algorithm to extract maximum possible ROI from palmprint image.

FEATURE EXTRACTION AND MATCHING

Palmprint Features

Feature extraction is to obtain effective features from preprocessed palmptint Image. The important issue of palmprint recognition is to define feature set to differentiate individuals from others and also to obtain similarity index to match two palmprints. Palmprint have large internal surface and contain several unique and stable characteristic features used to identify individuals. Generally, palmprint features

Figure 3. Coordinate system based in reference points in finger valleys. In a), finger web points are used as reference points (white X marks), on which a coordinate system is established. The resulting region of interest is depicted in b).

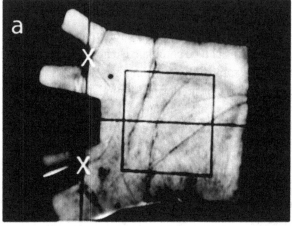
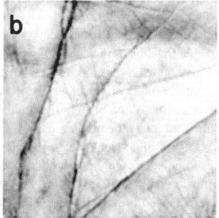

can be classified into two main types: Creases and ridges shown in Figure 4. Creases include principal line and wrinkles. In palmprint, there are three principal lines. This lines vary little over time and their location, length, width are most important physiological features for individual identification. Wrinkles are irregular and much thinner than principal lines. Therefore, the complex pattern of creases carries rich information for personal authentication. The low-resolution palmprint image(100dpi) generally use principal lines and wrinkles.

Ridges (Jain et al., 2007) can be divided into ridge pattern, minutia points, ridge contours and pores. Ridges can be acquired with high resolution scanner (500 or higher). In latent palmprint recognition and forensic application ridge features are used for suspect and victim identification. First ridge feature are utilized by Jain and Feng (2009) for palmprint matching. Crease-insensitive ridge orientation field are estimated and descriptor based minutiae matching are used. Several local feature descriptors have been studied and analyzed by Jain and Demirkus (2008) for latent palmprint recognition .Multi feature based palmprint recognition is proposed by Dia and Zhou(2011). They have combined minutiae, ridges and creases features to increase matching speed. In forensics and law enforcement, such as the FBI's Next Generation Identification (NGI) system [NIST 2008], the British national palm print database and searching tool [CNET 2006], latent palmprint recognition has shown great potential in identifying victims.

Recently, rapid progress in technical development of senor techniques, scan device and component hardware, 3D structure features and multispectral features of palmprint are developed. Table 1 represents palmprint features and characteristics.

1. **3D Structural Features:** 3D palmprint captures the depth information of palmprint. 2D palmprint are vulnerable to brute force attack where as it is difficult to counterfeit 3D palmprint . Highly

Figure 4. Palmprint features (a) a high resolution image and (b) a low resolution image

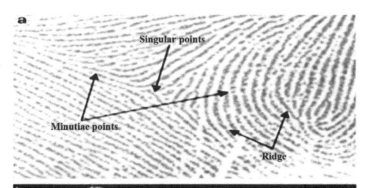

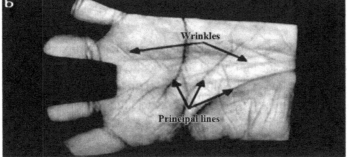

Table 1. Palmprint feature and characteristics

Type	Characteristics
Creses(Principle Line and Wrikles)	-100 dpi - Online low-resolution person recognition
Ridges(Ridge pattern, Minutia points, Ridge contours and Pores)	-500 dpi for ridge patterns and minutia - 1000 dpi for pores and ridge contours - Latent palmprint recognition - Forensics and law enforcement
3D structural information	-3D imaging - increases antispoof capability - 2D and 3D information fusion for a high accuracy and robust palmprint recognition system
Multispectral features	- Infrared spectral imaging - Multispectral data fusion for improving recognition accuracy - Palm vein information fusion for improving the capability of spoof detection

accurate and robust palmprint recognition system (Zhang et al., 2009, 2010) can be developed by combing 2D and 3D features. 3D palmprint data such as mean curvature, Gaussian curvature and surface type are extracted and score level fusion is used by Zhang et al. (2009) for fast matching.

2. **Multispectral Features:** Single spectrum based palmprint may not always achieve the desired performance. In multispectral palmprint recognition, effective features like principle lines, orientation fields, minutia, texture and density can be extracted using different spectral wave lengths(Rowe et al., 2007; Han et al., 2008 & Zhang et al., 2010).Then the fusion is performed to develop a high accuracy and robust palmprint recognition system. First on-line multispectral recognition system was developed by Han et al. (2008). Palmprint image is captured under different illumination including red, green, blue and infrared. Competitive coding is adopted for matching and wavelet based fusion is used to integrate the features. Zhang et al. (2010) acquired discriminative features from different bands. They have integrated multispectral features using score level fusion.

Palmprint Recognition Approaches

The palmprint image features can be extracted and represented as a standard template to store in the database. In the literature, several palmprint recognition methods to identify a person using palmprint have been reported. These approaches are classified into four categories: 1) line based 2) appearance based 3) statistical based and 4) coding based approaches.

Line Based Approaches

In palmprint image, Lines are the most observable features. The principal lines and wrinkles are called palm lines are stable and reliable for individual identification. Length, position, orientation, location, width, depth and size of various lines and wrinkles are taken as line features. In the literature, different edge detection or existing edge detectors and line tracing technique are used to extract line features from a palmprint.

Funada et al. (1998), Duta et al. (2002) and Chen et al. (2001) extracted line patterns like principle lines, wrinkles, ridges, and creases for recognition. Edge detection methods like Sobel operator (Wong et al., 2007), canny (Wu et al., 2002) morphological operator (Rafael Diaz et al., 2004) and modified radon transform (Huang et al., 2008) are used.

Wu et al. (2006) used first order derivative of Gaussian to detect the location of the lines and second derivative of Gaussian to represent line magnitude. Finally results are combined and encoded using chain code. Location and width of palm lines are extracted using isotropic non linear filter (Liu et al., 2007).

Travieso et al. (2011) and Liu et al. (2005) developed their own algorithm to extract the line patterns. Han et al. (2003) computed line features using magnitude of the image and they are enhanced by morphological operations. Palm lines are extracted by employing morphological operations and coarse to fine level strategy is used for matching (Wu & Wang 2004). Chih -Lung et al. (2005) employs hierarchical decomposition technique to extract principal features from palmprint's ROI and then extracted dominant points at different resolution. Two stage filters are used by Wang and Ruan et al. (2006c) to detect the palm lines.

Ali et al. (2011) employs Robust Orientation Hausdorff Similarity (ROHS) measure for palmprint recognition. When compared to traditional Hausdroff distance measure, ROHS used for matching is more resistant to noise and occlusion. Length of lines and distance between point of interception to endpoints where calculated by Rotinwa-Akinbile et al. (2011). And using Discrete Fourier Transformed technique is used to transform to frequency domain. The extracted coefficients are used as discriminative features for recognition. They used Correlative, Spectral, and Euclidean distance measure for matching.

Appearance Based Approaches

In appearance or subspace based approaches the entire palm image is represented as feature vector with intensities as its components. For subspace features, PCA (Guangming et al., 2003 and Kumar & Negi, 2007),2DPCA (Junwei et al., 2006 and Zhong-Qiu et al., 2007), LDA(Wu et al., 2003), ICA(Conne et al., 2005 & Li Shang et al., 2006),LPP(Jiwen Lu et al., 2008 & Wang et al., 2008), MPCA(Haiping Lu et al., 2008 & Wang et al.,2010) and MICA(Alex et al., 2005 & Wang et al., 2009) appear in the literature. Apart from these methods, kernel based techniques (Ekinci & Aykut, 2008; Deng et al.,2007 and Feng et al.,2006) was developed for low dimension representation. To analyze the appearance of palm, some researchers have developed their own algorithms (Yang et al,,2007; Zuo et al., 2005 & Deng et al,2008).

In Guangming et al. (2003) the original palmprint is decomposed into set of feature space called eigenpalms by using Karhunen–Loeve transform. Eigenvector represents the principal components of palmprint image and Euclidean distance is used for matching. Second order information is used by Junwei et al. (2006) to reduce the dimensions of feature vector. First, 2DPCA is applied to the palmprint image matrix and 1DPCA is applied for dimension reduction. Wu et al. (2003) efficiently discriminate the palms by projecting high dimensional original palmprint space to significantly lower dimensional feature space by using fishes linear discriminant technique.

Linear subspace projection techniques like principal component analysis (PCA), fisher discriminant analysis (FDA) and independent component analysis (ICA) are thoroughly tested and compared by Conne et al. (2005). Multi-resolution, multifrequency and wavelet transformation is adopted to analyze the palms and they are divided into different frequency sub bands and the best performing sub band is selected for further processing.

Li Shang et al. (2006) extracts features from palmprint using fast fixed-point algorithm for independent component analysis (FastICA). The orthogonal least square (OLS) algorithm is used to train Radial basis propoablistic neural network (RBPNN).The structure of RBPNN is optimized by the recursive OLS algorithm (ROLSA).

Deng et al. (2007) proposed wavelet-based PCA method. Mean and standard deviation are used to normalize the palmprint image and then wavelet transformed is used to decompose into sub bands. Low-resolution sub band coefficients are considered for palmprint representation and PCA technique is used for dimensional reduction of data. Finally, for similarity measure Euclidean linear distance based nearest-neighbor classifier is used.

Linear discriminant analysis (LDA) method is linear. Usually, palmprint data cannot be considered to be linear. For palmprint recognition, nonlinear subspace method kernel discriminant analysis (KDA) has been investigated. The problem with KDA is high computational cost is involved in decomposing eigen vectors when a large number of training samples is considered. Spectral regression kernel discriminant analysis (SRKDA) is proposed by Deng et al. (2007) to solve a set of regularize regression problems. Incremental implementation is used to reduce the computational cost.

Local preservative projection (LPP) subspace feature extraction method is linear and cannot extract nonlinear features. Feng et al. (2006) propose the algorithm consists of two steps: Kernel PCA and LPP to extract non-linear feature.

Subspace learning methods are very sensitive to the illumination, translation, and rotation variances in image recognition. Jia et al. (2013) proposed a method using a new descriptor of palmprint named histogram of oriented lines (HOL), which is a variant of histogram of oriented gradients (HOG). HOL is not very sensitive to changes of illumination, and has the robustness against small transformations because slight translations and rotations make small histogram value changes.

Further, to improve the performance of subspace approach image transformation methods can be used. The transformation cooeffients may be more effective for palmprint recognition. Several transformation technique such as Fourier (Jing et al., 2005), Gabor (Ekinci & Aykut,2007),discrete cosine(Jing et al.,2004) and wavelet transformations (Connie et al., 2003) are used.

Gabor wavelet and kernel PCA methods are used for palmprint recognition (Ekinci & Aykut, 2007). Features are extracted using Gabor wavelet. Then Kernel PCA is used to extract nonlinear features and reduces the dimensions of feature vectors.

Statistical Approaches

Statistical approaches are further divided into local and global statistics. In Local statistical method, palmprint ROI is transformed to another domain and divided into several regions Poon et al. (2004). For each region, mean and variance is calculated and considered as features. Different transformation such as Gabor, wavelet and Fourier are used. Square regions are commonly employed but some researchers used elliptical and circular (Poon et al., 2004 and Kumar & Shen, 2004). According to the collected papers, so far, no one investigates high order statistics for this approach.

Wu et al. (2004) employs a set of line detectors in different directions to extract directional lines. ROI image is divided in to several overlapping sub images and computes directional line energy features (DLEF). The similarity between two DLEFs is computed using Euclidean distance. Wang et al. (2006)

uses local binary pattern histogram to represent the local features of a palmprint image. Adaboast Calculation is utilized to choose those sub-windows that are more discriminative features for classification. To develop feeble classifiers, Chi-square system is utilized.

Local Binary pattern statistic (DLBPS) is used to represent palmprint features. Initially, palmprint is segmented into non-overlapping and equivalent regions. Each region defines local binary pattern (LBP).To reduce the feature vector, discriminative common vector (DCV) algorithm is utilized. At, last palmprint classification is done using Euclidean distance and nearest neighbor classifier.

Ribaric and Lopar (2012) employs Local Haralick features for palmprint identification system. The palmprint's ROI is isolated into N covering regions (sub images). Grey level co-occurrence matrices are computed for each subimage of ROI. The haralick features are obtained from normalized GLCM matrix. Further, score level fusion is done to improve performance.

Badrinath et al. (2011) segment the ROI into circular regions. Phase difference for each circular region using stock well transformation is obtained. A technique is proposed to group hand images into either right or left hand focused around their characteristic attributes and it is robust to translation and rotation on scanner..

Global statistical approaches compute global statistical features directly from the original image or Region of interest (ROI). Moments, centers of gravity and density have been regarded as the global statistical features. Pang et al. (2003) used Zernike moment invariants for palmprint verification. This procedure characterizes the statistical and geometrical features containing the line structural data about palmprint.

Zang et al. (2004) transform the palmprint image into wavelet domain. For each wavelet sub band, context modeling is used to collect dominant coefficients of principal line and wrinkles. To measure the characteristics of the palmprint, a set of statistical signatures is defined. The palmprint recognition method based on Hu invariant moment is proposed by Noh and Rhee (2005). The low-resolution (75dpi) palmprint image (135×135 Pixel) is used for the small scale database of the efficient palmprint recognition system.

Luo et al. (2011) proposes a unified framework to combine the local features and global features to improve the system's performance. The orientation information extracted using Gabor filters is considered as local features. The Fourier transform coefficients of the palmprint image are taken as global features.

Coding Approaches

Coding approaches encodes filter responses as feature. Coding based routines typically has low memory prerequisite and quick matching speed and therefore has been exceptionally effective in palmprint representation and matching. This approaches uses one matching function to search entire database. The advantage of this approach is to avoid introducing errors from hierarchical or classification systems. The major challenge is to design the matching function and to spot effective palmprint features for matching. The coding algorithm for palmprint is inspired by the iris code technique developed by Daugman, (1993). Bitwise hamming distance is employed by Iris Code for high speed matching in large databases (Daugman, 1993). First coding based technique for palmprint was developed by Zhang et al. (2003) and Zhang et al. (2002).

To generate Palm codes, first palmprint image is convolved with 2D Gabor filter and then encoded the phase of the filter response as bitwise (Kong and Zhang et al., 2003). Correlation between the two palm codes causes performance degradation. Fusion Code is proposed using fusion approach for improving the efficiency. Kong et al. (2006) encode the maximum magnitude of phase of filter response after convolving a palmprint image with Gabor filter. In addition, there are other coding approaches ordinal code (Sun et al., 2005) orientation code(Wu et al., 2005 and Wu et al., 2006) competitive code(Kong & Zhang, 2004 & Kong,2006) and line orientation code(Jia et al., 2008). A novel palmprint recognition using ordinal representation is proposed by Sun et al. (2005). Two line-like image regions that are orthogonal in orientation are compared and one bit feature code is produced. Wu et al. (2006) extract the palmprint orientation code(POC) using four directional templates with different directions. Hamming distance is used to measure the similarity between two POC. In their next research (Wu et al., 2006) they have used Fusion codes. The Fusion codes are generated by integrating the phase code, orientation code. The modified hamming distance (not bitwise) is used to measure the similarity of two fusion codes. Kong and Zhang (2003) extracted orientation feature from palm lines using multiple 2D Gabor filters. Coding scheme and bitwise angular distance is employed fir fast matching. In their later version, 25 translated templates are used to generate match code (Kong et al.,2006).

Jia et al. (2008) employed modified finite Radon transform (MFRAT) to extract line orientation features for palmprint more accurately.

Other Approaches

With exception of these three approaches, there are several other approaches which are difficult to classify. To extract palmprint feature, they integrated several image processing methods and employed standard classifications.

Doi et al. (2003) integrate finger geometry and crease features of palmprint to build fast and robust palmprint recognition. The intersection points of finger skeletal lines and finger creases and the intersection points of the extended finger skeletal lines and principal lines are considered as feature points (Doi et al.,2003). The differences between two features is calculated using root mean square deviation for matching.

The discrete Meyer wavelet transform is used to decompose the palmprint image into sub bands and from ridgelet transform is applied to each sub band. Curvelet coefficients are obtained for best coefficient threshold and filter to get correct recognition rate (Dong et al., 2004).

In Chen et al. (2006) dual-tree complex wavelet transformation is used to decompose the image into sub band and applied Fourier transform to each sub band, The spectrum magnitude are considered as features and finally support vector machine is utilized as a classifier. Dual tree complex wavelet transformation method has advantage of shift invariance over traditional wavelet transformation.

Series of local feature are extracted along the spiral (Chen et al.,2005) to represent a feature vector by employing symbolic aggregate approximation method. To compare two feature vectors minimum distance measure is used.

Zhang et al. (2007) motivated by the success of complex-wavelet structural similarity (CW-SSIM) index method used for image quality assessment(Wang et al., 2004) and proposed modified complex-wavelet structural similarity (CW-SSIM) index to calculate matching score (Zhang et al., 2007). The average of all local modified CW-SSIM is used for matching. This method has advantage of robust to translation, small rotation and distortion and a fast rough alignment of palmprint images

Zhou et al. (2006) decomposes the palmprint image into low sub band images using 2-diemensions 2- band and 3- band wavelet. The support vector machine (SVM) is used for classification of palmprint image. In this approach, middle frequency spectrum is not considered.

Koichi et al. (2006) propose phase based image matching. Rotation and scale differences of two ROI images are obtained using amplitude spectrum. To achieve highly robust palmprint recognition phase components in 2D (two-dimensional) discrete Fourier transforms is considered. Finally, to measure similarity band-limited phase-only correlation (BLPOC) is used. BLPOC only considers low to middle frequency information.

Hennings-Yeamans et al. (2007) uses multiple correlation filters per class for palmprint classification. Log-Gabor filter are used to assign scores to different location of palm. Top ranked regions are selected to train correlation filters. Optimal tradeoff synthetic discriminant function (OTSDF) filter are used as a classifiers. Vijay Kumar et al. (2004) and his coworkers extensively studied correlation filter. Several user-specific techniques (e.g. user-specific segmentation and user- specific threshold) are used to optimize the performance.

FUSION

Research have shown promising results on employing above mentioned (these) approaches individually. However, efforts are still require to achieve higher performance for their use in higher security application. These unimodal approaches rely on the evidence of a single source of information for authentication of person. Deformed data from sensor devices, variability, poor performance, non universality, Spoofing etc are imitations of unimodal. By integrating palmprint with other biometric modularity (multimodal system) or combine various classifiers (intramural system) limitations of unimodal can be overcome.

In multi modal system, various biometric traits including fingerprint(Rowe et al.,2007), palm vein (Wang et al.,2008), finger surface(Savic and Pavesic,2007), face(Jing et al., 2007 and Ribaric et al,2005, iris(Wu et al.,2007) and hand shape(Li et al., 2006) have been combined with palmprints

From single hand image, geometric features, finger surface features and palmprint feature can be extracted and integrated. Only one sensor is needed. Various fusion rules such as sum, maximum, average, minimum, SVM and neural networks are investigated by researcher. The availability of multiple sources of information can reduce the redundancy in unimodal system. Intra modal fusion (Sun et al., 2008 and Hao et al., 2007) has shown a promising result in palmprint authentication.

Multispectral palmprint images are represented by quaternion matrix (Xingpeng Xu et al., 2012). Then to extract features PCA and DWT are utilized. The dissimilarity between features is calculated using Euclidean distance and nearest neighbor classifier is used for taking the final decision.

Intra-modal palmprint authentication based on texture features is proposed by Prasad et al. (2014). Texture information is extracted using 2D-Gabor and 2D-LogGabor filters. Feature level fusion is used to combine two feature types.

Hyper spectral palmprint data is analyzed by Guo et al. (2010) to select the feature band. The statistical features are extracted from each band and compared . Score level fusion is performed to determine the best combination from all candidates. Ajay et al. (2005) extracts palmprint features using Gabor, line and appearance based methods and these features are integrated using the score and decision level fusion. Kumar et al. (2003) even fuse user identities.

IDENTIFICATION IN LARGE DATABASES

Biometric identification system, usually have huge underlying databases. In these large identification systems, the goal is to determine the identity of a subject from a large set of users already enrolled in biometric database. Though the state-of-art palmprint identification algorithm works really well for small databases in terms of accuracy and response time but fail to scale well for large databases. Reduction of search space in palmprint database thus remains the challenging problem. For example, as the number of subjects enrolled in the database increases, the response time increases and reduces the accuracy(Baveja et al., 2010 & Gyaourova & Ross,2012).More sophisticated matching algorithms are required to improve performance and accuracy. To reduce the search space certain hierarchical, classification and indexing approaches have been reported in literature.

In hierarchical approaches, searching is performed in layered fashion. Coarse-to fine matching is performed by Jan et al. (2004) using four-level features for large palmprint database. In You et al. (2002) texture-based dynamic selection is proposed to search the sample in the database in a hierarchical fashion. Although hierarchical approaches increases speed but reduces the accuracy. The drawback of this approach is that a target palm prints are possible to be removed by a classifier using simple features.

Classification is a process of assigning images into one of a set of predefined categories. The main idea of classification is to divide the database into groups where each group has homogenous characteristics. Palmprint classification in Li et al. (2006) uses novel representation derived from principal line structure is based on two stage classifier that classifies palmprint into ten evenly distributed categories. Wu et al. (2004) classify the palmprint database based on number of principal lines and number of their intersection into six classes. In Prasad et al. (2009) two level classifications is done. First palmprint database is divided into two categories (right hand group and left hand group). Then depending upon the distance travelled by the heart line it is further classified to each group.

In indexing palmprint feature vectors are indexed and assigned an index value using different indexing technique. The given query is compared to the template which have comparable index. In Yang et al. (2011) ridge orientation field and density map are used for indexing. These ridge features takes only 0.22 seconds for searching a query palmprint in the database, which is faster than minutiae matching.

Recently, fast palmprint identification for large database approaches has been reported in the literature. Fast iris searching algorithm using Beacon Guided Search (BGS) technique is proposed in Hao et al. (2008). Iris features are divided into number of beacon spaces and reduce the search space by using the multiple collisions principle. They have evaluated their method on huge database consisting of 632,500 iris templates and improvement in search speed with a negligible loss of accuracy is obtained.

Yue et al. (2009) used competitive code (Li et al., 2006) for fast feature extraction and matching .They have used set cover tree method to speed up the palmprint identification. Its identification results are the same as those obtained by brute-force search, while its identification speed is between 33% and 50% faster. Further, the performance is by using optimizing tree structure(Yue et al., 2011). While both approaches can reduce the average identification time without accuracy loss, their speedups over brute-force search are somewhat limited since at least one template per subject must be considered during the search. It is also evident that these approaches are not applicable for the identification systems where only one template per subject is available.

The palmprint image is convolved using six Gabor filter of different orientation to obtain competitive coding(Yue et al., 2011). They have used orientation feature to construct hash function to divide database into six bins. Then, for a given query image orientation patterns are compute and searching is performed using hash table.

Authors have extended their work (Yue et al., 2013) by exploring the Orientation pattern hashing method in more depth and introducing principal orientation pattern hashing. An Orientation feature corresponding to principal lines defines principal line orientation pattern. Both orientation hashing and principal orientation hashing are faster than brute-force searching.

CONCLUSION

Palmprint recognition is one of the emerging technologies for personal identification. Palmprint have much larger surface area and discriminative feature such as principal lines, ridges and wrinkles which are useful in biometric security. In this paper various existing methods and technique used for palmprint identification have been reviewed. Palmprint acquisition using CCD based scanners is recommended. Coding methods such as Palm code, fusion code, competitive code increases performance and require less memory space. Limitations of unimodal biometric can be overcome by integrating palmprint with other biometric modularity or combine various classifiers (intra modal). In intra-modal fusion, palmprint features like appearance based, line and texture features are fused to increase accuracy. More research is required for intra modal fusion.

For real-time large database identification, Competitive code or other coding methods, indexing and hashing techniques should be explored to increase matching speed. Recent work involves use of multi-scale, multi-resolution and 3D palmprint for efficient implementation of palmprint recognition. Existing palmprint technique has its own advantage and disadvantage based various factors such as cost, response time, robustness and accuracy. The techniques can be selected based on the requirement.

REFERENCES

Alex, M., & Vasilescu, O., & Demetri Terzopoulos, (2005). Multilinear independent components analysis. *IEEE Computer Society Conference on Computer Vision and Pattern Recognition, 1, 547–553.*

Ali, M., Ghafoor, M., Taj, I.A., & Hayat, K. (2011). Palm Print Recognition Using Oriented Hausdorff Distance Transform. *Frontiers of Information Technolog (FIT), 85 – 88.*

Alto, K., Aoki, T., Nakajima, H., Kobayashi, K., & Higuchi, T. (2006). A phase-based palmprint recognition algorithm and its experimental evaluation. In *Proceeding of International Symposium on Intelligent Signal Processing and Communications.*

Badrinath, G. S., & Gupta, P. (2011). Stockwell transform based palm-print recognition. *Applied Soft Computing, 11*(7), 4267–4281. doi:10.1016/j.asoc.2010.05.031

Chen, G. Y., Bui, T. D., & Krzyak, A. (2006). Palmprint classification using dual-tree complex wavelets. In *Proceeding of International Conference on Image Processing.*

Chen, J., Moon, Y., Wong, M., & Su, G. (2010). Palmprint authentication using a symbolic representation of images. *Image and Vision Computing, 28*(3), 343–351. doi:10.1016/j.imavis.2009.06.004

Chen, J., Zhang, C., & Rong, G. (2001). Palmprint recognition using creases. *Proceedings of International Conference of Image Processing, 3,* 234-237.

Chen, J. S., Moon, Y. S., & Yeung, H. W. (2005). Palmprint authentication using time series. In *Proceeding of Fifth International Conference on Audio- and Video-based Biometric Person Authentication.*

Connle, Teoh Beng Jin, Goh Kah Ong, & Ngo Chek Ling. (2005). An automated palmprint recognition system. *Image and Vision Computing, 23*(5), 501–515.

Connie, T., Jin, A., Ong, M., & Ling, D. (2003). An automated palmprint recognition system. *Image and Vision Computing, 23*(5), 501–515. doi:10.1016/j.imavis.2005.01.002

Dai, J. F., & Zhou, J. (2011). Multifeature-based high-resolution palmprint recognition. *IEEE Transaction. Pattern Analysis and Machine Inteligence, 33*(5), 945–957. doi:10.1109/TPAMI.2010.164

Daugman, J. G. (1993). High confidence visual recognition of persons by a test of statistical independence. *IEEE Transactions on Pattern Analysis and Machine Intelligence, 15*(11), 1148–1161. doi:10.1109/34.244676

Deng, C., Xiaofei, H., & Jiawei, H. (2007). Efficient kernel discriminant analysis via spectral regression. In *Proceedings of the Seventh International Conference on Data Mining.* IEEE.

Deng, W., Hu, J., Guo, J., Zhang, H., & Zhang, C. (1503–1504). C. (2008). Comment on globally maximizing locally minimizing: Unsupervised discriminant projection with applications to face and palm biometrics. *IEEE Transactions on Pattern Analysis and Machine Intelligence.*

Doi, J., & Yamanaka, M. (2003). Personal authentication using feature points on finger and palmar creases. In *Proceedings of 32nd Applied Imagery Patten Recognition Workshop.*

Dong, K., Feng, G., & Hu, D. (2004). Digital curvelet transform for palmprint recognition. Lecture Notes in Computer Science, Springer, 3338, 639–645.

Doublet, J., Revenu, M., & Lepetit, O. (2007). Robust grayscale distribution estimation for contactless palmprint recognition. In *Proceedings of the First IEEE International Conference on Biometrics: Theory, Applications, and Systems.* doi:10.1109/BTAS.2007.4401935

Duta, N., Jain, A., & Mardia, K. (2002). Matching of palmprint. *Pattern Recognition Letters, 23*(4), 477–485. doi:10.1016/S0167-8655(01)00179-9

Ekinci, M., & Aykut, M. (2007). Gabor-based kernel PCA for palmprint recognition. *Electronics Letters, 43*(20), 1077–1079. doi:10.1049/el:20071688

Ekinci, M., & Aykut, M. (2008). Palmprint recognition by applying wavelet based kernel PCA. *Journal of Computer Science and Technology, 23*(5), 851–861. doi:10.1007/s11390-008-9173-4

Funada, J., Ohta, N., Mizoguchi, M., Temma, T., Nakanishi, T., & Murai, K. et al.. (1998). Feature extraction method for palmprint considering elimination of creases. *Proceedings of the 14th International Conference of Pattern Recognition, 2,* 1849-1854. doi:10.1109/ICPR.1998.712091

Guangming, L., David, Z., & Kuanquan, W. (2003). Palmprint recognition using eigenpalms features. *Pattern Recognition Letters*, *24*(9-10), 1463–1467. doi:10.1016/S0167-8655(02)00386-0

Guiyu, F., Dewen, H., & David, Z. et al.. (2006). An alternative formulation of kernel LPP with application to image recognition. *Neurocomputing*, *69*(13-15), 1733–1738. doi:10.1016/j.neucom.2006.01.006

Guo, Z., Zhang, l., Zhang,D. (2010). Feature Band Selection for Multispectral Palmprint Recognition. *Proceedings of the 20th International Conference on Pattern Recognition*. doi:10.1109/ICPR.2010.284

Gyaourova, A., & Ross, A. (2012). Index codes for multibiometric pattern retrieval. *IEEE Trans. Information and Forensics Security*, *7*(2), 518–529. doi:10.1109/TIFS.2011.2172429

Han, C. C. (2004). A hand-based personal authentication using a coarse-to-fine strategy. *Image and Vision Computing*, *22*(11), 909–918. doi:10.1016/j.imavis.2004.05.008

Han, C. C., Chen, H. L., Lin, C. L., & Fan, K. C. (2003). Personal authentication using palmprint features. *Pattern Recognition*, *36*(2), 371–381. doi:10.1016/S0031-3203(02)00037-7

Han, C. C., Cheng, H. L., Lin, C. L., & Fan, K. C. (2003). Personal authentication using palm-print features. *Pattern Recognition*, *36*(2), 371–381. doi:10.1016/S0031-3203(02)00037-7

Han, D., Guo, Z., & Zhang, D. (2008). Multispectral palmprint recognition using wavelet-based image fusion. In *Proceedings of the 9th International Conference on Signal Processing*.

Hao, F., Daugman, H., & Zieliski, P. (2008). A fast search algorithm for a large fuzzy database. *IEEE Transaction Information and Forensics Security*, *3*(2), 203–212. doi:10.1109/TIFS.2008.920726

Hao, Y., Sun, Z., & Tan, T. (2007). Comparative Studies on Multispectral Palm Image Fusion for Biometrics. *Proceedings of the Asian Conference on Computer Vision*, *2*, 12-21. doi:10.1007/978-3-540-76390-1_2

Hennings, P., & Kumar, B. V. K. V. (2004). Palmprint recognition using correlation filter classifiers. *Conference Record of the 38th Asilomar Conference on Signal, Systems and Computers*, *1*, 567–571. doi:10.1109/ACSSC.2004.1399197

Hennings-Yeomans, P.H., Vijaya Kumar, B.V. K. & Savvides, M. Palmprint classification using multiple advanced correlation filters and palm-specific segmentation. *IEEE Transactions on Information Forensics and Security*, *2*(3), 613–622.

Huang, D., Jia, W., & Zhang, D. (2008). Palmprint verification based on principal lines. *Pattern Recognition*, *41*(4), 1316–1328. doi:10.1016/j.patcog.2007.08.016

Jain, A., Flynn, P., & Ross, A. (2007). *Handbook of Biometrics*. Springer.

Jain, A. K., & Feng, J. (2009). Latent palmprint matching. *IEEE Transactions on Pattern Analysis and Machine Intelligence*, *31*(6), 1032–1047. doi:10.1109/TPAMI.2008.242 PMID:19372608

Jia, W., & Hu, R. X., Lei, Zhao, Y.K., & Gui, J. (2013). Histogram of Oriented Lines for Palmprint Recognition. *IEEE Transactions on Systems, Man, and Cybernetics. Systems*, *44*(3), 385–395.

Jia, W., Huang, D. S., & Zhang, D. (2008). Palmprint verification based on robust line orientation code. *Pattern Recognition*, *41*(5), 1504–1513. doi:10.1016/j.patcog.2007.10.011

Jing, X., Tang, Y., & Zhang, D. (2005). A fourier-lDA approach for image recognition. *Pattern Recognition, 38*(3), 453–457. doi:10.1016/j.patcog.2003.09.020

Jing, X., & Zhang, D. (2004). A face and palmprint recognition approach based on discriminant DCT feature extraction, *IEEE Transaction. System and Man Cybernetic. Part B, 34*(6), 2405–2415.

Jing, X. Y., Yao, Y. F., Zhang, D., Yang, J. Y., & Li, M. (2007). Face and palmprint pixel level fusion and Kernel DCV-RBF classifier for small sample biometric recognition. *Pattern Recognition, 40*(11), 3209–3224. doi:10.1016/j.patcog.2007.01.034

Kekre, H. B., Sarode, T., & Vig, R. (2012). An effectual method for extraction of ROI of palmprints, *International Conference on Communication Information & Computing Technology (ICCICT)*. doi:10.1109/ICCICT.2012.6398207

Kong, A., Cheung, K. H., Zhang, D., Kamel, M., & You, J. (2006). An analysis of Biohashing and its variants. *Pattern Recognition, 39*(7), 1359–1368. doi:10.1016/j.patcog.2005.10.025

Kong, A., Zhang, D., & Kamel, M. (2006). Palmprint identification using feature-level fusion. *Pattern Recognition, 3*(3), 478–487. doi:10.1016/j.patcog.2005.08.014

Kong, A., Zhang, D., & Kamel, M. (2009). A survey of palmprint recognition. *Pattern Recognition, 42*(7), 1408–1418. doi:10.1016/j.patcog.2009.01.018

Kong, A. W. K., & Zhang, D. (2004).Competitive coding scheme for palmprint verification. *Proceedings of International Conference on Pattern Recognition, 1,* 520–523.

Kong, W., & Zhang, D. (2002). Palmprint texture analysis based on low-resolution images for personal authentication. *Proceedings of 16th International Conference on Pattern Recognition, 3,* 807–810. doi:10.1109/ICPR.2002.1048142

Kong, W., Zhang, D., & Li, W. (2003). Palmprint feature extraction using 2D gabor filters. *Pattern Recognition, 36*(10), 2339–2347. doi:10.1016/S0031-3203(03)00121-3

Kumar, Kalluri, Munagam, & Agarwal. (2012). *Dynamic ROI Extraction Algorithm for Palmprints.* Springer-Verlag Berlin Heidelberg.

Kumar, A., & Shen, C. (2004). Palmprint identification using PalmCodes. In *Proceedings of 3rd International Conference on Image and Graphics*. doi:10.1109/ICIG.2004.110

Kumar, A., Wong, D. C. M., Shen, H. C., & Jain, A. K. (2003). Personal verification using palmprint and hand geometry biometric. Lecture Notes in Computer Science, Springer, 2668, 668–678.

Kumar, A., & Zhang, D. (2003). Integrating palmprint with face for user authentication. In *Proceedings of Multi Modal User Authentication Workshop*.

Kumar, A., & Zhang, D. (2006). Personal recognition using hand shape and texture. *IEEE Transactions on Image Processing, 15*(8), 2454–2461. doi:10.1109/TIP.2006.875214 PMID:16900698

Kumar, K. V., & Negi, A. (2007). A novel approach to eigenpalm features using feature partitioning framework. *Conference on Machine Vision Applications.*

Kumara, A., & Zhang, D. (2005). Personal authentication using multiple palmprint representation. *Pattern Recognition, 38*(10), 1695–1704. doi:10.1016/j.patcog.2005.03.012

Leung, M., Fong, A., & Cheung, H. (2007). Palmprint verification for controlling access to shared computing resources. *IEEE Pervasive Computing / IEEE Computer Society [and] IEEE Communications Society, 6*(4), 40–47. doi:10.1109/MPRV.2007.78

Li, F., Leung, M. K., Shikhare, T., Chan, V., & Choon, K. F. (2006). Palmprint classification. *In Proc. IEEE Int. Conference on Systems Man and Cybernetics.*

Li, Q., Qiu, Z., & Sun, D. (2006).Feature-level fusion of hand biometrics for personal verification based on Kernel PCA. *International Conference on Biometrics.*

Li, W., Zhang, D., & Xu, Z. (2002). Palmprint identification by Fourier transforms. *International Journal of Pattern Recognition and Artificial Intelligence, 16*(4), 417–432. doi:10.1142/S0218001402001757

Li, W., Zhang, L., Zhang, D., & Yan, J. (2009). Principal line based ICP alignment for palmprint verification. In *Processing of 16th IEEE International Conference on Image Processing (ICIP).*

Lin, C.-L., Chuang, T. C., & Fan, K.-C. (2005). Palmprint Verification using hierarchical decomposition. *Pattern Recognition, 38*(12), 2639–2652. doi:10.1016/j.patcog.2005.04.001

Liu, L., & Zhang, D. (2005). Palm-line detection. *IEEE International Conference on Image Processing, 3,* 269-272.

Liu, L., Zhang, D., & You, J. (2007). Detecting wide lines using isotropic nonlinear filtering. *IEEE Transactions on Image Processing, 6*(6), 1584–1595. doi:10.1109/TIP.2007.894288 PMID:17547136

Lu, H. (2008). MPCA: Multilinear principal component analysis of tensor objects. *IEEE Transactions on Neural Networks, 19*(1), 18–39. doi:10.1109/TNN.2007.901277 PMID:18269936

Lu, J., Zhao, Y., Xue, Y., & Hu, J. (2008). Palmprint recognition via locality preserving projections and extreme learning machine neural network. *9th International Conference on Signal Processing.*

Luo, N., Guo, Z., Wu, G., Song, C., & Zhou, L. (2011). Local-global-based palmprint verification. *International Conference on Advanced Computer Control.*

Meiru, M., Ruan, Q., & Shen, Y. (2010). Palmprint Recognition Based on Discriminative Local Binary Patterns Statistic Feature. *International Conference on Signal Acquisition and Processing.*

Michael, G. K. O., & Connie, T. (2008). Touch-less palm print biometrics. *Novel design and implementation. Image and Vision Computing, 26*(12), 1551–1560. doi:10.1016/j.imavis.2008.06.010

Noh, J. S., & Rhee, K. H. (2005). Palmprint identification algorithm using Hu invariant moments and Otsu binarization. In *Proceeding of Fourth Annual ACIS International Conference on Computer and Information Science.*

Otsu, N. (1978). A threshold selection method from gray-scale histogram. *IEEE Transactions on Systems, Man, and Cybernetics, 8,* 62–66.

Pang, Y. H., Connie, T., Jin, A., & Ling, D. (2003) Palmprint authentication with Zernike moment invariants. In *Proceedings of the Third IEEE International Symposium on Signal Processing and Information Technology*.

Poon, C., Wong, D. C. M., & Shen, H. C. (2004). A New Method in Locating and Segmenting Palmprint into Region of Interest. IEEE. *Pattern Recognition, 4*, 533–536.

Poon, C., Wong, D. C. M., & Shen, H. C. (2004). Personal identification and verification: fusion of palmprint representations. In *Proceedings of International Conference on Biometric Authentication*. doi:10.1007/978-3-540-25948-0_106

Prasad, Pramod, & Sharma. (2009). Classification of Palmprint Using Principal Line. *Information Systems, Technology and Management*. Springer.

Prasad Munaga, V. N. K., Kavati, & Adinarayana, B. (2014). Palmprint Recognition Using Fusion of 2D-Gabor and 2D Log-Gabor Features. Communications in Computer and Information Science (CCIS 420). Springer.

Qin, A. K., Suganthan, N., Tay, C. H., & Pa, S. (2006). Personal Identification System based on Multiple Palmprint Features. *9th International Conference on Control, Automation, Robotics and Vision*. doi:10.1109/ICARCV.2006.345257

Rafael Diaz, M., Travieso, C., Alonso, J., & Ferrer, M. (2004). Biometric system based in the feature of hand palm. *Proceedings of 38th Annual International Carnahan Conference on Security Technology*.

Ribaric, S., & Fratric, I. (2005). A biometric identification system based on eigenpalm and eigenfinger features. *IEEE Transaction Pattern Analysis Machine Intelligence,* 1698–1709.

Ribaric, S., Fratric, I., & Kis, K. (2005). A biometric verification system based on the fusion of palmprint and face features. In *Proceeding of the 4th International Symposium on Image, Signal and Signal Processing and Analysis*. doi:10.1109/ISPA.2005.195376

Ribaric, S., & Lopar, M. (2012).Palmprint recognition based on local Haralick features. *IEEE Mediterranean Electrotechnical Conference*. doi:10.1109/MELCON.2012.6196517

Rotinwa-Akinbile, M. O., Aibinu, A. M., & Salami, M. J. E. (2011).Palmprint Recognition Using Principal Lines Characterization. *International Conference on Informatics and Computational Intelligence*.

Rowe, R., Uludag, U., Demirkus, M., Parthasaradhi, S., & Jain, A. (2007). A spectral whole-hand biometric authentication system. In *Proceedings of Biometric Symposium*.

Savic, T., & Pavesic, N. (2007). Personal recognition based on an image of the palmar surface of the hand. *Pattern Recognition, 40*(11), 3252–3163. doi:10.1016/j.patcog.2007.03.005

Shang, L., Huang, D.-S., Du, J.-X., & Zheng, C.-H. (2006). Palmprint recognition using FastICA algorithm and radial basis probabilistic neural network. *Neurocomputing, 69*(13-15), 1782–1786. doi:10.1016/j.neucom.2005.11.004

Su, C. (2009). Palm extraction and identification. *Expert Systems with Applications, 36*(2), 1082–1091. doi:10.1016/j.eswa.2007.11.001

Sun, Y. H. Z., Tan, T., & Ren, C. (2008). Multi-Spectral Palm Image Fusion for Accurate Contact-Free Palmprint Recognition. *Proceedings of the IEEE International Conference on Image Processing.*

Sun, Z., Tan, T., Wang, Y., & Li, S. Z. (2005). Ordinal palmprint representation for personal identification. Proceeding of Computer Vision and Pattern Recognition, 1, 279–284.

Tao, J., Jiang, W., Gao, Z., Chen, S., & Wang, C. (2006). Palmprint recognition based on 2-Dimension PCA. *First International Conference on Innovative Computing. Information and Control, 1,* 326–330.

Travieso, C. M., Fuertes, J. J., & Alonso, J. B. (2011). Derivative method for hand palm texture biometric verification. *IEEE International Carnahan Conference on Security Technology.* doi:10.1109/CCST.2011.6095889

Wang, J., Barreto, A., Wang, L., Chen, Y., Rishe, N., Andrian, J., & Adjouadi, M. (2010). Multilinear principal component analysis for face recognition with fewer features. *Neurocomputing, 73*(10-12), 1550–1555. doi:10.1016/j.neucom.2009.08.022

Wang, J. G., Yau, W. Y., Suwandy, A., & Sung, E. (2008). Person recognition by fusing palmprint and palm vein images based on Laplacian palm representation. *Pattern Recognition, 41*(5), 1514–1527. doi:10.1016/j.patcog.2007.10.021

Wang, X., Gong, H., Zhang, H., Li, B., & Zhuang, Z. (2006). Palmprint identification using boosting local binary pattern. *Proceedings of International Conference on Pattern Recognition, 3,* 503–506.

Wang, X., Jing, X., Zhu, X., Sun, S., & Hong, L. (2009). A novel approach of fingerprint recognition based on multilinear ICA. *IEEE International Conference on Network Infrastructure and Digital Content.* doi:10.1109/ICNIDC.2009.5360839

Wang, Y., & Ruan, Q. (2006). Palm-line extraction using steerable filters. *In Proceedings of the 8th International Conference on Signal Processing.*

Wang, Y., & Ruan, Q. (2006). Multispectral palmprint recognition using wavelet-based image fusion. In *Proceedings of the 18th International Conference on Pattern Recognition.*

Wang, Z., Bovik, C., Sheikh, H. R., & Simoncelli, E. P. (2004). Image quality assessment: From error to structural similarity. *IEEE Transactions on Image Processing, 13*(4), 600–612. doi:10.1109/TIP.2003.819861 PMID:15376593

Wong, K. Y. E., Sainarayanan, G., & Chekima, A. (2007). Palmprint Identification Using SobelCode. *Malaysia-Japan International Symposium on Advanced Technology (MJISAT).*

Wu, X., & Wang, K. (2004). A Novel Approach of Palm-line Extraction. *Proceedings of the Third International Conference on Image and Graphics (ICIG'04).*

Wu, X., Wang, K., & Zhang, D. (2002). Fuzzy directional element energy feature (FDEEF) based palmprint identification. *International Conference on pattern recognition.*

Wu, X., Wang, K., & Zhang, D. (2004). HMMs based palmprint identification. *Proceedings of International Conference on Biometric Authentication(ICBA), 3072,* 775–781. doi:10.1007/978-3-540-25948-0_105

Wu, X., Wang, K., & Zhang, D. (2004). Palmprint recognition using directional energy feature. *Proceedings of International Conference on Pattern Recognition, 4,* 475–478.

Wu, X., Wang, K., & Zhang, D. (2005). Palmprint authentication based on orientation code matching. *Proceeding of Fifth International Conference on Audio- and Video- based Biometric Person Authentication, 3546,* 555–562. doi:10.1007/11527923_57

Wu, X., Zhang, D., & Wang, K. (2003). Fisherpalms based palmprint recognition. *Pattern Recognition Letters, 24*(15), 2829–2838. doi:10.1016/S0167-8655(03)00141-7

Wu, X., Zhang, D., & Wang, K. (2006). Fusion of phase and orientation information for palmprint authentication. *Pattern Analysis & Applications, 9*(2-3), 103–111. doi:10.1007/s10044-005-0006-6

Wu, X., Zhang, D., Wang, K., & Huang, B. (2004). Palmprint classification using principal lines. *Pattern Recognition, 37*(10), 1987–1998. doi:10.1016/j.patcog.2004.02.015

Wu, X., Zhang, D., Wang, K., & Qi, N. (2007). Fusion of palmprit and iris for personal authentication. In *Proceedings of the Third International Conference on Advanced Data Mining and Applications.* doi:10.1007/978-3-540-73871-8_43

Xin, C. (2011). A Contactless Hand Shape Identification System. In *3rd International Conference on Advanced Computer Control (ICACC2011).* doi:10.1109/ICACC.2011.6016476

Xu, X., Guo, Z., Song, C., & Li, Y. (2012). Multispectral Palmprint Recognition Using a Quaternion Matrix. *Hand-Based Biometrics Sensors and Systems, 12,* 4633–4647. PMID:22666049

Yang, J., Zhang, D., Yang, J., & Niu, B. (2007, April). Globally Maximizing, Locally Minimizing: Unsupervised Discriminant Projection with Applications to Face and Palm Biometrics. *IEEE Transactions on Pattern Analysis and Machine Intelligence, 29*(4), 650–664, 664. doi:10.1109/TPAMI.2007.1008 PMID:17299222

You, J., Kong, W., Zhang, D., & Cheung, K. (2004). On hierarchical palmprint coding with multiple features for personal identification in large databases. *IEEE Transaction. IEEE Transactions on Circuits and Systems for Video Technology, 14*(2), 234–243. doi:10.1109/TCSVT.2003.821978

You, J., Li, W., & Zhang, D. (2002). Hierarchical palmprint identification via multiple feature extraction. *Pattern Recognition, 35*(4), 847–859. doi:10.1016/S0031-3203(01)00100-5

Yue, F., Li, B., Yu, M., & Wang, J. (2011).Fast palmprint identification using orientation pattern hashing. *In Proceedings. International. Conference on. Hand-based Biometrics.*

Yue, F., Li, B., Yu, M., & Wang, J. (2013). Hashing Based Fast Palmprint Identification for Large-Scale Databases. *IEEE Transactions On Information Forensics and Security, 8*(5), 769–778. doi:10.1109/TIFS.2013.2253321

Yue, F., Zuo, W., & Zhang, D. (2009). Competitive code-based fast palmprint identification using a set of cover trees. *Optical Engineering (Redondo Beach, Calif.), 48*(6), 1–7.

Yue, F., Zuo, W., Zhang, D., & Li, B. (2011). Fast palmprint identification with multiple templates per subject. *Pattern Recognition Letters, 32*(8), 1108–1118. doi:10.1016/j.patrec.2011.02.019

Zhang, D. (2004). *Palmprint Authentication.* Springer Science & Business Media.

Zhang, D., Guo, Z., Lu, G., Zhang, L., & Zuo, W. (2010). An online system of multi-spectral palmprint verification. *IEEE Transactions on Instrumentation and Measurement, 58*(2), 480–490. doi:10.1109/TIM.2009.2028772

Zhang, D., Kanhangad, V., Luo, N., & Kumar, A. (2010). Robust palmprint verification using 2D and 3D features. *Pattern Recognition, 43*(1), 358–368. doi:10.1016/j.patcog.2009.04.026

Zhang, D., Kong, W., You, J., & Wong, M. (2003). On-line palmprint identification. *IEEE Transactions on Pattern Analysis and Machine Intelligence, 25*(8), 1041–1050. doi:10.1109/TPAMI.2003.1227981

Zhang, D., Lu, G., Li, W., Zhang, L., & Luo, N. (2009). Palmprint recognition using 3-D information. *IEEE Transaction, Systems, Man, and Cybernetics, Part C: Applications and Reviews, 39*(5), 505–519.

Zhang, D., Lu, G., Li, W., & Lei, Z. N. L. (2009). Palmprint Recognition Using 3-D Information. *IEEE Transaction On Systems, Man, and Cybernetics-Part C. Applications and Reviews, 39*, 505–519.

Zhang, D., & Shu, W. (1999). Two novel characteristics in palmprint verification Datum point invariance and line feature matching. *Pattern Recognition, 32*(4), 691–702. doi:10.1016/S0031-3203(98)00117-4

Zhang, L., Guo, Z., Wang, Z., & Zhang, D. (2007). "Palmprint verification using complex wavelet transform. *Proceedings of International Conference on Image Processing, 2,* 417–420.

Zhang, L., & Zhang, D. (2004). Characterization of palmprints by wavelet signatures via directional context modeling. *IEEE Transactions on Systems, Man, and Cybernetics. Part B, Cybernetics, 34*(3), 1335–1347. doi:10.1109/TSMCB.2004.824521 PMID:15484907

Zhao, Z.-Q., Huang, D.-S., & Jia, W. (2007). Palmprint recognition with 2DPCA+PCA based on modular neural networks. *Neurocomputing, 71*(1-3), 448–454. doi:10.1016/j.neucom.2007.07.010

Zhou, X., Peng, Y., & Yang, M. (2006). Palmprint recognition using wavelet and support vector machines. *Proceeding of 9th Pacific Rim International Conference on Artificial Intelligence Guilin, 4099,* 385–393. doi:10.1007/978-3-540-36668-3_42

Zuo, W., Wang, K., & Zhang, D. (2005). Bi-directional PCA with assembled matrix distance metric. *Proceeding of IEEE International Conference on Image Processing, 2,* 958-961.

KEY TERMS AND DEFINITIONS

Authentication: A process that establishes the origin of information or determines an entity's identity.

Biometrics: The automated use of physiological or behavioral characteristics to determine or verify identity.

Enrollment: The process whereby a user's initial biometric sample or samples are collected, assessed, processed, and stored for ongoing use in a biometric system.

Identification: One to Many. Biometrics can be used to determine a person's identity even without his knowledge or consent.

Matching: The comparison of biometric templates to determine their degree of similarity or correlation.

Multimodal Biometrics: Multimodal biometric systems are those that utilize more than one physiological or behavioral characteristic for enrollment, verification, or identification.

Unimodal Biometric: A Unimodal biometric system uses only a single biometric characteristics.

Verification: One to One. Biometrics can also be used to verify a person's identity.

Chapter 13
Emotion Recognition Using Facial Expression

Santosh Kumar
Indian Institute of Technology (BHU),
Varanasi, India

Rahul Kumar
Indian Institute of Technology (BHU),
Varanasi, India

Shubam Jaiswal
Indian Institute of Technology (BHU),
Varanasi, India

Sanjay Kumar Singh
Indian Institute of Technology (BHU),
Varanasi, India

ABSTRACT

Recognition of facial expression is a challenging problem for machine in comparison to human and it has encouraged numerous advanced machine learning algorithms. It is one of the methods for emotion recognition as the emotion of a particular person can be found out by studying his or her facial expressions. In this paper, we proposes a generic algorithms for recognition of emotions and illustrates a fundamental steps of the four algorithms such as Eigenfaces (Principal Component Analysis [PCA]), Fisherfaces, Local Binary Pattern Histogram (LBP) and SURF with FLANN over two databases Cohn-kanade database and IIT BHU student face images as benchmark database. The objective of this book chapter is to recognize the emotions from facial images of individuals and compare the performances of holistic algorithms like Eigenfaces, Fisherfaces, and texture based recognition algorithms LBPH, hybrid algorithm SURF and FLANN. Matching efficiency of individual emotions from facial expression databases are labeled for training and testing phases. The set of features is extracted from labeled dataset for training purpose and test images are matched with discriminative set of feature points. Based on that comparison, we conclude that Eigenfaces and Fisherfaces yields good recognition accuracy on the benchmark database than others and the efficiency of SURF with FLANN algorithm can be enhanced significantly by changing the parameters.

1. INTRODUCTION

The automatic recognition of emotions from facial expression is a well-known problem in field of computer vision, pattern recognition and image analysis. The image analysis includes both computations and measurements from facial motion to recognize the expression. It is getting proliferations in the variety field of applications and uses. But it has major challenges problems due to large intra-class variation, varying

DOI: 10.4018/978-1-4666-8723-3.ch013

pose, illumination change, partial occlusion, and cluttered background in the field of computer vision. The research study of facial expression of emotion has long been the focus of theoretical controversy and empirical research (Allport, 1924) (Birdwhistell, 1963) (Coleman, 1949), (Darwin, 1872a,1998b), (Ekman, 1973a, 1994b) (Fridlund, 1999), (Hunt, 1941) (Landis, 1924), (Mead, 1975), (Munn, 1940), (Osgood, 1966), (Russell, 1994), (Schlosberg, 1954) (Woodworth, 1938), (Keltner et al., 2003). However, scientist and researchers have recently made momentous progresses on a particularly interesting subset of object recognition problems: face (Rowley, Baluja & Kanade, 1998), (Viola, & Jones., 2004), (Xiao et al., 2007) and human detection (Dalal N, & Triggs, 2005) achieving near 90% detection rate on the frontal face in real-time (Viola, & Jones, 2004) using a boosting based approach. Meanwhile, with the recent advance on robust facial expression detection, some major image search engines start to use high level image features to filter text based image search results (Cui et al., 2008). For example, recognition of facial expression form given database already integrated human face detection as a high level filter in computer vision approaches. However, designing of efficient algorithm for facial expression of human face is still a challenging problem.

2. BACKGROUND

In literature review, many methods for face and facial expression recognition have been presented; however each of them having their own limitations. In Eigenfaces and Fisherfaces, which are built on Principal Component Analysis (PCA) (Turk, & Pentland, 1991); the more recent 2D PCA and Linear Discriminant Analysis (Etemad, & Chellappa, 1997), (Martinez, & Kak, 2001) are also examples of holistic methods. Although these methods have been studied widely, local descriptors have gained attention because of their robustness to illumination and pose variations. Heiselee al. showed the validity of the component -based methods, and how they outperform holistic methods. The local-feature methods compute the descriptor from parts of the face, and then gather the information into one descriptor. Among these methods are Local Features Analysis Gabor features (Gabor wavelets (Lanitis et al., 1997), (Dailey, & Cottrell, 1999), Elastic Bunch Graph Matching (EBGM) (Wiskott et al. 1999), and Local Binary Pattern (LBPH) (Ahonen et al., 2006). The last one is an extension of the LBP feature, that was originally designed for texture description (Ahonen et al., 2006). applied to face recognition. LBP achieved better performance than previous methods, thus it gained popularity, and was studied extensively. Newer methods tried to overcome the shortcomings of LBP like Local Ternary Pattern (LTP) and Local Directional Pattern (LDiP). The last method encodes the directional information in the neighborhood, instead of the intensity. Zhang et al. (2003) explored the use of higher order local derivatives (LDEP) to produce better results than LBPH (Ahonen et al., 2006). Both methods use other information, instead of intensity, to overcome noise and illumination variation problems. In (Yang et al., 2004) proposed a novel approach of facial action units (AU) and expression recognition based on coded dynamical features and proposed a method which is implemented using 2D appearance-based local approach for the extraction of intransient facial features and recognition of four facial expressions (Sarode, & Bhatia, 2010) and discussed the paper about the various facial expression databases are available with different variations like illumination, expression, size, shape, color, and texture. Shih et al. (2008) compared the performance ratio on JAFFE database of facial expression recognition (Shih, et al, 2008). Wai Kin et al. (2008) proposed a method based on the 2-D Gabor filter which obtained palm print and texture feature extraction for authentication (Wang et al, 1998). They have described the five modules to get satisfactory results for palm print recognition

1.   Palm print acquisition,
2.   Pre-processing,
3.   Textured feature extraction,
4.   Matching, and
5.   Template database storage.

Table 1 illustrates facial feature extraction methods and overview of prominent deformation, motion extraction methods

3. FACE EXPRESSION: ISSUES AND CHALLENGES

In the computer vision community, the recognition of facial expression should not be confused with emotion recognition of human as is often completed. While it deals with the classification of facial feature deformation and motion into abstract classes of databases which are purely based on visual information, emotions are a result of many different factors and their state might or might not be revealed through a number of channels such as emotional voice, pose, gestures, gaze direction and facial expressions. Recognition of facial expression is a complex task because of the varying emotions of different individuals (Donato et. al., 1999), (Fase, & Lutin, 2000). Therefore, it is required to develop to an automatic system to mitigate the above mentioned challenges and to solve these problems, it is required develop efficient

Table 1. Facial feature extraction methods

S.N.	Deformation Extraction Approaches	Appearance Based Approaches	Local Texture Based Approaches
1	Image-based	Neural network (Lanitis A. et al., 1997), (Dailey M., Cottrell G., 1999) (Lisetti, & Rumelhart, 1998) Gabor wavelets (Lanitis et al., 1997), (Dailey, & Cottrell, 1999)	High gradient components (Lien J.,, 1998) Intensity profiles (Bartlett, 1998) PCA + Neural networks (Padgett, & Cottrell, 1999) (Cottrell & Metcalfe,1991)
2	Model-based	Active appearance model (Lanitis et al., 1997), (Cootes, & Edward., 2001, 1998) Point distribution model (Huang& Huang Y., 1997) Labeled graphs () Hong H., 1998), (Zhang et al., 1998) (Lyons et al., 1999)	Geometric face model (Kobayashi et al., 1997) Two view point-based models (Pantic &Rothkrantz, 2000)
S.N.	**Motion Extraction**	**Appearance Based Approaches**	**Local Texture Based Approaches**
3	Dense optical flow	Dense 2-D Flow fields (Lien, 1998) (Bartlett, 1998)	Region-based flow (Otsuka, 1998) (Yoneyama et. al., 1999)
4	Motion models	3D motion models (Yacoob M. et. al., 1996) 3D deformable models (Decalo &. Metaxas, 1996)	Parametric motion models (Yacoob et. al., 1996) 3D motion models (Basu, 1998)
5	Feature point tracking	-----	Feature tracking (Tian et. al., 2001), (Wang, 1998), (Otsuka & Ohya, 1998), (Roesnblum et. al., 1996)
6	Difference-images	Holistic difference-images (Donato et. al., 1999), (Fase & Lutin, 2000)	Region-based difference-images (Choudhury & Pentland, 2000)
7	Marker-based	--------	Highlighted facial features (Bascle & Blake, 1998) Dot markers (Suwa, Sugie &Fujimora1978), (Kaiser et. al., 1992).

machine learning approaches for computationally expensive and high memory consumption task. The algorithm involved in our study uses feature point as a basic algorithmic parameter for emotion matching procedure but the number of feature points to include for this task and to extract only those feature points which will clearly classify the image data set into mutually exclusive expression classes is still an active area of research. So, this problem is encountered in our study where we have computed efficiency of matching expressions of testing set with the training set as performance metric for comparison between the four algorithms that we have used and also for each algorithm variation of efficiency is evaluated with the variation of algorithmic parameter like feature points (see Figure 1).

Following are the challenges in recognition of emotion by using facial expression.

3.1. Difference in Lighting Conditions

The lighting conditions in which the pictures are taken are not always similar because the variations in time and place. The example of lighting variations could be the pictures taken inside the room and the pictures taken outside. Due to these variations, a same person with similar facial expressions may appear differently in different pictures. As a result, if the person has single image store in the database of face recognition, matching could be difficult with the face detection under different lighting conditions (Beymer, 1994).

3.2. Skin Colour Variations

Another challenge for skin based face recognition system is the difference in the skin color due to the difference in the races of the people. Due to this variation, sometimes the true skin pixels are filtered out along with the noise present in an image. In addition, the false skin background/non-background is not

Figure 1. Few sample image of facial expression
(Kanade, Cohn, & Tian, 2000).

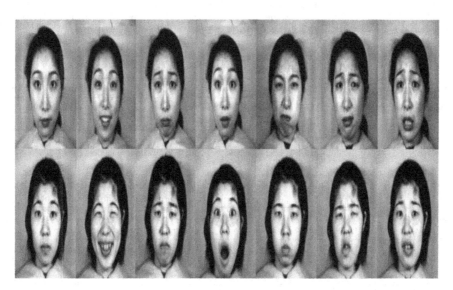

completely filtered out during noise filtering process. So, it is a tough task is to choose the filter which will cover the entire skin tones of different people and kick out false skin noise.

3.3. Variation in Face Angle or Orientation Variation

The angle of the human face from camera can be different in different situations. A frontal face detection algorithm can't work on non-frontal faces present in the image because the geometry of facial features in frontal view is always different than the geometry of facial features in non-frontal view. This is why orientation variation remains the difficult challenge in face detection system (Beymer, 1994).

4. DATABASE PREPARATION AND DESCRIPTION

To prepare the face images database of student, a 20 megapixel digital camera has been used to acquisition of face images from, IIT (BHU), Varanasi, India. It took more than 6 months to keep adequate number of subject images for training and testing purpose. The preparation of student database is taken in two different sessions. The size of face image database is 2000 (200 subject and 10 images per subject). However, the quality of images was not that high as compared to benchmark database which was expected as the students were not trained for posing with that accuracy. The device used for capturing is also became a challenge as after several testing the camera with high accuracy is selected.

In second database (extended Cohn-kanade) (Cohen et al., 2000), the emotions are given in label form for only those subject's expressions which were found to be unambiguous. Therefore, we were bound to not use all the expressions of the subjects included in the database however, only those images are used in training and testing whose emotions were clearly given. The ratio of inclusion of images for training and testing is 5:1 and since we have included 100 subjects in our database so our training file is consisting of 1500 images and we tested 300 images of 100 subjects of various expressions. The size of the database became an issue as the time and memory consumption in running the algorithms over the database was very high but with some programmatic optimization we solved this problem and then collected our results over different algorithmic parameter

5. PROPOSED METHODOLOGY

In proposed emotion recognition scheme, we have used Eigen face recognition approach Principal Component Analysis (PCA) (Turk & Pentland, 1999); (Kirby & Sirowich, 1990), Fisherfaces (Etemad, & chellapa, 1990) and texture feature approaches such as Local Binary Pattern Histogram (LPBH) (Ahonen et al., 2006),(Ojala, 2002), Speeded Up Robust Feature (SURF) (Bay & Van, 2006) with FLANN. For experimental result evaluation, the face images of student database were segmented into two parts: (i) training (Gallery) part. (ii) test (probe) part. The five images of each subject (student) were randomly selected for training part (total of 100 subject ×10 images per subject) and the remaining 500 face images were used as probe (test). The following steps are used in proposed approach for training and testing process:

1. Open Train and Test file.
2. **Initialize:** Create a model by calling corresponding algorithm constructor from face Recognizer APIfor training.
3. Scan Train File line by line and store images and labels in a vector data structure.
4. Call model->train (Images, Labels).
5. Open Test File.
6. While Testing image vector not empty) Call model -> predict (test image, actual label) and store its predicted label.b) Print whether prediction is correct or not.c) Store other information's in an output folder and output file.

In this experiment, the train file is having format with each line having image path followed their corresponding labels with a semicolon separator in between. Train and predict of database are symbolizing functions of the face Recognizer API model. Predicted label is checked whether it is matching with the actual label and that's how the efficiency is calculated.

5.1. Face Recognition Approaches

5.1.1. Eigenfaces

Eigenfaces is the name given to a set of eigenvectors when they are used in the computer vision for face recognition problem. The approach of using eigenfaces for recognition was developed by Sirovich & Kirby (1987). In real life captured image the dimensional reduction becomes important task in order to perform real time computation on high dimensional images. So, in Principal Component Analysis (PCA) we are looking for components that account for most of the information. The PCA expresses a set of possibly correlated variables into a smaller set of uncorrelated variables. The idea is, that a high-dimensional dataset is often described by correlated variables and therefore only a few meaningful dimensions account for most of the information. The PCA method finds the directions with the greatest variance in the data, called principal components.

Algorithm

Let $X=\{x, x,.....,..\}$ be a random vector with observations $x_j \in R^d$

1. Compute the mean $\mu = \dfrac{1}{n}\sum\nolimits_{i-1}^{n} x_i$ (1)

2. Compute the Covariance Matrix $S = \sum\nolimits_{i-1}^{n}\left(x_i - \mu\right)\left(x_i - \mu\right)^{T_i}$ (2)
3. Compute the eigenvalues λ_i and eigenvectors v_i of S.

i. $S v_i = \lambda_i v_i, i = 1,2,..., n$

4. Order the eigenvectors in descending order by their eigenvalue. The k principal components are the eigenvectors corresponding to the k largest eigenvalues.
5. The principal components of the observed vector are then given by:
6. y= $W(x-u)$where W= $(v_1, v_2 \ldots\ldots v_k)$. (3)

The Eigen faces method then performs facial expression recognition by following steps: For all testing images iterative perform step 2 and step 3.

1. Projecting all training samples into the PCA subspace.
2. Projecting the testing image into the PCA subspace.
3. Finding the nearest neighbor between the projected training images and the projected query image. The resulting eigenvectors are orthogonal and to get orthonormal eigenvectors they need to be normalized to unit length.

5.1.2. Fisherfaces

Fisherfaces is a supervised classification method used for face recognition. It is used to classify samples of unknown classes based on training samples with labelled classes. The goal of Fisherfaces is to maximize between-class (across users) variance and minimize within-class (within user) variance (Belhumeur et al., 1997). Here, C class is the face with mean of class j denoted by $\bar{N}_j$ and the ith image in class j denoted as x_i^j . These scatter matrix are s_b and s_w respectively and are calculated (eq. 4, 5 and 6) as follows:

$$S_b = \sum\nolimits_{j=1}^{C} \left(\bar{N}_j - N\right)\left(\bar{N}_j - N\right)^{T} \tag{4}$$

$$S_w = \sum\nolimits_{j=1}^{C} \sum\nolimits_{i=1}^{N_j} \left(x_i^j - \bar{N}_j\right)\left(x_i^j - \bar{N}_j\right)^{T} \tag{5}$$

$$W_{Frisher-Descriminat} = \arg\max \frac{\left|W^{T} S_b W\right|}{\left|W^{T} S_w W\right|} \tag{6}$$

Literature reviews shows that LDA is repeatedly superior to PCA and works well for distributed classes in databases that are small in size. LDA approach needs drastically more computation than PCA for larger datasets.

5.1.2. Local Binary Pattern (LBP)

LBP method uses the idea of describing only local features of an object instead of looking at the whole image as a high-dimensional vector. The features you extract this way will have a low dimensionality implicitly. Thus, this type of local description will be totally robust of things like scale, translation or rotation in images. The basic idea of LBP is to summarize the local structure in an image by comparing each pixel with its neighborhood. Take a pixel as center and threshold its neighbor against. If the intensity of the center pixel is greater-equal its neighbor, then denote it with 1 else with 0. Finally, we will end up getting a binary number for each pixel, just like 11001111. So with 8 surrounding pixels we'll end up with 2^8 possible combinations, called Local Binary Patterns or sometimes referred as LBP codes. The first LBPH operator described in literature actually used a fixed 3× ×3 neighborhoods just like this: The generic descriptor of LBP yields a discrete value to a pixel by thresholding a 3×3 neighborhood window of pixels with the center pixel value (C) and seeing the result as a binary number representation. If the gray level intensity of neighboring pixel is higher or equal, the value is set to one otherwise zero (see Figure 2).

$$C_{N,R}(p,q) = \sum_{i=0}^{N-1} Fn\left(n_i - n_c\right) \times 2^i \qquad (1)$$

where

$$F(x) = \begin{cases} 1 & if \left(n_i - n_c\right) \geq 0 \\ 0 & Otherwise \end{cases} \qquad (2)$$

where n_c corresponds to the gray level intensity of center pixel of the circle and n_i matches to the gray level intensities of N evenly spaced pixels on a circle of radius R (see Figure 2).

Figure 2. Generation of LBP code descriptor from a given image pixel values of 3×3 descriptor window

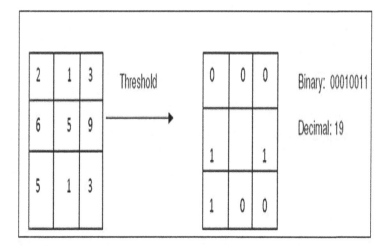

5.1.4. Speeded Up Robust Features (SURF)

It is a novel detector-descriptor approach and it is based on the Hessian matrix (Lindeberg, 1998) (Mikolajczyk and Schmid, 2001), however, it uses a very basic approximation, known as differentiation of Gaussian (DoG). It is a very basic Laplacian-based detector. It is based on integral face images to reduce the computation time. Therefore it called as 'Fast-Hessian' detector. The descriptor, on the other hand, describes a distribution of Haar-wavelet responses within the interest point neighborhood. It exploited integral images for speed. Moreover, only 64 dimensions are used, reducing the time for feature computation and matching, and increasing simultaneously the robustness. We also present a new indexing step based on the sign of the Laplacian, which increases not only the matching speed, but also the robustness of the descriptor (Bay et al., 2006). In a given image, SURF tries to find the interest points -The points where the variance is a maximum. It then constructs a 64-variable vector around it to extract the features (A 128-variable one is also possible, but it would consume more time for matching). In this way, there will be as many descriptors in an image as there are interest points. Now, when we use SURF for matching, we follow the below steps for every query image. For feature description, SURF uses Wavelet responses in horizontal and vertical direction. A neighbourhood of siz 20×20s is taken around the key point where sis the size. It is divided into 4×4 sub-regions. For each subregion, horizontal and vertical wavelet responses are taken and a vector is formed as $V = \sum dx, \sum dy, \sum |dx|, \sum |dy|$. This when represented as a vector give SURF feature descriptor with total 64 dimensions, lower the dimension, higher the speed of computation and matching, but better distinctiveness of features.

Another important improvement is the use of sign of Laplacian (trace of Hessian Matrix) for underlying interest point. It adds no computation cost since it is already computed during detection. The sign of the Laplacian distinguishes bright blobs on dark backgrounds from the reverse situation. In this matching stage, we only compare features if they have the same type of contrast (as shown in Figure 3.). This minimal information allows for faster matching, without reducing the descriptor's performance.

5.1.5. FLANN

Fast Library for Approximate Nearest Neighbors (FLANN) is a library that contains a collection of algorithms optimized for fast nearest neighbor search in large datasets and for high dimensional features.

Figure 3. Matching of same object based on feature

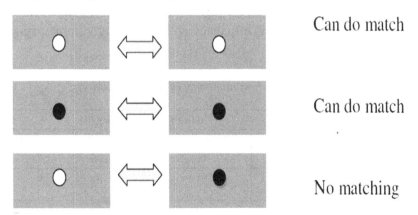

Can do match

Can do match

No matching

So, FLANN provides a library of feature matching methods. It can provide automatic selection of index tree and parameter based on the user's optimization on a particular data-set. They are chosen according to the user's preferences on the importance between build times, search time and memory footprint of the index trees. The type of index trees is KD, randomized KD and Hierarchical K-Means (Jain, 2010). The feature points are detected with SURF detectors and represented in SURF-128 descriptors. The program by default set up 4 Randomized KDTrees and search for 2-nearest-neighbours. The matched key-point is only counted when the second of the nearest-neighbors is doubly farther than the first.

Data Structure Used:

- **Randomized K-D Tree:** It improves the approximation of nearest neighbors from query point by searching simultaneously across a number of randomized trees. The trees are building from the same set of samples. Since in general practice it has been observed that variances among dimensions do not match very much. So randomly picking from the highest few will be enough to make the different trees.
- **Approximate Nearest Neighbor (ANN) Search:** The priority queue will be shared across all trees. In other words, the next cell to examine will be based on the closest cell-to-query-point distance among ALL trees.

6. EXPERIMENTATION RESULTS AND DISCUSSION

We have done our experiments on two databases: Cohen-Konade (cohen et al., 2000) and Student, IIT (BHU) facial expression databases. We have performed faces recognition approaches such as Eigenface Fisher faces, LBPH and SURF with FLANN. The identification accuracy of facial expression is illustrated in Table 2.

6.1. Performance Evaluation

Although Eigen faces, Fisher faces and SURF with FLANN approaches gave 100% efficiency and LBPH gave 96% recognition efficiency on Cohn-Kanade database but LBPH is faster. On student database Eigen faces, Fisher faces and LBP (Ahonen et al., 2006) gave 77%, 80% and 77% efficiency respectively but SURF with FLANN gave 88% efficiency when feature points are doubled which was giving 84% efficiency earlier but with more time and memory consumption. Therefore, we can see from above results that over the benchmark database, all the algorithms worked well. Eigenfaces and Fisherfaces gave 100% efficiency and LBPH gave 96% efficiency with default algorithmic parameter (maximum

Table 2. Illustrates the following identification accuracy of human emotion

Database	Identification Accuracy (%)			
	Eigenface	**Fisherfaces**	**LBPH**	**SURF with FLANN**
Cohn- Konade	100	100	96	99
IIT(BHU) Student, face database	80	80	77	80

feature points) but was much faster in comparison to Eigenfaces and Fisherfaces. As we have observed that the efficiency of SURF with FLANN approach increased by 4% when feature points are doubled which clearly indicates that feature points are deciding criteria for efficiency.

As we have observed that the efficiency decreased on the second database which was expected as untrained students are used in it so the ambiguity and forced way of expressing expression was observed in capturing images which was not the case with benchmark database. People were trained well and under the supervision of professional they performed the capturing of their showing expressions and also from the label file of that database we have observed that only those labels which were considered clear after multiple inspection were included in the label file which we have used in constructing our database of 100 individuals. So, this clarity of expression is totally missing in student database. Also, apart from supervision there are other factors that are causing the degradation in quality of expressions images database like camera quality, illumination etc.

After observing the above Figure 4, Eigenfaces, we have observed increase in efficiency with increase in feature points but the rate of increase keep on decreasing as we have increased feature points further and finally the efficiency is found to be attaining a constant which was expected as Eigenfaces algorithm is based on Principal Component Analysis method (PCA) which calculates maximum variance as a parameter for matching so not being a classification approach is the reason for its underperformance as comparison to other classification based method like Fisherfaces (Figure 5) but increasing algorithmic parameter (feature points) actually increases principal components which causes increase in efficiency up to an extent after that there is no effect of increase.

In the Figure 5 that is estimation of efficiency variation with variation in feature points for Fisherfaces, we observed that the efficiency doesn't changes at all on changing feature points (algorithmic parameter). This can be explained as Fisherfaces being a classification based method using Linear Discriminant Analysis (LDA) approach classifies the training images based on current algorithmic parameter which

Figure 4. Illustrates the variation of efficiency (on y-axis) with variation in feature points (on x-axis) for Eigenfaces algorithm

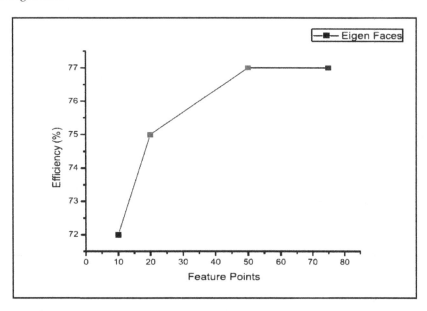

Figure 5. Illustrates the variation of efficiency (on y-axis) with variation in feature points (on x-axis) for Fisherfaces algorithm

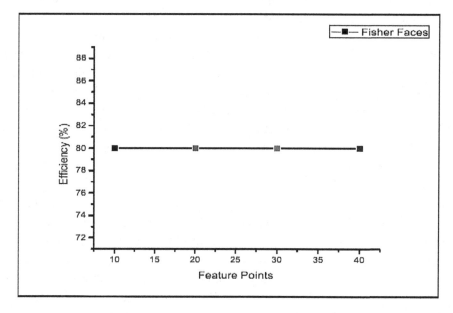

Figure 6. Illustrates the variation of efficiency (on y-axis) with variation in feature points (on x-axis) for SURF with FLANN algorithm

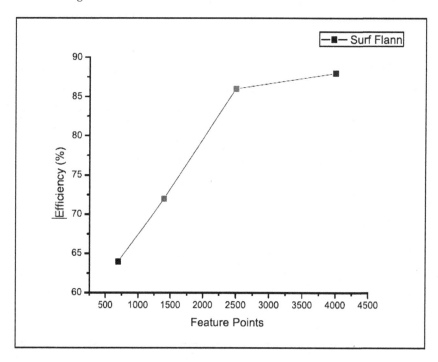

Figure 7. Illustrates the variation of efficiency (on y-axis) with variation in algorithmic parameter i.e. Radius of extended (circular) ring for LBPH operator for 16 neighbors (on x-axis) for LBPH algorithm

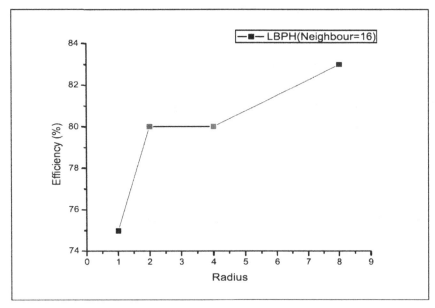

remains same even after changing that parameter. So, the efficiency that we have found for lower feature points is same as with higher feature points which are the maximum efficiency that we have found by classification based method for this unsupervised trained student database.

In the Figure 6 that is estimating the variation in efficiency on varying the feature points for SURF with FLANN algorithm we have observed that efficiency increases continuously with increase in feature points but the task becomes computationally more expensive and consuming more memory which was expected as this approach is somewhat naïve one to one matching approach with optimized feature extraction, keypoints description by SURF and optimized approximate nearest neighbor searching by FLANN. It uses one to one matching of every test image with every train image and finds the train image with the closest match with the test image and then assigning its label to that test image. So, with increase in feature points the efficiency is found to increase because of closer matching with more feature points to compare between the training and the testing image. In the next three graphs, we have shown variation in efficiency with the variation in algorithmic parameter like radius and neighbor for extended (or circular) LBPH operator of LBPH algorithm. With 16 neighbors increment in efficiency is found with increase in radius of circular ring for LBPH operator which was expected as with more neighbors and larger radius of the ring the matching will be more.

7. CONCLUSION

We have computed efficiency as the performance matric for comparison among four algorithms. All the algorithms worked extremely well for benchmark database but for student database the performance was satisfactory for student database. So, we varied algorithmic parameters like feature points in case of Eigenfaces, Fisherfaces and SURF with FLANN method and radius and neighbors for LBPH on student database. On comparison we have found that on benchmark database efficiency shown by Eigenfaces, Fisherfaces and SURF with FLANN is 100% for maximum feature points as algorithmic parameter and 96% for LBPH but the latter was faster than formers. Also, efficiency is found to increase in general with increase in feature points as in case of Eigenfaces, SURF with FLANN yet the task became more computationally expensive and memory consuming but for classification based method like Fisherfaces efficiency remain constant (Figure 7). For LBPH efficiency increased with increase in radius of circular ring with 16 neighbors but the variation was not monotonic for 8 neighbors and also for same radius efficiency first decreased for 12 neighbors then increased for 16 neighbors. So, the cause of this behavior can be found out in future research.

8. FUTURE DIRECTION

The precision of extracting appropriate feature points is very important in facial expression recognition. As we have seen in the results that with an increase in feature points, efficiency improves identification accuracy. However, recognition task takes more time execution and memory consuming. Future research can be done in optimizing the process of extracting feature points which is a critical step of facial expression recognition task. We have observed improvement areas like the iteration involved in testing images one by one. Since the testing process is independent for each test image. So, with parallelization techniques more efficiency can be achieved. Also, the automated approaches discussed in this paper can be implemented in places like psychotherapy center where observing the behavior or body language of patients can be used as major tool for knowing their mental situation. So, the approaches discussed here can be used to develop an automated tool for facial expression recognition that can aid in analyzing medical situation of patients just by observing them by some capturing devices that is installed in the patient's waiting room.

We concluded this research work by summarizing recognition results of human emotion and shortcomings of currently employed analysis methods and proposed possible future research directions. Different applications using automatic system for facial expression and analysis can be envisaged in the near future, fostering further interest in doing research in the fields of facial expression interpretation facial expression recognition and the facial expression animation. Non-verbal information transmitted by facial expressions of human is of enormous importance in different research areas such as: image understanding, analysis, psychological studies, pain assessment by using facial expression or emotion in medical research, face image compression and synthetic, face animation facial nerve grading in medicine, more engaging human–machine interfaces, view-indexing, robotics as well as virtual reality.

REFERENCES

Ahonen, T., Hadid, A., & Pietikainen, M. (2006). Face description with local binary patterns: Application to face recognition. *IEEE Transactions on Pattern Analysis and Machine Intelligence*, 28(12), 2037–2041. doi:10.1109/TPAMI.2006.244 PMID:17108377

Anitha, C., Venkatesha, M. K., & Adiga, B. S. (2010). A survey on facial expression databases. *International Journal of Engineering Science and Technology*, *2*(10), 5158–5174.

Bartlett, M. S. (1998). *Face image analysis by unsupervised learning and redundancy reduction*. (Doctoral dissertation). University of California, San Diego, CA.

Bascle, B., & Blake, A. (1998, January). Separability of pose and expression in facial tracking and animation. In *Proceedings Sixth IEEE International Conference on Computer Vision*. doi:10.1109/ICCV.1998.710738

Basu, S., Oliver, N., & Pentland, A. (1998, January). 3D modeling and tracking of human lip motions. *In Proceedings Sixth IEEE International Conference on Computer Vision*. doi:10.1109/ICCV.1998.710740

Bay, H., Tuytelaars, T., & Van Gool, L. (2006). Surf: Speeded up robust features. In *Computer vision–ECCV 2006* (pp. 404–417). Springer Berlin Heidelberg. doi:10.1007/11744023_32

Belhumeur, P., Hespanha, J., & Kriegman, D. (1991). Eigenfaces vs. Fisherfaces: Recognition using class speci0c linear projection. *IEEE Transactions on Pattern Analysis and Machine Intelligence*, *19*(7), 711–720. doi:10.1109/34.598228

Belhumeur, P. N., Hespanha, J., & Kriegman, D. (1997). Eigenfaces vs. Fisherfaces: Recognition Using Class Specific Linear Projection. *IEEE Transactions on Pattern Analysis and Machine Intelligence*, *19*(7), 711–720. doi:10.1109/34.598228

Black, M. J., & Yacoob, Y. (1997). Recognizing facial expressions in image sequences using local parameterized models of image motion. *International Journal of Computer Vision*, *25*(1), 23–48. doi:10.1023/A:1007977618277

Choudhury, T., & Pentland, A. (2000). Motion field histograms for robust modeling of facial expressions. In *Proceedings of the International Conference on Pattern Recognition (ICPR 2000)*. Barcelona, Spain.

Cootes, T., Edwards, G., & Taylor, C. (2001). Active appearance models. *IEEE Transactions on Pattern Analysis and Machine Intelligence*, *23*(6), 681–685. doi:10.1109/34.927467

Cottrell, G. W. (1990). Extracting features from faces using compression networks: Face, identity, emotion and gender recognition using holons. In Connectionist models: proceedings of the 1990 summer school (pp. 328-337).

Cui, J., Wen, F., & Tang, X. (2008). *Real time Google and live image searchre-ranking*. ACM Multimedia.

Dacher, K., Gian, Gonzaga, & Davidson. (2003). Facial expression of emotion. In Handbook of affective sciences. New York, NY: Oxford University Press.

Dalal, N., & Triggs, B. (2005, June). Histograms of oriented gradients for human detection. In *Proceedings of IEEE Computer Society conference on Computer Vision and Pattern Recognition, 2005(CVPR 2005)*, (Vol. 1, pp. 886-893). IEEE.

DeCarlo, D., & Metaxas, D. (1996). The integration of optical fow and deformable models with applications to human face shape and motion estimation. In *Proceedings of the International Conference on Computer Vision and Pattern Recognition (CVPR'96)*.

Edwards, G., Cootes, T., & Taylor, C. (1998). Face recognition using active appearance models. In *Proceedings of the Fifth European Conference on Computer Vision (ECCV)*. University of Freiburg.

Eisert, P., & Girod, B. (1997). Facial expression analysis for model-based coding of video sequences. *Picture Coding Symposium*. Berlin, Germany.

Etemad, K., & Chellappa, R. (1997). Discriminant analysis for recognition of human face images. *Journal of the Optical Society of America. A, Optics, Image Science, and Vision*, *14*(8), 1724–1733. doi:10.1364/JOSAA.14.001724

Fasel, B., & Luettin, J. (2000). Recognition of asymmetric facial action unit activities and intensities. In *Proceedings of the International Conference on Pattern Recognition (ICPR 2000)*. doi:10.1109/ICPR.2000.905664

Fasel, B., & Luettinb, J. (2003). Automatic facial expression analysis: A survey. *Pattern Recognition*, *36*(1), 259–275. doi:10.1016/S0031-3203(02)00052-3

Fellenz, W., Taylor, J., Tsapatsoulis, N., & Kollias, S. (1999). Comparing template-based, feature-based and supervised classification of facial expressions from static images. In *Proceedings of International Conference on Circuits, Systems, Communications and Computers (CSCC'99)*.

Heisele, B., Serre, T., & Poggio, T. (2007). A component-based framework for face detection and identification. *International Journal of Computer Vision*, *74*(2), 167–181. doi:10.1007/s11263-006-0006-z

Hong, H., Neven, H., & Von der Malsburg, C. (1998). Online facial expression recognition based on personalized galleries. In *Proceedings of the Second IEEE International Conference on Automatic Face and Gesture Recognition, (FG'98)*.

Huang, C., & Huang, Y. (1997). Facial expression recognition using model-based feature extraction and action parameters classification. *Journal of Visual Communication and Image Representation*, *8*(3), 278–290. doi:10.1006/jvci.1997.0359

Jain, A. K. (2010). Data clustering: 50 years beyond K-means. *Pattern Recognition Letters*, *31*(8), 651–666. doi:10.1016/j.patrec.2009.09.011

Kabir, M., Jabid, T., & Chae, O. (2010). A local directional pattern variance (LDPv) based face descriptor for human facial expression recognition. In *Proceedings 7th IEEE International Conference on Adv. Video Signal Based Surveill*.

Kaiser, S., & Wehrle, T. (1992). Automated coding of facial behavior in human–computer interactions with FACS. *Journal of Nonverbal Behavior*, *16*(2), 67–83. doi:10.1007/BF00990323

Kanade, T., Cohn, J., & Tian, Y. (2000). Comprehensive Database for Facial Expression Analysis. In *Proceedings of IEEE International Conference on Face and Gesture Recognition*.

Kobayashi, H., & Hara, F. (1997). Facial interaction between animated 3D face robot and human beings. In *Proceedings of the International Conference on Systems, Man and Cybernetics*. doi:10.1109/ICSMC.1997.633250

Lanitis, A., Taylor, C., & Cootes, T. (1997). Automatic interpretation and coding off ace images using *2exible models. IEEE Transactions on Pattern Analysis and Machine Intelligence, 19*(7), 743–756. doi:10.1109/34.598231

Liao, S., Jain, A. K., & Li, S. Z. (2014). A Fast and Accurate Unconstrained Face Detector. *arXiv preprint arXiv*:1408.1656.

Lien, J. (1998). *Automatic recognition of facial expression using hidden Markov models and estimation of expression intensity*. (Ph.D. Thesis). The Robotics Institute, CMU.

Lindeberg, T. (1998). Feature detection with automatic scale selection. *IJCV, 30*(2), 79–116. doi:10.1023/A:1008045108935

Lyons, M. J., Budynek, J., & Akamatsu, S. (1999). Automatic classification of single facial images. *IEEE Transactions on Pattern Analysis and Machine Intelligence, 21*(12), 1357–1362. doi:10.1109/34.817413

Martinez, A., & Benavente, R. (1998). *The AR Face Database*. Technical Report.

Mikolajczyk, K., & Schmid, C. (2001). Indexing based on scale invariant interest points. In *Proceedings 8th IEEE International Conference on Computer Vision, (ICCV)*.

Muja, M., & Lowe, D. G. (2009). Fast Approximate Nearest Neighbors with Automatic Algorithm Configuration. *VISAP,* (1), 2.

Ojala, T., Pietikäinen, M., & Harwood, D. (1996). A comparative study of texture measures with classification based on feature distributions. *Pattern Recognition, 29*(1), 51–59. doi:10.1016/0031-3203(95)00067-4

Otsuka, T., & Ohya, J. (1998). Extracting facial motion parameters by tracking feature points. In *Proceedings of First International Conference on Advanced Multimedia Content Processing*.

Otsuka, T., & Ohya, J. (1998). Spotting segments displaying facial expression from image sequences using HMM. In *Proceedings of Second IEEE International Conference on Automatic Face and Gesture Recognition (FG'98)*. doi:10.1109/AFGR.1998.670988

Padgett, C., & Cottrell, G. (n.d.). Representing face image for emotion classi0cation. In M. Mozer, M. Jordan, & T. Petsche (Eds.), Advances in Neural Information Processing Systems (vol. 9, pp. 894–900). Cambridge, MA: MIT Press.

Penev, P., & Atick, J. (1996). Local feature analysis: A general statistical theory for object representation. *Netw. Comput. Neural Syst., 7*(3), 477–500. doi:10.1088/0954-898X_7_3_002

Ramirez Rivera, A., Castillo, R., & Chae, O. (2013). Local directional number pattern for face analysis: Face and expression recognition. *IEEE Transactions on Image Processing, 22*(5), 1740–1752. doi:10.1109/TIP.2012.2235848 PMID:23269752

Raudys, S., & Jain, A. K. (1991). Small sample size effects in statistical pattern recognition: Recommendations for practitioners. *IEEE Transactions on Pattern Analysis and Machine Intelligence, 13*(3), 252–264. doi:10.1109/34.75512

Rosenblum, M., Yacoob, Y., & Davis, L. (1996). Human expression recognition from motion using a radial basis function network architecture. *IEEE Transactions on Neural Networks*, *7*(5), 1121–1138. doi:10.1109/72.536309 PMID:18263509

Rowley, H., Baluja, S., & Kanade, T. (1998). Neural network-based face detection. *IEEE Transactions on Pattern Analysis and Machine Intelligence*, *20*(1), 23–38. doi:10.1109/34.655647

Sarode, N., & Bhatia, S. (2010). Facial Expression Recognition. *International Journal on Computer Science and Engineering*, *2*(5), 1552–1557.

Shih, F. Y., Chuang, C. F., & Wang, P. S. (2008). Performance comparisons of facial expression recognition in JAFFE database. *International Journal of Pattern Recognition and Artificial Intelligence*, *22*(3), 445–459. doi:10.1142/S0218001408006284

Suwa, M., Sugie, N., & Fujimora, K. (1978). A preliminary note on pattern recognition of human emotional expression. In *Proceedings of the 4th International Joint Conference on Pattern Recognition*.

Tian, Y., Kanade, T., & Cohn, J. (2001). Recognizing action units for facial expression analysis. *IEEE Transactions on Pattern Analysis and Machine Intelligence*, *23*(2), 97–115. doi:10.1109/34.908962 PMID:25210210

Turk, M., & Pentland, A. (1991). Eigenfaces for recognition. *Journal of Cognitive Neuroscience*, *3*(1), 71–86. doi:10.1162/jocn.1991.3.1.71 PMID:23964806

Viola, P., & Jones, M. J. (2004). Robust real-time face detection. *International Journal of Computer Vision*, *57*(2), 137–154. doi:10.1023/B:VISI.0000013087.49260.fb

Wang, M., Iwai, Y., & Yachida, M. (1998). Expression recognition from time-sequential facial images by use of expression change model. In *Proceedings of the Second IEEE International Conference on Automatic Face and Gesture Recognition (FG'98)*. doi:10.1109/AFGR.1998.670969

Wiskott, L. M., Fellous, J., Kuiger, N., & von der Malsburg, C. (1997). Face recognition by elastic bunch graph matching. *IEEE Transactions on Pattern Analysis and Machine Intelligence*, *19*(7), 775–779. doi:10.1109/34.598235

Xiao, R., Zhu, H., Sun, H., & Tang, X. (2007). Dynamic cascades for face detection. In *Proceedings. IEEE Int. Conf. Computer Vision*.

Yacoob, Y., & Davis, L. S. (1996). Recognizing human facial expression from long image sequences using optical fow. *IEEE Transactions on Pattern Analysis and Machine Intelligence*, *18*(6), 636–642. doi:10.1109/34.506414

Yang, J., Zhang, D., Frangi, A. F., & Yang, J. Y. (2004). Two-dimensional PCA: A new approach to appearance-based face representation and recognition. *IEEE Transactions on Pattern Analysis and Machine Intelligence*, *26*(1), 131–137. doi:10.1109/TPAMI.2004.1261097 PMID:15382693

Yang, P., Liu, Q., & Metaxas, D. N. (2007, June). Boosting coded dynamic features for facial action units and facial expression recognition. In *Proceedings of IEEE Conference on Computer Vision and Pattern Recognition (CVPR'07)*. doi:10.1109/CVPR.2007.383059

Yoneyama, M., Iwano, Y., Ohtake, A., & Shirai, K. (1997). Facial expression recognition using discrete Hopfield neural networks. In *Proceedings of the International Conference on Image Processing (ICIP)*. doi:10.1109/ICIP.1997.647398

Zhang, B., & Gao Zhao, Y. (2010). Local derivative pattern versus local binary pattern: Face recognition with high-order local pattern descriptor. *IEEE Transactions on Image Processing*, *19*(2), 533–544. doi:10.1109/TIP.2009.2035882 PMID:19887313

Zhang, D., & Kong, L. W. et al.. (2003). Palmprint feature extraction using 2-D Gabor Filters. *Pattern Recognition*, *36*(10), 2339–2347. doi:10.1016/S0031-3203(03)00121-3

Zhang, Z., Lyons, M., Schuster, M., & Akamatsu, S. (1998). Comparison between geometry-based and Gabor wavelets-based facial expression recognition using multi-layer perceptron. In *Proceedings of the Second IEEE International Conference on Automatic Face and Gesture Recognition (FG'98)*. doi:10.1109/AFGR.1998.670990

KEY TERMS AND DEFINITIONS

Biometric Profile: Information used to represent an individual or group in an information system.

Biometric Traits: Class of phenotypic characteristics (e.g., face or stripe pattern) used as source for constructing a biometric profile.

Biometrics: Biometrics means "life measurement" but the term is usually associated with the use of unique physiological characteristics to identify an individual.

Classification: Classification refers to as assigning a physical object or incident into one of a set of predefined categories.

Identification: Process of retrieving identity by one to many (1 to M) matching of an unknown biometric profile against a set of known profiles.

Chapter 14
Facial Expression Analysis Using 3D Range Images

Parama Bagchi
RCC Institute of Information Technology, India

Debotosh Bhattacharjee
Jadavpur University, India

Mita Nasipuri
Jadavpur University, India

ABSTRACT

This proposed work deals with the uses and techniques of 3D range images for facial expression recognition. A 3D range image is basically a depth image (also called a 2.5D image), which contains depth information at each (x, y) pixel of the image. In the future, computer vision will become a part of our everyday life because of all of its extensive applications. Hence, the interactions between users and computers need to be more natural, and emphasizing as well as enumerating human-to-human communication to a larger extent. That is the reason why facial expressions find importance. Facial expression is an important factor of communication, and they reveal unknown facts about a person's feelings and emotions. There comes the need of a real facial expression detection system. Also, changes in expression are of great importance for the interpretation of human facial behavior as well as face recognition.

INTRODUCTION

Face recognition is an important issue today in the field of computer vision. Face recognition relies mainly on the quality of data resource. A face can be 2D or 3D, and static or dynamic. From the implementation task point of view, face data is used for face recognition, occlusion detection, expression recognition and similar other uses. Over the past few years, many related works have been based on expression recognition and authors have made efforts to build face recognition systems which can detect facial expressions like pain and mood, as well as of more subtle emotions such as embarrassment, amusement and shame. It is, therefore, indeed necessary, to develop a robust expression recognition system.

DOI: 10.4018/978-1-4666-8723-3.ch014

With the advancement of 3D technologies, compared to 2D faces, 3D faces have been used for face information analysis. The problem which lies with the majority of existing expression recognition systems is that, majority of existing recognition systems are based on 2D images. More specifically, advanced research has been conducted to model the temporal relationships of different expressions. But, none of the prevalent systems aims to use the nature of facial expressions and use this for recognition purpose. Of late, facial recognition systems have been developed that, explicitly recognize and model the temporal segments of either full expressions or components of expression such as facial action units. These systems make use of 2D face images, they also find the kind of motion between frames using feature based or appearance based methods to perform classification and modeling. Unfortunately, these systems present in history are sensitive to illumination, pose and occlusions like makeup, sunglasses, etc.In most cases, when 2D faces are used, it is necessary to maintain a frontal facial pose, in order to achieve a better recognition. Facial pose, hence, can simultaneously reduce the recognition rate of the existing systems. So, in order to address the challenges of accuracy and pose, extreme poses in case of 3D systems must be employed. Today, with the advances in 3D structured light scanning, stereo photogrammetric, the acquisition of 3D facial structure and capturing of facial pose is now, an easy task.

There have been previous works using the concept of 2Dface images for the reconstruction of 3D models, in order to extract 3D features that could be used for classification of the facial expression, but these methods are dominated and corrupted by problems of illumination and pose inherent to all 2D methods.

Our main contribution in this proposed work is to exploit, the geometry of 3D faces which deal with expressions e.g. sad, happy, exclamation, surprise, with an exclusive combination of expression and pose.

In this context, a review of the majority of work done in the field of 3D expression analysis using Hidden Markov's model, PCA, LDA, etc. will also be done.

Also, we shall propose a new system where we shall consider a combination of expression and pose, and we shall propose methods for recognizing 3D faces with expressions.

Normally, there is a devoid of systems in the field of 3D face recognition, which works with a combination of expression and pose. In analyzing facial expressions, it is indeed necessary to understand which facial features change under expressions and pose. For example, the nose region does not change under facial expressions but, the region surrounding mouth changes vigorously. Hence, it is needed to extract the areas surrounding the mouth, in order to analyze the expression.

In case of expression, faces become ill-posed, and so it is also necessary for 3D faces to be registered because the recognition rate diminishes if the 3D faces are not in frontal pose. Also, expression faces provide a rich set of features. By extracting those features, it is possible to demonstrate the efficiency of recognition rate.

In this present work, a framework for statistical shape analysis of facial surfaces for 3D expression faces has been proposed. Methods that make it appropriate for 3D face recognition in non-cooperative scenarios will also be discussed in this work. So, two major issues have been handled in this proposed work:

1. Firstly, to handle expressions with poses.
2. Secondly, to recognize faces in the presence of expressions.
3. Finally, to reconstruct registered neutral faces from expression faces.

BACKGROUND

In this Section, a literature review of the already existing works done in the field of 3D facial expressions has been discussed. In (Zhang, 1999), the author based their experiments on feature based facial expression recognition based on a two layer perceptron. In this work, two different types of features were extracted from the 3D face images:

1. Geometric positions of fiducial points, and
2. Feature detection technique using Gabor Wavelets.

In addition to this, the authors compared the recognition rate with different types of features. Experimental results showed that, Gabor wavelet coefficients gave better recognition rate than geometric areas. In (Shan et al, 2009), the authors have evaluated facial representation based on LBP (local binary patterns), for facial expression recognition. The authors also studied different machine learning methods and evaluated them on several databases. The test results illustrated that, LBP features are efficient for facial expression recognition. The authors in (Martinez & Du, 2012) have worked on a model, that which consists of distinct continuous spaces. The authors entailed that, more than one emotion categories can be recognized by a linear combination of these face spaces. According to the authors, the primary task for the recognition of faces with emotions was very precise. Henceforth, the authors in this proposed work provided an overview of how, the resulting model can be employed for expression recognition. In (Grafsgaard et al, 2013), the authors presented a facial recognition system to analyze a student's facial movements during tutoring sessions. Also, examinations of the extent to which these facial movements correspond to tutoring outcomes were also minutely observed after which, face models were constructed which depicted facial expressions while tutoring outcomes. Results demonstrated excellent outcome in this experiment. The authors in (Kaur et al, 2010), detected an unknown face based on his/her expressions. The main aim of the research was, to develop highly intelligent mind implemented robots. Here the authors suggested a system i.e. a facial expression recognition system which tackled the following problems:

1. Detection and location of faces.
2. Facial feature extraction.
3. Facial expression is classification.

The varieties of emotions present in the system were Angry, Happy, Sad, Disgust and Surprise along with neutral faces. Principal Component Analysis (PCA) was implemented for feature extraction to determine principal emotions. The experiments showed that, the facial expression recognition framework degraded in recognition rate due to facial occlusions or loss of feature points during tracking. In (Bettadapura, 2012), the authors experimented with the automatic recognition of facial expressions. The work in (Bettadapura, 2012), gave the advances made in this field of automatic face expression recognition. In this work, FACS Face Action Units (AUs) and MPEG-4 Facial Animation Parameters (FAPs) were used for face parameterization and also, the recent advances in face detection, tracking and feature extraction methods. In (Ryan et al, 2009), automatic facial expression recognition was discussed involving

2Dimagerywith problems due to inherent pose and illumination variations. Here, the authors surveyed 3D and 4D facial expression recognition including the recent developments in 3Dfacial data acquisition and tracking. The authors also surveyed the use of 3D and 4D face databases for facial expression recognition system. Also, the challenges in the field of face recognition were discussed. In (Sandbach et al, 2012), the authors considered the treatment of individuals, during interviews and interrogations, and how they react under various sensitive environments.

It is indeed true that, facial expression units have an enormous capability to recognize individuals. Over the past years, scientists have developed human observer based methods that can be used to classify facial expressions. However, the methods are very difficult to standardize, and there is no, one universal method which can solve all problems related to facial expressions. However, if a careful survey is conducted over all the previous works done in the field of 3D expression recognition, it can easily be seen that, not much work have been done in the field of mixed expressions and pose, which has been proposed in the present work.

MAIN FOCUS OF THE CHAPTER

Issues, Controversies and Problems

Most of the relevant works, done in the field of 3D expression recognition (Ryan et al, 2009), deals only with the expression faces. It is inevitably true that, expression faces are indeed tough to be recognized but, from the psychological point of view, it is still not known whether the information extracted from facial expressions actually helps in face recognition or not. Existing literary works suggest that, people recognized neutral expressions more, than happy and angry faces. There are inevitably several examples, and it is also true that, when a person has a particular severe expression face, it is indeed very difficult to be identified.

The main focus in this proposed work is, to deal with not only expression faces, but also pose problems, which hinders and actually degrades the face recognition rate. Expressions degrade the recognition rate, also pose does the same thing but in fact, pose detriments the recognition rate much more than what expression does. So, here a solution has been proposed to deal with the pose issue first, and then propose recognition of expression faces in case of 3D face images.

Before the present system would deal with faces with pose variation and expression, at first registration on3Dface image has to be performed. 3D face registration is an important step in face recognition. 3D registration is the process of aligning faces to a standard geometrical coordinate system. It is a crucial step in 3D modeling to find correspondences between two 3D faces (Alyuz et al, 2012) shape models. The main aim of 3D registration is to find out a rigid transformation which aligns 3D faces from any pose to a frontal pose. After registration, distances between frontal pose and the registered face are less than a minimum threshold.

Today, there are very few works which deal with extreme poses. Mostly all registration and recognition algorithms use faces in frontal pose. In contrast to that, the present method would be able to at first, register the 3D face in the frontal position, and then detect expressions and finally recognize the faces. The entire solution has been given in "Solutions and Recommendations", part in the following Section.

Solutions and Recommendations

There are not many databases (Yin et al, 2006) which have 3Dface images across combined pose and expressions (Moreno & Sanchez 2004). Currently let's discuss the following 3D face databases (Yin et al, 2008) that has been acquired:

- Frav3D 3D Face Database.
- GavabDB 3D Face Database.
- Bosphorus3D Face Database.
- Casia 3D Face Database.
- Texas 3D FRD Face Database.
- USF Human ID 3D Face Database.
- 3DMD face 3D Face Database.
- UND Database 3D Face Database.

Amongst these, expression faces were found but, mostly in frontal positions.

- **Frav3DFaceDatabase:** 3 to 4 expression face in frontal position/ individual.
- **GavabDB Face Database:** Has 2 to 3 expression face in frontal position/ individual.
- **Bosphorus Face Database:** Abundant expression faces: Up to 35 expressions per subject (Amongst the expressions, there were only 9 expression faces per subject across pose which is indeed too little).
- **Casia Face Database:** Only 5 expressions per subject but only in frontal pose (smile, laugh, anger, surprise, eye-close).
- **Texas 3D FRD Face Database:** 183 expression faces but strictly across pose.
- **USF Human ID 3D Database:** No face with an expression combined with the pose found.
- **3DMD face 3D Face Database:** 21 expression faces per individual but in frontal poses.
- **UND Database Face Database:** No expression faces found across pose.

Not many databases are found which has the rich combination of both pose and expression. In addition to that, the future aim is to collect and capture a set of databases where individuals both with extreme poses and expressions can be captured. David SLS- 1, Engine 3D scanners are commonly used acquisition devices for this purpose. The details of the acquisition device have been enlisted below:-

- **David SLS 1:** The scanner allows flexible adjustment. The 3D model can be used in different standard 3D formats e.g. OBJ, STL, PLY. They are stored and processed, e.g. for rapid prototyping, component testing, computer animation, games, etc.
- **Engine 3D Scanner:** NextEngine's Desktop 3D Scanner and ScanStudio™ software generates a 3D model, capturing even fine surface details of less than 0.2 millimeter.It scans all sides of the object separately, including top and bottom. In this scanner, a different standard 3D formats (Savran et al, 2008) is found e.g. .obj, .stl, .ply for computer animations, games, virtual 3D environments, etc. Now, our proposed system for expression and pose registration and recognition has been depicted in Figure 1.

Figure 1. A Block diagram is showing our proposed system of 3D expression recognition

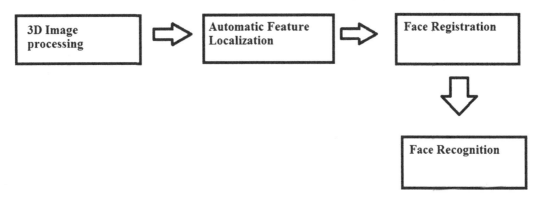

As could be clearly seen in Figure 1, the present system takes as input a mesh which is an expressive one as well as ill-posed. Ill-posed because it is oriented across 90°, in a manner in which it can never be recognized. The main idea is to register the mesh first, and then apply some algorithms which would convert the expression face into a neutral one, and then recognize it. Also, a second option exists and that is to recognize, the expression face without converting it into a neutral face. This would then indeed be quite challenging.

Our method for pose cum expression registration and recognition consists of the following steps:

1.   3D Image Acquisition,
2.   Image preprocessing by Trilinear interpolation,
3.   Landmark Localization,
4.   3D image Registration to obtain the Neutral Expression Face,
5.   Recognition of registered expression faces.

A broad discussion of steps 1 to 5 has been given below:

1.   **3D Image Acquisition:** In this initial step, 3D range image is generated using an acquisition device. A range image, more popularly termed as a depth image (also called a 2.5D image), contains the depth value at each (x, y) pixel on the image. Figure 2 shows the range images pose taken from the Bosphorus database.

Figure 2. Range Images for subjects taken from the Bosphorus Database across pose

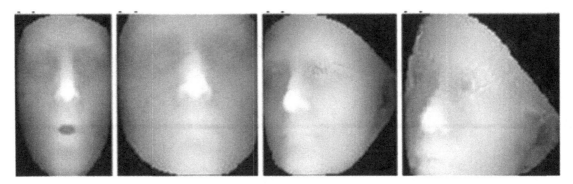

2. **Image Preprocessing by Trilinear Interpolation:** In this step, so as to remove the outliers, the entire 3D image as is obtained in step A is preprocessed first using an interpolation technique.

Surface interpolation maintains the continuity and smoothness of the surface, because raw 3D image (S.Berretti, A.D.Bimbo &P. Pala et. al, 2013) data is sometimes subjected to roughness. Hence, it has to be interpolated in order to make all the 3D data points maintain a smooth continuity.

Figure 3 shows, how the 3D surfaces look after applying Trilinear interpolation.

Next, the interpolated 3D images are then cropped in an elliptical style. The images are then smoothened by Gaussian filter. Snapshots of the images after smoothing have been shown in Figure 4.

3. **Landmark Localization:** Gaussian (K) and Mean (H) curvatures are widely feature detectors for range image analysis. HK segmentation was first used by Besl in 1986. Gaussian and mean curvatures are normally calculated from two principal curvatures k_1 and k_2. The Gaussian curvature K equals the sum of the principal curvatures, i.e., k_1 and k_2.

$$K = k_1 + k_2 \tag{1}$$

The mean curvature H is the average of principal curvatures k_1 and k_2

$$H = \frac{k_1 + k_2}{2} \tag{2}$$

The novelty of the present technique is that, we have detected almost all the regions across three different databases in the Convex ellipsoid region with H>0 and K>0.The range image is first considered

Figure 3. Figures showing a non-interpolated surface (a) and an interpolated surface (b) (Lee, 1992)

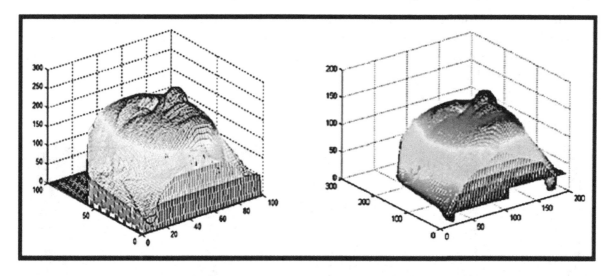

Figure 4. Images for the subjects after interpolation, smoothing, and cropping

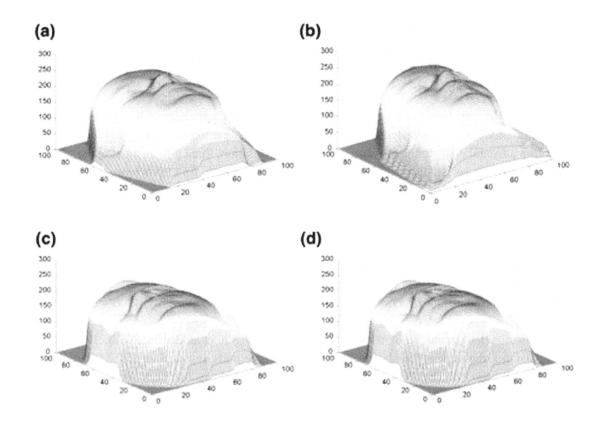

to be consisting of *N X M* points where *N* and *M* are the dimensions of the range image. For each (x_i, y_j) on the range image, a polynomial is fitted on the surface of the 3D face as shown in Equation 3.

$$g(i, j) = a_{ij} + b_{ij}\left(x - x_i\right) + c_{ij}\left(y - y_j\right) + d_{ij}\left(x - x_i\right)\left(y - y_j\right) + e_{ij}\left(x - x_i\right)^2 + f_{ij}\left(y - y_j\right)^2 \tag{3}$$

where i = *1......N, j =1...M*

The coefficients a_{ij}, b_{ij}, c_{ij}, d_{ij}, e_{ij}, f_{ij} are obtained by least squares fitting of points in the neighbourhood of (x_i, y_j). Finally, Gaussian and mean curvatures are calculated using second order derivatives as in Equation 4 and 5:

$$H(x, y) = \frac{\left(1 + f_y^2\right)f_{xx} - 2f_x f_y f_{xy} + \left(1 + f_x^2\right)f_{yy}}{2\left(1 + f_x^2 + f_y^2\right)^{3/2}} \tag{4}$$

$$K(x, y) = \frac{f_{xx}f_{xy} - f_{xy}^2}{\left(1 + f_x^2 + f_y^2\right)^2} \tag{5}$$

The results of the HK curvature detection (Bagchi et al, 2012b) shows that we have successfully detected the following key points as shown in Figure 5.

Now, only seven landmark points are proposed to be detected by HK curvatures namely:

1. Nose-tip, nose ridge and the point between nose-tip and nose ridge,
2. Inner and outer eye corners,
3. Mouth corners.
4. **3D Image Registration to Obtain the Neutral Face with Expression:** Mostly, in literature, the main aim of the registration algorithm is to find transformation matrices that will align all the data sets into a frontal pose. In the problem of 3D face recognition, three dimensional registration is an important issue. For 3D face which is oriented across any angle, for it to be correctly recognized, it has to be correctly registered. The method which has been used in this proposed work is, the algorithm takes as input a 3D face and returns the recorded images for poses from 0 to ± 90°.Now, the unregistered 3D range expression images (Stratou et al, 2011) across pose (Bagchi et al, 2013a; 2014a; 2014b) are given as input to the system and then registered (Bagchi et al, 2012a; 2013b) using either of the following two techniques:
    a. Finding out the angle of pose orientation (Bagchi et al, 2012b; 2012c; 2012d).
    b. Registration using extraction of vectors by Principal Component Analysis.

In (a), it is intended to find out by what angle a 3D face (Bagchi et al, 2012e; 2012f; 2014c) is actually oriented. Once the angle is found using some statistical methods, registration of the face can as well be done by the method. In (b), PCA vector extraction of the 3D faces has been proposed to be done, by extracting the vectors of 3D face. Next, registration of the 3D face is to be done based on the vector extraction. The above two proposals have actually been kept as part of our future work.

Figure 5. Feature points detected after HK classification

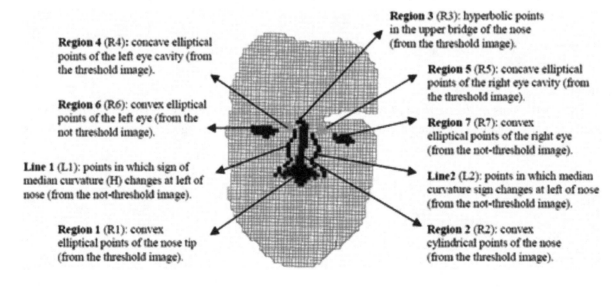

5. **Recognition of Expression Faces:** After registration of the faces as in step 4, the range images would be registered and would be neutral expression faces (Blanz & Vetter, 1999). The present work for the recognition of 3D expression faces (V. Blanz & T. Vetter, 1999) would be as follows:

    a. Fast and correct detection of facial expressions (Tsalakanidou & Malassiotis, 2010) is needed in image processing and computer applications. This problem is difficult specially when, there are subjects with unknown appearances and faces. To solve these problems, various registration methods have been designed based on local region descriptors and a non-rigid shape. So, after obtaining the registered expression faces as demonstrated in Step D, next building the neutral face from the expression faces (Benedikt et al, 2010) shall start. An expression face is shown in Figure 6.

    b. From the registered expression faces, as in Step (a), features need to be extracted for 3D expression analysis and recognition. From the initial work conducted in (Lee, 1992), it is proposed to extract the following features:

        i. It is being aimed to extract Normalized shape vector s_n, which refers to the vertex points for the x and y coordinates of the face shape and store them in a feature vector. These points are the vertex locations on the 3D image which has been registered. The similarity normalized shape s_n can be obtained by extracting a shape index of the registered 3D face image. An example of the normalized shape features is given in Figure 7.

Figure 8 shows the outline of the expression faces.

Figure 6. A diagram showing an expression face
(A.Ryan, J.F. Cohn, S.Lucey, J.Saragih, P.Lucey, F.D.L.Torre and A.Rossi et. al (2009)).

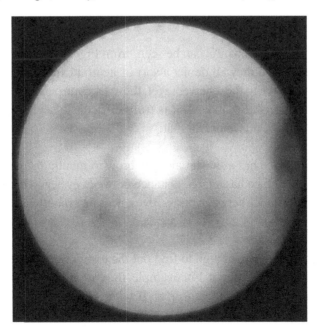

Figure 7. Diagrams showing normalized shape vectors for expression faces (A.M.S.Du et. al. 2012).

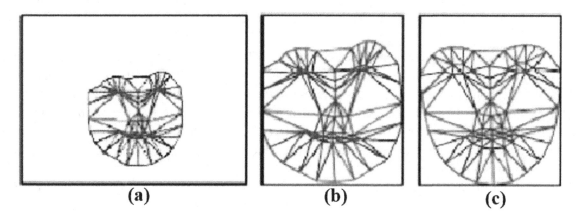

Figure 8. Diagrams showing outline of expression faces: Anger, Sad, Surprise, and Disgust

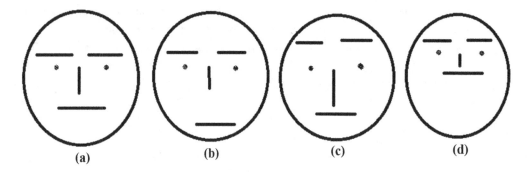

c.   Next is the analysis of expressions. As can be seen, from Figure 8, four faces and their expression figures are diagrammed, and they all depict a sort of neutral expression (i.e. the sender does not intend to convey any emotion to the receiver). Yet, these faces are said to interpret conveying anger, sadness, surprise and disgust. So, indeed, it is truly difficult to segregate as well as analyze the expressions. From Figure 8, it is apparent that:

i.   The angry looking face has a shorter average brow to mouth distance than a broad face.
ii.   The surprise looking face has a large distance between eyes and brows than a thinner face.
iii. There is a shorter distance between brows, eyes, nose and mouth in case of the disgust looking face.

But, only the above factors are not enough to find out the expressions which the faces depict. Some other feature detection technique is required. For example, the curvature of the mouth in joy or the opening of the eyes showing additional sclera in surprise. If taken into account, then, the surprise looking face in Figure 8 appears also to express sleepiness. Also, widely open eyes show surprise, which can only be achieved with changes in shape. Any face shape spaces include shape index, curvature based features. If expressions such as fear and disgust are taken into account, then it is quite clear that, these expressions are mostly based on shape changes thus making recognition less accurate.

d.   Henceforth, the six categories of emotions i.e. happy, sad, surprise, angry, fear and disgust could be analyzed by some statistical shape analysis of the 3D expression faces. So:

    i.   At first, the face and the shape of the primary facial components would be automatically detected. This includes manually separating each of the brows, eyes, nose, mouth and jaw line regions.

    ii.   The shape model would then be sampled with n equally spaced landmark points. The mean of all the points would then be computed.

    iii.   The 2D dimensional shape feature vector would then be given by the x and y coordinates of the n. Shape landmarks subtracted by the mean and divided by its norm. This would provide invariance to scaling and rotation both.

e.   Classification is the last step of the expression recognition system. A lot of work has been done in the field of expression recognition. Also, a lot of work has been done on classifiers for classifying expression faces. There are classifiers like static classifiers as the Naive Bayes (NB) Classification, Stochastic Structure Search and active classifiers like Single Hidden Markov Models (HMM) and Multi-Level Hidden Markov Models (ML-HMM) (Berretti et al, 2013; Akima, 1978). An experiment has been done with the use of Gaussian distribution and Cauchy distribution and it was found that using the Cauchy distribution gave better results (Akima, 1978) than Gaussian distribution.

Now, let's have a look at NB classifiers in more detail. NB classifiers are based on an assumption i.e. the independence assumption. Though, these are not true in many cases, but still, NB classifiers are known to work well. This is a violation of the assumption made about NB classifiers in recognizing 3D expression faces. A novel work proposed by Cohen (Cohen et al, 2004) was that, independence assumption problems exist because of the high degree of correlation between the display of emotions and facial motion (Akima, 1978). Sometimes later, the researchers found that the TAN classifiers were better than NB classifiers. They suggested, the use of NB classifier when data is insufficient because of the fact that, the TAN's learnt structure becomes unreliable when data is insufficient. The authors suggested the use of TAN when data is sufficiently available (Akima, 1978). Cohen et al. have also suggested the use of static classifiers and dynamic classifiers (Akima, 1978). Active classifiers are sensitive to change in the temporal patterns and the presence of expressions. So, they suggested the use of dynamic classifiers and static classifiers while performing person dependent tests. But differences do exist too, because static classifiers are easy to implement and train when compared to active classifiers. But, static classifiers provide poor performance when given expressive faces. Cohen found that NB and TAN algorithms gave an excellent performance with training data which is labeled. However, they performed poorly when unlabeled data was added to the training set. So, SSS algorithm (Berretti et al, 2013) which could outperform NB and TAN when presented with unlabeled data was discovered. In the case of dynamic classifiers, HMMs have traditionally been used to classify expressions. Cohen suggested an alternative use of HMMs by using it to segment long video sequences automatically into different expressions (Akima, 1978). Active appearances Modeling was used here. AAM uses a linear model, usually based on PCA. One limitation is that this model i.e. AAM is linear. So, the solution to this would be to implement Kernel PCA. In future, we propose to use the NB classifiers, decision tree classifier as well as the regression classifier. Table 1 depicts the various methodologies used in the field of 3D expression analysis.

Table 2 characterizes the various datasets used for 3D expression analysis in various existing work. The subjects which have been shown in Table 2 are the ones, which have been taken under uncontrolled environments.

In contrast to all the above methods discussed in Table 2 (Shan et al, 2009), we propose to register poses with expressions from 0 to 90°, which have not been much attempted till date. The database that, has been proposed here, to be collected as a part of our future work, would consist of 200 individuals, across pose and expressions, across pose and occlusions and across pose, occlusions and expressions.

FUTURE DIRECTIONS OF WORK

The following works have been proposed as part of the future work:

1. **An Approach to Register 3D Face Images Taking into Consideration Pose, Occlusions, and Expressions:** Face recognition has acquired substantiates importance in recent times because face is a non-touch biometric being one of the various methods used for identifying an individual. Some of the major factors affecting the face recognition system are pose, illumination, occlusion and expression. The factors which reduce the rate of face recognition are primarily illumination, expression, occlusion and viewing angle. Among the several factors that affect face recognition, illumination

Table 1. A comparative analysis of various 3D expression recognition techniques

Method	Advantages	Disadvantages
Non-rigid ICP	Able to handle variations in initial pose and occlusions well and gives dense correspondence	Vulnerable to noisy data.
FFDs	Fast and efficient to compute, and gives dense correspondence between meshes.	Vulnerable to errors in noisy data and variations in pose
Covariance Pyramids	Able to handle varying pose and provides correspondence between individuals.	Performed on a point-by-point basis, so difficult to scale to dense correspondence.
Harmonic maps	Robust to noise data does not suffer from local minima and gives dense correspondence	Fitting process is computationally expensive. Large differences between data and model may result in ambiguities in the correspondences.
Conformal maps	Able to handle occlusions and noisy data, and gives dense correspondence	Computationally expensive.
ASMs	Very fast fitting process and robustness to noise.	Cannot provide dense correspondence of mesh as restricted only to salient facial features
Morphable Models	Fitting method is robust to noise in the raw input and dense correspondence achieved	Variations allowed by model are restricted by range of data used to create it.
ADMs	Robust model fits that achieves good dense correspondence.	Fitting process is computationally expensive.
Present Method	A robust model that would first register images, detect expressions and finally recognize the images	Registration process is computationally expensive.

Table 2. Characteristics of various datasets for expression recognition techniques

Name	Size	Content	Landmarks
Chang et al. (1999)	6 adults	6 basic expressions	N/A
BU-3DFE (Yin et al, 2006)	100 adults	6 basic expressions at 4 intensity levels	83 facial points
BU-4DFE (Yin et al, 2008)	101 adults	6 basic expressions	83 facial points for every frame
Bosphorus (Savran et al, 2008)	105 adults are inc. actors	24 AUs, neutral, 6 basic expressions, occlusions	24 facial points
ICT-3DRFE (Stratou et al, 2011)	23 adults	15 expressions: 6 primary, 2 neutral, 2 eyebrow, 1 scrunched face, 4 eye gazes	N/A
(Tsalakanidou & Malassiotis, 2010)	52 adults	11 AUs and 6 basic expressions	N/A
Benedikt et al. (2010)	94 adults	Smiles and word utterance	N/A
(Blanz & Vetter, 1999)	200 adults	Neutral faces	N/A
GavabDB (Moreno & Sanchez, 2004)	61 adults	3 expressions: open/closed smiling and random	N/A
Present Dataset	200 adults (expected)	Across pose and expressions, across pose and occlusions and across pose, occlusion and expressions	N/A

and pose are the two major criterions. Next to pose and illumination, the major factors that affect the performance of face recognition are occlusion and expression. So, in order to overcome these issues, we propose to develop an efficient face recognition system based on occlusion, expression and pose as is demonstrated by the following steps:

a.   We first propose to register the 3D face oriented across any pose.

b.   GPCA classifier would then, be employed to remove occlusions.

c.   An expression detection and reconstruction mechanism would then be applied to the 3D range image which would consist of two different methods:

  i.   We propose to use a novel automatic feature selection method, which is based on the average entropy of class feature distributions, and apply it to complete pool of candidate features composed of normalized Euclidean distances between feature points in the 3D space of an expression face, after which some well known classifiers like ANN, LDA would be used for performance evaluation.

  ii.   Another method that we propose to use for expression analysis would be to compute the motion vector of the feature points on the expression face, perform geometric image-warping on the expression by extracting motion vectors of the feature values and, henceforth building the correspondence between the source and target face 3D image grids. Next, VTC (Vertex to coordinate) based expression mapping will be carried out to compute the pixel's luminance values in the warped target image. The variations in surface appearance across different facial expressions are mainly caused by local lighting changes due to skin deformation, e.g. in the vicinity of wrinkles. To produce the correct face shape and the right surface colors, we propose to combine the VTC-based deformation system with a geometric image warping approach. While the warping process generates the exact shape of the target face in the novel expression, VTC-based deformation system is used to correctly reproduce the changed surface appearance.

2. **An Approach to Register Images in the Presence of Occlusions and Expressions:** The uncontrolled conditions of real world biometric applications like expressions and occlusions detriments facial recognition. Uncontrolled acquisition of data from uncooperative subjects sometimes may result in 3D faces with significant pose variations such pose variations can cause occlusions which result in missing data. We propose to solve the problem of the automatic face expression using a unique combination of occlusions and expressions. We propose to solve this problem by the following approaches:

    a. At first, we propose to remove occlusions from the 3D range images using Gappy PCA
    b. Next, expression would be analyzed by an expression analyzer. We propose to extract features from the statistical shapes representation of facial expressions which are based on 3D face matching using a statistical shape model. After extracting the shape space vector, the shape model, which controls the change of form, is finally extracted as the significant feature for analysis of facial expressions. This feature models the high dimensional shape feature variations in the training data set. To extract the features the statistical model are to be constructed with the available dense point correspondences, and this is followed by the model fitting process, which would iteratively match the shapes of the new-built faces models to the input faces.

CONCLUSION

In real world, occlusions, expressions and pose affect facial recognition rate. Amongst some of these, the factors which affect 3D face recognition is pose, because when a person is oriented across extreme poses, maximum part of his face is unavailable. In a similar manner, expressions also, lower the recognition rate of individuals.

Normally, it is the nature of human beings that, we do not seem to recognize people in case of extreme expressions. Even under favorable conditions, but with extreme expressions, we do not seem to recognize people with expressions. It is a common phenomenon that, human beings are robust enough to detect surprise and joy from face images of people, regardless of the image conditions or resolution. But, we are not as good at recognizing anger and sadness and are worst at fear and disgust. Therefore, we believe that in this work, we seem to have addressed this issue. The problem in recognizing faces even aggravates when facial pose comes into consideration.

Also, we propose to develop a 3D dynamic facial expression database. So, in this work, we have also presented, an automated facial recognition approach, to analyze facial movements. Also, the subjects both exhibit pose as well as facial expressions. So, after registration of the subjects, the analysis will be made to detect and recognize the subjects in the presence of facial expressions.

ACKNOWLEDGMENT

Authors are thankful to a grant supported by DeitY, MCIT, Govt. of India, at Department of Computer Science and Engineering, Jadavpur University, India for providing necessary infrastructure to conduct experiments relating to this work.

REFERENCES

Akima, H. (1978). *A method of bivariate interpolation and smooth surface fitting for values given at irregularly distributed points*. ACM, TOMS.

Alyuz, N., Gokberk, B., &Akarun, L. (2012). *Adaptive Registration for Occlusion Robust 3D Face Recognition*. BeFIT'12 Workshop.

Bagchi, P., Bhattacharjee, D., Nasipuri, M., & Basu, D. K. (2012). A novel approach for nose-tip detection on 3D face images across pose. *International Journal of Computational Intelligence and Informatics, 2*(1).

Bagchi, P., Bhattacharjee, D., & Nasipuri, M. (2013). A Method for Nose-tip based 3D face registration using Maximum Intensity algorithm. *International Conference of Computation and Communication Advancement*. JIS College of Engineering.

Bagchi, P., Bhattacharjee, D., & Nasipuri, M. (2014, July 4). Robust 3D face recognition in presence of pose and partial occlusions or missing parts. *International Journal of Foundations of Computer Science & Technology, 4*(4), 21–35. doi:10.5121/ijfcst.2014.4402

Bagchi, P., Bhattacharjee, D., & Nasipuri, M. (2014). 3D Face Recognition across pose extremities. *2nd International Conference on Advanced Computing, Networking, and Informatics (ICACNI-2014)*.

Bagchi, P., Bhattacharjee, D., Nasipuri, M., & Basu, D. K. (2012). *A Novel approach to nose-tip and eye-corners detection using H-K Curvature Analysis in case of 3D images. In Proc of EAIT*. ISI Kolkata.

Bagchi, P., Bhattacharjee, D., Nasipuri, M., & Basu, D. K. (2012). A Novel approach in detecting pose orientation of a 3D face required for face registration. In *Proc of 47th Annual National Convention of CSI & 1st International Conference on Intelligent Infrastructure*. CSI Kolkata Chapter, Science City, Kolkata.

Bagchi, P., Bhattacharjee, D., Nasipuri, M., & Basu, D. K. (2012).A comparative Analysis of intensity based rotation invariant 3D facial landmarking system from 3D meshes. *Intl. conference on Multimedia processing, Communication and Computing Applications*. PES institute of Technology.

Bagchi, P., Bhattacharjee, D., Nasipuri, M., & Basu, D. K. (2012). A novel approach for registration of 3D face images. In *Proc of international Conference on Advances in Engineering, Science and Management (ICAESM)*. E.G.S. Pillay Engineering College.

Bagchi, P., Bhattacharjee, D., Nasipuri, M., & Basu, D. K. (2012). A novel approach for nose tip detection using smoothing by weighted median filtering applied to 3D face images in variant poses. In *Proc. of International Conference on Pattern Registration, Informatics and Medical Engineering*. Periyar University. doi:10.1109/ICPRIME.2012.6208357

Bagchi, P., Bhattacharjee, D., Nasipuri, M., & Basu, D. K. (2013). Detection of pose orientation across single and multiple axes in case of 3D face images. *CSI Journal of Computing, 1*(1-2).

Bagchi, P., Bhattacharjee, D., Nasipuri, M., & Basu, D. K. (2014). *Registration of Three Dimensional Human Face Images across Pose and their applications in Digital Forensic*. Computational Intelligence in Digital Forensics. doi:10.1007/978-3-319-05885-6_14

Benedikt, L., Cosker, D., Rosin, P., & Marshall, D. (2010). Assessing the uniqueness and permanence of facial actions for use in biometric applications. *IEEE Transactions on Systems, Manand Cybernetics, part A. Systems and Humans, 40*(3), 449–460. doi:10.1109/TSMCA.2010.2041656

Berretti, S., Bimbo, A. D., & Pala, P. (2013). Sparse Matching of Salient Facial Curves for Recognition of 3-D faces with missing parts. *IEEE Transactions on Information Forensics and Security, 8*(2), 374–389. doi:10.1109/TIFS.2012.2235833

Bettadapura,V., (2012). *Face Expression Recognition and Analysis: The State of the Art*. Tech Report.

Blanz, V., & Vetter, T. (1999). A morphable model for the synthesis of 3D faces. *26th Annual Conference on Computer Graphics and Interactive Techniques*. doi:10.1145/311535.311556

Cohen, I., Cozman, F. G., Sebe, N., Cirelo, M. C., & Huang, T. S. (2004). Semi-supervised Learning of Classifiers: Theory, Algorithms and Their Application to Human-Computer Interaction. *IEEE Transactions on Pattern Analysis and Machine Intelligence, 26*(12), 1553–1566. doi:10.1109/TPAMI.2004.127 PMID:15573817

Du, A. M. S. (2012). A Model of the Perception of Facial Expressions of Emotion by Humans: Research Overview and Perspectives. *Journal of Machine Learning Research, 13*(May), 1589–1608. PMID:23950695

Grafsgaard, J. F., Wiggins, J. B., Boyer, K. E., Wiebe, E. N., & Lester, J. C. (2013). Automatically Recognizing Facial Expression. *Predicting Engagement and Frustration.Intl. Conference on Educational Data Mining*, Memphis, TN.

Kaur, M., Vashisht, R., & Neeru, N. (2010). Recognition of Facial Expressions with Principal Component Analysis and Singular Value Decomposition. *International Journal of Computers and Applications*, 9–12.

Lee, J. T. (1992). *Evaluation of algorithms for surface interpolation over triangular patch.Intl*. Conf on International Society for Photography and Remote Sensing.

Moreno, A., & Sanchez, A. (2004). *GavabDB: a 3D face database*. 2ndCOST275 Workshop on Biometricson the Internet, Vigo, Spain.

Ryan, A., Cohn, J. F., Lucey, S., Saragih, J., Lucey, P., Torre, F. D. L., & Rossi, A. (October 2009). *Automated Facial Expression Recognition System*. IEEE International Carnahan Conference on Security Technology, NCIS, Washington, DC. doi:10.1109/CCST.2009.5335546

Sandbach, G., Zafeiriou, S., Pantic, M., & Yin, L. (2012). Static and dynamic 3D facial expression recognition: A comprehensive survey. *Image and Vision Computing, 30*(10), 683–689. doi:10.1016/j.imavis.2012.06.005

Savran, A., Alyuz, N., Dibeklioglu, H., Celiktutan, O., Gokberk, B., Sankur, B., & Akarun, L. (2008), *Bosphorus database for 3D face analysis*. 1stWorkshop on Biometrics and Identity Management, Roskilde University, Denmark.

Shan, C., Gong, S., & McOwan, P. W. (2009). Facial expression recognition based on Local Binary Patterns A comprehensive study. *Image and Vision Computing, 27*(6), 803–816. doi:10.1016/j.imavis.2008.08.005

Stratou, G., Ghosh, A., Debevec, P., & Morency, L. P. (2011). *Effect of illumination on automatic expression recognition: a novel 3D relightable facial database. 9th International Conference on Automatic Face and Gesture Recognition*, Santa Barbara, CA. doi:10.1109/FG.2011.5771467

Tsalakanidou, F., & Malassiotis, S. (2010). Real-time 2D + 3D facial action and expression recognition. *Pattern Recognition, 43*(5), 1763–1775. doi:10.1016/j.patcog.2009.12.009

Yin, L., Chen, X., Sun, Y., Worm, T., & Reale, M. (2008). A high-resolution 3D dynamic facial expression database. *8th Intl Conf.on AutomaticFace and Gesture Recognition.*

Yin, L., Wei, X., Sun, Y., Wang, J., & Rosato, M. (2006). 3D facial expression database for facial behavior research. *7th Intl. Conference on Automatic Face and Gesture Recognition.*

Zhang, Z. (1999). Feature-Based Facial Expression Recognition: Sensitivity Analysis and Experiments with a Multi-Layer Perceptron. *International Journal of Pattern Recognition and Artificial Intelligence, 13*(6), 893–911. doi:10.1142/S0218001499000495

KEY TERMS AND DEFINITIONS

Bosphorus Database: The Bosphorus Database is a highly rich collection of database for recognizing individuals which has the occlusion, expression and facial pose. It has a collection of both 3D and 2D images of men and women both, and face images under adverse conditions, deformable face modeling, and 3D face reconstruction. This database is unique in three aspects. The first is rich collections of expressions (35 expressions per subject), the second is changes in head poses (13 yaw and pitch rotations) and the third is face occlusions (related to beard & moustache, hair, hand, eyeglasses).

Curvature Analysis: In order to extract features from 3D face image, the surface texture is required to be analyzed. For this, the most fruitful candidate is to extract the curvatures of 3D surfaces namely the Mean-Gaussian curvature. Normally all features can be extracted from the convex or concave regions of 3D face.

Range Image: It is an image which contains a set of depth values at each (x, y) pixel of an image.

Structured Light: Mostly 3D scanners use the technology of structured light. It is done by illuminating a scene with a perfectly deigned light pattern and with this the depth can be determined using a single image of the reflected light. The structured lights are usually of the form of horizontal and vertical lines, points or checkerboard patterns.

Surface Interpolation: Surface Interpolation over a triangulation maintains the continuity and smoothness of the surface because raw 3D image data is sometimes subjected to roughness. Hence, it has to be interpolated in order to make all the 3D data points maintain a smooth continuity amongst themselves. Normally, in case of three dimensional surfaces Trilinear interpolation is done in order to smooth the surface and maintain a perfect continuity.

Weighted Median Filter: Median filter is windowed filter usually 3X3 used to smooth 3D facial surfaces. The advantage of this smoothing technique over the other available filters is that, it's inherent smoothing effect. It frequently gives a smooth smoothening effect all around 3D facial surface. The weights to be assigned to a weighted median filter can be +1 or -1. When a weight value of +1 is assigned, the smoothening effect is positive i.e. it smooths the surface. On the other hand, when the weight value of -1 is assigned, then the weighted median filter under smoothen the 3D facial surface.

Chapter 15
Scalable Video Watermarking:
A Survey

Nilkanta Sahu
Indian Institute of Technology Guwahati, India

Arijit Sur
Indian Institute of Technology Guwahati, India

ABSTRACT

In recent times, enormous advancement in communication as well as hardware technologies makes the video communication very popular. With the increasing diversity among the end using media players and its associated network bandwidth, the requirement of video streams with respect to quality, resolution, frame rate becomes more heterogeneous. This increasing heterogeneity make the scalable adaptation of the video stream in the receiver end, a real problem. Scalable video coding (SVC) has been introduced as a countermeasure of this practical problem where the main video stream is designed in such a hierarchical fashion that a set of independent bit streams can be produced as per requirement of different end using devices. SVC becomes very popular in recent time and consequently, efficient and secure transmission of scalable video stream becomes a requirement. Watermarking is being considered as an efficient DRM tool for almost a decade. Although video watermarking is regarded as a well focused research domain, a very less attention has been paid on the scalable watermarking in recent times. In this book chapter, a comprehensive survey on the scalable video watermarking has been done. The main objective of this survey work is to analyse the robustness of the different existing video watermarking scheme against scalable video adaptation and try to define the research problems for the same. Firstly, few existing scalable image watermarking schemes are discussed to understand the advantages and limitations of the direct extension of such scheme for frame by frame video watermarking. Similarly few video watermarking and some recent scalable video watermarking are also narrated by specifying their pros and cons. Finally, a summary of this survey is presented by pointing out the possible countermeasure of the existing problems.

DOI: 10.4018/978-1-4666-8723-3.ch015

INTRODUCTION

The rapid growth in Internet technology and media communication started a new era of video broadcasting and transmission. In this new era, the heterogeneity among end using display devises increased considerably with respect to the display resolution, processing power, network bandwidth etc. Depending on their computation power, display size or storage capacity, these devices have varying requirements in terms of video quality, frame rate, resolution etc. It has been observed that achieving these scalable adaptation at the receiving side for a variety of end user devices is a bit complicated process. Scalable video transmission provides a viable solution to this problem by doing these scalable adaptation at the multimedia servers rather than in the receiving ends. A hypothetical scalable video transmission scenario is depicted in Figure 1.

The widespread and easy accesses to digital contents and possibility to make unlimited copy without loss of considerable fidelity/quality make the multimedia content distribution more prone to the digital piracy and hacking. Thus the ownership as well as video content authentication become an important part of the efficient and secure multimedia communication and pose challenging research problems especially when scalable media is concern. Encryption and cryptographic hashes are proposed to meet the solutions. But it is observed that the scalability property of the bit stream is lost (Stutz & Uhl, 2012)

Figure 1. Use of scalable video

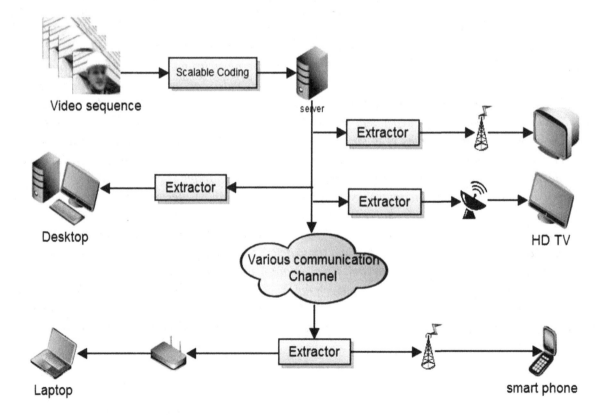

if the video bit stream is encrypted with conventional cryptographic ciphers like AES (National Institute of Standards and Technology, 2001). Some schemes used multiple keys for multiple layers, but it requires complicated key management to support application scenario.

Watermarking has been used (Cox, Kilian, Leighton, & Shamoon, 1997) (Hartley & Zisserman, 2003) (Kutter, Bhattacharjee, & Ebrahimi, 1999; Sun, He, Zhang, & Tian; Swanson, Kobayashi, & Tewfik, 1998) popularly in last two decades for copyright protection and content authentication of multimedia content. In this chapter a detailed survey of video watermarking concerning scalable video is given.

1. DIGITAL VIDEO WATERMARKING

Digital video watermarking is a technique which inserts a digital signature (number sequence, binary sequence, logo etc.) into the video stream which can be extracted or computed to authenticate the ownership of the media or the media itself. A fundamental video watermarking system is described Figure 2. As far as scalable video is concerned, basic (uncompressed domain, blind) watermarking scenario looks like Figure 3.

1.1 Evaluation Parameters

There are many parameters to evaluate the efficiency of a watermarking scheme. These parameters are often mutually conflicting. Few important parameters are described below:

Figure 2. Video watermarking

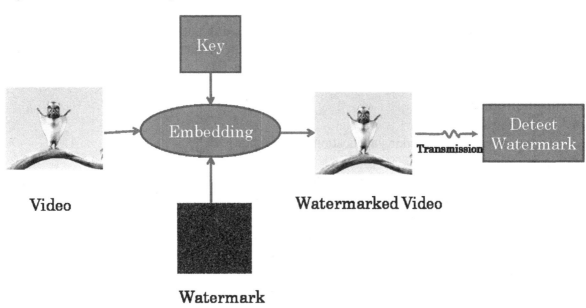

Figure 3. A basic scalable video watermarking scenario

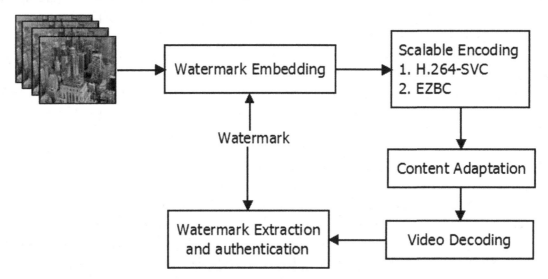

- **Robustness:** The robustness of a watermarking scheme is defined as how efficiently the watermarking scheme withstands against intentional and unintentional attacks.
- **Imperceptibility:** Imperceptibility implies that the watermark should not be perceptually noticeable in the watermarked video.
- **Payload:** Payload measures the number of bits or the size of the watermark which is embedded to the cover media.
- **Blindness:** A watermarking scheme is called blind if the original content is not required at the time of watermark extraction.
- **Bit Increase Rate:** The video bit rate may get increased due to embedding. An efficient watermarking scheme embeds watermark in such a way that bit increase rate (BIR) should not be increased considerably.

1.2 Applications

Some important video watermarking applications are as follows:

- **Ownership Authentication/Copyright Protection:** As video content is a valuable commodity ownership or copyright of the content must be protected. Watermarking resolves copyright issues of digital media by using copyright data as watermark information.
- **Video Authentication:** The content of digital media can easily be altered in such a way that it is very difficult to detect. Watermarking can be used to verify the authenticity of the content by identifying the possible video tampering or forgery.
- **Traitor Tracing:** Watermark can also be used to trace the source of pirated video content to stop the unauthorized content distribution.
- **Broadcast Monitoring:** Watermark can also be used to managing video broadcasting by putting unique watermark in each video clip and assessing broadcasts by an automated monitoring station.

- **Medical Application:** Names of the patients can be printed on the X-ray reports and MRI scans using techniques of visible watermarking. The medical reports play a very important role in the treatment offered to the patient. If there is a mix up in the reports of two patients this could lead to a disaster (Kutter et al., 1999).

2. SCALABLE VIDEO

A scalable video sequence is a single video bit stream having a hierarchical organization to provide different video sequence according to the specific requirement of the playing devices. In general, it consists of a mandatory bit-stream (base layer) along with a hierarchical set of optional bit stream (enhancement layers). A video bit stream of a particular resolution, quality, frame rate can be obtained as a composition of the mandatory stream with a specific subset of an optional streams by truncating the main bit stream in specific bit truncation points. The three most primitive scalable parameters are temporal scalability, resolution scalability and quality scalability as depicted in the Figure 4. There are several strategies to achieve scalability: layered coding which is followed by MPEG-4 and its predecessor, embedded coding used by 3D sub-band coder, such as MC-EZBC and hybrid coding used by MPEG4 FGS and H.264/ SVC(Meerwald & Uhl).

Scalable Video Coding (SVC) extension of the H.264/AVC was standardized by The Joint Video Team of the ITU-T VCEG and the ISO/IEC MPEG in 2007. SVC provides scalable bit streams having feature like graceful degradation in case transmission error to assure the seamless video transmission. To understand the challenges of scalable watermarking, it is important to understand the practical coding architecture of the existing recent standards. As an example, the scalable coding architecture of the H.264/SVC(Schafer, Schwarz, Marpe, Schierl, & Wiegand, 2005; Schwarz, Marpe, & Wiegand, 2007) is presented in this section.

The SVC extension is built on H.264 / MPEG-4-AVC and re-uses most of its innovative components. As a distinctive feature, SVC generates an H.264 / MPEG-4 AVC compliant, i.e., backwards-compatible base layer and one or several enhancement layer(s). The base layer bit stream corresponds to a minimum quality, frame rate, and resolution (e.g., QCIF video), and the enhancement layer bit streams represent the same video at gradually increased quality and/or increased resolution (e.g., CIF) and/or increased frame rate. Here a brief description of how different scalability is achieved in H.264 /SVC.

2.1 Temporal Scalability

Temporal scalability provides video content with different frame rates with the help of hierarchical prediction structure (Jung, Lee, & Lee, 2004) as illustrated in Figure 5. It is shown in Figure 5 that the hierarchically designed H.264/SVC GOP structure divides frames into distinct scalability layers (by jointly combining I, P and B frame types) (Unanue et al., 2011). In SVC, GOP is redefined as the set of pictures between two successive pictures of the temporal base layer together with the succeeding base layer picture in (Schwarz et al., 2007). Figure 5(a) shows a hierarchical prediction structure for dyadic enhancement layer for GOP size 4. It provides 3 independently decodable subsequences with full frame rate and 1/2 and 1/4 th of the full frame rate. But this is just a special case of temporal scalability. In

Figure 4. Different scalability: (a) temporal scalability (b) spatial scalability (c) quality scalability

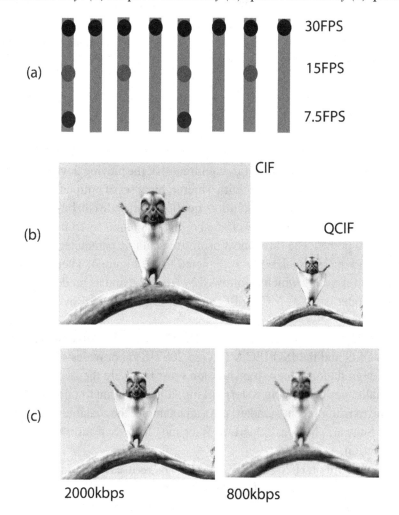

general concept of multiple reference picture from H.264 AVC can be always combined with hierarchical prediction structure. In that case a non-dyadic temporal scalability can be achieved as depicted in Figure 5(b) which provides 3 independently decodable subsequences.

2.2 Spatial Scalability

The spatial scalability provides the ability of representing video with different spatial resolutions. Spatial scalability is achieved by the conventional approach of multilayer coding where each layer corresponds to a specific spatial resolution. Each layer is encoded with the help of motion-compensated prediction and intra prediction. Moreover, an inter-layer prediction is also incorporated to make maximum use of the lower layer information. An enhancement layer is predicted from a layer with lower layer identifier. Three kind of inter layer predictions are used as follows,

Figure 5. Hierarchical prediction structure for enabling temporal scalability: (a) Hierarchical B-pictures (GOP size=4) (b) non-dyadic prediction (GOP size=9)
(Yan & Jiying).

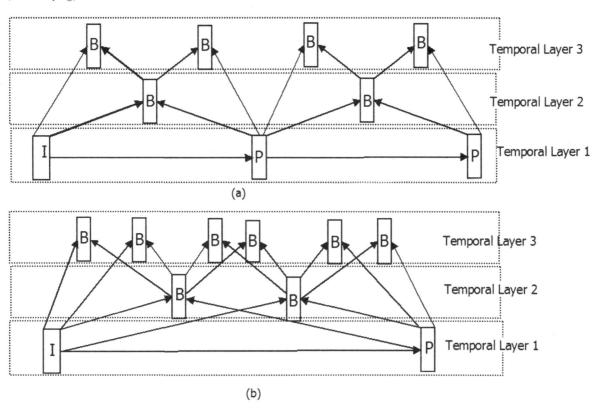

1.   Inter-Layer Motion Prediction.
2.   Inter-Layer Residual Prediction.
3.   Inter-Layer Intra Prediction.

Over all mechanism for spatial scalability for 2 spatial layer is depicted in Figure 6.

2.3 SNR / Quality Scalability

The SNR scalability (or quality scalability) arranges the bit stream in different layers in order to produce videos with distinct quality levels. In H.264/SVC, SNR scalability is implemented in the frequency domain (i.e. it is performed over the internal transform module). The quality scalability is implemented by adopting distinct quantization parameters for each layer. The H.264/SVC standard supports two distinct SNR scalability modes:

1.   **Coarse Grain Scalability (CGS):** CGS strategy can be regarded as a special case of spatial scalability when consecutive layers have the same resolution (Figure 7 (a)).
2.   **Medium Grain Scalability (MGS):** MGS uses more flexible prediction module to increase the efficiency (Figure 7 (b)).

Figure 6. Block diagram of a H.264/SVC encoder for two spatial layers
(Unanue et al., 2011).

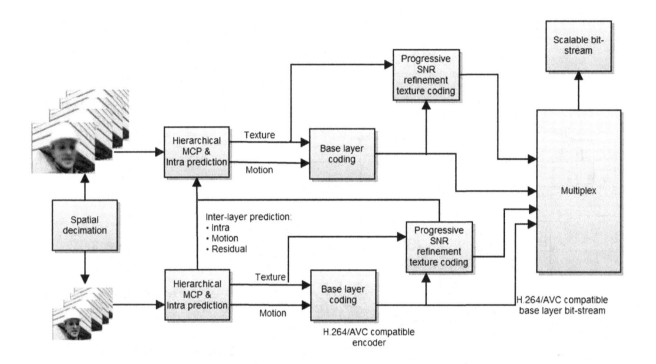

Figure 7. H.264/SVC SNR scalability granularity mode for a two-layer example
(Unanue et al., 2011).

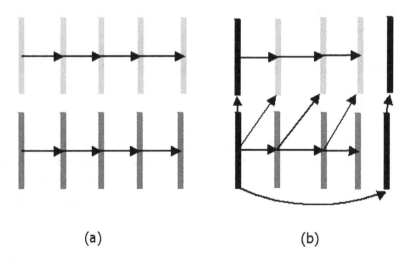

3. SCALABLE IMAGE WATERMARKING

It is observed in the literature that few video watermarking schemes are reported as a direct extension of the existing image watermarking scheme. More specifically, frame by frame video watermarking may be achieved by applying existing image watermarking scheme. Although, there exists few limitations of such extension, scalable image watermarking may be a good starting point to analyze the merits and demerits of state of the art scalable video watermarking.

3.1 Related Work

Piper et al. may be the first to explicitly propose a watermarking scheme for scalable coded image in (Piper, Safavi-Naini, & Mertins, 2004). They used different coefficient selection methods for the spread-spectrum embedding proposed in (Cox et al., 1997). Robustness of their scheme is evaluated against quality and resolution scalability. Later, Piper (Piper, Safavi-Naini, & Mertins, 2005) claimed that spatial resolution and quality scalable watermarking can be achieved by exploiting the characteristic of HVS. Seo et al. (Seo & Park) has proposed a scalable image watermarking scheme for protecting distant learning content and proposed a watermark embedding technique in wavelet based image coding.

Content-based watermarking schemes (Bas, Chassery, & Macq, 2002; Lee, Kim, & Lee, 2006) are generally proposed to resist the geometric attacks such as rotation, scaling, cropping etc. For example in (O'Ruanaidh & Pun, 1997; Radon, 2005), it has been shown that few transformation such as Fourier-Mellin, Radon are invariant to geometric attacks. In (Pereira & Pun, 2000), a reference pattern or template is embedded which can be used to synchronize the watermark during extraction whereas in (Sharma & Coumou, 2006), exhaustive search has been performed.

Feature point-based watermarking is one of the most promising approach because of its capability to handle different de-synchronization attacks such as spatial shifting, scaling, rotation etc. Kutter et al.(Kutter et al., 1999) argued that a watermark becomes more robust if the embedding is performed using these feature points as they can be viewed as the second-order information of the image.

Bas et al.(Bas et al., 2002) proposed a scheme where delaunay triangulation is computed on the set of feature points which are robust to geometric distortion. The water mark is then embedded into the resulting triangles and detection is done using the correlation properties on the different triangles. The main drawback of this method is that the extracted feature points from the original and distorted images may not be matched as the sets of triangles generated during watermark insertion and detection are different.

Scale Invariant Feature Transform (SIFT) (David G. Lowe, 2004) is an image descriptor developed by David Lowe. SIFT features have been used in many applications like Multi View Matching (Chen & Williams, 1993; Hartley & Zisserman, 2003), object recognition (D. G. Lowe, 1999), object classification (Bosch, Zisserman, & Muñoz, 2006; Mutch & Lowe, 2008), robotics (Saeedi, Lawrence, & Lowe, 2006) etc. It is also being used for robust image watermarking against geometric attacks (Jing, Gang, & Jiulong, 2009; Lee et al., 2006; Pham, Miyaki, Yamasaki, & Aizawa, 2007).

Miyaki et al.(Pham et al., 2007) proposed a RST invariant object based watermarking scheme where SIFT features are used for object matching. In the detection scheme, the object region is first detected by feature matching. The transformation parameters are then calculated, and the message is detected. Though the method produces quite promising results but it is a type of informed watermarking. The register file has to be shared between the sender and receiver which is a drawback. Kim et al.(Lee et al., 2006) inserted watermark into the circular patches generated by the SIFT. The detection ratio of the method varies from 60% to 90% depending upon the intensity of the attack. Under strong distortions due to attenuation and cropping, the additive watermarking method fails to survive for several images.

Jing et al.(Jing et al., 2009) used SIFT points to form a convex hull, which are then optimally triangulated. The watermark is then embedded into the circles centered around the centroid of each triangle. Here also the watermark fails to sustain when the image is scaled down considerably.

Priyatham et al. (Bollimpalli, Sahu, & Sur, 2014) proposed another SIFT based watermarking scheme where instead of embedding a message, message is generated by changing a patch intensity. Patch is selected by patch selection algorithm where they have chosen an object of suitable size. Changing the intensity of the patch generates new set of SIFT features which is registered as the watermark. As it uses SIFT feature itself as watermark instead of using it as a synchronization it is more robust than the other SIFT based scheme.

3.2 Problems with the Frame by Frame Watermarking

If these scalable image watermarking schemes are applied for scalable video to achieve resolution and quality adaptation by embedding watermark in every frame of the video sequence then following problems may arise:

- Frame by frame embedding may create flickering artifacts (Bhowmik & Abhayaratne, 2010)
- The embedded watermarks in each frame may be removed easily by a simple type I collusion attack if different watermark is inserted in each frame (Vinod & Bora, 2006) because the inter frame correlation in the close temporal neighborhood is generally very high.
- On the other hand if identical watermark is embedded in whole video sequence, it can be easily estimated using collusion attack of type II (Vinod & Bora, 2006).

4. SCALABLE VIDEO WATERMARKING

Although, general video watermarking has got a significant attention of the research community in the last decade, a very less attention has been paid to protect scalable video transmission. Lu (Lu, Safavi-Naini, Uehara, & Li) possibly the first characterized the scalable watermarking and argued that the watermark should be detected at every resolution and quality layer. Piper (Piper et al., 2005) mentioned another property to scalable watermarking scheme, named graceful improvement which means that with the improvement of video quality (with addition of enhancement layer) the watermark detection should become more and more reliable.

4.1 Challenges of Scalable Watermarking

The main problem of scalable watermarking is that the bit-budget for a scalable sub-stream is not known a-priory as main bit stream can be truncated at any spatio-temporal bit truncation point. In scalable watermark, it is required to protect base layer as well as enhancement layers which generally causes substantial bit increase for the watermarked video. Keeping low bit increase rate (BIR) for scalable video watermarking is a real challenging task (Meerwald & Uhl, 2010; C.-C. Wang, Lin, Yi, & Chen, 2006). As different scalable parameters like resolution, frame rate, quality etc. are different in nature, assuring combined watermarking security to all of them sometimes requires conflicting demands. Thus achieving combined scalable watermarking is a difficult task (Piper et al., 2005). It is also observed that the statistical distribution of the transform domain coefficients of the base layer is substantially different than that of enhancement layer. It makes the multi-channel detection more complicated for incremental detection performance. Finally, watermarking zone selection becomes challenging in presence of inter layer prediction structure of the scalable coding.

4.2 Existing Work

In the recent literature of the scalable video watermarking, a considerable number of works have been reported until recently. For example, Wang et al. (Wang, Lin, Yi, & Chen) have proposed a blind watermarking scheme for MPEG-4 where the watermark is embedded into FGS bit planes for authentication of enhancement layer. One bit is embedded by forcing the number of non-zero bits per bit plane to even or odd depending on the watermark. In another scheme, Chang et al. have combined encryption and watermarking to realize layered access control to a temporally scalable M-JPEG stream. They have encrypted enhancement layer and embedded the key needed to decrypt it in the base layer. So that, the key receives stronger error-protection than the content.

In schemes (Essaouabi & Ibnelhaj; yu, Ying, & ke, 2004), 3D wavelet coefficients are used for watermark embedding. Since the temporal motion is not considered in these schemes, they may suffer from the flickering artifact due to embedding and may produces visually degraded watermarked video(Bhowmik & Abhayaratne, 2010).

In (Jung et al., 2004), Jung et al. proposed a rotation scaling and translation (RST) invariant watermarking scheme where the content adaptive watermark signal is embedded in the Discrete Fourier Transform (DFT) domain of the video stream. Authors have used log polar projection to detect the watermark. The problem of extending this work for scalable video is that it may not withstand quality and temporal adaptation although it achieve desired robustness if only resolution scaling is considered. Moreover, visual artifacts may be generated due to logarithmic mapping during watermark embedding.

A RADON transformation based RST invariant watermarking scheme (Liu & Zhao, 2008) has been proposed by Liu and Zhao. In this scheme, authors have used temporal DFT and embedded the watermark using RADON transformation. Objectionable visual artifacts in the watermarked video may be caused due to embedding by altering the RADON coefficients. Since the embedded watermark in the base layer is same as in the different enhancement layers, the cross-layer collusion attack (Jung et al., 2004; Vinod & Bora, 2006) may be mounted over the watermarked video. Moreover, temporal motion may degrade the embedded watermark.

In another recent scheme, Y. Wang and A. Pearmain (Y. Wang & Pearmain, 2006) have proposed a blind scale-invariant watermarking scheme for MPEG-2. In this scheme, authors embeds the watermark in single frame (middle frame) of the GOP (Group of Picture) of 3 frames. It is observed that the scheme is vulnerable against type I collusion attack (Jung et al., 2004; Vinod & Bora, 2006) as watermark can easily be estimated by comparing watermarked frame and the two adjacent non-watermarked frame. The scheme may also be vulnerable against frame dropping attack as the watermark for a entire GOP has been lost if the single watermarked frame is dropped or replaced. The temporal artifacts due to watermark embedding may caused as the scheme is not using motion compensated embedding. Moreover, since the watermark can only be extracted from the base layer, base layer computation is always required for the watermark extraction from any of the enhancement layers.

However, these algorithms were not designed for SVC (Schwarz et al., 2007), and they did not introduced the concept of scaling detection into the scalable watermark model. In last few year, after standardization of SVC in 2007, very few works have been published in literature on watermarking of scalable video content. Some significant works are described here.

4.3 Watermarking Using MCTF

As we have seen that frame by frame watermarking is vulnerable to collusion attack and it creates flickering artifacts in watermarked video. To solve this problem, temporal direction has been exploited by many researchers. MCTF (Choi & Woods, 1999; Flierl & Girod, 2004; Verdicchio et al., 2004) has been used in many application to remove the temporal correlation between frames.

4.3.1 MCTF

MCTF is as its name suggests, a low pass filtering of the input frames along the temporal direction. It is used to remove temporal correlation within the sequence (Verdicchio et al., 2004). A basic MCTF model is depicted in Figure 8. To achieve efficient de-correlation, the input frames need to be aligned along the motion trajectories.

Every odd frame is predicted from even frames by this prediction (P) operator. The output of P is then subtracted from the current frame to obtain the residual error frame (high-pass temporal frame) or H-frame. This information is also added back to the reference frame by the U (Update) operator, which performs an additional MC stage using the reversed motion field, to generate a set of L-frames (or low-pass temporal frames).

Figure 8. Motion compensated temporal filtering
(Flierl & Girod, 2004).

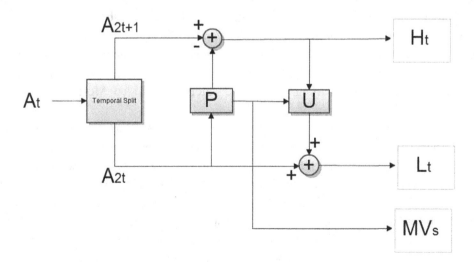

4.3.2 Video Watermarking Using Motion Compensated 2D+t+2D Filtering

Bhowmik et al. (Bhowmik & Abhayaratne, 2010) proposed a motion compensated temporal-spatial sub-band decomposition scheme, based on the MMCTF for video watermarking. They used a 2D+t+2D (Figure 9) decomposition framework, where they decomposed the video sequence into different temporal and spatial levels and choose best subband for embedding. The temporal decomposition is done using Modified MCTF. The embedding distortion performance (evaluated using MSE) and flicker difference metric shows superior performance the proposed sub-band decomposition also provides low complexity as MCTF (Figure 8) is performed only on those sub-bands where the watermark is embedded.

Watermark Embedding

In this paper non-blind watermarking is employed. Additive watermarking is chosen for non-blind case, coefficients are increased or decreased according to the Equation 1. Block diagram of embedding technique is shown in Figure 10.

$$C'_{s,t}[m,n] = C_{s,t}[m,n] + \alpha C_{s,t}[m,n]W \tag{1}$$

Figure 9. Example of a 2D+T+2D decomposition
(Bhowmik & Abhayaratne, 2010).

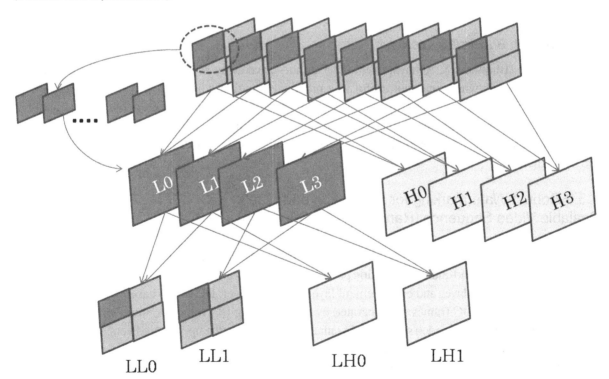

Figure 10. Block diagram for watermark embedding
(Bhowmik & Abhayaratne, 2010).

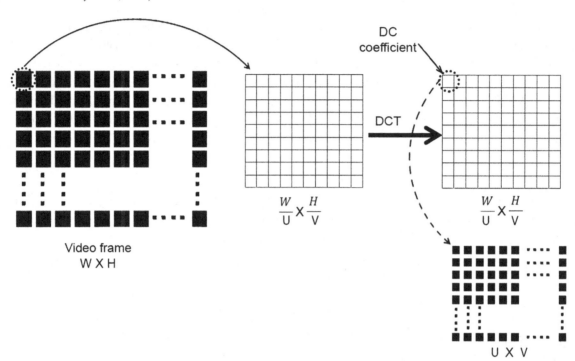

Problems with Bhowmik's Approach

In this scheme (Bhowmik & Abhayaratne, 2010) authors have evaluated the scheme against only quality scalability attack which may not useful in a practical situation where video will be scaled in any dimension according to the requirement. The watermarking evaluation parameters like Visual quality, Bit Increase Rate are not evaluated for watermarked video. Authors haven't considered any zone selection or coefficient selection method for the watermark embedding. Thus there is a scope for improving the said scheme.

4.3.3 Robust Watermarking for Resolution and Quality Scalable Video Sequence (Rana, Sahu, & Sur, 2014)

Recently Rana et al. (Rana et al., 2014) have proposed a robust watermarking scheme which can withstand spatial (i.e. resolution) and quality adaptation process for scalable video coding. In this scheme, watermark is inserted both in base layer and enhancement layers. In base layer, DC frame based watermarking has been employed where DC frames are generated by accumulating DC values of non-overlapping blocks for every frame in the input video sequence. In enhancement layers, the up-sampled version of the watermark signal is inserted in the corresponding residual frames which are generated in accordance with the DC frame. Before embedding, Discrete Cosine Transform (DCT) based temporal filtering is applied on DC as well as residual frame sequence and the respective watermark is embedded in low pass version of

Figure 11. Block diagram for watermark extraction (Bhowmik & Abhayaratne, 2010).

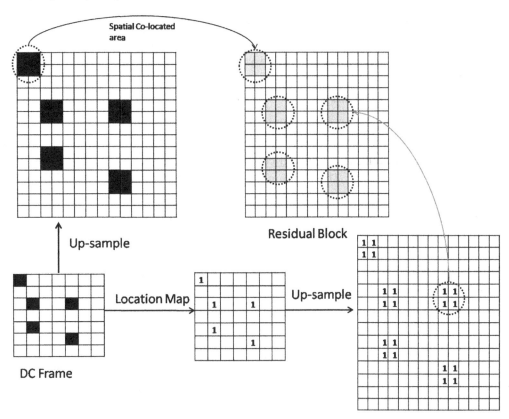

the DC frame or residual error frame. This embedding process not only resist temporal flickering due to temporal motion but helps to achieve a graceful improvement of the extracted watermark signal in successive enhancement layers. To maintain the spatial coherency of watermark embedding between every successive layers, a location map is used which helps in the spatial synchronization for the watermark embedding between base layer and successive enhancement layers.

In this work, authors have used Motion Compensated DCT based Temporal Filtering (MCDCT-TF) on the DC frames and selected low pass frames are used for embedding. Embedding in low pass frame spreads the watermark into all frames so that frame dropping attack can be prevented. Motion coherent embedding is employed to reduce the temporal flickering. During MCDCT-TF only temporally connected pixels are considered for watermark embedding.

DC Frame

In this scheme, authors have embedded the watermark in DC frame for base layer. They claimed that embedding in DC frames helps the spreading of watermark signal during the generation of the enhancement layer frames. In this scheme, a fixed size DC frame has been used which is partitioned into non overlapping blocks. The block size is determined based on the size of full resolution video frame size.

The DC frame formation in this scheme is illustrated in the Figure 12 which is taken from the paper itself (Rana et al., 2014) . For the fixed DC frame size ($U \times V$), the video frame ($W \times H$) is divided into ($\frac{W}{U} \times \frac{W}{V}$)non-overlapping blocks. All DC coefficients of such ($\frac{W}{U} \times \frac{W}{V}$) non-overlapping blocks after 2D block DCT are accumulated to form the respective DC frame.

Graceful Improvement of Watermark

In this scheme, authors have added a corresponding up-sampled version of the base layer watermark separately to the residual components of each enhancement layer. They have used a location map (M) in the proposed scheme to maintain the spatial coherency between base layer embedding and any of the enhancement layers embedding. The location map (M) based technique for achieving said spatial coherency is depicted in Figure 13 as described in the paper (Rana et al., 2014). The Figure 3 illustrates that the location map (M) as a binary matrix which is generated during the DC frame embedding. To get the required location map (M^U) for a particular enhancement layer, authors have up-sampled the location map (M) according to the resolution ratio of the base layer (DC frame) and the corresponding enhancement layer. According to the authors, this process helps to achieve the spatial synchronization of the embedding locations between DC frame and any of the enhancement layer residual error frames. Authors have claimed that maintaining spatial synchronization between base layer and enhancement layer not only reduces the chance of watermark destruction due to cross layer embedding but as a consequence, also helps to get improved watermark at extraction in successive enhancement layer. Thus the scheme proposed in (Rana et al., 2014) achieves the graceful improvement of the extracted watermark in subsequent enhancement layers.

Figure 12. Block DCT of video frame Ref
(Rana et al., 2014).

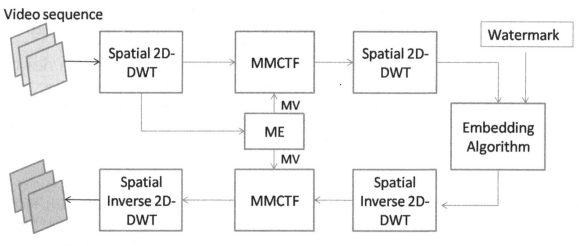

Figure 13. Location map based technique for spatial coherency (Rana et al., 2014).

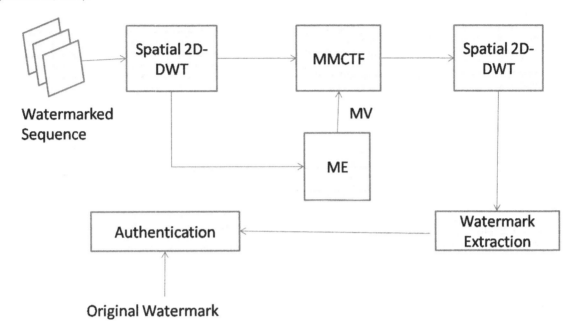

Watermark Zone Selection

Authors have partitioned the base layer frame (DC frame) as well as the residual frame sequence into non overlapping set of 3 residual frames in temporal direction. MCDCT-TF is done on every set of DC frames as well as residual frames. Then they have chosen corresponding low pass versions of base and residual layer for the watermark embedding.

They have applied some more restriction to control the visual degradation of the watermarked video. They have assumed that Ct1, Ct2, Ct3 are coefficients of low pass frames (base or residual), used for embedding one watermark bit. It may sometime happen that the difference of Ct2 with average of Ct1 and Ct3 (i.e. $|C t2 - (C t1 + C t3)/2|$) is relatively high. For this case, their embedding scheme adds relatively higher noise which may cause flickering artifacts. As a countermeasure authors have incorporated an adaptive threshold (Visual Quality Threshold Vth) to select the suitable coefficients to embed watermark such that embedding noise will be under an acceptable range. The value of the threshold is $(C t1 + C t3) *2\alpha$, where α is the robustness threshold which is used increase the embedding strength of the watermark to make it robust enough to prevent content adaptation attack. A location map (M) is derived during the time of base layer (DC frame) embedding which is used to select embedding coefficients during any enhancement layer embedding (Figure 13).

Base Layer Embedding

In (Rana et al., 2014), authors embeds the watermark into the motion compensated low pass DC frames in base layer. They have partitioned all selected coefficient into set of 3 consecutive coefficients ($Ct1$, $Ct2$, $Ct3$) for embedding watermark using Equation 2.

$$Ct_2' = \frac{Ct_1 + Ct_3}{2} + \left|\frac{Ct_1 + Ct_3}{2}\right| \times \alpha \times W_i \tag{2}$$

where $W_i \in (0, 1)$ is the watermark bit and α is the robustness threshold (watermarking strength) Ct'2 is the watermarked coefficient corresponding to Ct2 . The location map (M) is used to save the embedding location. As described in the previous section, the up-sampled version of the location map (M U) is used to maintain the spatial synchronization between base layer and the enhancement layer embedding.

Enhancement Layer Embedding

Before embedding in the residual layer authors have taken the Base layer location map (*M*) and up-sampled it according to the size of residual layer to detect the watermark regions in the low pass temporal residual layer.

Same as base layer embedding the watermarking region of the low pass residual frame is again partitioned into a non-overlapping set of 3 consecutive coefficients and embed the watermark using same equation. Over all embedding scheme is depicted in Figure 14.

Extraction Scheme

Watermark extraction for spatial scalable video is done from base layer as well as from each residual layer separately. The enhancement layer watermark is derived by using the base and enhancement layer

Figure 14. Watermark embedding model
(Rana et al., 2014).

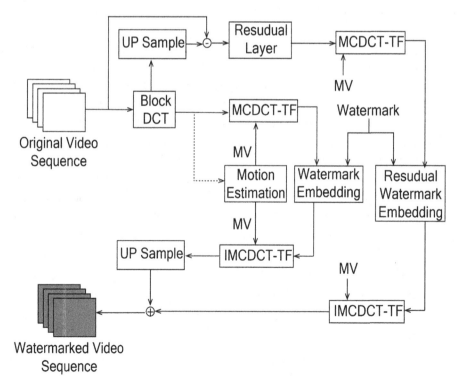

watermark. During extraction, first DC frame is formulated and then MCDCT -TF is done on those DC frames as well as the residual frames. Watermark extracted from base layer is added to the watermark extracted from the residual frames which causes the graceful improvement. Extraction rule used in the scheme is given in Equation 3.

$$
\left.\begin{array}{ll}
W'_{bi} = 0 & if\ Ct'_2 \leq \dfrac{Ct'_1 + Ct'_3}{2} \\[3mm]
W'_{bi} = 1 & if\ Ct'_2 > \dfrac{Ct'_1 + Ct'_3}{2}
\end{array}\right\}
\tag{3}
$$

4.4 Watermarking in Compressed Domain

Meerwald et al. (Meerwald & Uhl, 2010) proposed a compressed domain watermarking scheme for h.264/SVC. They extended a framework for robust watermarking of H.264-encoded video proposed by Noorkami et al. (Noorkami & Mersereau, 2007) to scalable video coding (SVC). Main focus was on spatial scalability. First they have shown that the watermark embedding in the base resolution layer of the video is insufficient to protect the decoded video of higher resolution. Watermark embedded in the base layer gets faded in higher resolution and bit rate of the enhancement layer gets increased. To solve this problem they up sampled the base layer watermark signal and embedded in the enhancement layer.

At first, the watermark is embedded in the base layer stream using the Equation 4 proposed in (Noorkami & Mersereau, 2007). Where $W_{i,j,k}$ is watermark signal, $S_{i,j,k}$ is location matrix, .. is base layer residual block.

$$
R_{i,j,k} = R_{i,j,k} + S_{i,j,k} W_{i,j,k}
\tag{4}
$$

Then up-sampled watermark signal is embedded in the enhance layer residual block R'^{E}_k using Equation 5.

$$
R''^{E}_k = R'^{E}_k + W^{E}_k
\tag{5}
$$

where W^{E}_k is up-sampled watermark and R'^{E}_k is given by Equation 6.

$$
R'^{E}_k = Q\left(T\left(o^{E}_k - H\left(o'^{B}_k\right)\right)\right)
\tag{6}
$$

Over all embedding scheme is depicted in Figure 15.

Figure 15. Block diagram of Meerwald's (Meerwald & Uhl, 2010) watermark embedding method for two spatial layers

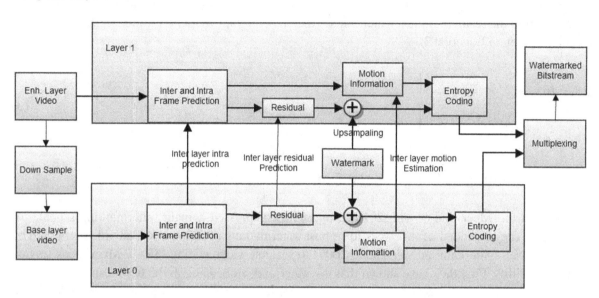

4.4.1 Drawbacks of the Approach

The main drawback of the scheme is that the base layer video is required for watermark extraction. So it does not obey the definition given in (Piper et al., 2004). Moreover, the bit rate of the enhancement layer increases significantly. It is also observed that the scheme becomes too complex for more than one enhancement layers.

4.5 Summary and Future Research

In overall study, it can be said that there is enough scope of doing research in scalable video watermarking. Firstly, there are very few attempts that have been made for resolution scalable watermarking especially when resolution are highly altered or aspect ratio has been changed. Although few works are reported to handle quality adaptation, but effect of these schemes on visual quality, bit increase rate etc. has not been explored properly. Finally, there is almost no work that has been presented regarding the combined scalable watermarking. As it is observed that watermarking for combined scalability required mutually conflicting demands, a careful investigation is required to resolve these issues.

REFERENCES

Bas, P., Chassery, J. M., & Macq, B. (2002). Geometrically invariant watermarking using feature points. *Image Processing, IEEE Transactions on, 11*(9), 1014-1028.

Bhowmik, D., & Abhayaratne, C. (2010). *Video watermarking using motion compensated 2D+t+2D filtering*. Paper presented at the 12th ACM workshop on Multimedia and security. doi:10.1145/1854229.1854254

Bollimpalli, P., Sahu, N., & Sur, A. (2014, sept). *SIFT Based Robust Image Watermarking Resistant To Resolution Scaling.* Paper presented at the Image Processing (ICIP), 2014 21st IEEE International Conference on. doi:10.1109/ICIP.2014.7026114

Bosch, A., Zisserman, A., & Muñoz, X. (2006). Scene Classification Via pLSA. In A. Leonardis, H. Bischof, & A. Pinz (Eds.), *Computer Vision? ECCV 2006* (Vol. 3954, pp. 517–530). Springer Berlin Heidelberg. doi:10.1007/11744085_40

Chen, S. E., & Williams, L. (1993). *View interpolation for image synthesis.* Paper presented at the 20th annual conference on Computer graphics and interactive techniques.

Choi, S.-J., & Woods, J. W. (1999). Motion-compensated 3-D subband coding of video. *Image Processing, IEEE Transactions on, 8*(2), 155-167.

Cox, I. J., Kilian, J., Leighton, F. T., & Shamoon, T. (1997). Secure spread spectrum watermarking for multimedia. *IEEE Transactions on Image Processing, 6*(12), 1673–1687. doi:10.1109/83.650120 PMID:18285237

Essaouabi, A., & Ibnelhaj, E. (2009). *A 3D wavelet-based method for digital video watermarking.* Paper presented at the Networked Digital Technologies, 2009. NDT '09. First International Conference on. doi:10.1109/NDT.2009.5272116

Flierl, M., & Girod, B. (2004). Video coding with motion-compensated lifted wavelet transforms. *Signal Processing Image Communication, 19*(7), 561–575. doi:10.1016/j.image.2004.05.002

Hartley, R., & Zisserman, A. (2003). *Multiple View Geometry in Computer Vision.* Cambridge University Press.

Jing, L., Gang, L., & Jiulong, Z. (2009). *Robust image watermarking based on SIFT feature and optimal triangulation.* Paper presented at the Information Technology and Applications, 2009. IFITA'09. International Forum on. doi:10.1109/IFITA.2009.110

Jung, H.-S., Lee, Y.-Y., & Lee, S. U. (2004). RST-resilient video watermarking using scene-based feature extraction. *EURASIP Journal on Applied Signal Processing, 2004*(14), 2113–2131. doi:10.1155/S1110865704405046

Kutter, M., Bhattacharjee, S. K., & Ebrahimi, T. (1999). *Towards second generation watermarking schemes.* Paper presented at the Image Processing. doi:10.1109/ICIP.1999.821622

Lee, H.-Y., Kim, H., & Lee, H.-K. (2006). Robust image watermarking using local invariant features. *Optical Engineering, 45*(3).

Liu, Y., & Zhao, J. (2008). *RST invariant video watermarking based on 1D DFT and Radon transform.* Paper presented at the Visual Information Engineering, 2008. VIE 2008. 5th International Conference on.

Lowe, D. G. (1999). *Object recognition from local scale-invariant features.* Paper presented at the Computer Vision. doi:10.1109/ICCV.1999.790410

Lowe, D. G. (2004). Distinctive Image Features from Scale-Invariant Keypoints. *International Journal of Computer Vision, 60*(2), 91–110. doi:10.1023/B:VISI.0000029664.99615.94

Lu, W., Safavi-Naini, R., Uehara, T., & Li, W. (2004). *A scalable and oblivious digital watermarking for images.* Paper presented at the Signal Processing.

Meerwald, P., & Uhl, A. (2008). *Toward robust watermarking of scalable video.* Paper presented at the SPIE, Security, Forensics, Steganography, and Watermarking of Multimedia Contents X.

Meerwald, P., & Uhl, A. (2010). *Robust Watermarking of H.264-Encoded Video: Extension to SVC.* Paper presented at the 2010 Sixth International Conference on Intelligent Information Hiding and Multimedia Signal Processing. doi:10.1109/IIHMSP.2010.28

Mutch, J., & Lowe, D. G. (2008). Object Class Recognition and Localization Using Sparse Features with Limited Receptive Fields. *International Journal of Computer Vision, 80*(1), 45–57. doi:10.1007/s11263-007-0118-0

National Institute of Standards and Technology. (2001). *Advanced Encryption Standard (AES) FIPS-197.*

Noorkami, M., & Mersereau, R. M. (2007). A Framework for Robust Watermarking of H.264-Encoded Video With Controllable Detection Performance. *Information Forensics and Security. IEEE Transactions on, 2*(1), 14–23.

O'Ruanaidh, J. J. K., & Pun, T. (1997). *Rotation, scale and translation invariant digital image watermarking.* Paper presented at the Image Processing. doi:10.1109/ICIP.1997.647968

Pereira, S., & Pun, T. (2000). Robust template matching for affine resistant image watermarks. *Image Processing. IEEE Transactions on, 9*(6), 1123–1129.

Pham, V.-Q., Miyaki, T., Yamasaki, T., & Aizawa, K. (2007). *Geometrically Invariant Object-Based Watermarking using SIFT Feature.* Paper presented at the Image Processing.

Piper, A., Safavi-Naini, R., & Mertins, A. (2004). Coefficient Selection Methods for Scalable Spread Spectrum Watermarking. In T. Kalker, I. Cox, & Y. Ro (Eds.), *Digital Watermarking* (Vol. 2939, pp. 235–246). Springer Berlin Heidelberg. doi:10.1007/978-3-540-24624-4_18

Piper, A., Safavi-Naini, R., & Mertins, A. (2005). *Resolution and quality scalable spread spectrum image watermarking.* Paper presented at the 7th workshop on Multimedia and security. doi:10.1145/1073170.1073186

Radon, Johann. (2005). 1.1 Über die Bestimmung von Funktionen durch ihre Integralwerte längs gewisser Mannigfaltigkeiten. *Classic papers in modern diagnostic radiology,* 5-5.

Rana, S., Sahu, N., & Sur, A. (2014). Robust watermarking for resolution and quality scalable video sequence. *Multimedia Tools and Applications,* 1–30.

Saeedi, P., Lawrence, P. D., & Lowe, D. G. (2006). Vision-based 3-D trajectory tracking for unknown environments. *Robotics. IEEE Transactions on, 22*(1), 119–136.

Schafer, R., Schwarz, H., Marpe, D., Schierl, T., & Wiegand, T. (2005). *MCTF and Scalability Extension of H.264/AVC and its Application to Video Transmission, Storage, and Surveillance.* Paper presented at the SPIE.

Schwarz, H., Marpe, D., & Wiegand, T. (2007). Overview of the Scalable Video Coding Extension of the H.264/AVC Standard. *Circuits and Systems for Video Technology. IEEE Transactions on, 17*(9), 1103–1120.

Seo, J. H., & Park, H. B. (2005). *Data Protection of Multimedia Contents Using Scalable Digital Watermarking*. Paper presented at the Fourth Annual ACIS International Conference on Computer and Information Science.

Sharma, G., & Coumou, D. J. (2006). *Watermark synchronization: Perspectives and a new paradigm*. Paper presented at the Information Sciences and Systems, 2006 40th Annual Conference on. doi:10.1109/CISS.2006.286644

Stutz, T., & Uhl, A. (2012). A Survey of H.264 AVC/SVC Encryption. *Circuits and Systems for Video Technology. IEEE Transactions on, 22*(3), 325–339.

Sun, Q., He, D., Zhang, Z., & Tian, Q. (2003/07). *A secure and robust approach to scalable video authentication*. Paper presented at the Multimedia and Expo.

Swanson, M. D., Kobayashi, M., & Tewfik, A. H. (1998). Multimedia data-embedding and watermarking technologies. *Proceedings of the IEEE, 86*(6), 1064–1087. doi:10.1109/5.687830

Unanue, I., Urteaga, I., Husemann, R., Ser, J. D., Roesler, V., Rodriguez, A., & Sanchez, P. (2011). A Tutorial on H.264/SVC Scalable Video Coding and its Tradeoff between Quality, Coding Efficiency and Performance. Javier Del Ser Lorente.

Verdicchio, F., Andreopoulos, Y., Clerckx, T., Barbarien, J., Munteanu, A., Cornelis, J., & Schelkens, P. (2004). *Scalable video coding based on motion-compensated temporal filtering: complexity and functionality analysis*. Paper presented at the ICIP. doi:10.1109/ICIP.2004.1421705

Vinod, P., & Bora, P. K. (2006). Motion-compensated inter-frame collusion attack on video watermarking and a countermeasure. *Information Security, IEE Proceedings, 153*(2), 61 - 73-73.

Wang, C.-C., Lin, Y.-C., Yi, S.-C., & Chen, P.-Y. (2006). *Digital Authentication and Verification in MPEG-4 Fine-Granular Scalability Video Using Bit-Plane Watermarking*. Paper presented at the IPCV.

Wang, Y., & Pearmain, A. (2006). Blind MPEG-2 video watermarking in DCT domain robust against scaling. *Vision, Image and Signal Processing, IEE Proceedings, 153*(5), 581-588.

Yan, L., & Jiying, Z. (2008). *RST invariant video watermarking based on 1D DFT and Radon transform*. Paper presented at the Visual Information Engineering.

Yu, Z. H., Ying, L., & Ke, W. C. (2004). *A blind spatial-temporal algorithm based on 3D wavelet for video watermarking*. Paper presented at the Multimedia and Expo.

Chapter 16
Digital Image Watermarking Based on Fractal Image Coding

Channapragada R. S. G. Rao
CMR Institute of Technology, India

Munaga V. N. K. Prasad
Institute for Development and Research in Banking Technology, India

ABSTRACT

This chapter proposes a watermarking technique using Ridgelet and Discrete Wavelet Transform (DWT) techniques. A wavelet transform is the wavelet function representation. A wavelet is a mathematical function which divides a continuous time signal into different scale components, where each scale components is assigned with a frequency range. Wavelets represent objects with point singularities, while ridgelets represents objects with line singularities. The Ridgelet transform Technique is a multi-scale representation for functions on continuous spaces that are smooth away from discontinuities along lines. The proposed technique applies Ridgelet transform on the cover image to obtain ridgelet coefficients. These coefficients are transformed by using 2-level DWT to get low frequency sub-bands – LL1 and LL2. The mutual similarities between LL1 and LL2 sub-bands are considered for embedding watermark. The obtained watermarked image has better quality when compared to a few exiting methods.

INTRODUCTION

The Berne Convention, is an international agreement governing copyright was first accepted by all Berne union member countries in Berne, Switzerland, in 1886 and modified at Paris in 1971 (Fitzgerald Brian et. al., 2011). The countries have realized the importance of intellectual property rights (IPR) after the establishment of the World Trade Organization (WTO) in 1995 (Hannibal Travis, 2008; Barbara Fox and Brian A. LaMacchia, 2003; Channapragada R. S. G. Rao et. al., 2014a). The advent of Wi-Fi technology has resulted in enormous increase in opportunities for creation and distribution of digital content. To protect the rights of creators of digital content and intended recipients while distributing over internet, the content is digitally watermarked so as to check the authenticity or copyright protection of the content. Digital watermarking has become an active and important area of research and development.

DOI: 10.4018/978-1-4666-8723-3.ch016

Digital watermarking is a proven and existing technology that has been deployed in a broad range of applications like, E-commerce, Counterfeit deterrence, Broadcast monitoring, Forensic, digital Rights management, Copy prevention, Content filtering and classification (I.J.Cox et. al., 2002; Christine I. Podilchuk and Edward J. Delp, 2001). A digital watermark is defined as secret/authentication information embedded in a noise-tolerant signal such as audio or image data. Digital Watermarking is the technique of inserting authentication content in a carrier signal (Ingemar J. Cox., 2008; I.J. Cox et. al., 2002). The digital signature embedded as a watermark should retain its integrity within the content even after various manipulation attacks. The embedded signature can easily be extracted using suitable techniques. A watermark can be unique to one image or common to multiple images. A watermarking life cycle, shown in Figure 1, is divided into three distinct steps, Watermark Insertion/ Embedding, Image Manipulation/ Attacks, and Watermark Extraction/Detection (I.J. Cox et. al., 2002; Vidyasagar M. Potdar et al.,2005). In Watermark Insertion, an algorithm inserts the watermark into cover image and produces a watermarked image. The watermarked image is stored in hard disk, shared or transmitted on Internet. If any user on Internet downloads this image and displays in his web site by making modifications without owner's permission then the image is said to be manipulated or attacked. These manipulations may distract watermark or may even remove the same. In the Watermark Extraction or Detection process, an algorithm is applied to the attacked image to extract the watermark from attacked watermarked image for proving the authentication (M. Kutter & F.A.P. Petitcolas, 1999).

There are many watermark techniques in terms of their characteristic, application areas and purposes. They have different insertion and extraction methods (I.J. Cox et. al., 2002; Christine I. Podilchuk and Edward J. Delp, 2001; R.S.G. Rao Channapragada et al., 2012a). Digital watermarking methods can be classified based on working domain, type of document, human perception or application area as shown in Figure 2.

The watermarking techniques can be categorized to Time and Spatial domain and Transform domain based on the algorithms applied. Enhancement of the input signal through filtering is the most acceptable processing approach in the time or space domain (I.J. Cox et. al., 2002; Christine I. Podilchuk and Edward J. Delp, 2001). To analyze the signal properties the frequency domain analysis is used. This allows studying the spectrum to determine which frequencies are present in the input signal and which are missing. Signals are converted from time or space domain to the frequency domain the transform techniques like Fourier Transform (FT), Discrete Fourier Transform (DFT), Fast Fourier Transform (FFT), Discrete Hadamard Transform (DHT), Walsh Hadamard Transform (WHT), Discrete Cosine Transform (DCT) etc. (M. Barni et. al.,1998; X. Kang et. al. 2008; R.S.G. Rao Channapragada et. al.,

Figure 1. Digital watermarking life cycle

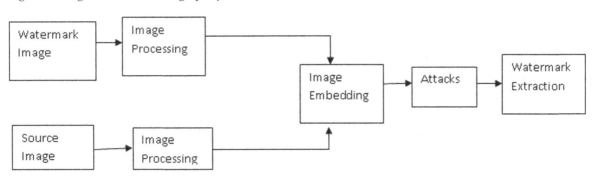

Figure 2. Digital Watermarking classification

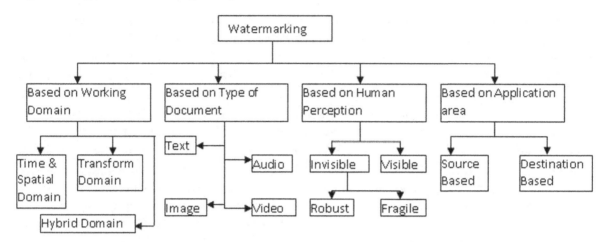

2012b, 2012c).These transform techniques converts the signal information to a magnitude and phase component of each frequency. The transformation of signal is converted to the power spectrum, which is the magnitude of each frequency component squared. In addition to frequency information, phase information is also obtained. In some applications, how the phase varies with frequency can be a significant consideration. Filtering, particularly in non-real time work can also be achieved by converting to the frequency domain, applying the filter and then converting back to the time domain. Frequency domain analysis is also called spectrum or spectral analysis.

The watermarking techniques can be classified based on the content on which watermark is applied i.e. watermark embedded into Text, Image, Audio or Video. Users are replicating the text information designed and developed by others by downloading through internet by causing copy right problems. To overcome this type of problem, text can be inserted into documents along with certain type of watermarking like number of spaces between words, page justification, pre formatted text style etc. (I.J. Cox et. al., 2002; Christine I. Podilchuk and Edward J. Delp, 2001).

The watermarks can be categorized to visible and invisible watermarks. Visible and invisible watermarks serve to prevent theft. Visible watermarks are useful for transmitting an immediate claim of ownership. The visible watermarks are perceptible to the human eye such as company logos and television channel logos etc. These watermarks can be extracted easily without any mathematical calculation and also can be destroyed easily. The invisible watermarks are not perceptible. And the type of watermark and the position of the watermark embedded are secret. Hence only the authorized people can extract the watermark through some mathematical calculations. This kind of watermarking is more secure and robust than visible watermarks. Fragile watermarks, which get destroyed with slightest modifications, are used for integrity proof. Semi-fragile watermarks, which resist the slightest transformation but get disturbed, are used to detect evil transformations. Robust watermarks are those which allows the author to prove their identity even after unacceptable transformations and are used in copyright applications and copy protection applications (I.J. Cox et. al., 2002; Christine I. Podilchuk and Edward J. Delp, 2001).

The application areas generally play a major role in classifying the watermarking techniques. According to application the watermarking techniques can be classified as source based and destination based watermarking techniques. The source based watermarks help to identify or authenticate ownership in a simple method. In this author identification gets embedded to the original image and its copies get circulated. In the destination based watermarking each distributed copy gets a unique watermark identifying the respective buyer. This helps the seller to trace the illegal reselling (I.J. Cox et. al., 2002; Christine I. Podilchuk and Edward J. Delp, 2001).

The rest of this chapter is organized as follows. The next section discusses various watermarking techniques, proposed watermarking technique section discusses a technique based on fractal image coding and ridgelet transformation techniques and the results obtained through the proposed technique. The last section discusses the conclusions and future development.

DIGITAL WATERMARKING TECHNIQUES

Many researchers have presented robust, fragile and semi fragile watermarking solutions (Channapragada R. S. G. Rao et. al., 2014a, 2014b, 2014c). Li and Wang (2000) have discussed a method to embed the watermark into spatial domain by using fractal image coding. Puate and Jordan (1997) have discussed a digital watermarking technique in which the original image was first compressed by using fractals and then the watermark was embedded. Barni.et. al. (1998). have presented a method to embed the watermark into transformed domain using Discrete Cosine Transform (DCT) technique. Jayamohan and Revathy (2012) have discussed a technique based on fractal theory and DWT. In the method, the original image was partitioned into small blocks and the local fractal dimension of each block is calculated by using differential box counting (DBC). The DWT coefficients of watermark are embedded into fractals to obtain the watermarked image. Fatemeh Daraee and Saeed Mozaffari (2014) have presented a technique in which the host image is coded by the fractal coding technique. Specific Range segments with predefined conditions are selected to insert the watermark uniformly over the entire host image. The watermark was embedded to the number of ones in the selected Range segments to obtain the watermarked Image. Rao and Prasad (2014d) have discussed a technique based on magic square and ridgelet transform techniques. The method expands the watermark by using magic square technique then embeds it into the ridgelets of the host image.

Jian Ping Huang (2008) has presented a novel digital watermarking technique using finite ridgelet transform (FRIT) technique. In this technique, the original watermark was decomposed into small blocks. These blocks were transformed using FRIT and then a sparse matrix was generated based on selected points, which is considered as watermark. The watermark extraction procedure has proven its robustness against tamper orientation. Yan Li et al. (2008) have presented a watermarking technique using low and middle level frequency ridgelet transform coefficients. The watermark was embedded in selected points by determining the most important energetic directions. Mangaiyarkarasi and Arulselvi (2011) have embedded the watermark into the most significant directional coefficients of ridgelet transformed original image. They have also proposed a blind extraction procedure using independent component analysis technique. Nima Khademi Kalantari and Seyed Mohammad Ahadi (2010) have proposed a watermarking technique in which the watermark data is embedded in selected blocks representing the most energetic direction of the host image by modifying the amplitude of the ridgelet coefficients. They have proposed watermark extraction procedure where it extracts the watermark data using the variance of the ridgelet coefficients of the most energetic direction in each block which uses a new robust noise estimation scheme. Hai Yan Yu and Xiao Li Zhang (2009) have presented a watermarking technique based on ridgelet transform and fuzzy logic C-Means clustering techniques. The original image was first segmented into small blocks and then transformed with ridgelet transform technique to obtain a sparse representation. The resultant blocks are classified into finite radon transform regions and texture regions by applying FCM clustering algorithm. The watermark was embedded into the middle ridgelet sub band in the highest energy directions of texture blocks. The authors have also presented a blind watermark extraction procedure.

Satoshi Ohga and Ryuji Hamabe (2014) have discussed a method to embed the watermark in fractals. They took 2D-DWT of original image and then by using fractal image coding the watermark was embedded in LL1. The quality of watermarked image was improved by using human visual model based on DWT presented by (M. Barni et. al., 2001). The model has proved that the DWT coefficients based on the weighting function affect the human eye with less perceptible noise. Even though the results obtained through this technique are acceptable, it is complex application in judging based on HVS model. So there is a need to improve the technique without HVS model. This has motivated to propose a technique making the modifications for improving the results.

PROPOSED WATERMARKING TECHNIQUE

This Chapter has proposed a watermarked technique based on fractal theory, ridgelet Transformation and DWT. Fractal Image coding is centered on Iterated Function System (IFS). IFS works on the idea that natural images exhibits some amount of Self Similarity (Arnaud E. Jacquin., 1992). This self similarity is used to code the image in fractal image coding. By applying DWT the image is partitioned into low and high frequency sub bands (H.J.M. Wang et. al., 1998). Wavelets detect objects with point singularities, while ridgelets are able to represent objects with line singularities. In 1999 Candes and Donoho have introduced the ridgelet transform Technique, which was a multi-scale representation for functions on continuous spaces that are smooth away from discontinuities along lines (Gaurav Bhatnagar et. al., 2013). The new transforms are more effective than the wavelet transform in approximating and de-noising images with straight edges (Jean-Luc Starck et. al., 2002; Rao C.R.S.G. and Munaga V.N.K. Prasad., 2014d,2015; David L. Donoho and Ana Georgina Flesia., 2003). It is very well known that the low frequency sub-band contains most of the important information of the original image and the other three sub-bands with high frequency HL1, LH1 and HH1 contains the edge components i.e details of the original image along horizontal axis, vertical axis and diagonal respectively. To attain higher level DWT i.e. 2-level, 3-level and so on, the Low frequency sub-band is taken and the transformation procedure is iterated. After decomposing LL1 into low frequency sub-band LL2 and high frequency sub-bands HL2, LH2 and HH2, to get 2-level DWT of original image.

Watermark Embedding Procedure

The method first applies the ridgelet Transform technique on the cover image. Taking the one-dimensional wavelet transform on the projections of the Radon Transform in a special way results in the ridgelet transformation, where ridgelet transform is invertible, non-redundant and computed via fast methods. Transverse to these ridges it is a wavelet (Minh N. Do and Martin Vetterli., 2003). The Eqn.1 evaluates the continuous ridgelet transformation (CRT) of the given image.

$$CRT(a,b,\theta) \quad = \quad \int_{R^2} \psi_{(a,b,\theta)}(x_1,x_2) f(x_1,x_2) \, dx_1 \, dx_2 \tag{1}$$

where as

$$\psi_{(a,b,\theta)}(x_1,x_2) \quad = \quad a^{-\frac{1}{2}} \psi\left(\frac{(x_1 \cos\theta \, x_2 \sin\theta \quad -b)}{a}\right) \tag{2}$$

and

$$f(x_1,x_2) \quad = \quad \int_0^{2\pi} \int_{-\infty}^{\infty} \int_0^{\infty} CRT_f(a,b,\theta) \psi(a,b,\theta)(x_1,x_2) \frac{da}{a^3} \, db \frac{d\theta}{4\pi} \tag{3}$$

The ridgelet function accepts L cells, where L is the scale of the ridgelet transform (Jean-Luc Starck et. al., 2002). The number of angles are computed by the ridgelet function is as follows. For a p x p pixel image, the number of possible center slices is $p + p = 2p$. Therefore, we get 2p angles. Each output in the cell corresponds to ridgelet transform coefficient at a particular angle (Rao C.R.S.G. and Munaga V.N.K. Prasad, 2014d).

The obtained transform coefficients are then divided into LL2 and LL1 sub-bands by applying 2-level DWT. LL1 is divided into non overlapping range blocks, R, of size m x m. LL2 is divided into overlapping domain blocks, D, of same size as range blocks i.e. m x m with a sliding step size, δ. The domain blocks are separated as even and odd blocks based on Eqn.4.

$$D_{i,j} \quad \in \quad \begin{cases} C_0 & if \; (i+j) \bmod 2 = 0 \\ C_1 & if \; (i+j) \bmod 2 \neq 0 \end{cases} \tag{4}$$

where i, j are index values, C0 and C1 are domain classes and D is domain blocks. The domain block, D, is transformed through a number of suitable affine transformations like identity transformation, reflection about vertical axis, reflection about horizontal axis, reflection about main diagonal, reflection about anti diagonal, rotation about centre of block (90^0 or 180^0 or 270^0). Then a candidate range block, R, is compared with transformed domain blocks and best match is considered whose mean square error is negligible. The transformed domain block is used to embed the watermark bit and positioned into the LL1 sub-band and the block, D, and index information is stored for extraction purpose as key. Then the modified ridgelet transform, MR, is constructed from the new LL1 sub-band. Finally, the watermarked image is constructed by performing inverse ridgelet Transform on the modified ridgelet transformed image, MR. The watermark can be embedded a number of times (U). If the number, U, increases the quality of watermarked image decreases.

Watermark Extraction Procedure

The watermarked image is transformed by applying ridgelet transform technique and then decomposed with 2-level DWT. LL1 sub-band is used to construct non over lapping range blocks and LL2 is used for constructing overlapping domain blocks of size m x m with a slide step δ respectively. The domain blocks are separated as even and odd blocks based on Eqn.4. Using key info stored in embedding process, select an appropriate range block, R, to extract the watermark bit embedded in that block by using Eqn.5.

$$W_b' = \begin{cases} 0 & if\ (i+j)\ \mathrm{mod}\ 2 = 0 \\ 1 & if\ (i+j)\ \mathrm{mod}\ 2 \neq 0 \end{cases} \tag{5}$$

where i, j, b are index values and W is Watermark .The process is repeated for extracting all watermark bits by using all the stored key values.

EXPERIMENTAL RESULTS

This section presents the results obtained by implementing the procedures discussed in previous section on standard color images of size 512 x 512 pixels to embed 32 bits binary sequence watermark (http://engineering.utsa.edu/~sagaian/lab/stegotestdata/testdata.html). The cover image, I, of size 512 X 512 is transformed by using ridgelet transform technique to obtain transformed image, RT. RT is transformed by applying 2-level DWT to obtain LL1 and LL2. LL1 is partitioned into non over lapping small blocks of size 4 X 4 known as range blocks, R. LL2 is partitioned into over lapping small blocks of size 4 X 4 with sliding step size δ=1, known as domain blocks, D. The domain blocks are portioned into two classes called C0 and C1 based on Eqn.4. The range blocks are sorted in descending order with respect to the block variance value. Based on the watermark bit the domain block, D, belonging to C0 or C1 is selected. The block D is transformed with affine transformation and then compared with range blocks. A range block, Ri, is selected whose mean square error with that of the transformed domain block D is negligible. The domain block D is modified with the watermark bit and the information is stored as key. The process is repeated for all watermark bits. Then the inverse transformation is applied to obtain the watermarked image.

Generally if there is an alteration in low frequency sub-bands, the change is reflected by degradation in image quality, which is minimal in the above procedure due to the watermark embedded in edges. Little degradation is compensated while taking inverse ridgelet transform. Also the degradation is low if watermark size is small and is embedded only a limited number of times. Because the watermark is embedded in LL1, the redundancy factor is less. When the watermark is embedded in LL1 for 3-4 times at maximum rather than embedding the watermark 10 times in high frequency sub-bands which takes most of toll in case of an attack. For smaller value of redundancy (U=1) the PSNR is as high as 60.13db (as shown in Figure 4) and for U=5 the PSNR is 53.26db and for U=10 the PSNR is found to be 50.27db for Lenna color image. Figure 3 is the original Lenna color image.

Table 1 gives the comparison between original and watermarked images for different images – Lenna, Baboon, Barbara, when U=1. The results are comparable with the results obtained through various meth-

Figure 3. Original Lena image

Figure 4. Watermarked image for redundancy factor U =1 (PSNR=60.13db)

Table 1. PSNR results for different images

S.No.	BMP Image Name Size 512 X 512	Proposed Method U=1	Satoshi Ohga. and Ryuji Hamabe. 2014		Jian Ping Huang., 2008	Yan Li, Shengqian Wang and Zhihua Xie., 2008	Nima Khademi Kalantari and Seyed Mohammad Ahadi., 2010;	Hai Yan Yu and Xiao Li Zhang., 2009
			With HVS	Without HVS				
1	Lenna	60.13	38.72	41.32	38.62	42.45	45	40.72
2	Baboon	56.22					45	
3	Barbara	61.16						

Table 2. PSNR results after attacks on Lena watermarked image 512 x 512

S.No.	Type Of Attack On 24 Bit Color Lenna Image	PSNR Obtained Proposed Method
1	Watermark extracted from bmp image	53.18
2	Bmp converted to gif format	52.39
3	Bmp converted to jpg format	50.87
4	Bmp converted to png format	53.18

ods presented in (Satoshi Ohga. and Ryuji Hamabe.,2014; Jian Ping Huang., 2008; Yan Li,Shengqian Wang and Zhihua Xie., 2008; P . Mangaiyarkarasi and S. Arulselvi., 2011; Nima Khademi Kalantari and Seyed Mohammad Ahadi., 2010; Hai Yan Yu and Xiao Li Zhang., 2009). The method given by Satoshi Ohga and Ryuji Hamabe has used 256 X 256 pixel size gray scale original lenna image for embedding 32 bit watermark through without and with HVS model applied techniques (Satoshi Ohga. and Ryuji Hamabe., 2014). The technique discussed by Jian Ping Huang has used 512 X 512 pixel gray scale lenna image and is embedded with its transformed image Jian Ping Huang., 2008). The technique discussed by Yan Li et al. has embedded a 48 X 48 pixel watermark into 512 X 512 pixel grey scale lenna image (Yan Li,Shengqian Wang and Zhihua Xie., 2008). Nima Khademi Kalantari and Seyed Mohammad Ahadi discussed a method in which 256 bits of watermark was embedded into 510 X 510 grey scale original image (Nima Khademi Kalantari and Seyed Mohammad Ahadi., 2010). Hai Yan Yu and Xiao Li Zhang have embedded a watermark sequence into 510 X 510 pixel grey scale original images (Hai Yan Yu and Xiao Li Zhang., 2009). Table 2 gives the PSNR results after attacks on Lena watermarked image.

It is observed that depending on the Ridgelet Transform of the image under consideration, the data hiding capacity and image quality varies. But in general, the watermark can be embedded in any image up to 5 times without visual degradation. Human eye cannot perceive the degradation very easily if the PSNR is more than 40 dB.

CONCLUSION

This chapter has presented an improved technique of digital watermarking based on fractal image coding using Ridgelet Transform and DWT. The method implants the watermark in low frequency sub-band of Ridgelets obtained after applying Ridgelet Transform to original image. The technique has used the self- similarity between LL2 and LL1 to embed watermark. As seen in the results section, the method is performing very well. The robustness performance is very high for watermark embedding method. However, the redundancy degree, i.e. the number of times the watermark can be embedded, is a complex problem as the redundancy increases the noise in watermarked image increases. It is compensated by stronger robustness performance against image compression attacks.

REFERENCES

Barni, M., Bartolini, F., Cappellini, V., & Piva, A. (1998). A DCT- domain system for robust image watermarking. *Signal Processing, 66*(8), 357–371. doi:10.1016/S0165-1684(98)00015-2

Barni, M., Bartolini, F., & Piva, A. (2001). Improved wavelet-based watermarking through pixel-wise masking. *IEEE Transactions on Image Processing, 10*(5), 783–791. doi:10.1109/83.918570 PMID:18249667

Bhatnagar, Wu, & Raman. (2013). Discrete fractional wavelet transform and its application to multiple encryption. *International Journal of Information Sciences, 223*, 297–316.

Cox, I. J. (2008). *Digital watermarking and steganography*. Burlington, MA, USA: Morgan Kaufmann.

Cox, I. J., Miller, M. L., & Bloom, J. A. (2002). *Digital Watermarking*. Academic Press.

Daraee, F., & Mozaffari, S. (2014). Watermarking in binary document images using fractal codes. *Pattern Recognition Letters*, *35*, 120–129. doi:10.1016/j.patrec.2013.04.022

Do, M. N., & Vetterli, M. (2003). The Finite Ridgelet Transform for Image Representation. *IEEE Transactions on Image Processing*, *12*(1), 16–28. doi:10.1109/TIP.2002.806252 PMID:18237876

Donoho, D. L., & Flesia, A. G. (2003). Digital Ridgelet Transform based on True Ridge Functions. *International Journal of Studies in Computational Mathematics*, *10*, 1–30.

Fitzgerald, Shi, Foong, & Pappalardo. (2011). Country of Origin and Internet Publication: Applying the Berne Convention in the Digital Age. *Journal of Intellectual Property (NJIP) Maiden Edition*, 38-73

Fox, B., & LaMacchia, B. A. (2003). Encouraging Recognition of Fair Uses in DRM Systems. *Communications of the ACM*, *46*(4), 61–63. doi:10.1145/641205.641233

Huang, P. (2008). A Fast Watermarking Algorithm for Image Authentication. *International Conference on Cyberworlds*. doi:10.1109/CW.2008.55

Jacquin, A. E. (1992). Image Coding Based on a Fractal Theory of Iterated Contractive Image Transformations. *IEEE Transactions on Image Processing*, *1*(1), 18–30. doi:10.1109/83.128028 PMID:18296137

Jayamohan & Revathy. (2012). A Hybrid Fractal-Wavelet Digital Watermarking Technique with Localized Embedding Strength. *6th International Conference on Information Processing*.

Kalantari, N. K., Ahadi, S. M., & Vafadust, M. (2010). A Robust Image Watermarking in the Ridgelet Domain Using Universally Optimum Decoder. *IEEE Transactions on Circuits and Systems for Video Technology*, *20*(3), 396–406. doi:10.1109/TCSVT.2009.2035842

Kang, X., Zeng, W., & Huang, J. (2008). A Multi-band Wavelet Watermarking Scheme. *International Journal of Network Security*, *6*(2), 121–126.

Kutter, M., & Petitcolas, F. A. P. (1999). A fair Benchmark for image Watermarking Systems, Security and Watermarking of Multimedia Contents. *Proceedings of the Society for Photo-Instrumentation Engineers*, *3657*, 1–14. doi:10.1117/12.344672

Li, Wang, & Xie. (2008). A Local Watermarking Scheme in the Ridgelet Domain Combining Image Content and JND Model. *International Conference on Computational Intelligence and Security*.

C. Li & S. Wang. (2000). Digital watermarking using fractal image coding. *IEICE Trans on Fundamentals E83-A*, *6*, 1268-1288.

Lin, P. L., Hsieh, C. K., & Huang, P. W. (2005). A hierarchical digital watermarking method for image tamper detection and recovery. *Pattern Recognition*, *38*(12), 2519–2529. doi:10.1016/j.patcog.2005.02.007

Mangaiyarkarasi, P., & Arulselvi, S. (2011). A new Digital Image Watermarking based on Finite Ridgelet Transform and Extraction using lCA. *International Conference on Emerging Trends in Electrical and Computer Technology*. doi:10.1109/ICETECT.2011.5760235

Ohga, & Hamabe. (2014). Digital Watermarking based on fractal image coding using DWT and HVS. *International Journal of Knowledge-based and Intelligent Engineering Systems, 18*, 81–89.

Podilchuk, C. I., & Delp, E. J. (2001). Digital Watermarking: Algorithms and Applications. *IEEE Signal Processing Magazine, 18*(4), 33–46. doi:10.1109/79.939835

Potdar, V. M., Han, S., & Chang, E. (2005). A Survey of Digital Image Watermarking Techniques. *Third IEEE International Conference on Industrial Informatics.* doi:10.1109/INDIN.2005.1560462

Puate, J., & Jordan, F. (1997). Using fractal compression scheme to embed a digital signature into an image. *SIPIE Photonics, 2915*, 108–118.

Rao, C. R. S. G., Mantha, A. N., & Prasad, M. V. N. K. (2012a). Study of Contemporary Digital watermarking Techniques. *International Journal of Computer Science Issues, 9*(6-1), 456-464.

Rao, C. R. S. G., Nukineedi, D. L., & Prasad, M. V. N. K. (2012b). Digital Watermarking Algorithm Based on CCC - FWHT Technique. *International Journal of Advancements in Computing Technology, 4*(18), 593–599. doi:10.4156/ijact.vol4.issue18.70

Rao, C. R. S. G., & Prasad, M. V. N. K. (2012c). Digital watermarking algorithm based on complete complementary code. *Third International Conference on Computing Communication & Networking Technologies (IEEE-ICCCNT).* doi:10.1109/ICCCNT.2012.6396038

Rao, C. R. S. G., & Prasad, M. V. N. K. (2014d). Digital Watermarking Based on Magic Square and Ridgelet Transform Techniques, Intelligent Computing, Networking, and Informatics. *Advances in Intelligent Systems and Computing, 243*, 143–161. doi:10.1007/978-81-322-1665-0_14

Rao, C. R. S. G., & Prasad, M. V. N. K. (2015). Digital Watermarking Techniques in Curvelet Transformation Domain. *Smart Innovation, Systems and Technologies, 31*, 199-211.

Rao, C. R. S. G., Ravi, V., Prasad, M. V. N. K., & Gopal, E. V. (2014a). Watermarking Using Artificial Intelligence Techniques. In *Encyclopedia of Business Analytics and Optimization.* Hershey, PA: IGI Global Publications.

Rao, C. R. S. G., Ravi, V., Prasad, M. V. N. K., & Gopal, E. V. (2014b). Digital Watermarking Techniques for Images – Survey. In *Encyclopedia of Business Analytics and Optimization.* Hershey, PA: IGI Global Publications.

Rao, C. R. S. G., Ravi, V., Prasad, M. V. N. K., & Gopal, E. V. (2014c). Watermarking Using Intelligent Methods – Survey. In *Encyclopedia of Business Analytics and Optimization.* Hershey, PA: IGI Global Publications.

Sang, J., & Alam, M. S. (2008). Fragility and robustness of binary phase-only-filter based fragile/semi-fragile digital watermarking. *IEEE Transactions on Instrumentation and Measurement, 57*(3), 595–606. doi:10.1109/TIM.2007.911585

Starck, , J.-LCandes, E. J., & Donoho, D. L. (2002). The Curvelet Transform for Image Denoising. *IEEE Transactions on Image Processing, 11*(6), 670–684. doi:10.1109/TIP.2002.1014998 PMID:18244665

Tewfik, A. H., & Swanson, M. (1997). Data hiding for multimedia personalization, interaction, & protection. *IEEE Signal Processing Magazine*, *14*(4), 41–44. doi:10.1109/79.598593

Travis, H. (2008). Opting Out of the Internet in the United States and the European Union: Copyright, Safe Harbors, and International Law. *The Notre Dame Law Review*, *83*(4), 331–408.

Wang, H. J. M., Su, P. C., & Kuo, C. C. J. (1998). Wavelet-based digital image watermarking. *Optics Express*, *3*(12), 491–496. doi:10.1364/OE.3.000491 PMID:19384400

Yu, H. Y., & Zhang, X. L. (2009). A Robust Watermark Algorithm Based on Ridgelet Transform and Fuzzy C-Means. *International Symposium on Information Engineering and Electronic Commerce*. doi:10.1109/IEEC.2009.30

KEY TERMS AND DEFINITIONS

Digital Rights Protection: The term refers to the protection of copyrights of digital media files, which can be implemented through encryption and decryption, steganography or digital watermarking.

Digital Watermarking: This is defined as inserting an authentication information into digital images.

Discrete Wavelet Transformation: A wavelet transform is the wavelet function representation. A wavelet is a mathematical function which divides a continuous time signal into different scale components, where each scale components is assigned with a frequency range.

Fractal Image Coding: Fractal Image coding is centered on Iterated Function System (IFS). IFS works on the idea that natural images exhibits some amount of Self Similarity. This self similarity is used to code the image in fractal image coding.

Ridgelet Transformation: The Ridgelet transform Technique is a multi-scale representation for functions on continuous spaces that are smooth away from discontinuities along lines.

Compilation of References

Kumar, Kalluri, Munagam, & Agarwal. (2012). *Dynamic ROI Extraction Algorithm for Palmprints*. Springer-Verlag Berlin Heidelberg.

Abbasi, S., Mokhtarian, F., & Kittler, J. (1999). Curvature scale space image in shape similarity retrieval. *Multimedia Systems*, *7*(6), 467–476. doi:10.1007/s005300050147

Achanta, R., Hemami, S., Estrada, F., & Susstrunk, S. (2009). Frequency-tuned salient region detection. In *Proc. of International Conference on Computer Vision and Pattern Recognition.*

Achanta, R., & Susstrunk, S. (2009). Saliency detection for content-aware image resizing. In *Proc. of 16th IEEE International Conference on Image Processing.*

Adams, J., Parulski, K., & Spaulding, K. (1998). Color processing in digital cameras. *IEEE Micro*, *18*(6), 20–30. doi:10.1109/40.743681

Ahmadlou, M., Adeli, H., & Adeli, A. (2010). New diagnostic EEG markers of the Alzheimer's disease using visibility graph. *Journal of Neural Transmission, 117*, 1099–1109. doi:10.1007/s00702-010-0450-3

Ahmadlou, M., & Adeli, H. (2012). Visibility graph similarity: A new measure of generalized synchronization in coupled dynamic systems. *Physica D. Nonlinear Phenomena*, *241*(4), 326–332. doi:10.1016/j.physd.2011.09.008

Ahonen, T., Hadid, A., & Pietikainen, M. (2006). Face description with local binary patterns: Application to face recognition. *IEEE Transactions on Pattern Analysis and Machine Intelligence*, *28*(12), 2037–2041. doi:10.1109/TPAMI.2006.244 PMID:17108377

Airplane crashes are very often caused by fatigue | L.A.Fuel. (n.d.). Retrieved May 26, 2014, from http://www.lafuel.com/2013/04/-3&d=78

Akaike, H. (1974). A new look at the statistical model identification. *IEEE Transactions on Automatic Control*, *19*(6), 716–723. doi:10.1109/TAC.1974.1100705

Akima, H. (1978). *A method of bivariate interpolation and smooth surface fitting for values given at irregularly distributed points*. ACM, TOMS.

Albano, A., & Mees, A. (1987). Data requirements for reliable estimation of correlation dimensions. *Chaos in Biological* .... Retrieved from http://link.springer.com/chapter/10.1007/978-1-4757-9631-5_24

Alex, M., & Vasilescu, O., & Demetri Terzopoulos, (2005). Multilinear independent components analysis. *IEEE Computer Society Conference on Computer Vision and Pattern Recognition, 1,547–553.*

Ali, M., Ghafoor, M., Taj, I.A., & Hayat, K. (2011). Palm Print Recognition Using Oriented Hausdorff Distance Transform. *Frontiers of Information Technolog (FIT),* 85 – 88.

Alto, K., Aoki, T., Nakajima, H., Kobayashi, K., & Higuchi, T. (2006). A phase-based palmprint recognition algorithm and its experimental evaluation. In *Proceeding of International Symposium on Intelligent Signal Processing and Communications.*

Álvarez Rueda, R. (2006, November 1). *Assessing alertness from EEG power spectral bands.* Retrieved from http://bibdigital.epn.edu.ec/handle/15000/9872

Aly, H. (2011). Data Hiding in Motion Vectors of Compressed Video Based on Their Associated Prediction Error. *IEEE Transactions on Information Forensics and Security,* 14-18.

Alyuz, N., Gokberk, B., &Akarun, L. (2012). *Adaptive Registration for Occlusion Robust 3D Face Recognition.* Be-FIT'12 Workshop.

Anitha, C., Venkatesha, M. K., & Adiga, B. S. (2010). A survey on facial expression databases. *International Journal of Engineering Science and Technology, 2*(10), 5158–5174.

Antonelli, M., Gibaldi, A., Beuth, F., Duran, A. J., Canessa, A., Solari, F., & Sabatini, S. P. et al. (2014). A hierarchical system for a distributed representation of the peripersonal space of a humanoid robot. *IEEE Transactions on Autonomous Mental Development, 6*(4), 259–273. doi:10.1109/TAMD.2014.2332875

Avidan, S., & Shamir, A. (2007). Seam carving for content-aware image resizing. *ACM Transactions on Graphics, 26*(3), 10. doi:10.1145/1276377.1276390

Bacchuwar, K. S., & Ramakrishnan, K. (2013). A Jump Patch-Block Match Algorithm for Multiple Forgery Detection. In *International Multi-Conference on Automation* (pp. 723–728). Computing, Communication, Control and Compressed Sensing. doi:10.1109/iMac4s.2013.6526502

Backer, G., Mertsching, B., & Bollmann, M. (2001). Data- and model-driven gaze control for an active-vision system. *IEEE Transactions on Pattern Analysis and Machine Intelligence, 23*(12), 1415–1429. doi:10.1109/34.977565

Badrinath, G. S., & Gupta, P. (2011). Stockwell transform based palm-print recognition. *Applied Soft Computing, 11*(7), 4267–4281. doi:10.1016/j.asoc.2010.05.031

Bagchi, P., Bhattacharjee, D., Nasipuri, M., & Basu, D. K. (2012). A novel approach for nose-tip detection on 3D face images across pose. *International Journal of Computational Intelligence and Informatics, 2*(1).

Bagchi, P., Bhattacharjee, D., Nasipuri, M., & Basu, D. K. (2012). A novel approach for registration of 3D face images. In *Proc of international Conference on Advances in Engineering, Science and Management (ICAESM).* E.G.S. Pillay Engineering College.

Bagchi, P., Bhattacharjee, D., Nasipuri, M., & Basu, D. K. (2012). A Novel approach in detecting pose orientation of a 3D face required for face registration. In *Proc of 47th Annual National Convention of CSI & 1st International Conference on Intelligent Infrastructure.* CSI Kolkata Chapter, Science City, Kolkata.

Bagchi, P., Bhattacharjee, D., Nasipuri, M., & Basu, D. K. (2012).A comparative Analysis of intensity based rotation invariant 3D facial landmarking system from 3D meshes. *Intl. conference on Multimedia processing, Communication and Computing Applications.* PES institute of Technology.

Bagchi, P., Bhattacharjee, D., Nasipuri, M., & Basu, D. K. (2013). Detection of pose orientation across single and multiple axes in case of 3D face images. *CSI Journal of Computing, 1*(1-2).

Bagchi, P., Bhattacharjee, D., & Nasipuri, M. (2013). A Method for Nose-tip based 3D face registration using Maximum Intensity algorithm. *International Conference of Computation and Communication Advancement.* JIS College of Engineering.

Bagchi, P., Bhattacharjee, D., & Nasipuri, M. (2014). 3D Face Recognition across pose extremities. *2nd International Conference on Advanced Computing, Networking, and Informatics (ICACNI-2014)*.

Bagchi, P., Bhattacharjee, D., & Nasipuri, M. (2014, July4). Robust 3D face recognition in presence of pose and partial occlusions or missing parts. *International Journal of Foundations of Computer Science & Technology, 4*(4), 21–35. doi:10.5121/ijfcst.2014.4402

Bagchi, P., Bhattacharjee, D., Nasipuri, M., & Basu, D. K. (2012). A novel approach for nose tip detection using smoothing by weighted median filtering applied to 3D face images in variant poses. In *Proc. of International Conference on Pattern Registration, Informatics and Medical Engineering*. Periyar University. doi:10.1109/ICPRIME.2012.6208357

Bagchi, P., Bhattacharjee, D., Nasipuri, M., & Basu, D. K. (2012). *A Novel approach to nose-tip and eye-corners detection using H-K Curvature Analysis in case of 3D images. In Proc of EAIT*. ISI Kolkata.

Bagchi, P., Bhattacharjee, D., Nasipuri, M., & Basu, D. K. (2014). *Registration of Three Dimensional Human Face Images across Pose and their applications in Digital Forensic*. Computational Intelligence in Digital Forensics. doi:10.1007/978-3-319-05885-6_14

Ballard, D. (1991). Animate vision. *Artificial Intelligence, 48*(1), 57–86. doi:10.1016/0004-3702(91)90080-4

Baluja, S., & Pomerleau, D. (1997b). Dynamic relevance: Vision-based focus of attention using artificial neural networks. *Artificial Intelligence, 97*(1-2), 381–395. doi:10.1016/S0004-3702(97)00065-9

Baluja, S., & Pomerleau, D. A. (1997a). Expectation-based selective attention for visual monitoring and control of a robot vehicle. *Robotics and Autonomous Systems, 22*(3-4), 329–344. doi:10.1016/S0921-8890(97)00046-8

Barari, A., & Dhavale, S. (2013). An Overview of Visual Cryptography based Video Watermarking Schemes: Techniques and Performance Comparison. In *Proceedings of International Conference on Advances in Computer Science, Association of Computer Electronics and Electrical Engineers*.

Barni, M., Bartolini, F., Cappellini, V., & Piva, A. (1998). A DCT- domain system for robust image watermarking. *Signal Processing, 66*(8), 357–371. doi:10.1016/S0165-1684(98)00015-2

Barni, M., Bartolini, F., & Piva, A. (2001). Improved wavelet-based watermarking through pixel-wise masking. *IEEE Transactions on Image Processing, 10*(5), 783–791. doi:10.1109/83.918570 PMID:18249667

Barranco, F., Díaz, J., Ros, E., & del Pino, B. (2009). Visual System Based on Artificial Retina for Motion Detection. *IEEE Transactions on Systems, Man, and Cybernetics. Part B, Cybernetics, 39*(3), 752–762. doi:10.1109/TSMCB.2008.2009067 PMID:19362896

Bar-Shalom, Y., & Foreman, T. (1988). *Tracking and Data Association: Mathematics in Science and Engineering*. San Diego, CA: Academic Press.

Bartlett, M. S. (1998). *Face image analysis by unsupervised learning and redundancy reduction*. (Doctoral dissertation). University of California, San Diego, CA.

Bas, P., Chassery, J. M., & Macq, B. (2002). Geometrically invariant watermarking using feature points. *Image Processing, IEEE Transactions on, 11*(9), 1014-1028.

Bascle, B., & Blake, A. (1998, January). Separability of pose and expression in facial tracking and animation. In *Proceedings Sixth IEEE International Conference on Computer Vision*. doi:10.1109/ICCV.1998.710738

Basha, T., Moses, Y., & Avidan, S. (2011). Geometrically consistent stereo seam carving. In *Proc. of IEEE International Conference on Computer Vision*.

Bassett, D. S., & Bullmore, E. (2006). Small-world brain networks. *The Neuroscientist, 12*(6), 512–523. doi:10.1177/1073858406293182 PMID:17079517

Basu, S., Oliver, N., & Pentland, A. (1998, January). 3D modeling and tracking of human lip motions.*In Proceedings Sixth IEEE International Conference on Computer Vision.* doi:10.1109/ICCV.1998.710740

Bayer, B. E. (1976). Color Imaging Array. *U.S. Patent 3971065.*

Bay, H., Tuytelaars, T., & Van Gool, L. (2006). Surf: Speeded up robust features. In *Computer vision–ECCV 2006* (pp. 404–417). Springer Berlin Heidelberg. doi:10.1007/11744023_32

Bayram, S., Sencar, H. T., & Memon, N. (2005). Source camera identification based on CFA interpolation. In *IEEE Int. Conf. Image Processing.* doi:10.1109/ICIP.2005.1530330

Begum, M., & Karray, F. (2011). Visual attention for robotic cognition: A survey. *IEEE Transactions on Autonomous Mental Development, 3*(1), 92–105. doi:10.1109/TAMD.2010.2096505

Begum, M., Karray, F., Mann, G. K. I., & Gosine, R. G. (2010). A probabilistic model of overt visual attention for cognitive robots. *IEEE Transactions on Systems, Man, and Cybernetics. Part B, Cybernetics, 40*(5), 1305–1318. doi:10.1109/TSMCB.2009.2037511 PMID:20089477

Begum, M., Mann, G. K. I., & Gosine, R. G. (2006). A biologically inspired Bayesian model of visual attention for humanoid robots. In *Proc. of 6th IEEE-RAS International Conference on Humanoid Robots,* (pp. 587–592). doi:10.1109/ICHR.2006.321333

Belhumeur, P., Hespanha, J., & Kriegman, D. (1991). Eigenfaces vs. Fisherfaces: Recognition using class speci0c linear projection. *IEEE Transactions on Pattern Analysis and Machine Intelligence, 19*(7), 711–720. doi:10.1109/34.598228

Bender, D. B., & Youakim, M. (2001). Effect of attentive fixation in macaque thalamus and cortex. *Journal of Neurophysiology, 85*(1), 219–234. PMID:11152722

Benedikt, L., Cosker, D., Rosin, P., & Marshall, D. (2010). Assessing the uniqueness and permanence of facial actions for use in biometric applications. *IEEE Transactions on Systems, Manand Cybernetics, part A. Systems and Humans, 40*(3), 449–460. doi:10.1109/TSMCA.2010.2041656

Berclaz, J., Fleuret, F., Turetken, E., & Fua, P. (2011). Multiple Object Tracking Using K-Shortest Paths Optimization. *Institute Of Electrical And Electronics Engineers Transactions On Pattern Analysis And Machine Intelligence, 33*(9), 1806–1819. PMID:21282851

Berretti, S., Bimbo, A. D., & Pala, P. (2013). Sparse Matching of Salient Facial Curves for Recognition of 3-D faces with missing parts. *IEEE Transactions on Information Forensics and Security, 8*(2), 374–389. doi:10.1109/TIFS.2012.2235833

Bettadapura,V., (2012). *Face Expression Recognition and Analysis: The State of the Art.* Tech Report.

Beuth, F., Jamalian, A., & Hamker, F. H. (2014). How Visual Attention and Suppression Facilitate Object Recognition? In *Proceedings of 24th International Conference on Artificial Neural Networks (ICANN)* (pp. 459-466). Hamburg, Germany: Springer. doi:10.1007/978-3-319-11179-7_58

Bhatnagar, Wu, & Raman. (2013). Discrete fractional wavelet transform and its application to multiple encryption. *International Journal of Information Sciences, 223,* 297–316.

Bhowmik, D., & Abhayaratne, C. (2010). *Video watermarking using motion compensated 2D+t+2D filtering.* Paper presented at the 12th ACM workshop on Multimedia and security. doi:10.1145/1854229.1854254

Bianchi, T., & Piva, A. (2013). Secure watermarking for multimedia content protection: A review of its benefits and open issues. *Signal Processing Magazine, IEEE, 30*(2), 87–96. doi:10.1109/MSP.2012.2228342

Bichot, N. P. (2001). Attention, eye movements, and neurons: Linking physiology and behavior. *Vision and Attention,* 209–232.

Black, M. J., & Yacoob, Y. (1997). Recognizing facial expressions in image sequences using local parameterized models of image motion. *International Journal of Computer Vision, 25*(1), 23–48. doi:10.1023/A:1007977618277

Blanz, V., & Vetter, T. (1999). A morphable model for the synthesis of 3D faces. *26th Annual Conference on Computer Graphics and Interactive Techniques.* doi:10.1145/311535.311556

Böhme, R., & Kirchner, M. (2012). Counter-forensics: Attacking image forensics. In Digital Image Forensics. Berlin, Germany: Springer.

Bollimpalli, P., Sahu, N., & Sur, A. (2014, sept). *SIFT Based Robust Image Watermarking Resistant To Resolution Scaling.* Paper presented at the Image Processing (ICIP), 2014 21st IEEE International Conference on. doi:10.1109/ICIP.2014.7026114

Bonaiuto, J., & Itti, L. (2006). The use of attention and spatial information for rapid facial recognition in video. *Image and Vision Computing, 24*(5), 557–563. doi:10.1016/j.imavis.2005.09.008

Borji, A., & Itti, L. (2013). State-of-the-art in Visual Attention Modeling. *IEEE Transactions on Pattern Analysis and Machine Intelligence, 35*(1), 185–207. doi:10.1109/TPAMI.2012.89 PMID:22487985

Born, R. T., & Bradley, D. C. (2005). Structure and function of visual area MT. *Annual Review of Neuroscience, 28*(1), 157–189. doi:10.1146/annurev.neuro.26.041002.131052 PMID:16022593

Bosch, A., Zisserman, A., & Muñoz, X. (2006). Scene Classification Via pLSA. In A. Leonardis, H. Bischof, & A. Pinz (Eds.), *Computer Vision? ECCV 2006* (Vol. 3954, pp. 517–530). Springer Berlin Heidelberg. doi:10.1007/11744085_40

Breazeal, C., Edsinger, A., Fitzpatrick, P., & Scassellati, B. (2001). Active vision for sociable robots. *IEEE Transactions on Systems. Man and Cybernetics: Part A, 31*(5), 443–453. doi:10.1109/3468.952718

Broida, T., & Chellappa, R. (1986). Estimation of object motion parameters from noisy images. *Institute Of Electrical And Electronics Engineers Transactions on Pattern Analysis and Machine Intelligence, 8*(1), 90–99. PMID:21869326

Brookings, J. B., Wilson, G. F., & Swain, C. R. (1996). Psychophysiological responses to changes in workload during simulated air traffic control. *Biological Psychology, 42*(3), 361–377. doi:10.1016/0301-0511(95)05167-8 PMID:8652753

Bruce, N. D. B., & Tsotsos, J. K. (2005). An attentional framework for stereo vision. In *Computer and Robot Vision, 2005. Proceedings. The 2nd Canadian Conference on,* (pp. 88–95). IEEE. doi:10.1109/CRV.2005.13

Bruce, N. D. B., & Tsotsos, J. K. (2009). Saliency, attention, and visual search: An information theoretic approach. *Journal of Vision, 9*(3).

Bruce, C. J., Goldberg, M. E., Bushnell, M. C., & Stanton, G. B. (1985). Primate Frontal Eye Fields. II. Physiological and Anatomical Correlates of Electrically Evoked Eye Movements. *Journal of Neurophysiology, 54*(3), 714–734. PMID:4045546

Bruce, N. D. B. (2005). Features that draw visual attention: An information theoretic perspective. *Neurocomputing, 65-66,* 125–133. doi:10.1016/j.neucom.2004.10.065

Bruce, N. D. B., & Tsotsos, J. K. (2009). Saliency, attention and visual search: An information theoretic approach. *Journal of Vision (Charlottesville, Va.), 9*(3), 1–24. doi:10.1167/9.3.5 PMID:19757944

Bruneau, D., Sasse, M. A., & McCarthy, J. (2002). The eyes never lie: The use of eye tracking data in HCI research. In *Proceedings of the CHI*, (vol. 2, p. 25). ACM.

Burt, P. J., & Adelson, E. H. (1983). The laplacian pyramid as a compact image code. *IEEE Transactions on Communications*, *31*(4), 532–540. doi:10.1109/TCOM.1983.1095851

Byrne, M. D., Anderson, J. R., Douglass, S., & Matessa, M. (1999). Eye tracking the visual search of click-down menus. In *Proceedings of the SIGCHI conference on Human Factors in Computing Systems*, (pp. 402–409). ACM. doi:10.1145/302979.303118

C. Li & S. Wang. (2000). Digital watermarking using fractal image coding. *IEICE Trans on Fundamentals E83-A, 6*, 1268-1288.

Cadieu, C., Kouh, M., Pasupathy, A., Connor, C. E., Riesenhuber, M., & Poggio, T. (2007). A model of V4 shape selectivity and invariance. *Journal of Neurophysiology*, *98*(3), 1733–1750. doi:10.1152/jn.01265.2006 PMID:17596412

Caffier, P. P., Erdmann, U., & Ullsperger, P. (2003). Experimental evaluation of eye-blink parameters as a drowsiness measure. *European Journal of Applied Physiology*, *89*, 319–325. doi:10.1007/s00421-003-0807-5

Cai, D., DeAngelis, G. C., & Freeman, R. D. (1997). Spatiotemporal receptive field organization in the LGN of cats and kittens. *Journal of Neurophysiology*, *78*, 1045–1061. PMID:9307134

Canny, J. A. (1986). Computational approach to edge detection. *Institute Of Electrical And Electronics Engineers Transaction Pattern Analysis and Machine Intelligence*, *8*(6), 679–698. PMID:21869365

Cao, L. (1997). Practical method for determining the minimum embedding dimension of a scalar time series. *Physica D. Nonlinear Phenomena*, *110*(1-2), 43–50. doi:10.1016/S0167-2789(97)00118-8

Cao, L., Mees, A., & Judd, K. (1998). Dynamics from multivariate time series. *Physica D. Nonlinear Phenomena*, *121*(1-2), 75–88. doi:10.1016/S0167-2789(98)00151-1

Cassin, B., Solomon, S., & Rubin, M. L. (1990). *Dictionary of eye terminology*. Wiley Online Library.

Cater, K., Chalmers, A., & Ward, G. (2003). Detail to attention: exploiting visual tasks for selective rendering. In *Proc. of 14th Eurographic Workshop on Rendering*.

Caumon, G., Collon-Drouaillet, P., Le Carlier de Veslud, C., Viseur, S., & Sausse, J. (2009). Surface - based 3D modeling of geological structures. *Math Geosci*, *41*(8), 927–945. doi:10.1007/s11004-009-9244-2

Cerf, M., Harel, J., Einhäuser, W., & Koch, C. (2008). Predicting human gaze using low-level saliency combined with face detection. *Advances in Neural Information Processing Systems*, 241–248.

Chamaret, C., Godeffroy, S., Lopez, P., & Le Meur, O. (2010). *Adaptive 3D rendering based on region-of-interest. In IS&T/SPIE Electronic Imaging* (p. 75240V). SPIE.

Chang, C.-H., Liang, C.-K., & Chuang, Y.-Y. (2011). Content-aware display adaptation and interactive editing for stereoscopic images. *IEEE Transactions on Multimedia*, *13*(4), 589–601. doi:10.1109/TMM.2011.2116775

Chang, S. G., Yu, B., & Vetterli, M. (2000). Spatially Adaptive Wavelet Thresholding with Context Modeling for Image Denoising. *IEEE Transactions on Image Processing*, *9*(9), 1522–1531. doi:10.1109/83.862630 PMID:18262990

Chelazzi, L., Duncan, J., Miller, E. K., & Desimone, R. (1998). Responses of Neurons in Inferior Temporal Cortex During Memory-Guided Visual Search. *Journal of Neurophysiology*, *80*, 2918–2940. PMID:9862896

Chen, J. S., Moon, Y. S., & Yeung, H. W. (2005). Palmprint authentication using time series. In *Proceeding of Fifth International Conference on Audio- and Video-based Biometric Person Authentication*.

Chen, M., Fridrich, J., Goljan, M., & Lukas, J. (2007). Source digital camcorder identification using sensor photo-response nonuniformity. In *Proc. of SPIE Electronic Imaging*. PhotonicsWest.

Chen, S. E., & Williams, L. (1993). *View interpolation for image synthesis*. Paper presented at the 20th annual conference on Computer graphics and interactive techniques.

Chen, D.-Y., Tyan, H.-R., Hsiao, D.-Y., Shih, S.-W., & Liao, H.-Y. M. (2008). Dynamic visual saliency modeling based on spatiotemporal analysis. In *Proc. of IEEE International Conference on Multimedia and Expo*.

Chen, G. Y., Bui, T. D., & Krzyak, A. (2006). Palmprint classification using dual-tree complex wavelets. In *Proceeding of International Conference on Image Processing*.

Cheni, X., Zhang, J., Zhengi, X., Gu, Z., & Lini, N. (2013). *A New Modeling for Visual Attention Calculation in Video Coding*. Paper presented at ICMEW. doi:10.1109/ICMEW.2013.6618329

Chen, J., Moon, Y., Wong, M., & Su, G. (2010). Palmprint authentication using a symbolic representation of images. *Image and Vision Computing*, *28*(3), 343–351. doi:10.1016/j.imavis.2009.06.004

Chen, J., Zhang, C., & Rong, G. (2001). Palmprint recognition using creases.*Proceedings of International Conference of Image Processing*, *3*,234-237.

Chen, L.-Q., Xie, X., Fan, X., Ma, W.-Y., Zhang, H.-J., & Zhou, H.-Q. (2003). A visual Attention model for adapting images on small displays. *Multimedia Systems*, *9*(4), 353–364. doi:10.1007/s00530-003-0105-4

Chen, M., Fridrich, J., Goljan, M., & Lukas, J. (2008). Determining image origin and integrity using sensor noise. *IEEE Transactions on Information Forensics and Security*, *3*(1), 74–90. doi:10.1109/TIFS.2007.916285

Chen, S., & Leung, H. (2008). Chaotic watermarking for video authentication in surveillance applications. *Circuits and Systems for Video Technology. IEEE Transactions on*, *18*(5), 704–709.

Chen, X. R., & Zhang, H. J. (2001). Text area detection from video frames, In *Proc. of 2nd IEEE Pacific-Rim Conference on Multimedia*.

Chialvo, D. R. (2004). Critical brain networks. *Physica A: Statistical Mechanics and its Applications* (Vol. 340, pp. 756–765). doi:10.1016/j.physa.2004.05.064

Chikkerur, S., Serre, T., Tan, C., & Poggio, T. (2010). What and where: A Bayesian inference theory of attention. *Vision Research*, *50*(22), 2233–2247. doi:10.1016/j.visres.2010.05.013 PMID:20493206

Choi, S.-B., Ban, S.-W., & Lee, M. (2004). Biologically motivated visual attention system using bottom-up saliency map and top-down inhibition. *Neural Information Processing-Letters and Reviews, 2*.

Choi, S.-J., & Woods, J. W. (1999). Motion-compensated 3-D subband coding of video. *Image Processing, IEEE Transactions on, 8*(2), 155-167.

Choi, K. S., Lam, E. Y., & Wong, K. K. Y. (2006). Source camera identification using footprints from lens aberration. *Proceedings of the Society for Photo-Instrumentation Engineers*, 60690J, 60690J-8. doi:10.1117/12.649775

Choudhury, T., & Pentland, A. (2000). Motion field histograms for robust modeling of facial expressions. In *Proceedings of the International Conference on Pattern Recognition (ICPR 2000)*. Barcelona, Spain.

Ciocca, G., Cusano, C., Gasparini, F., & Schettini, R. (2007). Self-adaptive image cropping for small displays. *IEEE Transactions on Consumer Electronics, 53*(4), 1622–1627. doi:10.1109/TCE.2007.4429261

Ciocca, G., Cusano, C., Gasparini, F., & Schettini, R. (2007a). Self-adaptive Image Cropping for Small Displays. In *Proc. of International Conference on Consumer Electronics*.

Cohen, I., Cozman, F. G., Sebe, N., Cirelo, M. C., & Huang, T. S. (2004). Semi-supervised Learning of Classifiers: Theory, Algorithms and Their Application to Human-Computer Interaction. *IEEE Transactions on Pattern Analysis and Machine Intelligence, 26*(12), 1553–1566. doi:10.1109/TPAMI.2004.127 PMID:15573817

Cohen, Y. E., & Andersen, R. (2002). A common reference frame for movement plans in the posterior parietal cortex. *Nature Reviews. Neuroscience, 3*(7), 553–562. doi:10.1038/nrn873 PMID:12094211

Comaniciu, D., & Meer, P. (2002). Mean shift: A robust approach toward feature space analysis. *Institute Of Electrical And Electronics Engineers Transactions on Pattern Analysis and Machine Intelligence, 24*(5), 603–619.

Comaniciu, D., Ramesh, V., & Meer, P. (2003). Kernel-based object tracking. *Institute Of Electrical And Electronics Engineers Transactions on Pattern Analysis and Machine Intelligence, 25*, 564–575.

Conn1e, Teoh Beng Jin, Goh Kah Ong, & Ngo Chek Ling. (2005). An automated palmprint recognition system. *Image and Vision Computing, 23*(5), 501–515.

Connie, T., Jin, A., Ong, M., & Ling, D. (2003). An automated palmprint recognition system. *Image and Vision Computing, 23*(5), 501–515. doi:10.1016/j.imavis.2005.01.002

Cootes, T., Edwards, G., & Taylor, C. (2001). Active appearance models. *IEEE Transactions on Pattern Analysis and Machine Intelligence, 23*(6), 681–685. doi:10.1109/34.927467

Corbetta, M., & Shulman, G. L. (2002). Control of goal-directed and stimulus-driven attention in the brain. *National Review, 3*(3), 201–215. doi:10.1038/nrn755 PMID:11994752

Cottrell, G. W. (1990). Extracting features from faces using compression networks: Face, identity, emotion and gender recognition using holons. In Connectionist models: proceedings of the 1990 summer school (pp. 328-337).

Courty, N., Marchand, E., & Arnaldi, B. (2003). A new application for saliency maps: synthetic vision of autonomous actors. In *Proc. of International Conference on Image Processing*. doi:10.1109/ICIP.2003.1247432

Cowen, L., Ball, L. J., & Delin, J. (2002). An eye movement analysis of web page usability. In People and Computers XVI-Memorable Yet Invisible, (pp. 317–335). Springer.

Cox, I. J. (2008). *Digital watermarking and steganography*. Burlington, MA, USA: Morgan Kaufmann.

Cox, I. J., Kilian, J., Leighton, F. T., & Shamoon, T. (1997). Secure spread spectrum watermarking for multimedia. *IEEE Transactions on Image Processing, 6*(12), 1673–1687. doi:10.1109/83.650120 PMID:18285237

Cox, I. J., Miller, M. L., & Bloom, J. A. (2002). *Digital Watermarking*. Academic Press.

Cox, I. J., Miller, M. L., Bloom, J. A., Fridrich, J., & Kalker, T. (2008). *Digital Watermarking and Steganography* (2nd ed.). Burlington: Morgan Kaufmann.

Cui, J., Wen, F., & Tang, X. (2008). *Real time Google and live image searchre-ranking*. ACM Multimedia.

Dacher, K., Gian, Gonzaga, & Davidson. (2003). Facial expression of emotion. In Handbook of affective sciences. New York, NY: Oxford University Press.

Dai, J. F., & Zhou, J. (2011). Multifeature-based high-resolution palmprint recognition. *IEEE Transaction. Pattern Analysis and Machine Inteligence, 33*(5), 945–957. doi:10.1109/TPAMI.2010.164

Dalal, N., & Triggs, B. (2005, June). Histograms of oriented gradients for human detection. In *Proceedings of IEEE Computer Society conference on Computer Vision and Pattern Recognition, 2005(CVPR 2005),* (Vol. 1, pp. 886-893). IEEE.

Daraee, F., & Mozaffari, S. (2014). Watermarking in binary document images using fractal codes. *Pattern Recognition Letters, 35,* 120–129. doi:10.1016/j.patrec.2013.04.022

Daugman, J. G. (1993). High confidence visual recognition of persons by a test of statistical independence. *IEEE Transactions on Pattern Analysis and Machine Intelligence, 15*(11), 1148–1161. doi:10.1109/34.244676

De Waard, D., & Brookhuis, K. A. (1991). Assessing driver status: A demonstration experiment on the road. *Accident; Analysis and Prevention, 23*(4), 297–307. doi:10.1016/0001-4575(91)90007-R PMID:1883469

DeAngelis, G., Ohzawa, I., & Freeman, R. D. (1995). Receptive-field dynamics in the central visual pathways. *Trends in Neurosciences, 18*(10), 451–458. doi:10.1016/0166-2236(95)94496-R PMID:8545912

DeCarlo, D., & Metaxas, D. (1996). The integration of optical fow and deformable models with applications to human face shape and motion estimation. In *Proceedings of the International Conference on Computer Vision and Pattern Recognition (CVPR'96).*

Deng, C., Xiaofei, H., & Jiawei, H. (2007). Efficient kernel discriminant analysis via spectral regression. In *Proceedings of the Seventh International Conference on Data Mining.* IEEE.

Deng, W., Hu, J., Guo, J., Zhang, H., & Zhang, C. (1503–1504). C. (2008). Comment on globally maximizing locally minimizing: Unsupervised discriminant projection with applications to face and palm biometrics. *IEEE Transactions on Pattern Analysis and Machine Intelligence.*

Desimone, R., & Duncan, J. (1995). Neural mechanisms of selective visual attention. *Annual Review of Neuroscience, 18*(1), 193–222. doi:10.1146/annurev.ne.18.030195.001205 PMID:7605061

Deubel, H., & Schneider, W. X. (1996). Saccade target selection and object recognition: Evidence for a common attentional mechanism. *Vision Research, 36*(12), 1827–1837. doi:10.1016/0042-6989(95)00294-4 PMID:8759451

Didier, B. (1990). *An Efficient Ray - Polygon Intersection. In Graphics Gems.* Academic Press.

Ding, Y., Xiao, J., & Yu, J. (2011). Importance filtering for image retargeting. In *Proc. of IEEE Conference on Computer Vision and Pattern Recognition.*

Doi, J., & Yamanaka, M. (2003). Personal authentication using feature points on finger and palmar creases. In *Proceedings of 32nd Applied Imagery Patten Recognition Workshop.*

Do, M. N., & Vetterli, M. (2003). The Finite Ridgelet Transform for Image Representation. *IEEE Transactions on Image Processing, 12*(1), 16–28. doi:10.1109/TIP.2002.806252 PMID:18237876

Dong, K., Feng, G., & Hu, D. (2004). Digital curvelet transform for palmprint recognition. Lecture Notes in Computer Science, Springer, 3338, 639–645.

Donoho, D. L., & Flesia, A. G. (2003). Digital Ridgelet Transform based on True Ridge Functions. *International Journal of Studies in Computational Mathematics, 10,* 1–30.

Doran, M. D., & Hoffman, J. E. (2010). The Role of Visual Attention in Multiple Object Tracking: Evidence from ERPs. *Attention, Perception & Psychophysics, 72*(1), 33–52. doi:10.3758/APP.72.1.33 PMID:20802834

Doublet, J., Revenu, M., & Lepetit, O. (2007). Robust grayscale distribution estimation for contactless palmprint recognition. In*Proceedings of the First IEEE International Conference on Biometrics: Theory, Applications, and Systems.* doi:10.1109/BTAS.2007.4401935

Driscoll, J. A., Peters, R. A. II, & Cave, K. R. (1998). A visual attention network for a humanoid robot. In *Proc. of IEEE/ RSJ International Conference on Intelligent Robots and Systems.* doi:10.1109/IROS.1998.724894

Driver Fatigue and Road Accidents. (n.d.). Retrieved May 26, 2014, from http://www.rospa.com/roadsafety/info/fatigue.pdf

Du, A. M. S. (2012). A Model of the Perception of Facial Expressions of Emotion by Humans: Research Overview and Perspectives. *Journal of Machine Learning Research, 13*(May), 1589–1608. PMID:23950695

Duchowski, A. T. (2002). A breadth-first survey of eye-tracking applications. *Behavior Research Methods, Instruments, & Computers, 34*(4), 455–470. doi:10.3758/BF03195475 PMID:12564550

Duchowski, A. T. (2007). *Eye tracking methodology: Theory and practice.* Springer Science & Business Media New York.

Du, H., He, S., Sheng, B., Ma, L., & Lau, R. W. H. (2015). Saliency-guided color-to-gray conversion using region-based optimization. *IEEE Transactions on Image Processing, 24*(1), 434–443. doi:10.1109/TIP.2014.2380172 PMID:25531949

Duta, N., Jain, A., & Mardia, K. (2002). Matching of palmprint. *Pattern Recognition Letters, 23*(4), 477–485. doi:10.1016/ S0167-8655(01)00179-9

Edwards, G., Cootes, T., & Taylor, C. (1998). Face recognition using active appearance models. In *Proceedings of the Fifth European Conference on Computer Vision (ECCV).* University of Freiburg.

Egenhofer, M. J., & Franzosa, R. (1991). Point-Set topological Relations, International Journal of *Geographical. Information Systems, 5*(2), 161–174.

Egenhofer, M. J., & Golledge, R. G. (1998). *Spatial and Temporal Reasoning in Geographic Information Systems.* Oxford University Press.

Eisert, P., & Girod, B. (1997). Facial expression analysis for model-based coding of video sequences.*Picture Coding Symposium.* Berlin, Germany.

Ejaz, N., Mehmood, I., & Baik, S. W. (2013). Efficient visual attention based framework for extracting key frames from videos. *Signal Processing Image Communication, 28*(1), 34–44. doi:10.1016/j.image.2012.10.002

Ekinci, M., & Aykut, M. (2007). Gabor-based kernel PCA for palmprint recognition. *Electronics Letters, 43*(20), 1077–1079. doi:10.1049/el:20071688

Ekinci, M., & Aykut, M. (2008). Palmprint recognition by applying wavelet based kernel PCA. *Journal of Computer Science and Technology, 23*(5), 851–861. doi:10.1007/s11390-008-9173-4

Elazary, L., & Itti, L. (2008). Interesting objects are visually salient. *Journal of Vision, 8*(3), 1-15.

Elgammal, A., Harwood, D., & Davis, L. (2000). Non-parametric Model for Background Subtraction.*European Conference on Computer Vision, 2 (June),* (pp. 751-767).

Eloe, N., Leopold, J. L., Sabharwal, C. L., & Yin, Z. (2012). Efficient Computation of Boundary Intersection and Error Tolerance in VRCC-3D+. In *Proceedings of the 18h International Conference on Distributed Multimedia Systems (DMS'12).* Academic Press.

Elsheikh, A. H., & Elsheikh, M. (2012). A reliable triangular mesh intersection algorithm and its application in geological modeling. *Engineering with Computers,* 1–15.

Engelke, U., Maeder, A., & Zepernick, H. J. (2010). Analysing inter-observer saliency variations in task-free viewing of natural images. In *Image Processing (ICIP), 2010 17th IEEE International Conference on,* (pp. 1085–1088). IEEE.

Engelke, U., Kaprykowsky, H., Zepernick, H.-J., & Ndjiki-Nya, P. (2011). Visual Attention in Quality Assessment. *Signal Processing Magazine, IEEE, 28*(6), 50–59. doi:10.1109/MSP.2011.942473

Eoh, H. J., Chung, M. K., & Kim, S. H. (2005). Electroencephalographic study of drowsiness in simulated driving with sleep deprivation. *International Journal of Industrial Ergonomics, 35*(4), 307–320. doi:10.1016/j.ergon.2004.09.006

Essaouabi, A., & Ibnelhaj, E. (2009). *A 3D wavelet-based method for digital video watermarking.* Paper presented at the Networked Digital Technologies, 2009. NDT '09. First International Conference on. doi:10.1109/NDT.2009.5272116

Etemad, K., & Chellappa, R. (1997). Discriminant analysis for recognition of human face images. *Journal of the Optical Society of America. A, Optics, Image Science, and Vision, 14*(8), 1724–1733. doi:10.1364/JOSAA.14.001724

Etz, S. P., & Luo, J. (2000). Ground truth for training and evaluation of automatic main subject detection. *Electronic Imaging,* 434–442.

Fang, D. Y., & Chang, L. W. (2006, May). Data hiding for digital video with phase of motion vector. In *Circuits and Systems, 2006. ISCAS 2006. Proceedings. 2006 IEEE International Symposium on.* IEEE.

Fang, Y., Lin, W., Chen, Z., Tsai, C. M., & Lin, C. W. (2014). A video saliency detection model in compressed domain. *Circuits and Systems for Video Technology. IEEE Transactions on, 24*(1), 27–38.

Fang, Y., Lin, W., Lau, C. T., & Lee, B.-S. (2011). A visual attention model combining top-down and bottom-up mechanisms for salient object detection. In *Proc. of IEEE International Conference on Acoustics, Speech and Signal Processing.* doi:10.1109/ICASSP.2011.5946648

Fang, Y., Zeng, K., Wang, Z., Lin, W., Fang, Z., & Lin, C.-W. (2014). Objective quality assessment for image retargeting based on structural similarity. *IEEE Journal on Emerging and Selected Topics in Circuits and Systems, 4*(1), 95–105. doi:10.1109/JETCAS.2014.2298919

Fan, X., Xie, X., Ma, W.-Y., Zhang, H.-J., & Zhou, H.-Q. (2003). Visual Attention Based Image Browsing on Mobile Devices. In *International Conference on Multimedia and Expo.*

Farid, H. (2006). *Digital image ballistics from JPEG quantization.* Dept. Computer Science, Dartmouth College, Tech. Rep. TR2006-583.

Farid, H. (2009). A Survey of image forgery detection. *IEEE Signal Processing Magazine, 26*(2), 16–25. doi:10.1109/MSP.2008.931079

Farid, H., & Lyu, S. (2003). Higher-order wavelet statistics and their application to digital forensics. *IEEE Workshop on Statistical Analysis in Computer Vision.* doi:10.1109/CVPRW.2003.10093

Fasel, B., & Luettinb, J. (2003). Automatic facial expression analysis: A survey. *Pattern Recognition, 36*(1), 259–275. doi:10.1016/S0031-3203(02)00052-3

Fasel, B., & Luettin, J. (2000). Recognition of asymmetric facial action unit activities and intensities. In *Proceedings of the International Conference on Pattern Recognition (ICPR 2000).* doi:10.1109/ICPR.2000.905664

Fatigue is a Major Cause in Truck Crashes. (n.d.). Retrieved May 26, 2014, from http://www.optalert.com/news/truck-crashes-fatigue

Felleman, D. J., & Van Essen, D. C. (1991). Distributed hierarchical processing in the primate cerebral cortex. *Cerebral Cortex, 1*(1), 1–47. doi:10.1093/cercor/1.1.1 PMID:1822724

Fellenz, W., Taylor, J., Tsapatsoulis, N., & Kollias, S. (1999). Comparing template-based, feature-based and supervised classification of facial expressions from static images. In *Proceedings of International Conference on Circuits, Systems, Communications and Computers (CSCC'99)*.

Fitzgerald, Shi, Foong, & Pappalardo. (2011). Country of Origin and Internet Publication: Applying the Berne Convention in the Digital Age. *Journal of Intellectual Property (NJIP) Maiden Edition*, 38-73

Flierl, M., & Girod, B. (2004). Video coding with motion-compensated lifted wavelet transforms. *Signal Processing Image Communication*, *19*(7), 561–575. doi:10.1016/j.image.2004.05.002

Forsyth, D. A., & Ponce, J. (2003). *Computer Vision: A Modern Approach*. Berkeley, CA: Prentice Hall.

Fox, B., & LaMacchia, B. A. (2003). Encouraging Recognition of Fair Uses in DRM Systems. *Communications of the ACM*, *46*(4), 61–63. doi:10.1145/641205.641233

Fridrich, A. J., Soukal, B. D., & Lukáš, A. J. (2003). Detection of copy-move forgery in digital images.*Proceedings of Digital Forensic Research Workshop*.

Fridrich, J. (2010). *Steganography in Digital Media*. Cambridge, UK: Cambridge University Press.

Fridrich, J., Chen, M., & Goljan, M. (2007). Imaging sensor noise as digital x-ray for revealing forgeries.*9th International Workshop on Information Hiding*.

Fridrich, J., Soukal, D., & Lukas, J. (2003). Detection of copy-move forgery in digital images. In *Proc. of Digital Forensic Research Workshop*.

Frintrop, S. (2005). *VOCUS: a visual attention system for object detection and goal-directed search*. (Ph.D. thesis). Rheinische Friedrich-Wilhelms-Universität Bonn, Germany.

Frintrop, S., & Kessel, M. (2009). *Most Salient Region Tracking*. Paper presented at IEEE International Conference on Robotics and Automation, Kobe, Japan.

Frintrop, S., Jensfelt, P., & Christensen, H. (2007). Simultaneous robot localization and mapping based on a visual attention system. *Attention in Cognitive Systems, Lecture Notes on Artificial Intelligence, 4840*.

Frintrop, S., Rome, E., & Christensen, H. I. (2010). Computational visual attention systems and their cognitive foundations: a survey. *Transactions on Applied Perceptions, 7*(1).

Frintrop, S. (2006). *VOCUS: A visual attention system for object detection and goal-directed search* (Vol. 3899). Springer-Verlag New York. doi:10.1007/11682110

Frintrop, S., & Jensfelt, P. (2008). Attentional Landmarks and Active Gaze Control for Visual SLAM. *IEEE Transactions on Robotics*, *24*(5), 1054–1065. doi:10.1109/TRO.2008.2004977

Frintrop, S., Rome, E., & Christensen, H. I. (2010). Computational Visual Attention Systems and their Cognitive Foundations: A Survey. *ACM Transactions on Applied Perception*, *7*(1), 1–46. doi:10.1145/1658349.1658355

Friston, K. J. (1994). Functional and effective connectivity in neuroimaging: A synthesis. *Human Brain Mapping*, *2*(1-2), 56–78. doi:10.1002/hbm.460020107

Friston, K. J., & Büchel, C. (2000). Attentional modulation of effective connectivity from V2 to V5/MT in humans. *Proceedings of the National Academy of Sciences of the United States of America*, *97*(13), 7591–7596. doi:10.1073/pnas.97.13.7591 PMID:10861020

Fritz, G., Seifert, C., & Paletta, L. (2004). Attentive object detection using an information theoretic saliency measure. In *Proceedings of 2nd Int'l Workshop on Attention and Performance in Computational Vision (WAPCV)* (pp 136–143). Prague, Czech Republic: WAPCV.

Funada, J., Ohta, N., Mizoguchi, M., Temma, T., Nakanishi, T., & Murai, K. et al.. (1998). Feature extraction method for palmprint considering elimination of creases.*Proceedings of the 14th International Conference of Pattern Recognition, 2,*1849-1854. doi:10.1109/ICPR.1998.712091

Galdino, L., & Borges, D. (2000). *A Visual Attention Model for Tracking Regions Based on Color Correlograms.* Paper presented at CGIP. doi:10.1109/SIBGRA.2000.883892

Gale, A., Haslum, M., & Penfold, V. (1971). EEG correlates of cumulative expectancy and subjective estimates of alertness in a vigilance-type task. *The Quarterly Journal of Experimental Psychology, 23*(3), 245–254. doi:10.1080/14640746908401818

Gao, D., Mahadevan, V., & Vasconcelos, N. (2008). On the plausibility of the discriminant center-surround hypothesis for visual saliency. *Journal of Vision, 8*(7).

Geradts, Z. J., Bijhold, J., Kieft, M., Kurosawa, K., Kuroki, K., & Saitoh, N. (2001). Methods for Identification of Images Acquired with Digital Cameras. In *Proc. of SPIE, Enabling Technologies for Law Enforcement and Security,* (vol. 4232). doi:10.1117/12.417569

Goferman, S., Zelnik-Manor, L., & Tal, A. (2012). Context-aware saliency detection. *IEEE Transactions on Pattern Analysis and Machine Intelligence, 34*(10), 1915–1926. doi:10.1109/TPAMI.2011.272 PMID:22201056

Goldberg, J. H., & Kotval, X. P. (1999). Computer interface evaluation using eye movements: Methods and constructs. *International Journal of Industrial Ergonomics, 24*(6), 631–645. doi:10.1016/S0169-8141(98)00068-7

Goldberg, J. H., Stimson, M. J., Lewenstein, M., Scott, N., & Wichansky, A. M. (2002). Eye tracking in web search tasks: design implications. In *Proceedings of the 2002 symposium on Eye tracking research & applications,* (pp. 51–58). ACM. doi:10.1145/507072.507082

Goldberg, M. E., Bisley, J. W., Powell, K. D., & Gottlieb, J. (2006). Saccades, salience and attention: The role of the lateral intraparietal area in visual behavior. *Progress in Brain Research, 155,* 157–175. doi:10.1016/S0079-6123(06)55010-1 PMID:17027387

Gopalakrishnan, V., Hu, Y., & Rajan, D. (2009). Random walks on graphs to model saliency in images. In *Proc. of IEEE Computer Society Conference on Computer Vision and Pattern Recognition.* doi:10.1109/CVPR.2009.5206767

Gou, H., Swaminathan, A., & Wu, M. (2007). Robust Scanner Identification based on Noise Features. *In Proc. of IS&TSPIE Conf on Security, Stego., and Watermarking ofMultimedia Contents IX.*

Gou, H., Swaminathan, A., & Wu, M. (2007). Noise features for image tampering detection and steganalysis.*IEEE International Conference on Image Processing.* doi:10.1109/ICIP.2007.4379530

Grafsgaard, J. F., Wiggins, J. B., Boyer, K. E., Wiebe, E. N., & Lester, J. C. (2013). Automatically Recognizing Facial Expression. *Predicting Engagement and Frustration.Intl. Conference on Educational Data Mining,* Memphis, TN.

Grandjean, E. (1979). Fatigue in industry. *British Journal of Industrial Medicine, 36,* 175–186. doi:10.2105/AJPH.12.3.212 PMID:40999

Greenspan, A. G., Belongie, S., Goodman, R., Perona, P., Rakshit, S., & Anderson, C. H. (1994). Overcomplete steerable pyramid filters and rotation invariance. In *Proceedings of IEEE International Conference on Computer Vision Pattern Recognition (CVPR)* (pp. 222–228). doi:10.1109/CVPR.1994.323833

Guangming, L., David, Z., & Kuanquan, W. (2003). Palmprint recognition using eigenpalms features. *Pattern Recognition Letters*, *24*(9-10), 1463–1467. doi:10.1016/S0167-8655(02)00386-0

Guigue, P., & Devillers, O. (2003). Fast and robust triangle - triangle overlap test using orientation predicates. *Journal of Graphics Tools*, *8*(1), 25–42.

Guironnet, M., Guyader, N., Pellerin, D., & Ladret, P. (2005). Spatio-temporal Attention Model for Video Content Analysis. In *Proc. of IEEE International Conference on Image processing*. doi:10.1109/ICIP.2005.1530602

Guiyu, F., Dewen, H., & David, Z. et al.. (2006). An alternative formulation of kernel LPP with application to image recognition. *Neurocomputing*, *69*(13-15), 1733–1738. doi:10.1016/j.neucom.2006.01.006

Guler, S., Silverstein, J., & Pushee, I. (2007). *Stationary Objects in Multiple Object Tracking*. Paper presented at AVSS. doi:10.1109/AVSS.2007.4425318

Guo, Z., Zhang, l., Zhang,D. (2010). Feature Band Selection for Multispectral Palmprint Recognition. *Proceedings of the 20th International Conference on Pattern Recognition*. doi:10.1109/ICPR.2010.284

Guo, C., & Zhang, L. (2010). A novel multiresolution spatiotemporal saliency detection model and its applications in image and video compression. *Image Processing. IEEE Transactions on*, *19*(1), 185–198.

Guo, D., Tang, J., Cui, Y., Ding, J., & Zhao, C. (2015). Saliency-based content-aware lifestyle image mosaics. *Journal of Visual Communication and Image Representation*, *26*, 192–199.

Guo, Y., Liu, F., Shi, J., Zhou, Z.-H., & Gleicher, M. (2009). Image retargeting using mesh parameterization. *IEEE Transactions on Multimedia*, *11*(5), 856–867. doi:10.1109/TMM.2009.2021781

Gyaourova, A., & Ross, A. (2012). Index codes for multibiometric pattern retrieval. *IEEE Trans. Information and Forensics Security*, *7*(2), 518–529. doi:10.1109/TIFS.2011.2172429

Hakkinen, J., Kawai, T., Takatalo, J., Mitsuya, R., & Nyman, G. (2010). What do people look at when they watch stereoscopic movies?. *Electronic Imaging*, *7524*, 75240E.

Hamker, F. H. (2005). The emergence of attention by population-based inference and its role in distributed processing and cognitive control of vision. *Computer Vision and Image Understanding*, *100*(1), 64–106. doi:10.1016/j.cviu.2004.09.005

Hamker, F. H. (2005b). The reentry hypothesis: The putative interaction of the frontal eye field, ventrolateral prefrontal cortex, and areas V4, IT for attention and eye movement. *Cerebral Cortex*, *15*(4), 431–447. doi:10.1093/cercor/bhh146 PMID:15749987

Han, C. C. (2004). A hand-based personal authentication using a coarse-to-fine strategy. *Image and Vision Computing*, *22*(11), 909–918. doi:10.1016/j.imavis.2004.05.008

Han, C. C., Chen, H. L., Lin, C. L., & Fan, K. C. (2003). Personal authentication using palmprint features. *Pattern Recognition*, *36*(2), 371–381. doi:10.1016/S0031-3203(02)00037-7

Han, D., Guo, Z., & Zhang, D. (2008). Multispectral palmprint recognition using wavelet-based image fusion. In *Proceedings of the 9th International Conference on Signal Processing*.

Hao, F., Daugman, H., & Zieliski, P. (2008). A fast search algorithm for a large fuzzy database. *IEEE Transaction Information and Forensics Security*, *3*(2), 203–212. doi:10.1109/TIFS.2008.920726

Hao, Y., Sun, Z., & Tan, T. (2007). Comparative Studies on Multispectral Palm Image Fusion for Biometrics.*Proceedings of the Asian Conference on Computer Vision*, *2*, 12-21. doi:10.1007/978-3-540-76390-1_2

Harel, J., Koch, C., & Perona, P. (2006). *Graph-based visual saliency.* Proc. of Neural Information Processing Systems.

Harel, J., Koch, C., & Perona, P. (2006). Graph-based visual saliency. *Advances in Neural Information Processing Systems, 19,* 2006.

Harris, C., & Stephens, M. (1988). A combined corner and edge detector.*4th Alvey Vision Conference,* (pp. 147–151).

Hartley, R., & Zisserman, A. (2003). *Multiple View Geometry in Computer Vision.* Cambridge University Press.

Hartung, F., & Kutter, M. (1999). Multimedia watermarking techniques. *Proceedings of the IEEE, 87*(7), 1079–1107. doi:10.1109/5.771066

Heinen, M. R., & Engel, P. M. (2009). NLOOK: A computational attention model for robot vision. *Journal of the Brazilian Computer Society, 15*(3), 3–17. doi:10.1007/BF03194502

Heisele, B., Serre, T., & Poggio, T. (2007). A component-based framework for face detection and identification. *International Journal of Computer Vision, 74*(2), 167–181. doi:10.1007/s11263-006-0006-z

He, K., Sun, J., & Tang, X. (2010). Guided image filtering. In *Proc. of European Conference on Computer Vision.*

Held, M. (1997). ERIT a collection of efficient and reliable intersection tests. *Journal of Graphics Tools, 2*(4), 25–44. doi:10.1080/10867651.1997.10487482

Hennings, P., & Kumar, B. V. K. V. (2004). Palmprint recognition using correlation filter classifiers. *Conference Record of the 38th Asilomar Conference on Signal, Systems and Computers, 1,* 567–571. doi:10.1109/ACSSC.2004.1399197

Hennings-Yeomans, P.H., Vijaya Kumar, B.V. K. & Savvides, M. Palmprint classification using multiple advanced correlation filters and palm-specific segmentation. *IEEE Transactions on Information Forensics and Security, 2*(3), 613–622.

Hillaire, S., Lecuyer, A., Regia-Corte, T., Cozot, R., Royan, J., & Breton, G. (2012). Design and application of real-time visual attention model for the exploration of 3D virtual environments. *IEEE Transactions on Visualization and Computer Graphics, 18*(3), 356–368. doi:10.1109/TVCG.2011.154 PMID:21931178

Hoffman, D. M., Girshick, A. R., Akeley, K., & Banks, M. S. (2008). Vergence–accommodation conflicts hinder visual performance and cause visual fatigue. *Journal of Vision (Charlottesville, Va.), 8*(3), 33. doi:10.1167/8.3.33 PMID:18484839

Hong, H., Neven, H., & Von der Malsburg, C. (1998). Online facial expression recognition based on personalized galleries. In *Proceedings of the Second IEEE International Conference on Automatic Face and Gesture Recognition, (FG'98).*

Horn, B., & Schunk, B. (1981). Determining optical flow. *Artificial Intelligence, 17*(1-3), 185–203. doi:10.1016/0004-3702(81)90024-2

Hou, X., & Zhang, L. (2007). Saliency detection: A spectral residual approach. In *Computer Vision and Pattern Recognition, 2007. CVPR'07. IEEE Conference on,* (pp. 1–8). IEEE.

Hou, X., & Zhang, L. (2007, June). Saliency detection: A spectral residual approach. In *Computer Vision and Pattern Recognition, 2007. CVPR'07. IEEE Conference on* (pp. 1-8). IEEE. doi:10.1109/CVPR.2007.383267

Hou, B., Yang, W., Wang, S., & Hou, X. (2013). SAR image ship detection based on visual attention model. In *Proc. of IEEE International Geoscience and Remote Sensing Symposium,* (pp. 2003-2006). doi:10.1109/IGARSS.2013.6723202

Houghton, E. G., Emnett, R. F., Factor, J. D., & Sabharwal, C. L. (1985). Implementation of A Divide and Conquer Method For Surface Intersections. *Computer Aided Geometric Design, 2,* 173–183. doi:10.1016/0167-8396(85)90022-6

Houmansadr, A., & Ghaemmaghami, S. (2006, April). A novel video watermarking method using visual cryptography. In *Engineering of Intelligent Systems, 2006 IEEE International Conference on* (pp. 1-5). IEEE. doi:10.1109/ICEIS.2006.1703171

Hou, X., & Zhang, L. (2007). Saliency detection: a spectral residual approach. In *Proc. of IEEE Conference on Computer Vision and Pattern Recognition*.

Hsu, C., Hung, T., Lin, C.-W., & Hsu, C. (2008). Video forgery detection using correlation of noise residue. In *Proceedings of IEEE 10th Workshop on Multimedia Signal Processing*. IEEE.

Hsu, C. C., & Dai, G. T. (2012). Multiple Object Tracking using Particle Swarm Optimization. *World Academy of Science. Engineering and Technology*, *6*(8), 29–32.

Hsu, C.-C., Lin, C.-W., Fang, Y., & Lin, W. (2013). *Objective quality assessment for image retargeting based on perceptual distortion and information loss*. Proc. of Visual Communications and Image Processing. doi:10.1109/VCIP.2013.6706443

Hsu, C.-C., Lin, C.-W., Fang, Y., & Lin, W. (2014). Objective quality assessment for image retargeting based on perceptual geometric distortion and information loss. *IEEE Journal of Selected Topics in Signal Processing*, *8*(3), 377–389. doi:10.1109/JSTSP.2014.2311884

Huang, C., & Huang, Y. (1997). Facial expression recognition using model-based feature extraction and action parameters classification. *Journal of Visual Communication and Image Representation*, *8*(3), 278–290. doi:10.1006/jvci.1997.0359

Huang, D., Jia, W., & Zhang, D. (2008). Palmprint verification based on principal lines. *Pattern Recognition*, *41*(4), 1316–1328. doi:10.1016/j.patcog.2007.08.016

Huang, H., Fu, T., Rosin, P. L., & Chun, Q. (2009). Real-time content-aware image resizing. *Science in China Series F: Information Sciences*, *52*(2), 172–182. doi:10.1007/s11432-009-0041-9

Huang, H., Guo, W., & Zhang, Y. (2008). Detection of copy-move forgery in digital images using SIFT algorithm. *IEEE Pacific-Asia Workshop on Computational Intelligence and Industrial Application*. doi:10.1109/PACIIA.2008.240

Huang, P. (2008). A Fast Watermarking Algorithm for Image Authentication. *International Conference on Cyberworlds*. doi:10.1109/CW.2008.55

Huang, R. S., Jung, T. P., Delorme, A., & Makeig, S. (2008). Tonic and phasic electroencephalographic dynamics during continuous compensatory tracking. *NeuroImage*, *39*(4), 1896–1909. doi:10.1016/j.neuroimage.2007.10.036 PMID:18083601

Huang, R. S., Tsai, L. L., & Kuo, C. J. (2001). Selection of valid and reliable EEG features for predicting auditory and visual alertness levels. *Proceedings of the National Science Council, Republic of China. Part B, Life Sciences*, *25*, 17–25. PMID:11254168

Hubel, D. H. (1995). *Eye, Brain and Vision*. New York, NY: Scientific American Library.

Hutchinson, J. E. (1981). Fractals and self-similarity. *Indiana University Mathematics Journal*, *3*(5), 713–747. doi:10.1512/iumj.1981.30.30055

Huynh-Thu, Q., Barkowsky, M., & Callet, P. L. (2011). The importance of visual attention in improving the 3D-TV viewing experience: Overview and new perspectives. *IEEE Transactions on Broadcasting*, *57*(2), 421–431. doi:10.1109/TBC.2011.2128250

Huynh-Thu, Q., Barkowsky, M., & Le Callet, P. et al. (2011). The Importance of Visual Attention in Improving the 3D-TV Viewing Experience: Overview and New Perspectives. *Broadcasting. IEEE Transactions on*, *57*(2), 421–431.

Hwang, D. S., & Chien, S. Y. (2008). Content-aware image resizing using perceptual seam carving with human attention model. In *Proc. of IEEE International Conference on Multimedia and Expo.*

Hwang, D.-S., & Chien, S.-Y. (2008). Content-aware image resizing using perceptual seam curving with human attention model. In *Proc. of IEEE International Conference on Multimedia and Expo.*

Itti, L., Dhavale, N., & Pighin, F. (2004). Realistic avatar eye and head animation using a neurobiological model of visual attention. In *Optical Science and Technology, SPIE's 48th Annual Meeting*, (pp. 64–78). SPIE.

Itti, L., Gold, C., & Koch, C. (2001). Visual attention and target detection on cluttered natural scenes. *Optical Engineering (Redondo Beach, Calif.)*, *40*(9), 1784–1793. doi:10.1117/1.1389063

Itti, L., & Koch, C. (2001). Computational modeling of visual attention. *Nature Reviews. Neuroscience*, *2*(3), 194–203. doi:10.1038/35058500 PMID:11256080

Itti, L., Koch, C., & Niebur, E. (1998). A model of saliency-based visual attention for rapid scene analysis. *Pattern Analysis and Machine Intelligence. IEEE Transactions on*, *20*(11), 1254–1259.

Itti, L., Koch, C., & Niebur, E. (1998). A model of saliency-based visual attention for rapid scene analysis. *IEEE Transactions on Pattern Analysis and Machine Intelligence*, *20*(11), 1254–1259. doi:10.1109/34.730558

Jacob, R. J. K., & Karn, K. S. (2003). Eye tracking in human-computer interaction and usability research: Ready to deliver the promises. *Mind*, *2*(3), 4.

Jacquin, A. E. (1992). Image Coding Based on a Fractal Theory of Iterated Contractive Image Transformations. *IEEE Transactions on Image Processing*, *1*(1), 18–30. doi:10.1109/83.128028 PMID:18296137

Jain, A. K. (2010). Data clustering: 50 years beyond K-means. *Pattern Recognition Letters*, *31*(8), 651–666. doi:10.1016/j.patrec.2009.09.011

Jain, A. K., & Feng, J. (2009). Latent palmprint matching. *IEEE Transactions on Pattern Analysis and Machine Intelligence*, *31*(6), 1032–1047. doi:10.1109/TPAMI.2008.242 PMID:19372608

Jain, A., Flynn, P., & Ross, A. (2007). *Handbook of Biometrics*. Springer.

Jain, R., & Nagel, H. (1979). On the analysis of accumulative difference pictures from image sequences of real world scenes. *Institute Of Electrical And Electronics Engineers Transactions on Pattern Analysis and Machine Intelligence*, *1*(2), 206–214. PMID:21868850

James, W., Burkhardt, F., & Skrupskelis, I. K. (1980). *The principles of psychology* (Vol. 1). Harvard Univ Press.

Jansen, L., Onat, S., & König, P. (2009). Influence of disparity on fixation and saccades in free viewing of natural scenes. *Journal of Vision*, *9*(1).

Jap, B. T., Lal, S., Fischer, P., & Bekiaris, E. (2009). Using EEG spectral components to assess algorithms for detecting fatigue. *Expert Systems with Applications*, *36*(2), 2352–2359. doi:10.1016/j.eswa.2007.12.043

Javed, O., Shafique, K., & Shah, M. (2002). A Hierarchical Approach to Robust Background Subtraction using Color and Gradient Information.*Institute Of Electrical And Electronics Engineers Workshop on Motion and Video Computing*, (pp. 22-27). doi:10.1109/MOTION.2002.1182209

Jayamohan & Revathy. (2012). A Hybrid Fractal-Wavelet Digital Watermarking Technique with Localized Embedding Strength. *6th International Conference on Information Processing.*

Jia, W., Huang, D. S., & Zhang, D. (2008). Palmprint verification based on robust line orientation code. *Pattern Recognition*, *41*(5), 1504–1513. doi:10.1016/j.patcog.2007.10.011

Jia, W., & Hu, R. X., Lei, Zhao, Y.K., & Gui, J. (2013). Histogram of Oriented Lines for Palmprint Recognition. *IEEE Transactions on Systems, Man, and Cybernetics. Systems*, *44*(3), 385–395.

Jing, L., Gang, L., & Jiulong, Z. (2009). *Robust image watermarking based on SIFT feature and optimal triangulation.* Paper presented at the Information Technology and Applications, 2009. IFITA'09. International Forum on. doi:10.1109/IFITA.2009.110

Jing, X. Y., Yao, Y. F., Zhang, D., Yang, J. Y., & Li, M. (2007). Face and palmprint pixel level fusion and Kernel DCV-RBF classifier for small sample biometric recognition. *Pattern Recognition*, *40*(11), 3209–3224. doi:10.1016/j.patcog.2007.01.034

Jing, X., Tang, Y., & Zhang, D. (2005). A fourier-lDA approach for image recognition. *Pattern Recognition*, *38*(3), 453–457. doi:10.1016/j.patcog.2003.09.020

Jing, X., & Zhang, D. (2004). A face and palmprint recognition approach based on discriminant DCT feature extraction, *IEEE Transaction. System and Man Cybernetic. Part B*, *34*(6), 2405–2415.

Jing, Z., Li, Z., Jingjing, G., & Zhixing, L. (2009). A study of top-down visual attention model based on similarity distance. In *Proc. of 2nd International Congress on Image and Signal Processing*.

Johnson, M. K., & Farid, H. (2006). Exposing digital forgeries through chromatic aberration. In *Proc. of International Multimedia Conference*.

Johnson, M. K., & Farid, H. (2006). Exposing digital forgeries through chromatic aberration. *ACM Multimedia and Security Workshop*.

Johnson, M., & Farid, H. (2005). Exposing digital forgeries by detecting inconsistencies in lighting. *Proc ACM Multimedia and Security Workshop*. doi:10.1145/1073170.1073171

Judd, K., & Mees, A. (1998). Embedding as a modeling problem. *Physica D. Nonlinear Phenomena*, *120*(3-4), 273–286. doi:10.1016/S0167-2789(98)00089-X

Jung, H.-S., Lee, Y.-Y., & Lee, S. U. (2004). RST-resilient video watermarking using scene-based feature extraction. *EURASIP Journal on Applied Signal Processing*, *2004*(14), 2113–2131. doi:10.1155/S1110865704405046

Jung, T. P., Makeig, S., Stensmo, M., & Sejnowski, T. J. (1997). Estimating alertness from the EEG power spectrum. *IEEE Transactions on Bio-Medical Engineering*, *44*(1), 60–69. doi:10.1109/10.553713 PMID:9214784

Just, M. A., & Carpenter, P. A. (1976). Eye fixations and cognitive processes. *Cognitive Psychology*, *8*(4), 441–480. doi:10.1016/0010-0285(76)90015-3

Kabir, M., Jabid, T., & Chae, O. (2010). A local directional pattern variance (LDPv) based face descriptor for human facial expression recognition. In *Proceedings 7th IEEE International Conference on Adv. Video Signal Based Surveill.*

Kadir, T., & Brady, M. (2001). Saliency, scale and image description. *International Journal of Computer Vision*, *45*(2), 83–105. doi:10.1023/A:1012460413855

Kadiyala, V., Pinneli, S., Larson, E. C., & Chandler, D. M. (2008). *Quantifying the perceived interest of objects in images: effects of size, location, blur, and contrast. In Electronic Imaging* (p. 68060S). SPIE.

Kaiser, S., & Wehrle, T. (1992). Automated coding of facial behavior in human–computer interactions with FACS. *Journal of Nonverbal Behavior*, *16*(2), 67–83. doi:10.1007/BF00990323

Kalantari, N. K., Ahadi, S. M., & Vafadust, M. (2010). A Robust Image Watermarking in the Ridgelet Domain Using Universally Optimum Decoder. *IEEE Transactions on Circuits and Systems for Video Technology*, *20*(3), 396–406. doi:10.1109/TCSVT.2009.2035842

Kanade, T., Cohn, J., & Tian, Y. (2000). Comprehensive Database for Facial Expression Analysis. In *Proceedings of IEEE International Conference on Face and Gesture Recognition.*

Kandel, E. R., Schwartz, J. H., & Jessell, T. M. (2000). *Principles of Neural Science* (Vol. 4). McGraw-Hill New York.

Kang, J., Cohen, I., & Medioni, G. (2004). Object reacquisition using geometric invariant appearance, model.*International Conference on Pattern Recognition (ICPR)*, (pp. 759–762).

Kang, X., Zeng, W., & Huang, J. (2008). A Multi-band Wavelet Watermarking Scheme. *International Journal of Network Security*, *6*(2), 121–126.

Kar, S., Bhagat, M., & Routray, A. (2010). EEG signal analysis for the assessment and quantification of driver's fatigue. *Transportation Research Part F: Traffic Psychology and Behaviour*, *13*(5), 297–306. doi:10.1016/j.trf.2010.06.006

Karsh, R., & Breitenbach, F. (1983). Looking at looking: The amorphous fixation measure. *Eye Movements and Psychological Functions: International Views*, 53–64.

Karthikeyan, S., Jagadeesh, V., & Manjunath, B. S. (2013). *Learning top down Scene context for Visual Attention modeling in Natural Images.* Paper presented at IEEE International Conference on Image Processing. doi:10.1109/ICIP.2013.6738044

Kaur, M., Vashisht, R., & Neeru, N. (2010). Recognition of Facial Expressions with Principal Component Analysis and Singular Value Decomposition. *International Journal of Computers and Applications*, 9–12.

Kee, E., & Farid, H. (2010). Digital image authentication from thumbnails.*SPIE Symposium on Electronic Imaging.*

Kekre, H. B., Sarode, T., & Vig, R. (2012). An effectual method for extraction of ROI of palmprints, *International Conference on Communication Information & Computing Technology (ICCICT)*. doi:10.1109/ICCICT.2012.6398207

Kelley, T. A., Serences, J. T., Giesbrecht, B., & Yantis, S. (2008). Cortical mechanisms for shifting and holding visuospatial attention. *Cerebral Cortex*, *18*(1), 114–125. doi:10.1093/cercor/bhm036 PMID:17434917

Ke, Y., Min, W., Qin, F., & Shang, J. (2014). Image Forgery Detection based on Semantics. *International Journal of Hybrid Information Technology*, *10*(1), 109–124. doi:10.14257/ijhit.2014.7.1.09

Khan, Z. H., Gu, I. Y. H., & Backhouse, A. G. (2011). Robust Visual Object Tracking Using Multi-Mode Anisotropic Mean Shift and Particle Filters. *Institute Of Electrical And Electronics Engineers Transactions On Circuits And Systems For Video Technology*, *21*(1), 74–87.

Kharrazi, M., Sencar, H. T., & Memon, N. (2004) Blind source camera identification.*InProceedings of the IEEE International Conference on Image Processing.*

Kienzle, W., Wichmann, F. A., Scholkopf, B., & Franz, M. O. (2006). A non-parametric approach to bottom-up visual saliency. *Advances in Neural Information Processing Systems*, 19.

Kiess, J., Gracia, R., Kopf, S., & Effelsberg, W. (2012). Improved image retargeting by distinguishing between faces in focus and out of focus. In *Proc. of IEEE International Conference on Multimedia and Expo Workshops*. doi:10.1109/ICMEW.2012.32

Kim, J.-S., Kim, J.-H., & Kim, C.-S. (2009). Adaptive image and video retargeting technique based on fourier analysis. In *Proc. of IEEE Conference on Computer Vision and Pattern Recognition.*

Kim, K., Chalidabhongse, T. H., Harwood, D., & Davis, L. (2005). Real-time Foreground-Background Segmentation using Codebook Model. *Real-Time Imaging*, *11*(3), 167–256. doi:10.1016/j.rti.2004.12.004

Kim, W., & Kim, C. (2011). A texture-aware salient edge model for image retargeting. *IEEE Signal Processing Letters*, *18*(11), 631–634. doi:10.1109/LSP.2011.2165337

Kitagawa, G. (1987). Non-gaussian state-space modeling of nonstationary time series. *Journal of the American Statistical Association*, *82*(400), 1032–1041.

Kiymik, M. K., Akin, M., & Subasi, A. (2004). Automatic recognition of alertness level by using wavelet transform and artificial neural network. *Journal of Neuroscience Methods*, *139*(2), 231–240. doi:10.1016/j.jneumeth.2004.04.027 PMID:15488236

Klimesch, W. (1996). Memory processes, brain oscillations and EEG synchronization. *International Journal of Psychophysiology*, *24*(1-2), 61–100. doi:10.1016/S0167-8760(96)00057-8 PMID:8978436

Klimesch, W. (1999). EEG alpha and theta oscillations reflect cognitive and memory performance: A review and analysis. *Brain Research. Brain Research Reviews*, *29*(2-3), 169–195. doi:10.1016/S0165-0173(98)00056-3 PMID:10209231

Kobayashi, H., & Hara, F. (1997). Facial interaction between animated 3D face robot and human beings. In *Proceedings of the International Conference on Systems, Man and Cybernetics*. doi:10.1109/ICSMC.1997.633250

Kobayashi, M., Okabe, T., & Sato, Y. (2009). *Detecting Video Forgeries Based on Noise Characteristics. Pooc.of.* Springer-Verlag Berlin Heidelberg.

Kobayashi, M., Okabe, T., & Sato, Y. (2010). Detecting Forgery From Static-Scene Video Based on Inconsistency in Noise Level Functions. *IEEE Transactions on Information Forensics and Security*, *5*(4), 883–892. doi:10.1109/TIFS.2010.2074194

Koch, C., & Ullman, S. (1987). Shifts in selective visual attention: towards the underlying neural circuitry. In Matters of intelligence, (pp. 115–141). Springer.

Koch, C., & Ullman, S. (1985). Shifts in selective visual attention: Towards the underlying neural circuitry. *Human Neurobiology*, *4*, 219–227. PMID:3836989

Koch, C., & Ullman, S. (1985). Shifts in selective visual attention: Towards the underlying neural circuitry. *Human Neurobiology*, *4*, 219–227. PMID:3836989

Kokui, T., Takimoto, H., Mitsukura, Y., Kishihara, M., & Okubo, K. (2013). Color image modification based on visual saliency for guiding visual attention. In *Proc. of the 22nd IEEE International Symposium on Robot and Human Interactive Communication*. doi:10.1109/ROMAN.2013.6628548

Kong, A. W. K., & Zhang, D. (2004).Competitive coding scheme for palmprint verification.*Proceedings of International Conference on Pattern Recognition*, *1*,520–523.

Kong, A., Cheung, K. H., Zhang, D., Kamel, M., & You, J. (2006). An analysis of Biohashing and its variants. *Pattern Recognition*, *39*(7), 1359–1368. doi:10.1016/j.patcog.2005.10.025

Kong, A., Zhang, D., & Kamel, M. (2006). Palmprint identification using feature-level fusion. *Pattern Recognition*, *3*(3), 478–487. doi:10.1016/j.patcog.2005.08.014

Kong, A., Zhang, D., & Kamel, M. (2009). A survey of palmprint recognition. *Pattern Recognition*, *42*(7), 1408–1418. doi:10.1016/j.patcog.2009.01.018

Kong, W., & Zhang, D. (2002). Palmprint texture analysis based on low-resolution images for personal authentication. *Proceedings of 16th International Conference on Pattern Recognition, 3,*807–810. doi:10.1109/ICPR.2002.1048142

Kong, W., Zhang, D., & Li, W. (2003). Palmprint feature extraction using 2D gabor filters. *Pattern Recognition, 36*(10), 2339–2347. doi:10.1016/S0031-3203(03)00121-3

Kootstra, G., Nederveen, A., & De Boer, B. (2008). Paying attention to symmetry. In *Proceedings of the British Machine Vision Conference (BMVC2008)*, (pp. 1115–1125). BMVC.

Kumar, A., Wong, D. C. M., Shen, H. C., & Jain, A. K. (2003). Personal verification using palmprint and hand geometry biometric. Lecture Notes in Computer Science, Springer, 2668, 668–678.

Kumar, A., & Shen, C. (2004). Palmprint identification using PalmCodes. In *Proceedings of 3rd International Conference on Image and Graphics*. doi:10.1109/ICIG.2004.110

Kumar, A., & Zhang, D. (2003). Integrating palmprint with face for user authentication. In *Proceedings of Multi Modal User Authentication Workshop*.

Kumar, A., & Zhang, D. (2006). Personal recognition using hand shape and texture. *IEEE Transactions on Image Processing, 15*(8), 2454–2461. doi:10.1109/TIP.2006.875214 PMID:16900698

Kumara, A., & Zhang, D. (2005). Personal authentication using multiple palmprint representation. *Pattern Recognition, 38*(10), 1695–1704. doi:10.1016/j.patcog.2005.03.012

Kumar, K. V., & Negi, A. (2007). A novel approach to eigenpalm features using feature partitioning framework.*Conference on Machine Vision Applications*.

Kutter, M., Bhattacharjee, S. K., & Ebrahimi, T. (1999). *Towards second generation watermarking schemes*. Paper presented at the Image Processing. doi:10.1109/ICIP.1999.821622

Kutter, M., & Petitcolas, F. A. P. (1999). A fair Benchmark for image Watermarking Systems, Security and Watermarking of Multimedia Contents. *Proceedings of the Society for Photo-Instrumentation Engineers, 3657,* 1–14. doi:10.1117/12.344672

Lacasa, L., Luque, B., Ballesteros, F., Luque, J., & Nuño, J. C. (2008). From time series to complex networks: The visibility graph. *Proceedings of the National Academy of Sciences of the United States of America, 105*(13), 4972–4975. doi:10.1073/pnas.0709247105 PMID:18362361

Lalonde, J. F., & Efros, A. A. (2007). Using color compatibility for assessing image realism.*Proceedings of the International Conference on Computer Vision*. doi:10.1109/ICCV.2007.4409107

Lal, S. K. L., & Craig, A. (2001). A critical review of the psychophysiology of driver fatigue. *Biological Psychology, 55*(3), 173–194. doi:10.1016/S0301-0511(00)00085-5 PMID:11240213

Lanitis, A., Taylor, C., & Cootes, T. (1997). Automatic interpretation and coding off ace images using *2exible models*. *IEEE Transactions on Pattern Analysis and Machine Intelligence, 19*(7), 743–756. doi:10.1109/34.598231

Le Meur, O., & Le Callet, P. (2009). What we see is most likely to be what matters: visual attention and applications. In *Image Processing (ICIP), 2009 16th IEEE International Conference on*, (pp. 3085–3088). IEEE.

Le Meur, O., & Chevet, J. C. (2010). Relevance of a feed-forward model of visual attention for goal-oriented and free-viewing tasks. *Image Processing. IEEE Transactions on, 19*(11), 2801–2813.

Le Meur, O., Le Callet, P., & Barba, D. (2007). Predicting visual fixations on video based on low-level visual features. *Vision Research, 47*(19), 2483–2498. doi:10.1016/j.visres.2007.06.015 PMID:17688904

Le Meur, O., Le Callet, P., Barba, D., & Thoreau, D. (2006). A coherent computational approach to model bottom-up visual attention. *Pattern Analysis and Machine Intelligence. IEEE Transactions on, 28*(5), 802–817.

Lee, H.-Y., Kim, H., & Lee, H.-K. (2006). Robust image watermarking using local invariant features. *Optical Engineering, 45*(3).

Lee, S.-J., & Jung, S.-H. (2001). A survey of watermarking techniques applied to multimedia. In *Proc. of IEEE International Symposium on Industrial Electronics*, (*vol. 1*, pp. 272–277). IEEE.

Lee, J. T. (1992). *Evaluation of algorithms for surface interpolation over triangular patch.Intl.* Conf on International Society for Photography and Remote Sensing.

Lee, J., & Maunsell, J. H. R. (2009). A Normalization Model of Attentional Modulation of Single Unit Responses. *PLoS ONE, 4*(2), e4651. doi:10.1371/journal.pone.0004651 PMID:19247494

Lee, J., & Maunsell, J. H. R. (2010). Attentional Modulation of MT Neurons with Single or Multiple Stimuli in Their Receptive Fields. *The Journal of Neuroscience, 30*(8), 3058–3066. doi:10.1523/JNEUROSCI.3766-09.2010 PMID:20181602

Lee, J.-S., Simone, F. D., & Ebrahimi, T. (2011). Efficient video coding based on audio-visual focus of attention. *Journal of Visual Communication and Image Representation, 22*(8), 704–711. doi:10.1016/j.jvcir.2010.11.002

Lee, K. W., Buxton, H., & Feng, J. (2005). Cue-guided search: A computational model of selective attention. *Neural Networks. IEEE Transactions on, 16*(4), 910–924.

Lee, K.-Y., Chung, C.-D., & Chuang, Y.-Y. (2012). Scene warping: Layer based stereoscopic image resizing. In *Proc. of IEEE Conference on Computer Vision and Pattern Recognition.*

Lee, S., Kim, K., Kim, J.-Y., Kim, M., & Yoo, H.-J. (2010). Familiarity based unified visual attention model for fast and robust object recognition. *Pattern Recognition, 43*(3), 1116–1128. doi:10.1016/j.patcog.2009.07.014

Lenné, M. G., Triggs, T. J., & Redman, J. R. (1997). Time of day variations in driving performance. *Accident; Analysis and Prevention, 29*(4), 431–437. doi:10.1016/S0001-4575(97)00022-5 PMID:9248501

Leung, M., Fong, A., & Cheung, H. (2007). Palmprint verification for controlling access to shared computing resources. *IEEE Pervasive Computing / IEEE Computer Society [and] IEEE Communications Society, 6*(4), 40–47. doi:10.1109/MPRV.2007.78

Li, S., & Lee, M. (2007). *Fast Visual Tracking Using Motion Saliency in Video.* Paper presented at ICASSP. doi:10.1109/ICASSP.2007.366097

Li, W., Zhang, L., Zhang, D., & Yan, J. (2009). Principal line based ICP alignment for palmprint verification. In *Processing of 16th IEEE International Conference on Image Processing (ICIP).*

Li, Wang, & Xie. (2008). A Local Watermarking Scheme in the Ridgelet Domain Combining Image Content and JND Model. *International Conference on Computational Intelligence and Security.*

Liang, Y., Liu, Y.-J., Luo, X.-N., Xie, L., & Fu, X. (2013). Optimal-scaling-factor assignment for patch-wise image retargeting. *IEEE Computer Graphics and Applications, 33*(5), 68–78. doi:10.1109/MCG.2012.123 PMID:24808083

Liang, Y., Su, Z., & Luo, X. (2012). Patchwise scaling method for content-aware image resizing. *Signal Processing, 92*(5), 1243–1257. doi:10.1016/j.sigpro.2011.11.018

Liao, S., Jain, A. K., & Li, S. Z. (2014). A Fast and Accurate Unconstrained Face Detector. *arXiv preprint arXiv*:1408.1656.

Lien, J. (1998). *Automatic recognition of facial expression using hidden Markov models and estimation of expression intensity.* (Ph.D. Thesis). The Robotics Institute, CMU.

Li, F., Leung, M. K., Shikhare, T., Chan, V., & Choon, K. F. (2006). Palmprint classification.*InProc. IEEE Int. Conference on Systems Man and Cybernetics.*

Li, J., Tian, Y., Huang, T., & Gao, W. (2010). Probabilistic multi-task learning for visual saliency estimation in video. *International Journal of Computer Vision, 90*(2), 150–165. doi:10.1007/s11263-010-0354-6

Lin, C.-L., Chuang, T. C., & Fan, K.-C. (2005). Palmprint Verification using hierarchical decomposition. *Pattern Recognition, 38*(12), 2639–2652. doi:10.1016/j.patcog.2005.04.001

Lindeberg, T. (1996a). *Feature detection with automatic scale selection. Technical Report.* Dept. of Numerical Analysis and Computing Science, Royal Institute of Technology.

Lindeberg, T. (1996b). *Edge detection and ridge detection with automatic scale selection. Technical report.* Dept. of Numerical Analysis and Computing Science, Royal Institute of Technology.

Lindeberg, T. (1998). Feature detection with automatic scale selection. *IJCV, 30*(2), 79–116. doi:10.1023/A:1008045108935

Lin, P. L., Hsieh, C. K., & Huang, P. W. (2005). A hierarchical digital watermarking method for image tamper detection and recovery. *Pattern Recognition, 38*(12), 2519–2529. doi:10.1016/j.patcog.2005.02.007

Lin, S.-S., Lin, C.-H., Chang, S.-H., & Lee, T.-Y. (2014). Object-coherence warping for stereoscopic image retargeting. *IEEE Transactions on Circuits and Systems for Video Technology, 25*(5), 759–768.

Lin, Z., Wang, R., Tang, X., & Shum, H.-Y. (2005). Detecting doctored images using camera response normality and consistency. In *Proc. of IEEE Computer Society Conference on Computer Vision and Pattern Recognition*, (vol. 1, pp. 1087–1092). IEEE.

Li, Q., Qiu, Z., & Sun, D. (2006).Feature-level fusion of hand biometrics for personal verification based on Kernel PCA. *International Conference on Biometrics.*

Li, S. Z., Zhu, L., Zhang, Z. Q., Blake, A., Zhang, H. J., & Shum, H. (2002). Statistical learning of multi-view face detection, In *Proc. of 7th European Conference on Computer Vision.*

Li, S., & Lee, M.-C. (2007). An efficient spatiotemporal attention model and its application to shot matching. *IEEE Transactions on Circuits and Systems for Video Technology, 17*(10), 1383–1387. doi:10.1109/TCSVT.2007.903798

Liu, C., Szeliski, R., Kang, S. B., Lawrence Zitnick, C., & Freeman, W. T. (2006). *Automatic estimation and removal of noise from a single image.* Technical Report MSR-TR-2006-180. Microsoft Research.

Liu, F., & Wu, C. K. (2011). Robust visual cryptography-based watermarking scheme for multiple cover images and multiple owners. *IET Information Security, 5*(2), 121-128.

Liu, Y., & Zhao, J. (2008). *RST invariant video watermarking based on 1D DFT and Radon transform.* Paper presented at the Visual Information Engineering, 2008. VIE 2008. 5th International Conference on.

Liu, C., Yuen, J., & Torralba, A. (2011). SIFT flow: Dense correspondence across scenes and its applications. *IEEE Transactions on Pattern Analysis and Machine Intelligence, 33*(5), 978–994. doi:10.1109/TPAMI.2010.147 PMID:20714019

Liu, F., & Gleicher, M. (2005). Automatic image retargeting with fisheye-view warping. In *Proc. of the 18th Annual ACM Symposium on User Interface Software and Technology.* doi:10.1145/1095034.1095061

Liu, H., & Heynderickx, I. (2009). Studying the added value of visual attention in objective image quality metrics based on eye movement data. In *Proc. of 16th IEEE International Conference on Image Processing.* doi:10.1109/ICIP.2009.5414466

Liu, H., & Heynderickx, I. (2011). Visual Attention in Objective Image Quality Assessment: Based on Eye-Tracking Data. *Circuits and Systems for Video Technology. IEEE Transactions on, 21*(7), 971–982.

Liu, H., & Heynderickx, I. (2011). Visual attention in objective image quality assessment: Based on eye-tracking data. *IEEE Transactions on Circuits and Systems for Video Technology, 21*(7), 971–982. doi:10.1109/TCSVT.2011.2133770

Liu, H., Jiang, S., Huang, Q., & Xu, C. (2008). A generic virtual content insertion system based on visual attention analysis. In *Proc. of the 16th ACM International Conference on Multimedia.* doi:10.1145/1459359.1459410

Liu, H., Xie, X., Ma, W.-Y., & Zhang, H.-J. (2003). Automatic browsing of large pictures on mobile devices. In *Proc. of 11th ACM International Conference on Multimedia.* doi:10.1145/957013.957045

Liu, L., & Zhang, D. (2005). Palm-line detection.*IEEE International Conference on Image Processing, 3,*269-272.

Liu, L., Zhang, D., & You, J. (2007). Detecting wide lines using isotropic nonlinear filtering. *IEEE Transactions on Image Processing, 6*(6), 1584–1595. doi:10.1109/TIP.2007.894288 PMID:17547136

Liu, X., Sun, J., & Liu, J. (2013). Visual attention based temporally weighting method for video hashing. *IEEE Signal Processing Letters, 20*(12), 1253–1256. doi:10.1109/LSP.2013.2287006

Liu, Y., Cormack, L. K., & Bovik, A. C. (2010). Natural scene statistics at stereo fixations.*Proceedings of the 2010 Symposium on Eye-Tracking Research & Applications,* 161–164. ACM. doi:10.1145/1743666.1743706

Liu, Z., Yan, H., Shen, L., Ngan, K. N., & Zhang, Z. (2010). Adaptive image retargeting using saliency-based continuous seam carving. *Optical Engineering (Redondo Beach, Calif.), 49*(1).

Li, W., Zhang, D., & Xu, Z. (2002). Palmprint identification by Fourier transforms. *International Journal of Pattern Recognition and Artificial Intelligence, 16*(4), 417–432. doi:10.1142/S0218001402001757

Li, X., & Ling, H. (2009). Learning based thumbnail cropping. In *Proc. of IEEE International Conference on Multimedia and Expo.*

Li, Y., Ma, Y.-F., & Zhang, H.-J. (2003). Salient region detection and tracking in video. In *Proc. of International Conference on Multimedia and Expo.*

Logothetis, N. K., Pauls, J., & Poggio, T. (1995). Spatial reference frames for object recognition, tuning for rotations in depth. Cambridge, MA: MIT.

Logothetis, N. K., Pauls, J., Bülthoff, H. H., & Poggio, T. (1994). View-dependent object recognition by monkeys. *Current Biology, 4*(5), 401–414. doi:10.1016/S0960-9822(00)00089-0 PMID:7922354

Longfei, Z., Yuanda, C., Gangyi, D., & Yong, W. (2008). A computable visual attention model for video skimming. In *Proc. of Tenth IEEE Symposium on Multimedia.* doi:10.1109/ISM.2008.117

Long, Y., & Huang, Y. (2006). Image based source camera identification using demosaicing.*Proceedings of MSP,* 419–424.

Lou, D. C., Tso, H. K., & Liu, J. L. (2007). A copyright protection scheme for digital images using visual cryptography technique. *Computer Standards & Interfaces, 29*(1), 125–131. doi:10.1016/j.csi.2006.02.003

Lowe, D. G. (1999). *Object recognition from local scale-invariant features.* Paper presented at the Computer Vision. doi:10.1109/ICCV.1999.790410

Lowe, D. (2004). Distinctive image features from scale-invariant keypoints. *International Journal of Computer Vision, 60*(2), 91–110. doi:10.1023/B:VISI.0000029664.99615.94

Lu, W., Safavi-Naini, R., Uehara, T., & Li, W. (2004). *A scalable and oblivious digital watermarking for images.* Paper presented at the Signal Processing.

Lucas, B. D., & Kanade, T. (1981). An iterative image registration technique with an application to stereo vision.*7th International Joint Conference on Artificial Intelligence.*

Lu, H. (2008). MPCA: Multilinear principal component analysis of tensor objects. *IEEE Transactions on Neural Networks, 19*(1), 18–39. doi:10.1109/TNN.2007.901277 PMID:18269936

Lu, J., Zhao, Y., Xue, Y., & Hu, J. (2008). Palmprint recognition via locality preserving projections and extreme learning machine neural network.*9th International Conference on Signal Processing.*

Luk'aˇs, J., Fridrich, J., & Goljan, M. (2006) Detecting digital image forgeries using sensorpattern noise. In *Proc. of Society of Photo-Optical Instrumentation Engineers Conference*, (vol. 6072, pp. 362–372).

Lukas, J., Fridrich, J., & Goljan, M. (2006). Detecting digital image forgeries using sensor pattern noise. *Proc of Security, Steganography, and Watermarking of Multimedia Contents VIII, part of EI SPIE.*

Lukas, J., Fridrich, J., & Goljan, M. (2005). Determining digital image origin using sensor imperfections. In *Proc. of Society of Photo-Optical Instrumentation Engineers Conference*, (vol. 5685, pp. 249–260).

Lum, P. Y., Singh, Lehman, Ishkanov, Vejdemo-Johansson, Alagappan, Carlsson, & Carlsson. (2013). Extracting insights from the shape of complex data using topology. *Scientific Reports, 3*(1236). DOI: 10.1038/srep01236

Luo, J. (2007). Subject content-based intelligent cropping for digital photos.*IEEE International Conference on Multimedia and Expo.* doi:10.1109/ICME.2007.4285126

Luo, J., & Singhal, A. (2000). On measuring low-level saliency in photographic images. In *Proc. of IEEE Conference on Computer Vision and Pattern Recognition.* doi:10.1109/CVPR.2000.855803

Luo, N., Guo, Z., Wu, G., Song, C., & Zhou, L. (2011). Local-global-based palmprint verification.*International Conference on Advanced Computer Control.*

Lyons, M. J., Budynek, J., & Akamatsu, S. (1999). Automatic classification of single facial images. *IEEE Transactions on Pattern Analysis and Machine Intelligence, 21*(12), 1357–1362. doi:10.1109/34.817413

Macdonald, W. A. (1985). *Human factors & road crashes - A review of their relationship.* Academic Press.

Maeder, A. J. (1995). Importance maps for adaptive information reduction in visual scenes. In *Intelligent Information Systems, 1995. ANZIIS-95.Proceedings of the Third Australian and New Zealand Conference on*, (pp. 24–29). IEEE. doi:10.1109/ANZIIS.1995.705709

Mahadevan, V., & Vasconcelos, N. (2013). Biologically-inspired Object Tracking Using Center-surround Mechanisms. *IEEE Transactions on Pattern Analysis and Machine Intelligence, 35*(3), 541–554. doi:10.1109/TPAMI.2012.98 PMID:22529325

Mahdian, B., & Saic, S. (2010). A bibliography on blind methods for identifying image forgery. *Signal Processing Image Communication, 25*(6), 389–399. doi:10.1016/j.image.2010.05.003

Makeig, S., & Jung, T. P. (1995). Changes in alertness are a principal component of variance in the EEG spectrum. *Neuroreport* (Vol. 7, pp. 213–216). doi:10.1097/00001756-199512290-00051

Maki, A., Nordlund, P., & Eklundh, J. O. (1996). A computational model of depth-based attention. *Pattern Recognition, 1996, Proceedings of the 13th International Conference on*, (vol. 4, pp. 734–739). IEEE.

Maki, A., Nordlund, P., & Eklundh, J. O. (2000). Attentional scene segmentation: Integrating depth and motion. *Computer Vision and Image Understanding, 78*(3), 351–373. doi:10.1006/cviu.2000.0840

Ma, M., & Guo, J. K. (2004). Automatic Image Cropping for Mobile Devices with Built-in Camera. In *First IEEE Consumer Communications and Networking Conference*. doi:10.1109/CCNC.2004.1286964

Mancas, M., Mancas-Thillou, C., Gosselin, B., & Macq, B. (2006). A rarity-based visual attention map – application to texture description. In *Proc. IEEE International Conference on Image Processing*. doi:10.1109/ICIP.2006.312489

Mangaiyarkarasi, P., & Arulselvi, S. (2011). A new Digital Image Watermarking based on Finite Ridgelet Transform and Extraction using lCA. *International Conference on Emerging Trends in Electrical and Computer Technology*. doi:10.1109/ICETECT.2011.5760235

Manjunath, B. S., Ohm, J. R., Vasudevan, V. V., & Yamada, A. (2001). Color and Texture Descriptors. *IEEE Transactions on Circuits and Systems for Video Technology, 11*(6), 703–715. doi:10.1109/76.927424

Marchesotti, L., Cifarelli, C., & Csurka, G. (2009). A framework for visual saliency detection with applications to image thumbnailing. In *Proc. of IEEE 12th International Conference on Computer Vision*. doi:10.1109/ICCV.2009.5459467

Marques, O., Mayron, L. M., Borba, G. B., & Gamba, R. H. (2006). Using visual attention to extract regions of interest in the context of image retrieval. In *Proc. of the 44th Annual Southeast Regional Conference*. doi:10.1145/1185448.1185588

Marshall, S. P. (2000). *Method and apparatus for eye tracking and monitoring pupil dilation to evaluate cognitive activity*. Google US Patents.

Martinez, A., & Benavente, R. (1998). *The AR Face Database*. Technical Report.

Matas, J., Chum, O., Urban, M., & Pajdla, T. (2002). Robust wide baseline stereo from maximally stable extremal regions. In *Proc. of British Machine Vision Conference*. doi:10.5244/C.16.36

Mather, G. (2009). *Foundations of sensation and perception* (Vol. 10). Psychology Press.

Matsushita, Y., & Lin, S. (2007). Radiometric calibration from noise distributions. In *Proc. of IEEE Computer Society Conference on Computer Vision and Pattern Recognition*, (pp. 1–8). IEEE.

Matthews, G., Davies, D. R., Westerman, S. J., & Stammers, R. B. (2000). Human performance: Cognition, stress, and individual differences. Psychology Press East Sussex Cap 9 – 12 (p. 416).

Ma, Y.-F., Lu, L., Zhang, H.-J., & Li, M. (2002). A user attention model for video summarization. In *Proc. of the 10th ACM International Conference on Multimedia*. doi:10.1145/641007.641116

Ma, Y.-F., & Zhang, H.-J. (2003). Contrast-based image attention analysis by using fuzzy growing. In *Proc. of 11th ACM International Conference on Multimedia*. doi:10.1145/957013.957094

Maycock, G. (1997). Sleepiness and driving: The experience of U.K. car drivers. *Accident; Analysis and Prevention, 29*(4), 453–462. doi:10.1016/S0001-4575(97)00024-9 PMID:9248503

Mcfarlane, N., & Schofield, C. (1995). Segmentation and tracking of piglets in images. *Machine Vision and Applications, 8*(3), 187–193. doi:10.1007/BF01215814

Meerwald, P., & Uhl, A. (2008). *Toward robust watermarking of scalable video*. Paper presented at the SPIE, Security, Forensics, Steganography, and Watermarking of Multimedia Contents X.

Meerwald, P., & Uhl, A. (2010). *Robust Watermarking of H.264-Encoded Video: Extension to SVC.* Paper presented at the 2010 Sixth International Conference on Intelligent Information Hiding and Multimedia Signal Processing. doi:10.1109/IIHMSP.2010.28

Meiru, M., Ruan, Q., & Shen, Y. (2010). Palmprint Recognition Based on Discriminative Local Binary Patterns Statistic Feature.*International Conference on Signal Acquisition and Processing.*

Miau, F., Papageorgiou, C., & Itti, L. (2001). Neuromorphic algorithms for computer vision and attention. In *Proceedings of Annual Int'l Symposium on Optical Science and Technology* (pp 12–23). Academic Press.

Michael, G. K. O., & Connie, T. (2008). Touch-less palm print biometrics. *Novel design and implementation. Image and Vision Computing, 26*(12), 1551–1560. doi:10.1016/j.imavis.2008.06.010

Mikolajczyk, K., & Schmid, C. (2001). Indexing based on scale invariant interest points. In *Proceedings 8th IEEE International Conference on Computer Vision, (ICCV).*

Milanese, R., Wechsler, H., Gil, S., Bost, J., & Pun, T. (1994). Integration of bottom-up and top-down cues for visual attention using nonlinear relaxation. In *Proc. of IEEE Computer Society Conference on Computer Vision and Pattern Recognition.* doi:10.1109/CVPR.1994.323898

Mishra, R., Chouhan, M. K., & Nitnawre, D., Dr. (2012). Multiple Object Tracking by Kernel Based Centroid Method for Improve Localization. *International Journal of Advanced Research in Computer Science and Software Engineering, 2*(7), 137–140.

Mitri, S., Frintrop, S., Pervolz, K., Surmann, H., & Nuchter, A. (2005). Robust Object Detection at Regions of Interest with an Application in Ball Recognition. In *Proceedings of IEEE International Conference on Robotics and Automation (ICRA)*(pp 125–130). Barcelona, Spain: IEEE. doi:10.1109/ROBOT.2005.1570107

Möller, T. (1997). A fast triangle - triangle intersection test. *Journal of Graphics Tools, 2*(2), 25–30. doi:10.1080/10867651.1997.10487472

Montabone, S., & Soto, A. (2010). Human detection using a mobile platform and novel features derived from a visual saliency mechanism. *Image and Vision Computing, 28*(3), 391–402. doi:10.1016/j.imavis.2009.06.006

Montez, T., Linkenkaer-Hansen, K., van Dijk, B. W., & Stam, C. J. (2006). Synchronization likelihood with explicit time-frequency priors. *NeuroImage, 33*(4), 1117–1125. doi:10.1016/j.neuroimage.2006.06.066 PMID:17023181

Moore, T., Armstrong, K. M., & Fallah, M. (2003). Visuomotor origins of covert spatial attention. *Neuron, 40*(4), 671–683. doi:10.1016/S0896-6273(03)00716-5 PMID:14622573

Moreno, A., & Sanchez, A. (2004). *GavabDB: a 3D face database.* 2ndCOST275 Workshop on Biometricson the Internet, Vigo, Spain.

Mori, T., Inaba, M., & Inoue, H. (1996). *Visual Tracking Based on Cooperation of Multiple Attention Regions.* Paper presented at ICRA. doi:10.1109/ROBOT.1996.509156

Motwani, M. C., Gadiya, M. C., Motwani, R. C., & Harris, F. C. Jr. (2004). Survey of image denoising techniques. In *Proc. of Global Signal Processing Expo.*

Muja, M., & Lowe, D. G. (2009). Fast Approximate Nearest Neighbors with Automatic Algorithm Configuration. *VISAP, (1),* 2.

Murthy, O. V. R., Muthuswamy, K., Rajan, D., & Tien, C. L. (2010). Image retargeting in compressed domain. In *Proc. of 20th International Conference on Pattern Recognition.*

Mutch, J., & Lowe, D. G. (2008). Object Class Recognition and Localization Using Sparse Features with Limited Receptive Fields. *International Journal of Computer Vision*, *80*(1), 45–57. doi:10.1007/s11263-007-0118-0

Naor, M., & Shamir, A. (1995). Visual cryptography. In Advances in Cryptology—EUROCRYPT'94 (pp. 1-12). Springer Berlin/Heidelberg. doi:10.1007/BFb0053419

National Institute of Standards and Technology. (2001). *Advanced Encryption Standard (AES) FIPS-197*.

Navalpakkam, V., Arbib, M., & Itti, L. (2005). Attention and scene understanding. In L. Itti, G. Rees, & J. K. Tsotsos (Eds.), *Neurobiology of Attention* (pp. 197–203). doi:10.1016/B978-012375731-9/50037-9

Navalpakkam, V., & Itti, L. (2006). Optimal cue selection strategy. *Advances in Neural Information Processing Systems*, *19*, 987–994.

Navalpakkam, V., & Itti, L. (2006a). An integrated model of top-down and bottom-up attention for optimizing detection speed. In *Proceedings of International Conference on Computer Vision and Pattern Recognition (CVPR)*. doi:10.1109/CVPR.2006.54

Ng, T. T., & Chang, S. F. (2004). *Classifying photographic and photorealistic computer graphic images using natural image statistics. Technical report, ADVENT Technical Report*. Columbia University.

Nguyen, H., & Bhanu, B. (2009). Multi-Object Tracking In Non-Stationary Video Using Bacterial Foraging Swarms. *Proceedings of the 16th Institute Of Electrical And Electronics Engineers international conference on Image processing*, (pp. 873-876).

Niu, Y., Liu, F., Feng, W. C., & Jin, H. (2012). Aesthetics-based stereoscopic photo cropping for heterogeneous displays. *IEEE Transactions on Multimedia*, *14*(3), 783–796. doi:10.1109/TMM.2012.2186122

Noh, J. S., & Rhee, K. H. (2005). Palmprint identification algorithm using Hu invariant moments and Otsu binarization. In *Proceeding of Fourth Annual ACIS International Conference on Computer and Information Science*.

Noorkami, M., & Mersereau, R. M. (2007). A Framework for Robust Watermarking of H.264-Encoded Video With Controllable Detection Performance. *Information Forensics and Security. IEEE Transactions on*, *2*(1), 14–23.

Nothdurft, H. C. (2005). Salience of feature contrast. In L. Itti, G. Rees, & J. K. Tsotsos (Eds.), *Neurobiology of Attention* (pp. 233–239). Amsterdam, Netherlands: Elsevier Academic Press. doi:10.1016/B978-012375731-9/50042-2

Ohga, & Hamabe. (2014). Digital Watermarking based on fractal image coding using DWT and HVS. *International Journal of Knowledge-based and Intelligent Engineering Systems*, *18*, 81–89.

Ojala, T., Pietikäinen, M., & Harwood, D. (1996). A comparative study of texture measures with classification based on feature distributions. *Pattern Recognition*, *29*(1), 51–59. doi:10.1016/0031-3203(95)00067-4

Okada, Y., Ukai, K., Wolffsohn, J. S., Gilmartin, B., Iijima, A., & Bando, T. (2006). Target spatial frequency determines the response to conflicting defocus-and convergence-driven accommodative stimuli. *Vision Research*, *46*(4), 475–484. doi:10.1016/j.visres.2005.07.014 PMID:16198392

Oliva, A., & Torralba, A. (2001). Modeling the shape of the scene: A holistic representation of the spatial envelope. *International Journal of Computer Vision*, *42*(3), 145–175. doi:10.1023/A:1011139631724

Oliva, A., Torralba, A., Castelhano, M. S., & Henderson, J. M. (2003). Top-down control of visual attention in object detection. In *Proc. of International Conference on Image Processing*. doi:10.1109/ICIP.2003.1246946

Orabona, F., Metta, G., & Sandini, G. (2005). Object-based Visual Attention: a Model for a Behaving Robot. In *Proc IEEE Computer Society Conference on Computer Vision and Pattern Recognition*. doi:10.1109/CVPR.2005.502

O'Ruanaidh, J. J. K., & Pun, T. (1997). *Rotation, scale and translation invariant digital image watermarking.* Paper presented at the Image Processing. doi:10.1109/ICIP.1997.647968

Osberger, W., & Maeder, A. J. (1998). Automatic identification of perceptually important regions in an image. In *Pattern Recognition, 1998. Proceedings. Fourteenth International Conference on,* (vol. 1, pp. 701–704). IEEE.

Otsuka, T., & Ohya, J. (1998). Extracting facial motion parameters by tracking feature points. In *Proceedings of First International Conference on Advanced Multimedia Content Processing.*

Otsuka, T., & Ohya, J. (1998). Spotting segments displaying facial expression from image sequences using HMM. In *Proceedings of Second IEEE International Conference on Automatic Face and Gesture Recognition (FG'98).* doi:10.1109/AFGR.1998.670988

Otsu, N. (1978). A threshold selection method from gray-scale histogram. *IEEE Transactions on Systems, Man, and Cybernetics, 8,* 62–66.

Ouerhani, N. (2003). *Visual attention: From bio-inspired modeling to real-time implementation.* (Ph.D. thesis). Institut de Microtechnique Université de Neuchâtel, Switzerland.

Ouerhani, N., & Hugli, H. (2000). Computing visual attention from scene depth. In *Pattern Recognition, 2000. Proceedings. 15th International Conference on,* (vol. 1, pp. 375–378). IEEE.

Ouerhani, N., & Hugli, H. (2003). *A Model of Dynamic Visual Attention for Object Tracking in Natural Image Sequences.* Paper presented at CMNM. doi:10.1007/3-540-44868-3_89

Padgett, C., & Cottrell, G. (n.d.). Representing face image for emotion classi0cation. In M. Mozer, M. Jordan, & T. Petsche (Eds.), Advances in Neural Information Processing Systems (vol. 9, pp. 894–900). Cambridge, MA: MIT Press.

Pal, R., Mitra, P., & Mukhopadhyay, J. (2008). ICam: maximizes viewers attention on intended objects. In *Proc. of Pacific Rim Conference on Multimedia* (LNCS), (vol. 5353, pp. 821-824). Berlin: Springer. doi:10.1007/978-3-540-89796-5_90

Palomino, A. J., Marfil, R., Bandera, J. P., & Bandera, A. (2011). A Novel Biologically Inspired Attention Mechanism for a Social Robot. *EURASIP Journal on Advances in Signal Processing, 2011,* 1–10. doi:10.1155/2011/841078

Pal, R. (2013). Computational models of visual attention: a survey. In R. Srivastava, S. K. Singh, & K. K. Shukla (Eds.), *Recent Advances in Computer Vision and Image Processing: Methodologies and Applications* (pp. 54–76). IGI Global.

Pal, R., Mitra, P., & Mukherjee, J. (2012) Image retargeting using controlled shrinkage. In: *Proc. of ICVGIP.* doi:10.1145/2425333.2425404

Pal, R., Mitra, P., & Mukherjee, J. (2012). Image retargeting using controlled shrinkage. In *Proc. of the Eighth Indian Conference on Vision, Graphics, and Image Processing.*

Pal, R., Mukherjee, A., Mitra, P., & Mukherjee, J. (2010). Modelling visual saliency using degree centrality. *IET Computer Vision, 4*(3), 218–229. doi:10.1049/iet-cvi.2009.0067

Pal, R., Mukhopadhyay, J., & Mitra, P. (2011). Image retargeting through constrained growth of important rectangular partitions. In *Proc. of 4th International Conference on Pattern Recognition and Machine Intelligence.* doi:10.1007/978-3-642-21786-9_19

Pan, F., Chen, J. B., & Huang, J. W. (2009). Discriminating between photorealistic computer graphics and natural images using fractal geometry. *Science in China Series F: Information Sciences, 52*(2), 329–337. doi:10.1007/s11432-009-0053-5

Pang, Y. H., Connie, T., Jin, A., & Ling, D. (2003) Palmprint authentication with Zernike moment invariants. In *Proceedings of the Third IEEE International Symposium on Signal Processing and Information Technology.*

Pan, X., & Lyu, S. (2010). Detecting image duplication using SIFT features. *Proceedings of IEEE ICASSP.*

Papadelis, C., Kourtidou-Papadeli, C., Bamidis, P. D., Chouvarda, I., Koufogiannis, D., Bekiaris, E., & Maglaveras, N. (2006). Indicators of sleepiness in an ambulatory EEG study of night driving. In *Conference Proceedings : ... Annual International Conference of the IEEE Engineering in Medicine and Biology Society. IEEE Engineering in Medicine and Biology Society* (vol. 1, pp. 6201–6204). doi:10.1109/IEMBS.2006.259614

Papadelis, C., Chen, Z., Kourtidou-Papadeli, C., Bamidis, P. D., Chouvarda, I., Bekiaris, E., & Maglaveras, N. (2007). Monitoring sleepiness with on-board electrophysiological recordings for preventing sleep-deprived traffic accidents. *Clinical Neurophysiology, 118*(9), 1906–1922. doi:10.1016/j.clinph.2007.04.031 PMID:17652020

Parkhurst, D., Law, K., & Niebur, E. (2002). Modeling the role of salience in the allocation of overt visual attention. *Vision Research, 42*(1), 107–123. doi:10.1016/S0042-6989(01)00250-4 PMID:11804636

Pelz, J. B., & Canosa, R. (2001). Oculomotor behavior and perceptual strategies in complex tasks. *Vision Research, 41*(25-26), 3587–3596. doi:10.1016/S0042-6989(01)00245-0 PMID:11718797

Penev, P., & Atick, J. (1996). Local feature analysis: A general statistical theory for object representation. *Netw. Comput. Neural Syst., 7*(3), 477–500. doi:10.1088/0954-898X_7_3_002

Pereira, S., & Pun, T. (2000). Robust template matching for affine resistant image watermarks. *Image Processing. IEEE Transactions on, 9*(6), 1123–1129.

Perreira Da Silva, M. (2010). *Modèle computationnel d'attention pour la vision adaptative.* Université de La Rochelle.

Pessoa, L., & Exel, S. (1999). Attentional strategies for object recognition. In *Proceedings of International Work-Conference on Artificial and Natural Neural Networks (IWANN '99)* (Vol. 1606, pp. 850–859). Alicante, Spain: Springer.

Peterson, M. S., Kramer, A. F., & Irwin, D. E. (2004). Covert shifts of attention precede involuntary eye movements. *Attention, Perception & Psychophysics, 66*(3), 398–405. doi:10.3758/BF03194888 PMID:15283065

Peters, R. J., & Itti, L. (2007). Beyond bottom-up: incorporating task-dependent influences into a computational model of spatial attention. In *Proc. of IEEE Conference on Computer Vision and Pattern Recognition.* doi:10.1109/CVPR.2007.383337

Petitcolas, F. A. (2000). Watermarking schemes evaluation. *Signal Processing Magazine, IEEE, 17*(5), 58–64. doi:10.1109/79.879339

Pham, V.-Q., Miyaki, T., Yamasaki, T., & Aizawa, K. (2007). *Geometrically Invariant Object-Based Watermarking using SIFT Feature.* Paper presented at the Image Processing.

Pinneli, S., & Chandler, D. M. (2008). A Bayesian approach to predicting the perceived interest of objects. In *Image Processing, 2008. ICIP 2008. 15th IEEE International Conference on,* (pp. 2584–2587). IEEE.

Piper, A., Safavi-Naini, R., & Mertins, A. (2005). *Resolution and quality scalable spread spectrum image watermarking.* Paper presented at the 7th workshop on Multimedia and security. doi:10.1145/1073170.1073186

Piper, A., Safavi-Naini, R., & Mertins, A. (2004). Coefficient Selection Methods for Scalable Spread Spectrum Watermarking. In T. Kalker, I. Cox, & Y. Ro (Eds.), *Digital Watermarking* (Vol. 2939, pp. 235–246). Springer Berlin Heidelberg. doi:10.1007/978-3-540-24624-4_18

Podilchuk, C. I., & Delp, E. J. (2001). Digital Watermarking: Algorithms and Applications. *IEEE Signal Processing Magazine, 18*(4), 33–46. doi:10.1109/79.939835

Poole, A., & Ball, L. J. (2006). *Eye tracking in HCI and usability research. In Encyclopedia of Human Computer Interaction* (Vol. 1, pp. 211–219). IGR. doi:10.4018/978-1-59140-562-7.ch034

Poon, C., Wong, D. C. M., & Shen, H. C. (2004). A New Method in Locating and Segmenting Palmprint into Region of Interest. IEEE. *Pattern Recognition, 4,* 533–536.

Poon, C., Wong, D. C. M., & Shen, H. C. (2004). Personal identification and verification: fusion of palmprint representations. In *Proceedings of International Conference on Biometric Authentication.* doi:10.1007/978-3-540-25948-0_106

Popescu, A. C., & Farid, H. (2005). Exposing digital forgeries by detecting traces of re-sampling. *IEEE Transactions on Signal Processing, 53*(2), 758–767. doi:10.1109/TSP.2004.839932

Popescu, A. C., & Farid, H. (2005). Exposing digital forgeries in color filter array interpolated images. *IEEE Transactions on Signal Processing, 53*(10), 3948–3959. doi:10.1109/TSP.2005.855406

Posner, M. I., Snyder, C. R., & Davidson, B. J. (1980). Attention and the detection of signals. *Journal of Experimental Psychology. General, 109*(2), 160–174. doi:10.1037/0096-3445.109.2.160 PMID:7381367

Posner, M., & Petersen, S. (1990). The attention system of the human brain. *Annual Review of Neuroscience, 13*(1), 25–42. doi:10.1146/annurev.ne.13.030190.000325 PMID:2183676

Potapova, E., Zillich, M., & Vincze, M. (2011). Learning What Matters: Combining Probabilistic Models of 2D and 3D Saliency Cues. In Computer Vision Systems, (pp. 132–142). Springer.

Potapova, E., Zillich, M., & Vincze, M. (2012). Attention-driven segmentation of cluttered 3D scenes. In *Proceedings of International Conference on Pattern Recognition (ICPR 2012),* (pp 3610-3613). ICPR.

Potdar, V. M., Han, S., & Chang, E. (2005). A Survey of Digital Image Watermarking Techniques. *Third IEEE International Conference on Industrial Informatics.* doi:10.1109/INDIN.2005.1560462

Prasad Munaga, V. N. K., Kavati, & Adinarayana, B. (2014). Palmprint Recognition Using Fusion of 2D-Gabor and 2D Log-Gabor Features. Communications in Computer and Information Science (CCIS 420). Springer.

Prasad, Pramod, & Sharma. (2009). Classification of Palmprint Using Principal Line. *Information Systems, Technology and Management.* Springer.

Privitera, C. M., & Stark, L. W. (2000). Algorithms for defining visual regions-of-interest: Comparison with eye fixations. *Pattern Analysis and Machine Intelligence. IEEE Transactions on, 22*(9), 970–982.

Puate, J., & Jordan, F. (1997). Using fractal compression scheme to embed a digital signature into an image. *SIPIE Photonics, 2915,* 108–118.

Pushpa, D., & Sheshadri, H. S. (2012). Multiple Object Detection and Tracking in Cluttered Region with Rational Mobile Area. *International Journal of Computers and Applications, 39*(10), 14–17. doi:10.5120/4855-7125

Qadir, G., Yahay, S., & Ho, A. T. S. (2012). Surrey university library for forens ic analys is (SULFA) of video content. In *Proc. of IET Conference on Image Processing.*

Qin, A. K., Suganthan, N., Tay, C. H., & Pa, S. (2006). Personal Identification System based on Multiple Palmprint Features.*9th International Conference on Control, Automation, Robotics and Vision.* doi:10.1109/ICARCV.2006.345257

Qiu, G., Gu, X., Chen, Z., Chen, Q., & Wang, C. (2007). An information theoretic model on spatiotemporal visual saliency. In *Proc. of IEEE International Conference on Multimedia and Expo.* doi:10.1109/ICME.2007.4285023

Radon, Johann. (2005). 1.1 Über die Bestimmung von Funktionen durch ihre Integralwerte längs gewisser Mannigfaltigkeiten. *Classic papers in modern diagnostic radiology,* 5-5.

Rafael Diaz, M., Travieso, C., Alonso, J., & Ferrer, M. (2004). Biometric system based in the feature of hand palm. *Proceedings of 38th Annual International Carnahan Conference on Security Technology.*

Ramasamy, C., House, D. H., Duchowski, A. T., & Daugherty, B. (2009). *Using eye tracking to analyze stereoscopic filmmaking. In SIGGRAPH'09: Posters* (p. 28). ACM.

Ramirez Rivera, A., Castillo, R., & Chae, O. (2013). Local directional number pattern for face analysis: Face and expression recognition. *IEEE Transactions on Image Processing, 22*(5), 1740–1752. doi:10.1109/TIP.2012.2235848 PMID:23269752

Ramstrom, O., & Christensen, H. I. (2002). *Visual attention using game theory.* Biologically Motivated Computer Vision.

Rana, S., Sahu, N., & Sur, A. (2014). Robust watermarking for resolution and quality scalable video sequence. *Multimedia Tools and Applications*, 1–30.

Randell, D. A., Cui, Z., & Cohn, A. G. (1992). A Spatial Logic Based on Regions and Connection. *KR, 92*, 165–176.

Rao, C. R. S. G., & Prasad, M. V. N. K. (2015). Digital Watermarking Techniques in Curvelet Transformation Domain. *Smart Innovation, Systems and Technologies, 31*, 199-211.

Rao, C. R. S. G., Mantha, A. N., & Prasad, M. V. N. K. (2012a). Study of Contemporary Digital watermarking Techniques. *International Journal of Computer Science Issues, 9*(6-1), 456-464.

Rao, C. R. S. G., Nukineedi, D. L., & Prasad, M. V. N. K. (2012b). Digital Watermarking Algorithm Based on CCC - FWHT Technique. *International Journal of Advancements in Computing Technology, 4*(18), 593–599. doi:10.4156/ijact.vol4.issue18.70

Rao, C. R. S. G., & Prasad, M. V. N. K. (2012c). Digital watermarking algorithm based on complete complementary code.*Third International Conference on Computing Communication & Networking Technologies (IEEE-ICCCNT).* doi:10.1109/ICCCNT.2012.6396038

Rao, C. R. S. G., & Prasad, M. V. N. K. (2014d). Digital Watermarking Based on Magic Square and Ridgelet Transform Techniques, Intelligent Computing, Networking, and Informatics. *Advances in Intelligent Systems and Computing, 243*, 143–161. doi:10.1007/978-81-322-1665-0_14

Rao, C. R. S. G., Ravi, V., Prasad, M. V. N. K., & Gopal, E. V. (2014a). Watermarking Using Artificial Intelligence Techniques. In *Encyclopedia of Business Analytics and Optimization.* Hershey, PA: IGI Global Publications.

Rao, C. R. S. G., Ravi, V., Prasad, M. V. N. K., & Gopal, E. V. (2014b). Digital Watermarking Techniques for Images – Survey. In *Encyclopedia of Business Analytics and Optimization.* Hershey, PA: IGI Global Publications.

Rao, C. R. S. G., Ravi, V., Prasad, M. V. N. K., & Gopal, E. V. (2014c). Watermarking Using Intelligent Methods – Survey. In *Encyclopedia of Business Analytics and Optimization.* Hershey, PA: IGI Global Publications.

Rapantzikos, K., Tsapatsoulis, N., & Avrithis, Y. (2004). Spatiotemporal visual attention architecture for video analysis. In *Proc. of IEEE 6th Workshop on Multimedia Signal Processing.* doi:10.1109/MMSP.2004.1436423

Raudys, S., & Jain, A. K. (1991). Small sample size effects in statistical pattern recognition: Recommendations for practitioners. *IEEE Transactions on Pattern Analysis and Machine Intelligence, 13*(3), 252–264. doi:10.1109/34.75512

Rawat, S., & Raman, B. (2012). A blind watermarking algorithm based on fractional Fourier transform and visual cryptography. *Signal Processing, 92*(6), 1480–1491. doi:10.1016/j.sigpro.2011.12.006

Rayner, K., Pollatsek, A., Ashby, J., & Clifton, C. Jr. (2012). *Psychology of Reading.* Psychology Press.

Read, J. C. A. (2005). Early computational processing in binocular vision and depth perception. *Progress in Biophysics and Molecular Biology, 87*(1), 77–108. doi:10.1016/j.pbiomolbio.2004.06.005 PMID:15471592

Redi, J., Taktak, W., & Dugelay, J. L. (2011). Digital Image Forensics: A Booklet for Beginners. *Multimedia Tools and Applications, 51*(1), 133–162. doi:10.1007/s11042-010-0620-1

Remagnino, P. (1997). An integrated traffic and pedestrian model-based vision system.*Proceedings of the Eighth British Machine Vision Conference*, (pp. 380-389).

Ren, T., Liu, Y., & Wu, G. (2010). Rapid image retargeting based on curve-edge grid representation. In *Proc. of IEEE 17th International Conference on Image Processing.* doi:10.1109/ICIP.2010.5654031

Rensink, R. A., O'Regan, J. K., & Clark, J. J. (1997). To see or not to see: The need for attention to perceive changes in scenes. *Psychological Science, 8*(5), 368–373. doi:10.1111/j.1467-9280.1997.tb00427.x

Reynolds, J. H., Chelazzi, L., & Desimone, R. (1999). Competitive Mechanisms Subserve Attention in Macaque Areas V2 and V4. *The Journal of Neuroscience, 19*(5), 1736–1753. PMID:10024360

Reynolds, J. H., & Heeger, D. J. (2009). The normalization model of attention. *Neuron, 61*(2), 168–185. doi:10.1016/j.neuron.2009.01.002 PMID:19186161

Ribaric, S., & Fratric, I. (2005). A biometric identification system based on eigenpalm and eigenfinger features. *IEEE Transaction Pattern Analysis Machine Intelligence,* 1698–1709.

Ribaric, S., Fratric, I., & Kis, K. (2005). A biometric verification system based on the fusion of palmprint and face features. In *Proceeding of the 4th International Symposium on Image, Signal and Signal Processing and Analysis.* doi:10.1109/ISPA.2005.195376

Ribaric, S., & Lopar, M. (2012).Palmprint recognition based on local Haralick features.*IEEE Mediterranean Electrotechnical Conference.* doi:10.1109/MELCON.2012.6196517

Roberto, G., Ardizzone, E., & Pirrone, R. (2011). Springs-based simulation for image retargeting. In *Proc. of 18th IEEE International Conference on Image Processing.*

Rosenblum, M., Pikovsky, A., & Kurths, J. (1996). Phase synchronization of chaotic oscillators. *Physical Review Letters, 76*(11), 1804–1807. doi:10.1103/PhysRevLett.76.1804 PMID:10060525

Rosenblum, M., Yacoob, Y., & Davis, L. (1996). Human expression recognition from motion using a radial basis function network architecture. *IEEE Transactions on Neural Networks, 7*(5), 1121–1138. doi:10.1109/72.536309 PMID:18263509

Rosin, P. L. (2009). A simple method for detecting salient regions. *Pattern Recognition, 42*(11), 2363–2371. doi:10.1016/j.patcog.2009.04.021

Rotinwa-Akinbile, M. O., Aibinu, A. M., & Salami, M. J. E. (2011).Palmprint Recognition Using Principal Lines Characterization.*International Conference on Informatics and Computational Intelligence.*

Rousselet, G. A., Thorpe, S. J., & Fabre-Thorpe, M. (2004). How parallel is visual processing in the ventral pathway? *Trends in Cognitive Sciences, 8*(8), 363–370. doi:10.1016/j.tics.2004.06.003 PMID:15335463

Rowe, R., Uludag, U., Demirkus, M., Parthasaradhi, S., & Jain, A. (2007). A spectral whole-hand biometric authentication system. In *Proceedings of Biometric Symposium.*

Rowley, H., Baluja, S., & Kanade, T. (1998). Neural network-based face detection. *IEEE Transactions on Pattern Analysis and Machine Intelligence, 20*(1), 23–38. doi:10.1109/34.655647

Rubinov, M., & Sporns, O. (2010). Complex network measures of brain connectivity: Uses and interpretations. *NeuroImage*, *52*(3), 1059–1069. doi:10.1016/j.neuroimage.2009.10.003 PMID:19819337

Rubinstein, M., Gutierrez, D., Sorkine, O., & Shamir, A. (2010). A comparative study of image retargeting. *ACM Transactions on Graphics*, *29*(6), 1. doi:10.1145/1882261.1866186

Russel, A. R., Mihalaş, S., von der Heydt, R., Niebur, E., & Etienne-Cummings, R. (2014). A model of proto-object based saliency. *Vision Research*, *94*, 1–15. doi:10.1016/j.visres.2013.10.005 PMID:24184601

Ryan, A., Cohn, J. F., Lucey, S., Saragih, J., Lucey, P., Torre, F. D. L., & Rossi, A. (October 2009). *Automated Facial Expression Recognition System*. IEEE International Carnahan Conference on Security Technology, NCIS, Washington, DC. doi:10.1109/CCST.2009.5335546

Sabharwal, C. L., & Leopold, J. L. (2011). Reducing 9-Intersection to 4-Intersection for Identifying Relations in Region Connection Calculus. In *Proceedings of the 24th International Conference on Computer Applications in Industry and Engineering* (CAINE 2011). IEEE.

Sabharwal, C. L., & Leopold, J. L. (2013). A Fast Intersection Detection Algorithm For Qualitative Spatial Reasoning. In *Proceedings of the 19h International Conference on Distributed Multimedia Systems*. Academic Press.

Sabharwal, C. L., Leopold, J. L., & Eloe, N. (2011). A More Expressive 3D Region Connection Calculus. In *Proceedings of the 2011 International Workshop on Visual Languages and Computing (in conjunction with the 17th International Conference on Distributed Multimedia Systems (DMS'11)*. Academic Press.

Sabharwal, Leopold, & McGeehan. (2013). Triangle-Triangle Intersection Determination and Classification to Support Qualitative Spatial Reasoning, Polibits. *Research Journal of Computer Science and Computer Engineering with Applications*, (48), 13–22.

Saeedi, P., Lawrence, P. D., & Lowe, D. G. (2006). Vision-based 3-D trajectory tracking for unknown environments. *Robotics. IEEE Transactions on*, *22*(1), 119–136.

Salah, A., Alpaydin, E., & Akrun, L. (2002). A selective attention based method for visual pattern recognition with application to handwritten digit recognition and face recognition.[PAMI]. *IEEE Transactions on Pattern Analysis and Machine Intelligence*, *24*(3), 420–425. doi:10.1109/34.990146

Salvucci, D. D. (1999). *Mapping eye movements to cognitive processes*. Carnegie Mellon University.

Salvucci, D. D., & Anderson, J. R. (1998). *Tracing eye movement protocols with cognitive process models*. Lawrence Erlbaum Associates, Inc.

Salvucci, D. D., & Goldberg, J. H. (2000). Identifying fixations and saccades in eye-tracking protocols. In *Proceedings of the 2000 symposium on Eye tracking research & applications*, (pp. 71–78). ACM. doi:10.1145/355017.355028

Sandbach, G., Zafeiriou, S., Pantic, M., & Yin, L. (2012). Static and dynamic 3D facial expression recognition: A comprehensive survey. *Image and Vision Computing*, *30*(10), 683–689. doi:10.1016/j.imavis.2012.06.005

Sang, J., & Alam, M. S. (2008). Fragility and robustness of binary phase-only-filter based fragile/semifragile digital watermarking. *IEEE Transactions on Instrumentation and Measurement*, *57*(3), 595–606. doi:10.1109/TIM.2007.911585

Santella, A., Agrawala, M., DeCarlo, D., Salesin, D., & Cohen, M. (2006). Gaze-based interaction for semi-automatic photo cropping. In *Proc. of the SIGCHI Conference on Human Factors in Computing Systems*. doi:10.1145/1124772.1124886

Sarode, N., & Bhatia, S. (2010). Facial Expression Recognition. *International Journal on Computer Science and Engineering*, *2*(5), 1552–1557.

Savic, T., & Pavesic, N. (2007). Personal recognition based on an image of the palmar surface of the hand. *Pattern Recognition*, *40*(11), 3252–3163. doi:10.1016/j.patcog.2007.03.005

Savran, A., Alyuz, N., Dibeklioglu, H., Celiktutan, O., Gokberk, B., Sankur, B., & Akarun, L. (2008), *Bosphorus database for 3D face analysis.* 1stWorkshop on Biometrics and Identity Management, Roskilde University, Denmark.

Schafer, R., Schwarz, H., Marpe, D., Schierl, T., & Wiegand, T. (2005). *MCTF and Scalability Extension of H.264/AVC and its Application to Video Transmission, Storage, and Surveillance.* Paper presented at the SPIE.

Schall, J. D. (2004). On the role of frontal eye field in guiding attention and saccades. *Vision Research*, *44*(12), 1453–1467. doi:10.1016/j.visres.2003.10.025 PMID:15066404

Schleicher, R., Galley, N., Briest, S., & Galley, L. (2008). Blinks and saccades as indicators of fatigue in sleepiness warnings: Looking tired? *Ergonomics*, *51*(7), 982–1010. doi:10.1080/00140130701817062 PMID:18568959

Schwarz, H., Marpe, D., & Wiegand, T. (2007). Overview of the Scalable Video Coding Extension of the H.264/AVC Standard. *Circuits and Systems for Video Technology. IEEE Transactions on*, *17*(9), 1103–1120.

Schweitzer, H., Bell, J. W., & Wu, F. (2002) Very fast template matching.*European Conference on Computer Vision (ECCV).* (pp. 358–372).

Sencar, H. T., & Memon, N. (2008). Overview of state-of-the-art in digital image forensics. In *Indian Statistical Institute Platinum Jubilee Monograph series titled Statistical Science and Interdisciplinary Research.* Singapore: World Scientific. doi:10.1142/9789812836243_0015

Sencar, H. T., & Memon, N. (Eds.). (2013). *Digital Image Forensics: There is More to a Picture than Meets the Eye.* New York, NY, USA: Springer. doi:10.1007/978-1-4614-0757-7

Seo, J. H., & Park, H. B. (2005). *Data Protection of Multimedia Contents Using Scalable Digital Watermarking.* Paper presented at the Fourth Annual ACIS International Conference on Computer and Information Science.

Serby, D., Koller-Meier, S., & Gool, L. V. (2004). Probabilistic object tracking using multiple features.*Institute Of Electrical And Electronics Engineers International Conference of Pattern Recognition (ICPR)*, (pp. 184–187).

Setlur, V., Takagi, S., Raskar, R., Gleicher, M., & Gooch, B. (2005). Automatic Image Retargeting. In *Proc. of 4th International Conference on Mobile and Ubiquitous Multimedia.* doi:10.1145/1149488.1149499

Shanableh, T. (2012). Data hiding in MPEG video files using multivariate regression and flexible macroblock ordering. *Information Forensics and Security. IEEE Transactions on*, *7*(2), 455–464.

Shan, C., Gong, S., & McOwan, P. W. (2009). Facial expression recognition based on Local Binary Patterns A comprehensive study. *Image and Vision Computing*, *27*(6), 803–816. doi:10.1016/j.imavis.2008.08.005

Shang, L., Huang, D.-S., Du, J.-X., & Zheng, C.-H. (2006). Palmprint recognition using FastICA algorithm and radial basis probabilistic neural network. *Neurocomputing*, *69*(13-15), 1782–1786. doi:10.1016/j.neucom.2005.11.004

Sharma, G., & Coumou, D. J. (2006). *Watermark synchronization: Perspectives and a new paradigm.* Paper presented at the Information Sciences and Systems, 2006 40th Annual Conference on. doi:10.1109/CISS.2006.286644

Sheikh, Y., & Shah, M. (2005). Bayesian Modeling of Dynamic Scenes for Object Detection. *Institute Of Electrical And Electronics Engineers Transactions on Pattern Analysis and Machine Intelligence*, *27*(11), 1778–1792. PMID:16285376

Shih, F. Y. (2007). *Digital Watermarking and Steganography: Fundamentals and Techniques.* BocaRaton. CRC Press.

Shih, F. Y., Chuang, C. F., & Wang, P. S. (2008). Performance comparisons of facial expression recognition in JAFFE database. *International Journal of Pattern Recognition and Artificial Intelligence*, *22*(3), 445–459. doi:10.1142/S0218001408006284

Shuai, B., Zhang, Q., Liu, J., Liu, X., & Feng, X. (2011, October). Saliency region extraction for MPEG video method based on visual selective attention. In *Image and Signal Processing (CISP), 2011 4th International Congress on* (Vol. 1, pp. 560-564). IEEE. doi:10.1109/CISP.2011.6099990

Shulman, G., Remington, R., & McLean, J. (1979). Moving attention through visual space. *Journal of Experimental Psychology. Human Perception and Performance*, *5*(3), 522–526. doi:10.1037/0096-1523.5.3.522 PMID:528957

Siagian, C., & Itti, L. (2007). Rapid biologically-inspired scene classification using features shared with visual attention. *IEEE Transactions on Pattern Analysis and Machine Intelligence*, *29*(2), 300–312. doi:10.1109/TPAMI.2007.40 PMID:17170482

Simakov, D., Caspi, Y., Shechtman, E., & Irani, M. (2008). Summarizing visual data using bidirectional similarity.*Proc. of IEEE Conference on Computer Vision and Pattern Recognition*.

Simons, D. J. (2000). *Change blindness and visual memory*. Philadelphia, PA: Psychology Press.

Singh, T. R., Singh, K. M., & Roy, S. (2013). Video watermarking scheme based on visual cryptography and scene change detection.*AEÜ. International Journal of Electronics and Communications*,*67*(8),645–651. doi:10.1016/j.aeue.2013.01.008

Smith, K. J., Valentino, D. A., & Arruda, J. E. (2003). Rhythmic oscillations in the performance of a sustained attention task. *Journal of Clinical and Experimental Neuropsychology*, *25*(4), 561–570. doi:10.1076/jcen.25.4.561.13869 PMID:12911107

Song, K. Y., Kittler, J., & Petrou, M. (1996). Defect detection in random color textures. *Image and Vision Computing*, *14*(9), 667–683. doi:10.1016/0262-8856(96)84491-X

Sporns, O., & Zwi, J. D. (2004). The small world of the cerebral cortex. *Neuroinformatics*, *2*(2), 145–162. doi:10.1385/NI:2:2:145 PMID:15319512

Srivastava, A., & Biswas, K. K. (2008). Fast content aware image retargeting. In *Proc. of Sixth Indian Conference on Computer Vision, Graphics, & Image Processing*. doi:10.1109/ICVGIP.2008.44

Srivastava, A., Lee, A. B., Simoncelli, E. P., & Zhu, S. C. (2003). On advances in statistical modeling of natural images. *Journal of Mathematical Imaging*, *18*(1), 17–33. doi:10.1023/A:1021889010444

Stam, C. J. (2004). Functional connectivity patterns of human magnetoencephalographic recordings: A "small-world" network? *Neuroscience Letters*, *355*(1-2), 25–28. doi:10.1016/j.neulet.2003.10.063 PMID:14729226

Stam, C. J. (2005). Nonlinear dynamical analysis of EEG and MEG: Review of an emerging field. *Clinical Neurophysiology*, *116*(10), 2266–2301. doi:10.1016/j.clinph.2005.06.011 PMID:16115797

Stam, C. J., de Haan, W., Daffertshofer, A., Jones, B. F., Manshanden, I., van Cappellen van Walsum, A. M., & Scheltens, P. et al. (2009). Graph theoretical analysis of magnetoencephalographic functional connectivity in Alzheimer's disease. *Brain. Journal of Neurology*, *132*, 213–224. doi:10.1093/brain/awn262 PMID:18952674

Stam, C. J., Jones, B. F., Nolte, G., Breakspear, M., & Scheltens, P. (2007). Small-world networks and functional connectivity in Alzheimer's disease. *Cerebral Cortex*, *17*(1), 92–99. doi:10.1093/cercor/bhj127 PMID:16452642

Stam, C. J., & Reijneveld, J. C. (2007). Graph theoretical analysis of complex networks in the brain. *Nonlinear Biomedical Physics*, *1*(1), 3. doi:10.1186/1753-4631-1-3 PMID:17908336

Stam, C. J., & Van Dijk, B. W. (2002). Synchronization likelihood: An unbiased measure of generalized synchronization in multivariate data sets. *Physica D. Nonlinear Phenomena, 163*(3-4), 236–251. doi:10.1016/S0167-2789(01)00386-4

Starck, , J.-LCandes, E. J., & Donoho, D. L. (2002). The Curvelet Transform for Image Denoising. *IEEE Transactions on Image Processing, 11*(6), 670–684. doi:10.1109/TIP.2002.1014998 PMID:18244665

Stauffer, C., & Grimson, W. E. L. (2000). Learning Patterns of Activity Using Real-Time Tracking. *Institute Of Electrical And Electronics Engineers Transactions on Pattern Analysis and Machine Intelligence, 22*(8), 747–757.

Stentiford, F. (2001). An estimator for visual attention through competitive novelty with application to image compression. In *Proc. Picutre Coding Symposium.*

Stratou, G., Ghosh, A., Debevec, P., & Morency, L. P. (2011). *Effect of illumination on automatic expression recognition: a novel 3D relightable facial database. 9th International Conference on Automatic Face and Gesture Recognition,* Santa Barbara, CA. doi:10.1109/FG.2011.5771467

Strogatz, S. H. (2001). Exploring complex networks. *Nature, 410*(6825), 268–276. doi:10.1038/35065725 PMID:11258382

Stutz, T., & Uhl, A. (2012). A Survey of H.264 AVC/SVC Encryption. *Circuits and Systems for Video Technology. IEEE Transactions on, 22*(3), 325–339.

Subramanian, S., Kumar, K., Mishra, B. P., Banerjee, A., & Bhattacharya, D. (2008). Fuzzy logic based content protection for image resizing by seam curving. In *Proc. of IEEE Conference on Soft Computing and Industrial Applications.*

Su, C. (2009). Palm extraction and identification. *Expert Systems with Applications, 36*(2), 1082–1091. doi:10.1016/j.eswa.2007.11.001

Suh, B., Ling, H., Bederson, B. B., & Jacobs, D. W. (2003). Automatic Thumbnail Cropping and Its Effectiveness. In *Proc. of 16th Annual Symposium on User Interface Software and Technology.* doi:10.1145/964696.964707

Sun, J., & Liu, J. (2005, September). A temporal desynchronization resilient video watermarking scheme based on independent component analysis. In *Image Processing, 2005. ICIP 2005. IEEE International Conference on* (Vol. 1, pp. I-265). IEEE.

Sun, Q., He, D., Zhang, Z., & Tian, Q. (2003/07). *A secure and robust approach to scalable video authentication.* Paper presented at the Multimedia and Expo.

Sun, Z., Tan, T., Wang, Y., & Li, S. Z. (2005). Ordinal palmprint representation for personal identification. Proceeding of Computer Vision and Pattern Recognition, 1, 279–284.

Sun, J. (2003). *Hierarchical object-based visual attention for machine vision.* Edinburgh, UK: University of Edinburgh.

Sun, Y. H. Z., Tan, T., & Ren, C. (2008). Multi-Spectral Palm Image Fusion for Accurate Contact-Free Palmprint Recognition.*Proceedings of the IEEE International Conference on Image Processing.*

Sun, Y., Fisher, R., Wang, F., & Gomes, H. (2008). A Computer Vision Model for Visual-object-based Attention and Eye Movements. *Computer Vision and Image Understanding, 112*(2), 126–142. doi:10.1016/j.cviu.2008.01.005

Sur, A., Sagar, S. S., Pal, R., Mitra, P., & Mukhopadhyay, J. (2009). A new image watermarking scheme using saliency based visual attention model, In *Proc. of IEEE Indicon.* doi:10.1109/INDCON.2009.5409402

Suwa, M., Sugie, N., & Fujimora, K. (1978). A preliminary note on pattern recognition of human emotional expression. In *Proceedings of the 4th International Joint Conference on Pattern Recognition.*

Swaminathan, A., Wu, M., & Liu, K. J. R. (2008). Digital image forensics via intrinsic fingerprints. *IEEE Transactions on Information Forensics and Security, 3*(1), 101–117. doi:10.1109/TIFS.2007.916010

Swanson, M. D., Kobayashi, M., & Tewfik, A. H. (1998). Multimedia data-embedding and watermarking technologies. *Proceedings of the IEEE, 86*(6), 1064–1087. doi:10.1109/5.687830

Tagare, H. D., Toyama, K., & Wang, J. G. (2001). A maximum-likelihood strategy for directing attention during visual search. *IEEE Transactions on Pattern Analysis and Machine Intelligence, 23*(5), 490–500. doi:10.1109/34.922707

Takens, F. (1981). Detecting strange attractors in turbulence. In Dynamical Systems and Turbulence, Lecture Notes in Mathematics (pp. 366– 381). Springer-Verlag. doi:10.1007/BFb0091924

Takens, F. (1993). Detecting nonlinearities in stationary time series. *International Journal of Bifurcation and Chaos.* Retrieved from http://www.worldscientific.com/doi/pdf/10.1142/S0218127493000192

Tao, J., Jiang, W., Gao, Z., Chen, S., & Wang, C. (2006). Palmprint recognition based on 2-Dimension PCA. *First International Conference on Innovative Computing. Information and Control, 1*, 326–330.

Tatler, B. W. (2007). The central fixation bias in scene viewing: Selecting an optimal viewing position independently of motor biases and image feature distributions. *Journal of Vision, 7*(14).

Teng, W.-C., Kuo, Y.-C., & Tara, R. Y. (2013). A teleoperation system utilizing saliency-based visual attention. In *Proc. of IEEE International Conference on Systems, Man, and Cybernetics.*

Tewfik, A. H., & Swanson, M. (1997). Data hiding for multimedia personalization, interaction, & protection. *IEEE Signal Processing Magazine, 14*(4), 41–44. doi:10.1109/79.598593

Tian, Y., Kanade, T., & Cohn, J. (2001). Recognizing action units for facial expression analysis. *IEEE Transactions on Pattern Analysis and Machine Intelligence, 23*(2), 97–115. doi:10.1109/34.908962 PMID:25210210

Torralba, A. (2003). Modeling global scene factors in attention. *JOSA A, 20*(7), 1407–1418. doi:10.1364/JOSAA.20.001407 PMID:12868645

Torralba, A., Oliva, A., Castelhano, M. S., & Henderson, J. M. (2006). Contextual guidance of eye-movements and attention in real-world scenes: The role of global features in object search. *Psychological Review, 113*(4), 766–786. doi:10.1037/0033-295X.113.4.766 PMID:17014302

Travieso, C. M., Fuertes, J. J., & Alonso, J. B. (2011). Derivative method for hand palm texture biometric verification. *IEEE International Carnahan Conference on Security Technology.* doi:10.1109/CCST.2011.6095889

Travis, H. (2008). Opting Out of the Internet in the United States and the European Union: Copyright, Safe Harbors, and International Law. *The Notre Dame Law Review, 83*(4), 331–408.

Treisman, A. M., & Gelade, G. (1980). A feature-integration theory of attention. *Cognitive Psychology, 12*(1), 97–136. doi:10.1016/0010-0285(80)90005-5 PMID:7351125

Treisman, A. M., & Gormican, S. (1988). Feature analysis in early vision: Evidence from search asymmetries. *Psychological Review, 95*(1), 15–48. doi:10.1037/0033-295X.95.1.15 PMID:3353475

Tropp, O., Tal, A., & Shimshoni, I. (2006). A fast triangle to triangle intersection test for collision detection. *Computer Animation and Virtual Worlds, 17*(50), 527–535. doi:10.1002/cav.115

Tsalakanidou, F., & Malassiotis, S. (2010). Real-time 2D + 3D facial action and expression recognition. *Pattern Recognition, 43*(5), 1763–1775. doi:10.1016/j.patcog.2009.12.009

Tseng, P.-H., Carmi, R., Cameron, I. G. M., Munoz, D. P., & Itti, L. (2009). Quantifying center bias of observers in free viewing of dynamic natural scenes. *Journal of Vision, 9*(7).

Tsotsos, J. K. (1990). Analyzing vision at the complexity level. *Behavioral and Brain Sciences, 13*(03), 423–469. doi:10.1017/S0140525X00079577

Tsotsos, J. K. (2008). What Roles can Attention Play in Recognition? In *Proceedings of 7th IEEE International Conference on Development and Learning (ICDL)* (pp. 55–60). IEEE. doi:10.1109/DEVLRN.2008.4640805

Tsotsos, J. K., Culhane, S. M., Kei Wai, W. Y., Lai, Y., Davis, N., & Nuflo, F. (1995). Modeling visual attention via selective tuning. *Artificial Intelligence, 78*(1), 507–545. doi:10.1016/0004-3702(95)00025-9

Turk, M., & Pentland, A. (1991). Eigenfaces for recognition. *Journal of Cognitive Neuroscience, 3*(1), 71–86. doi:10.1162/jocn.1991.3.1.71 PMID:23964806

Unanue, I., Urteaga, I., Husemann, R., Ser, J. D., Roesler, V., Rodriguez, A., & Sanchez, P. (2011). A Tutorial on H.264/SVC Scalable Video Coding and its Tradeoff between Quality, Coding Efficiency and Performance. Javier Del Ser Lorente.

Ungerleider, L. G., & Desimone, R. (1986). Cortical connections of visual area MT in the macaque. *The Journal of Comparative Neurology, 248*(2), 190–222. doi:10.1002/cne.902480204 PMID:3722458

University of Illinois at Chicago (UIC). (n.d.). Retrieved from http://www.cs.cf.ac.uk/Dave/Multimedia/Lecture_Examples/Compression/ mpegproj/

Utsugi, K., Shibahara, T., Koike, T., Takahashi, K., & Naemura, T. (2010). Seam carving for stereo images. In *Proc. of 3DTV-Conference*. doi:10.1109/3DTV.2010.5506316

Utsugi, K., Shibahara, T., Koike, T., & Naemura, T. (2009). Proportional constraint for seam carving. In *Proc. of International Conference on Computer Graphics and Interactive Techniques*.

van de Sande, K. E. A., Uijlings, J. R. R., Gevers, T., & Smeulders, A. W. M. (2011). Segmentation as selective search for object recognition. In *Proceedings of International Conference on Computer Vision* (pp. 1879–1886). Barcelona, Spain: IEEE. doi:10.1109/ICCV.2011.6126456

Van Dongen, H. P. A., & Dinges, D. F. (2000). Circadian Rhythms in Fatigue, Alertness and Performance. In *Principles and Practice of Sleep Medicine* (pp. 391–399). Retrieved from http://www.nps.navy.mil/orfacpag/resumepages/projects/fatigue/dongen.pdf

Van Essen, D. C., Newsome, W. T., Maunsell, J. H. R., & Bixby, J. L. (1986). The projections from striate cortex (V1) to areas V2 and V3 in the macaque monkey: Asymmetries, areal boundaries, and patchy connections. *The Journal of Comparative Neurology, 244*(4), 451–480. doi:10.1002/cne.902440405 PMID:3958238

Van Lanh, T., Chong, K.-S., Emmanuel, S., & Kankanhalli, M. S. (2007) A survey on digital camera image forensic methods. In *Proc. of IEEE International Conference on Multimedia and Expo*. doi:10.1109/ICME.2007.4284575

Vashistha, A., Nallusamy, R., Das, A., & Paul, S. (2010, July). Watermarking video content using visual cryptography and scene averaged image. In *Multimedia and Expo (ICME), 2010 IEEE International Conference on* (pp. 1641-1646). IEEE. doi:10.1109/ICME.2010.5583256

Veenman, C., Reinders, M., & Backer, E. (2001). Resolving motion correspondence for densely moving points. *Institute Of Electrical And Electronics Engineers Transactions on Pattern Analysis and Machine Intelligence, 23*(1), 54–72.

Verdicchio, F., Andreopoulos, Y., Clerckx, T., Barbarien, J., Munteanu, A., Cornelis, J., & Schelkens, P. (2004). *Scalable video coding based on motion-compensated temporal filtering: complexity and functionality analysis.* Paper presented at the ICIP. doi:10.1109/ICIP.2004.1421705

Vijayakumar, S., Conradt, J., Shibata, T., & Schaal, S. (2001). Overt visual attention for a humanoid robot. In *Intelligent Robots and Systems, 2001. Proceedings. 2001 IEEE/RSJ International Conference on,* (vol. 4, pp. 2332–2337). IEEE.

Vijayakumar, S., Conradt, J., Shibata, T., & Schaal, S. (2001) Overt visual attention for a humanoid robot. In *Proc IEEE/ RSJ International Conference on Intelligent Robots and Systems.* doi:10.1109/IROS.2001.976418

Vikram, T. N., Tscherepanow, M., & Wrede, B. (2011). A random center-surround bottom-up visual attention model useful for salient region detection. In *Proc. of IEEE Workshop on Applications of Computer Vision.* doi:10.1109/ WACV.2011.5711499

Vinod, P., & Bora, P. K. (2006). Motion-compensated inter-frame collusion attack on video watermarking and a countermeasure. *Information Security, IEE Proceedings, 153*(2), 61 - 73-73.

Vinod, S., & Gopi, E. S. (2013). Neural Network Modelling of Color Array Filter for Digital Forgery Detection using Kernel LDA.*Proceedings of International Conference on Computational Intelligence: Modeling Techniques and Applications (CIMTA), 10,* 498-504.

Viola, P., & Jones, M. (2001). Rapid object detection using a boosted cascade of simple features. In *Proc. of International Conference on Computer Vision and Pattern Recognition.* doi:10.1109/CVPR.2001.990517

Viola, P., & Jones, M. J. (2004). Robust real-time face detection. *International Journal of Computer Vision, 57*(2), 137–154. doi:10.1023/B:VISI.0000013087.49260.fb

Vu, K., Hua, K. A., & Tavanapong, W. (2003). Image retrieval based on regions of interest. *Knowledge and Data Engineering. IEEE Transactions on, 15*(4), 1045–1049.

Wallace, G. (1991). The JPEG still picture compression standard. *IEEE Transactions on Consumer Electronics, 34*(4), 30–44.

Walther, D., Edgington, D. R., & Koch, C. (2004). Detection and tracking of objects in underwater video. In *Proceedings of International Conference on Computer Vision and Pattern Recognition (CVPR),* (pp 544–549). doi:10.1109/ CVPR.2004.1315079

Walther, D., & Koch, C. (2006). Modeling attention to salient proto-objects. *Neural Networks, 19*(9), 1395–1407. doi:10.1016/j.neunet.2006.10.001 PMID:17098563

Wandell, B. A. (1995). *Foundations of vision.* Sinauer Associates.

Wang, C.-C., Lin, Y.-C., Yi, S.-C., & Chen, P.-Y. (2006). *Digital Authentication and Verification in MPEG-4 Fine-Granular Scalability Video Using Bit-Plane Watermarking.* Paper presented at the IPCV.

Wang, J., Le Callet, P., Ricordel, V., & Tourancheau, S. (2011). Quantifying depth bias in free viewing of still stereoscopic synthetic stimuli. In *Proceedings of16th European Conference on Eye Movements.*

Wang, Y., & Pearmain, A. (2006). Blind MPEG-2 video watermarking in DCT domain robust against scaling. *Vision, Image and Signal Processing, IEE Proceedings, 153*(5), 581-588.

Wang, D., Li, G., Jia, W., & Luo, X. (2011). Saliency-driven scaling optimization for image retargeting. *The Visual Computer, 27*(9), 853–860. doi:10.1007/s00371-011-0559-x

Wang, H. J. M., Su, P. C., & Kuo, C. C. J. (1998). Wavelet-based digital image watermarking. *Optics Express*, *3*(12), 491–496. doi:10.1364/OE.3.000491 PMID:19384400

Wang, H., Liu, G., & Dang, Y. (2012). The target quick searching strategy based on visual attention. In *Proc. of International Conference on Computer Science and Electronics Engineering*. doi:10.1109/ICCSEE.2012.442

Wang, J. G., Yau, W. Y., Suwandy, A., & Sung, E. (2008). Person recognition by fusing palmprint and palm vein images based on Laplacian palm representation. *Pattern Recognition*, *41*(5), 1514–1527. doi:10.1016/j.patcog.2007.10.021

Wang, J., Barreto, A., Wang, L., Chen, Y., Rishe, N., Andrian, J., & Adjouadi, M. (2010). Multilinear principal component analysis for face recognition with fewer features. *Neurocomputing*, *73*(10-12), 1550–1555. doi:10.1016/j.neucom.2009.08.022

Wang, J., Chandler, D. M., & Le Callet, P. (2010). *Quantifying the relationship between visual salience and visual importance. In IS&T-SPIE Electronic Imaging* (p. 75270K). SPIE.

Wang, J., Da Silva, M. P., Le Callet, P., & Ricordel, V. (2013). A Computational Model of Stereoscopic 3D Visual Saliency. *Image Processing. IEEE Transactions on*, *22*(6), 2151–2165.

Wang, J., Ying, Y., Guo, Y., & Peng, Q. (2006). Automatic foreground extraction of head shoulder images. In *Proc. of 24th Computer Graphics International Conference*. doi:10.1007/11784203_33

Wang, M. S., & Chen, W. C. (2009). A hybrid DWT-SVD copyright protection scheme based on k-means clustering and visual cryptography. *Computer Standards & Interfaces*, *31*(4), 757–762. doi:10.1016/j.csi.2008.09.003

Wang, M., Iwai, Y., & Yachida, M. (1998). Expression recognition from time-sequential facial images by use of expression change model. In *Proceedings of the Second IEEE International Conference on Automatic Face and Gesture Recognition (FG'98)*. doi:10.1109/AFGR.1998.670969

Wang, N., & Doube, W. (2011). How real is really a perceptually motivated system for quantifying visual realism in digital images.*Proceedings of the IEEE International Conference on Multimedia and Signal Processing 2*, 141–149. doi:10.1109/CMSP.2011.172

Wang, X. L. K., Wang, W., & Yang Li, A. (2010). Multiple Object Tracking Method Using Kalman Filter.*Proceedings of the 2010 Institute Of Electrical And Electronics Engineers International Conference on Information and Automation*.

Wang, X., Gong, H., Zhang, H., Li, B., & Zhuang, Z. (2006). Palmprint identification using boosting local binary pattern. *Proceedings of International Conference on Pattern Recognition*, *3*, 503–506.

Wang, X., Jing, X., Zhu, X., Sun, S., & Hong, L. (2009). A novel approach of fingerprint recognition based on multilinear ICA.*IEEE International Conference on Network Infrastructure and Digital Content*. doi:10.1109/ICNIDC.2009.5360839

Wang, Y., & Ruan, Q. (2006). Multispectral palmprint recognition using wavelet-based image fusion. In *Proceedings of the 18th International Conference on Pattern Recognition*.

Wang, Y., & Ruan, Q. (2006). Palm-line extraction using steerable filters.*InProceedings of the 8th International Conference on Signal Processing*.

Wang, Y.-S., Tai, C.-L., Sorkine, O., & Lee, T.-Y. (2008). Optimized scale-and-stretch for image resizing. *ACM Transactions on Graphics*, *27*(5), 1. doi:10.1145/1409060.1409071

Wang, Z., Bovik, A. C., Sheikh, H. R., & Simoncelli, E. P. (2004). Image quality assessment: From error visibility to structural similarity.*IEEE Transactions on Image Processing*, *13*(4), 600–612. doi:10.1109/TIP.2003.819861 PMID:15376593

Watts, D. J., & Strogatz, S. H. (1998). Collective dynamics of "small-world"networks. *Nature, 393*(6684), 440–442. doi:10.1038/30918 PMID:9623998

Wedel, M., & Pieters, R. (2007). A review of eye-tracking research in marketing. *Review of Marketing Research, 4,* 123–147. doi:10.1108/S1548-6435(2008)0000004009

Widdel, H. (1984). Operational problems in analysing eye movements. *Advances in Psychology, 22,* 21–29. doi:10.1016/S0166-4115(08)61814-2

Williams, G. W. (1963). Highway hypnosis: An hypothesis. *The International Journal of Clinical and Experimental Hypnosis, 11*(3), 143–151. doi:10.1080/00207146308409239 PMID:14050133

Wiskott, L. M., Fellous, J., Kuiger, N., & von der Malsburg, C. (1997). Face recognition by elastic bunch graph matching. *IEEE Transactions on Pattern Analysis and Machine Intelligence, 19*(7), 775–779. doi:10.1109/34.598235

Wismeijer, D., Erkelens, C., van Ee, R., & Wexler, M. (2010). Depth cue combination in spontaneous eye movements. *Journal of Vision (Charlottesville, Va.), 10*(6), 25. doi:10.1167/10.6.25 PMID:20884574

Wolfe, J. M. (1994). Guided search 2.0: A revised model of visual search. *Psychonomic Bulletin & Review, 1*(2), 202–238. doi:10.3758/BF03200774 PMID:24203471

Wolfe, J. M. (2000). Visual attention. *Seeing, 2,* 335–386. doi:10.1016/B978-012443760-9/50010-6

Wolfe, J. M., & Horowitz, T. S. (2004). What attributes guide the deployment of visual attention and how do they do it?. *Nature Reviews. Neuroscience, 5*(6), 495–501. doi:10.1038/nrn1411 PMID:15152199

Wong, K. Y. E., Sainarayanan, G., & Chekima, A. (2007). Palmprint Identification Using SobelCode. *Malaysia-Japan International Symposium on Advanced Technology (MJISAT).*

Wren, C., Azarbayejani, A., & Pentland, A. (1997). Pfinder: Real-time tracking of the human body. *Institute Of Electrical And Electronics Engineers Transactions on Pattern Analysis and Machine Intelligence, 19*(7), 780–785.

Wu, X., Wang, K., & Zhang, D. (2005). Palmprint authentication based on orientation code matching. *Proceeding of Fifth International Conference on Audio- and Video- based Biometric Person Authentication, 3546,* 555–562. doi:10.1007/11527923_57

Wu, C.-Y., Leou, J.-J., & Chen, H.-Y. (2009). Visual attention region determination using low-level features. In *Proc. of IEEE International Symposium on Circuits and Systems.* doi:10.1109/ISCAS.2009.5118478

Wu, H., Wang, Y.-S., Feng, K.-C., Wong, T.-T., Lee, T.-Y., & Heng, P.-A. (2010). Resizing by symmetry-summarization. *ACM Transactions on Graphics, 29*(6), 1. doi:10.1145/1882261.1866185

Wu, J., Kamath, M. V., & Poehlman, S. (2006). Detecting differences between photographs and computer generated images.*Proceedings of the 24th IASTED International conference on Signal Processing, Pattern Recognition, and Applications,* 268–273.

Wu, L., Gong, Y., Yuan, X., Zhang, X., & Cao, L. (2012). Semantic aware sports image resizing jointly using seam carving and warping. *Multimedia Tools and Applications.*

Wu, X., & Wang, K. (2004). A Novel Approach of Palm-line Extraction.*Proceedings of the Third International Conference on Image and Graphics (ICIG'04).*

Wu, X., Wang, K., & Zhang, D. (2002). Fuzzy directional element energy feature (FDEEF) based palmprint identification. *International Conference on pattern recognition.*

Wu, X., Wang, K., & Zhang, D. (2004). HMMs based palmprint identification.*Proceedings of International Conference on Biometric Authentication(ICBA), 3072,* 775–781. doi:10.1007/978-3-540-25948-0_105

Wu, X., Wang, K., & Zhang, D. (2004). Palmprint recognition using directional energy feature.*Proceedings of International Conference on Pattern Recognition, 4,*475–478.

Wu, X., Zhang, D., & Wang, K. (2003). Fisherpalms based palmprint recognition. *Pattern Recognition Letters, 24*(15), 2829–2838. doi:10.1016/S0167-8655(03)00141-7

Wu, X., Zhang, D., & Wang, K. (2006). Fusion of phase and orientation information for palmprint authentication. *Pattern Analysis & Applications, 9*(2-3), 103–111. doi:10.1007/s10044-005-0006-6

Wu, X., Zhang, D., Wang, K., & Huang, B. (2004). Palmprint classification using principal lines. *Pattern Recognition, 37*(10), 1987–1998. doi:10.1016/j.patcog.2004.02.015

Wu, X., Zhang, D., Wang, K., & Qi, N. (2007). Fusion of palmprit and iris for personal authentication. In *Proceedings of the Third International Conference on Advanced Data Mining and Applications.* doi:10.1007/978-3-540-73871-8_43

Xiao, R., Zhu, H., Sun, H., & Tang, X. (2007). Dynamic cascades for face detection. In *Proceedings. IEEE Int. Conf. Computer Vision.*

Xin, C. (2011). A Contactless Hand Shape Identification System. In *3rd International Conference on Advanced Computer Control (ICACC2011).* doi:10.1109/ICACC.2011.6016476

Xu, C., Ping, X., & Zhang, T. (2006, August). Steganography in compressed video stream. In *Innovative Computing, Information and Control, 2006. ICICIC'06. First International Conference on* (Vol. 1, pp. 269-272). IEEE.

Xu, X., Guo, Z., Song, C., & Li, Y. (2012). Multispectral Palmprint Recognition Using a Quaternion Matrix. *Hand-Based Biometrics Sensors and Systems, 12,* 4633–4647. PMID:22666049

Yacoob, Y., & Davis, L. S. (1996). Recognizing human facial expression from long image sequences using optical fow. *IEEE Transactions on Pattern Analysis and Machine Intelligence, 18*(6), 636–642. doi:10.1109/34.506414

Yan, L., & Jiying, Z. (2008). *RST invariant video watermarking based on 1D DFT and Radon transform.* Paper presented at the Visual Information Engineering.

Yan, B., Li, K., Yang, X., & Hu, T. (2014). Seam searching based pixel fusion for image retargeting. *IEEE Transactions on Circuits and Systems for Video Technology.*

Yang, J., & Yang, M. (2012). *Top-Down Visual Saliency via Joint CRF and Dictionary Learning.* Paper presented at International Conference on Computer Vision and Pattern Recognition. doi:10.1109/CVPR.2012.6247940

Yang, J., Zhang, D., Frangi, A. F., & Yang, J. Y. (2004). Two-dimensional PCA: A new approach to appearance-based face representation and recognition. *IEEE Transactions on Pattern Analysis and Machine Intelligence, 26*(1), 131–137. doi:10.1109/TPAMI.2004.1261097 PMID:15382693

Yang, J., Zhang, D., Yang, J., & Niu, B. (2007, April). Globally Maximizing, Locally Minimizing: Unsupervised Discriminant Projection with Applications to Face and Palm Biometrics. *IEEE Transactions on Pattern Analysis and Machine Intelligence, 29*(4), 650–664, 664. doi:10.1109/TPAMI.2007.1008 PMID:17299222

Yang, P., Liu, Q., & Metaxas, D. N. (2007, June). Boosting coded dynamic features for facial action units and facial expression recognition. In *Proceedings of IEEE Conference on Computer Vision and Pattern Recognition (CVPR'07).* doi:10.1109/CVPR.2007.383059

Yanulevskaya, V., Uijlings, J., Geusebroek, J. M., Sebe, N., & Smeulders, A. (2013). A proto-object-based computational model for visual saliency. *Journal of Vision, 13*(27), 1-19.

Yarbus, A. L. (1967). *Eye movements and vision.* New York: Plenum. doi:10.1007/978-1-4899-5379-7

Yee, H., Pattanaik, S., & Greenberg, D. P. (2001). Spatiotemporal sensitivity and visual attention for efficient rendering of dynamic environments. *ACM Transactions on Graphics, 20*(1), 39–65. doi:10.1145/383745.383748

Ye, S., Sun, Q., & Chang, E.-C. (2007). Detecting digital image forgeries by measuring inconsistencies of blocking artifact. In *Proc. of IEEE International Conference on Multimedia and Expo.* doi:10.1109/ICME.2007.4284574

Yilmaz, A., Javed, O., & Shah, M. (2006). Object tracking: A survey. Association for Computing Machinery Computer Survey, 38(4).

Yilmaz, A., Li, X., & Shah, M. (2004). Contour based object tracking with occlusion handling in video acquired using mobile cameras. *Institute Of Electrical And Electronics Engineers Transactions on Pattern Analysis and Machine Intelligence, 26*(11), 1531–1536. PMID:15521500

Yin, L., Chen, X., Sun, Y., Worm, T., & Reale, M. (2008). A high-resolution 3D dynamic facial expression database. *8th Intl Conf.on AutomaticFace and Gesture Recognition.*

Yin, L., Wei, X., Sun, Y., Wang, J., & Rosato, M. (2006). 3D facial expression database for facial behavior research. *7th Intl. Conference on Automatic Face and Gesture Recognition.*

Yoneyama, M., Iwano, Y., Ohtake, A., & Shirai, K. (1997). Facial expression recognition using discrete Hopfield neural networks. In *Proceedings of the International Conference on Image Processing (ICIP).* doi:10.1109/ICIP.1997.647398

You, J., Kong, W., Zhang, D., & Cheung, K. (2004). On hierarchical palmprint coding with multiple features for personal identification in large databases. *IEEE Transaction. IEEE Transactions on Circuits and Systems for Video Technology, 14*(2), 234–243. doi:10.1109/TCSVT.2003.821978

You, J., Li, W., & Zhang, D. (2002). Hierarchical palmprint identification via multiple feature extraction. *Pattern Recognition, 35*(4), 847–859. doi:10.1016/S0031-3203(01)00100-5

You, J., Perkis, A., & Gabbouj, M. (2010). Improving image quality assessment with modeling visual attention. In *Proc. of 2nd European Workshop on Visual Information Processing.* doi:10.1109/EUVIP.2010.5699102

Yu, Z. H., Ying, L., & Ke, W. C. (2004). *A blind spatial-temporal algorithm based on 3D wavelet for video watermarking.* Paper presented at the Multimedia and Expo.

Yue, F., Li, B., Yu, M., & Wang, J. (2011).Fast palmprint identification using orientation pattern hashing.*In Proceedings. International. Conference on. Hand-based Biometrics.*

Yue, F., Li, B., Yu, M., & Wang, J. (2013). Hashing Based Fast Palmprint Identification for Large-Scale Databases. *IEEE Transactions On Information Forensics and Security, 8*(5), 769–778. doi:10.1109/TIFS.2013.2253321

Yue, F., Zuo, W., & Zhang, D. (2009). Competitive code-based fast palmprint identification using a set of cover trees. *Optical Engineering (Redondo Beach, Calif.), 48*(6), 1–7.

Yue, F., Zuo, W., Zhang, D., & Li, B. (2011). Fast palmprint identification with multiple templates per subject. *Pattern Recognition Letters, 32*(8), 1108–1118. doi:10.1016/j.patrec.2011.02.019

Yu, H. Y., & Zhang, X. L. (2009). A Robust Watermark Algorithm Based on Ridgelet Transform and Fuzzy C-Means. *International Symposium on Information Engineering and Electronic Commerce.* doi:10.1109/IEEC.2009.30

Yu, Y., Gu, J., Mann, G. K. I., & Gosine, R. G. (2013). Development and Evaluation of Object-Based Vosual Attention for Automatic Perception of Robots. *IEEE Transactions on Automation Science and Engineering, 10*(2), 365–379. doi:10.1109/TASE.2012.2214772

Yu, Y., Mann, G. K. I., & Gosine, R. G. (2008). An Object-based Visual Attention Model for Robots. In *Proceedings of IEEE International Conference on Robotics and Automation (ICRA)* (pp. 943–948). Pasadena, CA: IEEE.

Yu, Y., Mann, G. K. I., & Gosine, R. G. (2010). An Object-based Visual Attention Model for Robotic Applications. *IEEE Transactions on Systems, Man, and Cybernetics, 40*(5), 1398–1412. doi:10.1109/TSMCB.2009.2038895 PMID:20129865

Yu, Z., & Wong, H.-S. (2007). A rule based technique for extraction of visual attention regions based on real time clustering. *IEEE Transactions on Multimedia, 9*(4), 766–784. doi:10.1109/TMM.2007.893351

Zach, F., Riess, C., & Angelopoulou, E. (2012). Automated Image Forgery Detection through Classification of JPEG Ghosts.*Proceedings of the German Association for Pattern Recognition (DAGM 2012)*, 185–194. doi:10.1007/978-3-642-32717-9_19

Zeng, Y. C., & Pei, S. C. (2008, May). Automatic video diagnosing method using embedded crypto-watermarks. In *Circuits and Systems, 2008. ISCAS 2008. IEEE International Symposium on* (pp. 3017-3020). IEEE.

Zhai, Y., & Shah, M. (2006). Visual attention detection in video sequences using spatiotemporal cues. In *Proc. of the 14th Annual ACM International Conference on Multimedia.* doi:10.1145/1180639.1180824

Zhang, D., Lu, G., Li, W., Zhang, L., & Luo, N. (2009). Palmprint recognition using 3-D information. *IEEE Transaction, Systems, Man, and Cybernetics, Part C: Applications and Reviews, 39*(5), 505–519.

Zhang, Y., Jiang, G., Yu, M., & Chen, K. (2010). Stereoscopic Visual Attention Model for 3D Video. In *Advances in Multimedia Modeling*, (pp. 314–324). Springer Berlin.

Zhang, B., & Gao Zhao, Y. (2010). Local derivative pattern versus local binary pattern: Face recognition with high-order local pattern descriptor. *IEEE Transactions on Image Processing, 19*(2), 533–544. doi:10.1109/TIP.2009.2035882 PMID:19887313

Zhang, D. (2004). *Palmprint Authentication.* Springer Science & Business Media.

Zhang, D., Guo, Z., Lu, G., Zhang, L., & Zuo, W. (2010). An online system of multi-spectral palmprint verification. *IEEE Transactions on Instrumentation and Measurement, 58*(2), 480–490. doi:10.1109/TIM.2009.2028772

Zhang, D., Kanhangad, V., Luo, N., & Kumar, A. (2010). Robust palmprint verification using 2D and 3D features. *Pattern Recognition, 43*(1), 358–368. doi:10.1016/j.patcog.2009.04.026

Zhang, D., Kong, W., You, J., & Wong, M. (2003). On-line palmprint identification. *IEEE Transactions on Pattern Analysis and Machine Intelligence, 25*(8), 1041–1050. doi:10.1109/TPAMI.2003.1227981

Zhang, D., Lu, G., Li, W., & Lei, Z. N. L. (2009). Palmprint Recognition Using 3-D Information. *IEEE Transaction On Systems, Man, and Cybernetics-Part C. Applications and Reviews, 39*, 505–519.

Zhang, D., & Shu, W. (1999). Two novel characteristics in palmprint verification Datum point invariance and line feature matching. *Pattern Recognition, 32*(4), 691–702. doi:10.1016/S0031-3203(98)00117-4

Zhang, L., Guo, Z., Wang, Z., & Zhang, D. (2007). "Palmprint verification using complex wavelet transform.*Proceedings of International Conference on Image Processing, 2*,417–420.

Zhang, L., Tong, M. H., Marks, T. K., Shan, H., & Cottrell, G. W. (2008). SUN: A Bayesian framework for saliency using natural statistics. *Journal of Vision (Charlottesville, Va.), 8*(7), 32. doi:10.1167/8.7.32 PMID:19146264

Zhang, L., & Zhang, D. (2004). Characterization of palmprints by wavelet signatures via directional context modeling. *IEEE Transactions on Systems, Man, and Cybernetics. Part B, Cybernetics, 34*(3), 1335–1347. doi:10.1109/TSMCB.2004.824521 PMID:15484907

Zhang, X., Hu, W., Qu, W., & Maybank, S. (2010). Multiple Object Tracking Via Species-Based Particle Swarm Optimization. *Institute Of Electrical And Electronics Engineers Transactions On Circuits And Systems For Video Technology, 20*(11), 1590–1602.

Zhang, Z. (1999). Feature-Based Facial Expression Recognition: Sensitivity Analysis and Experiments with a Multi-Layer Perceptron. *International Journal of Pattern Recognition and Artificial Intelligence, 13*(6), 893–911. doi:10.1142/S0218001499000495

Zhang, Z., Lyons, M., Schuster, M., & Akamatsu, S. (1998). Comparison between geometry-based and Gabor wavelets-based facial expression recognition using multi-layer perceptron. In *Proceedings of the Second IEEE International Conference on Automatic Face and Gesture Recognition (FG'98)*. doi:10.1109/AFGR.1998.670990

Zhan, W., Cao, X., Zhang, J., Zhu, J., & Wang, P. (2009). Detecting photographic composites using shadows. *IEEE International Conference on Multimedia and Expo*, 1042–1045.

Zhao, Q., & Koch, C. (2011). Learning a saliency map using fixated locations in natural scenes. *Journal of Vision (Charlottesville, Va.), 11*(3), 9. doi:10.1167/11.3.9 PMID:21393388

Zhao, Z.-Q., Huang, D.-S., & Jia, W. (2007). Palmprint recognition with 2DPCA+PCA based on modular neural networks. *Neurocomputing, 71*(1-3), 448–454. doi:10.1016/j.neucom.2007.07.010

Zhou, X., Peng, Y., & Yang, M. (2006). Palmprint recognition using wavelet and support vector machines. *Proceeding of 9th Pacific Rim International Conference on Artificial Intelligence Guilin, 4099*, 385–393. doi:10.1007/978-3-540-36668-3_42

Zhu, G., Li, Y., & Wen, P. P. (2014). Analysis and Classification of Sleep Stages Based on Difference Visibility Graphs from a Single Channel EEG Signal. *IEEE Journal of Biomedical and Health Informatics*, (99), 1–1. doi:10.1109/JBHI.2014.2303991

Zund, F., Pritch, Y., Sorkine-Hornung, A., Mangold, S., & Gross, T. (2013). Content-aware compression using saliency-driven image retargeting. In *Proc. of 20th IEEE International Conference on Image Processing*.

Zuo, W., Wang, K., & Zhang, D. (2005). Bi-directional PCA with assembled matrix distance metric. *Proceeding of IEEE International Conference on Image Processing, 2*, 958-961.

About the Contributors

Rajarshi Pal is working as an Assistant Professor at Institute for Development and Research in Banking Technology (IDRBT), Hyderabad, India since 2011. His primary research interests include visual attention models and their applications, watermarking, and cheque fraud detection from image analysis. He has obtained his Ph. D. form Indian Institute of Technology, Kharagpur, India in 2011. Prior to joining in IDRBT, he has served as a Research Associate at Center for Soft Computing Research, Indian Statistical Institute, Kolkata, India.

* * *

Parama Bagchi received B.Tech (CSE)and M.Tech (Computer Technology) degree from BCET under WBUT and Jadavpur University in 2005 and 2010 respectively. Her current research interests include Image Processing, Pattern Recognition and Face Recognition. She is pursuing her research work in Jadavpur University. Currently she is working as an Assistant Professor in CSE Department of RCC Institute of Information Technology, Beliaghata, Kolkata.

Adrita Barari received her B.Tech. degree in Electronics and Communication Engineering from the West Bengal University of Technology, Kolkata, India, in 2010. In June 2012, she joined the Defence Institute of Advanced Technology, Pune, India, as a scholarship student to pursue her M.Tech degree in Signal Processing and Communication from the Dept. of Electronics Engineering. She is currently associated with research in Image Processing Algorithms. Her interest areas include Image Processing, Augmented Reality and Digital Watermarking.

Debotosh Bhattacharjee received the MCSE and Ph.D (Engg.) degrees from Jadavpur University, India, in 1997 and 2004 respectively. He was associated with different institutes in various capacities until March 2007. After that he joined his Alma Mater, Jadavpur University. His research interests pertain to the applications of computational intelligence techniques like Fuzzy logic, Artificial Neural Network, Genetic Algorithm, Rough Set Theory, Cellular Automata etc. in Face Recognition, OCR, and Information Security. He is a life member of Indian Society for Technical Education (ISTE, New Delhi), Indian Unit for Pattern Recognition and Artificial Intelligence (IUPRAI), and senior member of IEEE (USA).

Rajat Subhra Chakraborty is an Assistant Professor in the Computer Science and Engineering Department of Indian Institute of Technology Kharagpur. He has a Ph.D. in Computer Engineering from Case Western Reserve University and a B.E. (Hons.) in Electronics and Telecommunication Engineering from Jadavpur University (India) in 2005. He has work experience at National Semiconductor and AMD. His research interests include: Hardware Security, VLSI Design and Design Automation, and Reversible Watermarking for digital content protection. He is the co-author of two published books (CRC Press, Springer), two more books are forthcoming (World Scientific, Springer), four book chapters, and close to 50 publications in international journals and conferences of repute. He is one of the recipients of the "IBM Faculty Award" for 2012, and a "Royal Academy of Engineering (U.K.) Fellowship" in 2014. He holds 1 U.S. patent, and 2 more international patents and 3 Indian patents have been filed based on his research work. Dr. Chakraborty is a member of IEEE and ACM.

Kingshuk Chatterjee was a project linked scientist at Electronics and communication Sciences Unit at Indian statistical Institute, 203 B. T. Road, Kolkata-108. At present Mr. Chatterjee is a research scholar at Indian Statistical Institute and working towards its PhD in Computer Science. His general areas of research interest include computer vision, theoretical aspects of DNA computing and quantum computing.

Matthieu Perreira Da Silva is associate professor in the IVC team of the IRCCyN Lab. Apart from his research activities in the team, he is also teaching in the computer science department of Polytech Nantes engineering school. He received aM.Sc in image processing in 2001 and a Ph.D. in computer science and applications in 2010, both from the University of La Rochelle, France. From 2001 to 2006 he worked as a R&D engineer in a private company dealing with biometric identification. From 2006 to mid-2011, he was successively engineer, Ph.D. student and teaching assistant at the University of La Rochelle. His research interests include human perception, visual attention, human computer interaction, artificial curiosity, autonomous machine learning, image processing, and computer vision.

Sunita V. Dhavale received the M.E. degree in Computer Engineering from Pune University in 2009 and currently pursuing the PhD degree in Computer Engineering. In March 2011, she joined the faculty of Department of Computer Engineering, Defence Institute of Advanced Technology at Pune, India, as an Assistant Professor. Her research areas include Digital Watermarking, Steganography, Network Security, etc.

Debi Prosad Dogra is an Assistant Professor in the School of Electrical Sciences, IIT Bhubaneswar, India. Prior to joining IIT Bhubaneswar, Dr. Dogra was with Advanced Technology Group, Samsung Research Institute Noida, India for a period of two years (2011-2013). In SRI Noida, Dr. Dogra was leading a research team with areas of focus were in designing applications in the domains of healthcare automation, gesture recognition, augmented reality with the help of video object tracking and image segmentation, visual surveillance. Prior to joining SRI Noida, he obtained his Ph.D. degree from IIT Kharagpur in the year of 2012. He received his M.Tech degree from IIT Kanpur in 2003 after completing his B.Tech. (2001) from HIT Haldia, India. After finishing his masters, he joined Haldia Institute of Technology as a faculty members in the Department of Computer Sc. & Engineering (2003-2006). He worked with ETRI, South Korea during 2006-2007 as a researcher. Dr. Dogra has published more than 15 international journal and conference papers in the areas of computer vision, image segmentation, and healthcare analysis. He is a member of IEEE.

Debayan Ganguly is working as a project linked scientist at Electronics and communication Sciences Unit at Indian statistical Institute, 203 B. T. Road, Kolkata-108. At present Mr. Ganguly is a research scholar of CSIR and working towards his PhD in Computer Science. His general areas of research interest include computer vision, theoretical aspects of DNA computing and quantum computing. He has total three publications in international journals.

Soma Ghosh is working as a project linked scientist at Electronics and communication Sciences Unit at Indian statistical Institute, 203 B. T. Road, Kolkata-108. Her research interest includes video image processing for indoor and outdoor scenes.

Fred H. Hamker is professor of Artificial Intelligence at the Department of Computer Science of the Chemnitz University of Technology. He received his diploma in Electrical Engineering from the University of Paderborn in 1994 and his PhD in Computer Science at the TU Ilmenau in 1999. He was a Post-Doc at the J.W. Goethe University of Frankfurt and the California Institute of Technology (Pasadena, USA). In 2008 he received his venia legendi from the Department of Psychology at the Westf. Wilhelms-University Muenster.

Shubam Jaiswal received his B. Tech. degree in the Department of Computer Engineering at the Indian Institute of Technology, Varanasi, India. His research interests include Computer vision, Pattern Recognition, machine learning.

Amirhossein Jamalian has received his Bachelor and Master degrees in Computer Engineering from Islamic Azad University, South Tehran Branch, Iran in 2004 and Sharif University of Technology, Tehran, Iran in 2007, respectively. He has been recruited as a full-time faculty member at Islamic Azad University, Sama Organization, Andisheh Branch, Iran since February 2009 until September 2013. Currently, he is a Ph.D. candidate in Artificial Intelligence at the Department of Computer Science of the Chemnitz University of Technology, Germany. His research interests are Computational Neuroscience, Machin/Robot Vision, Object Recognition and Machine Learning.

Sibsambhu Kar completed his B.E. in Electrical Engineering in 2001 from Jadavpur University, Kolkata, India, M. Tech. degree in Power System Engineering in 2005 from Indian Institute of Technology, Kharagpur, India and PhD in Signal and Image Processing from Indian Institute of Technology, Kharagpur in the year 2011. He worked as a Lecturer in Siliguri Institute of Technology, Siliguri, India from January 2002 to July 2003 and in Future Institute of Engineering and Management, Kolkata, India from May 2005 to January 2008. Currently, he is working in Samsung R&D Institute, Bangalore as Sr. Chief Engineer in the domain of Image Processing. His research interest includes Signal Processing, Image Processing and Data Analytics.

Rahul Kumar received his B. Tech. degree in the Department of Computer Engineering at the Indian Institute of Technology, Varanasi, India. His research interests include computer vision, image processing, pattern recognition, cloud computing security, and information security.

Santosh Kumar completed his B. Tech. from Department of Computer Science and Engineering from Ajay Kumar Garg Engineering, Ghaziabad, Uttar Pradesh Technical University (UPTU) in 2008 and M. Tech. in Computer Science & Engineering from Birla Institute of Technology, Mesra, Ranchi (Jharkhand, India) in 2012. Currently he is pursuing Ph.D. from Department of Computer Science and Engineering, Indian Institute of Technology, Varanasi. His research interests span a wide range of spectrum including computer vision, pattern recognition, digital image processing, digital video processing, swarm intelligence, bio-inspired computing, artificial Intelligence, operating systems and theoretical computer science.

Y. L. Malathi Latha received Master of Computer Engineering and Terchnology Degree in 2008 from Osmania University, Hyderabad, India. She is currently a Ph.D. student and Associate Professor of Swami Vivekananda Institute of Technology (SVIT), Hyderabad, India. Her research interests are pattern recognition, biometrics and information fusion.

Patrick Le Callet was born in 1970. He received both an M.Sc. and a PhD degree in image processing from Ecole Polytechnique de l'Université de Nantes. He was also a student at the Ecole Normale Superieure de Cachan where he sat the "Aggrégation" (credentialing exam) in electronics of the French National Education. He worked as an Assistant Professor from 1997 to 1999 and as a full time lecturer from 1999 to 2003 at the Department of Electrical Engineering of Technical Institute of the University of Nantes (IUT). Since 2003 he teaches at Ecole Polytechnique de l'Université de Nantes (Engineering School) in the Electrical Engineering and the Computer Science departments where is now a Full Professor. Since 2006, he is the head of the Image and Video Communication lab at CNRS IRCCyN, a group of more than 35 researchers. He is mostly engaged in research dealing with the application of human vision modeling in image and video processing. His current centers of interest are 3D image and video quality assessment, watermarking techniques and visual attention modeling and applications. He is co-author of more than 200 publications and communications and co-inventor of 13 international patents on these topics. He also co-chairs within the VQEG (Video Quality Expert Group) the "HDR Group" and "3DTV" activities. He serves or has served as associate editor for many journals such as IEEE transactions on Image Processing, IEEE transactions on Circuit System and Video Technology, SPRINGER EURASIP Journal on Image and Video Processing, and SPIE Electronic Imaging.

Jennifer L. Leopold was born in Kansas City, Missouri, USA, in 1959. She received her B.S. (Math) in 1981, M.S. (Computer Science) in 1986, and Ph.D. (Computer Science) in 1999, all from the University of Kansas, USA. She is associate professor (2008-) of Computer Science at Missouri University of Science and Technology. She started as assistant professor (2002-2008) at Missouri University of Science and Technology. Previous to that appointment she was a research associate at the University of Kansas Biodiversity Research Institute (1999-2002). She also has worked in industry for over ten years as a systems analyst. She has several publications in end-user programming, with particular focus on database accessibility and scientific visualization. She has received over $2.5M in NSF funding, predominantly for bioinformatics research to develop and study software tools that allow end-users to use powerful information technology to enhance their research without the need for traditional programming training. Dr. Leopold has been a member of IEEE Computer Society and ACM. She has been a reviewer for numerous books, journals, and conferences. She has served as conference co-chair for the International Conference on Distributed Multimedia Systems (2012) and the International Workshop on Visual Languages and Computing (2013 and 2014), and proceedings chair for the IEEE Symposium on Bioinformatics and Computational Biology (2014). She has served as an invited participant in several NSF-funded workshops, particularly in bioinformatics.

Pankaj Malviya is presently an M.Tech. student in the Department of Computer Science and Engineering of National Institute of Technology, Rourkela. His specialization is Computer Science. His research interests include: Cryptography, Digital Forensics, Artificial Intelligence, and Image Processing. His recent research work has been published by LNCS in the Proceedings of International Conference on Information Systems Security.

Mita Nasipuri received her B.E.Tel.E., M.E.Tel.E, and Ph.D. (Engg.) degrees from Jadavpur University, in 1979, 1981 and 1990, respectively. Prof. Nasipuri has been a faculty member of Jadavpur University since 1987. Her current research interest includes image processing, pattern recognition, and multimedia systems. She is a senior member of the IEEE, U.S.A., Fellow of I.E (India) and W.B.A.S.T, Kolkata, India.

Ruchira Naskar has received a Ph.D. in Computer Science and Engineering from Indian Institute of Technology, Kharagpur. Currently, she is an Assistant Professor in the Department of Computer Science and Engineering of National Institute of Technology, Rourkela. She has over 20 publications in international journals and conferences and one Indian Patent filed. Her research interests include Digital Forensics, Digital Rights Management and Cryptography.

Ramesh Chand Pandey is a research scholar in Department of Computer science & Engineering at Indian Institute of Technology, Varanasi, India. He has following area of interest: Image Forensic, Video Forensic, Image Processing, Video Processing etc.

Munaga V. N. K. Prasad received his PhD from the Institute of Technology (then Benaras Hindu University), Varanasi, India. He is currently working as an Associate Professor at the Institute for Development and Research in Banking Technology (IDRBT), Hyderabad, India. His research interests include biometrics, digital watermarking and payment system technologies. There are nearly 50 international journal and conference papers to his credit.

Channapragada R. S. G. Rao is having 20 years of experience out of which he has 5 years in software industry and 15 years in reputed engineering colleges at various positions. He has submitted his PhD thesis in the area of Digital watermarking for evaluation in JNTUH. He has obtained PG degree in Master of Information Technology (1998) from N.T.U.(presently known as Charles Darwin University, Australia), and M.Tech (2008) from JNTUH, Hyderabad. He has studied B.E.(1991) in Computer Science Engineering from Gulbarga University, Karnataka. He has published 16 papers in International and National Journals/ conferences, which includes prestigious IEEE and Springer conferences. He has guided many M.Tech and B.Tech mini and major projects. He has experience in computer network design and implementation and training and placements activities. He has attended many workshops organized by both industry and academic institutions.

Kumar S. Ray, PhD, is a Professor in the Electronics and Communication Sciences Unit at Indian Statistical Institute, Kolkata, India. He is an alumnus of University of Bradford, UK. He was a visiting faculty member under UNDP fellowship program, at University of Texas, Austin, USA. Prof. Ray was a member of task force committee of the Government of India, Department of Electronics (DoE/MIT), for the application of AI in power plants. He is the founder member of Indian Society for Fuzzy Mathematics and Information Processing (ISFUMIP) and member of Indian Unit for Pattern Recognition and Artificial Intelligence (IUPRAI). In 1991, he was the recipient of the K.S. Krishnan memorial award for the best system oriented paper in Computer Vision. Biographical sketch of Prof. Kumar Sankar Ray has been published in Marquis Who's Who in the World 2007 and Marquis Who's Who in Asia. He has written a number of research articles published in international journals and has presented at several professional meetings. He serves as a reviewer of several International journals. His current research interests include artificial intelligence, computer vision, commonsense reasoning, soft computing, non-monotonic deductive database systems, and DNA computing. He is the co-author of two edited volumes on approximate reasoning and fuzzy logic and fuzzy computing, published by, Elsevier, North-Holland. Also he is the co-author of Case studies in intelligent computing-Achievements and trends, CRC Press Taylor and Francis group, USA. He is the author of two research monographs viz, Soft Computing Approach to Pattern Classification and Object Recognition, a unified concept, Springer, New York, and Polygonal Approximation and Scale-Space Analysis of closed digital curves, Apple Academic Press, Canada, 2013.

Vincent Ricordel received the Ph.D degree in Signal Processing and Telecommunication from the University of Rennes, France, in 1996. After a post-doc in 1997 at the Tampere University of Technology (TUT), Finland, he has been, from 1998 to 2002, an associate professor at Technical Institute of the University of Toulon (IUT), France. Since 2002, he holds an associate professor position at Ecole Polytechnique de l'Université de Nantes (Engineering school), France, where he joined the Image and Video Communication lab at CNRS IRCCyN. His research interests include video coding and image sequence analysis. His current center of interest is perceptual video coding.

Aurobinda Routray received the B.E. degree from the National Institute of Technology Rourkela, Rourkela, India, in 1989, the M.Tech. degree from the Indian Institute of Technology Kanpur, Kanpur, India, in 1991, and the Ph.D. degree from Sambalpur University, Sambalpur, India, in 1999. During 2003–2004, he visited Purdue University, West Lafayette, IN, as a Better Opportunities for Young Scientists in Chosen Areas of Science and Technology Fellow sponsored by the Department of Science and Technology, Government of India. His a Professor with the Department of Electrical Engineering, Indian Institute of Technology Kharagpur, Kharagpur, India. His research interests include nonlinear and statistical signal processing, signal-based fault detection and diagnosis, real-time and embedded signal processing, numerical linear algebra, and data-driven diagnostics.

Anwesha Sengupta received the B.E. and M.S. degrees in Electrical Engineering from Jadavpur University and Indian Institute of Technology in 2005 and 2011 respectively. She served as a Lecturer in the Department of Electronics at the Institute of Technology and Marine Engineering, Sarisha, Diamond Harbour (presently Neotia Institute of Technology, Management and Science, NITMAS) from November 2010-June 2011. She is currently pursuing her Ph.D in the Department of Electrical Engineering at the Indian Institute of Technology, Kharagpur since 2011. Her research interests include signal processing, EEG analysis etc.

Chaman L. Sabharwal was born at Ludhiana, Punjab, India, in 1937. He received his B.A.(Hons) in 1959, M.A.(Math) in 1961 from Panjab University, Chandigarh, India. He received his M.S.(Math) in 1966 and Ph.D.(Math) from the University of Illinois, Urbana, Champaign, Illinois, USA, in 1967. He is professor of Computer Science at Missouri University of Science and Technology (1986-). He was assistant professor (1967-971), associate professor (1971-9175), full professor (1975-1982) at Saint Louis University. He was Senior Programmer Analyst (1982), Specialist (1983), Senior Specialist(1984) Lead Engineer(1985) at Boeing Corporation. He published several technical reports and journal articles on CAD/CAM. He was consultant at Boeing (1986-1990). He was National Science Foundation fellow (1979) at Boeing and NSF Image Databases Panelist (1996). Dr. Sabharwal has been member of American Mathematical Society, Mathematical Society of America, IEEE Computer Society, ACM, and ISCA. He has been on editorial board of International Journal of Zhejiang University Science (JZUS), Editorial Board CAD (Computer Aided Design), Progress In Computer Graphics Series, Modeling and Simulation, Instrument Society of America. He has been a reviewer for numerous books, journals and conferences. He was awarded service awards by NSF Young Scholars George Engelmann Institute, and ACM Symposium on Applied Computing for Multimedia and Visualization track.

Nilkanta Sahu received his M. Tech degree in Computer Science and Engineering from Department of Computer Science and Engineering, NIT Rourkela, India and his B. Tech. degree in Information Technology from Jalpaiguri Govt. Engineering College, West Bengal, India. He is currently pursuing his PhD on Multimedia Security at Department of Computer Science and Engineering, Indian Institute of Technology, Guwahati. His Research interests include video watermarking, Information hiding and multimedia security.

K. K. Shukla is a Professor and Head of the Department in Department of Computer science &Engineering at Indian Institute of Technology, Varanasi, India. He has more than 20 years of academic experience and published 180papers in Journals, Conferences and Book Chapters. He has following area of interest: Data mining, Software Engineering, Networking, Image Processing, Video Processing, Image Forensic, Video Forensic, Biometric Security, Biomedical image Processing etc.

Sanjay Kumar Singh is an Associate Professor in Department of Computer science & Engineering at Indian Institute of Technology, Varanasi, India. He has more than ten years academic experience and published more than 40 papers in Journals, Conferences and Book chapters. He has following area of interest: Image Processing, Video Processing, Image Forensic, Video Forensic, Biometric Security, Biomedical Image Processing etc.

Arijit Sur received his Ph. D. degree in Computer Science and Engineering from Department of Computer Science and Engineering, Indian Institute of Technology Kharagpur. He has received his M. Sc. in Computer and Information Science and M. Tech in Computer Science and Engineering both from Department of Computer Science and Engineering, University of Calcutta, India. He is currently working as an Assistant Professor at Department of Computer Science and Engineering, Indian Institute of Technology, Guwahati. He is a recipient of Infosys Scholarship during his Ph. D. tenure at Indian Institute Technology, Kharagpur. He has received Microsoft Outstanding Young Faculty Program Award at Dept. of CSE, Indian Institute of Technology, Guwahati. His current research interest is Multimedia Security such as Image and Video Watermarking, Steganography & Steganalysis and Reversible Data Hiding.

Prasun Chandra Tripathi is currently studying M. Tech. at University of Hyderabad, India. The topic of his M. Tech. Thesis is image retargeting.

Junle Wang received his M.S. degrees in Signal Processing (South China University of Technology, China), and Electronic Engineering (University of Nantes, France) in 2009, and the PhD degree in computer science from University of Nantes in 2012. He then became an ATER (assistant professor) in the Department of Electronic and Digital Technologies, at Ecole Polytechnique de l'Universié de Nantes. Currently he is in charge of the R&D division at ArsNova Systems, France. His research interests include image classification, visual attention, quality of experience of stereoscopic-3D, image quality assessment, human visual perception and psychophysical experimentation.

Index

Become an IRMA Member

Members of the **Information Resources Management Association (IRMA)** understand the importance of community within their field of study. The Information Resources Management Association is an ideal venue through which professionals, students, and academicians can convene and share the latest industry innovations and scholarly research that is changing the field of information science and technology. Become a member today and enjoy the benefits of membership as well as the opportunity to collaborate and network with fellow experts in the field.

IRMA Membership Benefits:

- **One FREE Journal Subscription**

- **30% Off Additional Journal Subscriptions**

- **20% Off Book Purchases**

- Updates on the latest events and research on Information Resources Management through the IRMA-L listserv.

- Updates on new open access and downloadable content added to Research IRM.

- A copy of the Information Technology Management Newsletter twice a year.

- A certificate of membership.

IRMA Membership $195

Scan code to visit irma-international.org and begin by selecting your free journal subscription.

Membership is good for one full year.

Printed in the United States
By Bookmasters